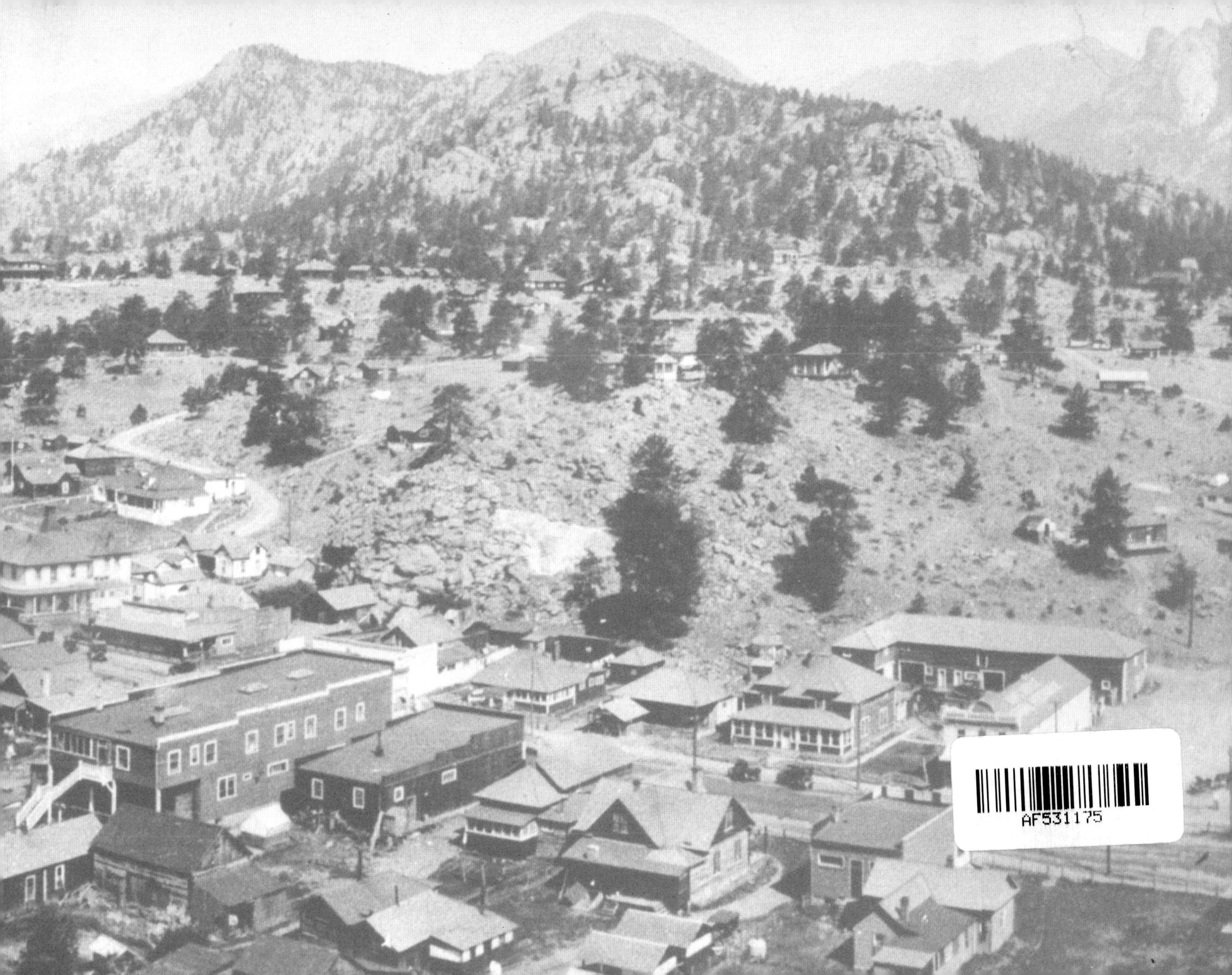

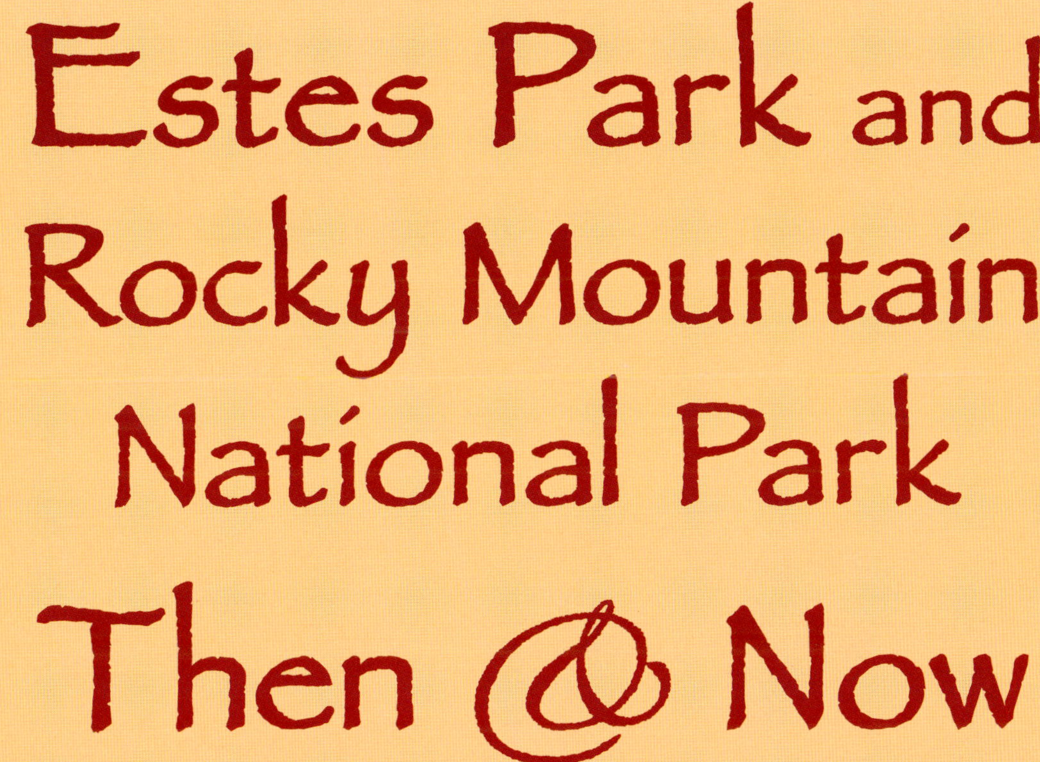

Estes Park and Rocky Mountain National Park Then & Now

Contemporary Rephotography by Mic Clinger

Text by James H. Pickering and Carey Stevanus

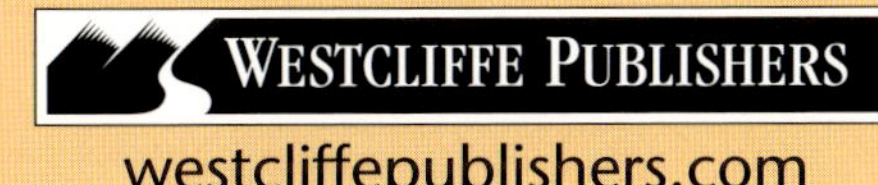
Westcliffe Publishers

westcliffepublishers.com

Contents

Photographic Portfolios

Site Maps

Estes Valley Scenes and Sites

1. Estes Park from Park Hill
2. "Rocky Mountain Jim" Cabin Site
3. Estes Park from Mount Olympus
4. Estes-Evans-Dunraven Ranch
5. Charles Partridge Adams House
6. Dunraven Cottage and Estes Park Hotel
7. Estes Park Hotel
8. Estes Park Country Club
9. Front Range from Prospect Mountain
10. Longs Peak from Dollar Lake
11. Cheley Colorado Camps
12. Marys Lake
13. Beaver Point
14. Rocky Mountain National Park 1923 Headquarters
15. The Lone Pine
16. The Y–Big Thompson Entrance to Rocky Mountain National Park
17. Holland Inn
18. YMCA of the Rockies
19. Mountainside Lodge
20. Wigwam Tea Room
21. F. O. Stanley House
22. Estes Park Fish Hatchery
23. Stanley Power Plant
24. McCreery Cabin
25. North St. Vrain Road (Highway 36)
26. South St. Vrain Road (Highway 7)
27. Big Thompson Road (Highway 34)

The Village

28. Panoramic View
29. Al Birch House
30. Estes Park from the Birch Ruins
31. Sam Service Store
32. Original 1915 Rocky Mountain National Park Headquarters
33. John Edward Macdonald Home and Store
34. Josephine Hotel
35. Riverside Amusement Park
36. National Park Hotel
37. William T. Parke Store
38. Rocky Mountain Parks Transportation Company
39. Hupp Hotel

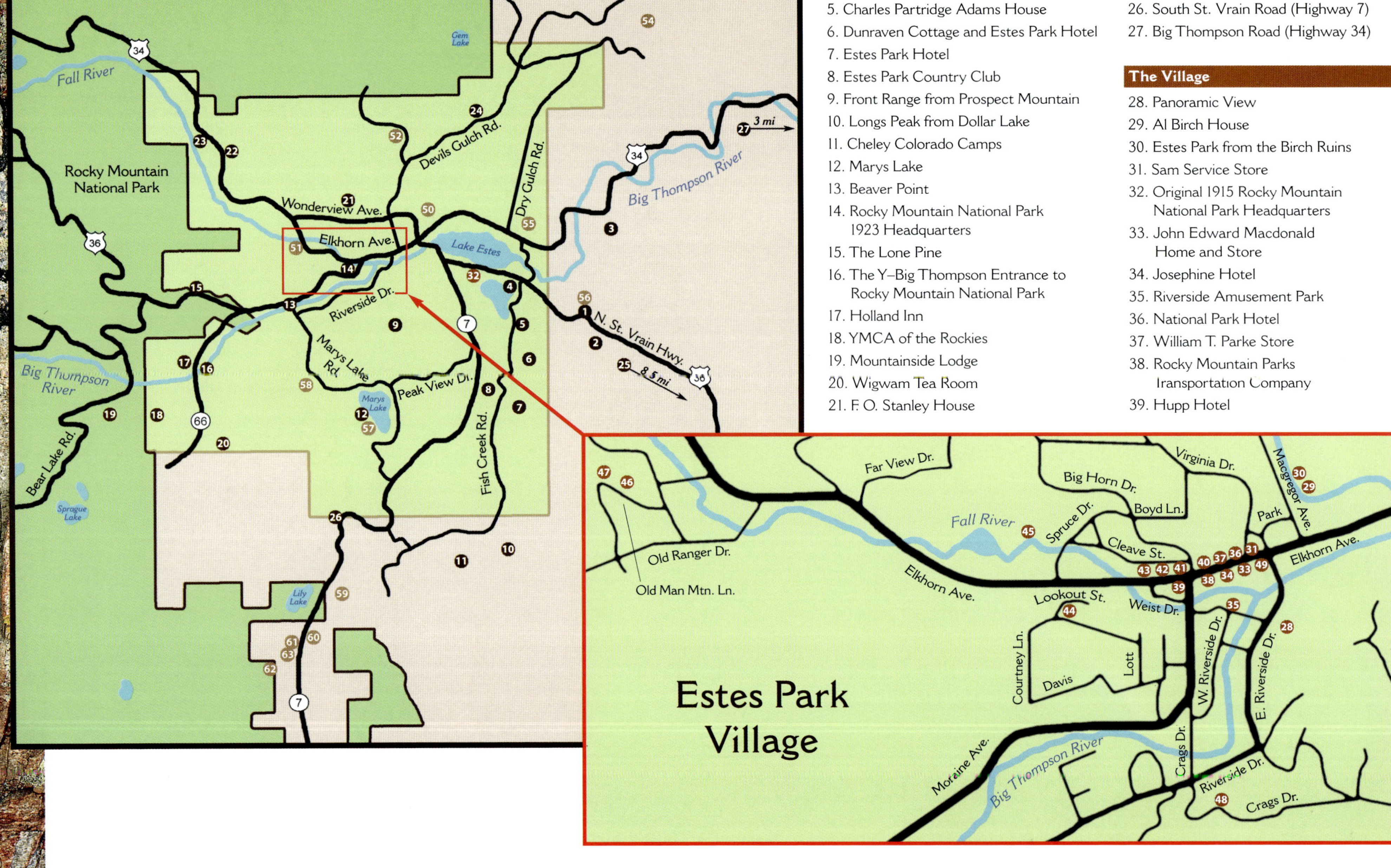

The Village continued

40. Manford Hotel
41. Estes Park Bank
42. Ye Lyttel Shop
43. Estes Park Church
44. Estes Park from the West End
45. Lewiston Hotel
46. Estes Park from Oldman Mountain
47. Oldman Mountain Ski Site
48. Crags Hotel
49. Boyd House

Hotels, Lodges, and Ranches

50. Stanley Hotel
51. Elkhorn Lodge
52. MacGregor Ranch
53. McGraw Ranch
54. Rustic Hotel
55. Olympus Lodge
56. Crocker Ranch
57. Estes Park Chalets
58. Ferguson's Highlands Hotel
59. Baldpate Inn
60. Wind River Ranch
61. Columbine Lodge
62. Hewes-Kirkwood Inn
63. Lambs Ranch and Longs Peak Inn

Rocky Mountain National Park: East of Continental Divide

64. Rocky Mountain National Park Dedication Site in Horseshoe Park
65. Fall River Lodge
66. Convict Cabins
67. March Homestead Cabin
68. Cascade Lodge
69. Richmond Homestead and Horseshoe Inn
70. CCC Camp in Little Horseshoe Park
71. Deer Ridge Chalet
72. Hupp Homestead
73. Hondius Ranch
74. Camping in Moraine Park
75. Chapman Ranch
76. Eaton House
77. William Allen White Cabin
78. The Scottage
79. Moraine Lodge
80. Sprague's Ranch and Stead's Ranch and Hotel
81. Brinwood Ranch and Hotel
82. Forest Inn
83. Fern Lake Lodge
84. CCC Camps in Hollowell Park
85. Rocky Mountain Boys Camp
86. Spragues Lodge
87. Bear Lake and Bear Lake Lodge

Rocky Mountain National Park: West of Continental Divide

88. Old Fall River Road
89. Trail Ridge Road
90. Grand Lake
91. Grand Lake Lodge
92. Holzwarth Trout Lodge and Never Summer Ranch
93. Camp Wheeler (Squeaky Bob's)
94. Lulu City

Rocky Mountain National Park: Longs Peak Region

95. Eugenia Mine
96. Timberline Cabin
97. Agnes Vaille Shelter
98. The Keyhole

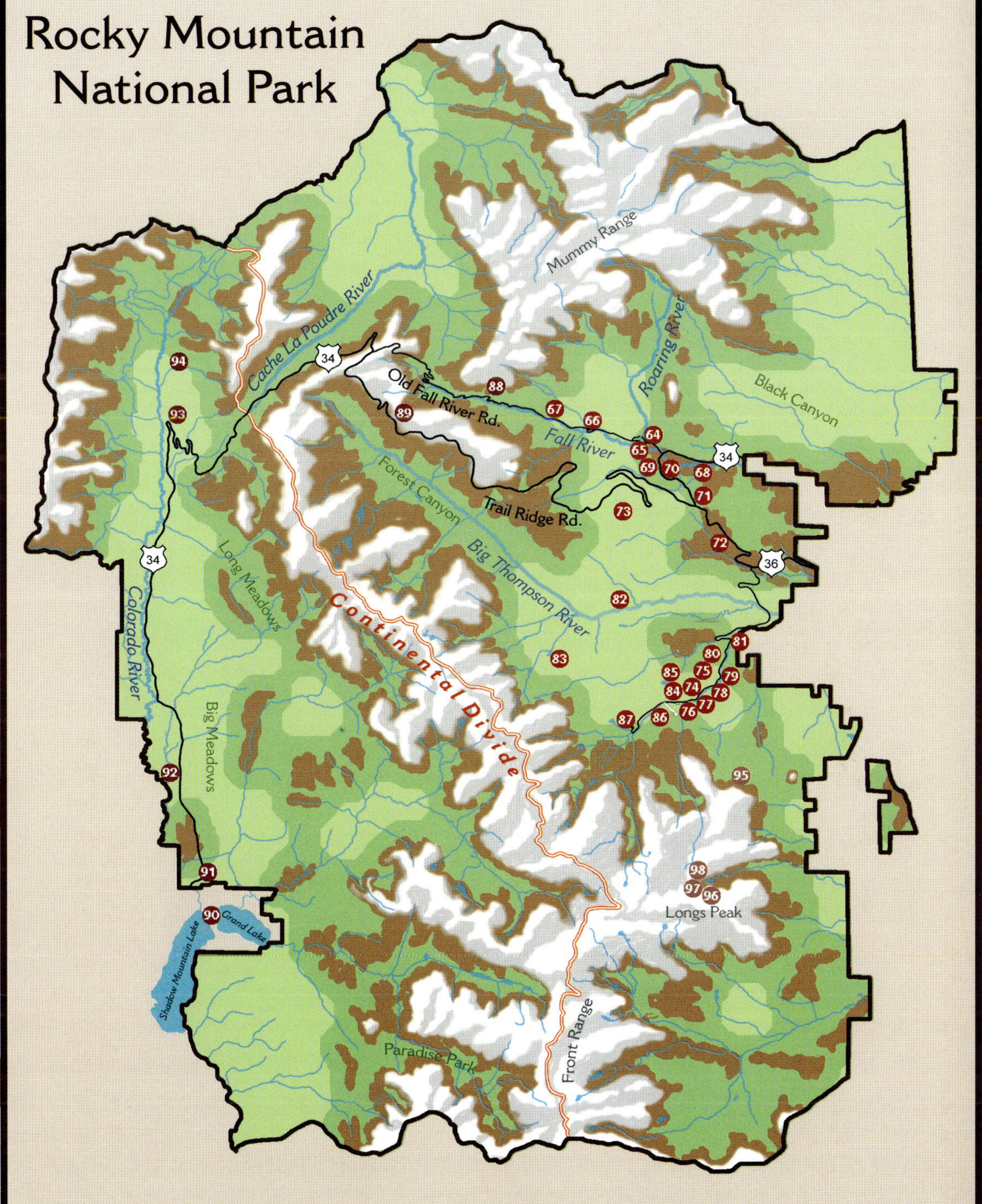

Preface

As early as November 1916, *The Denver Post* warned its readers that the marks of Estes Park's earliest pioneers were being fast "obliterated" by "the enormous development of the country as a summer resort" and that "within another year or two the last vestiges of the region's early history will have disappeared completely." Fortunately, the *Post*'s prediction has not proven totally correct. To be sure, many of the structures associated with the early history of the Estes Valley, the town of Estes Park, and adjacent Rocky Mountain National Park have disappeared—some the victim of fire, others at the hands of individuals who believed that "progress" and "modernity" required replacing old buildings with new, or, in the case of the National Park Service, that inholdings, regardless of historic value, should be removed in order to return the park to its natural condition. In other cases, historic buildings have been so transformed by successive occupants that their original appearance and purpose are no longer easily recognized.

Losing such important artifacts is regrettable for any number of reasons, not the least of which is what they have to tell us about the historical development of the town and region and the tourist industry that encouraged both, a complex and rich heritage that deserves to be preserved. As a historian, I have tried during the last 20 years to retell the story of Estes Park in a number of traditional histories. These books provide a fairly comprehensive history of Estes Park and Rocky Mountain National Park from October 1859, the month and year that pioneer Joel Estes first stumbled upon the valley that now bears his name, to the end of the Second World War.

What they fail to provide, except indirectly, is a guide to the historic structures of the Estes Park region: its hotels, ranches, and resorts; its shops and other commercial and governmental buildings; and its private residences. They do not serve as guides that both tell and show us where these landmarks once stood and reveal what the ones still standing look like today. This photographic history seeks to remedy that deficiency. The goal has been to produce a book for readers interested in Colorado's regional history, and in the way that the Estes Valley and Rocky Mountain National Park looked to residents and visitors of an earlier day, and for those who will find it a useful field guide to take with them while visiting the sites.

In achieving this mission, I have had two wonderful partners and coauthors. In Mic Clinger of Parker, Colorado, a talented photographer with a true love of history, and Carey Stevanus, a year-round resident of Estes Park who has also researched the valley's past, I fortunately found individuals whose love of place

MacGregor ranch, circa 1892

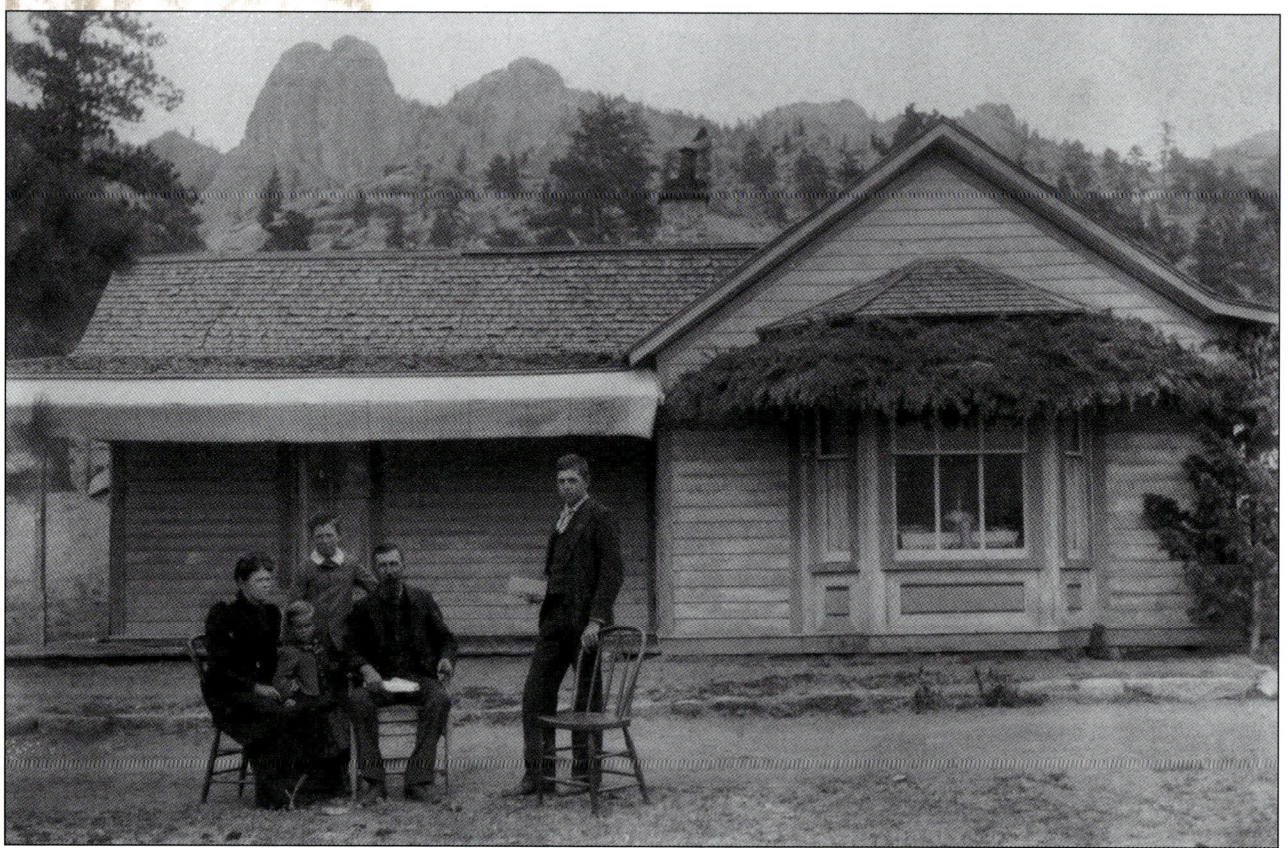

and desire to preserve its memory match my own. Our days "in the field" during the three years we worked on this project are ones that I will always remember, not only because of the discoveries we made and what we learned about the very history we were pursuing, but because of the companionship and fun they provided. "Doing history" became something other than a scholar's lonely enterprise.

On more than one occasion, our study of early photographs led us directly to the identifiable remains of the foundations of buildings long since forgotten and previously overlooked. Our search for the "exact" locations from which the original photographs were taken (Mic Clinger was a stickler on this point—and had an unerring eye) also taught us valuable lessons about how the appearance of Estes Park and Rocky Mountain National Park has changed over time. Not the least of these lessons had to do with now-mature trees that had seemingly sprouted in places where there once had been none, as if, we joked, some unknown "Johnny Appleseed" had trailed early photographers through the valley to frustrate those who might try to follow in their footsteps.

There were other surprises, as well, as some of our photographic retakes clearly demonstrate. Perhaps the most difficult to contend with were changes in road locations. This was true in Horseshoe Park, where we tried to locate the original sites from which several photographs of the September 1915 dedication of Rocky Mountain National Park were taken. It was even more troubling and disconcerting as we tried to duplicate photographs of the complex of buildings on lower Fish Creek Road that encompassed the original Joel Estes–Griff Evans ranch, which the Earl of Dunraven and resident manager Theodore Whyte added to during the following three decades. As our contemporary photographs make clear, the original road along Fish Creek, which wound directly between the buildings of the ranch complex, was moved and significantly raised in the late 1940s when the Big Thompson River was dammed to create Lake Estes as part of the Colorado–Big Thompson transmountain irrigation project. Farther up Fish Creek Road, on the hillside directly across from the site of the Estes Park Hotel, we discovered that several huge boulders, on which hotel guests in Victorian attire had been photographed, have vanished beneath the elevated 10th green of the Estes Park Golf Course.

We also learned a good deal about early photographers, the cameras and techniques that they employed, and the dramatic changes in the art of photography since the time when many of the original photographs were first taken. When William Henry Jackson first entered Estes Park in

"We Three": The authors pose before the 1882 A.Q. House at the MacGregor ranch.

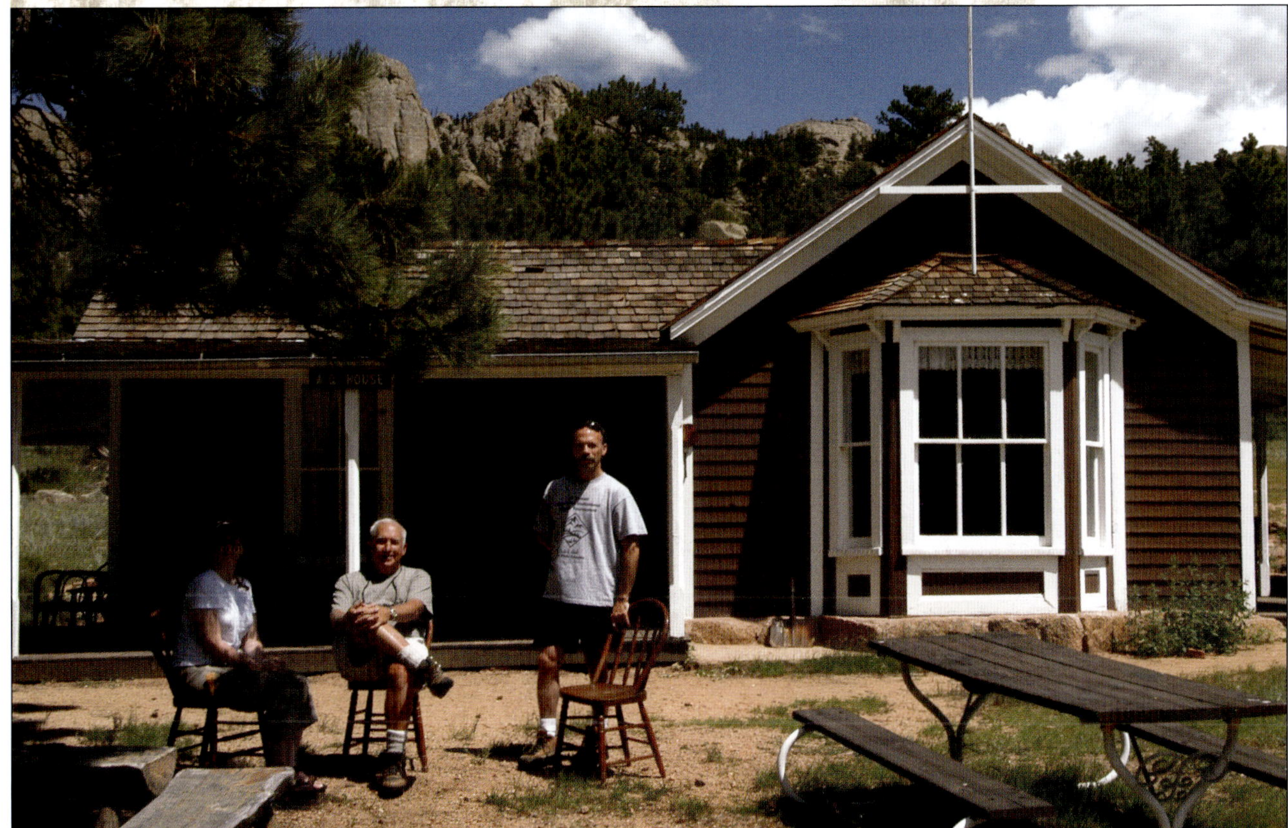

Photo by Skip Szilagyi

1873 as a member of the photographic division of the Hayden survey, he brought with him the cumbersome equipment of the contemporary professional photographer. This included a large camera and tripod, a darkroom, fragile glass plates on which the negatives were taken, colloidal solution for preparing the plates, and developer, wash, varnish, and other chemicals to preserve his images for printing. That equipment, carried on the back of a mule or horse, weighed some 300 pounds, for Jackson took with him into the field two cameras (one with double lenses for taking stereo photos) and enough chemicals and glass for 400 plates. A further difficulty was the fact that in Jackson's day, exposure of the plate took from 20 seconds to 5 minutes, depending on the chemical process and the amount of light entering through the lens. It was tough work, even for a professional such as Jackson.

Connecticut druggist Frederick H. Chapin, by contrast, had a somewhat easier time when he photographed Estes Park 15 years later. Thanks to the introduction of commercially available "dry" plates during the 1880s (which replaced the "wet plate" process with which Jackson had to contend), mountain photography had by then been brought within the abilities of the adept amateur, though Chapin still had to take with him a heavy camera and tripod and a supply of fragile glass plates. Inevitably there were accidents. Attempting to take a photograph of three bighorn sheep while climbing on Hallett Peak, Chapin became so excited that he "took a slide out of one plate-holder before putting the cap on." As he ruefully tells the reader, "That ruined piece of glass now lies among the rocks to amuse the conies and ptarmigan."

In taking our photographs, we had all the advantages of modern technology. We used lightweight, handheld digital cameras, occasionally supplemented by an equally lightweight tripod. At the end of a day of shooting, we downloaded the results onto a laptop computer, on which we could sort and edit the images as needed. Our most unwieldy equipment was a variety of ropes and bungee cords that we sometimes needed to tie back tree limbs to secure a clear shot.

Other than the trees that all too often got in our way, the biggest problem we faced in retaking photographs had to do with the lenses of the early cameras and how they affected the images they took, particularly with respect to background and foreground objects. On some occasions we would locate what seemed to the eye the exact location from which the original photograph was taken, then retake the photograph, only to discover that while the foreground was "right" (the size of nearby rocks or other objects), the background objects became small and distant. A case in point was our attempt to retake a frontal view of the Earl of Dunraven's Estes Park Hotel on Fish Creek Road (see p. 34). The rocks in the foreground of the original photograph provided an obvious clue to location, and we found those rocks directly below the 10th green of the Estes Park Golf Course, flanked by two pine trees. We walked to the point where we thought the foreground and background objects matched the original picture. But when Mic retook the photograph of the hotel from that spot, the hills behind the hotel looked much farther away. This is because our brains tend to compress visual information in order to process as much as possible. Therefore, when Mic lined up the original photograph with what he saw, it looked "right." Only afterward did the discrepancy become obvious.

Early photographers did not have the zoom lenses we have today. All their lenses had a fixed focal length, and even then their choices were limited. This made photography much more challenging. Today, we simply adjust the zoom to fill the picture from wherever we might be standing. But in those days the photographer had to think about his lenses, and he had to move the bulky tripod and other heavy equipment to where his picture looked best, regardless of the terrain or obstacles. We learned a great deal about early photography, in fact, as we worked with the photographs of William Henry Jackson, F. E. Baker, William T. Parke, Fred Payne Clatworthy, and others. We learned that like contemporary photographers, they had a variety of techniques at their disposal to control their views—from their choice of lens, which could deepen or make shallow their image, to their choice of time of day to control light and shadow and cloud effects, to their choice of where to position their cameras in relation to scene. We learned from them that an act so simple and obvious as tilting the camera up or down, or taking the picture from an angle as opposed to straight on, could make an amazing difference in the quality, character, suggestiveness, and dramatic power of the final photograph.

Common sense, it should be noted, also frequently came into play. Putting ourselves in the place of the original photographer and trying to imagine how he might have visualized the scene before him often allowed us to discover the spot from which his photograph was taken. Sometimes this was simply a matter of looking around for the convenient rock or area on which he placed his heavy tripod.

All this helped in our efforts at rephotography. But in making a final determination about a given location, Mic employed a complex set of calculations known as "triangulation," using vertical and horizontal lines of coincidence much in the way that members of Ferdinand V. Hayden's survey party did when mapping Colorado's rugged country in the 1870s. For example, using the original photograph of the Al Birch ruins on the Knoll property (see p. 84), he drew horizontal lines from the chimney to see where they intersected with the mountains and other background objects. He then drew vertical lines from other distinct points on the structure to see where they intersected. Visually, these lines and their coincidences had to be successfully lined up on the site in order to determine the azimuth (the angle along the horizon) and the distance of the camera from the object. Azimuth is fairly easy to determine; distance is not. As mentioned previously, the human eye tends to compress and distort what is actually there. While the focal length of our camera lens determines the amount of information in a snapshot, our eyes (with the help of our brain) have the uncanny ability to include, exclude, and compress what we see before us. To be more technical, our eyes have roughly the focal length of 58mm, as compared to the field view of a 35mm camera system. When taking a "now" photograph of a given site, it is therefore helpful to adjust the zoom lens of the camera and take a quick look through the viewfinder to see what the camera sees at that focal length. Next, if there are objects in the foreground, it is helpful to estimate their relative size in the viewfinder in comparison to the objects in the background. These two pieces of information are essential in rephotography: While keeping the previously established lines of coincidence lined up, they tell you if you need to be farther away or closer to your subject.

In the pages that follow, readers will find a photographic record of the most important historic sites and structures of the Estes Valley and in adjacent Rocky Mountain National Park. Each site includes one or more historical photographs of what it looked like to early visitors and residents, a photograph of what it looks like today, and a brief discussion of its history. In the back of the book are site locations (including GPS readings, except for those sites where the photographs were taken from private property), the archive or source from which each historical image was obtained, and suggestions for further reading. Our wish is that what we have provided here will be useful in helping others to understand the colorful past of the area in and near Joel Estes' valley and the places where that history occurred.

Four final notes, the first three cautionary ones: A number of the historical sites identified and photographed in Estes Park and in the Estes Valley are on private property, whose owners have rights that should be respected as a matter of courtesy. Roughly 40 percent are within Rocky Mountain National Park, where the National Park Service has a mandate to conserve the integrity of the natural landscape. Still others were taken at high places from which it would be dangerous to try to duplicate, quite apart from the permissions required. The fourth note takes the form of a request. It is our hope that this book will provide the occasion for individuals who have early photographs of the structures included in this book—or any others, as well—to make them available to one or more of the museums and repositories listed in the back. Recovering the history of Estes Park, and preserving and protecting it, are cumulative, ongoing tasks—ones that require the active help of all who care.

—James H. Pickering
Estes Park, Colorado

Introduction

Encompassing an area of nearly 32 square miles, the valley of Estes Park has been inhabited by humans for nearly 10,000 years, beginning in Paleolithic times. Evidence abounds that Native Americans used the park (the word "park" in the parlance of the mountains means "valley") on a seasonal basis for hunting. Projectile points, scrapers and other tools, and pottery shards have been found at various places throughout the valley. Game drives—low stone walls behind which hunters crouched in ambush—have been located on the tundra of Trail Ridge, and archaeologists have unearthed a series of stone ovens in Bodes Draw off Dry Gulch Road. Archaeologists also tell us that Oldman Mountain, the stone knob that rises immediately to the west of the village, was once a vision quest site. According to a tradition first reported in 1914, when three Arapaho revisited the area from Wyoming to help identify original Indian names of features within the proposed national park, the Arapaho and Apache fought a spirited battle in Upper Beaver Meadows, making use of a crude fort built of mountain boulders close to what would later become the Pieter Hondius ranch.

The first known white man to visit Estes Park was Kentuckian Joel Estes, who camped in the eastern part of the valley with his son, Milton, during a hunting expedition in mid-October 1859. "We did not know what we had found....," Milton Estes later wrote. "We were monarchs of all we surveyed, mountains, valleys, and streams. There was absolutely nothing to dispute our sway. We had a little world all to ourselves." By the next summer, Joel Estes had decided to use the park to make a living raising cattle. He built several crude log buildings near the base of Park Hill (where Highway 36 today comes in from Lyons) on a site now covered by the smaller arm of Lake Estes, and in 1863 moved his wife, Patsy, and family up from their ranch at Fort Lupton on the South Platte to live year-round.

Within a short time, the Esteses had visitors, some of whom briefly stopped for food, lodging, and directions. One of these was William Byers, the energetic editor of the *Rocky Mountain News*, who came up from Denver in August 1864 with several companions to attempt to reach the summit of Longs Peak in August, then "the chief climbing goal in the Colorado territory." Byers failed. "Not a living creature, unless it had wings to fly, was ever upon its summit," he later wrote, "and we believe we run no risk in predicting that no man will ever be." But in reporting their journey to *News* readers, Byers named the mountain valley after his host. William Byers left impressed, confidently predicting that "eventually this park will become a favorite pleasure resort."

The Estes family did not stay. By April 1866, following several harsh winters that made grazing difficult and at times impossible, Joel Estes was gone, leaving only his squatter's cabin, outbuildings, and name as evidence of his pioneering. The valley was not vacant for long. The next year the Estes holdings were taken up by Welshman Griffith J. "Griff" Evans, his wife, Jane, and their family, who brought all their worldly goods up by wagon from Lyons over the crude cart path that was opened by Joel Estes and his sons. The jovial Evans was a true impresario, and it was not long before the Evanses, like their predecessors, found themselves putting up visitors who in increasing numbers found their way into the park to hunt, prospect, and recreate on vacation while escaping the summer heat of the valley towns. By 1872, Estes Park's reputation as a sportsman's paradise was becoming increasingly well-known, even as far away as London.

Among the first to take advantage of Griff Evans' hospitality was the Earl of Dunraven (Windham Thomas Wyndham-Quin), an Irish-born, Oxford-educated, moneyed nobleman who came up from Denver to hunt the week after Christmas in 1872. Charmed by everything he saw, the earl decided to gain control of as much of the park as he could for his own uses. In the spring of 1874, having managed to get the land surveyed by the U.S. government so that it could be opened for legal settlement, Dunraven then went quietly to work. Employing a young and clearly talented Irish-Canadian mining engineer named Theodore Whyte, and resorting to methods that were at best questionable (and probably illegal), the earl soon gained direct title to some 5,000 acres of choice land, claims he would add to and not relinquish until 1908. Dunraven's plan was, in fact, a brilliant one. Control the springs and rivers and you control the land, and by carefully doing just that with the homestead titles he paid others to obtain, the Earl of Dunraven was able to claim ownership of much of the Estes Valley. In the years to come, Dunraven would be credited with the grandiose idea of carving a large hunting preserve out of the mountain wilderness to be used exclusively by himself and his aristocratic friends. There would even be tales of a cache of whiskey carefully hidden for future use.

While Dunraven's land grabbing was real enough, his principal motive was a practical one: the desire to secure the financial future of his three daughters (the earl had no direct male heir to inherit his ancestral estates) by investing in activities that would pay. Raising cattle in a generally temperate mountain valley was one way. Taking care of tourists was another. By the summer of 1877, the Earl of Dunraven had built and opened his Estes Park (or "English") Hotel on lower Fish Creek Road and established a sizable cattle ranching operation, using a site near the old Estes-Evans buildings.

Despite the Earl of Dunraven, there was ample room for others—and those others came. By 1875, a number of pioneer families had arrived to take up claims: the Jameses on Fall River, the MacGregors in the Black Canyon, the Fergusons above Marys Lake, the Hupps in Beaver Meadows, the Spragues in Moraine Park, and the Lambs in the Tahosa Valley at the foot of Longs Peak. Though they came like Joel Estes to ranch and farm, all but the Hupps were soon busy taking care of the needs of summer tourists, an activity that added substantially to their annual incomes. "The hotel business was forced upon us," Abner Sprague would later write. "We came here for small ranch operations, but guests and visitors became so numerous, at first wanting eggs, milk, and other provisions, then wanting lodging, and finally demanding full accommodations, that we had to go into the hotel business or go bankrupt from keeping free company!"

Estes Park, circa 1903

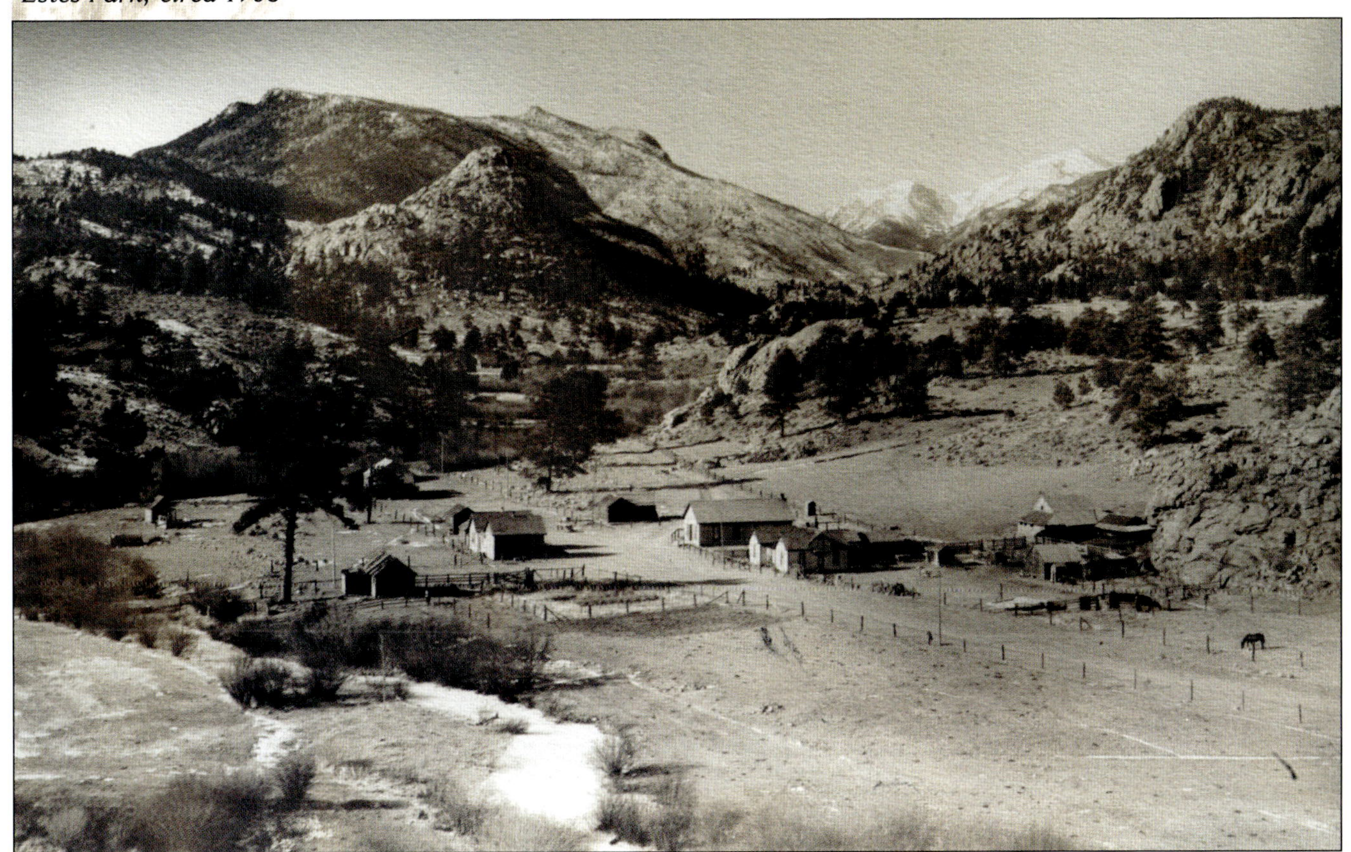

Initially there was a little friction between Theodore Whyte, who now was Dunraven's resident overseer, and the so-called "pioneers of '75." Whyte and his cowboys would try to intimidate the new arrivals into giving up their claims. But once they had resisted, peace and accommodation followed. Both Whyte and the settlers decided that they could live profitably side by side. "We began to neighbor," to quote Sprague once again, "as our jawing back and forth made us better acquainted, and as much friends as possible under the circumstances. We all began to see that the holding of so much of the Park by one company, even if it had been secured unlawfully, was the best thing for the place, particularly after it was proven that the place was only valuable on account of its location and its attraction for lovers of the out-of-doors...." By the end of the 1870s, Estes Park had a reputation as "the gem of the Rockies" and was attracting seasonal visitors from all over the world.

Estes Park received much more prominence and publicity in 1879 with the publication in London of Isabella Lucy Bird's *A Lady's Life in the Rocky Mountains*. In her sprightly book, the intrepid Victorian adventurer writes about her stay in Estes Park during the fall and early winter of 1873, when she boarded with the Evans family and participated in Griff Evans' cattle drives. She also told about her romantic interlude with the "desperado" known as "Rocky Mountain Jim," a mysterious hunter-rancher named James Nugent, who made his home in Muggins Gulch near the entrance to the park. It was Nugent who had half-dragged, half-carried Bird to the summit of Longs Peak, giving her the honor of being the second woman (after Eastern lyceum lecturer Anna Dickinson) to have officially made the strenuous trip. A year later Rocky Mountain Jim was fatally wounded by Griff Evans in a quarrel, for reasons that remain somewhat of a mystery, but whose roots are plain enough to see in the pages of Isabella Lucy Bird's remarkable book.

In the decade that followed, others would arrive and share the record of their visits by word and picture. These included the famous photographer William Henry Jackson, who first visited Estes Park in 1873 as head of the photographic party of Ferdinand V. Hayden's United States Geological and Geographical Survey of the Territories, and later on his own, leaving a rich legacy of striking black-and-white photographs of the Estes region. Jackson, however, was probably not the first one. That honor likely belongs to William G. Chamberlain, who began taking pictures in Denver in June 1861 and during the next 15 years, it is said, produced more photographs than any other photographer in Colorado. It was probably Chamberlain's stereo photograph of the Estes-Evans ranch that became the source of the illustration published in Bird's *A Lady's Life in the Rocky Mountains*.

There was also the equally remarkable Frederick Hastings Chapin, the partner in a Connecticut drug wholesale business who brought his camera and glass plates to Estes Park during the summers of 1887 and 1888, and then wrote about his adventures in *Mountaineering in Colorado: The Peaks About Estes Park*, published by Boston's famous Appalachian Mountain Club in 1889, complete with his own photographs. Other early photographers whose pictures captured scenes of Estes Park include F. E. Baker, Henry C. Rogers, William T. Parke, Enos A. Mills, Louis C. McClure, and, of course, Fred Payne Clatworthy, who had pioneered the photographic process known as "autochrome" and gained nationwide attention for the photographs that appeared regularly in the pages of *National Geographic*. Their collective legacy was to help establish the spectacular beauty of Estes Park and the Colorado West firmly in the minds of increasingly mobile and vacation-oriented Americans.

The first decade of the 20th century brought some important and exciting changes to the valley of Estes Park. In 1902, a young mountain guide and budding naturalist named Enos A. Mills, who had arrived in Estes Park in 1884 as a sickly youth of 14 from the family farm in eastern Kansas, bought the Lambs' Longs Peak House and renamed it Longs Peak Inn. Despite a disastrous fire in 1906, Mills rebuilt his rustic inn into one of the best-known mountain resorts in the nation and then, beginning in 1909, turned his attention, energy, and considerable talents to lobbying for the creation of a new national park in the Estes region.

Freelan O. Stanley, the coinventor with his identical twin brother F. E. Stanley of the famous Stanley Steamer, came to Estes Park in June 1903, stricken with tuberculosis. Stanley not only recovered his health, but began building a spacious "cottage" on Wonderview. Estes Park became Stanley's summer home. By 1907, he had begun construction of the 11 buildings that make up the world-famous "all-electric" Stanley Hotel, one of the great resort hotels of Colorado and the West. In 1909, he built a small hydroplant on Fall River to power his hotel complex.

The third important event of the decade occurred in 1905, when Cornelius H. Bond of Loveland, together with several of his associates, purchased the John Cleave quarter section situated at the confluence of the Big Thompson River and Fall River for the purpose of establishing a new town. Platted that spring, commercial and residential lots sold briskly, building began, and by the end of the decade a small village was substantially in place.

Until the 20th century, the roads into and out of the Estes Valley remained almost as problematic as in Joel Estes' and Griff Evans' time: difficult in all seasons, impassable in some, and totally unprepared to handle the new age of the automobile. In 1904, this began to change, when a new road from Loveland was forced through the wilderness of the Big Thompson Canyon. We have a marvelous photographic record of that first summer thanks to the work of Fred Payne Clatworthy, who came up from Loveland with his mother and sister, camping and taking views along the way. The road remained single-tracked until 1919, forcing drivers to seek pullouts to avoid oncoming traffic. By the summer of 1907 David Osborn and his sons were using the road to bring visitors in

Stanley Steamers to and from the valley. The next year, F. O. Stanley established an auto stage line of his own on the North St. Vrain road from Longmont and Lyons, which he had previously reconstructed for the purpose. Within a few years, both routes were making use of the Stanley Mountain Wagon, a big, sturdy 12-seater designed by F. O. Stanley specifically for hauling large loads of passengers and freight over the mountain roads of Colorado. These larger automobiles had come just in time, for the establishment of Rocky Mountain National Park in 1915 brought thousands of visitors bound for Estes Park to Denver and the valley railheads.

The early years of the new century also saw the establishment of additional accommodations for tourists, beginning in 1906 with the building of the steam-heated Hupp Hotel in the very center of the newly platted village and its across-the-street neighbor, the Manford, erected in 1908. The Stanley Hotel opened with considerable fanfare in June of the next year with the arrival by steamer caravan of some 125 members of the Colorado Pharmacal Association.

A new burst of hotel and resort building followed the dedication of the national park in September 1915. In addition to the now greatly expanded lodges and ranches of the "pioneers of '75," by 1920 visitors had many choices. These included the Rustic on the rim of Devils Gulch in the north end; Horseshoe Lodge and Fall River Lodge in Horseshoe Park; Spragues Lodge on Glacier Creek (Abner Sprague had turned his original resort in Moraine Park over to Chicagoan James Stead in 1904); the Brinwood Hotel and Moraine Park Lodge in Moraine Park; The Crags Hotel on Prospect Mountain near town; Baldpate Inn, Hewes-Kirkwood Inn, and the Columbine Lodge in the Tahosa Valley; and the Lewiston, Josephine, Sherwood, and National Park Hotels and Prospect Inn in the village. By the mid-1920s, in fact, the footprint of the village of Estes Park, much as we know it today, was very much in place.

Despite the impact of the Depression on many resort communities, Estes Park in the 1930s—thanks to its close proximity to Denver and the Midwest—continued to enjoy its reputation as a summer vacation destination. But there were also some significant changes. The decade saw the major reconstruction of the Big Thompson, North St. Vrain, and South St. Vrain roads (known today as Highways 34, 36, and 7), which transformed the problematic mountain roads into wide, dust-free modern highways. It also ushered in the beginnings of the Colorado–Big Thompson Project, which brought badly needed water from Grand Lake and the new Shadow Mountain Reservoir built in Middle Park across the Continental Divide (and under Rocky Mountain National Park) by means of the world's longest transmountain

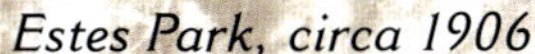

Estes Park, circa 1906

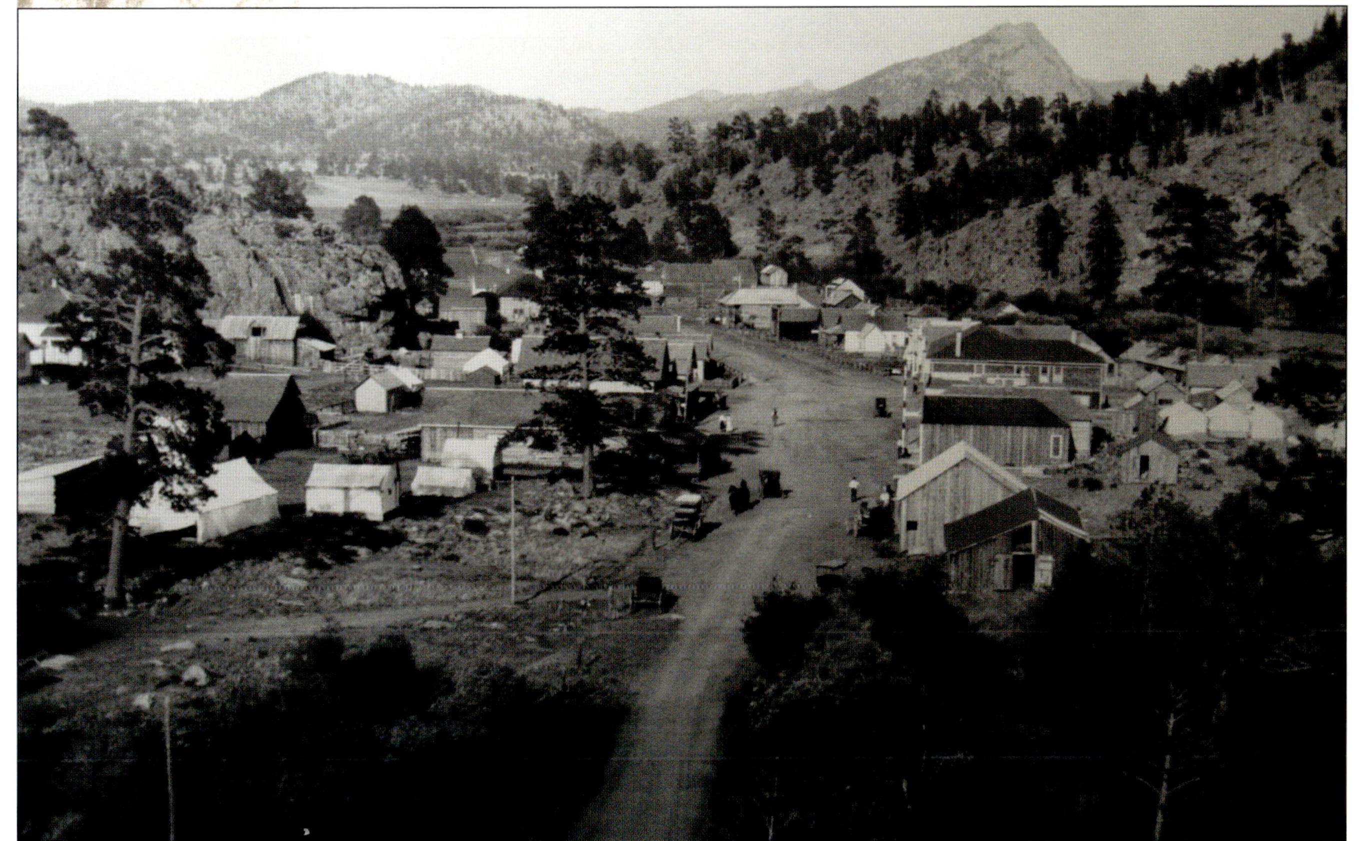

Photo by C. A. Graves

irrigation tunnel. The 13-mile Alva B. Adams Tunnel was successfully "holed through" in 1944, and four years later the completion of Olympus Dam, the creation of Lake Estes, and the construction of new power plants at Marys Lake and Lake Estes dramatically changed the view from Park Hill that so enchanted Joel Estes and other early visitors.

The decade of the 1930s also saw the beginning of major changes within Rocky Mountain National Park, as for the first time resources became available for the acquisition of private property, or "inholdings," including land that contained many of the lodges and resorts that decades of visitors had come to identify fondly with the "national park experience." These private holdings were considerable. They consisted of more than 11,000 acres that had been homesteaded before the park was created in 1915, plus an additional 2,000 acres that were subsequently added to the park through boundary changes. East of the Continental Divide, these private lands were for the most part concentrated in Beaver Meadows and in Moraine, Horseshoe, Tuxedo, and Hollowell Parks. On the west side of the park, they extended roughly from the site of Lulu City on the Colorado River south to Grand Lake. Owners were given the option of selling their lands outright, or selling and retaining control through 20-year leases.

The first inholding purchase came in October 1931, when for $32,500 the Park Service acquired the 120-acre tract in Horseshoe Park containing the Horseshoe Inn. This was followed in the spring of 1932 by additional purchases, including the Chapman and Sprague homesteads and Moraine Park Lodge in Moraine Park, Abner Sprague's lodge on Glacier Creek in Glacier Basin, and Jack Wood's cabin camp in Tuxedo Park near what was then the park's Big Thompson River entrance adjacent to the YMCA. By the end of 1932, the Park Service had concluded some 20 separate transactions and acquired 4,414 acres of land for a total of $435,316. The largest purchase was the old Hondius ranch in Beaver Meadows and Horseshoe Park and the Brinwood Hotel in Moraine Park. The most important acquisition on the western side of the park occurred in September 1940, when the Park Service obtained the Harbison estate, with its 226 acres of meadow- and timberland along the Colorado River that had once been the homesteads of sisters Annie and Kitty Harbison.

Whenever lodge and resort owners sold outright, the Park Service almost immediately began to raze buildings and obliterate footprints, in a number of instances making use of the young men from the park's Civilian Conservation Corps (CCC) camps. Within months, Horseshoe Park Inn, a fixture at the mouth of Endovalley for more than two decades, disappeared. So, too, did Moraine Park Lodge, where only the recreation hall was retained for later use as a museum. This was but the beginning. One by one as their leases ran out, or through subsequent purchase, the historic old wooden lodges passed into history, with even their locations difficult to recall: Bear Lake Lodge and Camp Woods in 1958; Forest Inn at The Pool and Fall River Lodge in 1959; the Brinwood Hotel, Deer Ridge Chalet, and Spragues Lodge in 1960; Stead's Ranch in 1963; and Fern Lake Lodge in 1976. Many of these structures had become the victims of time and the elements, and their passing, though regretted by old-timers, seemed barely worthy of notice. Their disappearance nonetheless brought to a close an important chapter in park history.

Changes to downtown Estes Park, though in the aggregate just as dramatic, came far more slowly. As one can tell from the panoramic view of the village and from other photographs included here, the vacant lots and downtown residences have disappeared. Parking lots and stores have replaced the liveries that once anchored Elkhorn Avenue (where the horses, turned loose by their riders at the end of a day on the trail, trotted home alongside automobiles, further congesting traffic). Many of the original store buildings and hotels have new facades and new purposes. Other businesses and amusements—including the once very popular Riverside Amusement Park, with its dance pavilion, swimming pool, and Dark Horse Tavern—have come and gone.

The biggest changes to the village are not its widened and paved streets, its decorative street lighting, or the fact that the telephone and electrical poles that once lined Elkhorn Avenue have been relocated to the rear alley—all of which were accomplished by 1930. The village's most dramatic change since the 1920s came in a few hours' time. It occurred on the morning of July 15, 1982, when a wall of water, sweeping down Fall River from a ruptured farmer's cooperative dam at Lawn Lake high in Rocky Mountain National Park, devastated the downtown area, caused millions of dollars in damage, and forced the town and its citizens to contemplate new beginnings. From the tragedy of the Lawn Lake flood came the creation of an urban renewal district (EPURA) with sufficient taxing authority to recreate and beautify the center of Estes Park, and add new parks and an east-west riverwalk along the Big Thompson and Fall Rivers. All this makes for a town very different from the years when F. O. Stanley was allowed to leave his parked automobile in front of the Estes Park Bank, or anyplace else he chose, simply by virtue of the fact that he was "Mr. Stanley, the Grand Old Man of Estes Park."

In short, Estes Park, its surrounding valley, and its adjacent national park have changed a great deal in the century and a half since Joel and Milton Estes stood at the crest of Park Hill and surveyed the open scene below. The following pages are dedicated to documenting those changes by using photographs to measure "what was" with "what is"—and by so doing, to help promote a better understanding of the rich and complex history of Estes Park and Rocky Mountain National Park.

Estes Park village, circa 1923

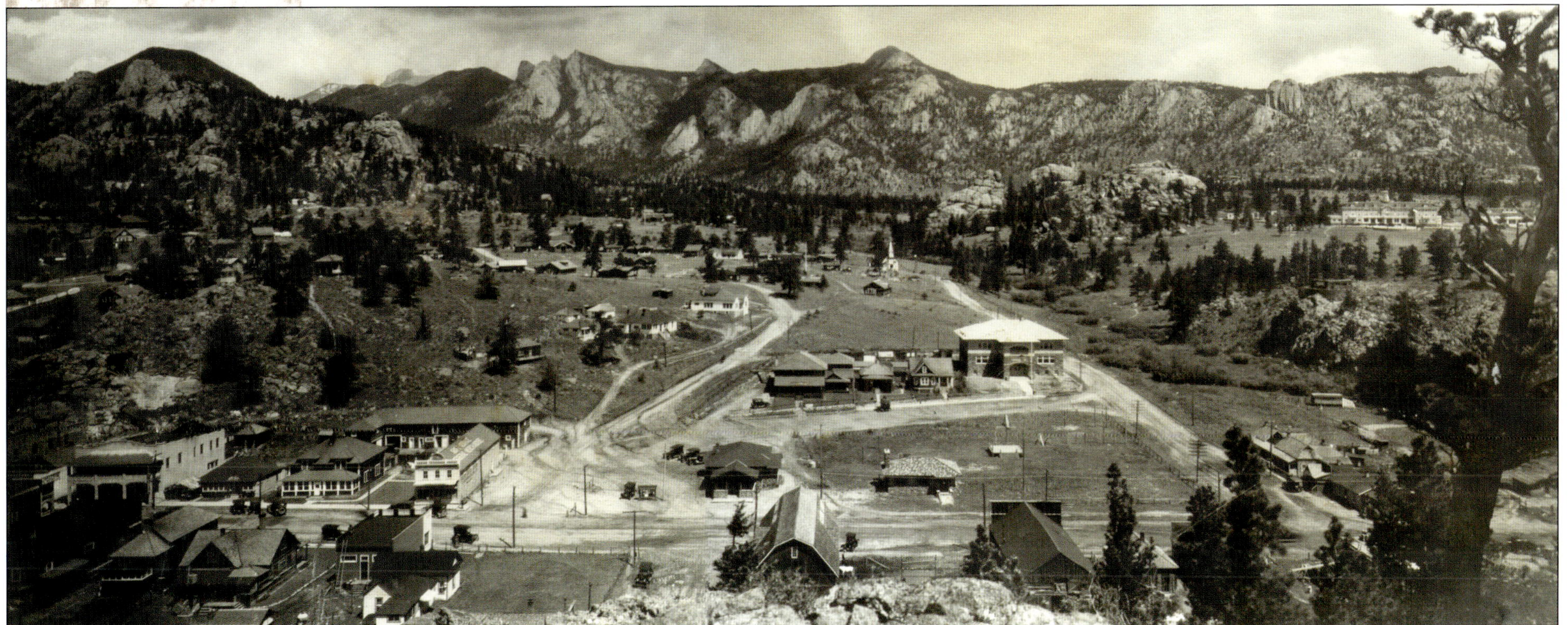

Estes Valley Scenes and Sites

1. Estes Park from Park Hill, circa 1900

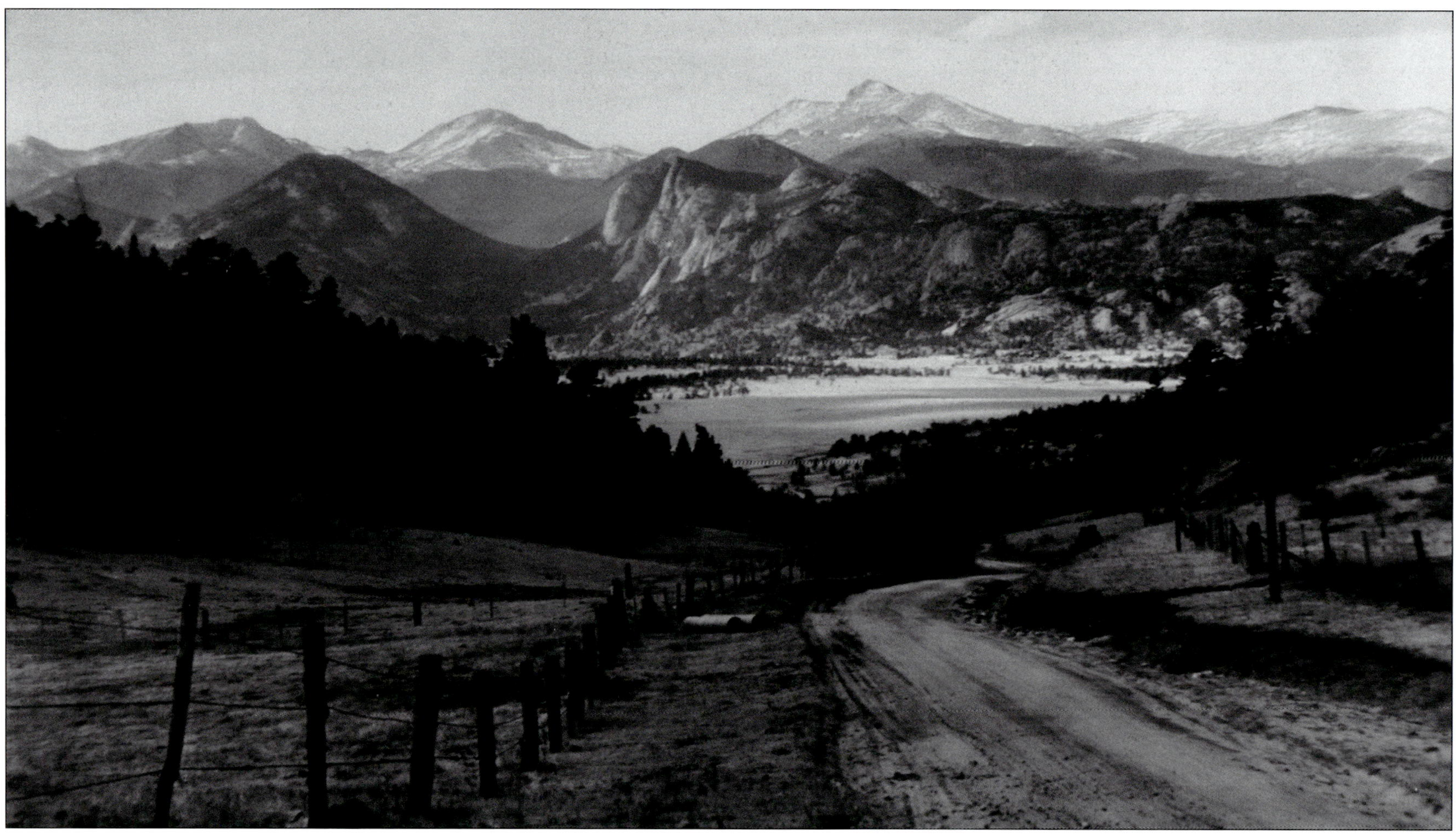

It was from here, the crest of Park Hill on today's Highway 36, that Joel Estes and his son, Milton, first looked down on the valley in mid-October 1859. Framed by the spectacular peaks of the Front Range, the region would soon bear their name. Milton Estes later wrote of the awe and wonder with which father and son surveyed the scene below, calling it "a grand sight and a great surprise," emotions that today's travelers often share. This view quickly became a favorite subject for photographers, professional and amateur alike. As if to add to the picturesqueness, and to force travelers to stop and take advantage of the view, a gated fence stood for some years at the crest of the hill to prevent cattle grazing in the gulch below from wandering too far from home. This grassy,

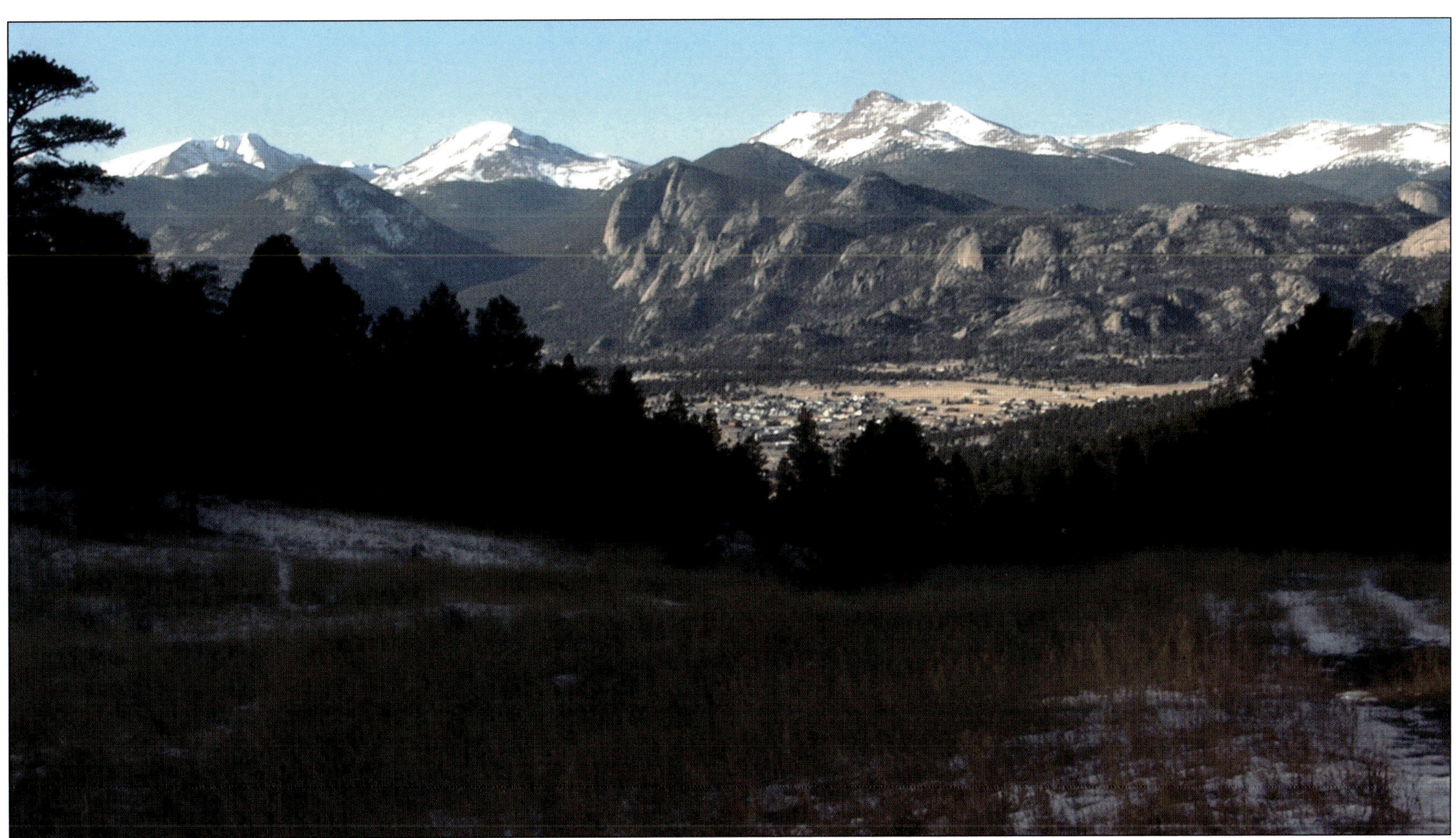

tree-lined gulch, known as Muggins Gulch after the nickname of an early tenant, also was the home of the famous "Rocky Mountain Jim" (see p. 16).

The original road coming up Muggins Gulch and across Park Hill was located immediately to the left of the present road. That road, once it reached the top of the hill, crossed today's Highway 36, and then ran down to enter Estes Park through the long draw that comes through the Crocker ranch. Both draw and road are still clearly visible as one begins the descent to the valley floor. The most obvious difference between the two photographs is the mushrooming development that now greets visitors as they obtain their first view of Joel Estes' valley.

2. "Rocky Mountain Jim" Cabin Site

Close by the gates of the park we discovered an open cabin. It was built of unhewn logs, and covered with earth. The door and window were gone, and the paths that once led to it were overgrown with bramble. We learned that this had once been the home of Mountain Jim, who, during his life, had been known as trapper, hunter, fisherman, and guide.... The desolate cabin still serves as a monument to his memory; and it is pointed out to strangers, the thrilling events of his strange life and tragic death are related; all of which have become historically associated with the park.

So wrote visitor S. Anna Gordon in her 1879 book *Camping in Colorado*. By then, James Nugent, better known as "Rocky Mountain Jim," had been dead for five years, fatally shot in April 1874 by the usually welcoming Welshman, Griffith J. "Griff" Evans, in what remains one of Estes Park's great mysteries.

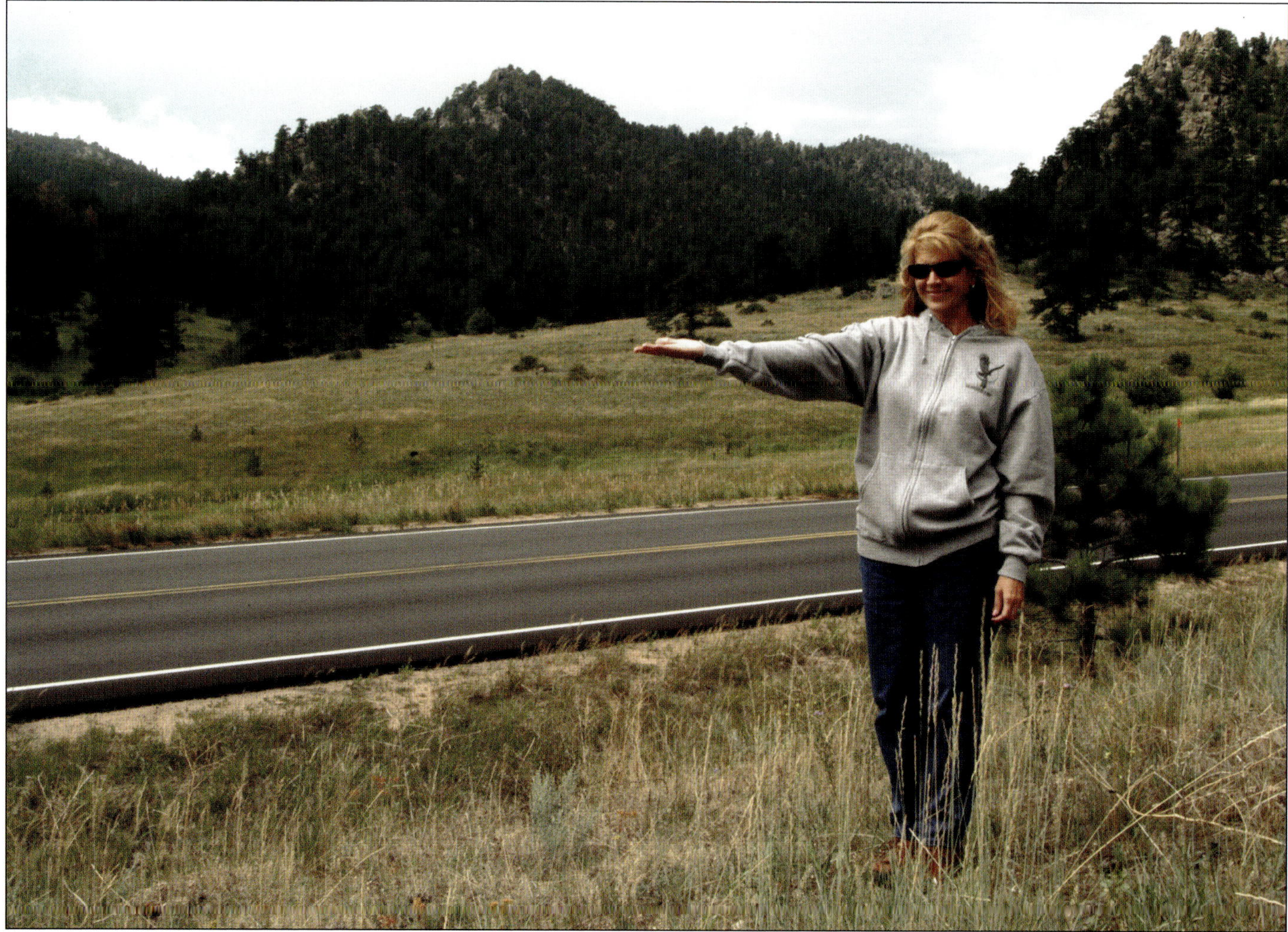

Rocky Mountain Jim lives on in the pages of Isabella Bird's famous 1879 volume, *A Lady's Life in the Rocky Mountains*, as a "desperado" and "ruffian," two things he probably was not. We know that Nugent lost an eye to a bear in Middle Park in July 1871. He soon took up a squatter's claim in Muggins Gulch, building his cabin just below the old Meadowdale Ranch, which is today's Harvest House for Women. Tradition says Jim's cabin was sited so he could keep an eye on anyone coming from or going to Estes Park. As seen in our photographs, Nugent chose well. We believe his cabin was located near the tree and rock that Denise Clinger, photographer Mic Clinger's wife, points to in the upper center of the first photograph. The second photograph is of the area believed to be where Nugent's

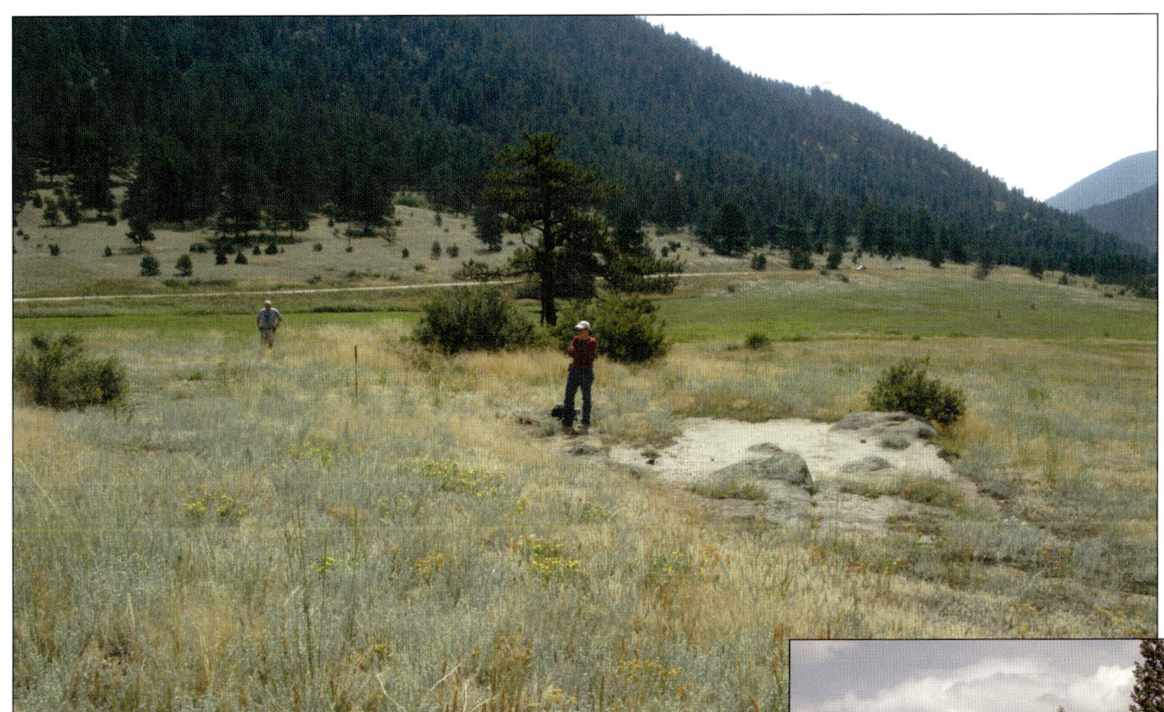

barn was located, where coauthor Carey Stevanus is seen standing. Coauthor Jim Pickering is standing near the probable location of his rustic cabin; Highway 36 can be seen in the distance. Nugent's water source, "Jim's Spring," is north of the cabin site, as seen in the third photograph. Now enclosed by a wooden springhouse, it is visible near Highway 36.

We do not know what Nugent's cabin looked like. His "den," as Bird calls it, was in decay by Gordon's time. Soon it was gone, its site all but forgotten. In Gordon and Bird's day, the cabin site was located "not far from the track" up Muggins Gulch. When Highway 36 was reconstructed in the 1930s, it was relocated to higher ground to provide a better roadbed. The site itself provides few clues that it was briefly the home of one of the most famous, and tragic, figures in early Estes Park history.

3. Estes Park from Mount Olympus, circa 1903

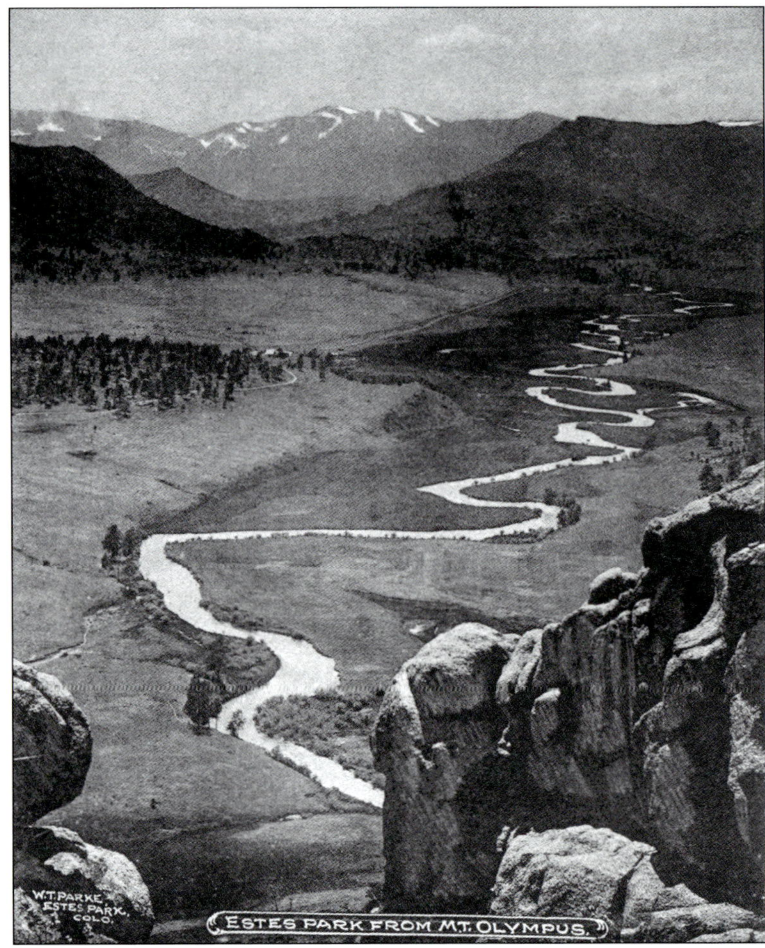

Photo by William T. Parke

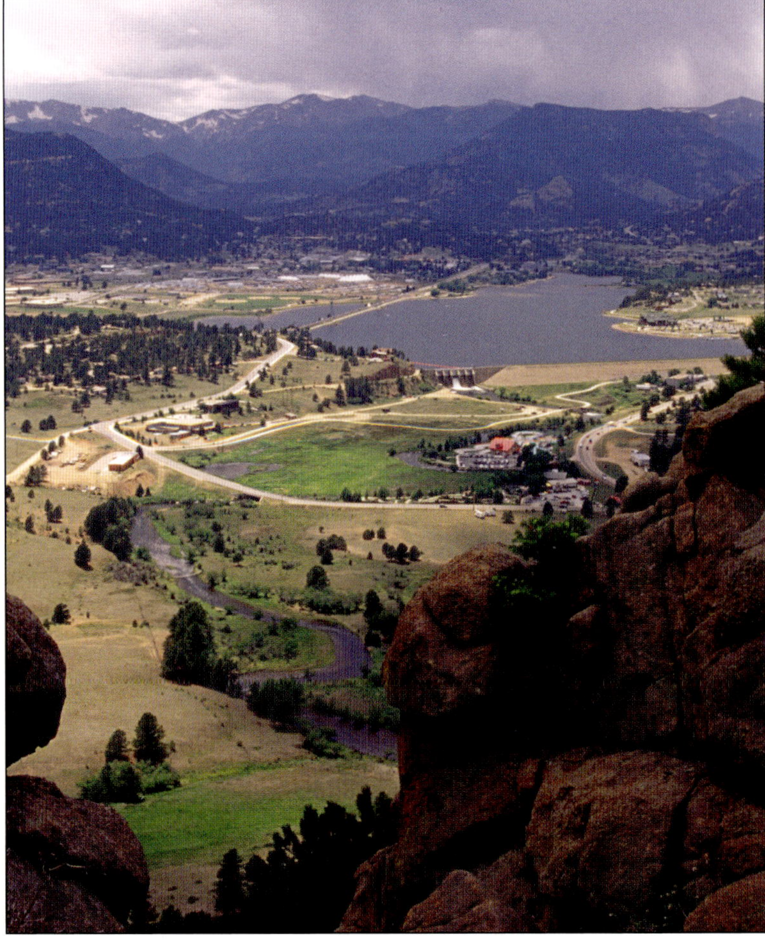

These photographs were shot from Mount Olympus, which at an elevation of 8,806 feet guards the eastern portal of the Estes Valley. The mountain apparently was named by Fernando C. Willett, who gave up the position of high school principal in Evansville, Indiana, because of ill health to come to Estes Park to tutor Griff Evans' children in May 1873. The photograph was taken around 1903 by Estes Park photographer William T. Parke, who ran a photo and curio shop (see p. 100) and produced his own line of postcard views of local scenes. (The unmistakable design of the postcard's caption identifies the photograph as Parke's work.) The site was a popular one for such early photographers as Enos A. Mills, Fred Payne Clatworthy, and J. R. Riddle of Topeka, Kansas.

Parke's turn-of-the-century photograph shows Estes Park with the Big Thompson River meandering through an open meadow. The only sign of civilization is the road from Lyons, which descended Park Hill through what is now the Crocker ranch, swung left past the Dunraven ranch (which is just visible in the photograph), and then turned west toward the small cluster of buildings that then constituted all there was of the future village.

The contemporary photograph shows how much the Estes Valley has changed. What was open grassy meadow is now dominated by Lake Estes, built in 1948 as part of the Colorado–Big Thompson Project. When the lake was created, the North St. Vrain road from Lyons (today's Highway 36) was redirected across the causeway dike visible here. The eastern arm of the lake hides the site of the Dunraven ranch buildings in the original photograph. Seen in the new photo are the buildings in Stanley Park, a gift of F. O. Stanley to the town.

4. Estes-Evans-Dunraven Ranch

When English traveler Isabella Bird visited Estes Park in 1873, she lodged with the Griff Evans family at the ranch at the base of Park Hill, which Griff had taken over from Joel Estes in 1867 and then enlarged and opened to tourists. What Estes' first buildings looked like we can only surmise, but from the reports of early visitors we know that they consisted of several crude log cabins with corral and barn nearby. It was probably Griff Evans, however, who dammed Fish Creek to create the small lake seen in later photographs.

By the time of Bird's arrival, other cabins had been added, including the poorly chinked cabin by the lake in which she stayed. She describes the Evans ranch as consisting of a "very trim-looking log cabin, with a flat mud roof, with four smaller ones." Nearby, "picturesquely dotted" along the stream issuing from the lake, were "two corrals, a long shed, [and] a log dairy with a waterwheel." The drawing she provides her readers, *My Home in the Rocky Mountains* (p. 21), seems to have been made from an early stereographic view such as the one reproduced here (p. 20), titled "Long's Peak from Evan's [sic] Ranch," by Denver photographer William G. Chamberlain. It shows only a central cabin with a chimney, enlarged by additions, and two nearby cabins. Neither Bird's drawing nor Chamberlain's photograph shows the corrals, shed, or dairy mentioned in her description, although these structures undoubtedly were located to the north and east, as they were in later days. Moreover, in both sketch and photograph, the central Estes-Evans cabin has a peaked roof rather than the flat mud one which Bird describes, though this discrepancy may be due to improvements made to the roof since Bird's visit of 1873. Since Chamberlain references Griff Evans in the title of his photograph, it can probably be dated 1876 or 1877. A brief December

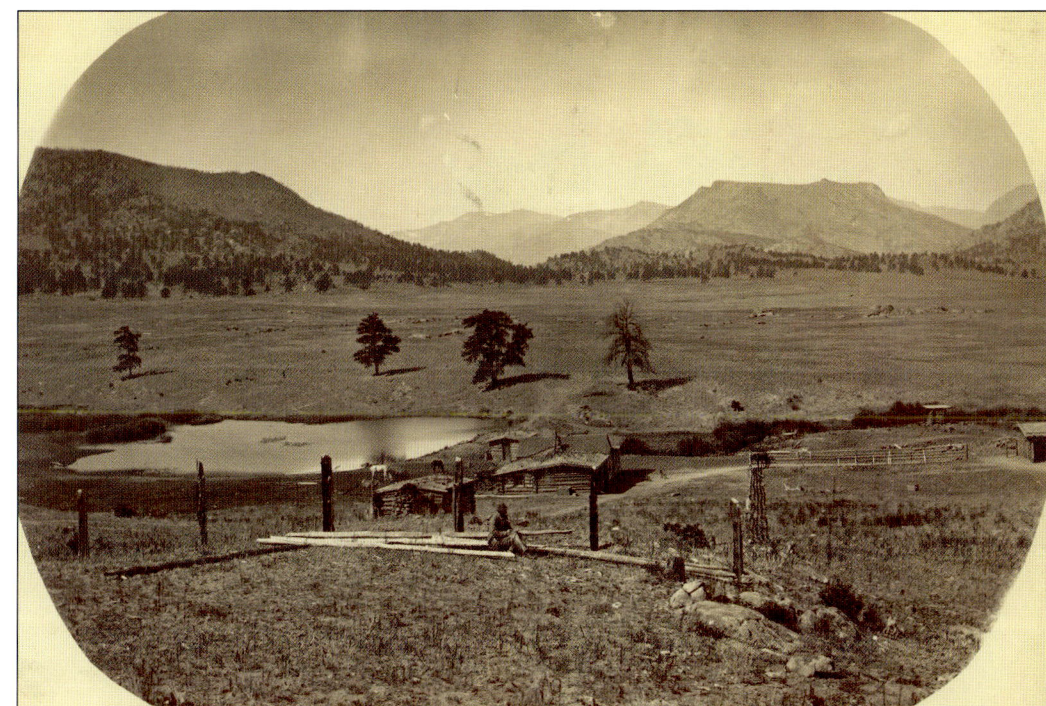

Estes-Evans ranch, circa 1876–1877

Photos by William G. Chamberlain

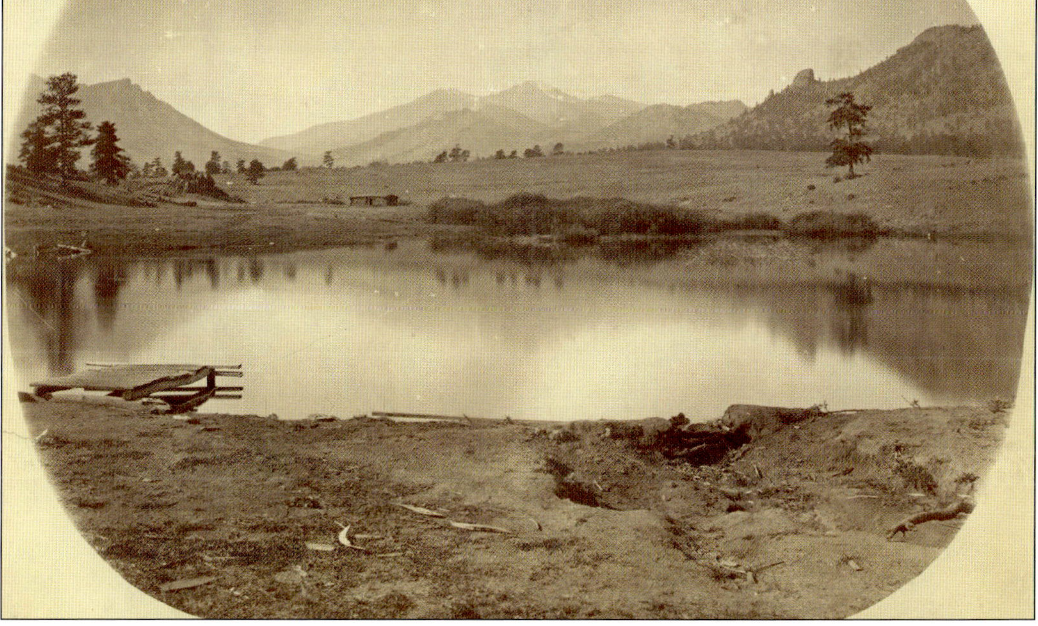

"Long's Peak from Evan's Ranch," 1877 or 1878 (originally a stereoscopic view)

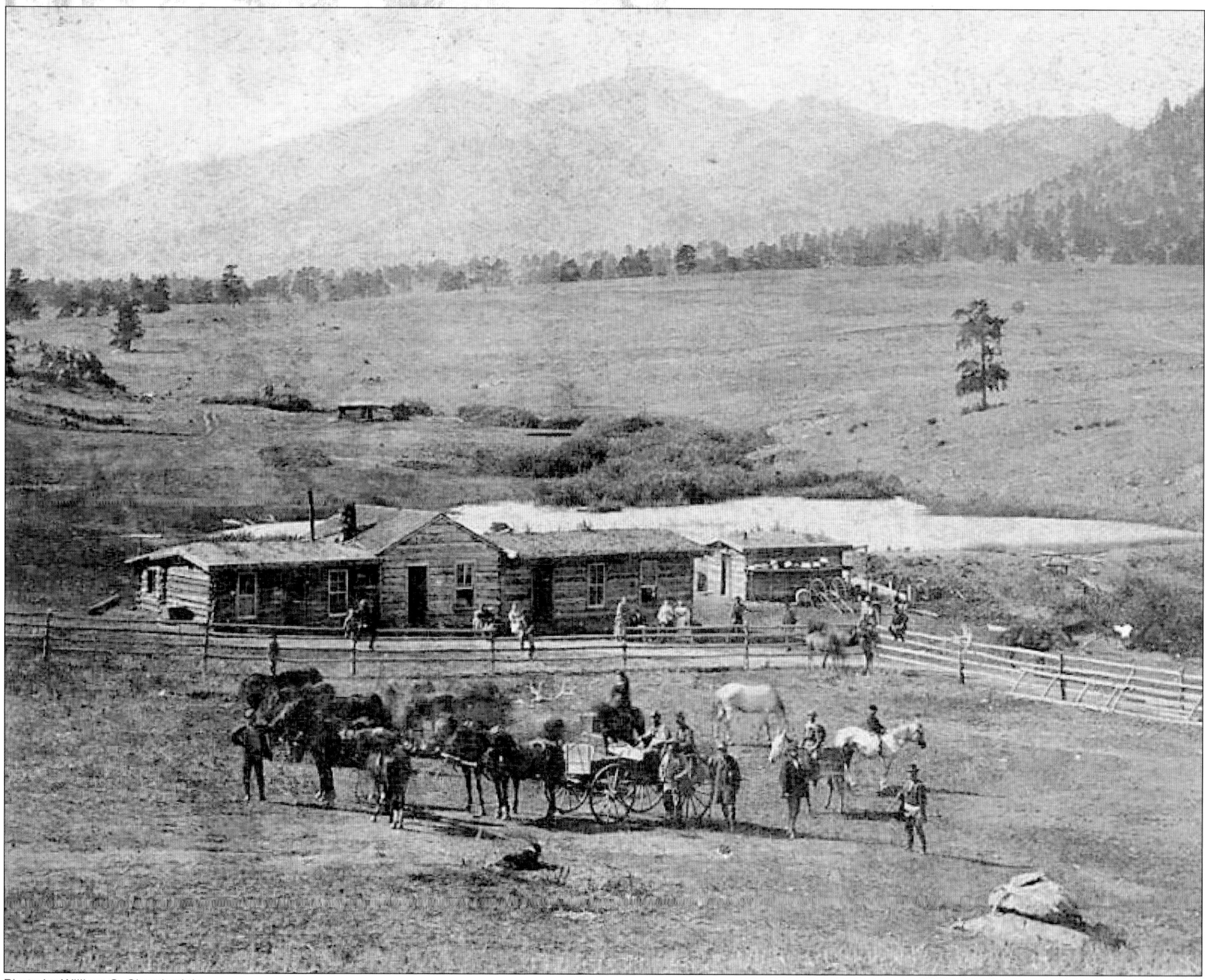

Photo by William G. Chamberlain

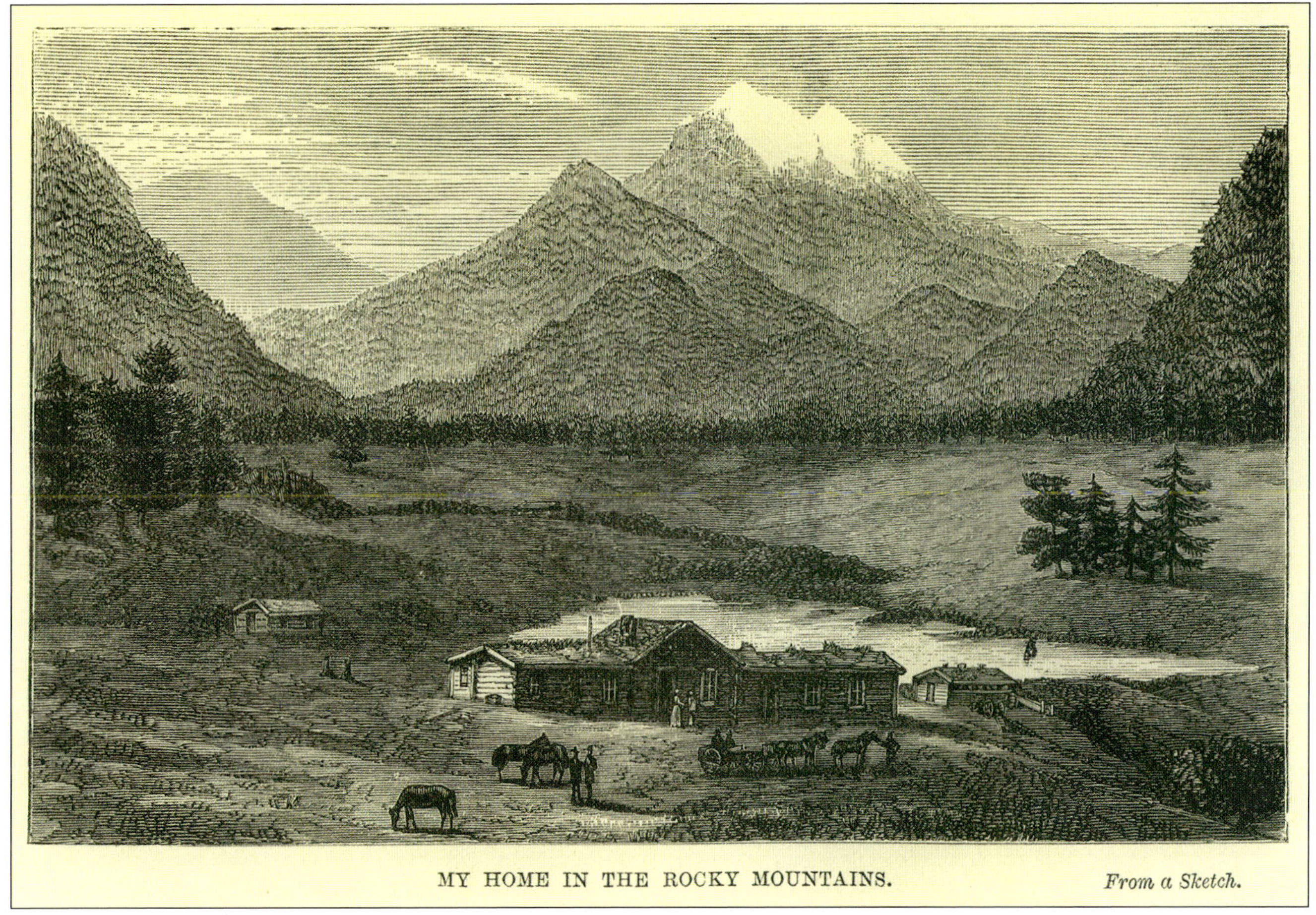

MY HOME IN THE ROCKY MOUNTAINS. *From a Sketch.*

1877 article in the *Greeley Tribune* reported that Evans' house and post office had been destroyed by fire, presumably late the previous month. Two other early photographs of the Estes-Evans ranch have also survived. Again, both come from Chamberlain's camera and appear to have been taken at an even earlier date, for there are as yet no fences in front of the ranch house.

Evans sold his holdings to the Earl of Dunraven in the fall of 1878. Dunraven's foreman, Theodore Whyte, then expanded them into the Dunraven ranch, which the earl and his overseers used in connection with their sizable cattle operation, and with the resort business begun a year earlier with the construction of the Estes Park Hotel farther south on Fish Creek. The original Estes-Evans cabin was soon replaced by a new and somewhat larger house with peaked roof and two wings located to the north of its predecessor. This building is clearly visible in subsequent photographs, including the panoramic view that was taken in 1935 (see pp. 28–29).

The photograph taken from the south looking down upon the ranch (p. 22) clearly shows that, well before 1900, the Estes-Evans ranch had been expanded, with a number of new buildings added. The two largest, both located east of Fish Creek, across and slightly south of the Estes-Evans cabins and its successor, were the manager's house and a building called the Dunraven chapel. The latter caught fire and burned to the ground in 1905. The tent in the foreground most likely belongs to the tubercular colony operated during the mid-1890s by celebrated Swiss physician Dr. Carl Ruedi, a well-published expert on the effect of climate on consumption. Ruedi had come to Denver in 1891 from Davos, Switzerland, where he had supervised a world-famous sanitarium. We know

Estes-Evans ranch, circa 1895

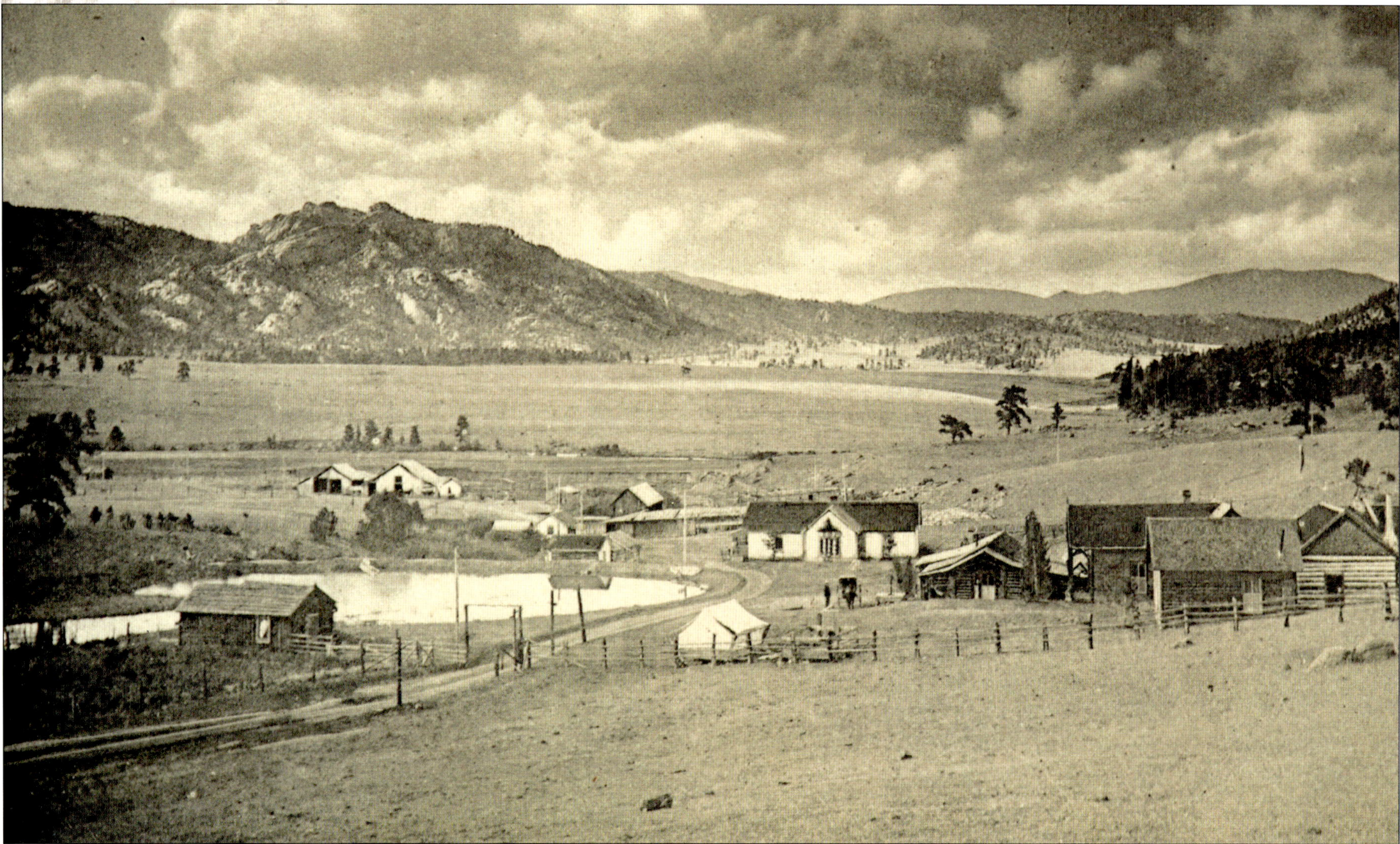

that his tent camp, which drew a number of patients from the sanitarium in Hygiene near Lyons, was located a sufficient distance from the Estes Park Hotel so as not to disturb or alarm the regular customers. Interestingly enough, a number of the fence posts on the hillside seen in the photograph still remain in place.

After the purchase of the Dunraven holdings in 1907 by Burton Sanborn and F. O. Stanley, the Dunraven ranch was operated by a series of individuals on a lease basis until 1947, when the remaining buildings were removed to make way for the construction of Lake Estes. The lake was one of the final components of the Colorado–Big Thompson Project, whose waters soon obliterated

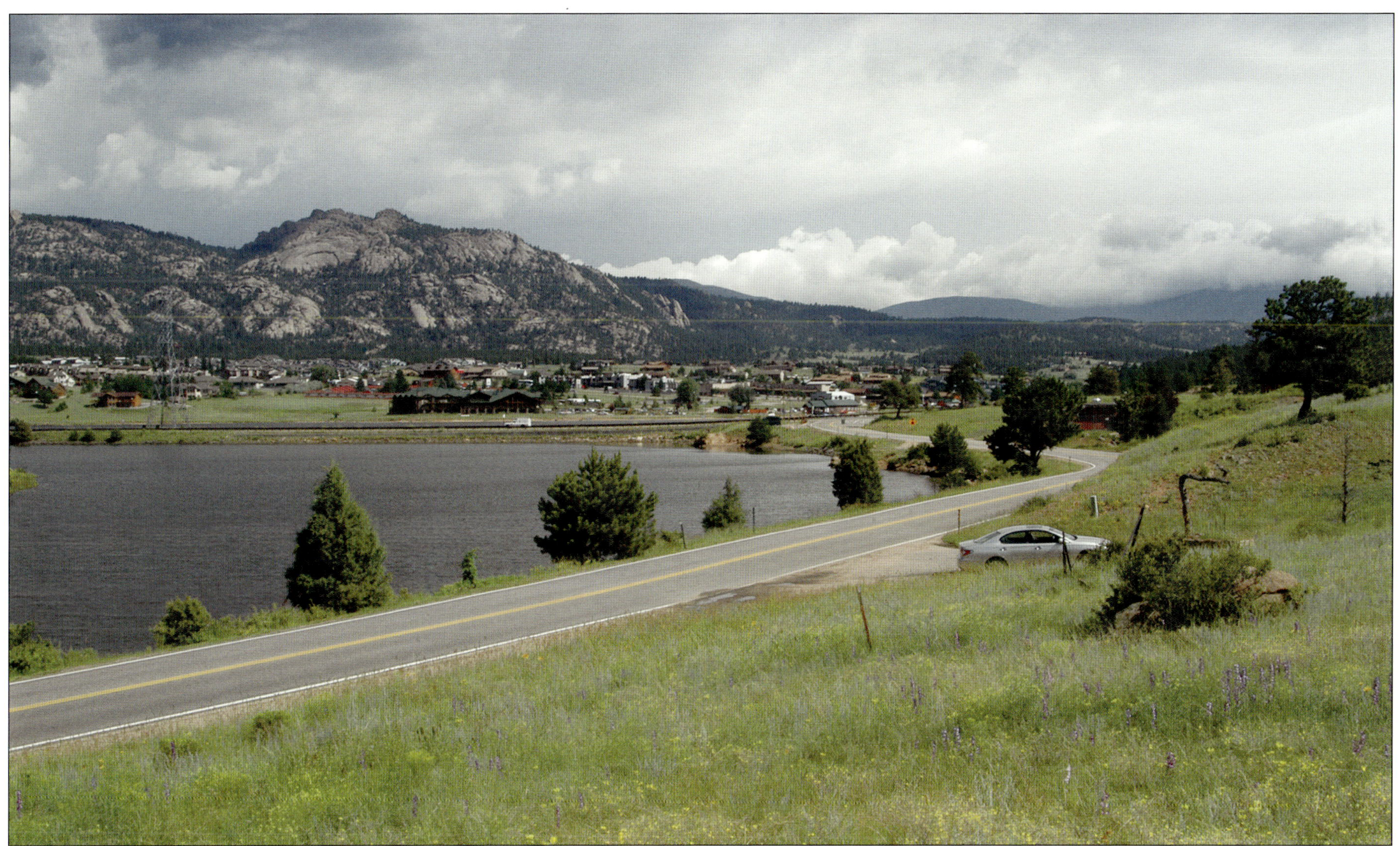

the site. The buildings of the Estes-Evans-Dunraven ranch against the mountains of the Front Range are clearly visible in the panoramic view taken in January 1935 by ranger John Preston of Rocky Mountain National Park as a series of three separate photographs.

It becomes clear when the old and new photographs are juxtaposed that Fish Creek Road has been relocated to the east on higher ground, and its roadbed somewhat altered after it curves around the large outcropping of rocks across from today's high school building. It was while coming down this road from the south on an April morning in 1874 that "Rocky Mountain Jim" was fired upon and mortally wounded by Griff Evans. The alteration of Fish Creek Road occurred in the late 1940s when Lake Estes was constructed, forever submerging the footings of the Estes-Evans-Dunraven ranch in the muddy bottom of the lake bed.

Estes-Evans-Dunraven ranch, circa 1900

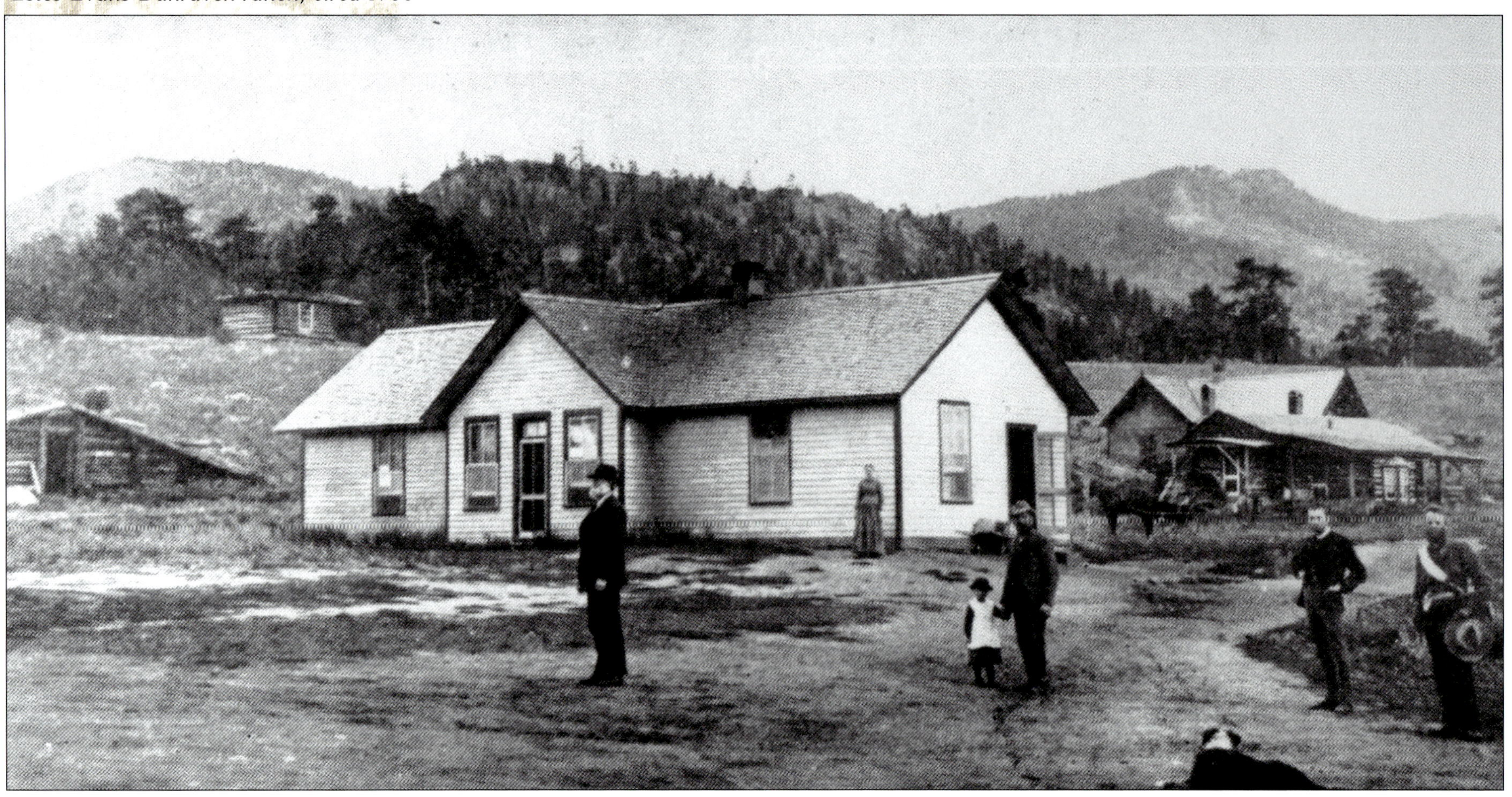

Identifying the photographs and illustrations: On page 19 are early photographs taken by Denver photographer William G. Chamberlain. They come from a scrapbook album of Denver and Colorado views dated 1861–1881 and given by Chamberlain's family to the Denver Public Library. *Page 20:* The Chamberlain photograph of the Evans ranch (originally a stereoptic view), probably taken in 1877 or 1878. *Page 21:* Isabella Bird's sketch, *My Home in the Rocky Mountains,* included in her book, *A Lady's Life in the Rocky Mountains* (1879). *Page 22:* A photograph taken in the mid-1890s looking north down the hillside on the Estes-Evans ranch with a tent in the foreground. *Above and opposite:* A photograph of the house that replaced the Evans house, taken from what is now Lake Estes, circa 1900, and juxtaposed with a contemporary view of the site. The figure standing in the center foreground is said to be Englishman John Cleave, who had

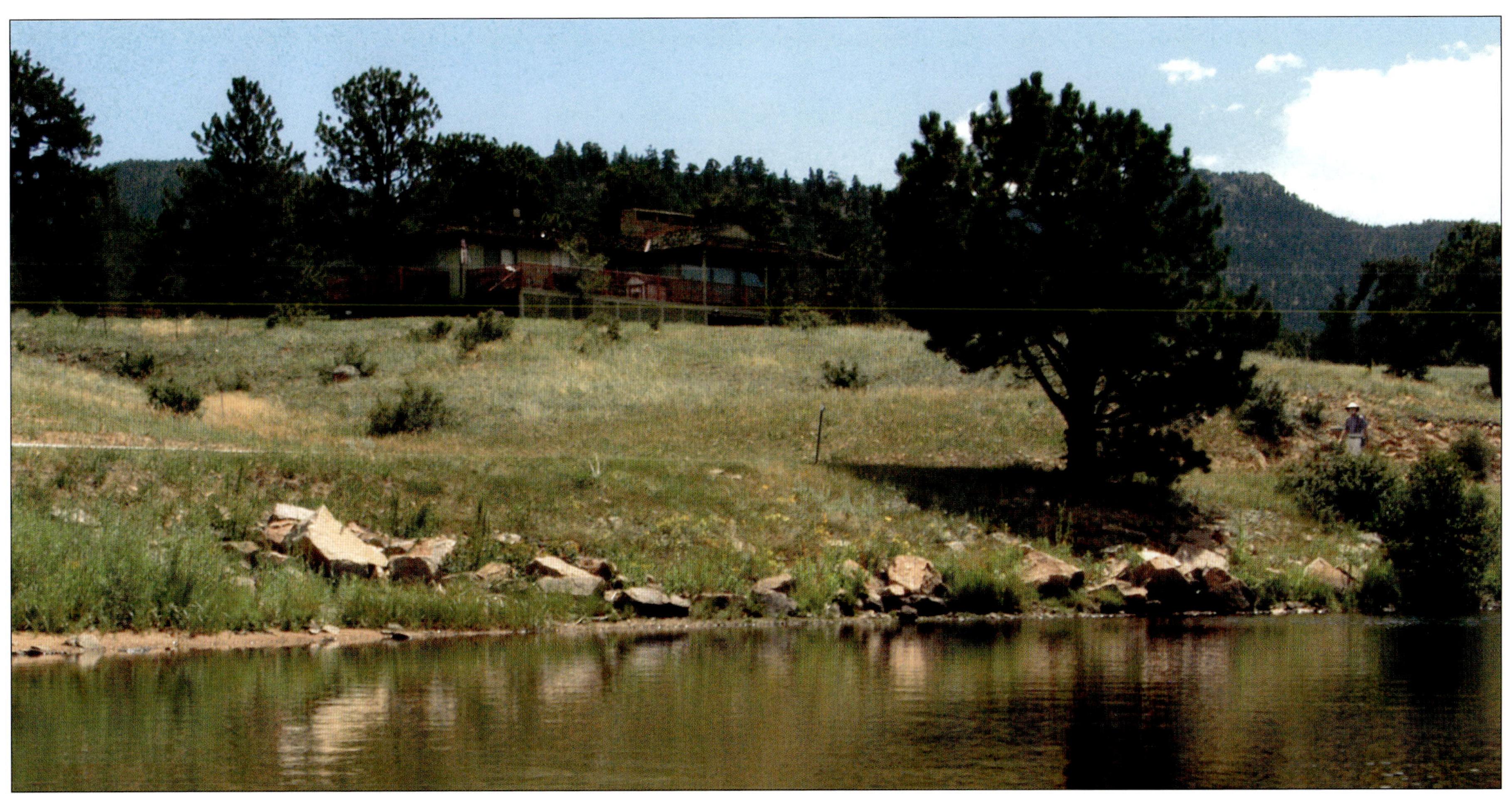

come to Estes Park from Chicago to help build Dunraven's cottage and hotel. *Page 26:* A photograph of the Evans House taken by Fred Payne Clatworthy in 1904. It was then called Lake View House, and was being managed, together with the Earl of Dunraven's Estes Park interests, by Frank G. Bartholf. Bartholf had homesteaded what would become the city of Loveland, and at his death in 1923 was said to be the richest man in Larimer County. *Pages 28–29:* John Preston's 1935 panoramic view of the buildings of the Estes-Evans-Dunraven ranch and a contemporary photograph of the same scene. The barns at the far right are those of the Dunraven ranch, which like the rest of the site were sacrificed to the needs of the Colorado–Big Thompson transmountain irrigation project of the 1930s and 1940s.

Lake View House, 1904

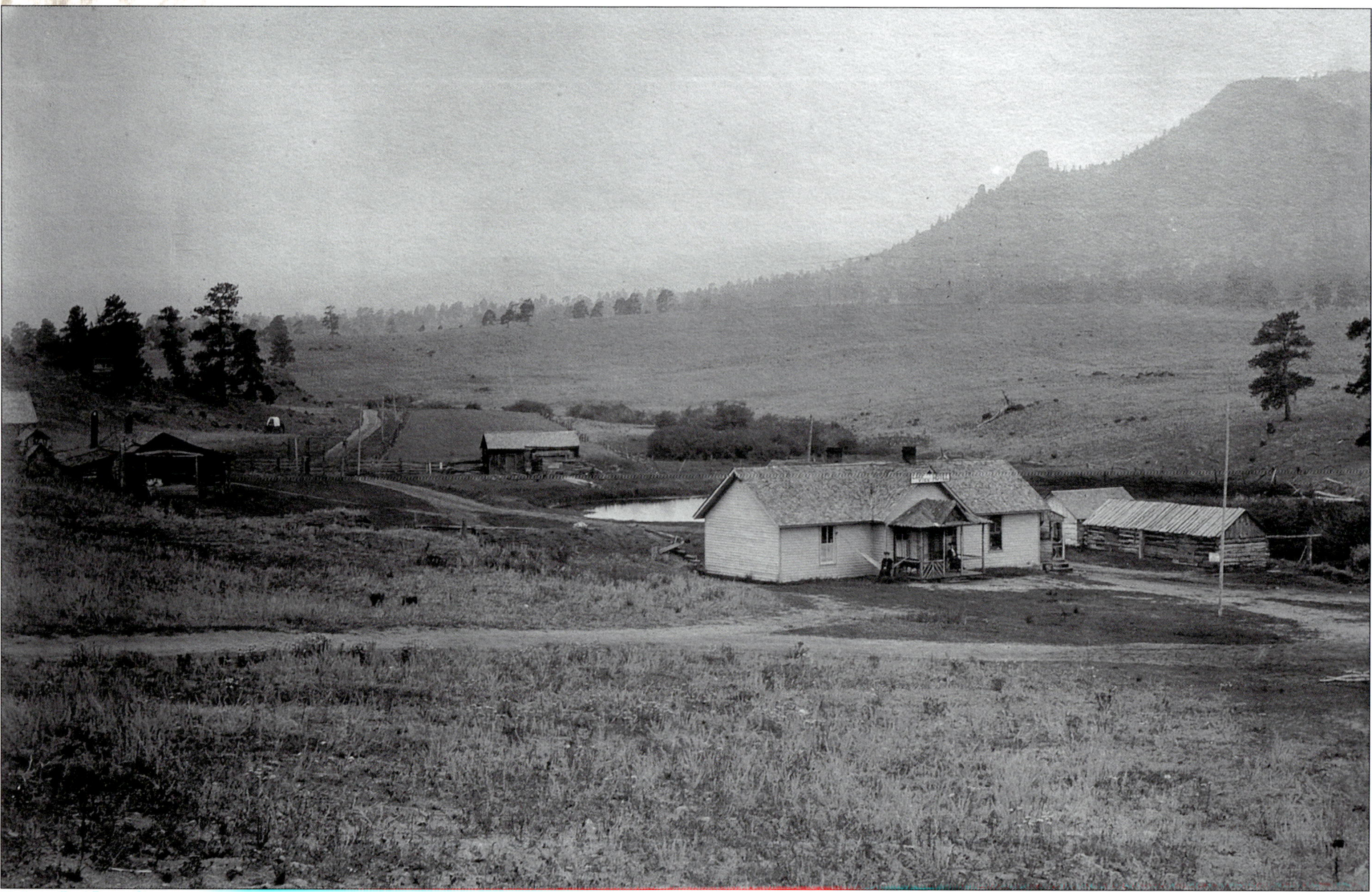

Photo by Fred Payne Clatworthy

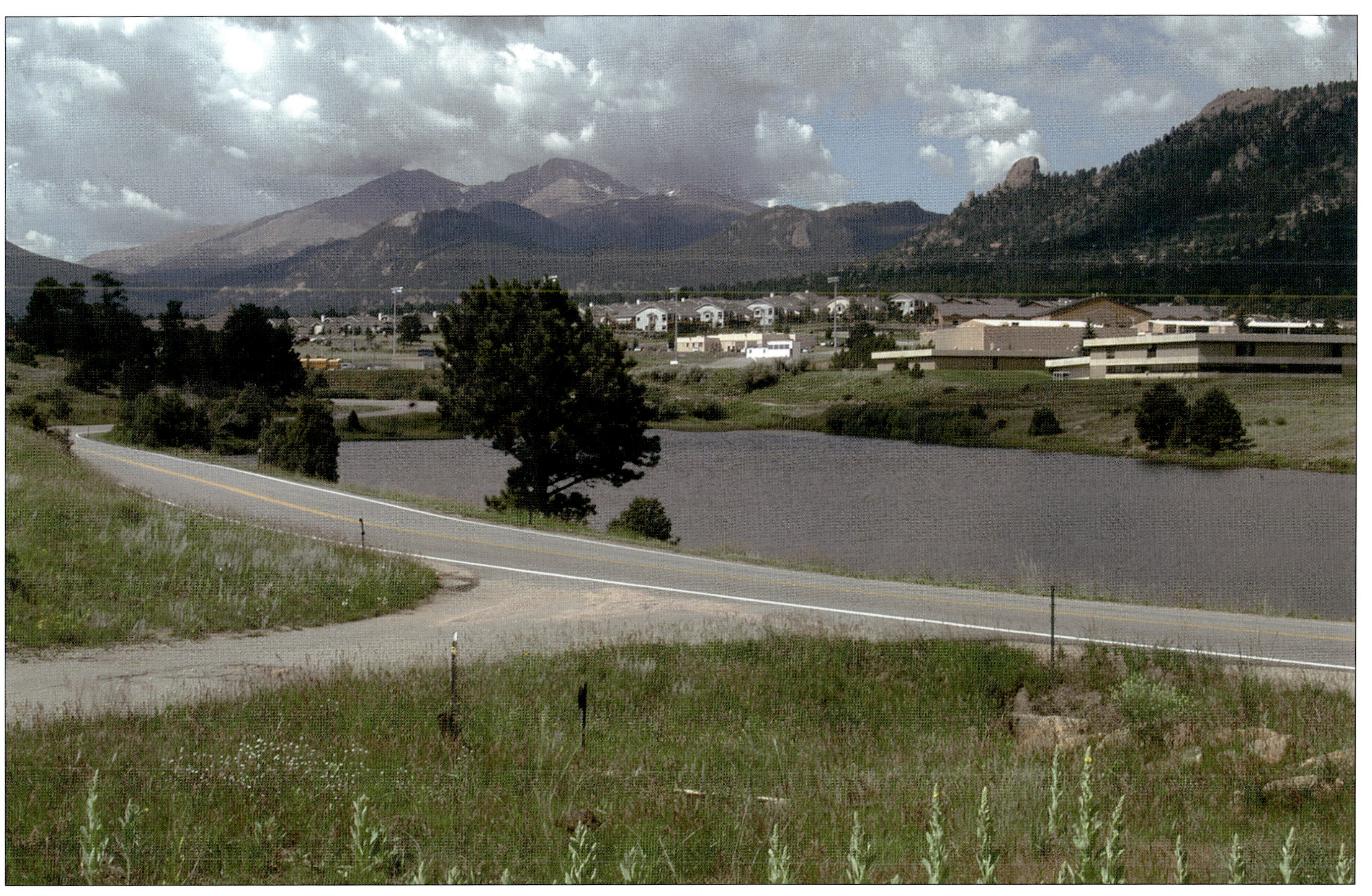

1935 panorama of the Estes-Evans-Dunraven ranch

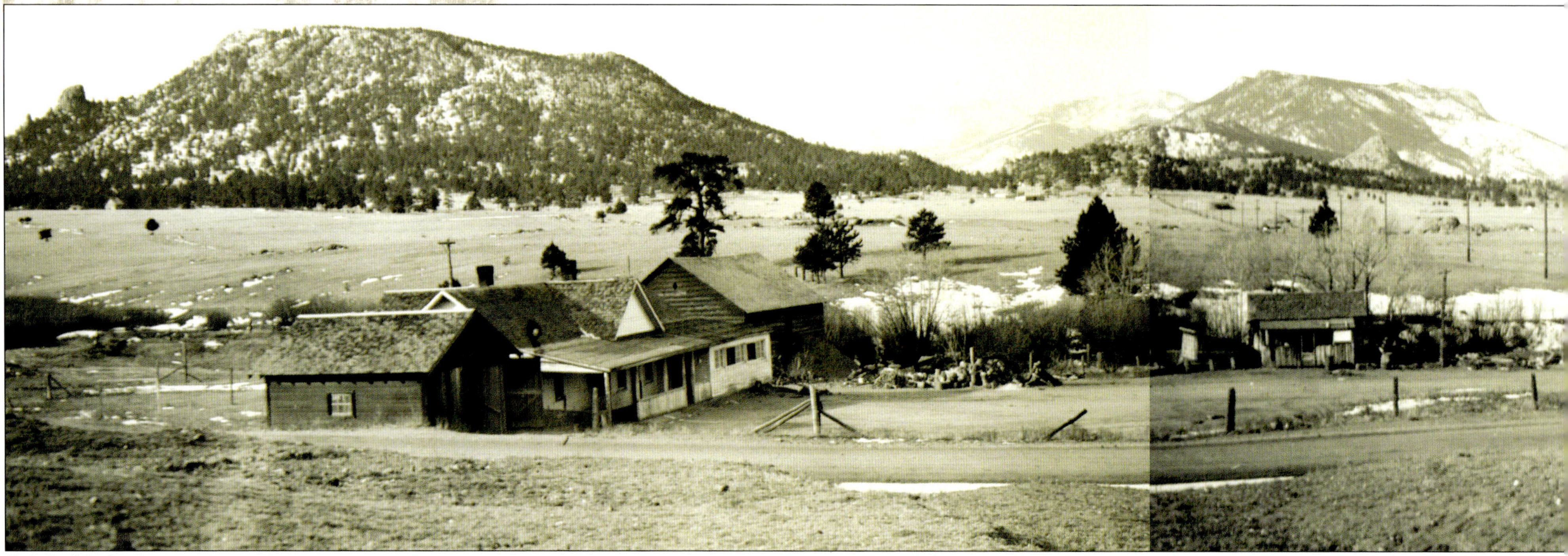

Photo by John Preston

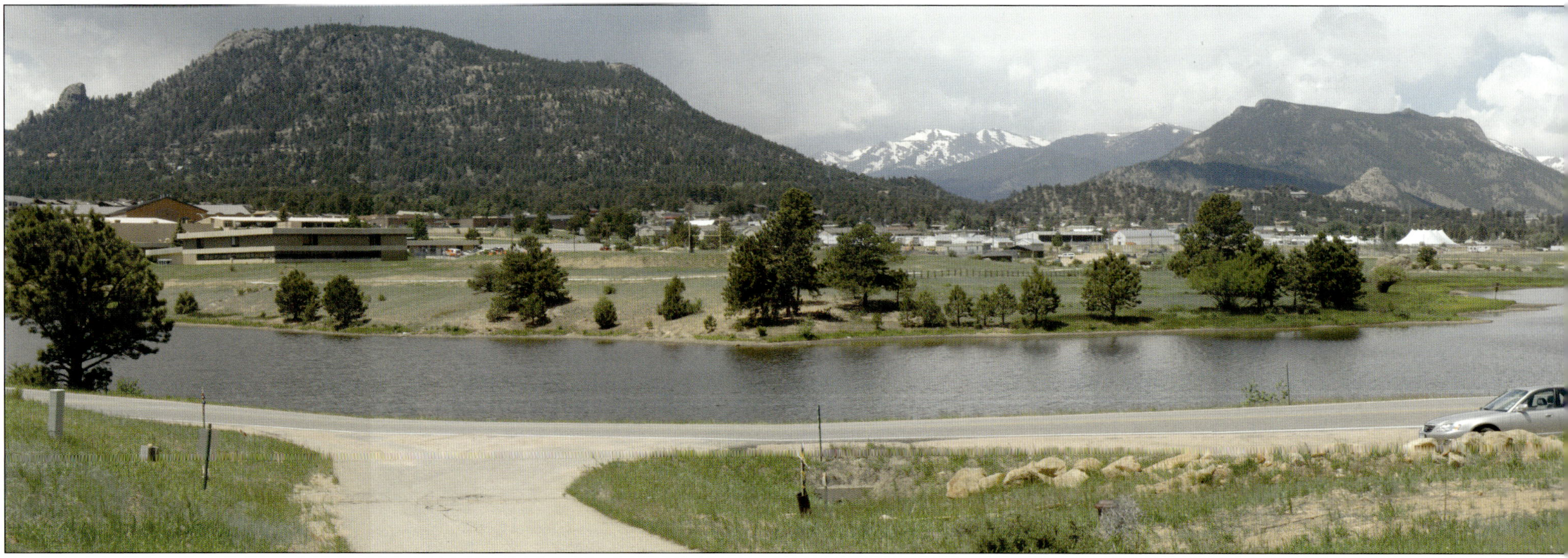

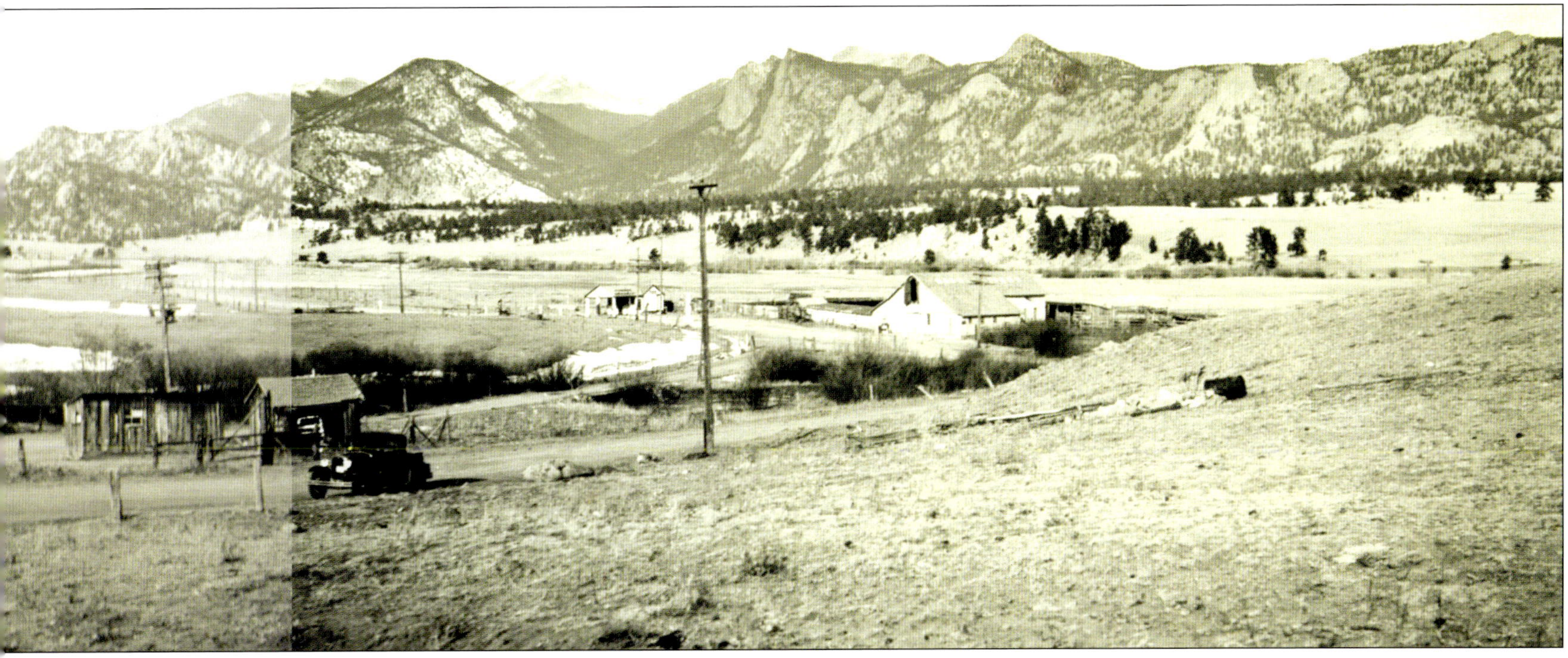

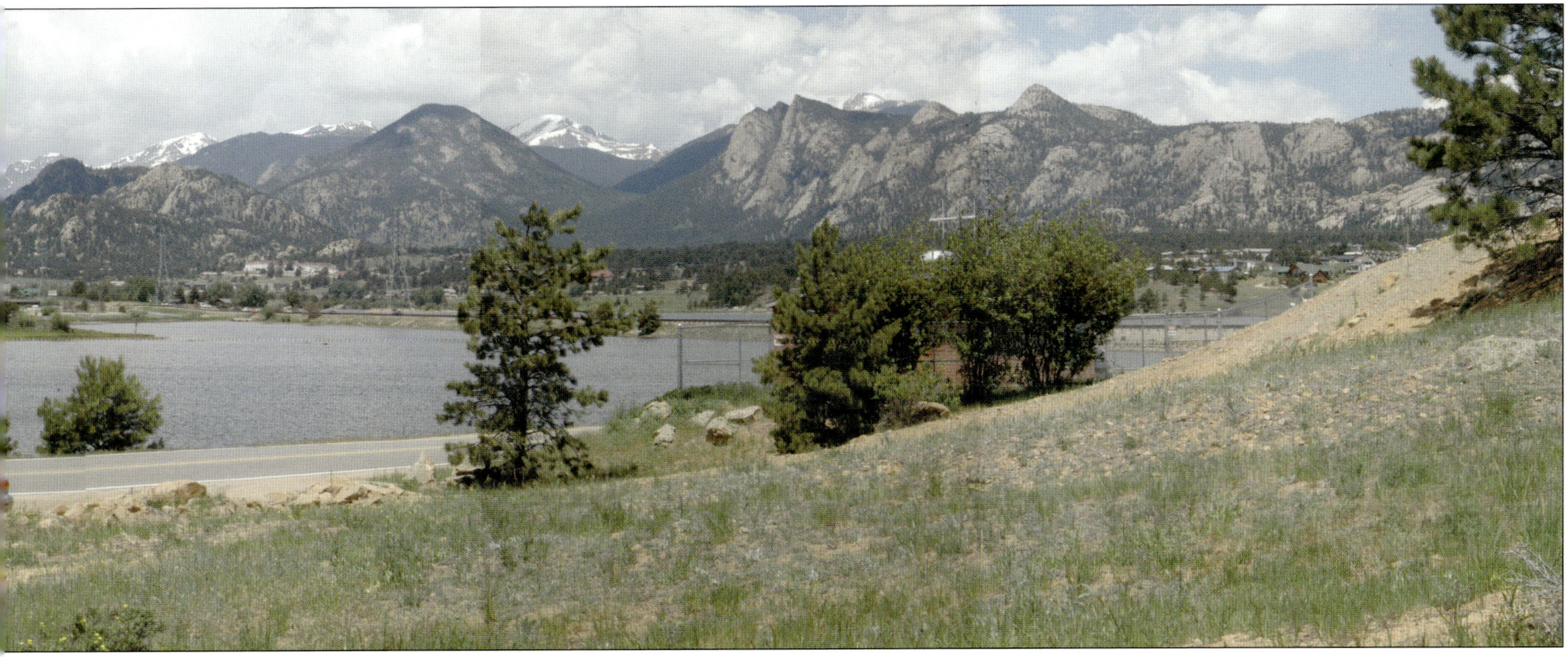

5. Charles Partridge Adams House

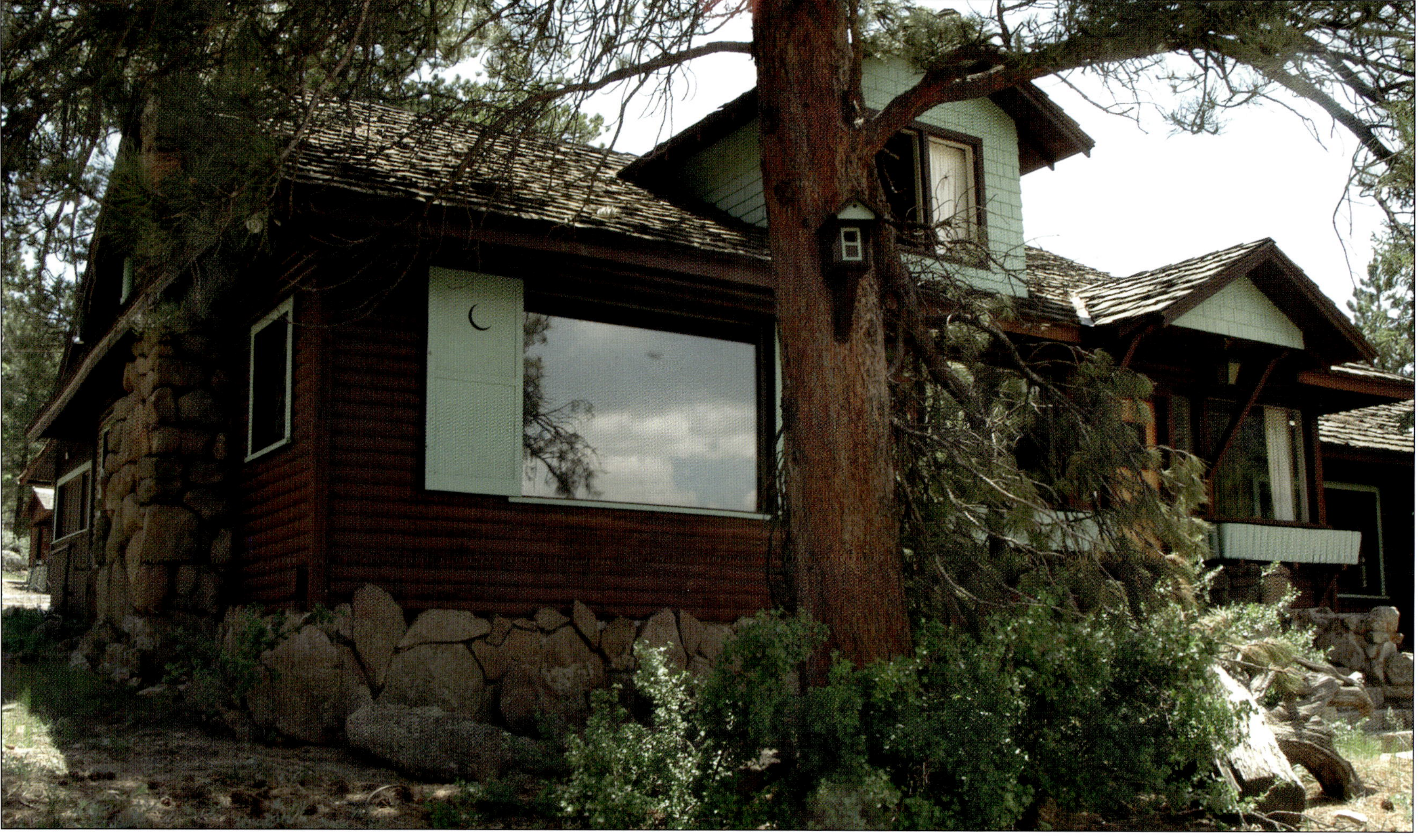

Landscape painter Charles Partridge Adams already enjoyed a regional reputation for his oils and watercolors when he first came to Estes Park in 1890 to honeymoon at Sprague's ranch in Moraine Park. Born in Massachusetts, Adams had come to Denver in 1876 with his mother and two sisters, hoping to find a cure for the girls' tuberculosis. In Denver, Adams received his only formal artistic training. By 1893, he had his own studio-gallery on Lamar Street.

By 1904, if not before, Adams and his family were summering in Estes Park, where they rented "a cozy log house" near the Dunraven ranch. That fall, he persuaded the Earl of Dunraven to sell him several acres on lower Fish Creek Road for the permanent summer home he named "The Sketch Box." Finished in July 1905, the building, with its fine views of Prospect Mountain and Longs Peak, provided Adams with a 14-by-28-foot studio, lighted by three north-facing windows. "The Studio," Adams later wrote, "was finished up to the roof rafters with a brownish-yellow stain, and seemed quite spacious, as it was more than twenty feet to the highest part of the room. Up to the plate rail I covered it with branches of our own native pine in monochrome, and added

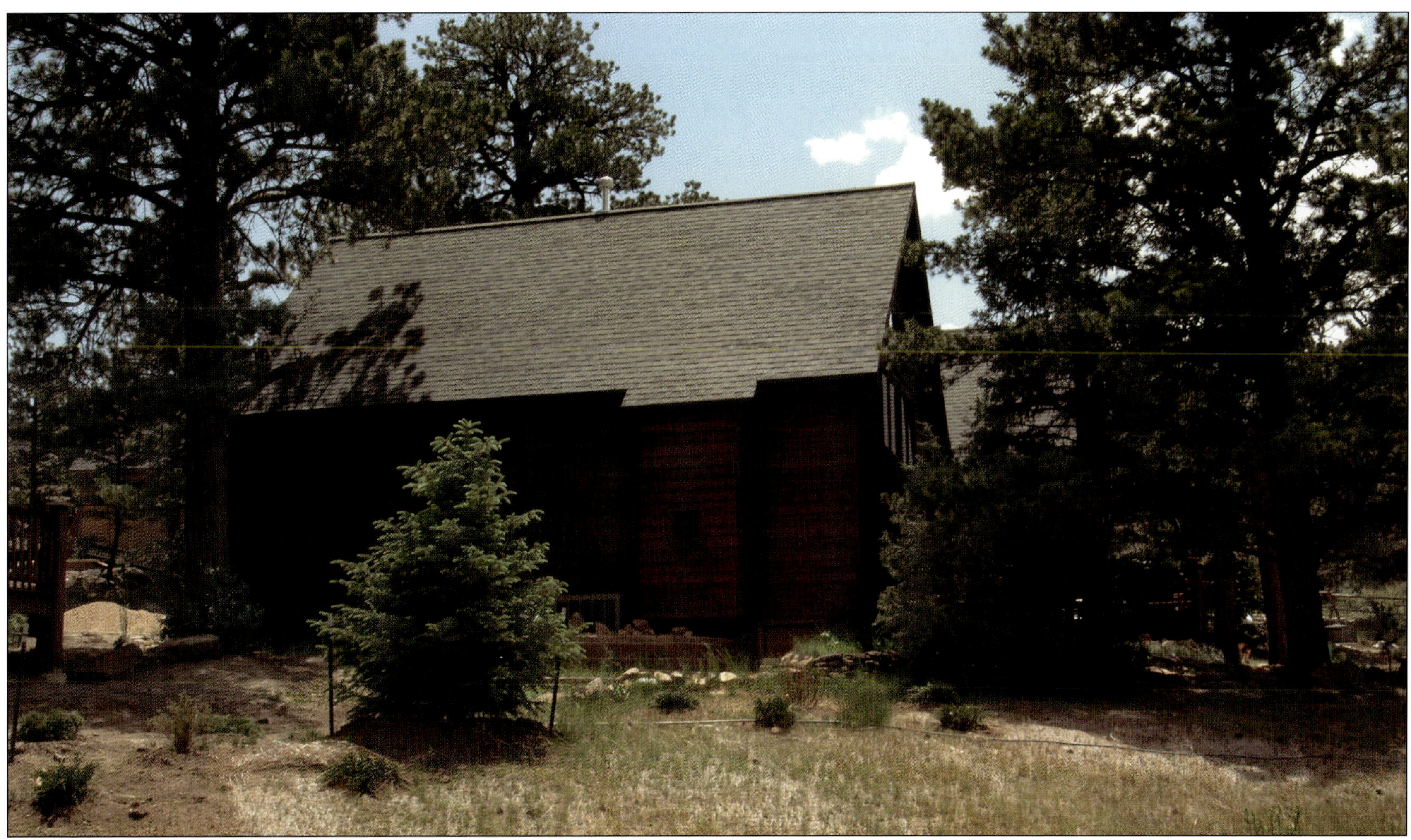

two or three bright colored and rather artificial birds for a bit of color." There was also a living room, kitchen, an upstairs bedroom, and a screened-in porch on both south and west sides. Oddly, there are no known photographs or drawings of the original house.

Adams and his family moved to California in 1920, where he would enjoy a second career painting seascapes. The house and studio in Estes Park then became the summer home of Denver attorney Edward Ring, who renamed it "Windy Willows," no doubt because of the willow stands along nearby Fish Creek. The home, once regarded as "one of the prettiest places of the Park," suffered additions and lost its porches, but retained its brown exterior and moss-green roof. The Partridge Adams house was torn down during the summer of 2003, but not before a central panel from the studio room, containing Adams' painting of a bird in flight, was removed and preserved. Our comparison photo was taken just before the house was demolished to make way for a condominium.

6. Dunraven Cottage and Estes Park Hotel, circa 1910

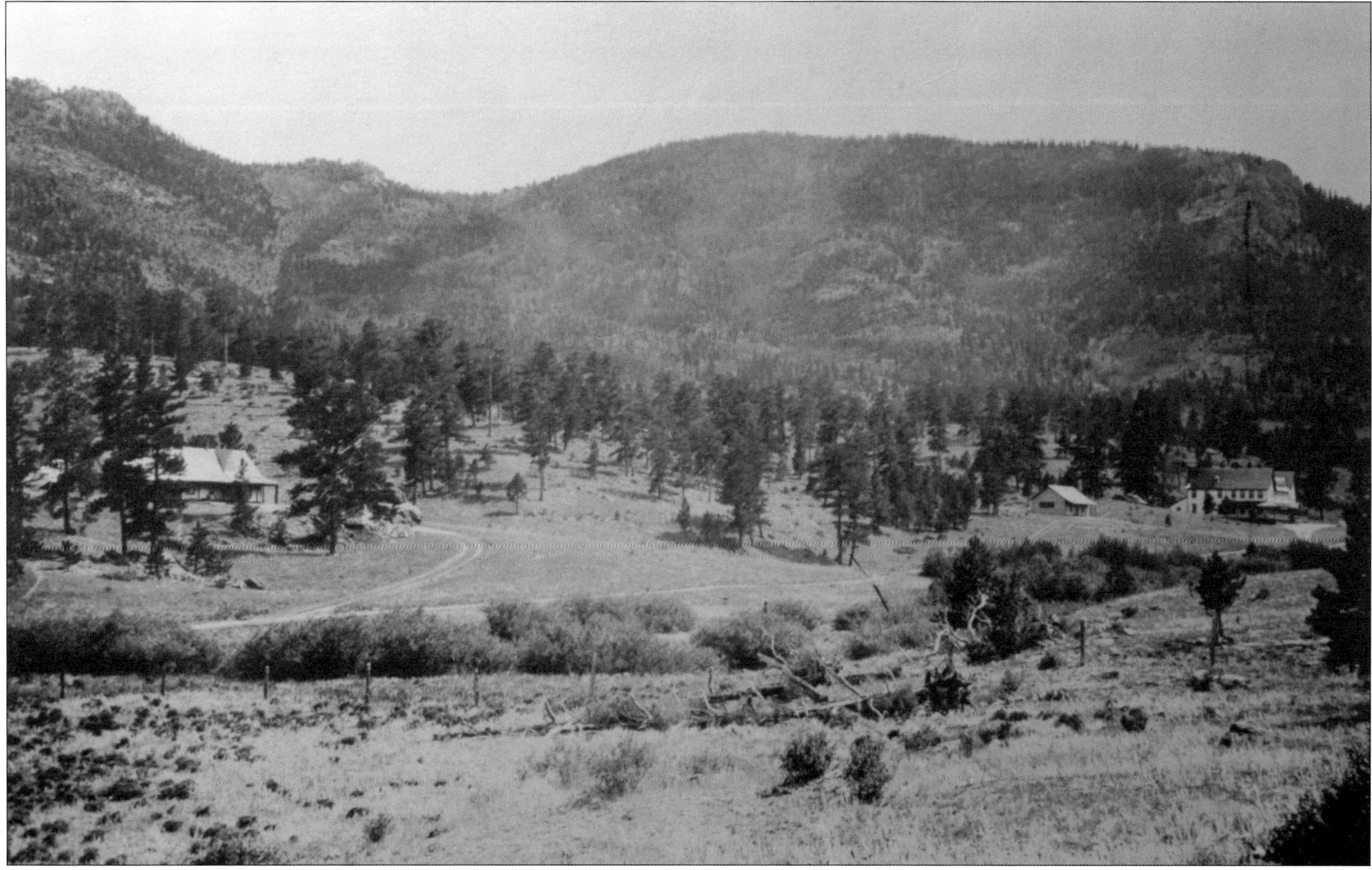

Windham Thomas Wyndham-Quin, the Fourth Earl of Dunraven, dominated the early history of Estes Park. Hunting in the valley after Christmas 1872, Dunraven became enchanted by its nearly untouched wilderness and determined to own as much of it as possible. This he managed to accomplish, by means that were questionable if not illegal. By 1876, when he formed the Estes Park Company Limited to consolidate and operate his holdings, Dunraven effectively controlled some 10,000 acres. There he ranched and cared for tourists. In 1876, a sawmill was brought in to build the octagonal cottage on Fish Creek (or Willow Creek as it was then known), which was to serve as Dunraven's home. This was followed by an even more ambitious project: the Estes Park (or "English") Hotel, built just far enough away to ensure privacy. The photographs here show the two buildings in their relationship to one another.

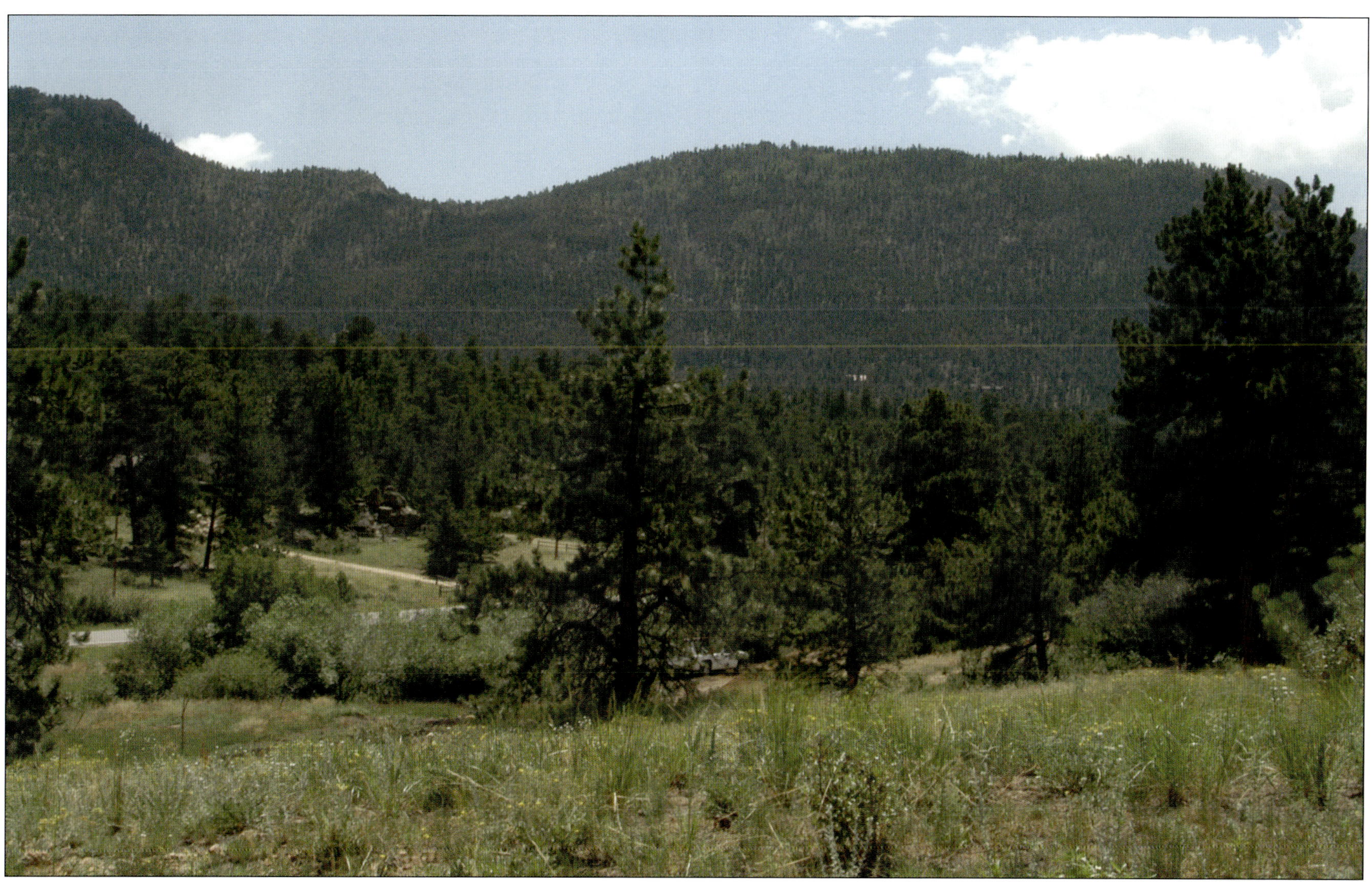

Dunraven's octagonal Queen Anne–style cottage, with its deeply pitched irregular roof and tower, extensive porches, bay window, and porch entrance, was built in 1876 by Englishman John Cleave. While the hotel was under construction, the cottage was used to house Cleave's workers. The hotel opened in the summer of 1877, and beyond that date the Earl of Dunraven seldom visited Estes Park. Both cottage and hotel were included in the holdings that Burton Sanborn and F. O. Stanley purchased from the earl in 1908. In 1923, cottage and grounds were sold by Carl Sanborn, Burton Sanborn's son, who now owned the property, to the Camp Fire Girls of Northern Colorado, which operated Camp Dunraven on the site. The cottage is now once again back in private hands.

7. Estes Park Hotel, circa 1877

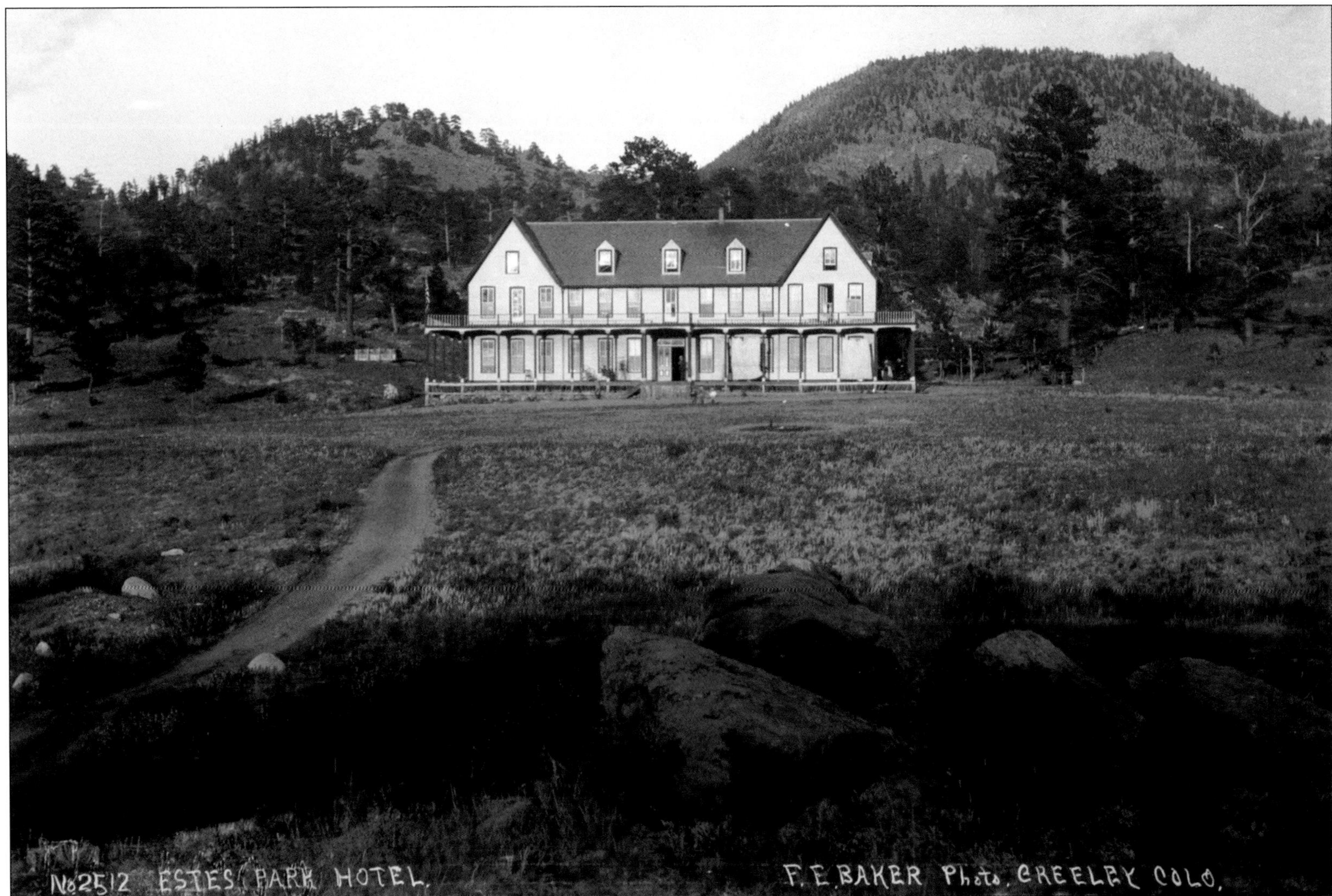

Photo by F. E. Baker

The Estes Park (or "English") Hotel, which became the centerpiece of the Earl of Dunraven's Estes Park Company, was built on a site selected by German-born artist Albert Bierstadt for its view of Longs Peak. Constructed of wood, brick, and stone, the 40-by-100-foot, three-story, white framed hotel, with its 14-foot verandas on the south and west sides, was dedicated in July 1877 with a grand ball that brought people from as far away as Denver. The hotel was designed to cater to the well-to-do who wished to vacation in the comfort of subdued elegance, as opposed to the ruder fare provided by the valley's family-operated ranches. For those not inclined to "rough it," the Estes Park Hotel offered manicured lawns, an artificial lake large enough to float small boats, tennis courts, and a nine-hole golf course. Nearby were a series of other buildings, as well as tent-cottages. During its later years, a clubhouse building, "the Dunraven Club," was added nearby, with billiard tables, private rooms, and an area for musical concerts.

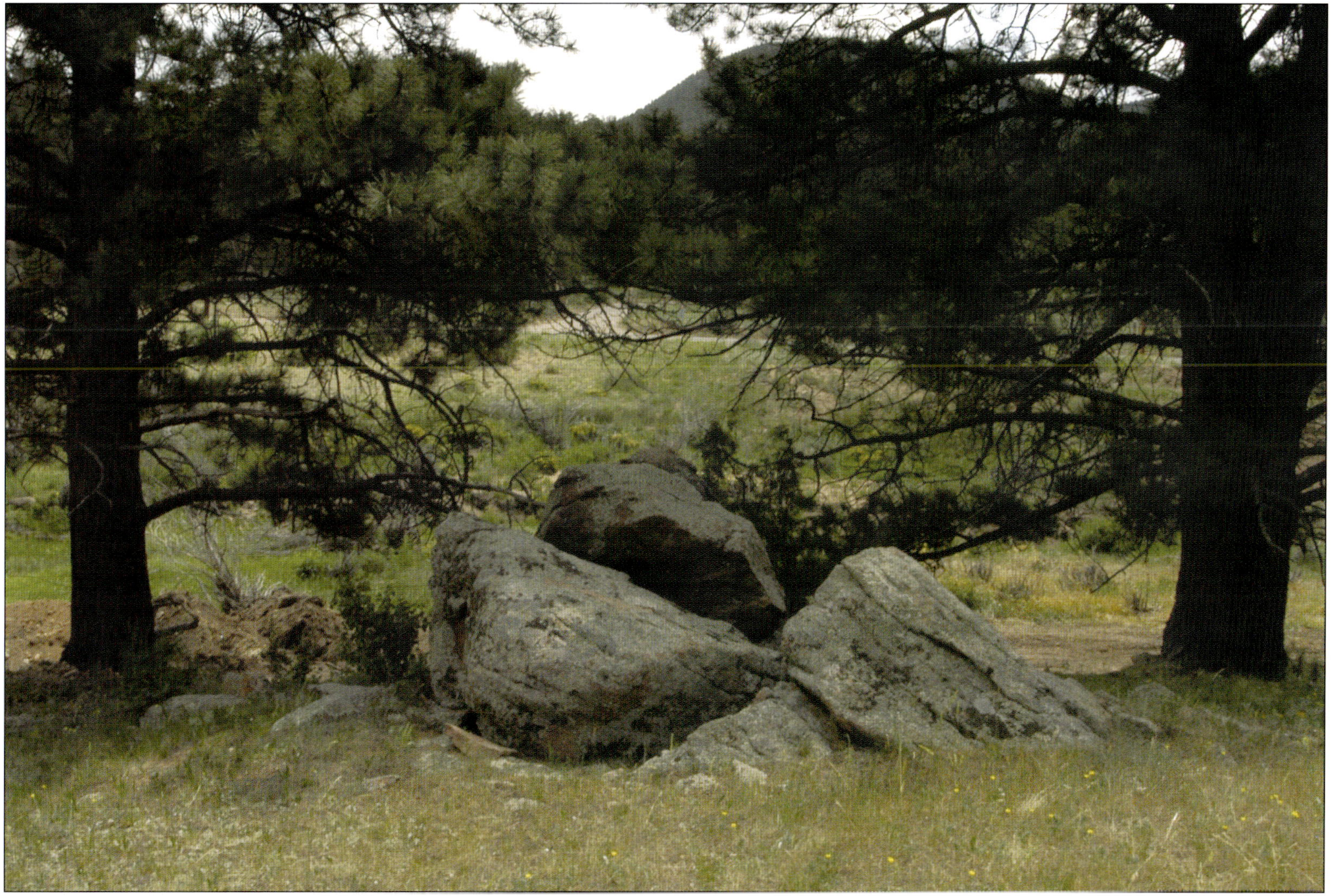

The views of the hotel in these photographs show something of the hotel's evolution. The first was taken shortly after the hotel's construction, for the lake that directly fronted the building is not yet in evidence. The boulders in the foreground of both photographs are located just below the 11th tee box of the Estes Park Golf Course. Over the years, the hotel would undergo a number of structural changes. The first of these converted the original second-story balcony to a roof (in order, it has been suggested, to reduce the possibility of late-night festivities). In 1908, a wing containing 20 additional rooms was added to the north end, which extended the veranda to a full 170 feet and brought the total number of rooms to 50. A side view of this addition is visible in the second of the paired photographs, which also suggests why the site Bierstadt selected caught the earl's fancy. The Estes Park Hotel was destroyed by fire on the morning of August 4, 1911. It was never rebuilt.

Estes Park Hotel and Longs Peak, circa 1910

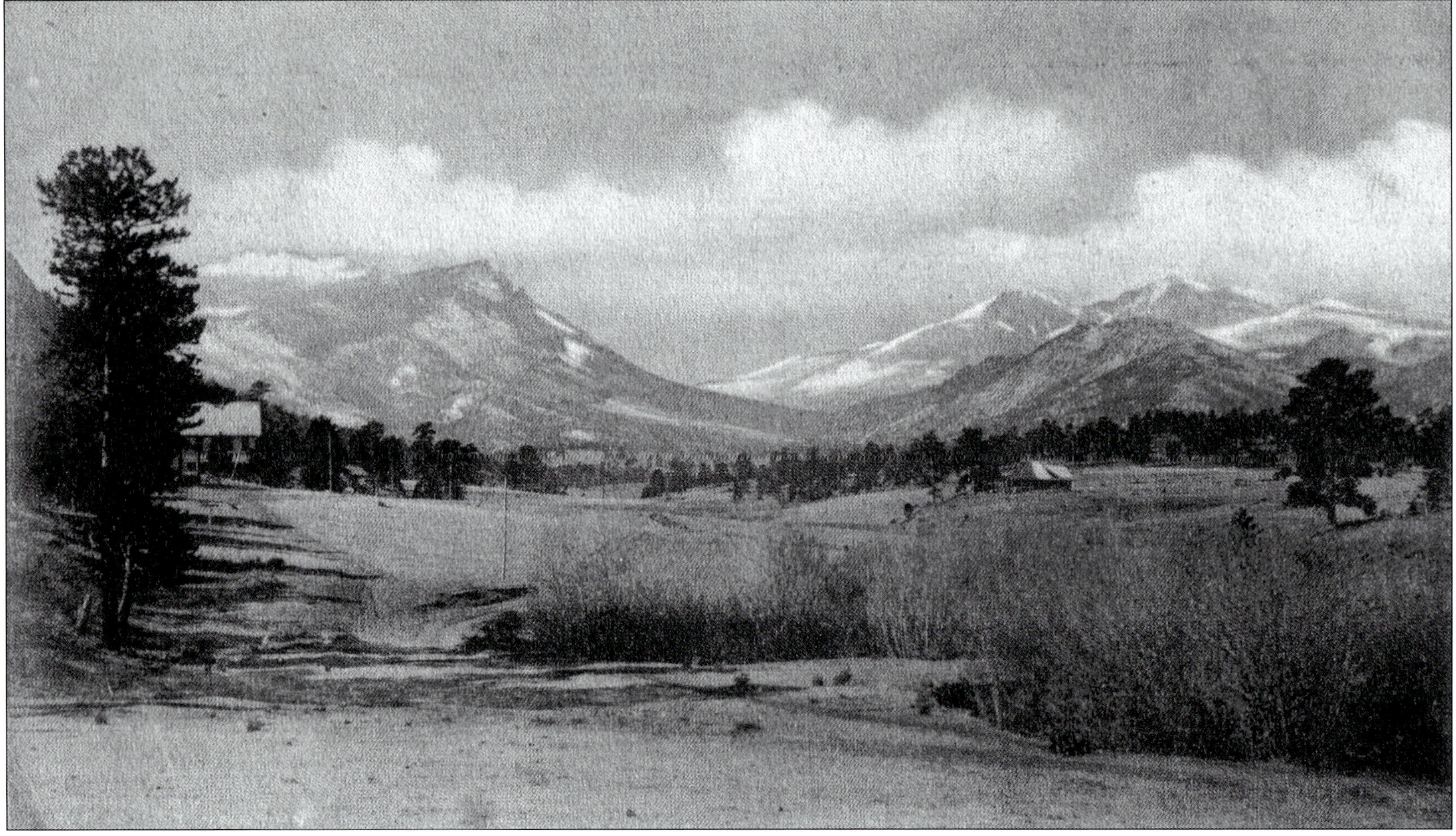

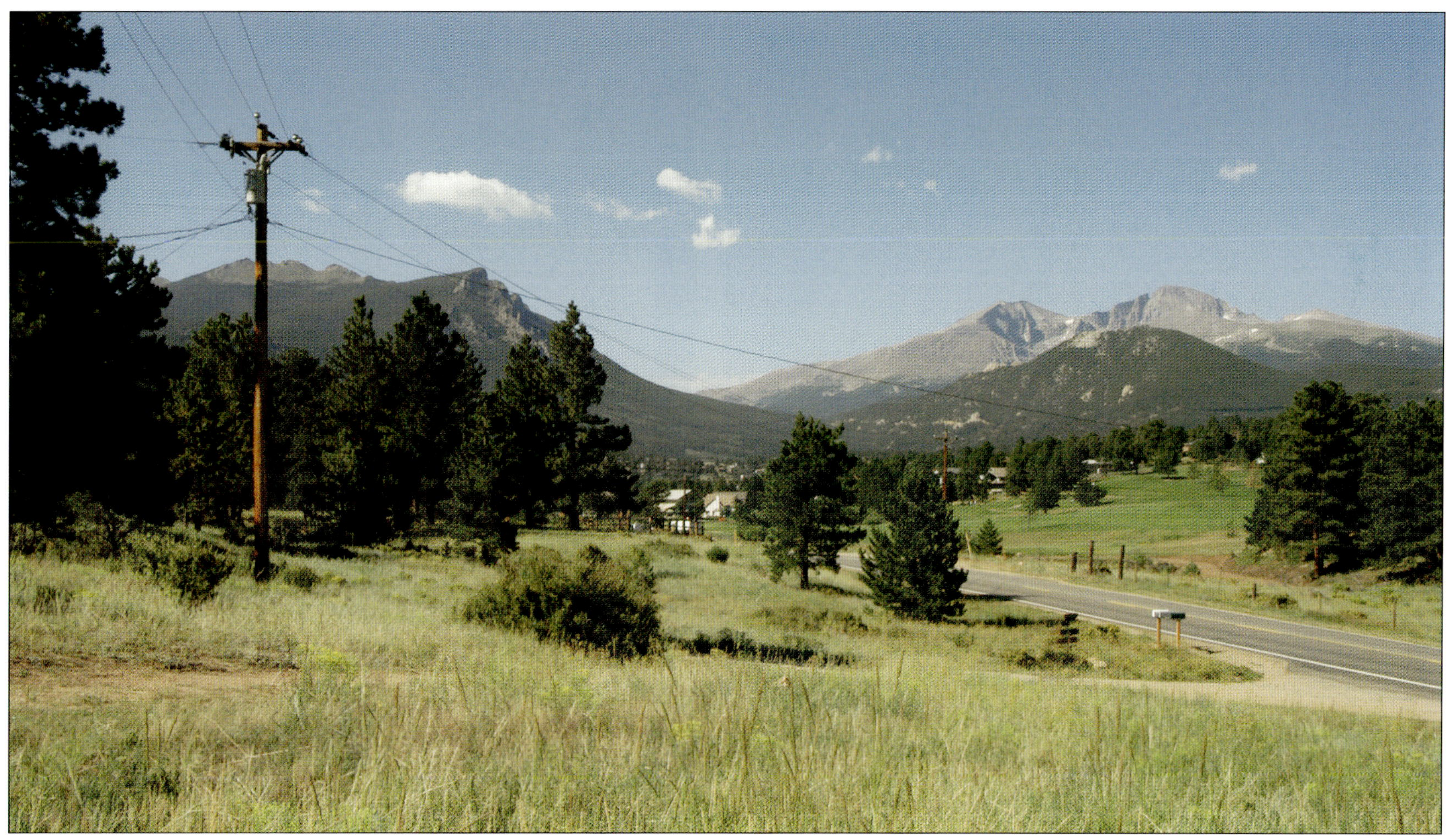

8. Estes Park Country Club, circa 1925

The Earl of Dunraven built the first golf course in Estes Park for guests of his Estes Park Hotel, which opened in 1877. The nine-hole course, among Colorado's earliest, began and ended in front of the hotel, and reportedly was designed with the help of "a golf expert from Scotland." After the hotel building burned in 1911, the golf course was abandoned. By then, Estes Park golfers could use the nine-hole course that F. O. Stanley had installed below the Stanley Hotel two years earlier.

The Stanley course proved extremely popular with hotel guests, visitors, and local residents, so much so that by 1916 another facility was needed. That year, Stanley and two fellow summer residents, Denverites Thomas B. Stearns and Frank L. Woodward, paid $20,000 for 120 acres that contained the old Dunraven course for the purpose of laying out a new "model" 18-hole golf course. Stanley and his partners turned the land over to local golf enthusiasts, who in 1916 organized the Estes Park Country Club. Thirty local residents invested $15,000 to underwrite the cost of building a log clubhouse with a large stone fireplace and a new 6,000-yard, par 73 course, to be ready by the 1918 season.

As the juxtaposed photographs suggest, the original clubhouse building has been enlarged several times, the first in 1923 when an addition was built on the west side to provide a refreshment area and a "lounging room" for the golfers. Two years later, in 1925, it was enlarged again, this time to accommodate expanded kitchen facilities. Since 1944, the Estes Park Golf Course has been owned and operated by the Town of Estes Park. The layout of the golf course itself has been changed several times over the past six decades, notably in August 1944, to accommodate a 3,000-foot-long airfield with a hard-packed granite runway. The runway was laid out on the west side of the course parallel to Highway 7. Until the early 1950s, the greens were sand and the fairways lacked grass. A number of stone-outlined tee boxes, remnants of the original 1918 course, are still visible, as is the small stone building that served as a cistern, which is perched on the rocks near the front entrance.

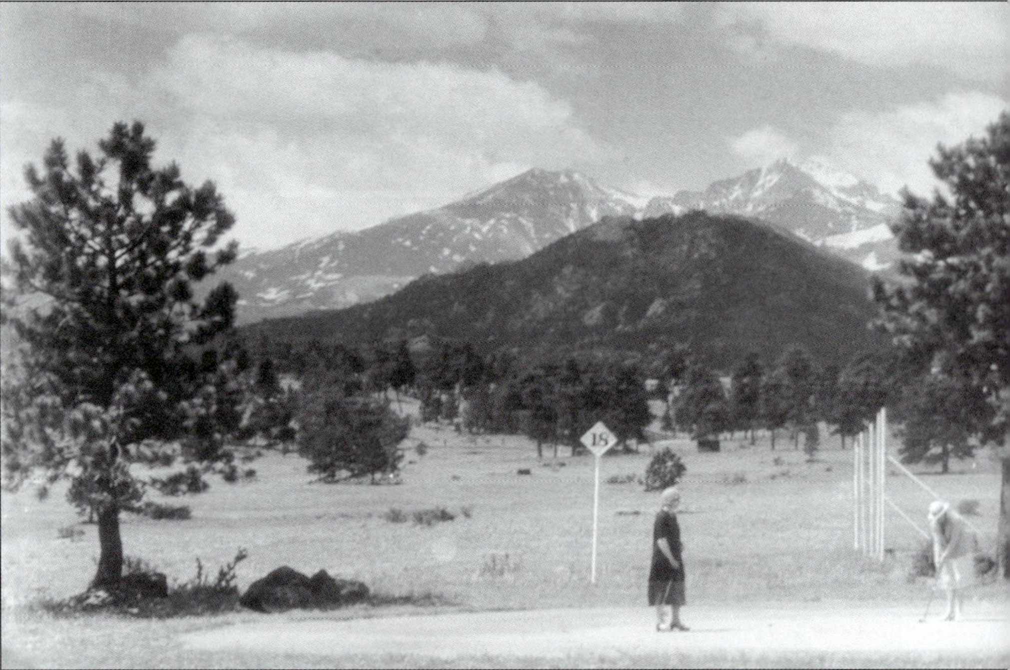

Photo by Fred Payne Clatworthy

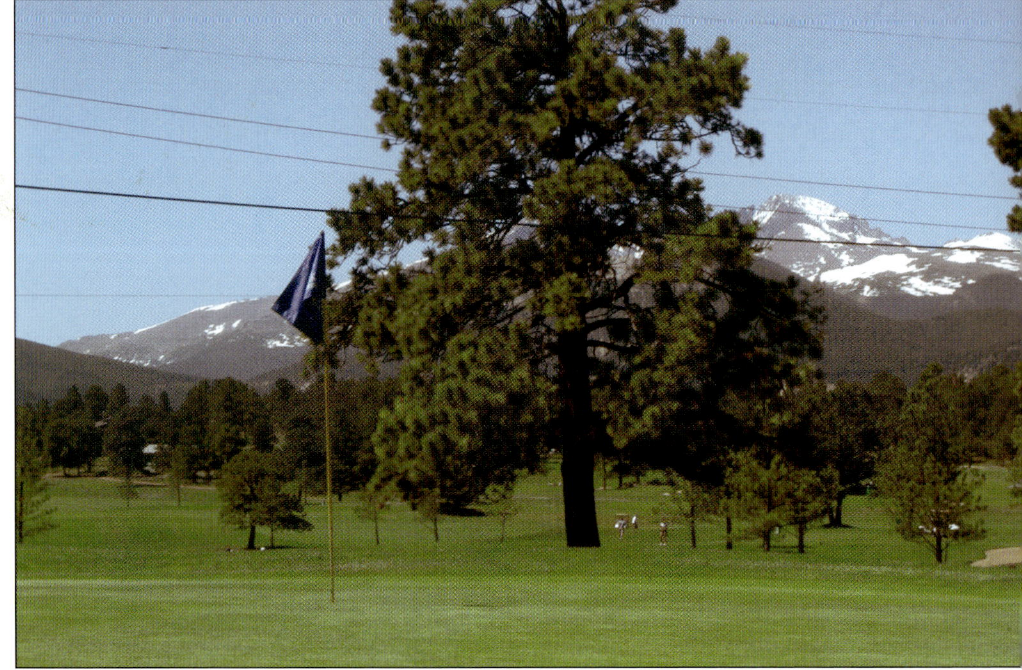

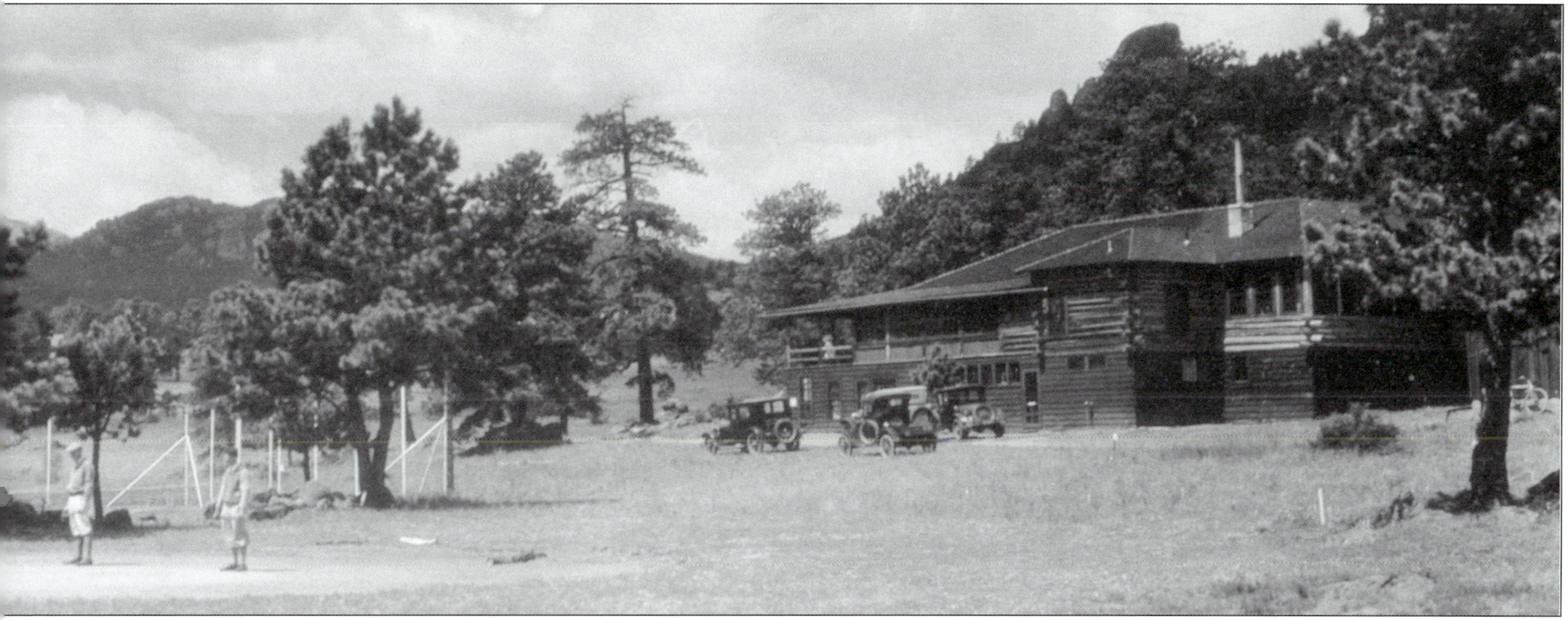

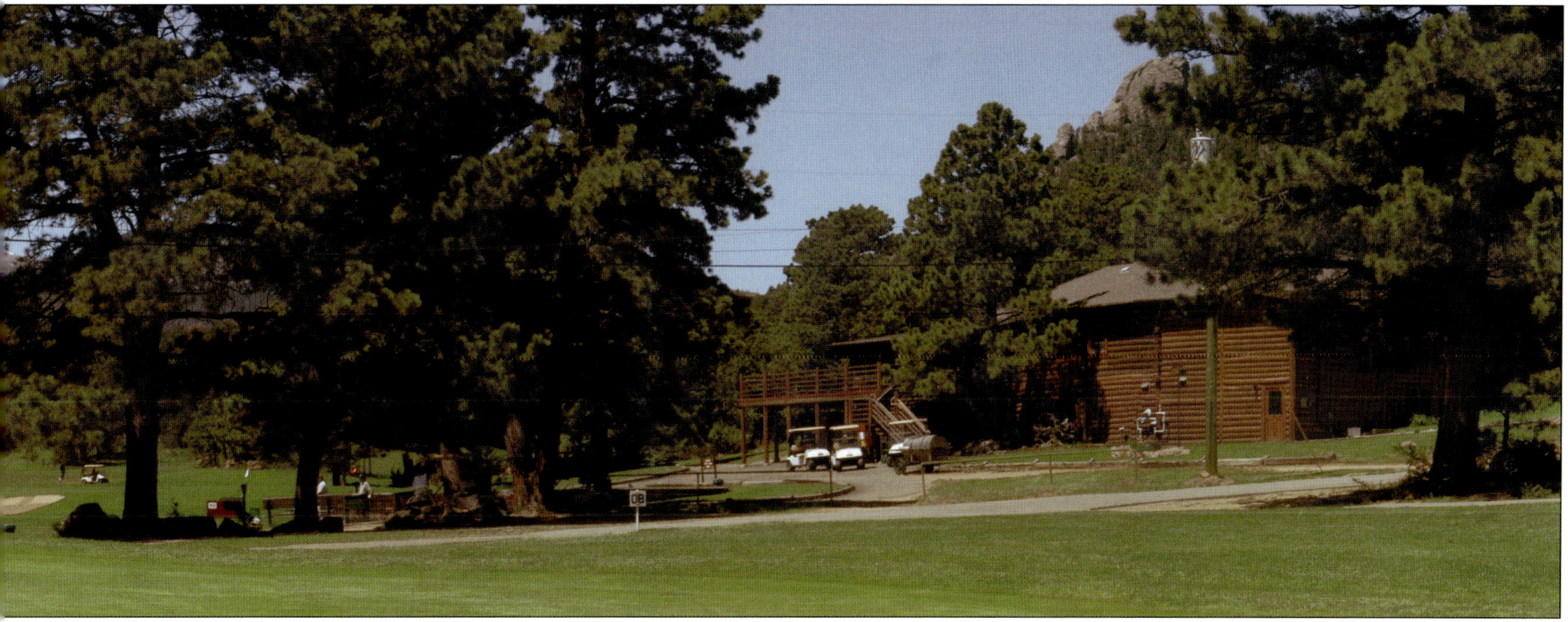

9. Front Range from Prospect Mountain, 1873
10. Longs Peak from Dollar Lake, circa 1882 (pages 42-43)

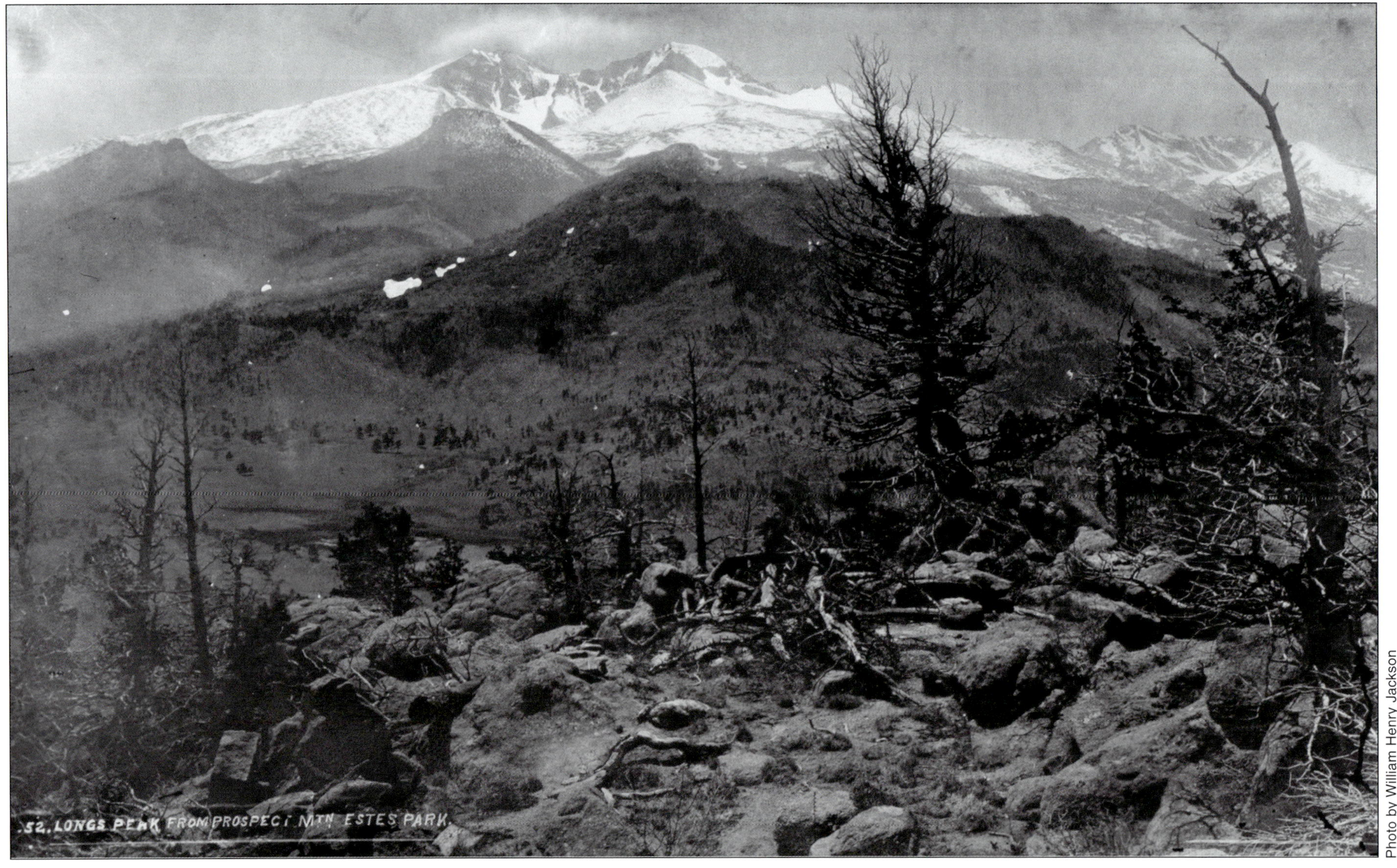

Photo by William Henry Jackson

William Henry Jackson, whose stunning black-and-white photographs of the American West helped introduce, and "sell," its then largely unknown wonders to the nation and the world, made several trips to Estes Park. The first was in May 1873 with Ferdinand V. Hayden's Geological and Geographical Survey. On May 30, 1873, Jackson climbed Prospect Mountain intent on taking photographs of Longs Peak and the other peaks of the Front Range (or "Snowy Range" as it was then often called). Although the "morning promised well," and Jackson had no difficulty making the ascent, by the time he was ready to take photographs it had clouded and "the wind commenced to blow so that there was no earthly use attempting anything." Determined to get his photographs, Jackson left his

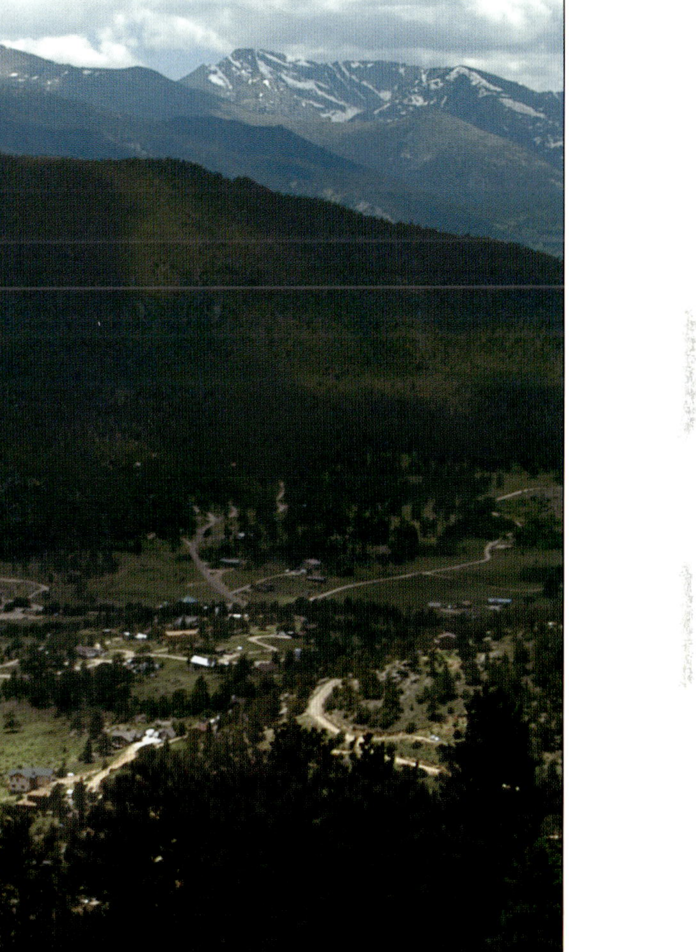

equipment on the mountain and returned to camp on the Big Thompson near the base of what is now Park Hill.

The next day was fair and Jackson returned to Prospect Mountain where he took several photographs, including the one reproduced here, although, he subsequently noted in his diary, he "had considerable trouble in working from one cause or another & did not secure as many negatives as I wished." On June 1, Jackson's photographic party broke camp and moved south, making camp that night at the foot of Longs Peak.

Though Jackson's first visit to Estes Park was brief, the photographs he took are among the very first views we have of the region. As his view from

10. Longs Peak from Dollar Lake, circa 1882

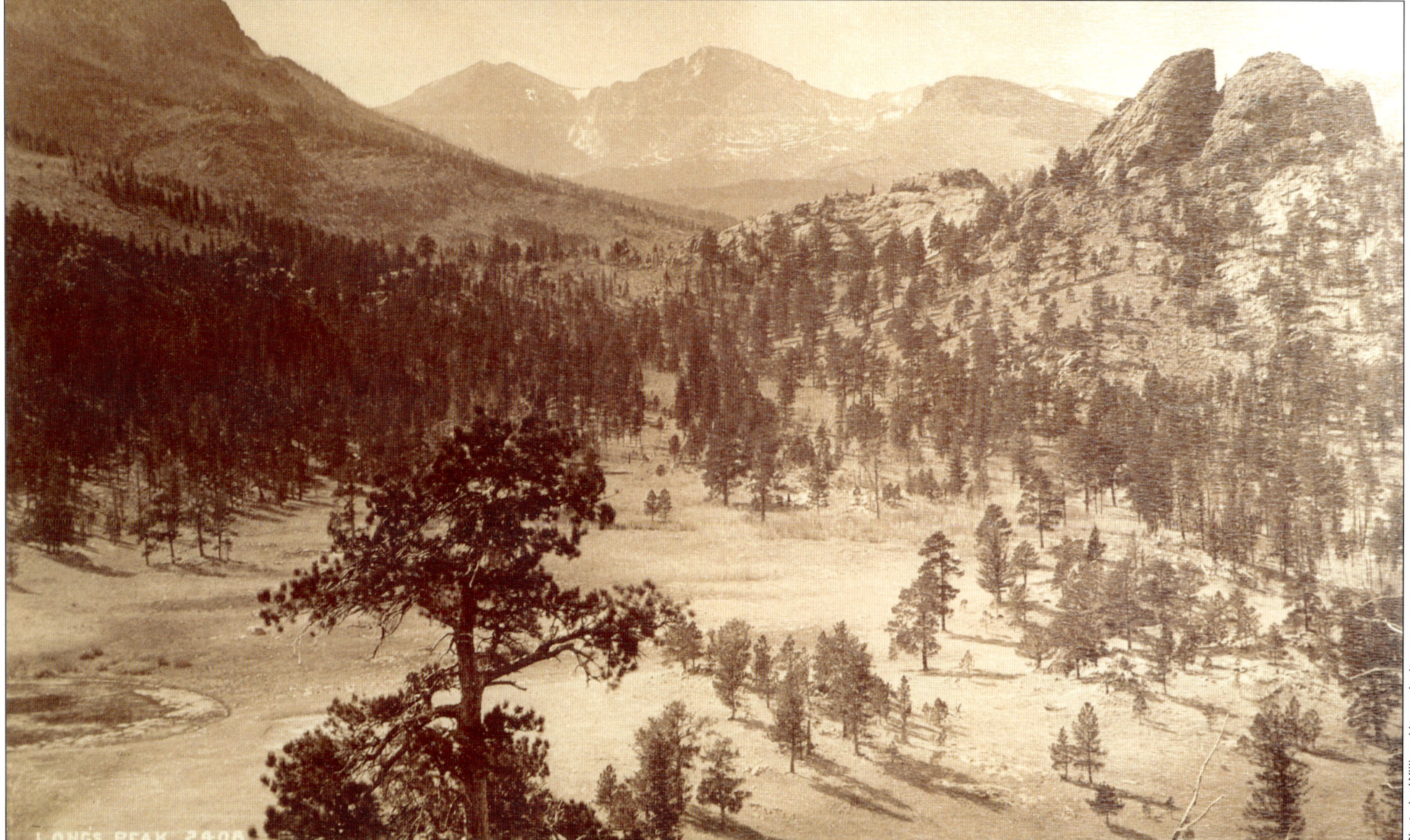

Photo by William Henry Jackson

Prospect Mountain suggests, Jackson had already mastered the conventions of landscape to provide that romantic sense of awe and wonder that many of us have felt on first seeing Longs Peak and its companions along the Front Range.

Jackson would return to Estes Park on one or more subsequent visits, when he presumably stayed at Dunraven's Estes Park Hotel on Fish Creek. It was then that he took the second of the photographs reproduced here. But how Jackson managed to find the small body of water known today as Dollar Lake, and the location from which the second photograph was taken, is not at all clear. Even today its location is hidden away, well off the beaten path. Presumably, Jackson left the hotel one morning, intent on taking interesting views of Longs Peak,

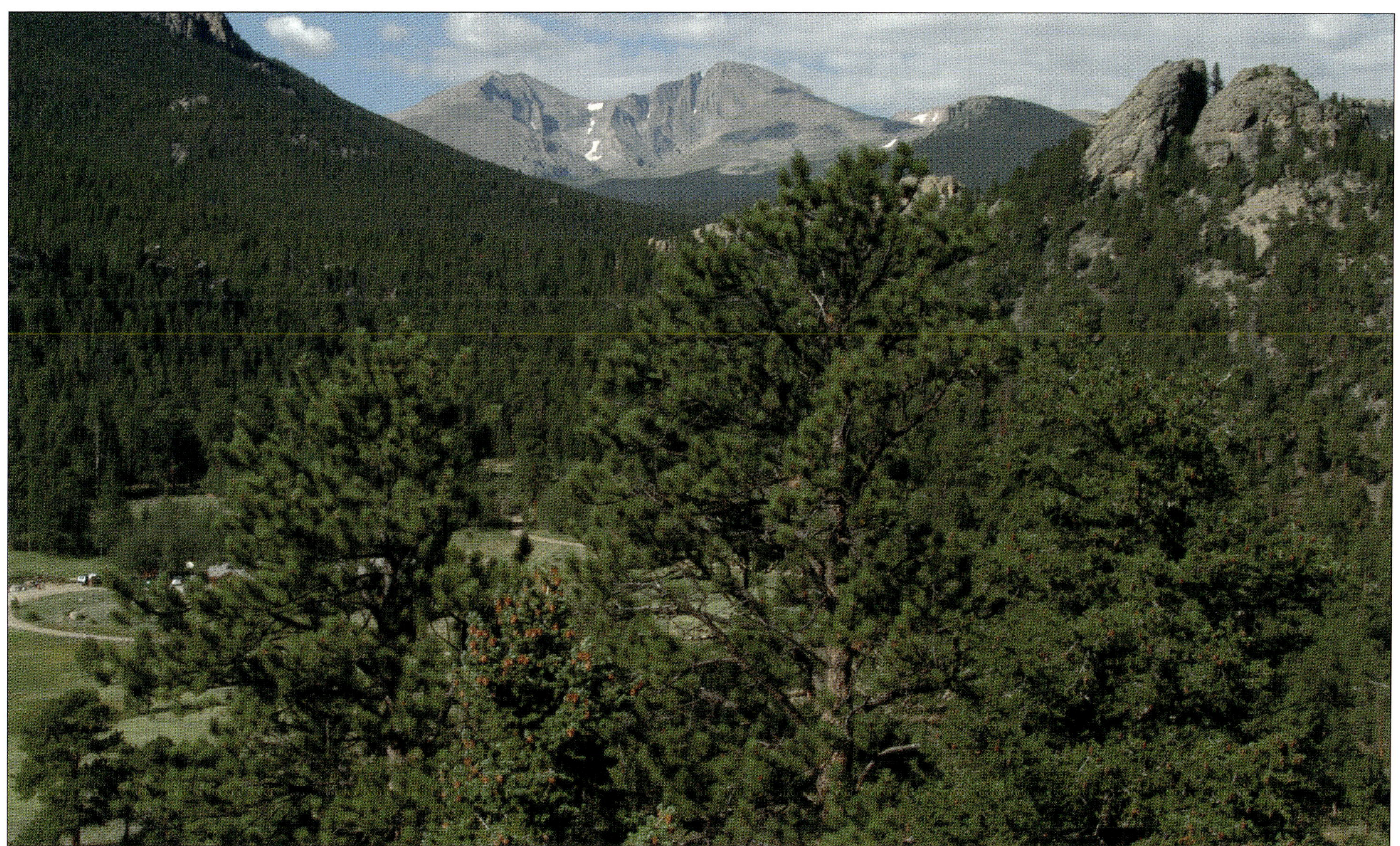

and wandered south on a route that took him, roughly, up today's Little Valley Road to the ridge near where St. Francis of Assisi Church now stands. Moving west along this ridge (as we did) brought him to the place from which the photograph was taken, with Dollar Lake below, Christmas Tree Rock on the right, and Longs Peak looming spectacularly above.

Interestingly enough, some copies of the photograph of Dollar Lake bear the name of California photographer Isaiah West Taber. In 1871, Taber opened a gallery in San Francisco, where he developed a highly successful business printing and selling Western views, many of them unacknowledged works of other photographers, including William Henry Jackson.

11. Cheley Colorado Camps, circa 1930

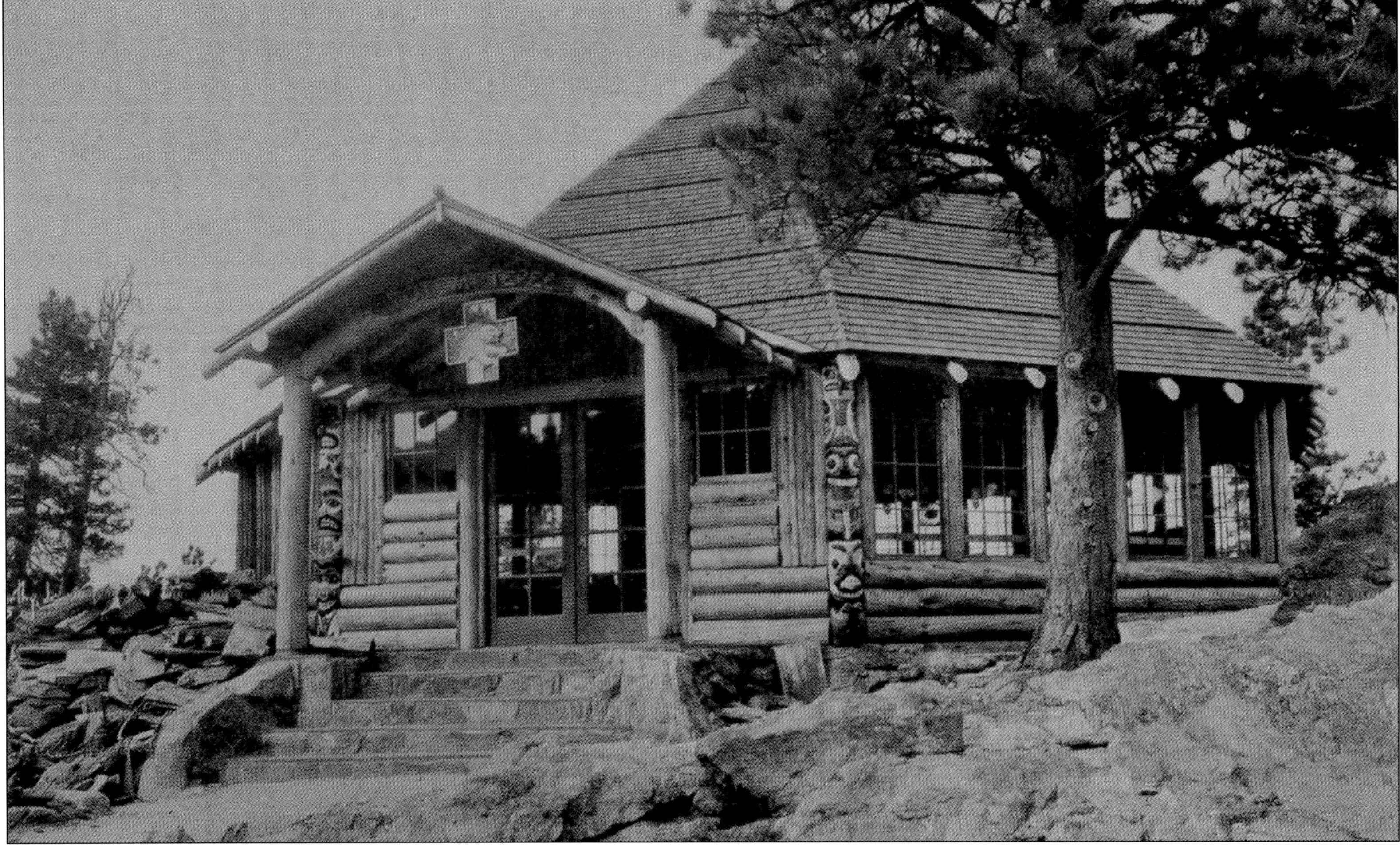

Photo by Fred Payne Clatworthy

Cheley Colorado Camps, the Estes Park region's best-known summer camp, began in 1921, when Frank H. Cheley opened Bear Lake Trail School on property that was leased from resort owner Frank W. Byerly along the shores of Bear Lake (see p. 226). His "alpine summer camp for boys" operated that first season with nine campers. Cheley, a veteran YMCA camping program director, had developed a philosophy that stressed physical activity and character building through outdoor recreation ("learning by doing").

Cheley intended to operate a camp for boys. Camp tradition says one brave little girl asked the director why he did not allow girls to come to his camp. Not sure he had an answer, Cheley rectified the situation in 1926 by opening Camp Chipeta, "a vigorous camp for vigorous girls," at Scotts Heights situated above the YMCA Camp.

The Cheley idea became an immediate success, and by 1926 it had become clear that the facilities at Bear Lake were insufficient for Cheley's growing camp organization. That year Cheley relocated Camp Haiyaha, as his Bear Lake Trail School was now named, to a new 160-acre site on the wooded northern slopes of Twin Sisters Mountain above Fish Creek, where he erected nine new buildings to house not only Camp Haiyaha but two new camps for younger

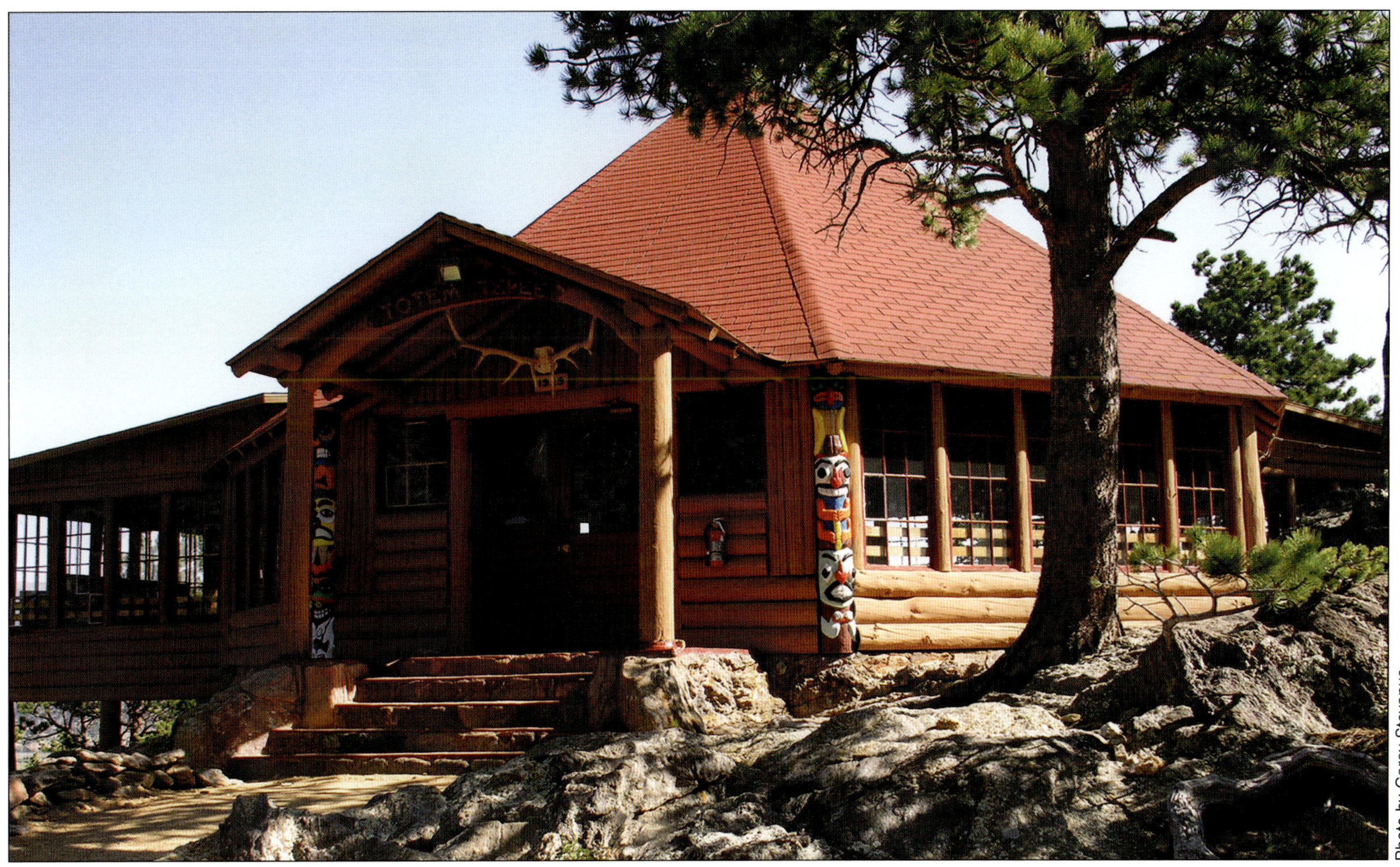

Photo by Carey Stevanus

boys and girls, Ski Hi and Chipeta, as well. Two additional adjacent tracts of 75 acres and 140 acres were later acquired with the purchase of Jacob Christian's Fish Creek Ranch and Amanda Blocker Byrd's homestead claim.

The most impressive of the buildings at Cheley's Land O' Peaks Camp, as Cheley renamed the entire camping operation, is Totem Tepee, built in 1928 and photographed here. Its unique design was inspired by Cheley camper Hugh Davis, who had spent a winter studying Alaskan totems, and then directed the carving of a series of totem poles that set this building apart from the rest. The eight totems are held together by a chain—the only support for the building.

Cheley Colorado Camps continues to provide the outdoor experience that Frank Cheley first introduced at Bear Lake. It serves some 1,000 campers each summer on more than 750 acres. Cheley remains very much a family enterprise, having passed in 1941 from Frank Cheley to his son, Jack. Now Jack's son, Don, and his wife, Carole, together with their children, Brooke, Austin, and Jeff, carry on the Cheley "Fun-Plus" tradition.

12. Marys Lake, circa 1886

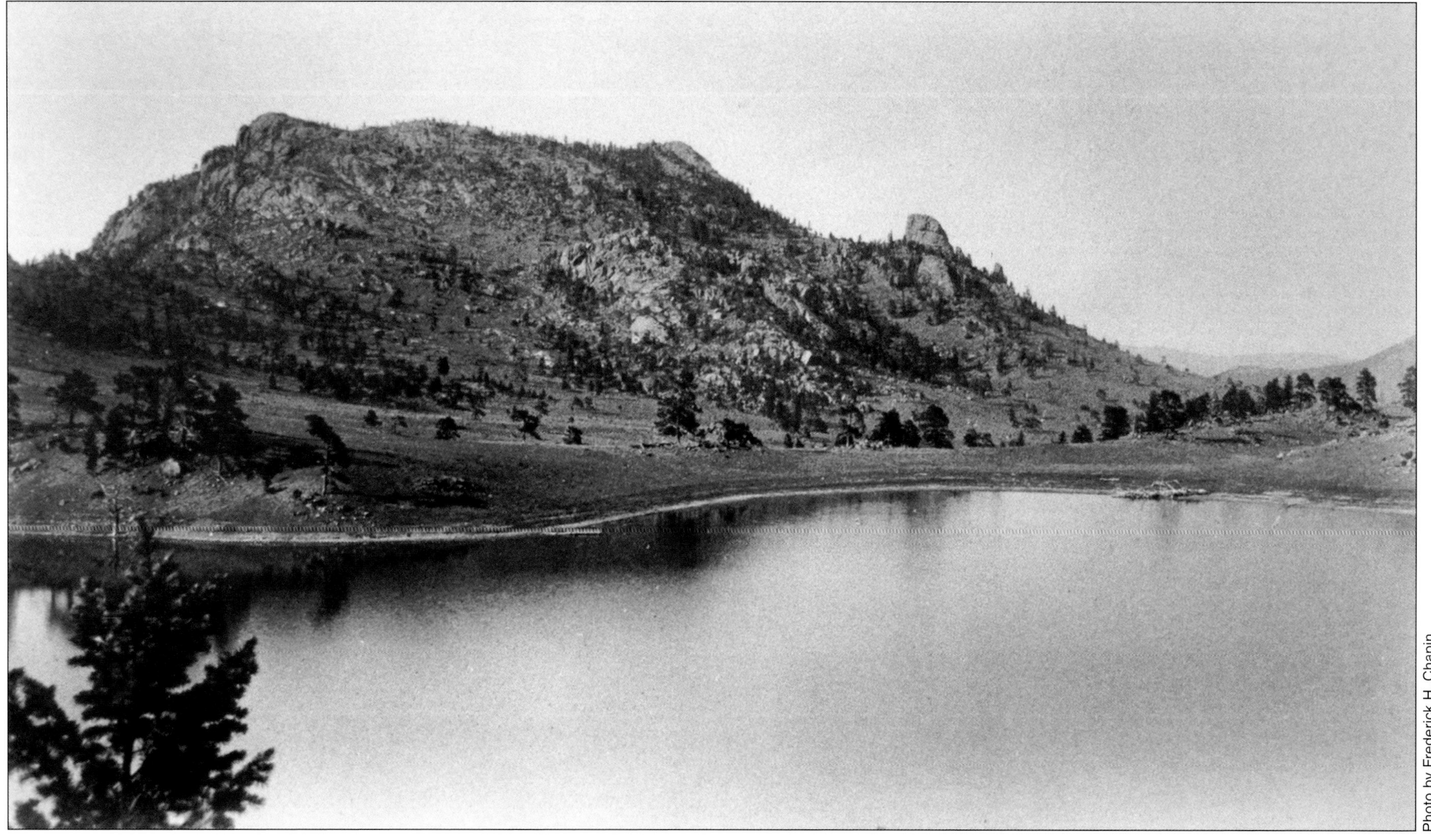

Photo by Frederick H. Chapin

Hartford, Connecticut, druggist Frederick H. Chapin took the original photograph of Marys Lake and Prospect Mountain. Chapin made three trips to Estes Park between 1886 and 1888, staying at Horace Ferguson's nearby Highlands Hotel resort. The lake, he wrote, is "a little sheet of alkaline water, Lily [Twin Sisters] Mountain rising on the south, Sheep Mountain on the west, and Prospect Mountain on the east. It was formerly a great resort for big-horn, elk, and deer, which came in great numbers to the lake, as they would a salt-lick; and many have been shot there." In 1914, several Arapaho visiting Estes Park identified an "old Indian camp" with tepee rings near the lake, suggesting that it had been used for hunting in earlier times.

The lake, which the Earl of Dunraven refers to in his writings as St. Mary's Lake, was apparently named either for Mary L. Fleming, the wife of Joel Estes'

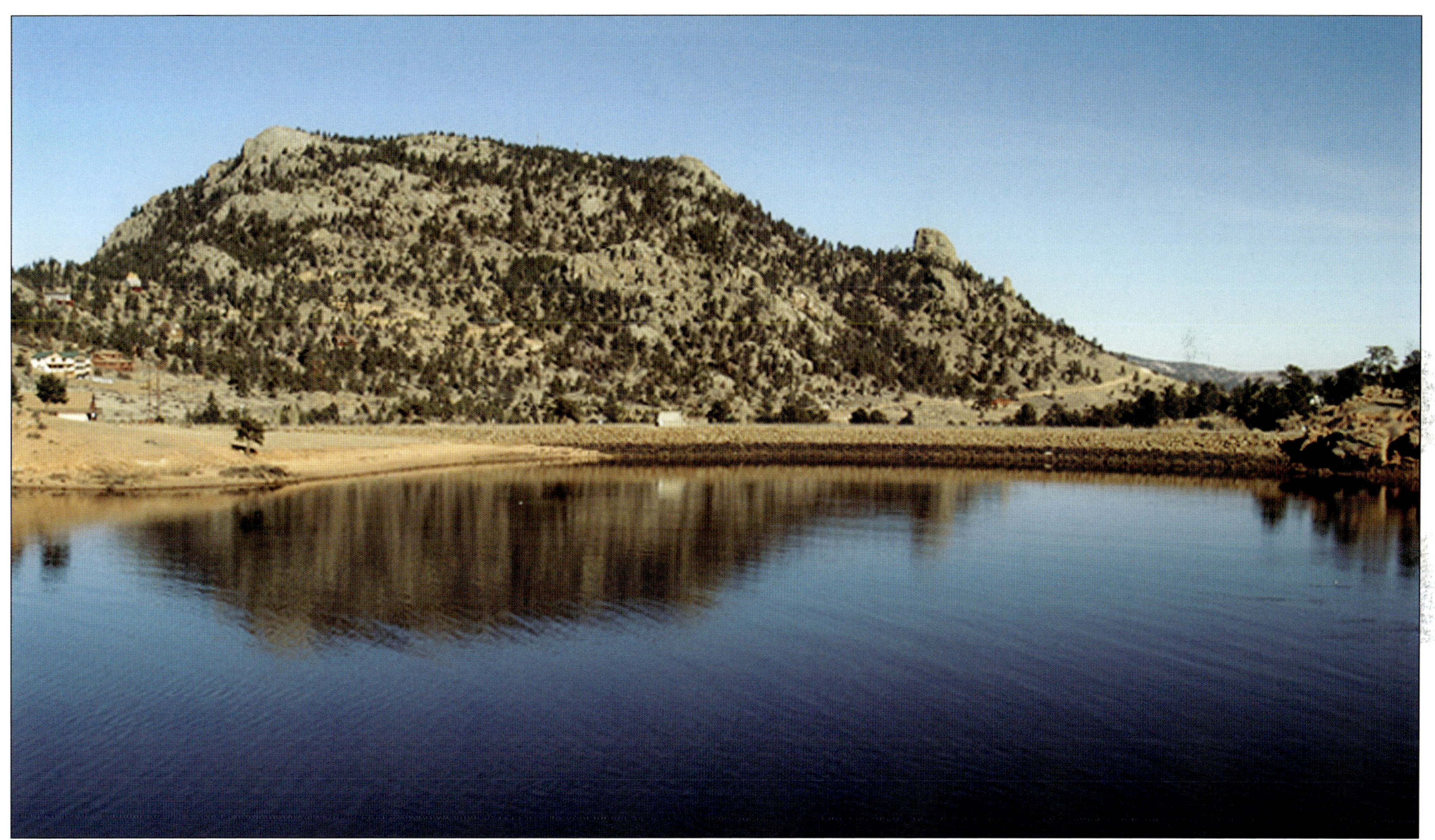

son, Milton, or for Griff Evans' niece, Mary Jane Buchanan, the wife of nearby homesteader John Buchanan. One story has "Rocky Mountain Jim" Nugent bestowing Mary Jane's first name on the lake when he encountered her headed there on a birthday ride with her husband.

In the late 1940s, the lake was deepened 25 to 30 feet by the construction of dikes on its east and northeast sides. This gave sufficient pondage to regulate the flow of water coming through the 13-mile Alva B. Adams Tunnel from Grand Lake before being sent on to the Estes Park Power Plant by a conduit through Prospect Mountain. Construction of the 8,100-kilowatt power plant and the enlargement of the lake required rerouting the road from the lake's south side (from where both Chapin's photograph and the present one were taken) across the tops of the dikes.

13. Beaver Point, November 1937

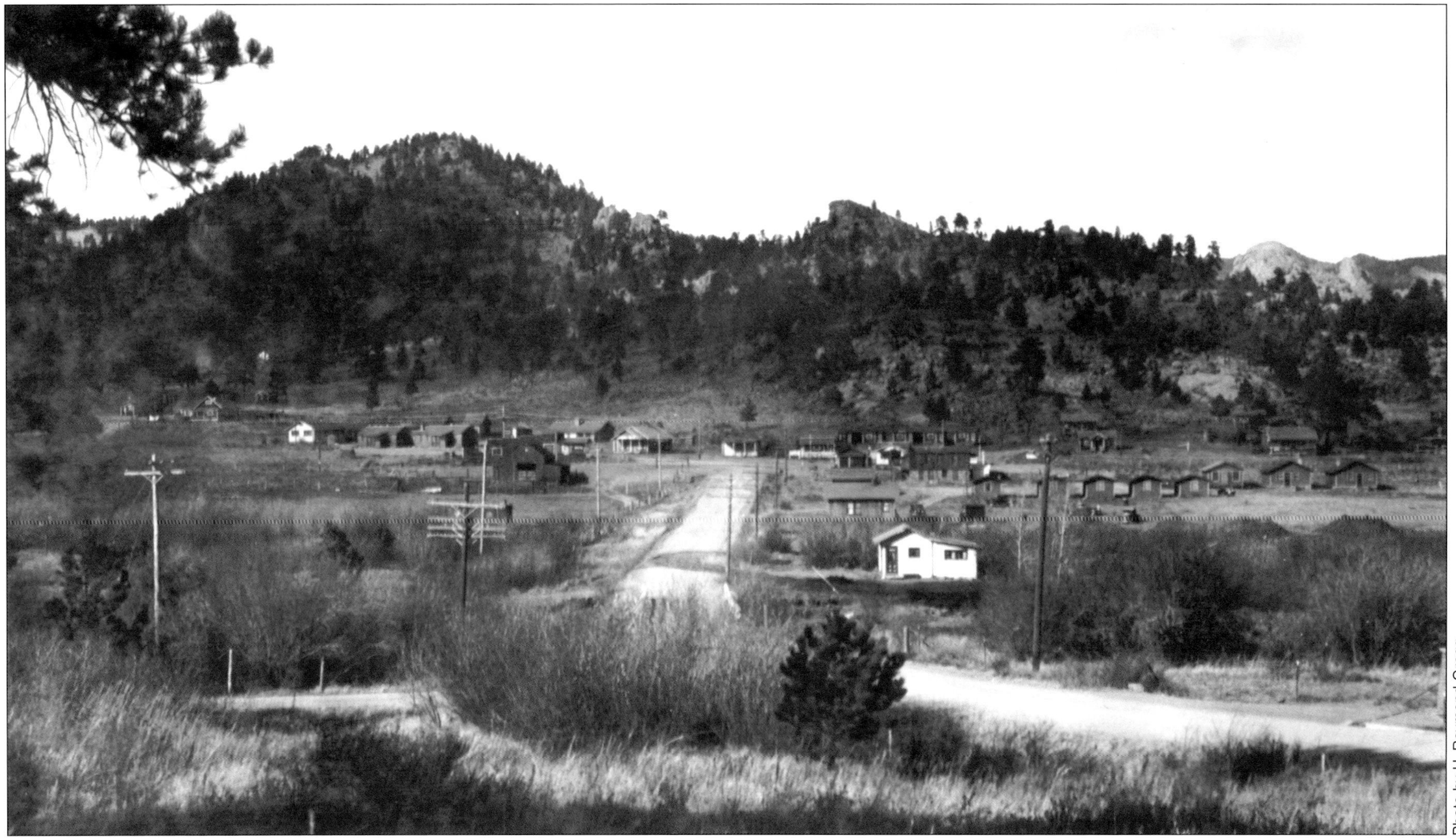

Photo by H. Raymond Gregg

Beaver Point is the name given to the intersection of High Drive and Marys Lake Road with CR 66. It takes its name from Beaver Brook, which runs southeast through Beaver Meadows and empties into the Big Thompson River nearby. For many years, Beaver Point has been a busy place. In the late 19th and early 20th centuries, horse-drawn wagons and stages, filled with newly arrived passengers and luggage, turned left at Beaver Point to go up what was then called Highlands Hill to deposit passengers at Horace Ferguson's Highlands Hotel (see p. 150) or continue on to Lamb's Longs Peak House (later the Longs Peak Inn) up in the Tahosa Valley (see p. 164). Since 1915, the road past Beaver Point has served as one of the principal entrances to Rocky Mountain National Park.

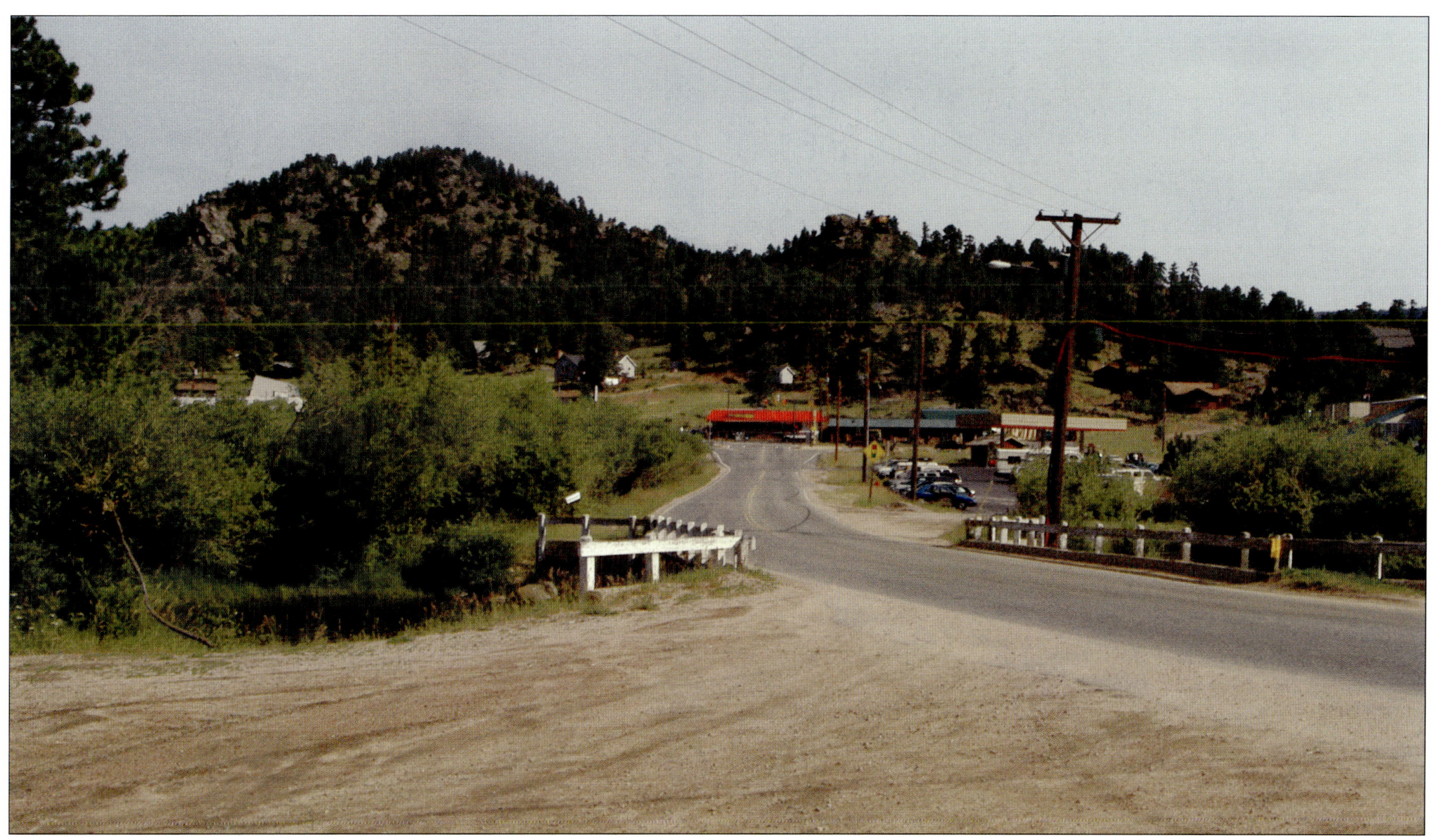

Here at Beaver Point also begins historic High Drive, angling northwest. The area served by this road, which once extended into the national park to reach the lower slopes of Deer Mountain and Beaver Meadows, is the site of many early cabins and buildings. Among the latter, on the site of what has long been the Sundeck Restaurant, was Anna Wolfrom's curio store. Located farther up High Drive, past the place where it enters the park, once stood the famous Lone Pine (see p. 52).

14. Rocky Mountain National Park 1923 Headquarters

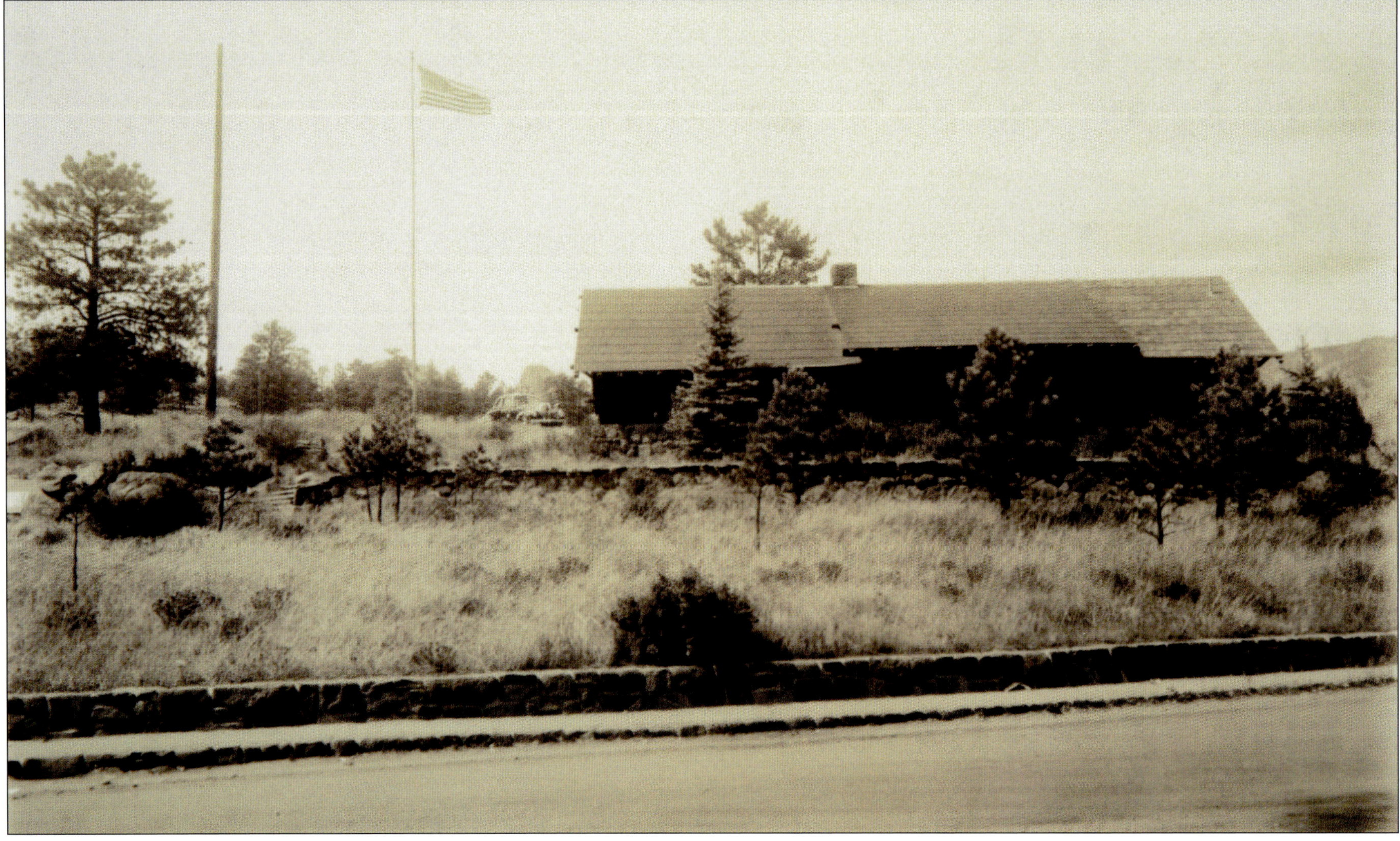

Until 1923, Rocky Mountain National Park maintained its administrative offices in a small white frame building on Elkhorn Avenue in the village, across the street from Sam Service's general store. That October they were transferred to a new headquarters building on what was then the outskirts of Estes Park, on the southern slope of Davis Hill where Moraine Avenue swings west along the Big Thompson River. The 26-by-45-foot masonry and lumber building, with an 8-foot porch extending halfway across the front, was built on land donated to the Park Service in May 1921 by the Estes Park Woman's Club. With its large stone fireplace, the lobby served as an information bureau, while the rest of the new building contained office space for the park's superintendent, rangers, and business office.

In June 1931, a small museum building, the park's first, was opened directly below the administration building. Much to the consternation of several superintendents and not a few visitors, the Park Service's across-the-street neighbor

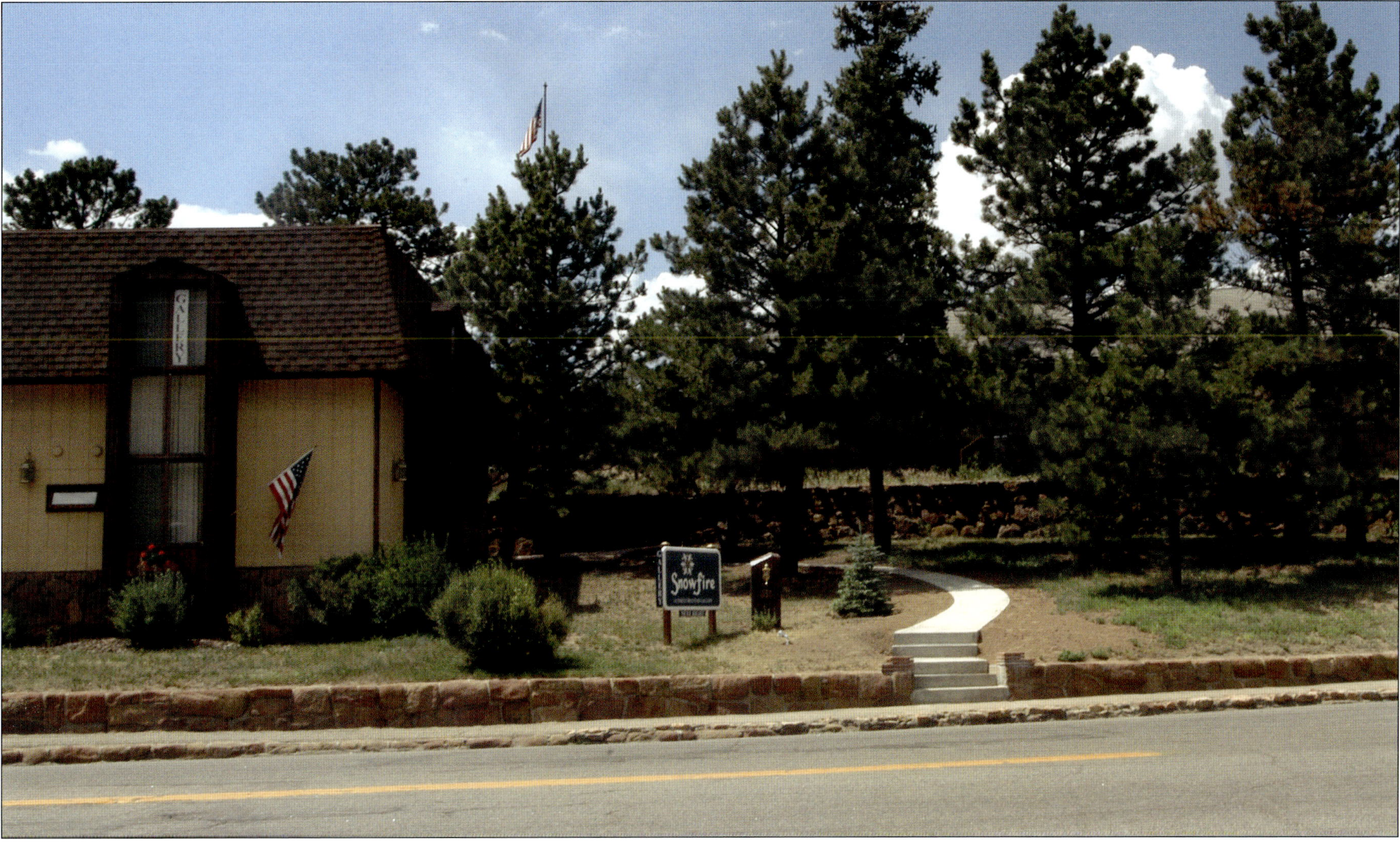

for years was the malodorous-smelling Blue Ribbon Livery which was operated by Harold Alps and a bane to visitors and residents nearby.

Park headquarters stayed on this site until 1967, when it was transferred to a new building located in lower Beaver Meadows constructed under the directives of "Mission 66," the National Park Service's 10-year plan to upgrade facilities in national parks across the nation. The Frank Lloyd Wright style of architecture that inspired the design for the new building is clearly very different from the style of the 1923 building, which is often lovingly referred to as "Park Service Rustic," with its decorative exterior stonework and extended pole rafters.

15. The Lone Pine, circa 1915

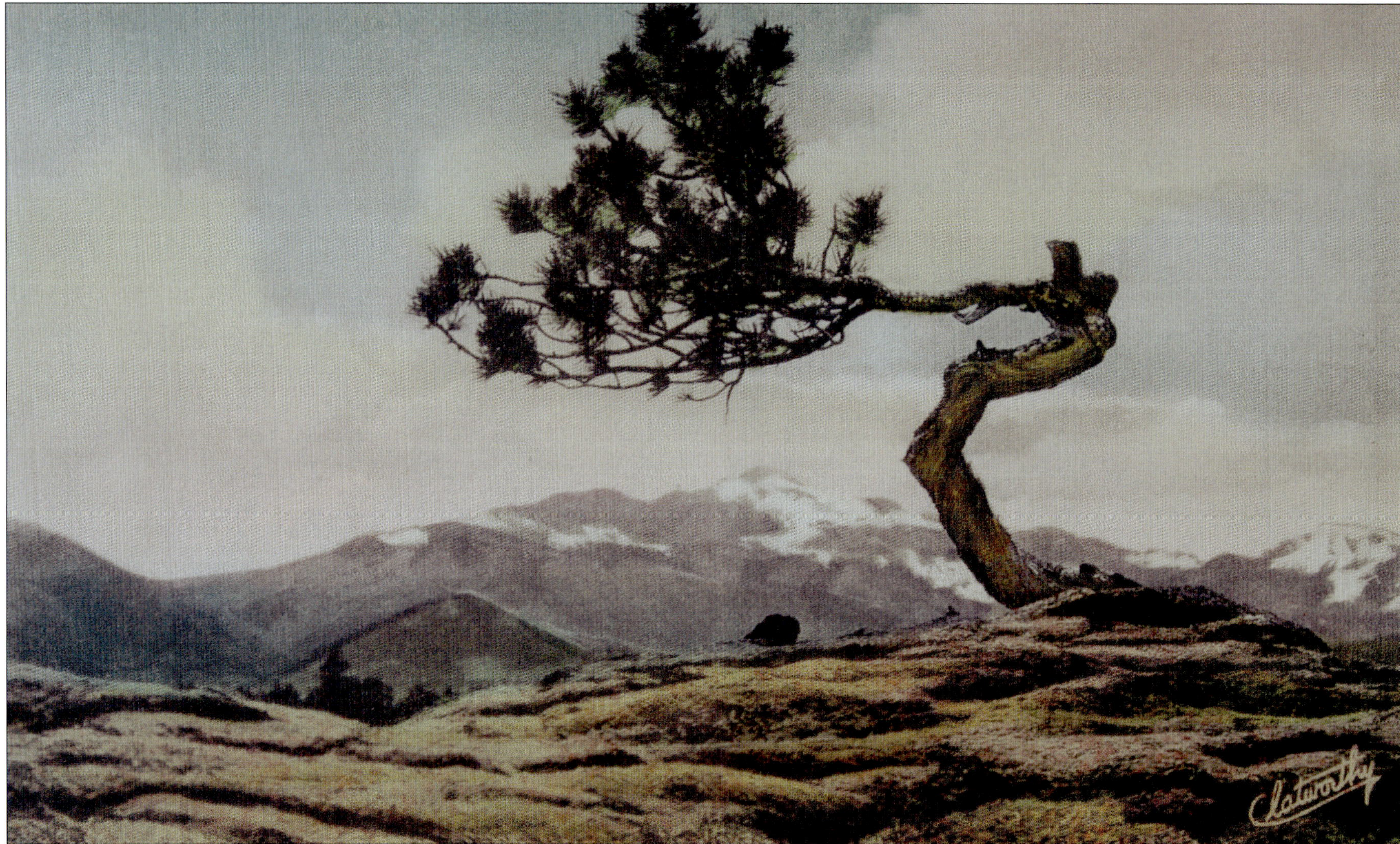

Photo by Fred Payne Clatworthy

One of the most unusual historic sites in Rocky Mountain National Park was a much-viewed, much-photographed tree on High Drive that once captured the imagination of local residents and tourists alike.

High Drive, originally built to bring out timber, once provided direct access to the park. Along this highly traveled road, in the crevice of a large rock, grew a small ponderosa pine. As it grew, its twisted, windblown shape somehow defied and defeated the forces of nature, and the "Lone Pine" became a landmark. The Lone Pine became so popular as a tourist stop that a gift store was built across the road offering commemorative souvenirs, including views taken by local photographers William T. Parke, Frank J. Francis, and Fred Payne Clatworthy,

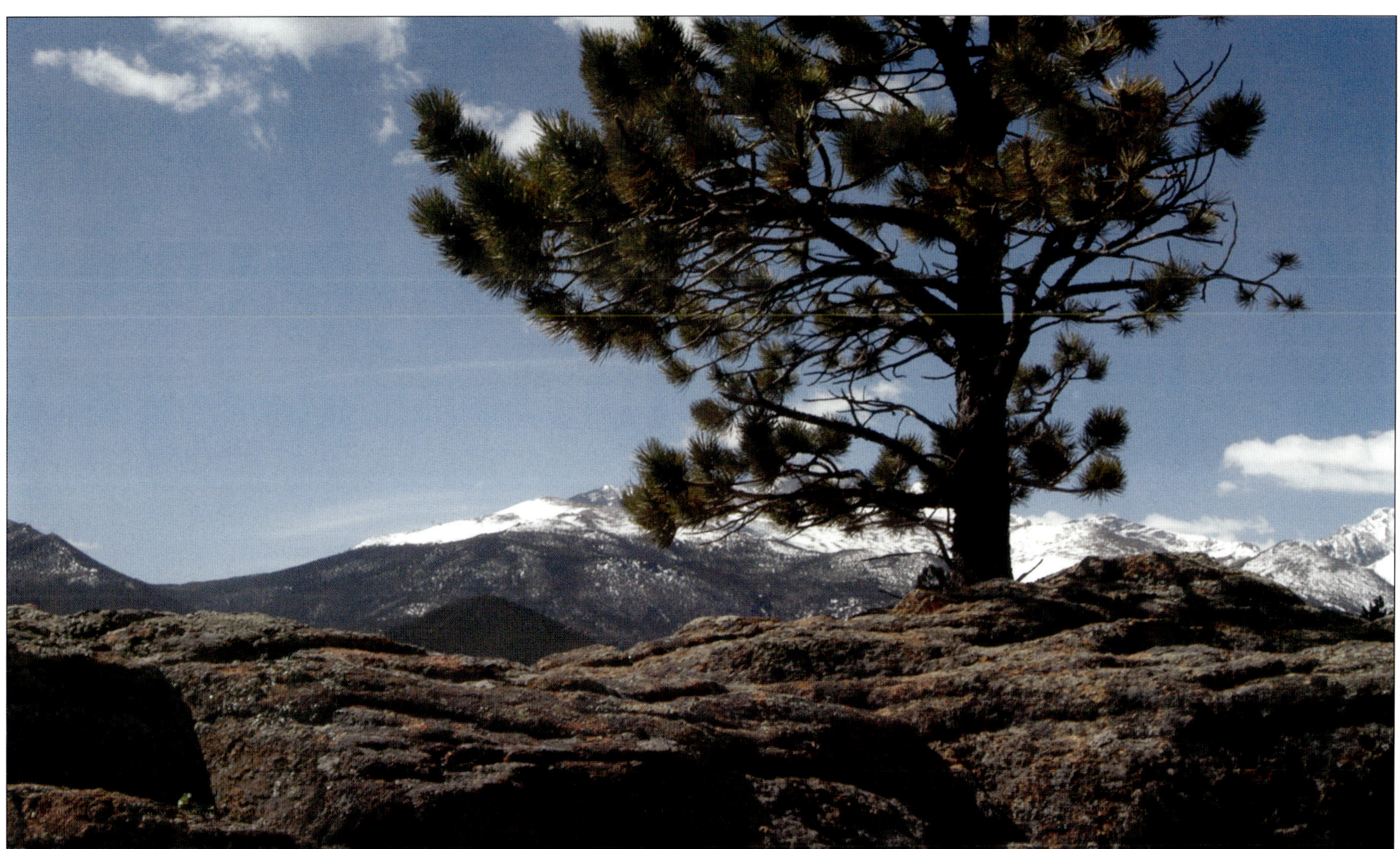

who took the original photograph shown here. The Lone Pine Trading Post, built in 1928, was a two-room log cabin owned by Blanche E. Bugh of Ohio.

The Lone Pine suffered a tragic fate. Visitors to the site of the tree started to pick off its needles and bark for keepsakes. A sign was posted at the base of the tree pleading, "Please, do not molest the tree," but tourists literally picked the Lone Pine to death. In 1949, the tree succumbed at last to humankind, and the *Estes Park Trail* ran an obituary of sorts for another piece of local history that was no more. Another tree was planted in its place, but the natural wonder that was the Lone Pine could not be duplicated: Its would-be successor grows straight toward the sky just like other trees.

16. The Y–Big Thompson Entrance to Rocky Mountain National Park, December 1939

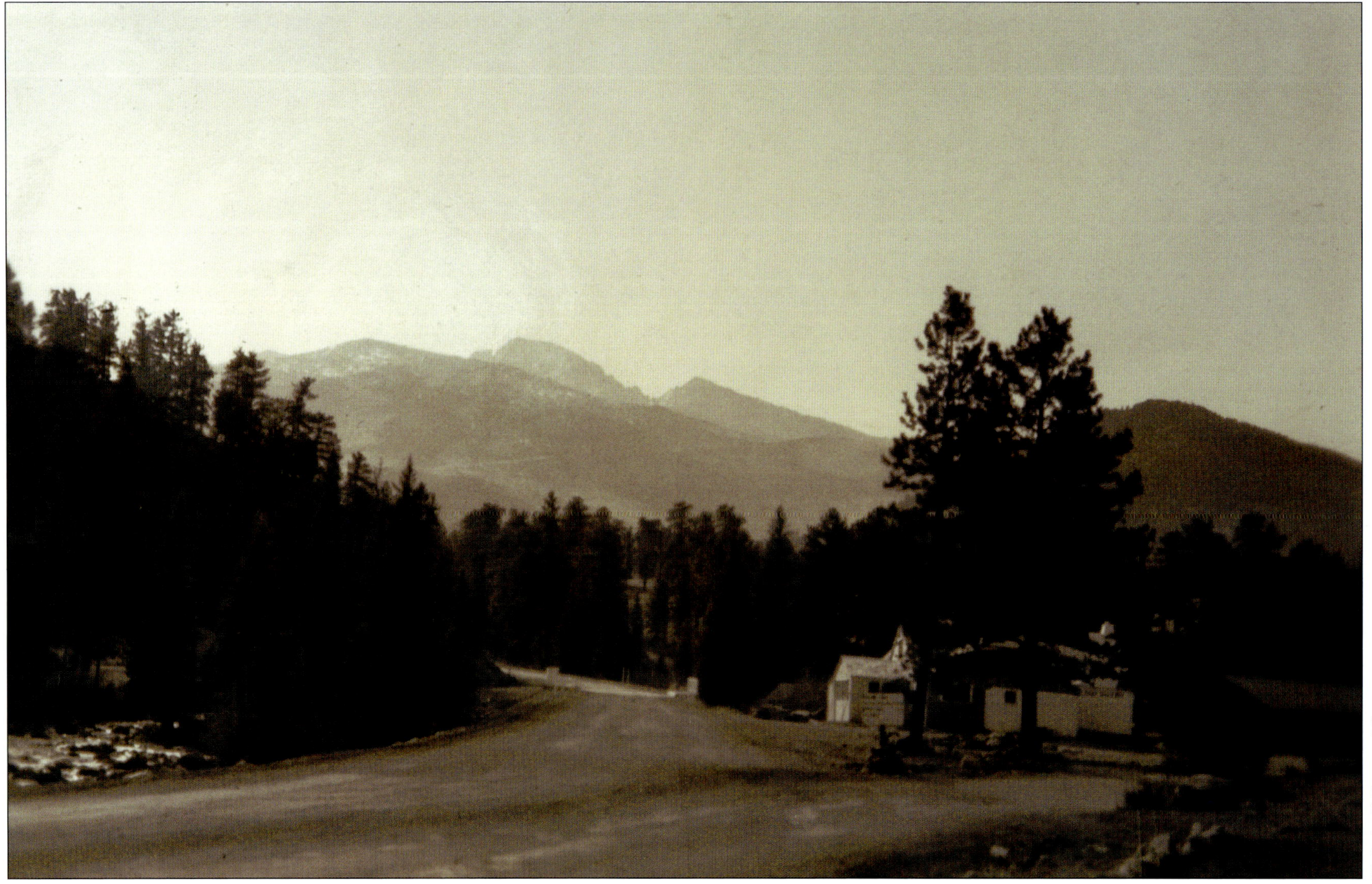

Photo by H. Raymond Gregg

Until 1960, the Big Thompson entrance to Rocky Mountain National Park was located between the south slope of Eagle Cliff Mountain and the Big Thompson River just off of today's Highway 66, the road to the YMCA of the Rockies. Before reaching the bridge, visitors turned right to enter the park, proceeding northwest following the river and then going up the lower slope of Eaton Hill (named for Benjamin H. Eaton, Colorado's governor from 1885–1887) whose family had a summer home there (see p. 196). Reaching an intersection, drivers could choose to either turn right and enter Moraine Park, or turn left and travel

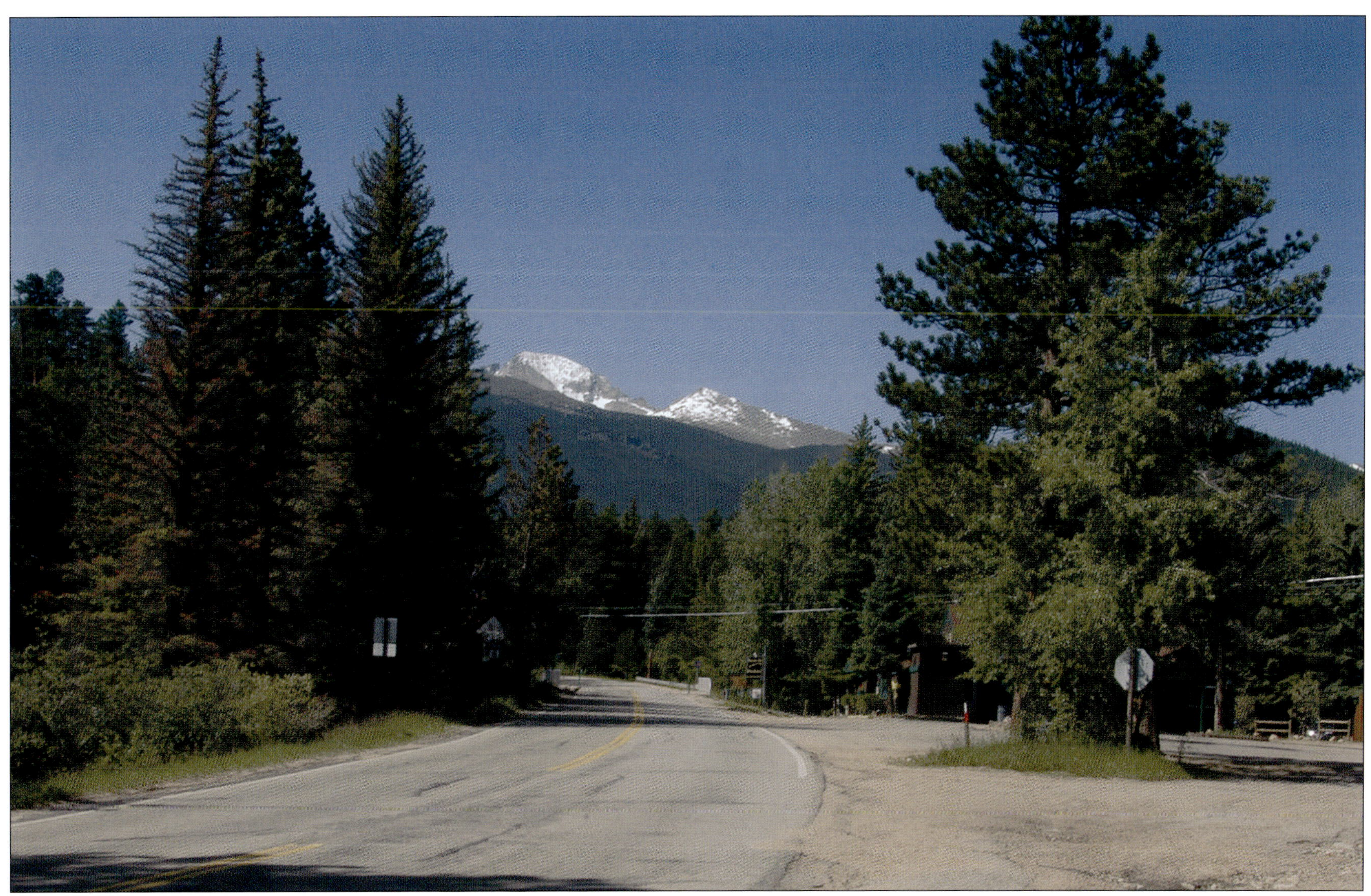

on to Hollowell Park, Sprague Lake, and the Bear Lake region. Simple tourist accommodations could be found in nearby Tuxedo Park, first at an auto campground operated by F. O. Stanley and later at Jack Woods' cabin camp called Camp Woods.

Today, the "Y junction" is a relatively quiet place. Early photographs show, however, that it became increasingly congested over the years, crowded with rental cabins, a store, mailboxes, and a restaurant, the Holland Inn (see p. 56), making the relocation of the park entrance to Beaver Meadows long overdue.

17. Holland Inn, circa 1935

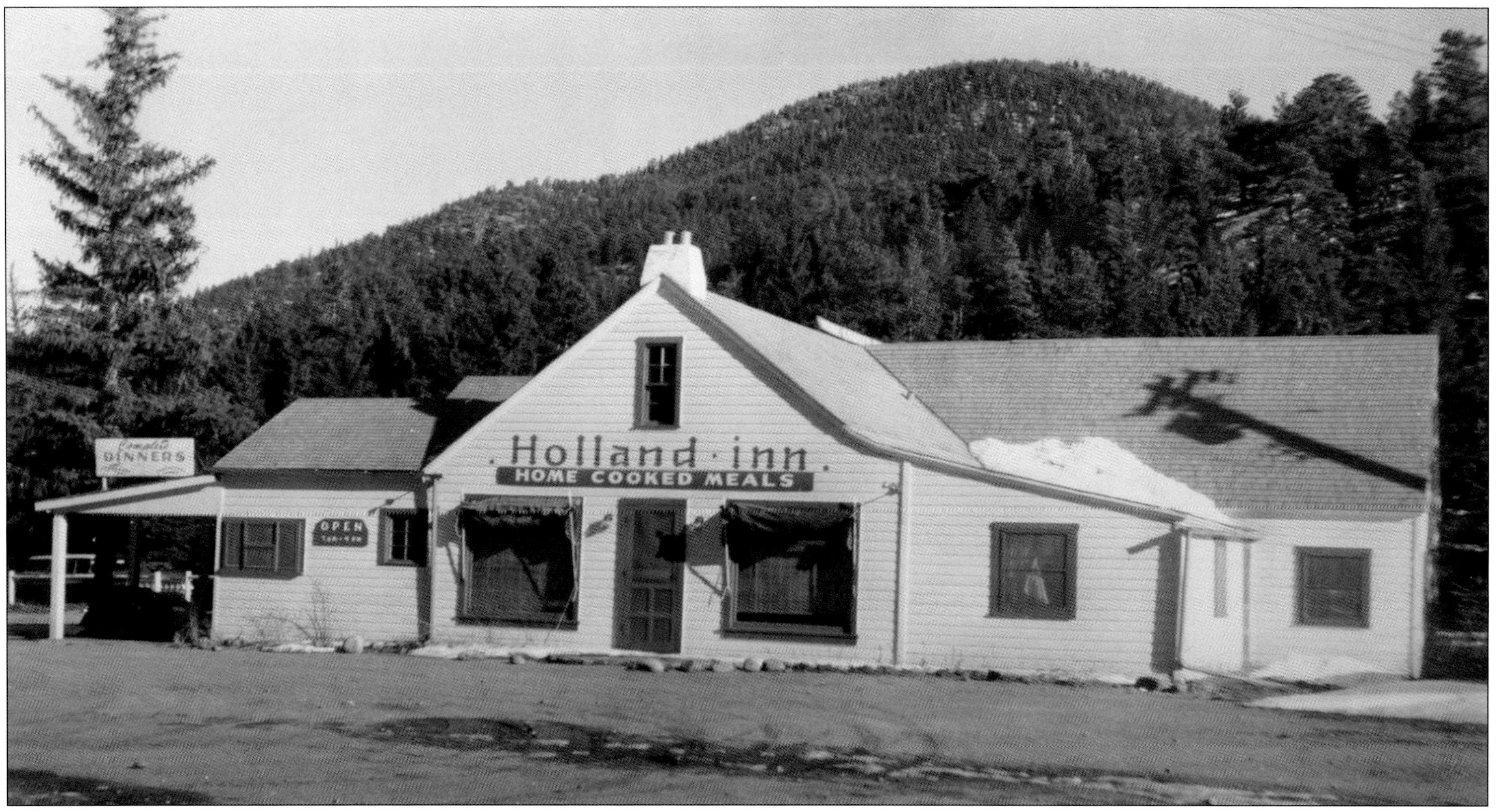

As the historic photograph, probably taken in the 1930s, tells us, the Dunraven Inn was first called the Holland Inn. We know from contemporary newspapers that the Holland Inn, built in 1907, was painted blue and white, and that its intersection was called "the Crossroads." There, roads led to the YMCA grounds and into Moraine Park (and, after 1915, Rocky Mountain National Park). Until the Big Thompson entrance to the park was relocated to its present location in Beaver Meadows, the Crossroads was a very busy place, making the restaurant's location ideal.

In 1971, the old Holland Inn was renamed the Dunraven Inn, after the Earl of Dunraven, for 30 years the Estes Valley's most famous landlord. The name is clearly ironic, for the Dunraven Inn's décor consists of examples of Leonardo da Vinci's famous portrait of Mona Lisa, *La Gioconda*. There are also dollar bills

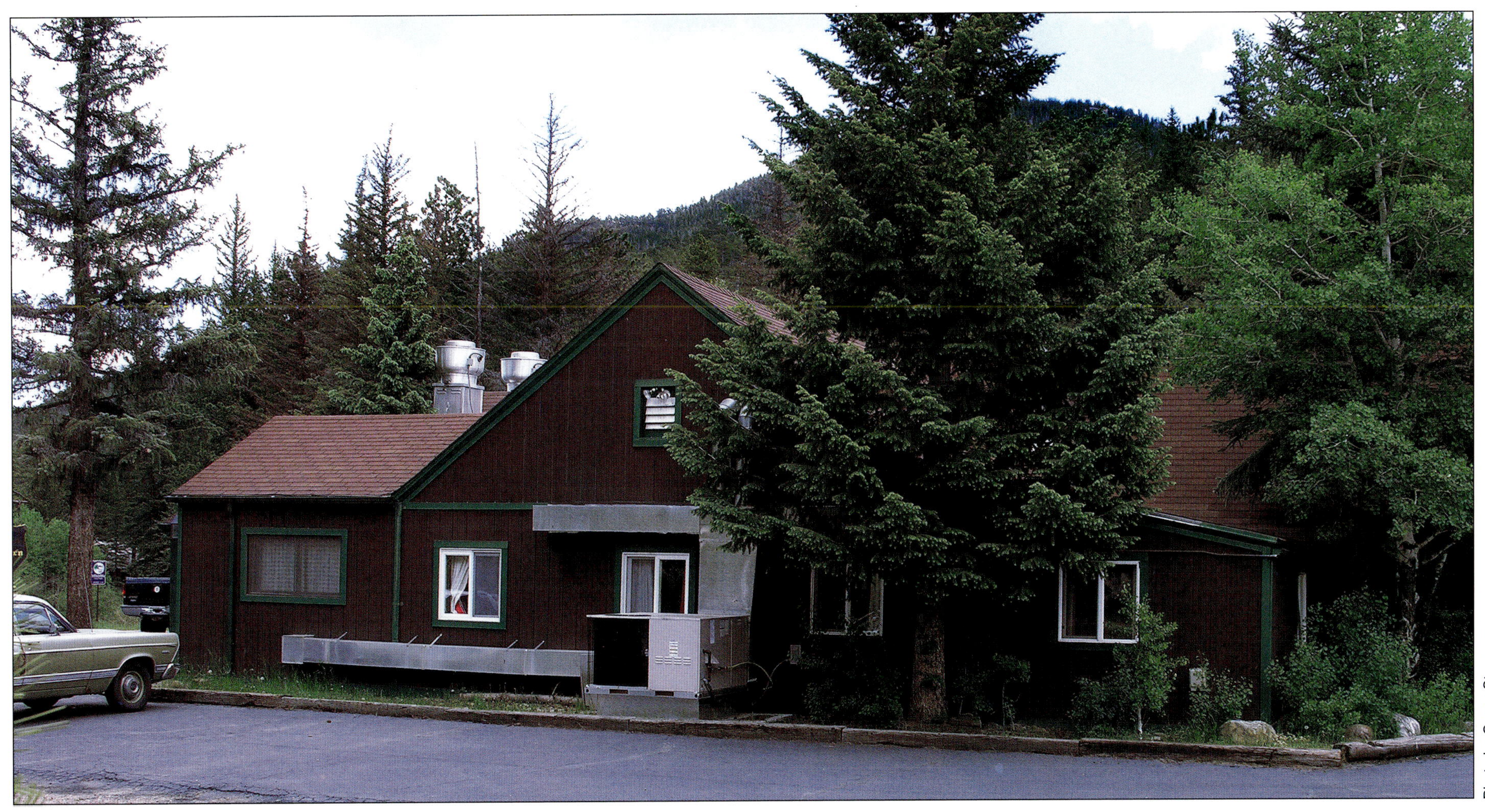

Photo by Carey Stevanus

affixed to the ceiling and walls of the barroom by several generations of patrons. The wealthy earl, who according to popular legend loved his whiskey, would no doubt have found this touch amusing.

On retaking the photograph, we discovered that the inn's original entrance faced the road into the national park a few feet away, not Highway 66 as it does now. This explains why today's kitchen is located in the front of the restaurant. The *Estes Park Trail* described its "Old English theme," featuring a large fireplace, timbering, and exposed beams. Its cocktail lounge, the Ship's Tavern, contained the original bar from the Dark Horse Tavern at Riverside Amusement Park, which had been torn down in 1970. Three days after opening, a malfunctioning floor heater caused a fire that damaged both bar and restaurant. The building was quickly repaired and the Dunraven was ready for the 1971 tourist season.

18. YMCA of the Rockies, 1923

The YMCA of the Rockies traces its origins to an encampment by Grand Lake in 1907, when a group of Y leaders decided to establish a permanent summer facility in the Rocky Mountains. As the story goes, the encampment was cut short by mosquitoes, giving the six delegates the opportunity to cross the Continental Divide to Estes Park to survey sites for their 1908 conference. They chose Wind River Lodge, a two-story gabled lodge and six adjacent cottages built on the lower slopes of Emerald Mountain. The site, near the Big Thompson River, offered the assurance of the glaciated "Y" on Mount Ypsilon across the moraines.

The first new structure, completed in 1910, was the Dining and Social Hall. Its Western-style Stick architecture's latticework, rustic posts, low gables, and and railings would be employed in future buildings. Fred Payne Clatworthy took the original photograph in 1923. By then, the Dining and Social Hall had become today's administration building. At the far left is Hyde Memorial Chapel, built in 1913. Its bell tower was added in 1956. To the right of the administration building is the post office, completed about 1923, and the dining hall, today's Walnut Room. The dining hall, which was built in 1911 as a gymnasium, was converted in 1912–1913, only to be almost destroyed by December 1913's epic snowstorm. It was repaired in time for the 1914 season.

The final building in the Clatworthy photograph (at far right, the site of what is now Walter G. Ruesch Auditorium) is Wind River Lodge, which had been moved by log rollers from its original site on the side of Buena Vista (today's Bible Point). Wind River Lodge, once again relocated, now serves as the Lula W. Dorsey Museum.

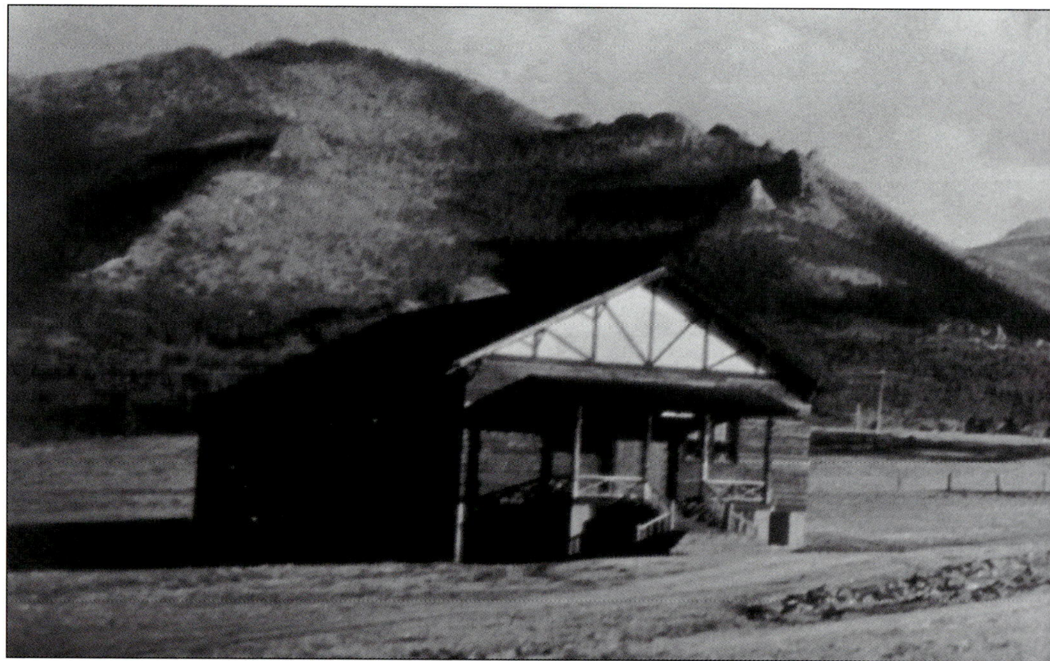

Photo by Fred Payne Clatworthy

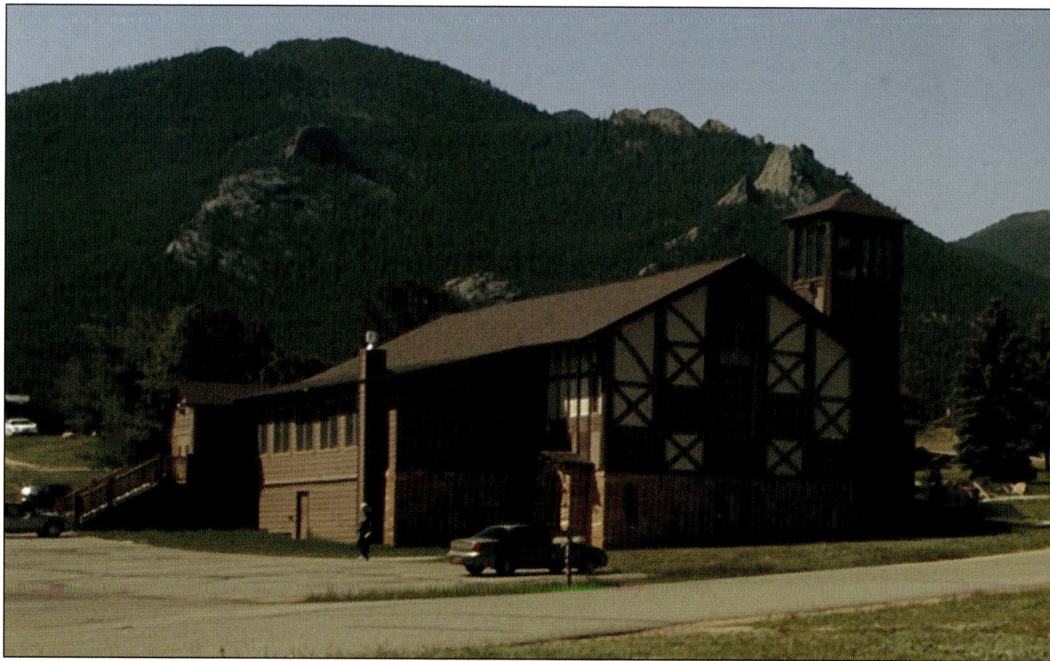

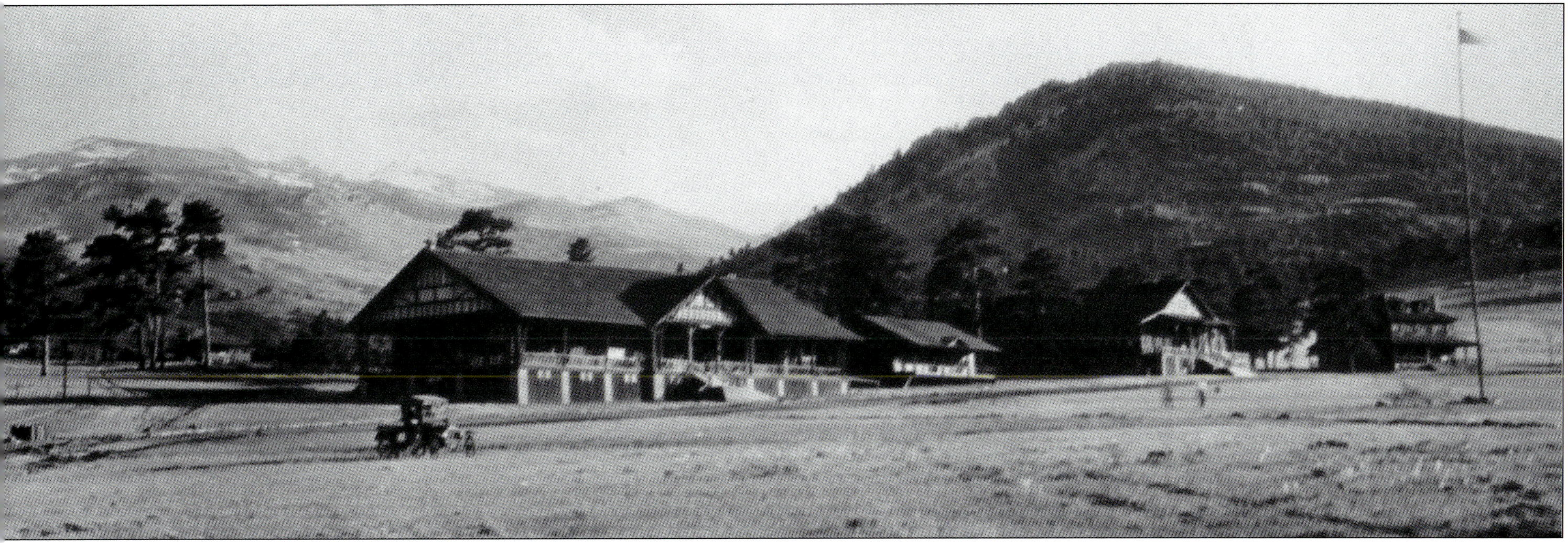

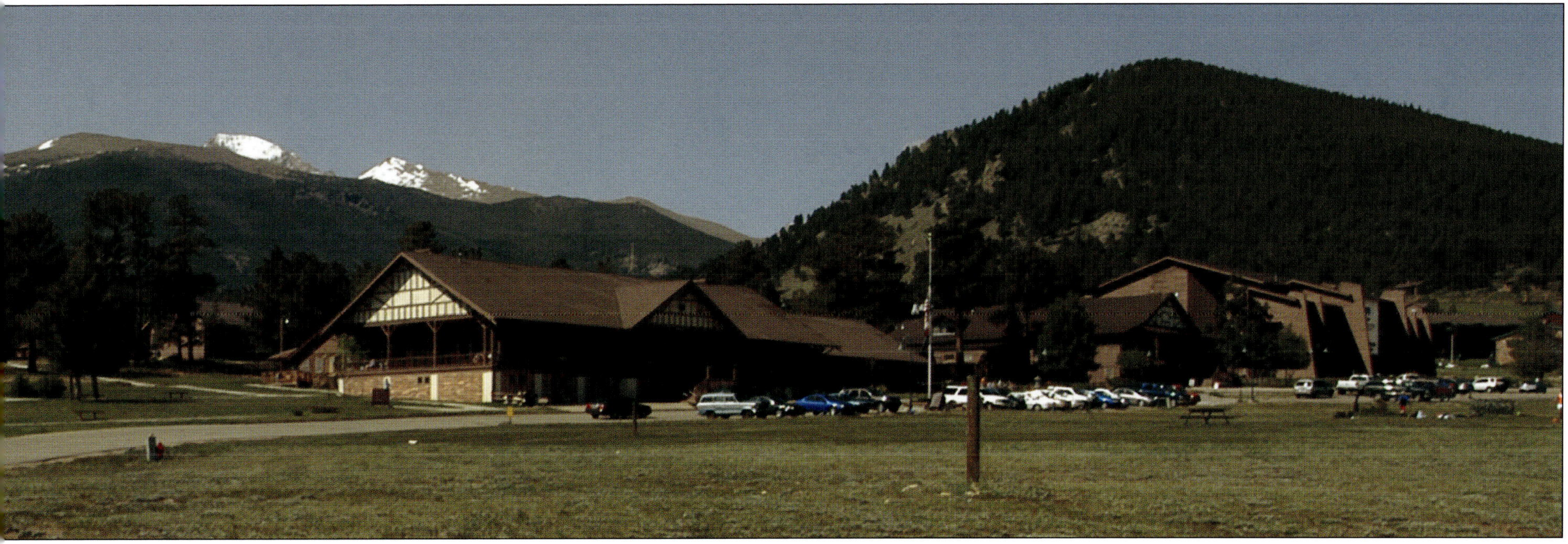

19. Mountainside Lodge, circa 1925

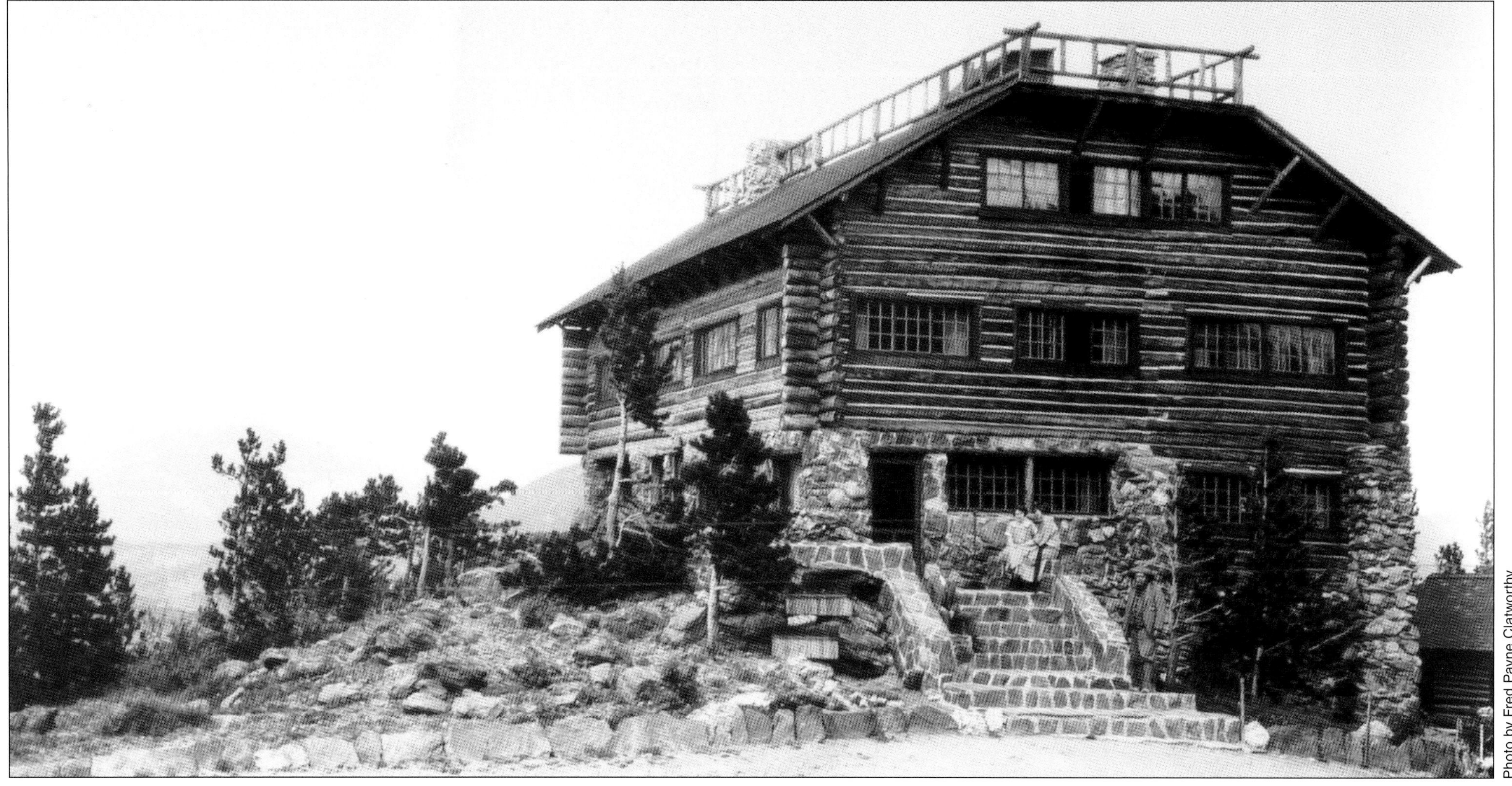

Photo by Fred Payne Clatworthy

Mountainside Lodge was the realized dream of Dr. John Timothy Stone, the energetic pastor of Chicago's Fourth Presbyterian Church and later president of that city's McCormick Theological Seminary. Stone first came to the Y in 1909 to give sermons and lectures and quickly became one of its most important supporters, serving on the board of directors with future Colorado governor William E. Sweet. In 1917, he purchased the Emerald Mountain site, first building a study for himself on a rocky outcropping to the west and then completing the main lodge building in 1920. Both were constructed of native stone and lodgepole pine, which was cut on the site. "The house is lovely," Stone wrote, "and the view beyond words in glory."

Stone and his family used Mountainside Lodge for only three seasons. In 1924, he reluctantly sold the property to finance a yearlong world mission tour.

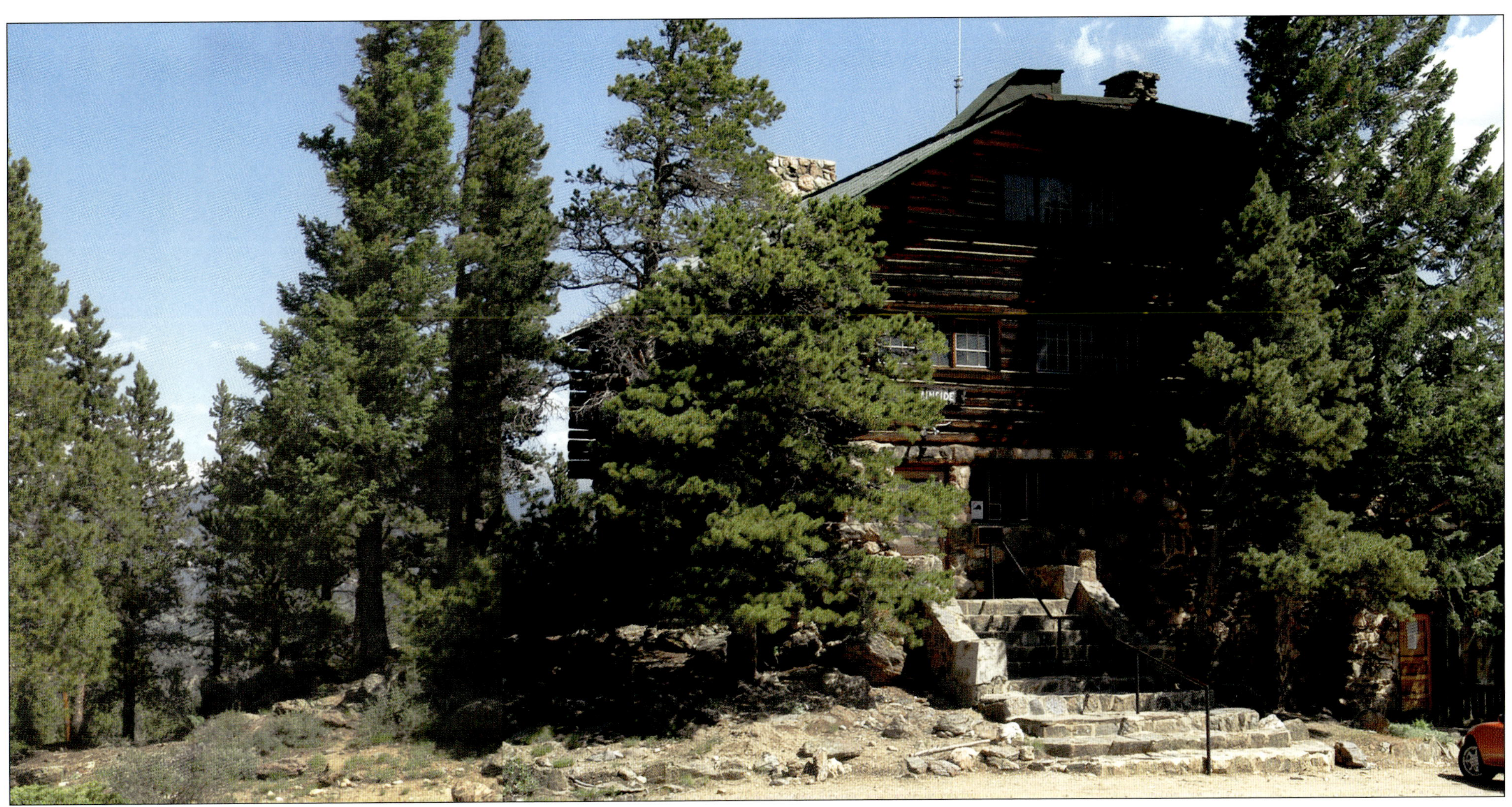

For a time, the lodge was operated as a hotel; later, from 1934 to 1939, it became the Camp Allsebrook girls' camp.

Purchased by the YMCA in 1956, the lodge and its cabins were later used between 1962 and 1994 for family reunions and church retreats. The lodge was then closed for repair and restoration. Thanks to the efforts of Jack R. Melton, director of the Y's Lula W. Dorsey Museum, and members of the Stone family, Mountainside Lodge was placed on the Colorado Register of Historic Places in 1997 and, in 2000, on the National Register of Historic Places. Today, Dr. John Stone's mountainside retreat awaits the conclusion of a $1.35 million capital campaign, designed to finish rehabilitation of the lodge building and its adjacent Bighorn Annex bunkhouse, and to construct new facilities on the site, including an outdoor wedding chapel.

20. Wigwam Tea Room, circa 1915

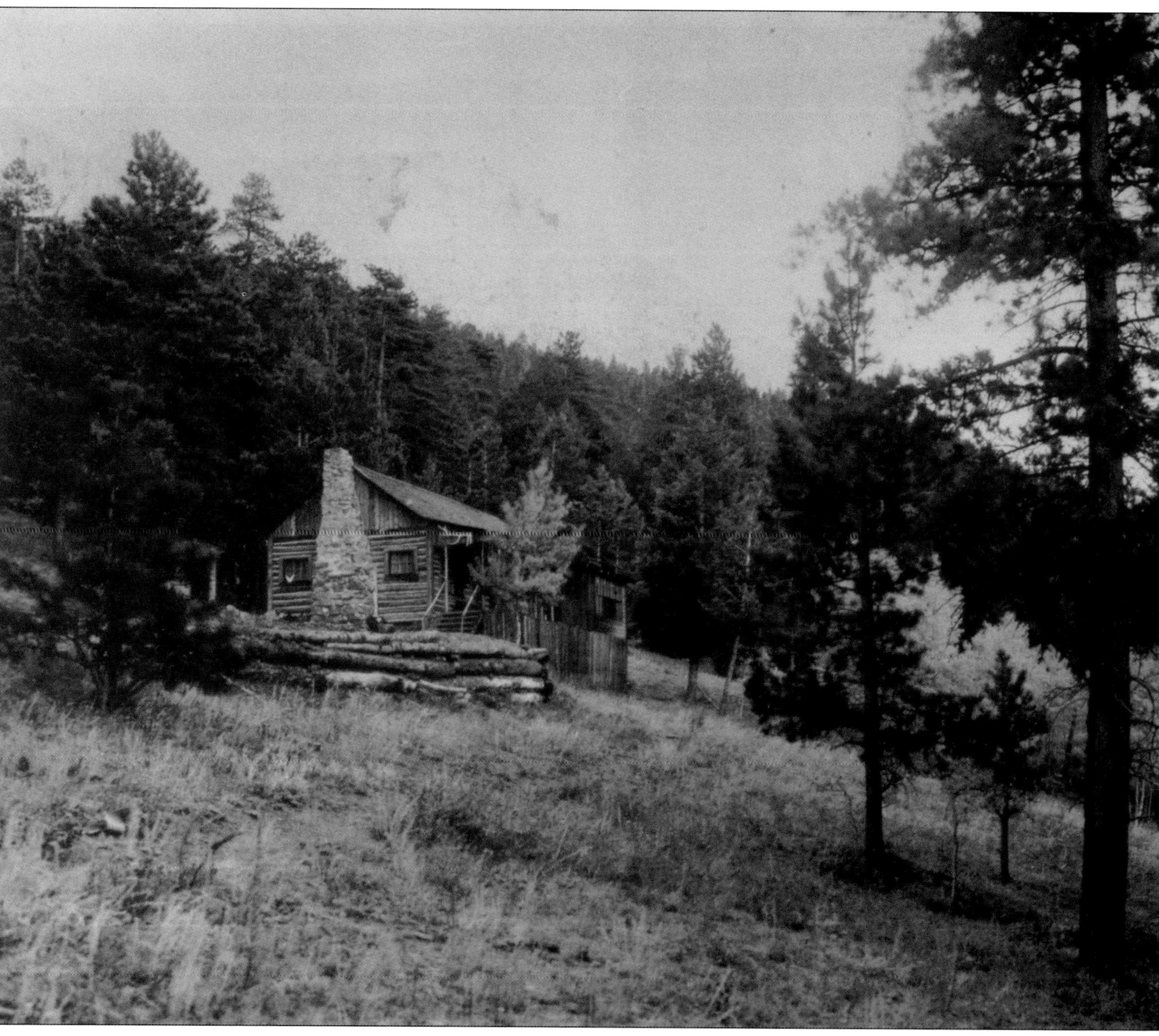

Many single women sought to find their independence out in the American West. Anna Wolfrom, a Kansas City, Missouri, school teacher who was not interested in the conventional life she saw before her, became the very first woman homesteader in the Estes Valley in 1907.

Wolfrom was only 35 when she submitted her application to homestead 160 acres along the Wind River Trail, and then built her cabin with little help. At the time, Wind River Trail was not accessible by wagon or by auto, forcing her to bring supplies in by a wheelbarrow. In 1914, Wolfrom expanded her home and opened the Wigwam Tea Room, an arts and crafts shop said to serve the best teas and cakes in the region. That September, Anna improved the trail to accommodate automobiles, and the Wigwam with its screened porch became the resting spot for as many as 200 guests a day.

By 1921, Anna Wolfrom had to double the size of the building and hire help. She then turned the Wigwam over to a manager and opened up a new business at

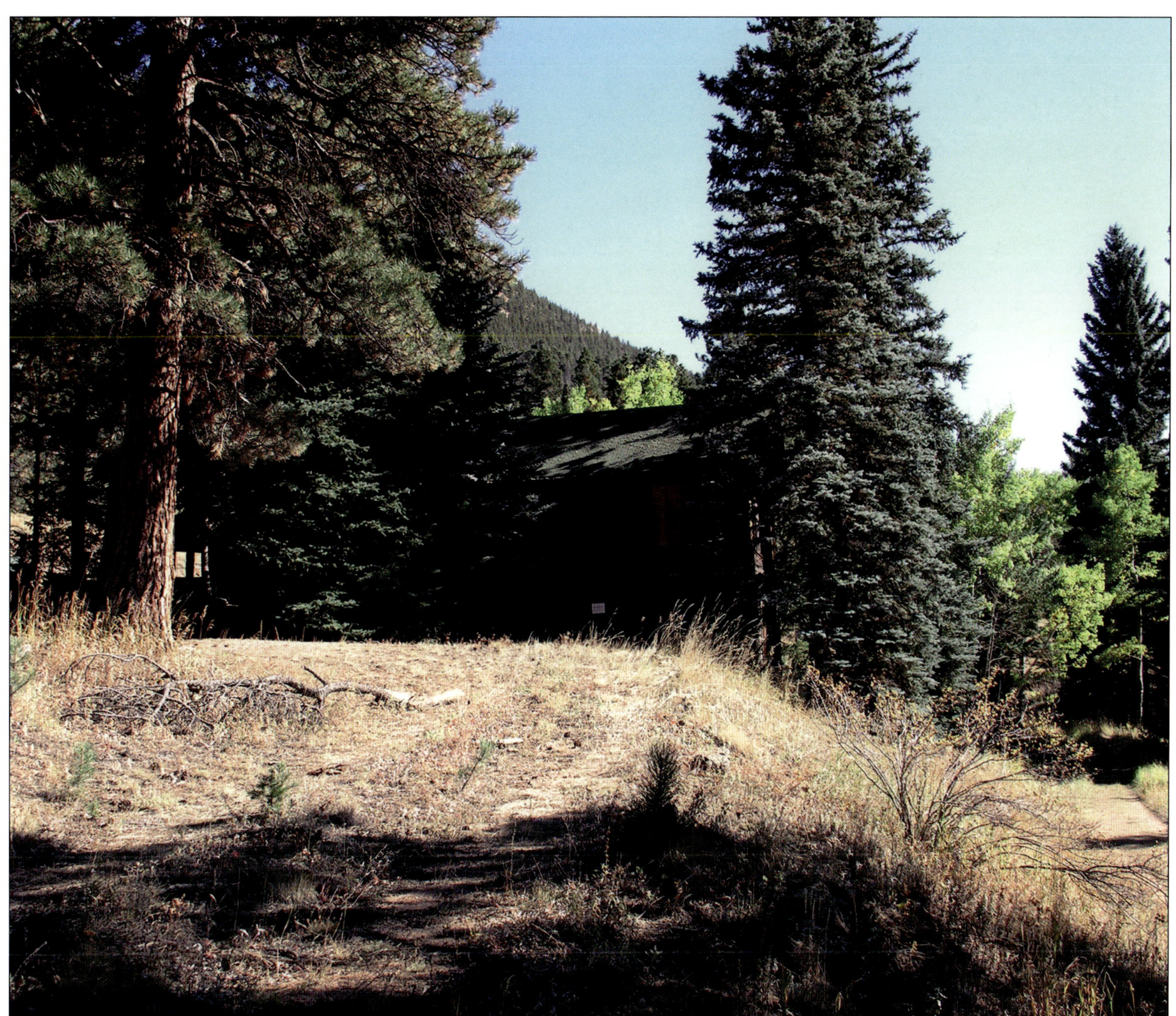

Photo by
Carey Stevanus

Beaver Point, one of the valley's busiest intersections (see p. 48). Here she had a store and a filling station built. After her 1923 marriage to Dr. Orville Dove of Kansas City, she continued to expand her business enterprises and opened up a new shop on Elkhorn Avenue near the Sam Service store (see p. 88).

In 1948, two years before her death, Anna Wolfrom Dove sold the Wigwam. The national park acquired the property in 1989 through a donation from The Nature Conservancy. But both time and vandals have now taken their toll. Because of Park Service regulations that say old buildings may remain standing only if they can be put to use, a decision will soon have to be made about the future of this historic structure.

21. F. O. Stanley House, circa 1940

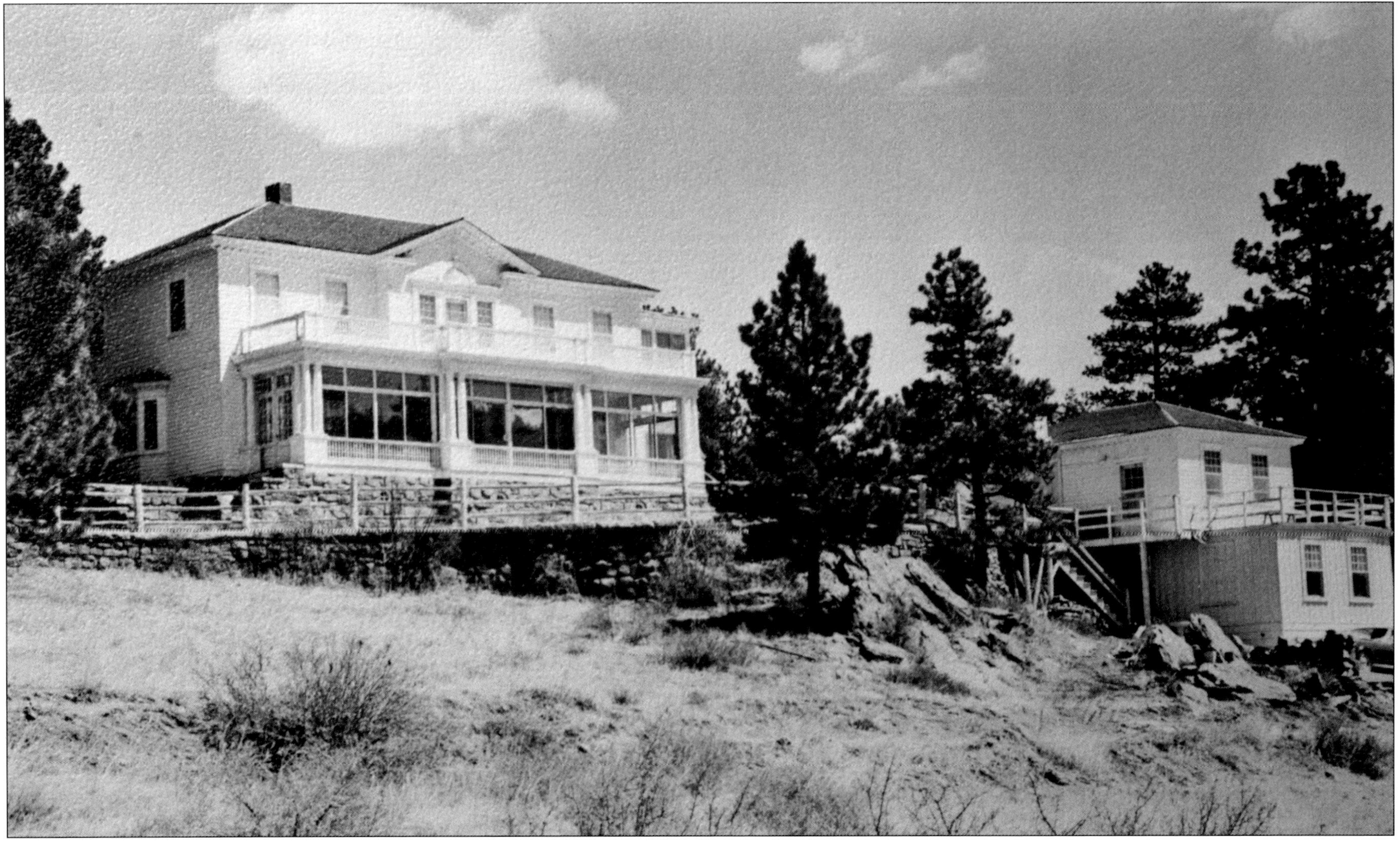

Freelan O. Stanley was a man ill with consumption, or tuberculosis, when he came to Estes Park to convalesce in the summer of 1903. Estes Park did wonders for his health, and before the season was over, Stanley and his wife Flora purchased 8.4 acres for a summer home in an area called "Rockside," just north of the future village of Estes Park. The setting was magnificent: a sloping hillside facing Longs Peak and the Front Range. During the winter that followed, work began on the 5,240-square-foot "cottage" that would be Stanley's summer home for the next 36 years. The house, with its high foundation, imposing entrance, and Doric columns, was built in the same Georgian Colonial Revival style as the Stanley Hotel, completed five years later.

The Stanley home featured a 40-foot veranda opening into an illuminated front hall with a central staircase above a two-story rotunda. Below the house,

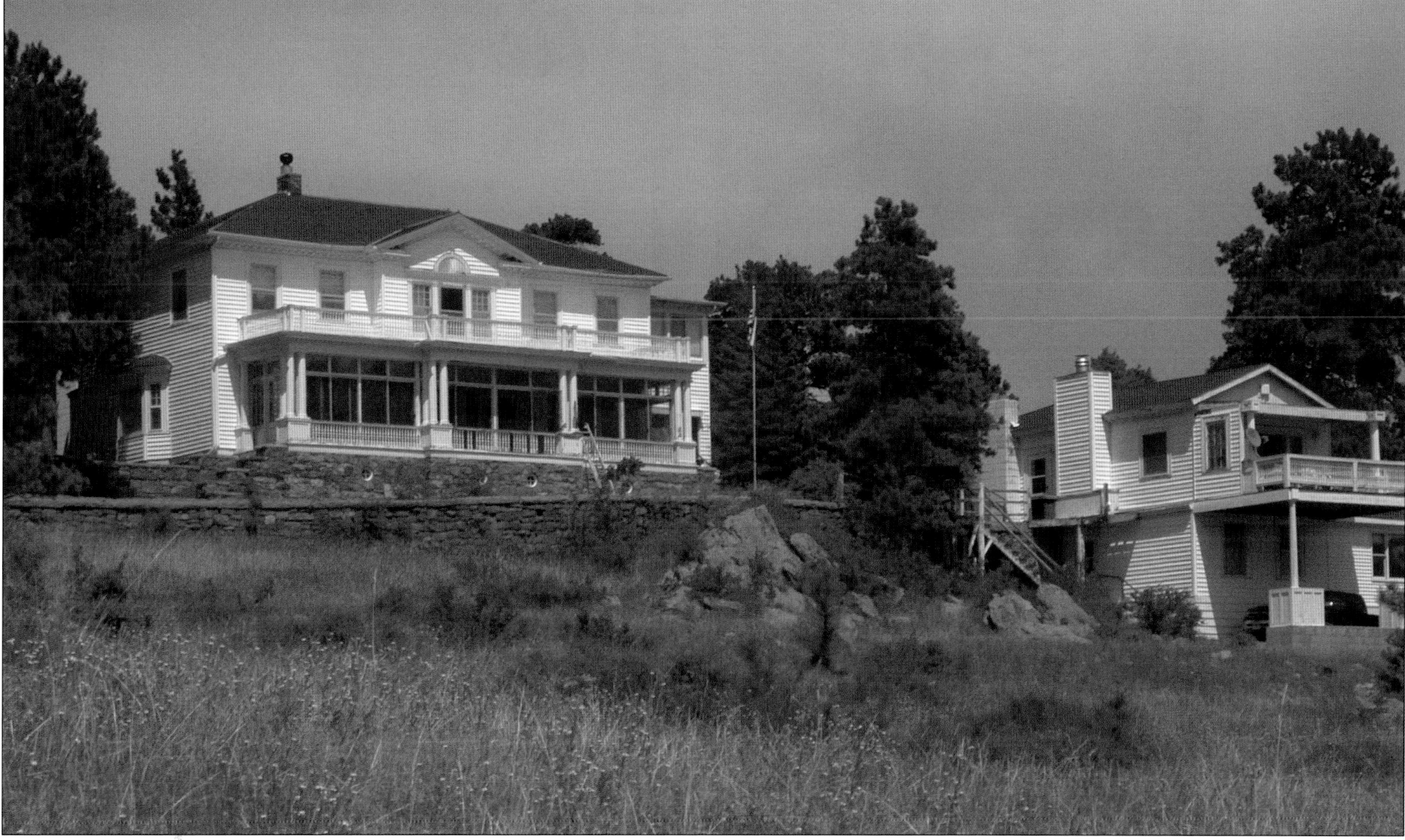

Stanley built a two-story carriage house with a garage and workshop. The garage had a built-in turntable, so that he would never have to drive his car in reverse. The lower level of the building contained his billiard table, Stanley's only form of competitive recreation. Behind the house was a path through boulders leading to a level outcropping. There, using bolts affixed to the rock, Mr. Stanley built a bench where he could play his violin or meditate on the view before him.

As the contemporary photograph shows, time has treated the Stanley House well, thanks to the quality that Stanley insisted on and the attentiveness of subsequent owners. About the only thing that has changed is the color. Just like the Stanley Hotel, its mustard yellow paint has long since given way to white.

22. Estes Park Fish Hatchery, circa 1930

Built and opened in spring of 1907, the Estes Park Fish Hatchery was a community effort to promote tourism undertaken by the Estes Park Protective and Improvement Association. The land, which was a gift from rancher Pieter Hondius, was located next to the Fall River, where an ample spring offered the constant temperatures needed to raise trout. The EPPIA raised the $3,352 needed to build and equip the fish hatchery, with much of the construction work done by association members. By mid-July, the new hatchery was ready to receive its first shipment of eggs.

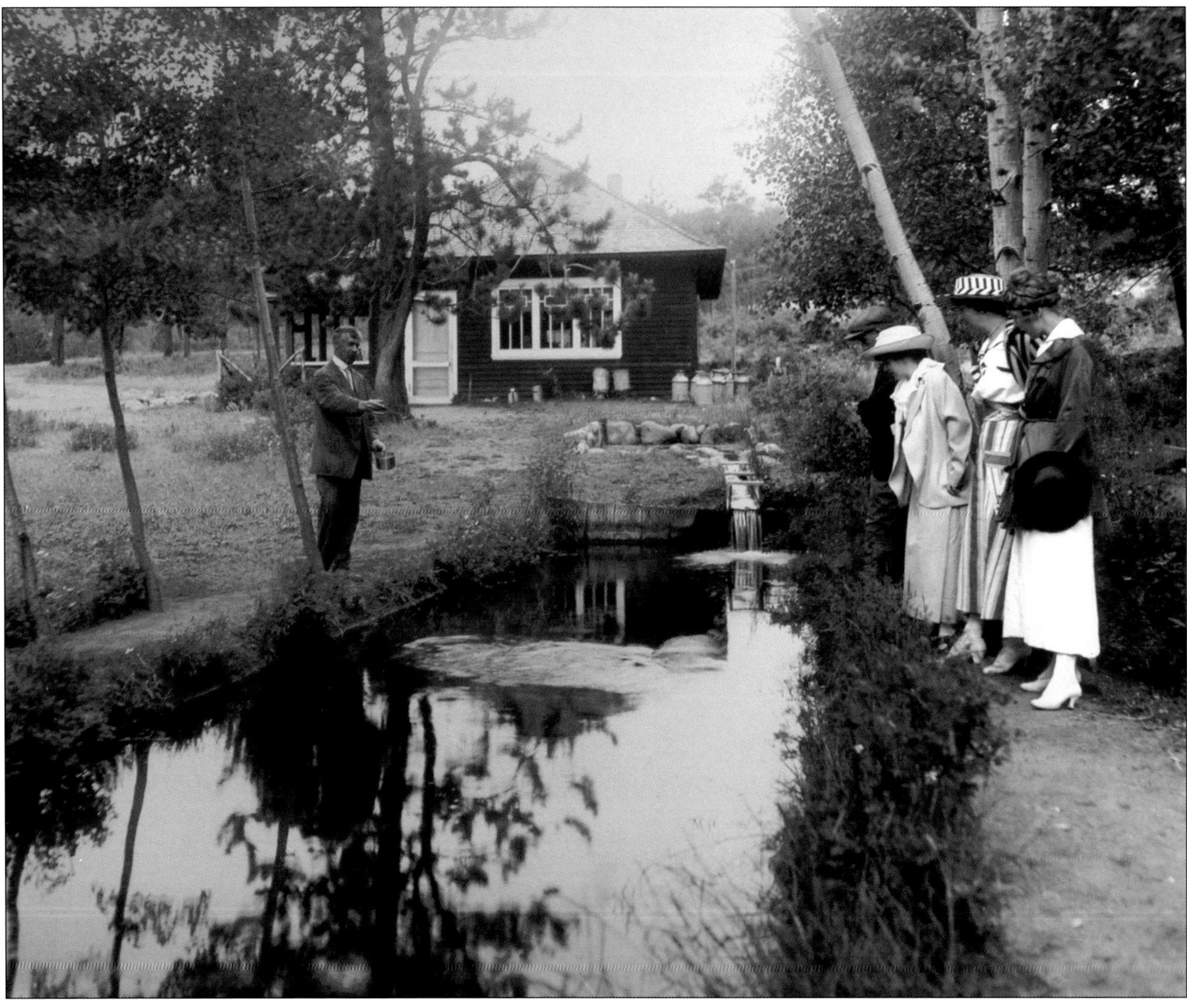

The Estes Park Fish Hatchery was an immediate success, much of it due to the efforts of its knowledgeable and genial superintendent, Gaylord Thomson, and his pet fish "Sunbeam," which allowed itself to be removed from the water and handled. The location of the hatchery also helped, for like the Stanley Power Plant to the west (see p. 68), it sat on the road then leading into Horseshoe Park.

The improvement association built a cottage nearby in 1909 for

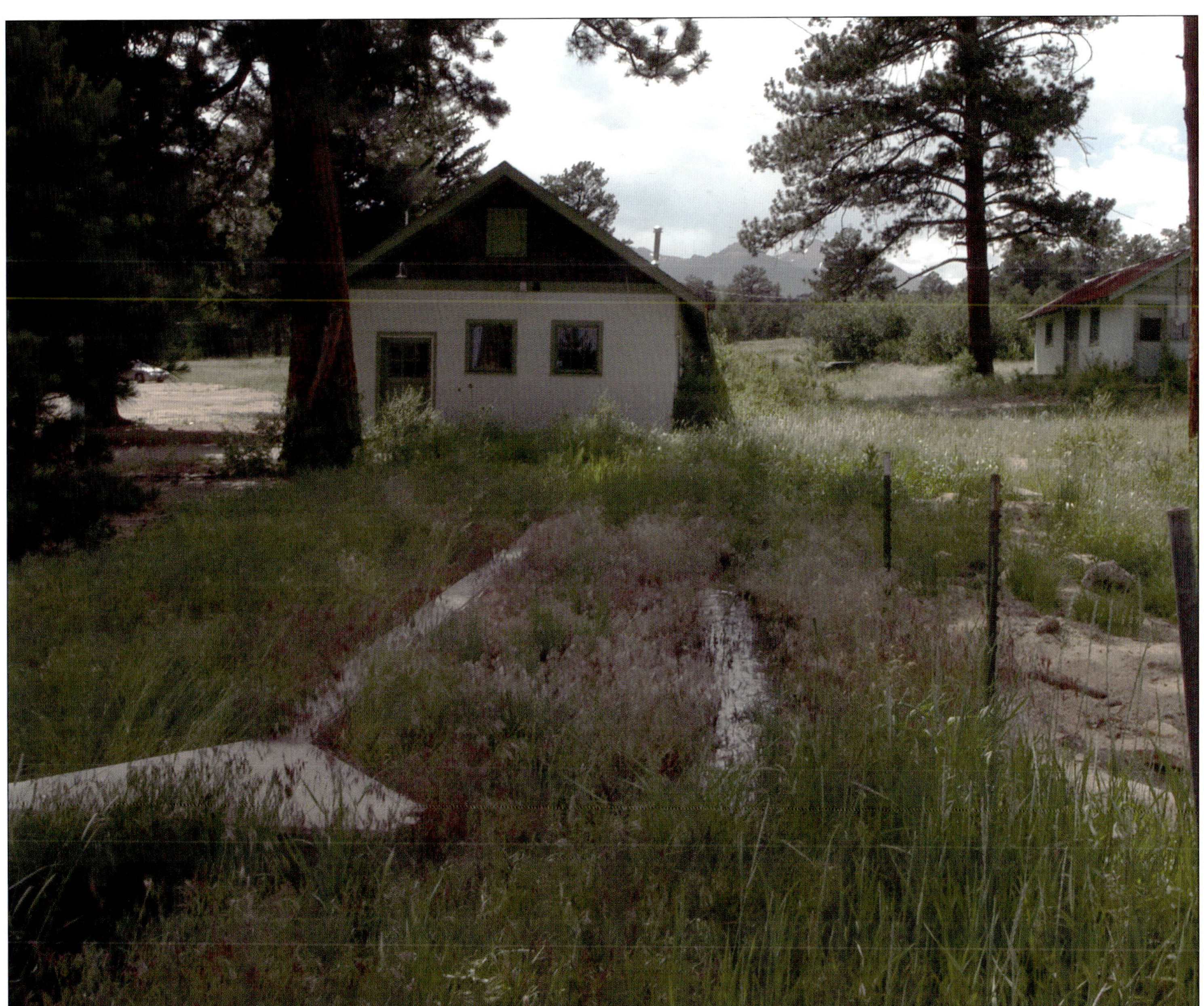

Thomson's family and also added four sizing ponds. In 1928–1929, major renovations came when the State of Colorado, then operating the facility, removed the old building, erected a structure that was about twice its size on the site, and added concrete nursing and sizing ponds to the east. It was those new ponds that attracted the visitors in the original photograph; they're still in evidence in the contemporary photo. In its heyday, the work of the hatchery was assisted by a series of earthen ponds that were built to the southwest, to which water flowed through a concrete diversion, which is also still in evidence.

The Estes Park Fish Hatchery operated until 1982, when rushing water from a burst dam at Rocky Mountain National Park's Lawn Lake roared down the Fall River and put out of commission both the hatchery and the nearby Stanley Power Plant.

23. Stanley Power Plant

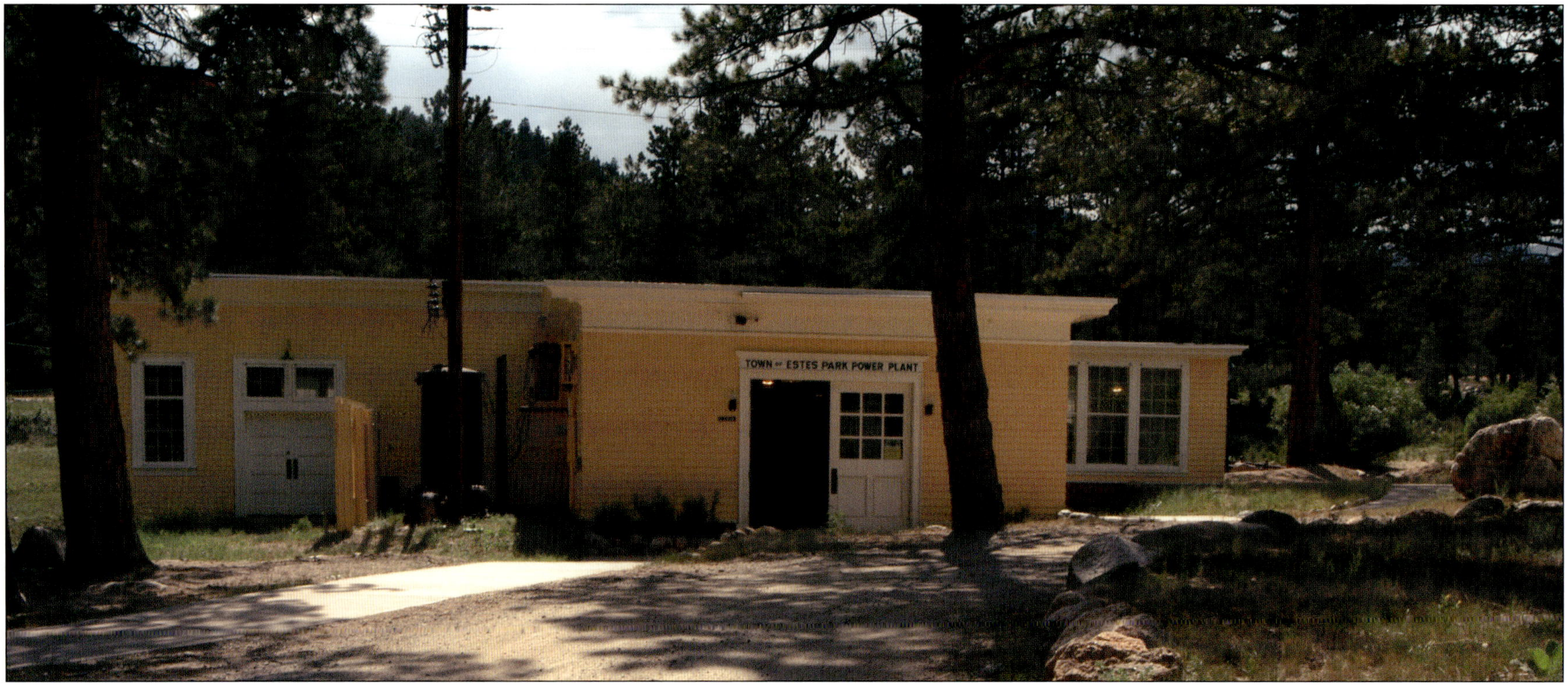

No known early photographs of the Stanley Power Plant exist, despite the plant's importance to the development of Estes Park's infrastructure, as well as its popularity as a tourist stop. Yet no attempt to document photographically the history of early Estes Park would be complete without it. Built in 1909 by F. O. Stanley for his "all-electric" Stanley Hotel, the plant was enlarged in stages over the next three decades. The first photograph in this series shows the outside of the main building.

Initially, there was but a single generator powered by a waterwheel. Water to drive the turbine came through a pipe leading from an intake on the north bank of Fall River at Cascade Lake, an earth-and-log diversion that was 5,300 feet upriver from the plant, dropping 400 feet en route. The second photo is of the remains of a section of this pipe. Stanley constructed a wood-frame building to house the unit. This is the core of the present building. Nearby, he erected a small house for the plant's operator. The total cost of plant and equipment was about $69,000.

The plant had problems from the beginning. Fall River simply could not provide a sufficient amount of water year-round to meet rising demand. In 1921, in an attempt to improve the power plant's hydrogenerating capacity, a second generator and turbine were installed in a room added to the northwest side of the original building. In 1931, when a third unit, a diesel engine and generator, was added, the building was expanded once again, this time with a 28-by-15-foot addition to the west, giving us the structure that exists today. A fourth unit, another diesel engine and generator, was added in 1938.

In 1928, the Public Service Company of Colorado bought the plant; in 1945, the Town of Estes Park acquired it. The Stanley Power Plant operated until July 15, 1982, when it was hit by a wall of water from the burst dam at Lawn Lake. The third photo shows the clock on the plant's west wall, stopped at the moment of impact. Like the Estes Park Fish Hatchery, the Stanley Power Plant never operated again.

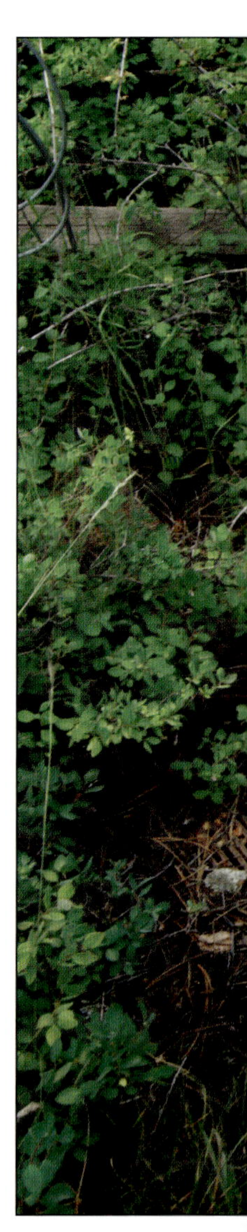

Thanks, however, to the Town of Estes Park and the Colorado State Historical Fund, the plant has been restored. Today, it is operated by the Estes Park Museum, and serves as an interpretive center with exhibits on hydropower as well as the plant's history. The Stanley Power Plant is listed on the National Register of Historic Places.

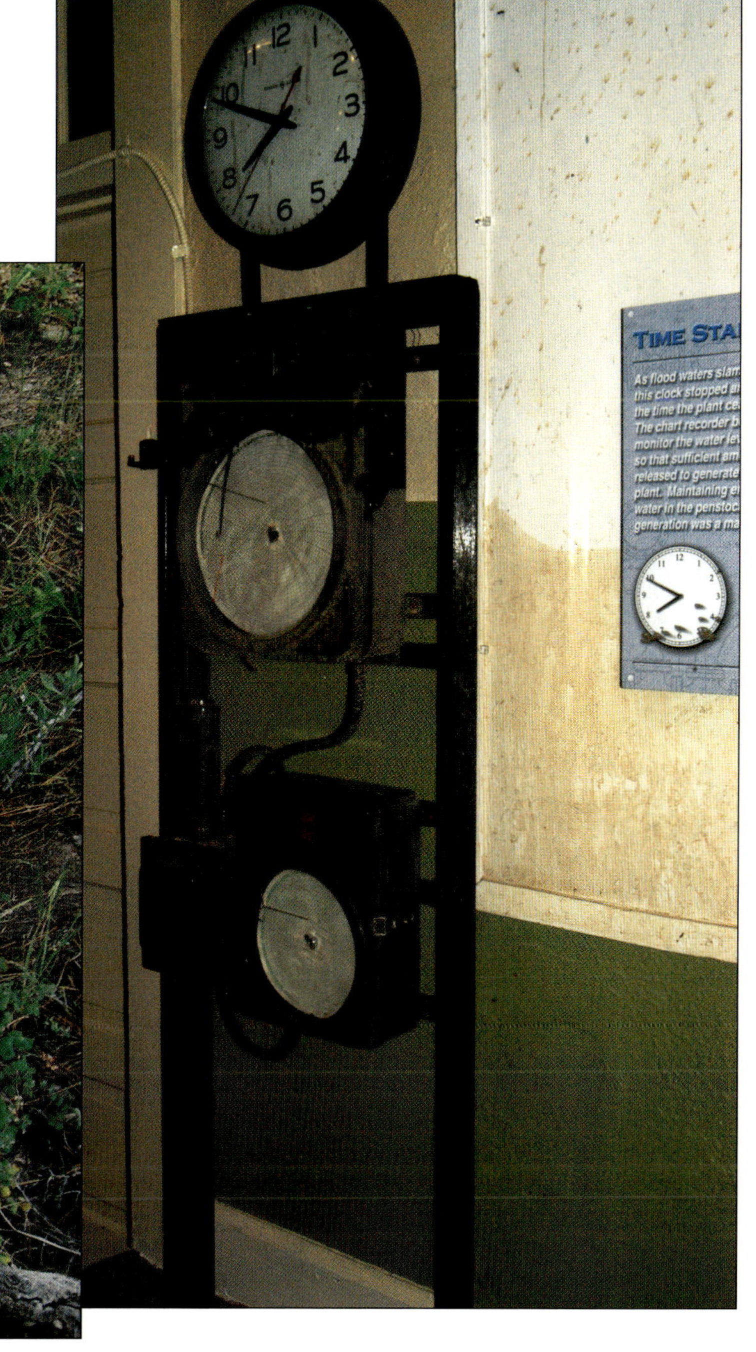

24. McCreery Cabin, circa 1892

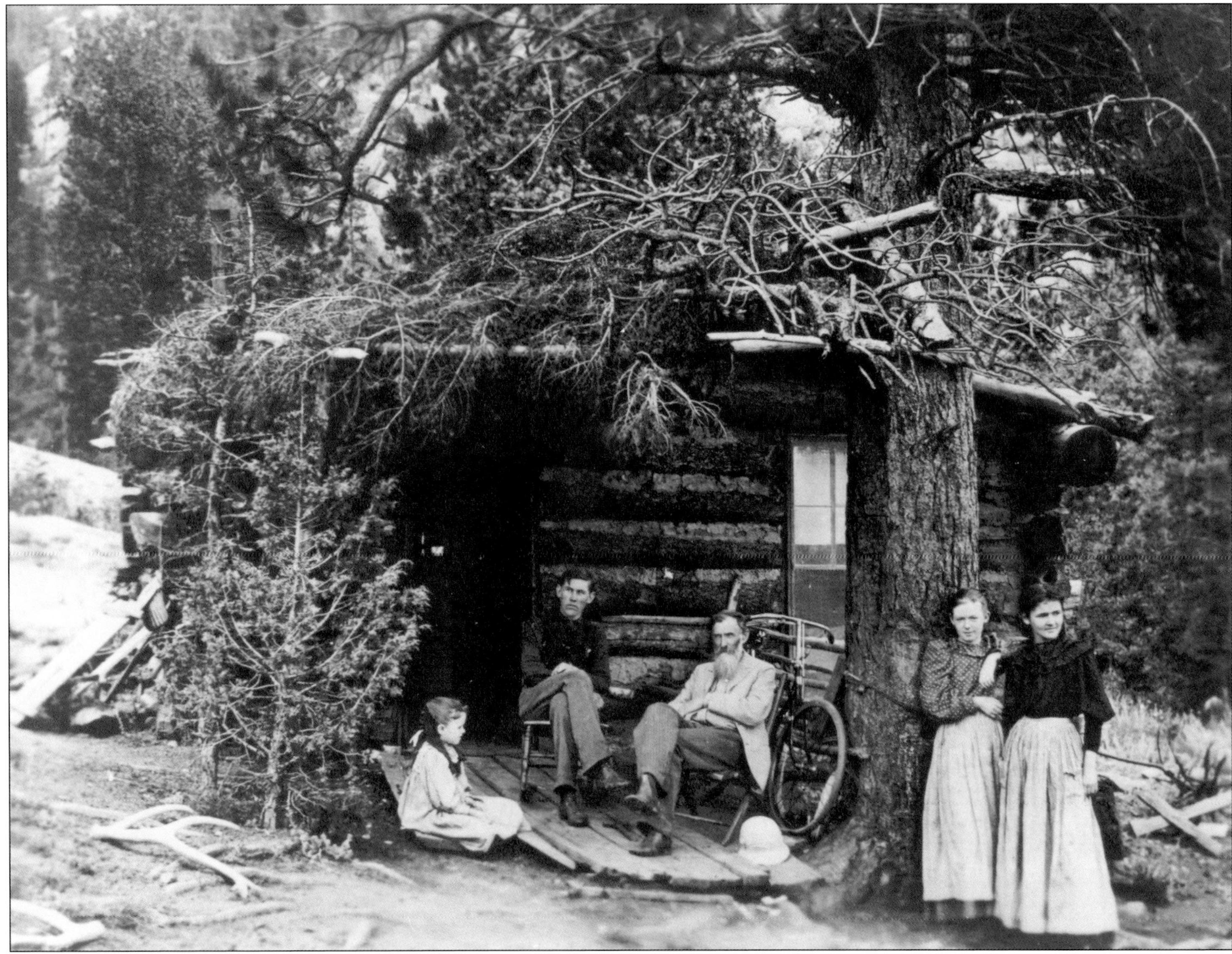

Just how William E. James happened to build a hunter's cabin in this remote spot off Devils Gulch Road, close to the boulders of Lumpy Ridge, is anything but clear. Perhaps he was attracted by the availability of water from what would become known as McCreery Spring. Or perhaps, since the Estes Valley had been platted that spring and nearly 5,000 acres "claimed" by the Earl of Dunraven's hirelings, James was forced to choose such a lonely and isolated spot.

James immediately built himself a cabin and filed a homestead claim. He then brought his wife and three boys for the winter. To Ella James' disgust, the cabin's sod roof had a tendency to leak muddy water when it snowed. Today, that cabin may be the oldest surviving structure in the Estes Valley.

In 1876, James decided to enter the hotel business and swapped the land with the Reverend William H. McCreery for land along Fall River, the future site

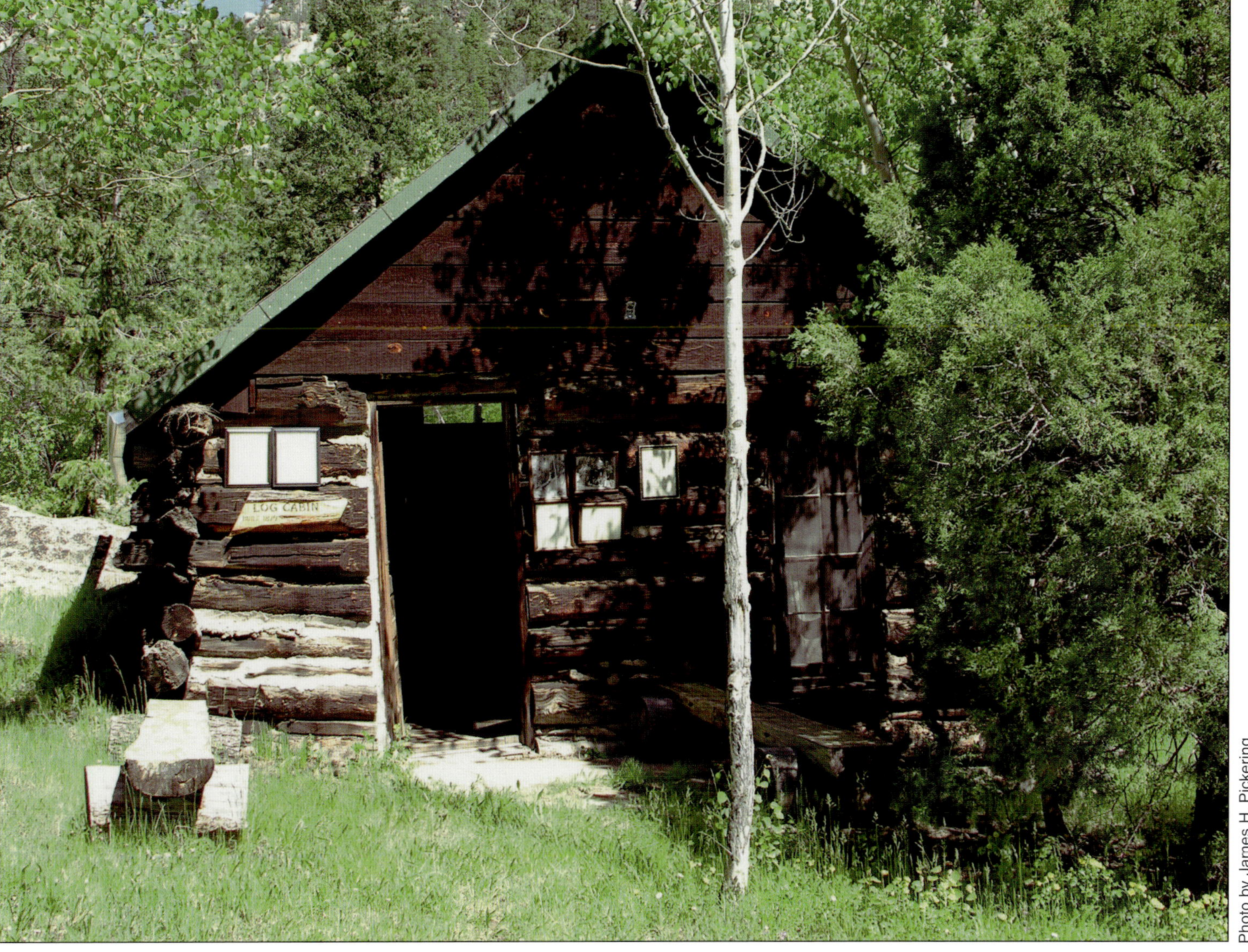

Photo by James H. Pickering

of the Elkhorn Lodge (see p. 130). McCreery, a Presbyterian minister who wintered in Loveland, coveted the privacy of James' cabin. He had come West in 1874 with his wife and daughter for health reasons. Soon, he discovered Estes Park and filed on the Elkhorn site.

McCreery used the cabin only as a summer retreat, since during these early years he was kept busy organizing churches in Loveland and Denver. In 1879, due to health reasons, he resigned his Loveland pastorate and entered business. In 1882, William McCreery was appointed superintendent of Larimer County schools.

The original photograph of the McCreery cabin, taken in 1892, shows McCreery (center) flanked by family members. The contemporary photograph shows the cabin with its "new" roof, added in 1910. Both cabin and spring are still owned by the McCreery family, now in its sixth generation in Estes Park.

25. North St. Vrain Road (Highway 36), 1907

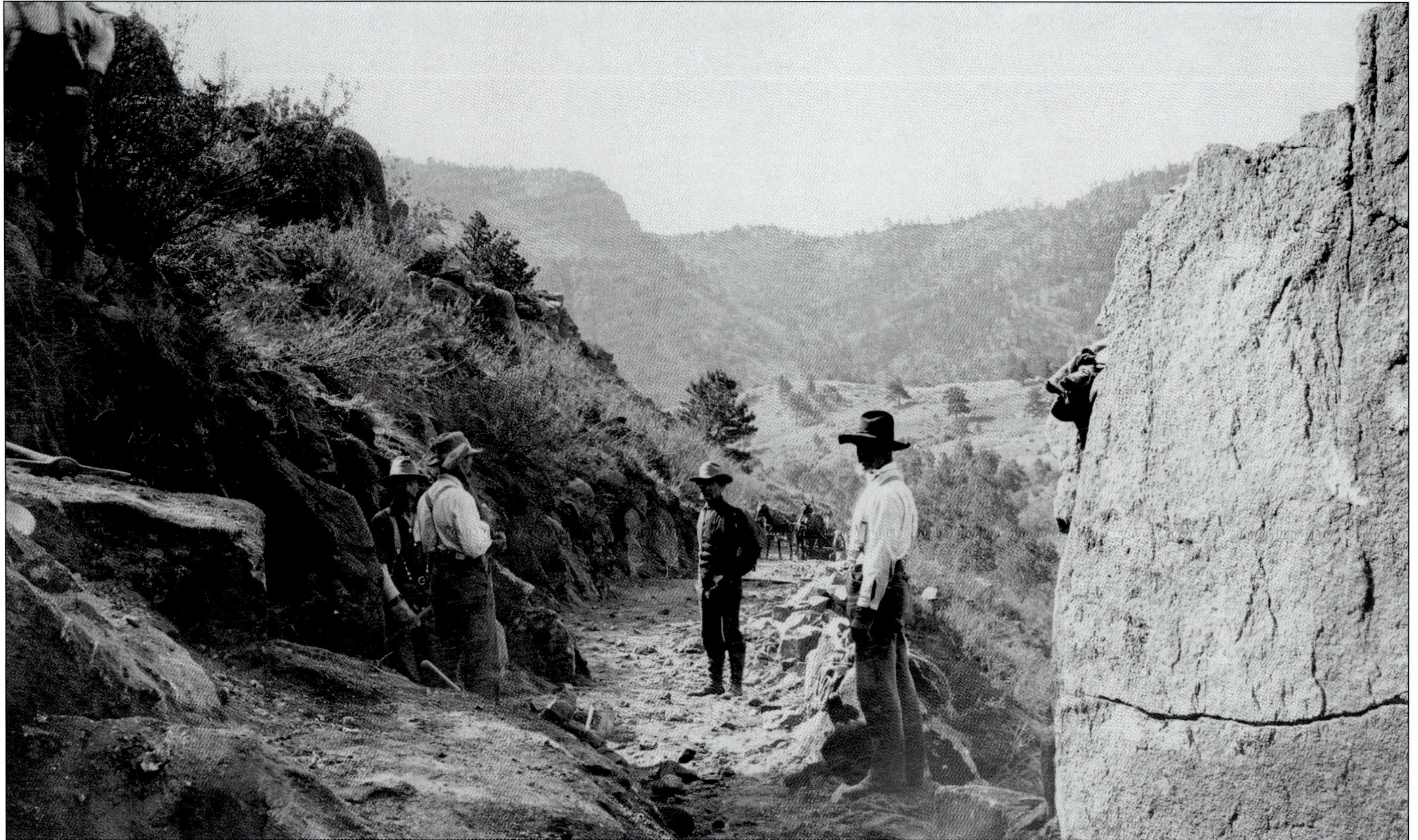

In 1907, F. O. Stanley decided to reconstruct the North St. Vrain road to Estes Park to achieve "a first class automobile road" for his Stanley Steamer auto stage line. To do the work, he called upon John B. Hall and his son, Charles Byron Hall, whose homestead in Lyons was located close by today's Apple Valley Road bridge. At the Lyons end, near where this historical photograph was taken, the Halls built essentially a new road through the old Welch resort (today's Shelley's Cottages) and along what is now the Longmont Dam Road. This route avoided the perils of Rowell ("Roll Over") Hill to the north with its 2,200-foot elevation gain. The Halls' road left the Dam Road to run west along St. Vrain Creek, ascending into the mountains to leave Boulder County near Pinewood Springs. Its course can still be traced along and below Highway 36 by looking for the rock "rip-rap," the rock walls that the Halls' workers installed

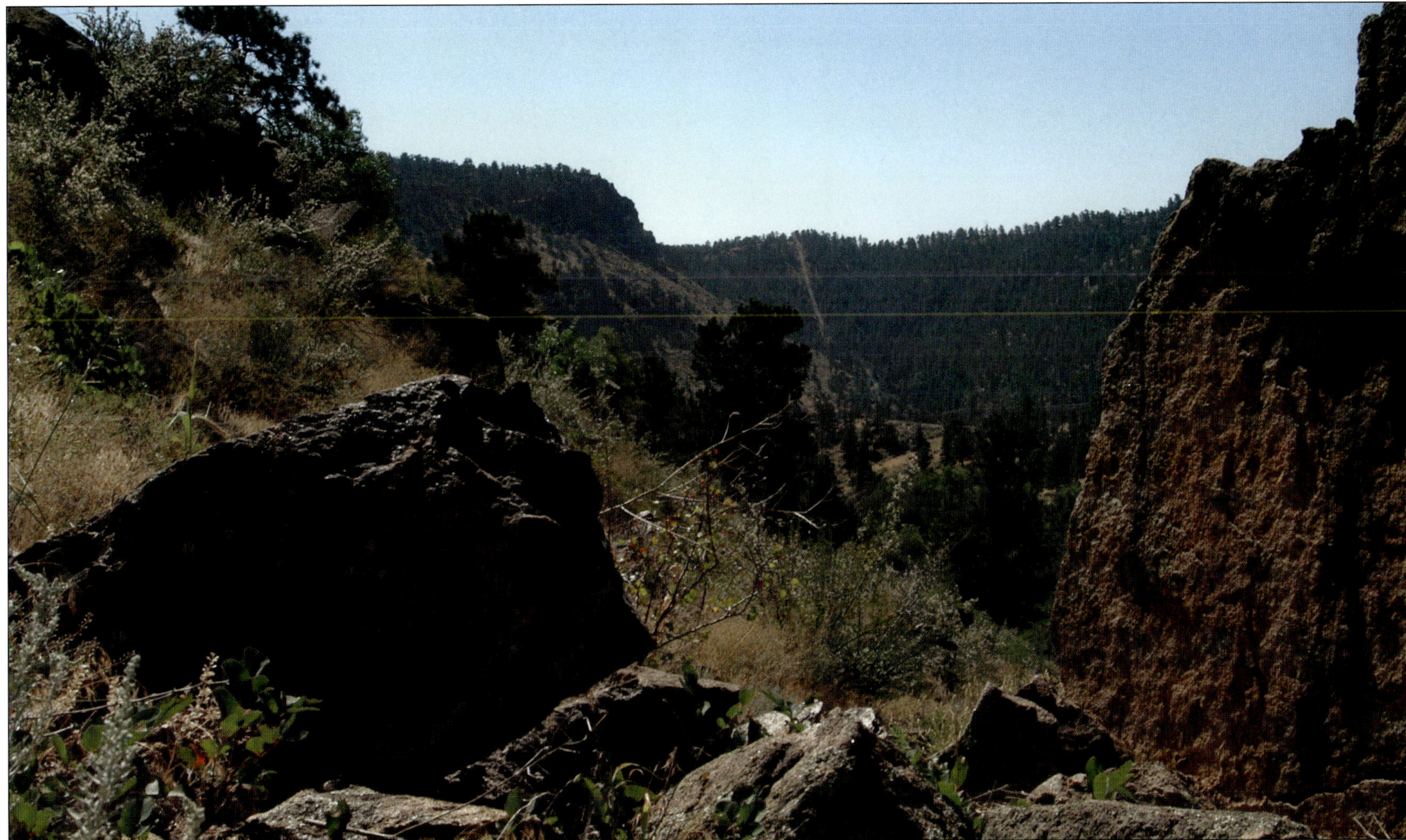

at various places to reinforce the roadbed and prevent erosion. Manual laborers did most of the work, as this photograph suggests, avoiding large boulders rather than blasting them away.

Although narrow, this road served Stanley well, and remained in service until the mid-1930s, when the State of Colorado financed the reconstruction that provided the mostly new and much wider North St. Vrain road (Highway 36) that we know today. The most difficult part of the construction work took place just to the east of where these photographs were taken. Extensive blasting was required to relocate the entire roadbed to the hillside above the old Hall road. The new and dust-free North St. Vrain highway from Lyons to Estes Park was formally accepted by the U.S. Bureau of Roads in May 1938.

26. South St. Vrain Road (Highway 7), circa 1936

Photographed here is the rock cut on the South St. Vrain highway (Highway 7) as it ascends the east side of Lily Mountain from the floor of the Estes Valley to enter the Tahosa Valley near Lily Lake. Constructed in 1935 as part of a decade-long project to widen and expand the South St. Vrain road through Allenspark, it replaced the original road to the Tahosa Valley built in 1875–1876 by the Reverend Elkanah J. Lamb and his son, Carlyle, to their ranch at the foot of Longs Peak (see p. 164). Their road, which followed an old hunting trail, climbed the heavily wooded western slope of Twin Sisters Mountain and passed directly in front of what is now the Baldpate Inn before turning south. The old Lamb road has now been incorporated into the Homer Rouse Trail, which begins not far from the entrance gate to Cheley Colorado Camps.

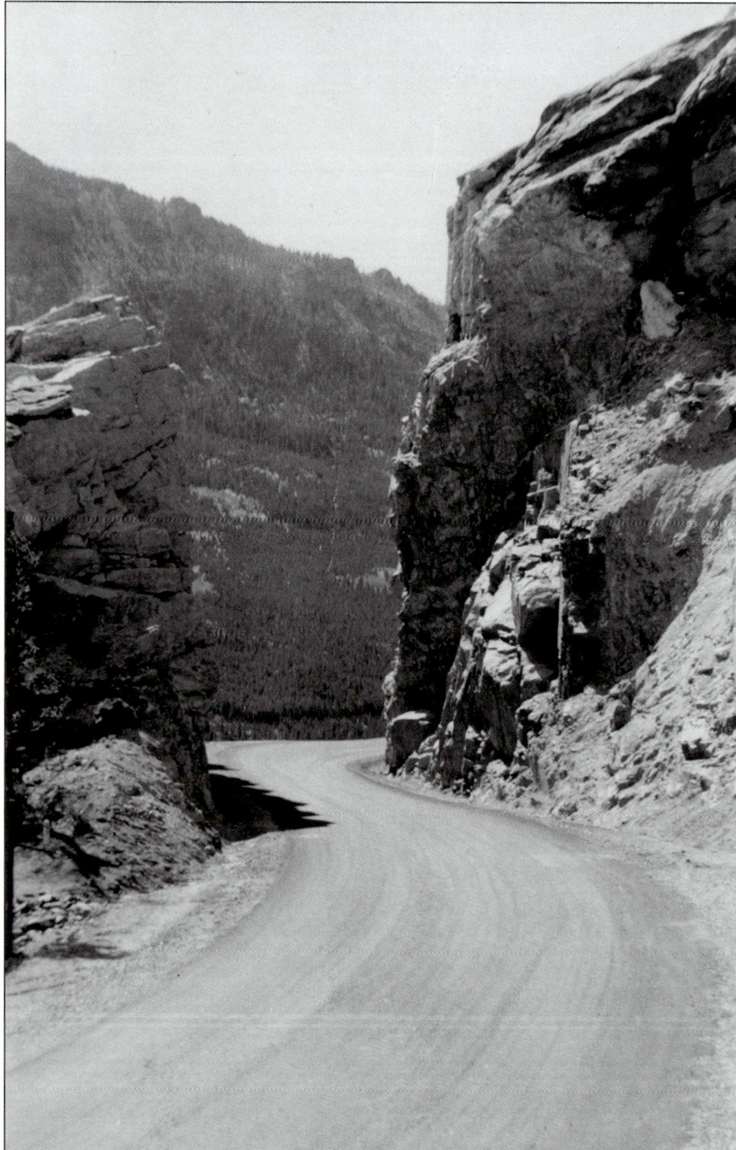

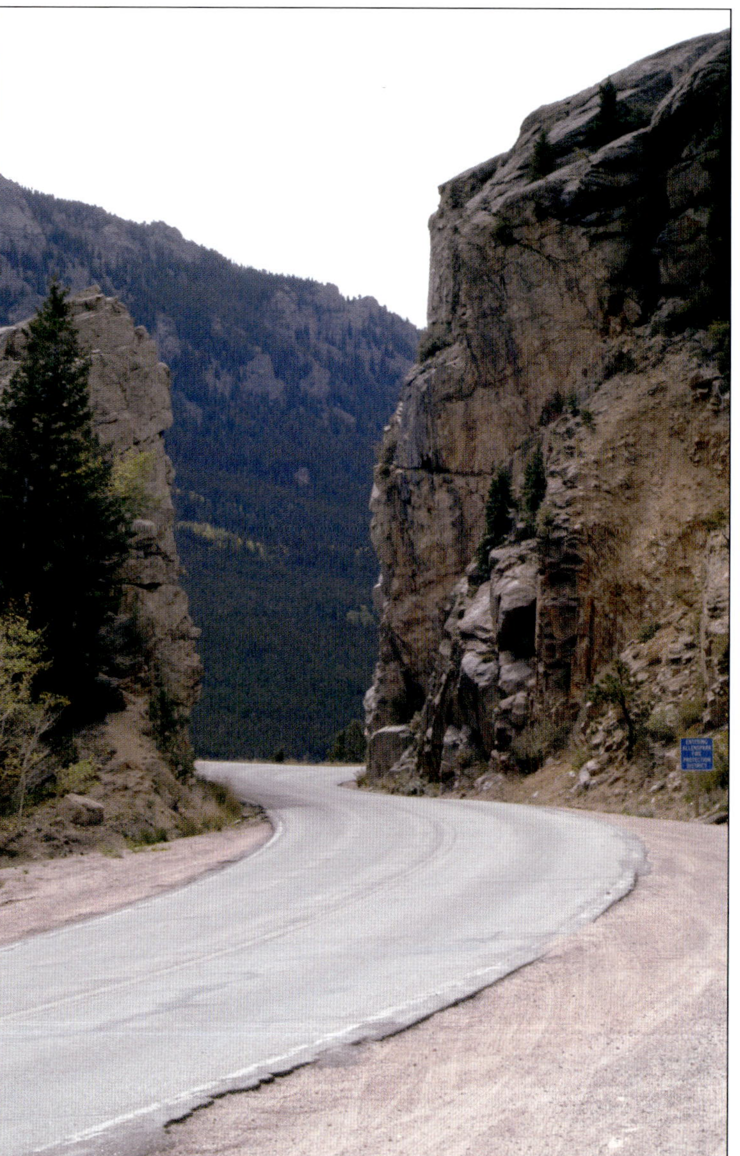

The new South St. Vrain road offers motorists splendid, unobstructed views of the floor of the Estes Valley 500 to 600 feet below. The road's rock cuts, created by blasting through granite, were the subject of picturesque postcard views celebrating the opening of the new highway: the first paved, and hence dust-free, road from the towns along the Front Range to Estes Park.

27. Big Thompson Road (Highway 34), circa 1910

The residents of Loveland and Fort Collins and suffering travelers had long lobbied for a new and improved road to Estes Park to replace the original Bald Mountain–Pole Hill Road completed in 1876. That road, with its rough hills and 11 percent grade, entered the mountains south of the Big Thompson Canyon, came through a picturesque valley named Rattlesnake Park, and entered the Estes Valley through the Crocker ranch. They got their wish in 1904 with the opening of the road up the Big Thompson Canyon. Although it would remain single-tracked until 1919, forcing cars meeting one another to seek a turnout, the new road was considered a major success. Residents of Loveland were so happy with the road's scenic wonders that they tried, without success, to have its eastern end named the "Loveland Grand Canyon."

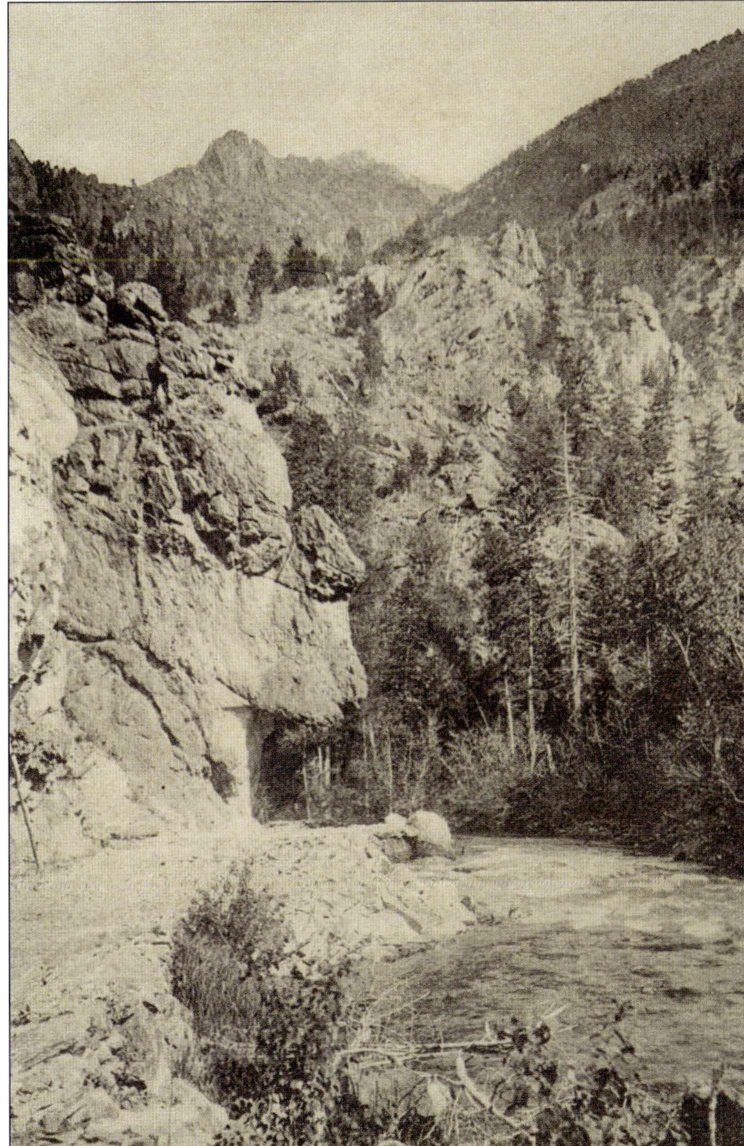

Photo by William T. Parke

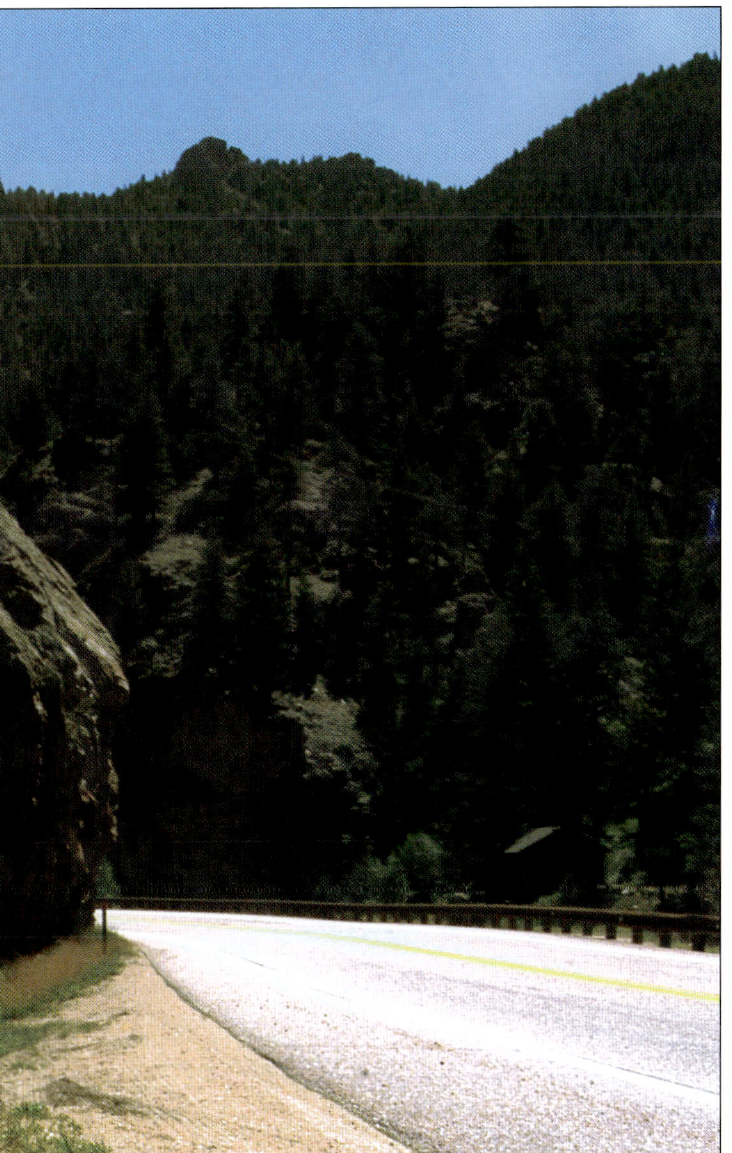

Despite their enthusiasm, it soon became clear that the new Big Thompson Road was ill equipped to handle the heavy automobile traffic to which it was soon subjected. Not only was the road too narrow and in several places too steep, but in many places its roadbed was too close to the river, resulting in flooding and washouts.

Between 1919 and 1938, road improvement happened in stages with the most dramatic taking place at the road's lower end, between The Narrows' steep cliffs at the mouth of the canyon and at Dickson Gulch

Big Thompson Road, circa 1935

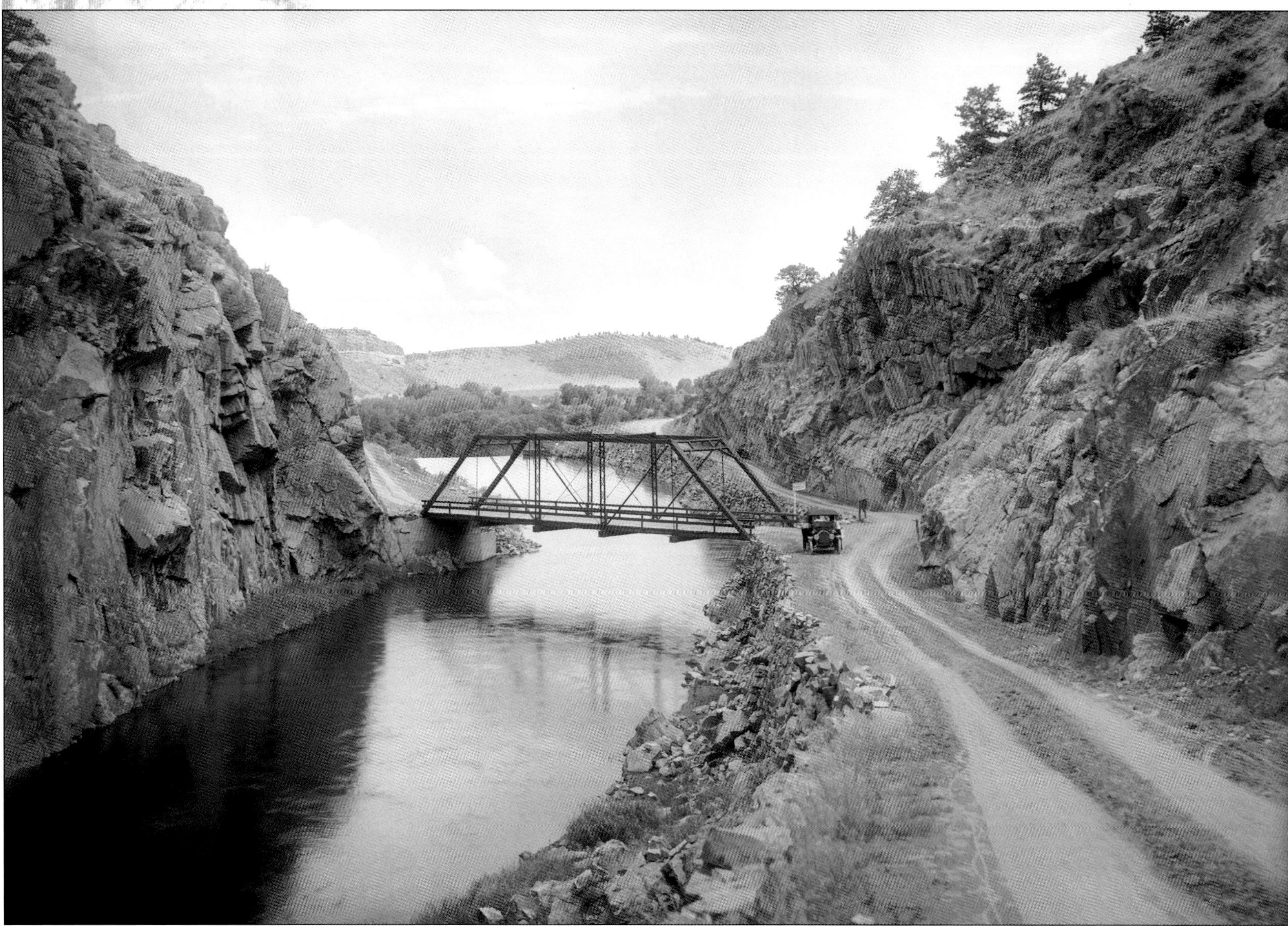

Photo by Louis C. McClure

some 3 miles west. Here, in 1934, in order to raise the roadbed, whole sections of the canyon wall were blasted away. Farther west, the road was redirected away from the river itself, eliminating some of the scenic sections celebrated in the views taken by Denver photographer Louis C. McClure.

All these changes drastically altered the traveler's experience. No longer did motorists enter the Big Thompson Canyon across the bridge on the old road to Fort Collins (shown above), or pass beneath the distinctive outcropping above Drake known as Sheeps Head Rock (shown in the first photograph). However scenic, this much-photographed landmark became the subject of complaints that it might fall down. Shortly after county commissioners investigated and pronounced it safe, Sheeps Head Rock collapsed into the road. The event proved fortuitous for road crews because, as our contemporary photograph shows,

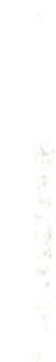

improving the road at this curve required not only widening the road to accommodate two lanes of traffic but raising its bed above the adjacent river.

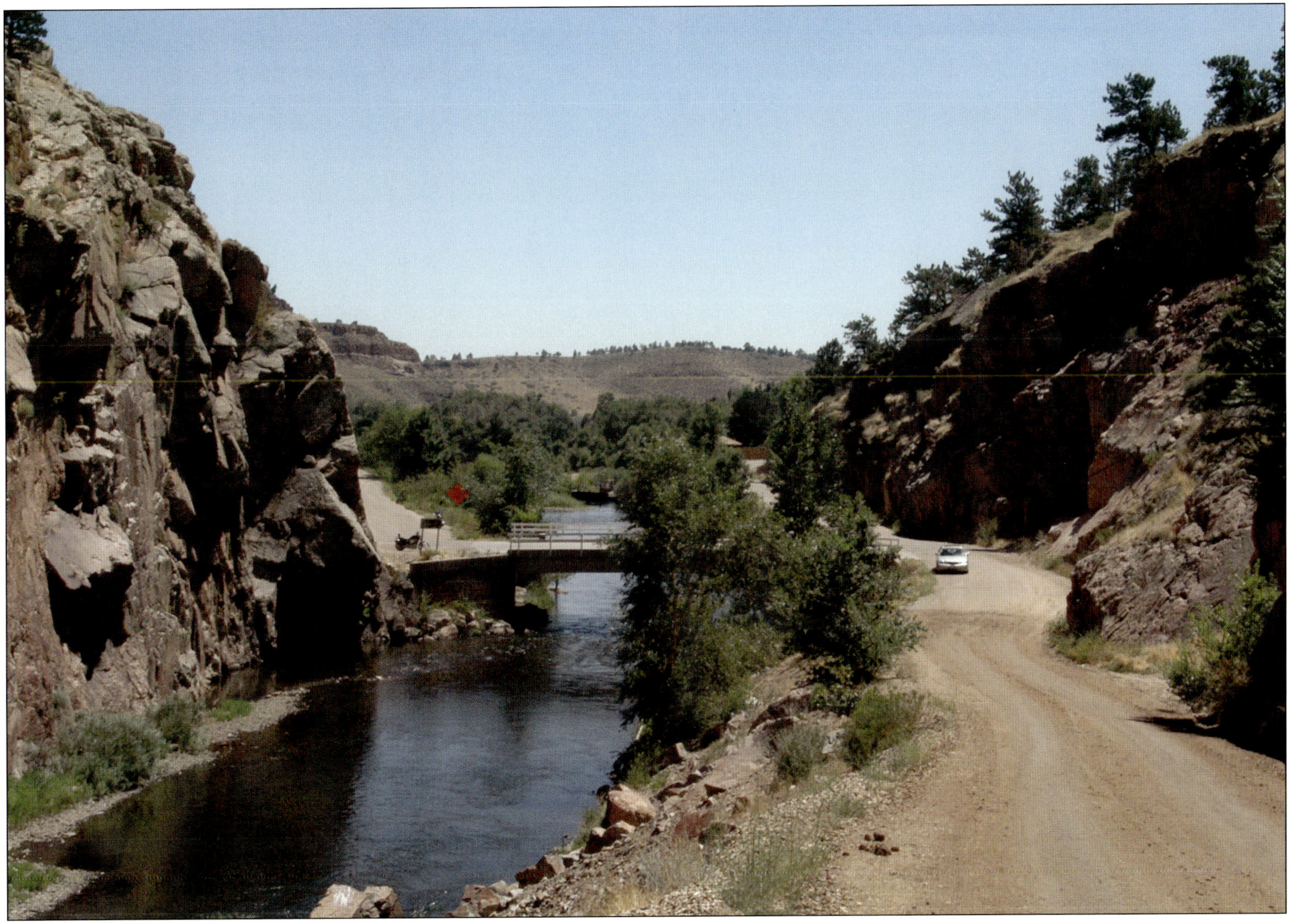

The Dam Store, another familiar Big Thompson Road landmark, suffered a kinder fate. Originally, it was located a mile down the old Loveland–Fort Collins Road, just beyond the bridge in our photograph (see p. 79). The building, dating from the early years of the 20th century, is still there. A new building at its present location was constructed in 1933 to take advantage of the new road and the adjacent dam site. The east and west wings visible in today's photograph were added later, as was the porch on the west end of the store that allows travelers to view the dam and falls.

The Dam Store, circa 1935

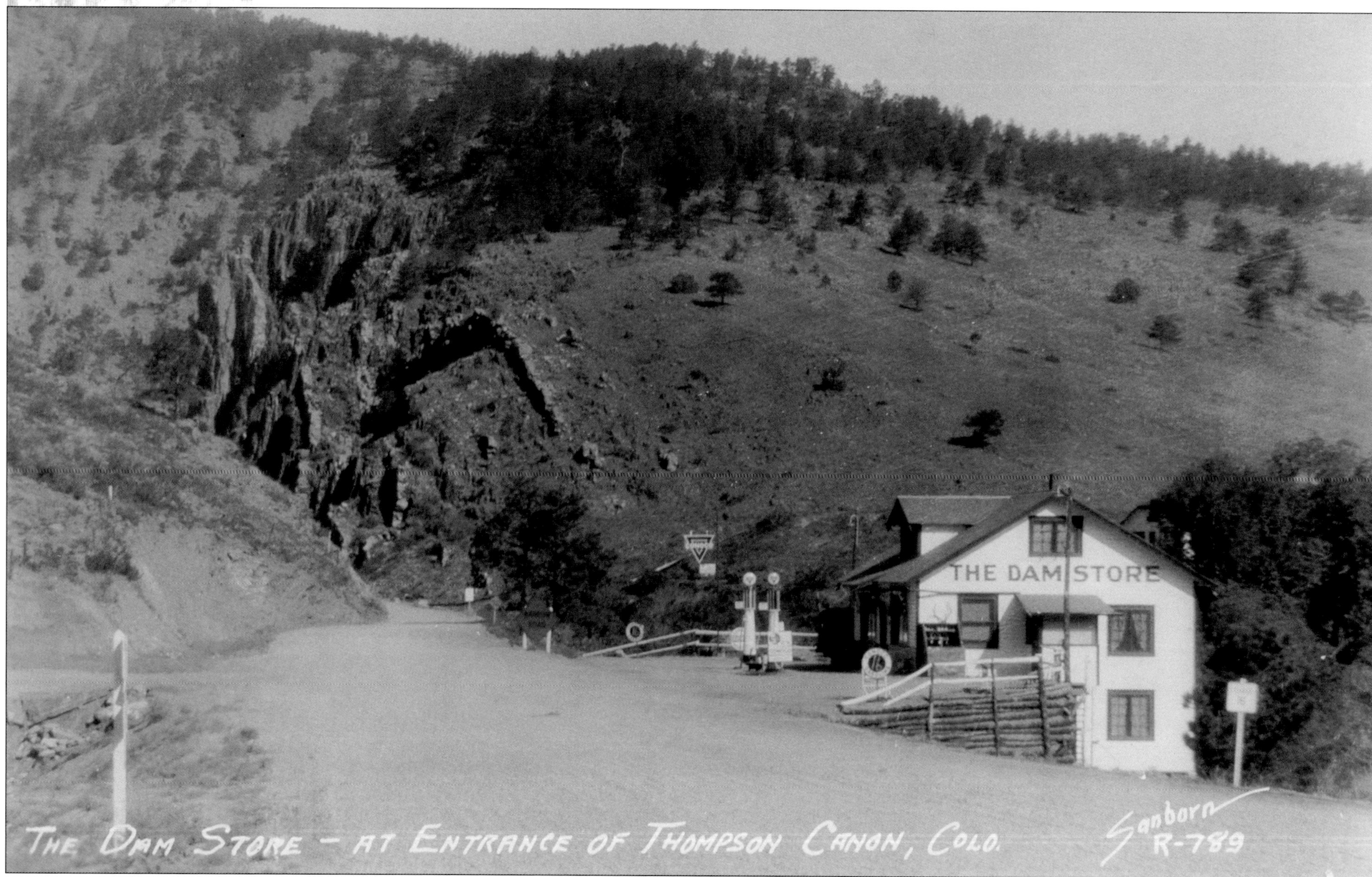

Photo by Sanborn Souvenir Company

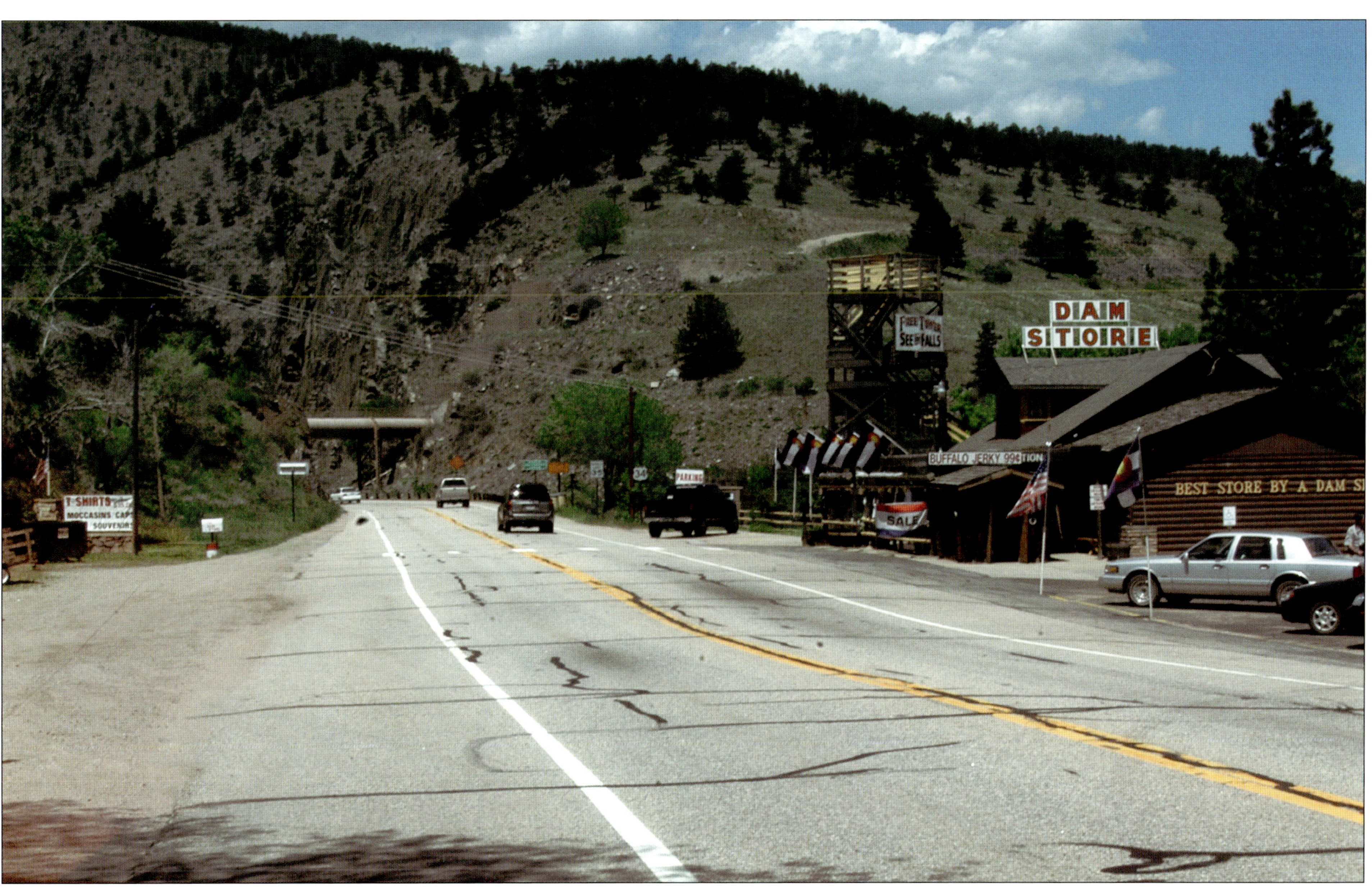
DAM
STORE
BUFFALO JERKY 99¢
BEST STORE BY A DAM
PARKING
SALE
T-SHIRTS

28. Panoramic View, 1919

The original panorama reproduced here was taken around 1919 by an unknown photographer from the Miller Studio in Baltimore, who positioned himself on the lower slopes of Little Prospect Mountain. His photograph captures almost the entire town, from Moraine Avenue on the left to the length of Elkhorn Avenue in the center and on the right. A contemporary photograph taken from the same spot provides clear evidence of the changes that have taken place in the last 80 years. As you will note, many of the original buildings remain, altered by successive facelifts and remodeling, and now put to different uses.

The site chosen in 1905 by Cornelius H. Bond and his partners for the purposes of laying out a town, though limited geographically by the terrain, was a natural one. Here, near the confluence of the Big Thompson and Fall Rivers, at the intersection of what would become Elkhorn and Moraine Avenues, were clustered the small group of buildings known as "the Corners." These included John Cleave's home and post office and the community building, which served as church, school, and meeting hall. Generally quiet enough through the year, summers transformed the Corners into a busy place, for it was here that the stages brought their passengers from the valley to rendezvous with the wagons and rigs sent by outlying tourist ranches and resorts.

Thanks to the camera's placement, the buildings along middle and lower Elkhorn Avenue are the ones most clearly visible. They include the

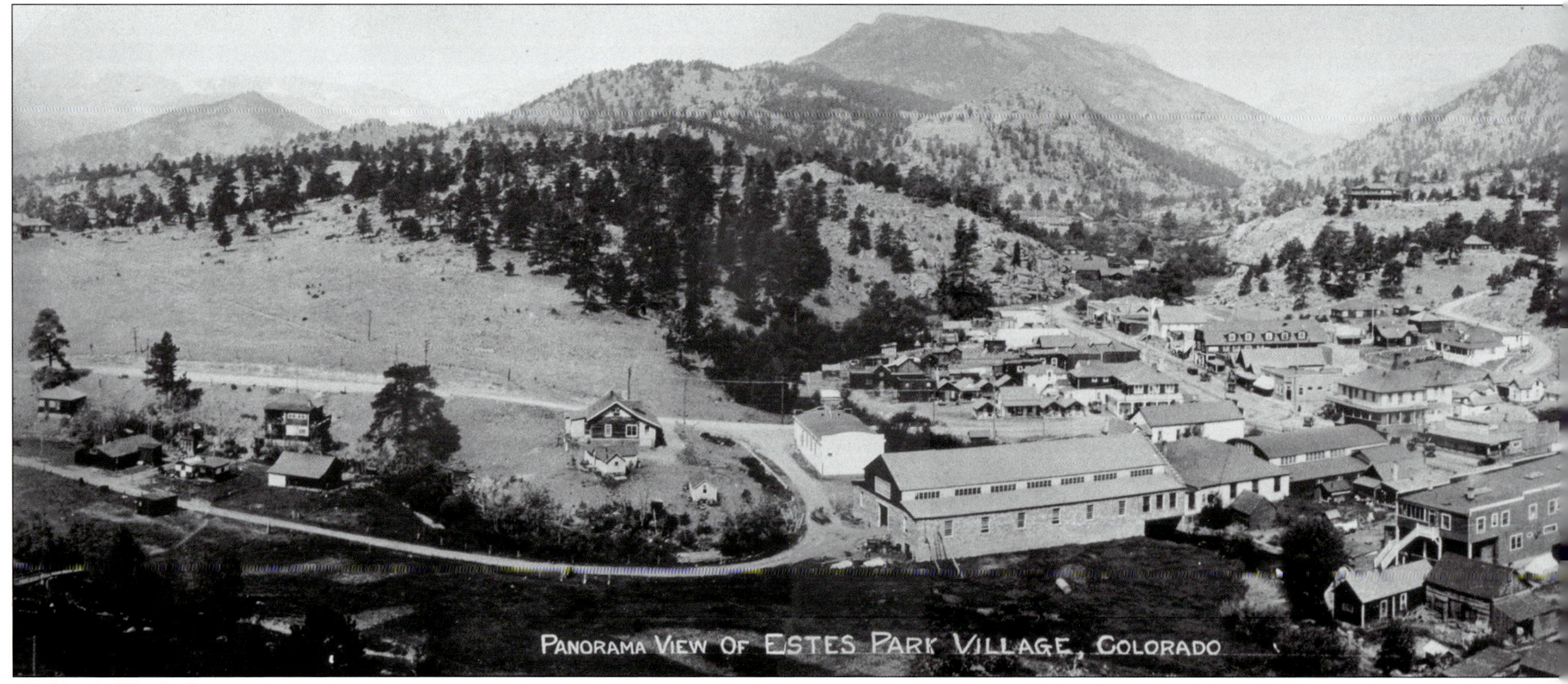

 Photo by Miller Studio

stream-cobble-and-stucco school building, built in 1916 behind the vacant lot being reserved for a park. The schoolhouse replaced the village's second school, built in 1907 of logs on the same site. Today, the site is occupied by the First National Bank. Clearly visible on the sloping hill behind the schoolhouse is the white steeple of Estes Park's first Catholic church, St. Walter's, built in 1915. Several hundred yards to the right of that building, framed by Lumpy Ridge, is the Stanley Hotel, together with the Manor House and the Casino (today's Stanley Hall). Immediately to the left of the school, separated by private houses, is Prospect Inn, also completed in 1915. All these buildings remain.

Sam Service's store and his adjacent home and storage warehouse dominate the center of the picture. Across the street, its white front facade clearly visible, is the building that served as the first administrative offices of Rocky Mountain National Park. To the right of the Service building, across the street, is the Estes Park post office, erected in 1914 on land leased by the town to the federal government. Directly across the street is the "Big Red Barn" livery, owned by J. Frank Grubb.

To the left of Grubb's livery, across the street that is now East Riverside, is the facade of Jim Boyd's blacksmith and wagon repair shop. By 1919, Boyd was repairing automobiles as well. Nearby, set back from the street and immediately

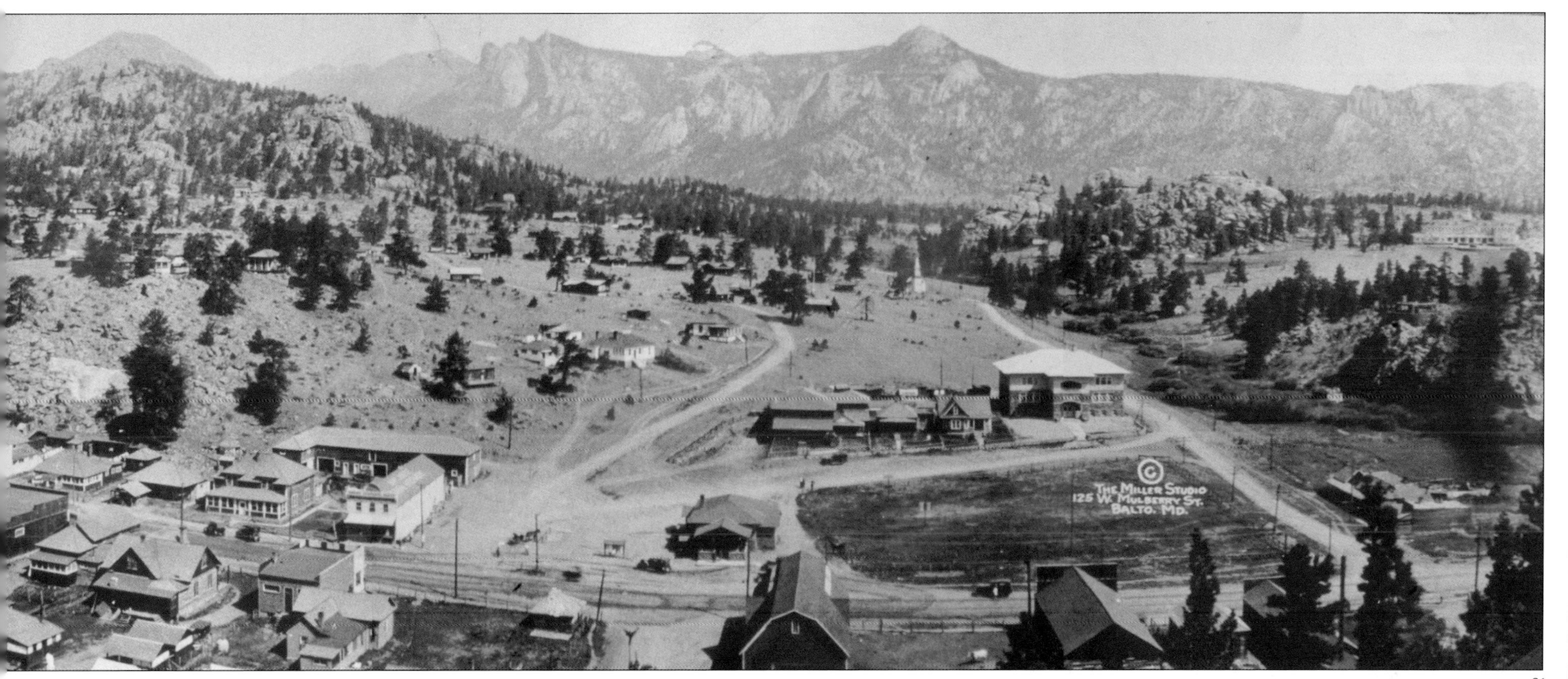

behind the national park office, is the Boyd house, later moved to make way for the group of stores (called the "Boyd block") that occupies the site today.

Farther up Elkhorn Avenue at its intersection with Moraine, the Hupp Hotel (known in 1919 as the Park Hotel) and the Manford Hotel (then known as the Hupp) faced each other across the street. E. M. A. Foot's mercantile store and the Estes Park Bank occupy the other two corners. By the date of the original photograph, these two "downtown" hotels had been joined by two others, both visible in the photograph. The first is the Sherwood Hotel, located three doors west of the bank and two doors down from the community church, which began life in 1915 as the Brown Tea Pot and, at the time of the photograph, was named the Aksarben ("Nebraska" spelled backwards). The second is the Josephine Hotel, halfway down Elkhorn in the middle of the block and built and opened in 1916. The Sherwood Hotel burned in 1956, but with the exception of Foot's store, the other buildings remain. The community church, later enlarged, is today's Old Church Shops.

The largest structure in the 1919 photograph, dominating its right-center portion, is actually a series of structures joined together. These are the depot, storage facilities, workshops, dormitory space, and offices of Roe Emery's Rocky

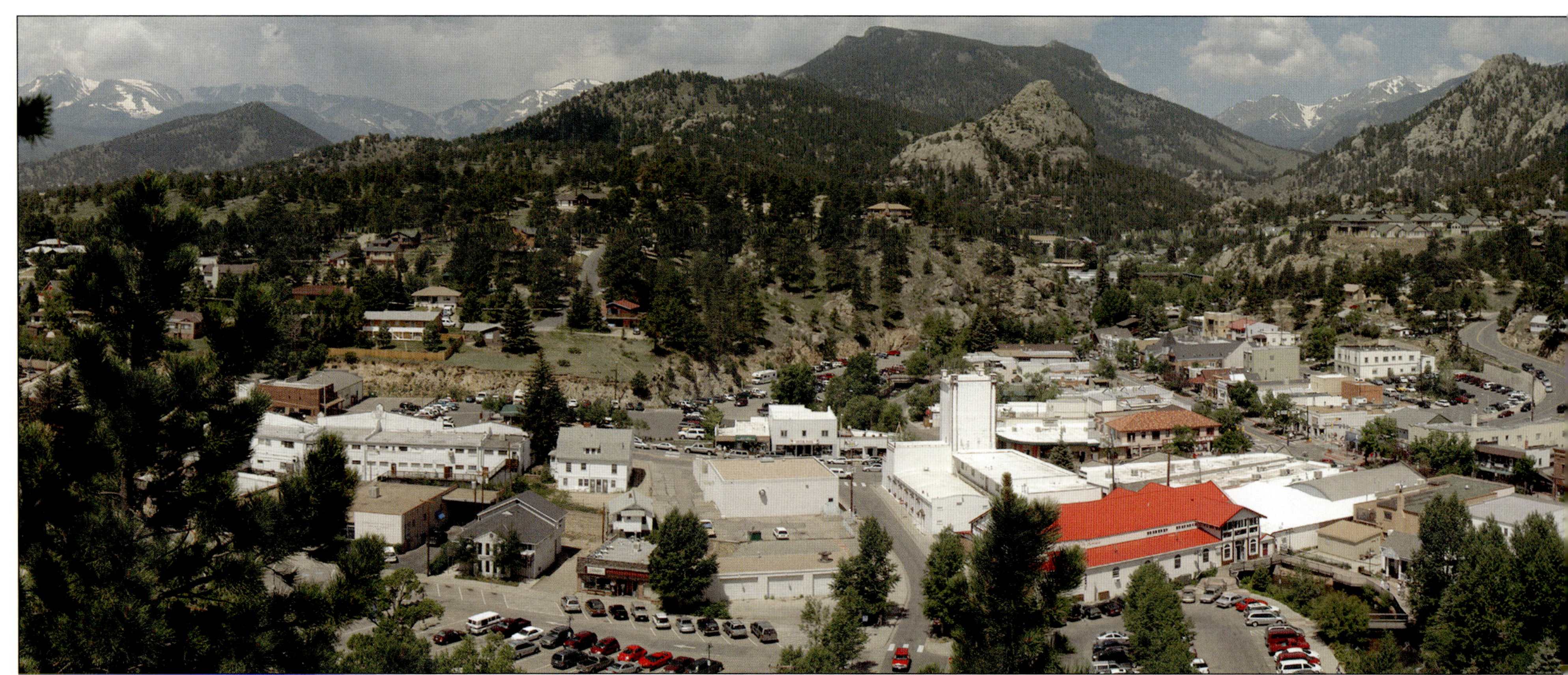

Mountain Parks Transportation Company. Today, this is the Park Theatre Mall. The Park Theatre is the large white building standing nearby. Its distinctive tower, so visible in today's photograph, was added in 1926 and its neon lights in 1938.

Three other buildings in the 1919 photograph also are worthy of note because of their visibility and their residents. The first is the house built by banker Sidney Sherman in 1908. It stands directly east of the theater. The second is the original home of postmaster John Cleave, which had been moved to a lot on Anderson Lane (today's Big Horn Drive) directly behind the Manford Hotel. The third is the log home of Estes Park merchant J. Edward Macdonald, two doors east of the Josephine Hotel on east Elkhorn. The back porch of this building is recognizable as the rear entrance to the Macdonald Book Shop, to which the house was converted in 1928.

The site above the town, where the new photograph was taken on a quiet Sunday morning in May, was a favorite one of early Estes Park photographers, including Fred Payne Clatworthy and William T. Parke. Access, however, is difficult, and we do not recommend a visit.

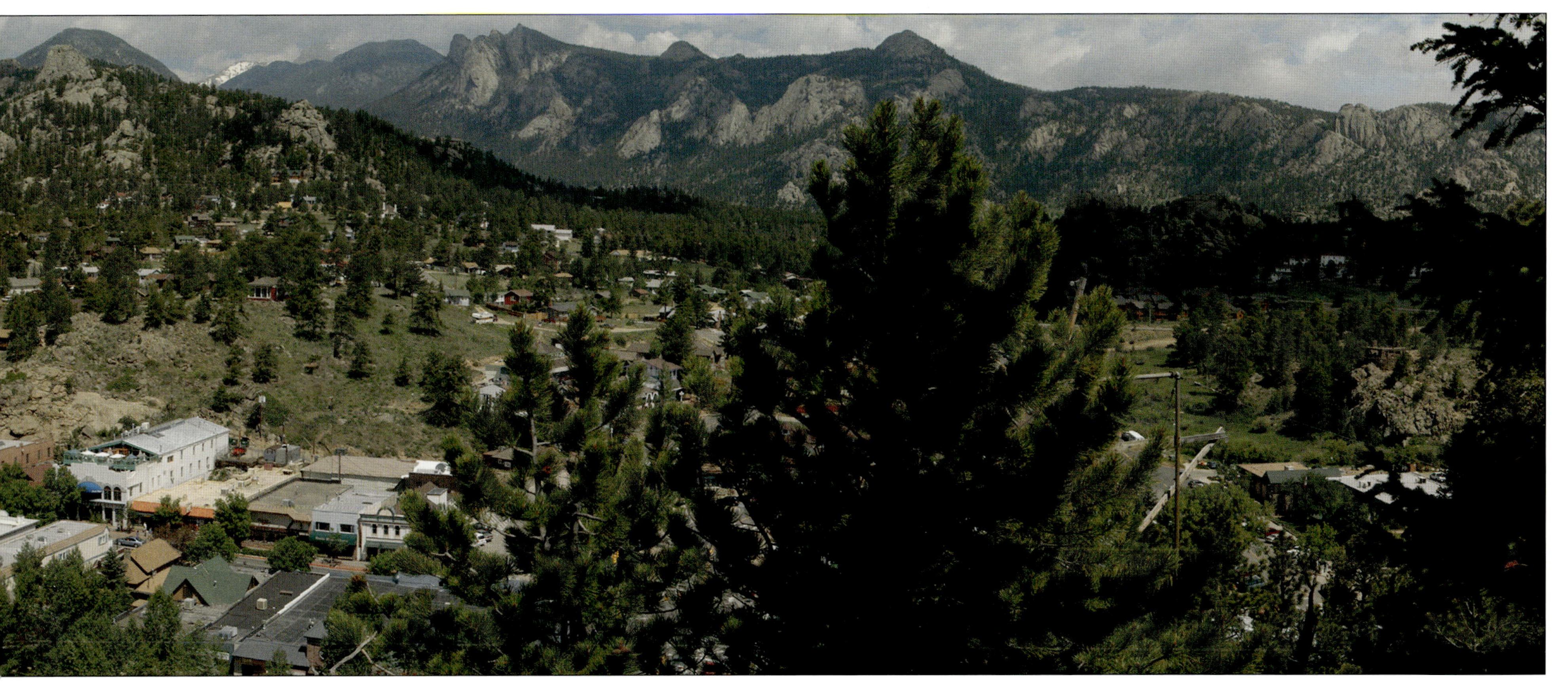

29. Al Birch House, circa 1910

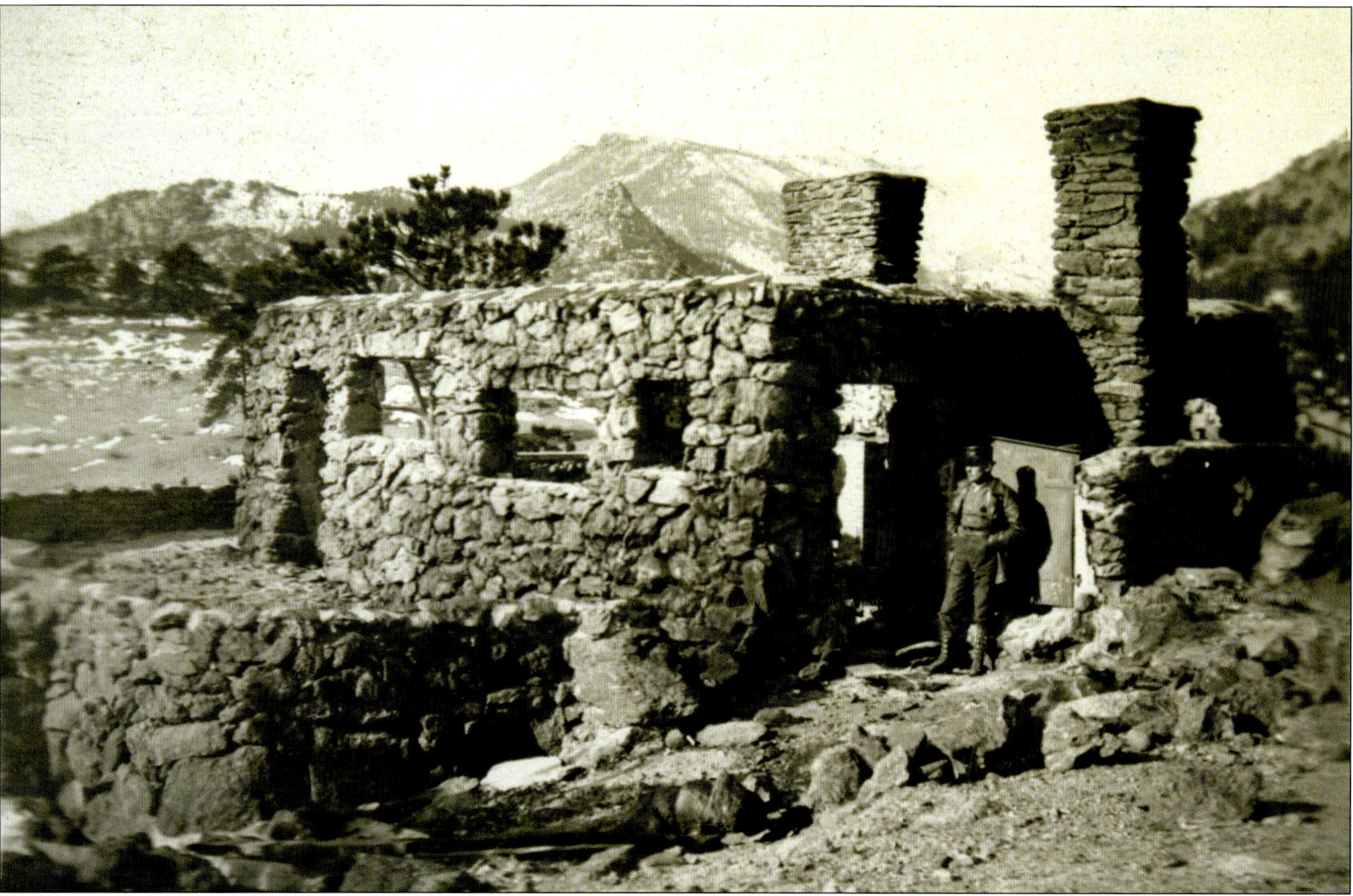

The original photograph above captures the stone ruins on the knoll behind and above the Municipal Building on Elkhorn Avenue. This was once the house of *Denver Post* writer Al Birch. Birch came to Estes Park in 1902 at age 20, and with two other young men cut a trail to Bear Lake and spent the summer there. Having fallen in love with the region, he decided to make it his summer home.

Completed in 1907, the stone house stood daringly perched on the knoll. Birch called it "Jacob's Ladder" because when the colors refracted through its leaded-glass front door it reminded him of Joseph's biblical coat of many colors.

Birch employed Estes Park mason Carl Piltz to do the stonework. Piltz, who would become famous for the many fireplaces he built for early residents of the village, did his work well, as the contemporary photograph shows. But the carpenter employed to do the interior work ran floor joists under the fireplace with only 4 inches of cement above the timbers. In December 1907, these joists were heated up by the firebox, caught fire, and left Birch's home a blackened ruin. Jacob's Ladder never was rebuilt. "I could not live up there enough to justify the expense," Birch later said.

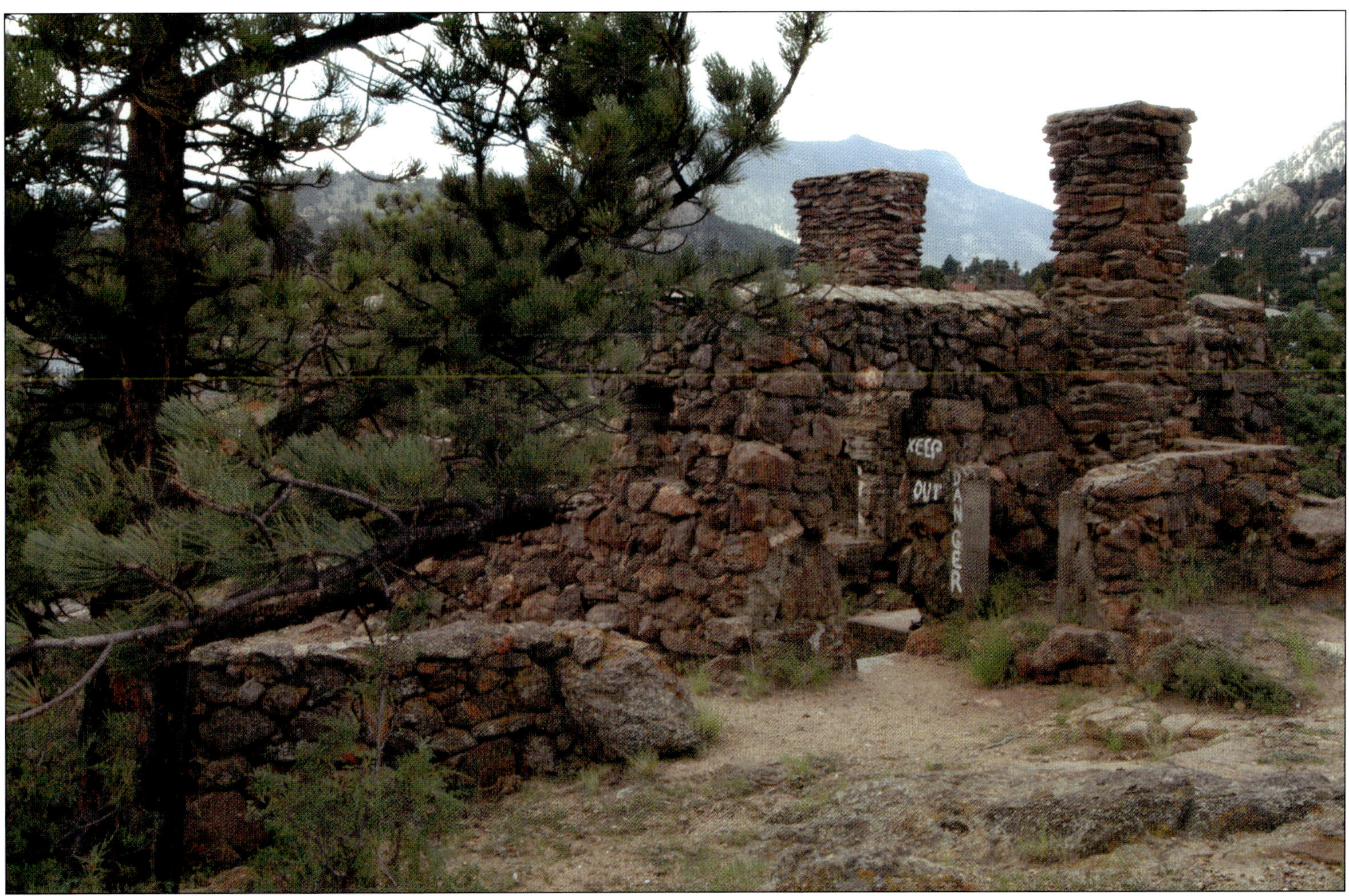

Its ruins nonetheless remain one of Estes Park's most visible and historic landmarks. The Town of Estes Park owns the land on which it sits, as well as the adjacent 20-acre property now known as the Knoll-Willows. The town has turned the scenic knoll, with its views of Longs Peak and the Front Range, into a quiet place for visitors and residents alike. A nature trail connects the ruins to a small parking lot across the road from the Stanley Hotel. The Estes Park Valley Land Trust holds a conservation easement on the land, further protecting its wildlife and natural beauty.

Although Al Birch did not rebuild on the knoll, he did erect another summer home below the cliff on Black Canyon Creek. His log cabin is conventional, albeit sturdy and well preserved, and is a wonderful example of mountain resort architecture. The Birch cabin also is now Town of Estes Park property.

30. Estes Park from the Birch Ruins, circa 1908

By the summer of 1908, Estes Park was becoming quite a busy place. We can date the original photograph, taken from the Birch ruins, by the addition of a new warehouse at the rear of Sam Service's general store (center). Note that the colors of the building's front and rear do not yet match. A closer inspection shows a man with a wagon and team of horses near the warehouse entrance. The general store is in evidence in the contemporary photograph, although it long since has been transformed to other purposes.

The photograph also can be dated by bank cashier Sidney Sherman's 1908 six-room log house, standing all alone below Davis Hill. What appears to be a construction ladder is propped against the side of the house.

Some of the other buildings in the original photograph include Estes Park school, completed in 1907 and sitting across from the fenced, but as yet unimproved, village park. Just next to the school is the house of George Johnson, who operated the Loveland-Estes Park Stage and later on a garage on upper Elkhorn Avenue, the longtime site of Bob's Amoco, which was converted in 2005 into shops.

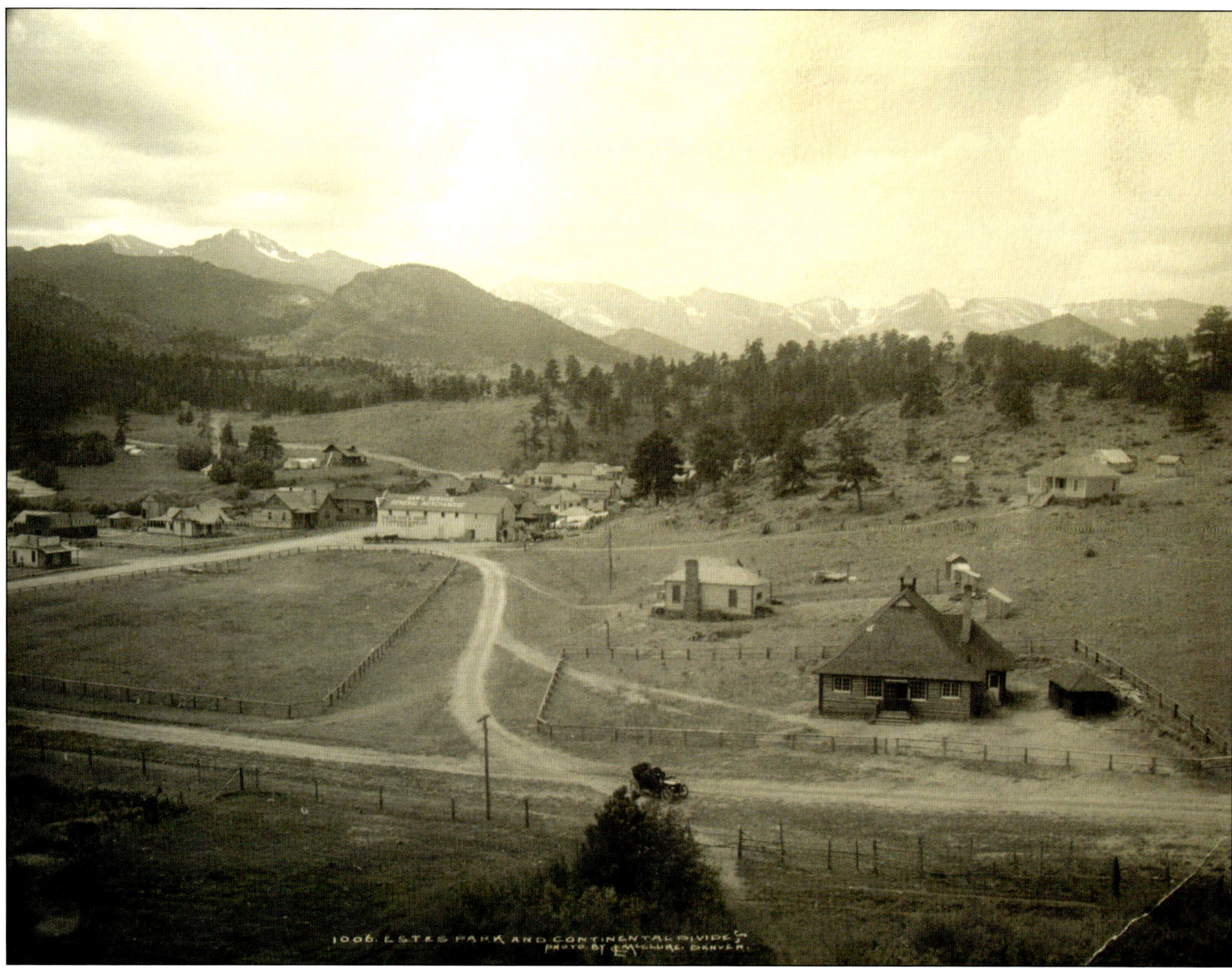

Photo by Louis C. McClure

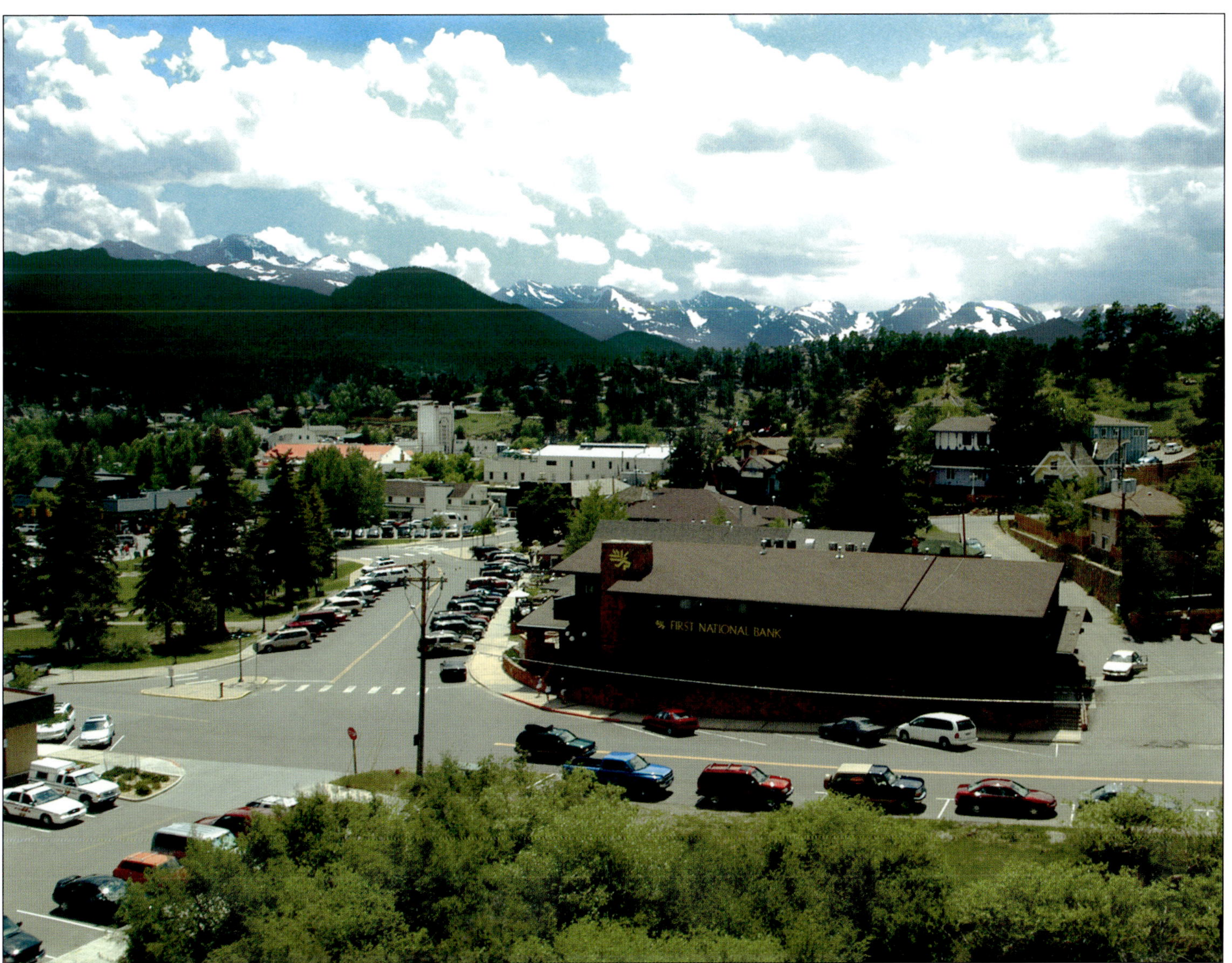

James Boyd, Service's brother-in-law, occupied the house across from the Service store (see p. 88). To its rear, fronting what is today's East Riverside Drive, is Boyd's blacksmith shop, which is identifiable by its facade.

Two more historically important buildings can be seen in the original. The one that is located opposite the park is William T. Parke's first store (see p. 100). It was then purchased by newcomer Sam Service in 1901. The Parke-Service store had Estes Park's very first telephone, and from it F. O. Stanley made his historic 1903 phone call announcing that he and his steam car had arrived from Lyons safely and in record time. Two years later, after the village was platted, Service relocated to the new, much larger building across the street.

The second historic building is the log structure that is just visible two doors west of the Boyd house. It was built by the Forest Service and became the home of merchant J. Edward Macdonald, who arrived in 1908. Twenty years later his home became the Macdonald Book Shop.

31. Sam Service Store, circa 1950

This building, among the first to be built on Elkhorn Avenue, was erected in 1905–1906 by Samuel Service shortly after the village of Estes Park was platted and its lots were offered for sale. Service, a native of Ireland's County Antrim, had moved to Estes Park from Lyons, where he had owned a grocery business and quarry and also served briefly as mayor. Service purchased the William T. Parke general store farther down Elkhorn, the first Estes Park business that was open year-round. But Service wanted to expand, and seized the opportunity to relocate his business to the corner of Elkhorn Avenue and Virginia Drive. Sam Service's store, with its frescoed front and its sign, "Sam'l Service General Merchandise," boldly painted like a billboard with large, white block letters across the roof, anchored the Estes Park business district for over 20 years. The store was also something more, for with its gas illumination and its large, potbellied stove, it became a favorite gathering place for the town's male residents, especially in cold weather.

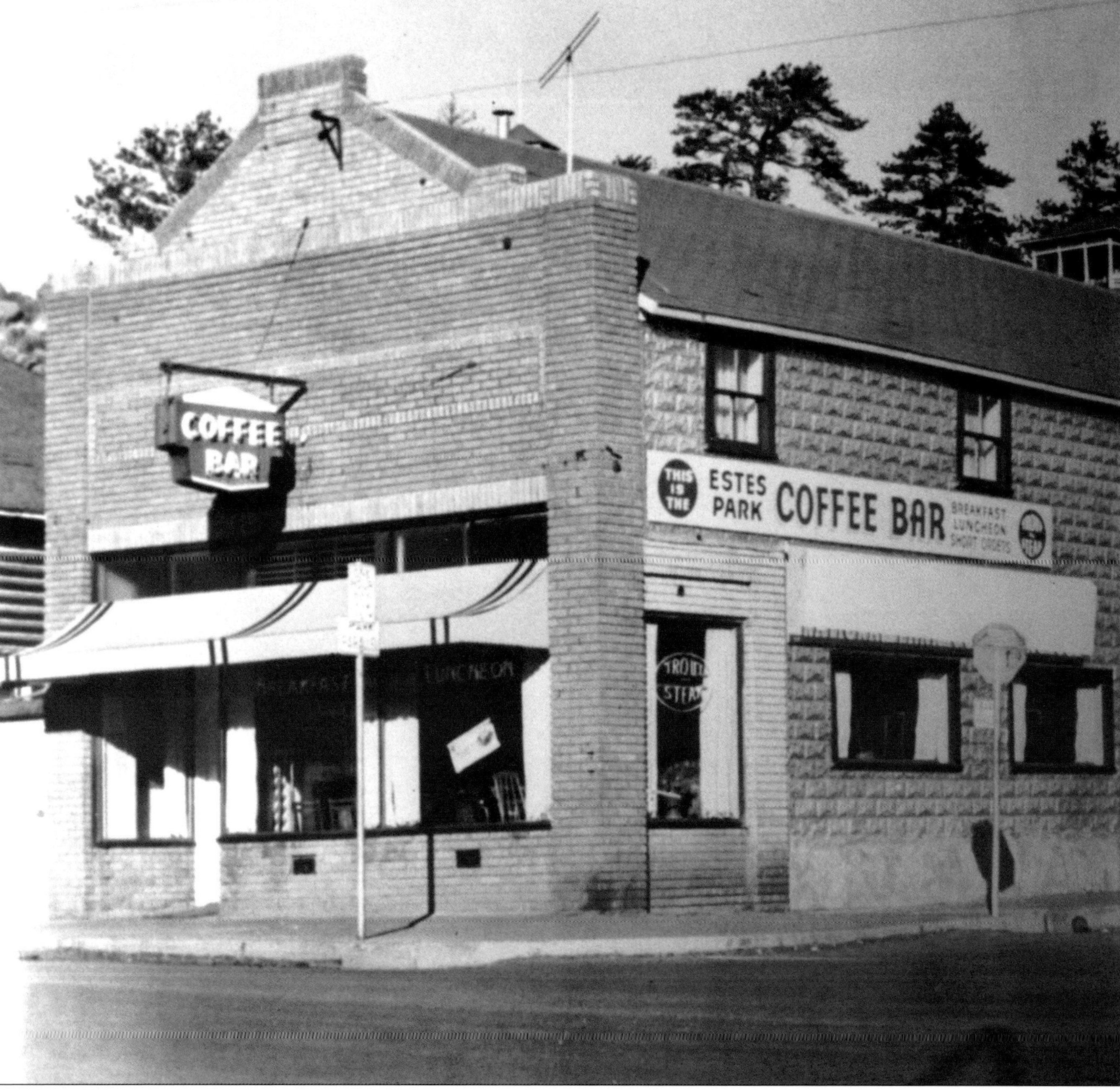

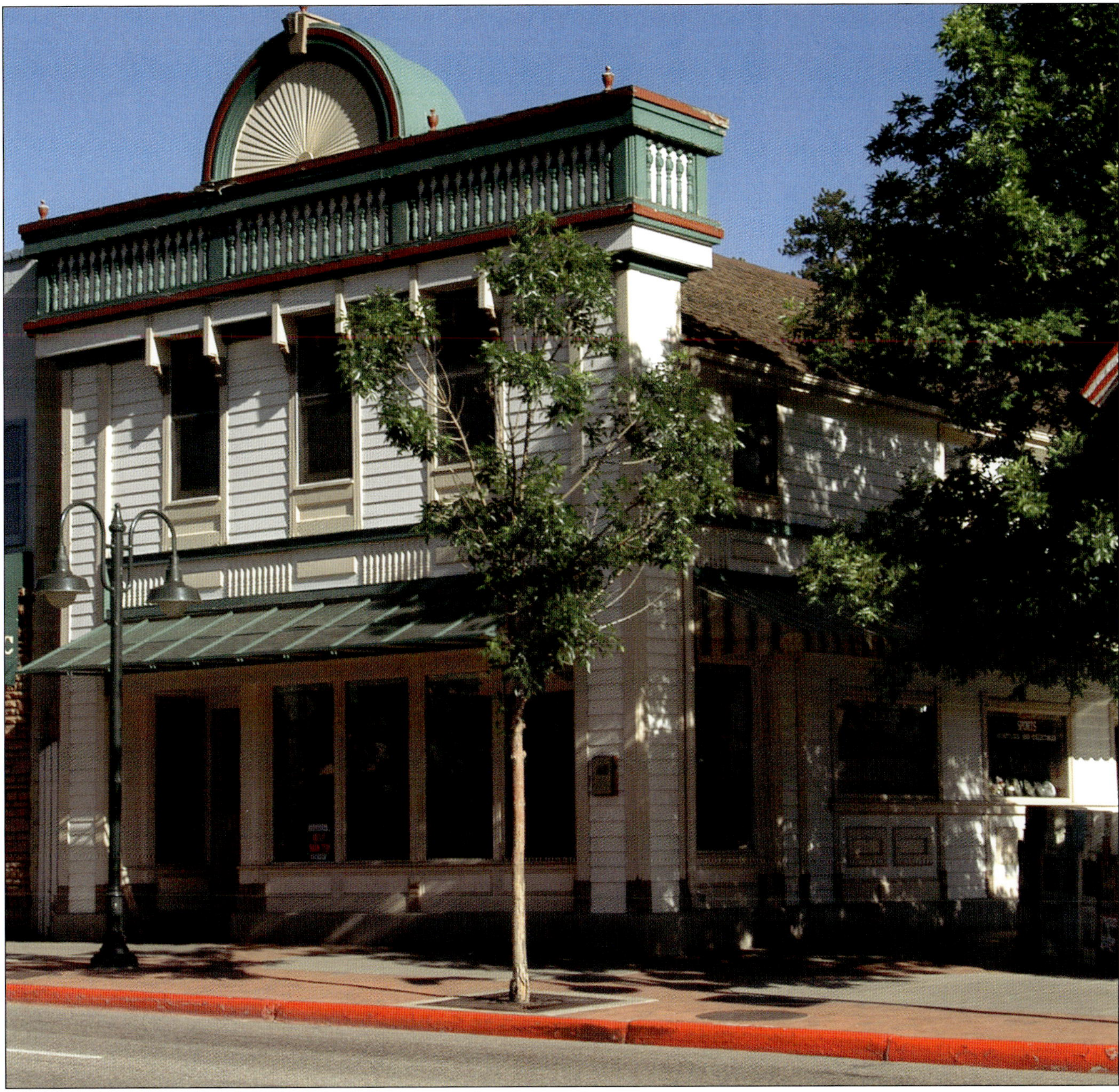

Sam Service operated his store up until 1928. In subsequent years, it became an Honor Brite Grocery Store and in 1938 the town's first Safeway store. In more recent years, it was the Coffee Bar, a popular local hangout. Because there are few if any good photographs of the original store, the "then" photograph comes from its Coffee Bar days. The front of the building resembles that of the original Service store, although it's been cut off, pushed back 18 inches, and remodeled. This occurred in the 1920s, when the town imposed uniformity in sidewalks and curbing on the buildings along Elkhorn. As the contemporary photograph attests, Sam Service's store once again has been turned to new uses.

32. Original 1915 Rocky Mountain National Park Headquarters, circa 1920

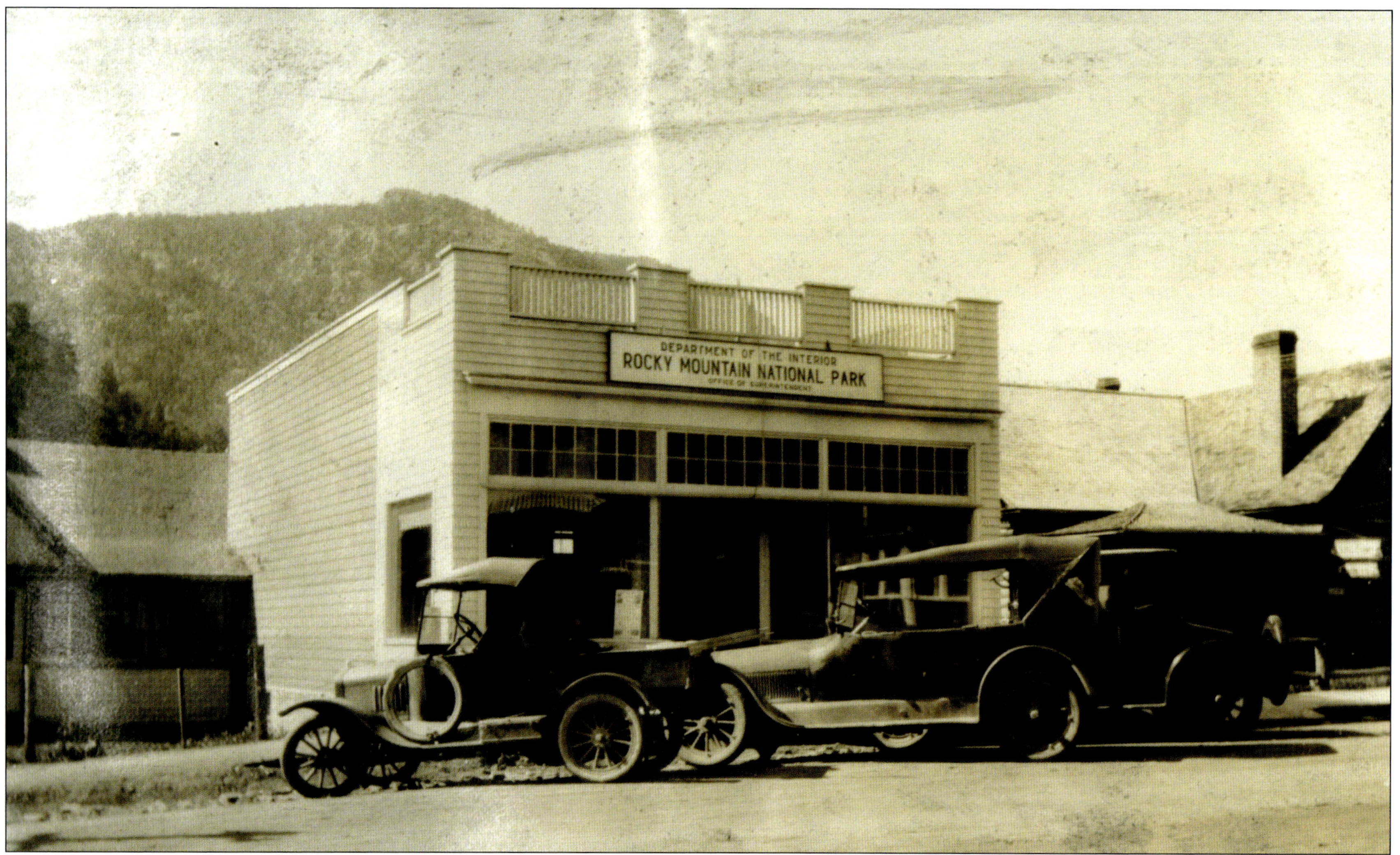

When Charles Russell Trowbridge, the first superintendent of the new national park, arrived in Estes Park in 1915, one of his first acts was to rent space to serve as park headquarters. Available was a small frame building that stood on lower Elkhorn Avenue and was across the street from Sam Service's general store. Though small and cramped, it served as headquarters for eight years, until October 1923, when the park's administrative offices were moved west to a new building located on Moraine Avenue, near its junction with West Riverside Drive (see p. 50). The original building (the one that appears in the photograph here) remained on Elkhorn Avenue until late 1924 or early 1925, when it was moved around the corner to East Riverside Drive. This new location was just north of

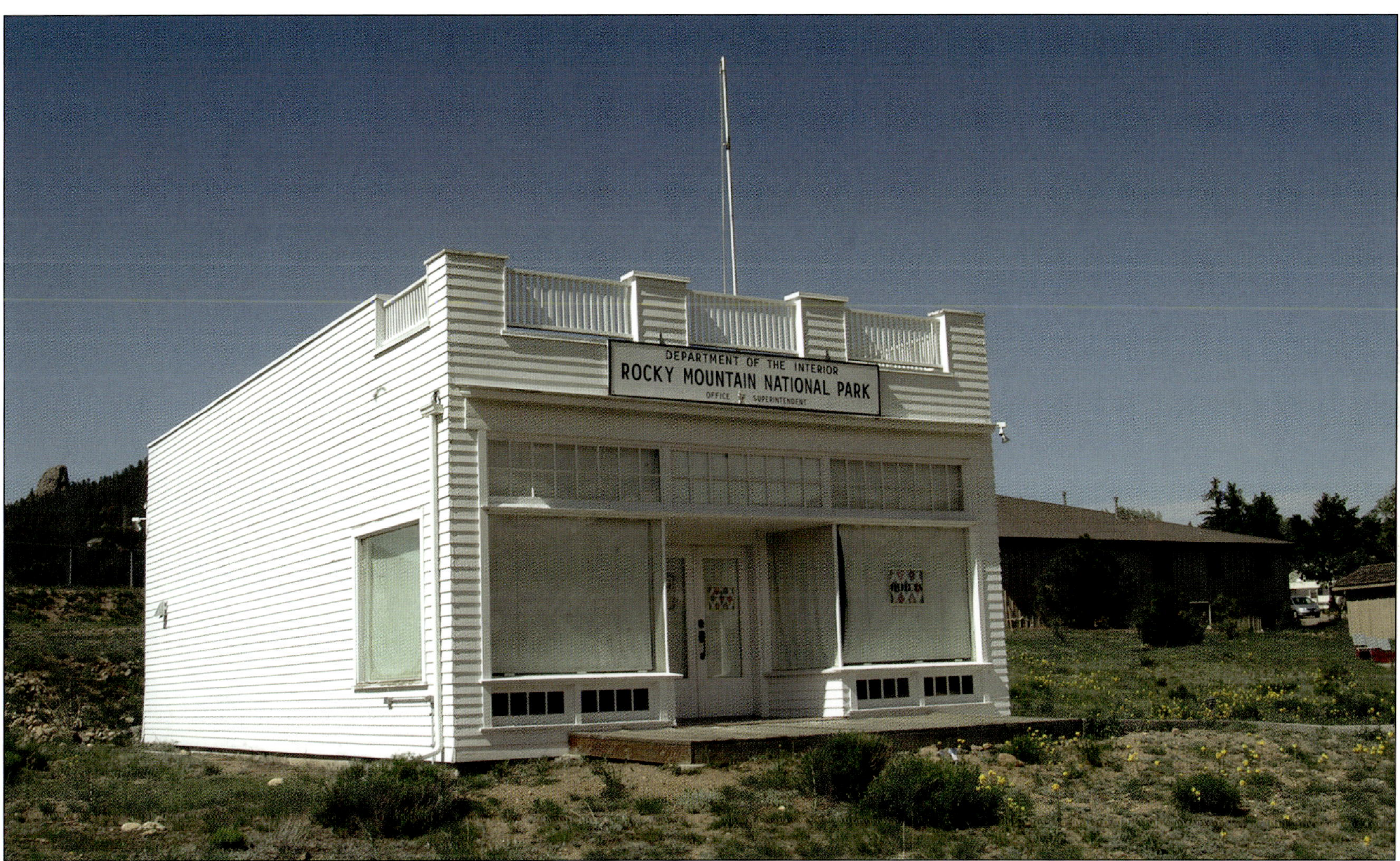

the bridge over the Big Thompson River. The building was moved in order to make way for a new block of stores, another architectural change in Estes Park.

The old building remained on that site with a variety of tenants, including a laundry and Estes Park's first Radio Shack store, until 1990, when after three years of fund-raising, the Estes Park Area Historical Museum relocated the historic building to museum grounds and restored it to its original 1915 appearance. It was rededicated on June 2, 1990 in connection with Rocky Mountain National Park's 75th anniversary. It now serves as a gallery for museum exhibits and is open to the public.

33. John Edward Macdonald Home and Store, circa 1914

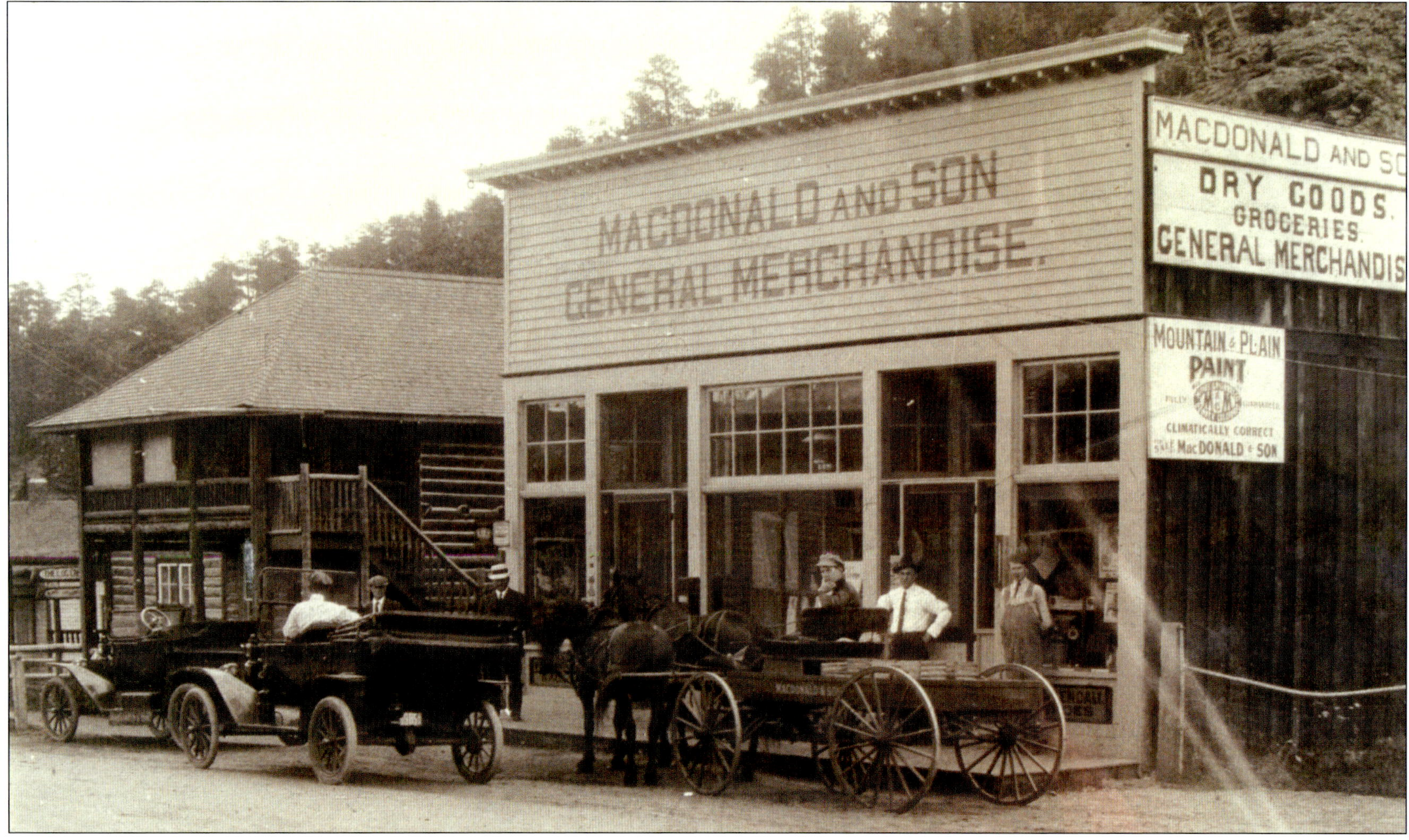

What since 1928 has been the Macdonald Book Shop was once the home of merchant J. Edward Macdonald. Macdonald came to Estes Park in 1908 to visit his brother-in-law, the painter R. H. Tallant, and decided to stay, purchasing and remodeling the log building on Elkhorn Avenue built by the Forest Service as its district headquarters. In 1909, Macdonald and his son Ralph went into business by purchasing the stock and goodwill of E. M. A. Foot's mercantile store at the corner of Elkhorn and Moraine Avenues. Their sign read, "The Popular Shop Macdonald and Son."

In 1910, Foot decided not to renew their lease, and Ed Macdonald erected a building of his own on two lots adjacent to his home farther down Elkhorn. Ralph Macdonald left the business in 1915 to operate a laundry down the street, while his father operated a dry goods, grocery, and general merchandise business until retiring in 1932. In 1938, the former Macdonald store was purchased by Ted Jelsema, who owned both the Riverside Hotel next door (the old Josephine Hotel) and the Riverside Amusement Park across Fall River (see p. 96). Jelsema promptly moved the west wall of the old store to the east, to provide a wider

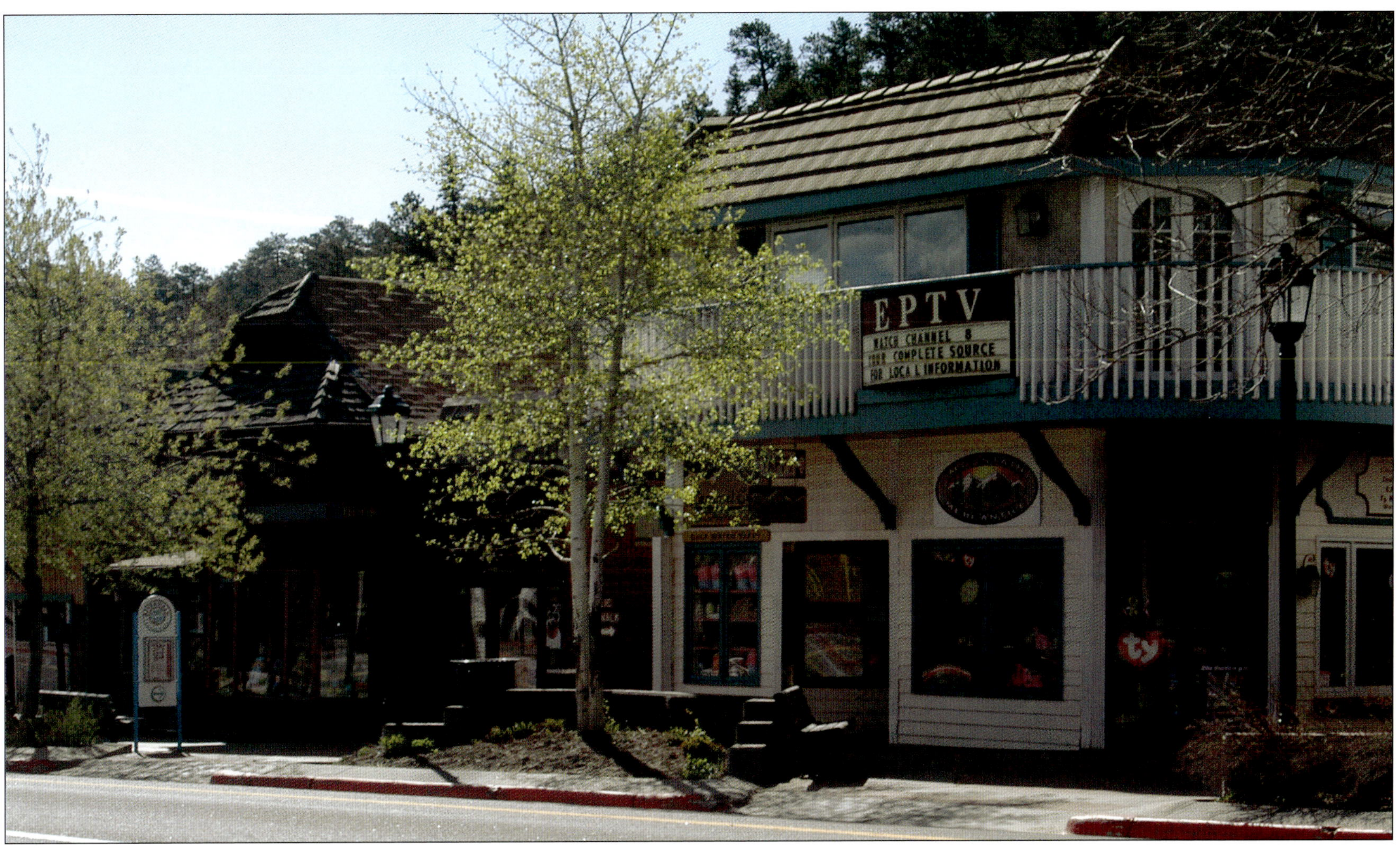

alley entrance to his amusement complex. The original building, extensively remodeled, remains. The Macdonald home also has undergone remodeling since the original photograph.

In the late 1920s, Ed Macdonald removed 8 feet from the buildings' fronts to comply with the village's newly mandated standards. Macdonald also removed one of the store's entrances and installed a new plate-glass front, and removed the sidewalk overhang from his adjacent home and bookstore. The footings for the posts that once supported the overhang are still visible in the sidewalk.

Macdonald Book Shop and the more recent Macdonald Papeterie behind the bookstore are owned and operated by Ed Macdonald's descendants.

34. Josephine Hotel, circa 1920

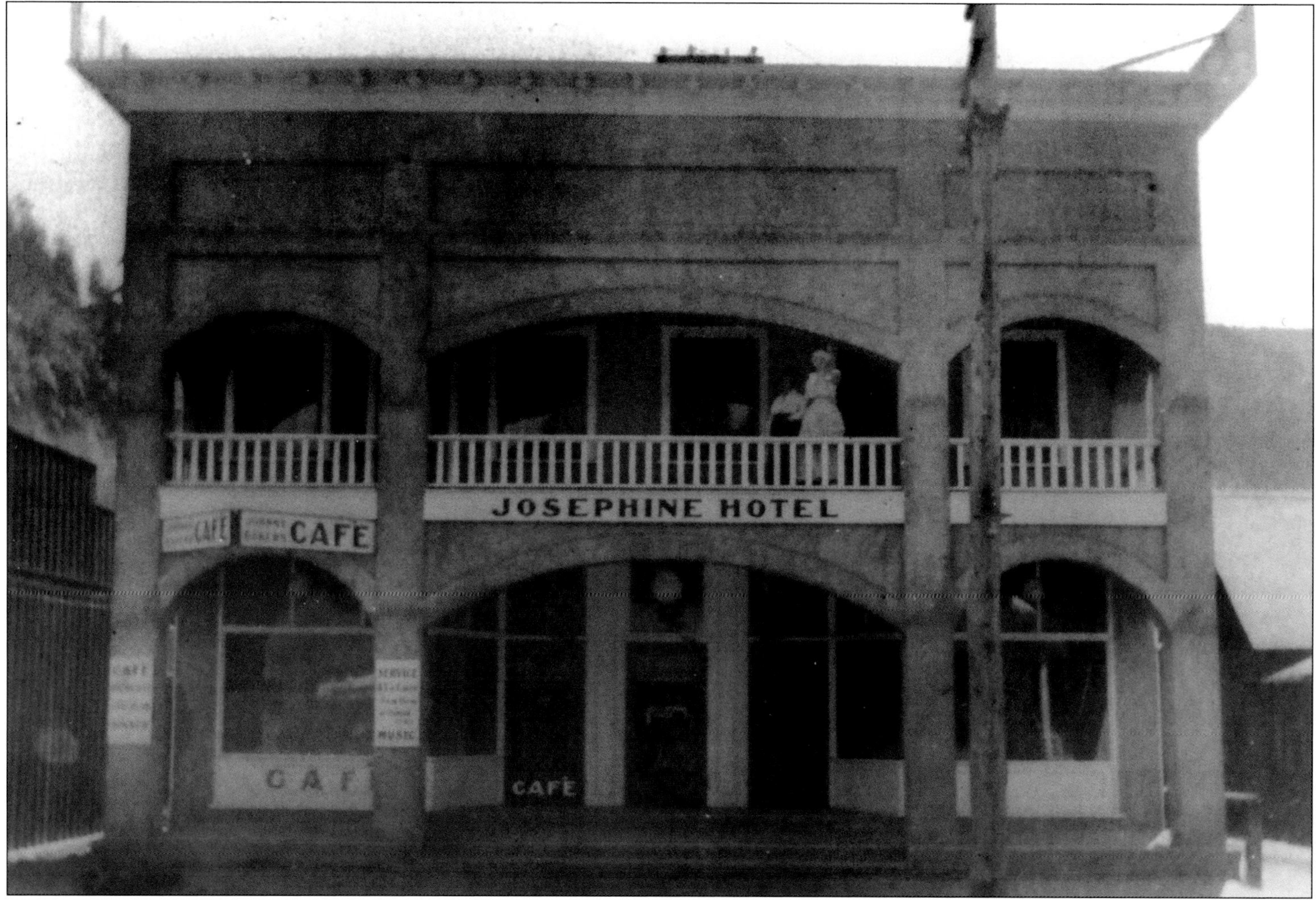

The Josephine Hotel was the second downtown hotel built by Josephine "Josie" Hupp, one of a number of enterprising women who were involved with the development of Estes Park's downtown business community. At one time, Hupp owned four downtown hotels: the Hupp (see p. 104), the Manford (see p. 106), the Josephine, and the Sherwood (which once stood farther up Elkhorn, just east of the old church). Born in Michigan, she came to Estes Park with her husband, Henry Hupp, the son of Estes Park pioneers John and Eliza Hupp, who homesteaded in Beaver Meadows (see p. 186). Josie Hupp seized the opportunity as soon as the village was platted in 1905, and a year later built and opened Estes Park's first downtown hotel.

Josie Hupp built the three-story, wood-frame Josephine Hotel in 1916. Four years later, she sold it to the Lewiston Hotel Company, only to repurchase the hotel in 1926. In 1930, she sold it permanently, this time to Ted Jelsema, another early entrepreneur. Jelsema owned Riverside Amusement Park, which

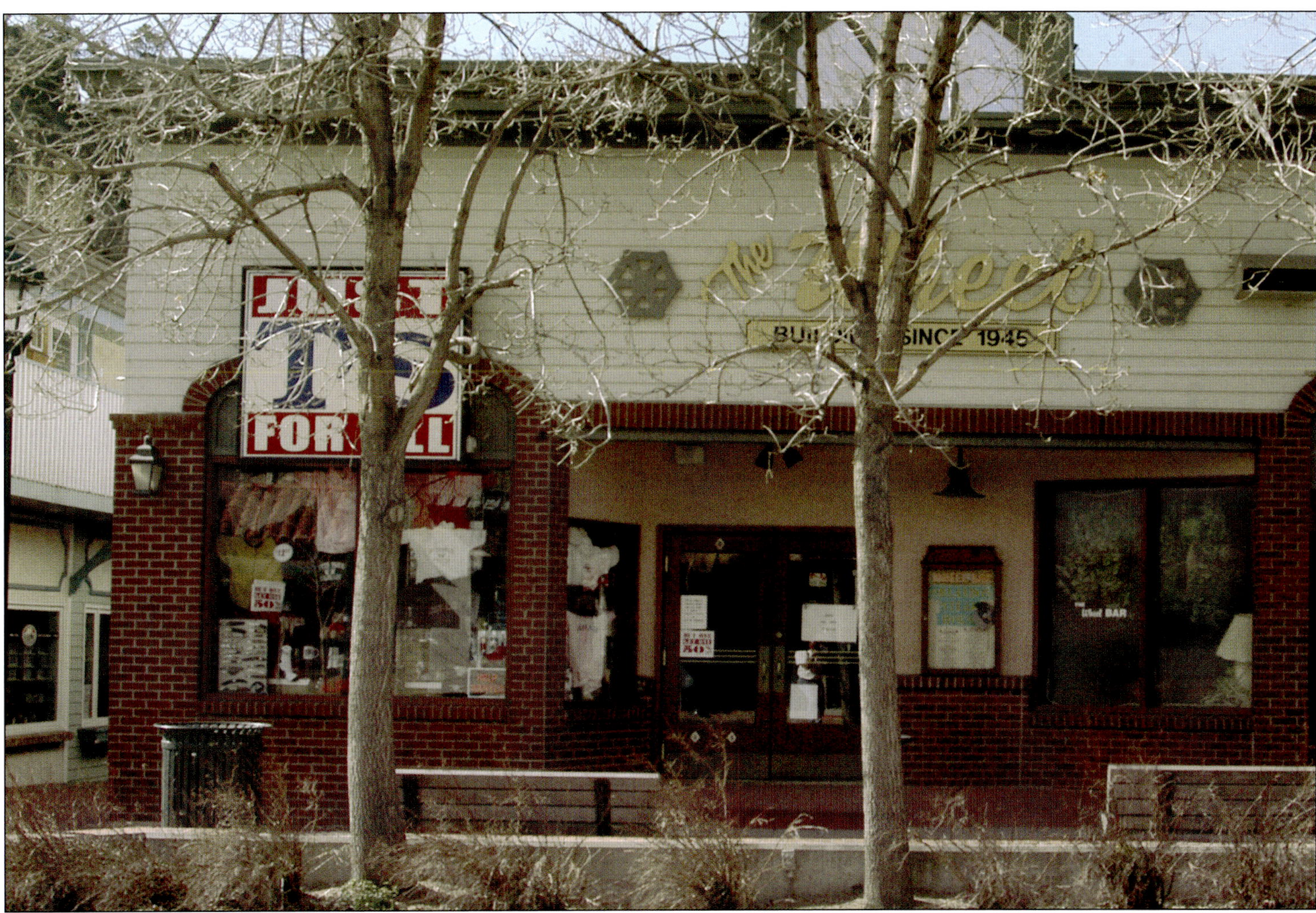

stood directly behind the hotel across Fall River (see p. 96). Jelsema celebrated his purchase by giving his new building a new coat of ornamental stucco and renaming it the Riverside Hotel. The hotel operation was gradually discontinued.

In 1945, the first floor, then housing the Estes Park Beer Parlor, was leased to O. M. Nagl. Renamed the Wheel Bar, the establishment has been run by the Nagl family ever since. In December 1956, a fire gutted the upper level. At the time, the Wheel occupied the west side of the building, Woody Wilson's electric shop occupied the east, and but a single tenant remained on the second floor. That portion of the building was never replaced.

In 1969, Nagl added the Other Room to the rear of the bar and a restaurant above named Orlando's, after its owner. In 1985, the family replaced the stucco exterior with brick and added new windows and doors.

35. Riverside Amusement Park, circa 1923

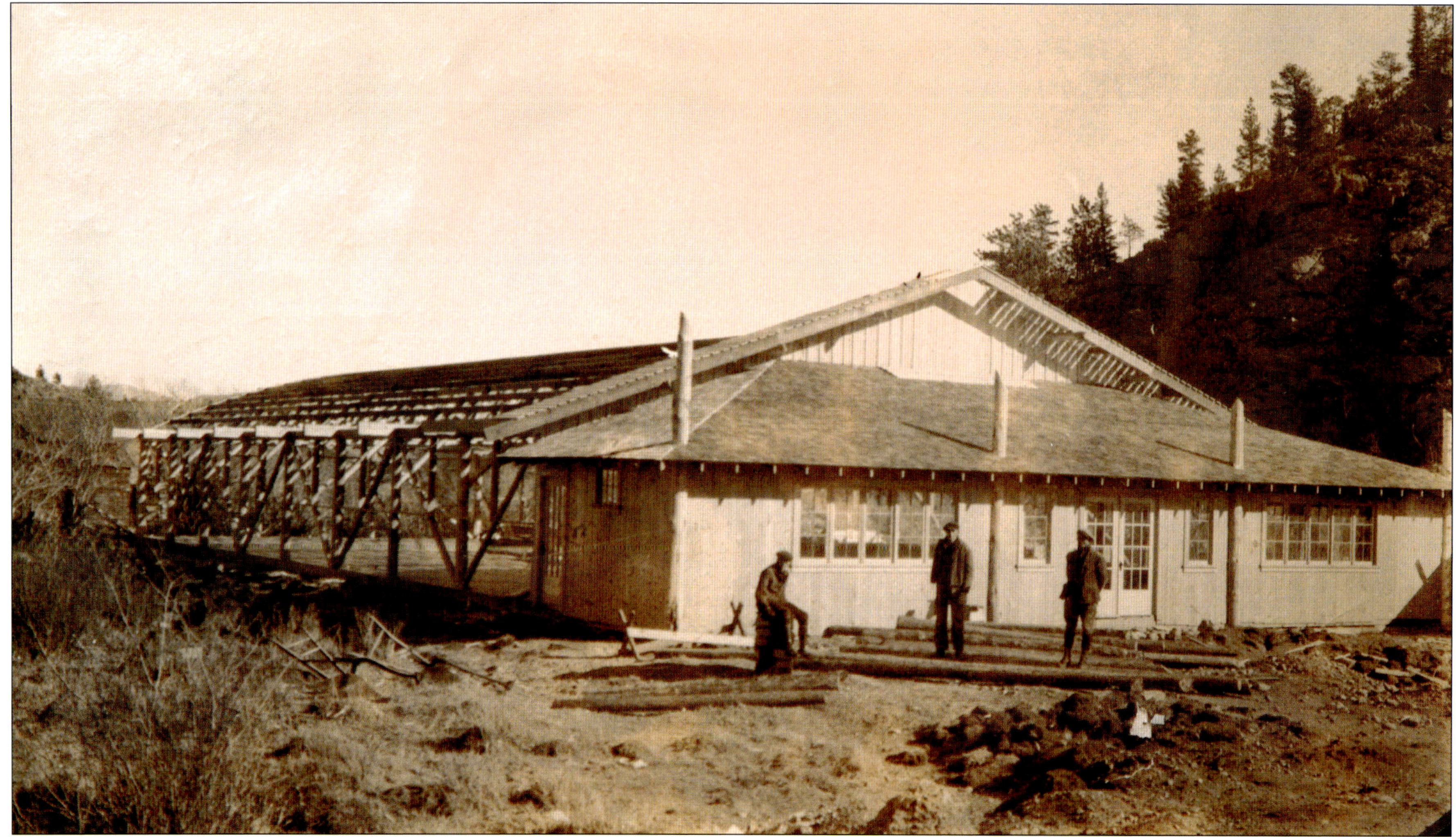

This parking lot near the confluence of Fall River and the Big Thompson was once the center of Estes Park's summer nightlife. Here stood the Riverside Dance Hall and Amusement Park, constructed in 1922–1923 by two entrepreneurial young men, Ted Jelsema and Frank Bond, on land obtained from Bond's father, village founder Cornelius H. Bond.

Riverside initially consisted of a 160-by-60-foot wooden pavilion containing a lobby with a large stone fireplace, ice cream and lunch parlor, and a large, rustic, booth-lined dance hall. To the east was a steam-heated swimming pool, enclosed by changing rooms and lockers. At the south end was a sand beach. A boiler kept the Fall River water at 84 degrees. Other attractions included a bowling alley and shooting gallery.

The main entrance to Riverside was located on Elkhorn Avenue next to the Josephine Hotel (see p. 94), then via a 6-foot-wide log bridge. Across the river was an auto entrance and fenced parking lot. Riverside, with its carnival-like

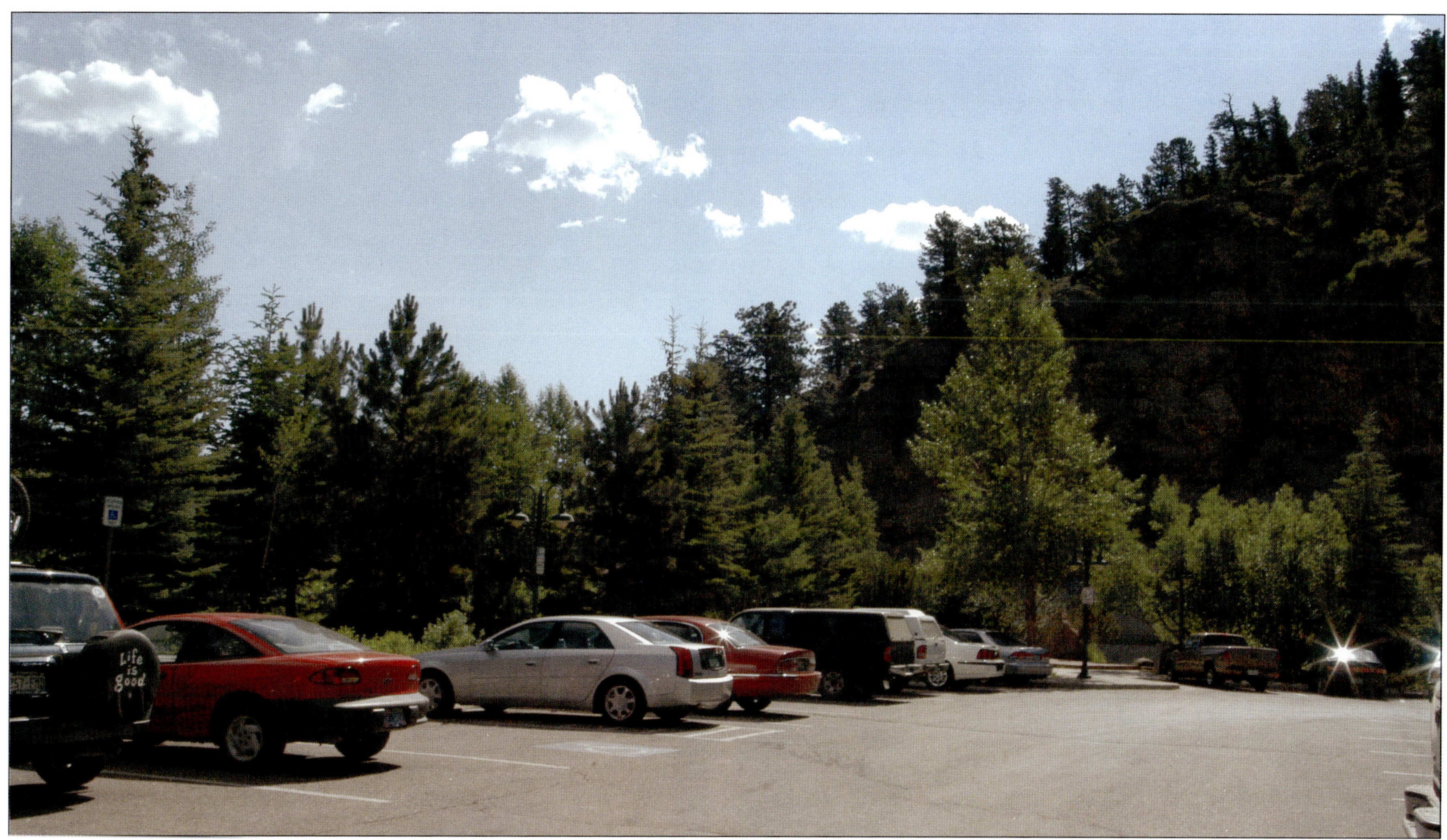

atmosphere, opened July 4, 1923. It was an immediate success, and the entrepreneurial Jelsema soon bought out Frank Bond's interest.

A favorite longtime feature at Riverside was its Wednesday night theme dances, which were repeated season after season by popular demand. In 1933, after Prohibition, Jelsema added the Dark Horse Inn, a tavern that used wooden merry-go-round horses for barstools. Riverside remained a fixture in Estes Park into the 1950s, although Jelsema sold it in January 1946. The swimming pool was soon closed and converted to a roller skating rink. Between 1958 and 1969, the Dark Horse Theater offered theatricals on a stage built over the pool. The end came in October 1969: The town of Estes Park, badly in need of more space for parking, entered into a lease-purchase agreement. After a farewell dance on January 31, 1970, Riverside Amusement Park and its Dark Horse Tavern were razed, and passed into memory.

36. National Park Hotel, 1972

Today's Park Place Mall, at 145 East Elkhorn Avenue, began life in 1919 as Harriet Rogers Byerly's National Park Hotel. Byerly had first come to Estes Park in 1912 to attend a conference at the YMCA camp, but stayed on to marry the photographer and resort owner Frank W. Byerly. They divorced in 1916, and Harriet Byerly opened up the Pine Cone Tea Room which was on Elkhorn just west of Sam Service's store and home. Three years later, in the fall of 1919, she had the tearoom building moved to the property's rear to allow for the construction of a 10-bedroom hotel. Business was good in Estes Park through the early 1920s, and in 1926, Harriet Byerly expanded and renovated her hotel with the construction of a two-story addition that contained 30 bedrooms, giving it the appearance shown in the early photograph.

Harriet Byerly operated the National Park Hotel until she died in 1955. Harriet's children carried on through the 1972 season, after which the hotel was sold. The new

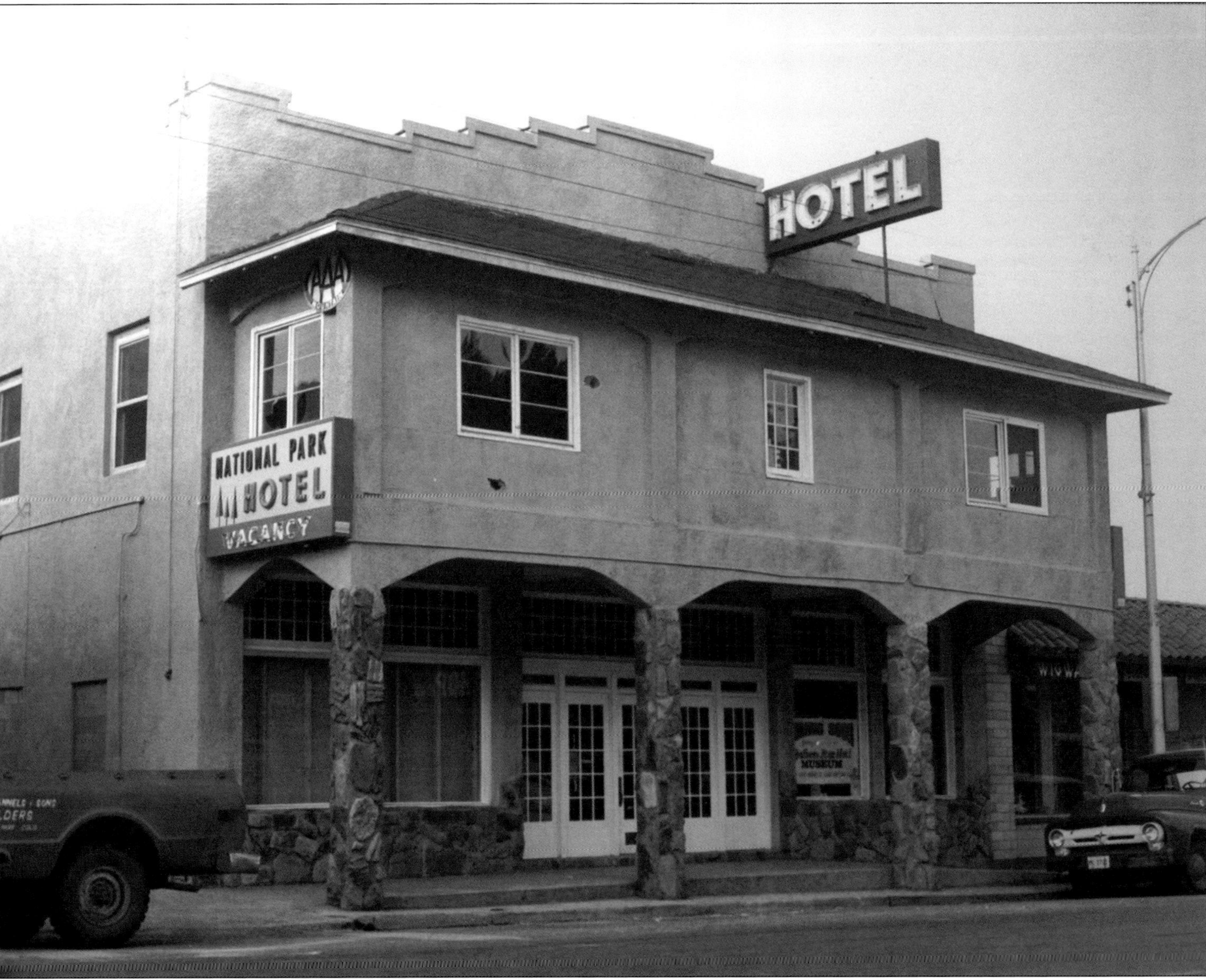

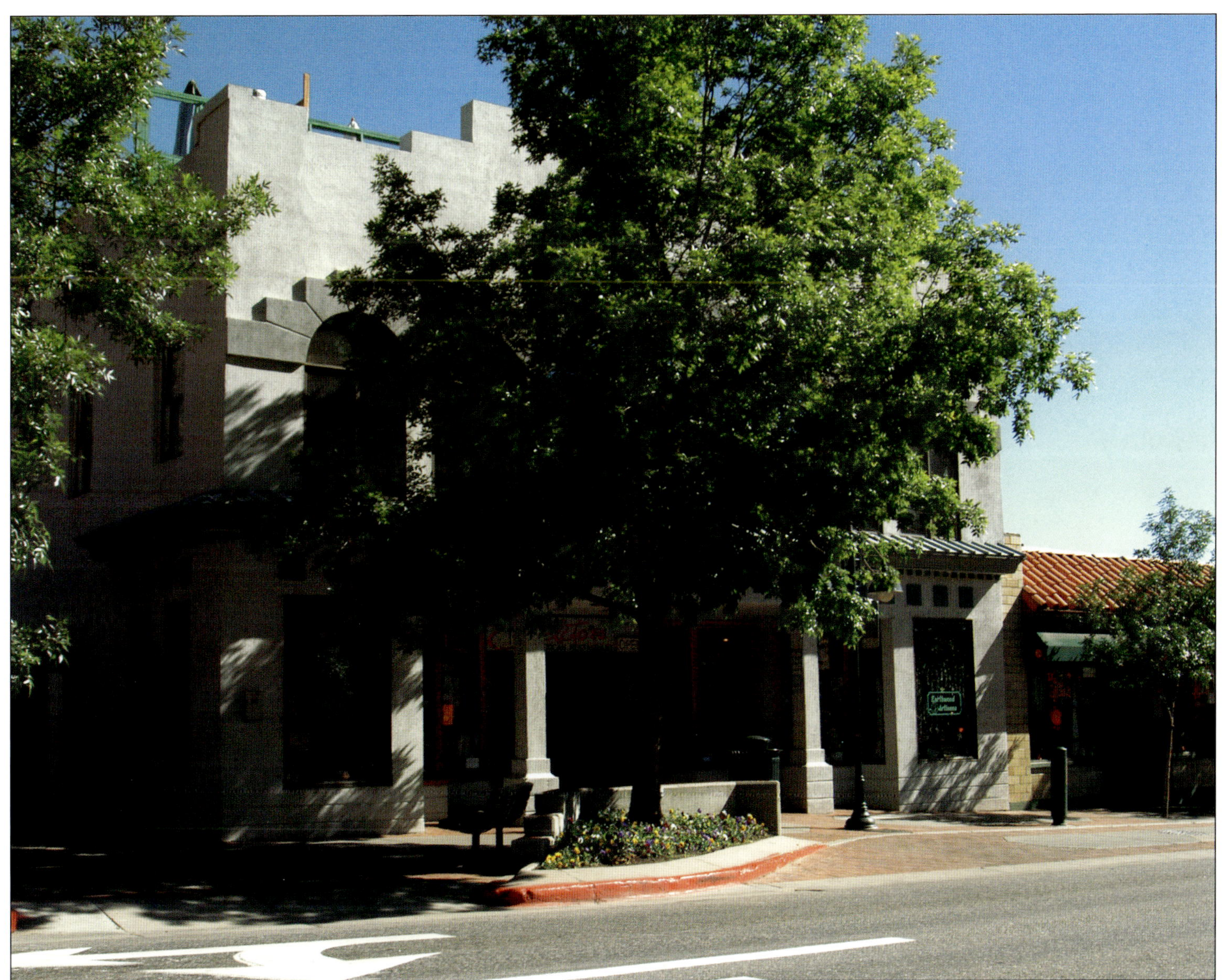

owners invested almost $1 million to convert the 40-room building into a Ripley's Believe It or Not! museum catering to people interested in "the strange, the unusual, the interesting, the odd and the just plain weird." On exhibit were oddities such as the "Man Eating Clam," "The Human Unicorn," "The Mummified Monk," as well as "Buttons—The World's Only 3-Legged Horse." This odd little museum opened in 1973, and for the next decade offered mountain tourists an interesting place for their kids to spend time on a rainy afternoon. It was closed in the early 1980s, and the old hotel was converted once again, this time into a mall with space for 14 tenants. Although, as seen in our contemporary photograph, the front overhang has been taken down and the front entrance has changed, the building's original architectural integrity is still pretty much the same as it was in Harriet Byerly's day.

37. William T. Parke Store, circa 1906

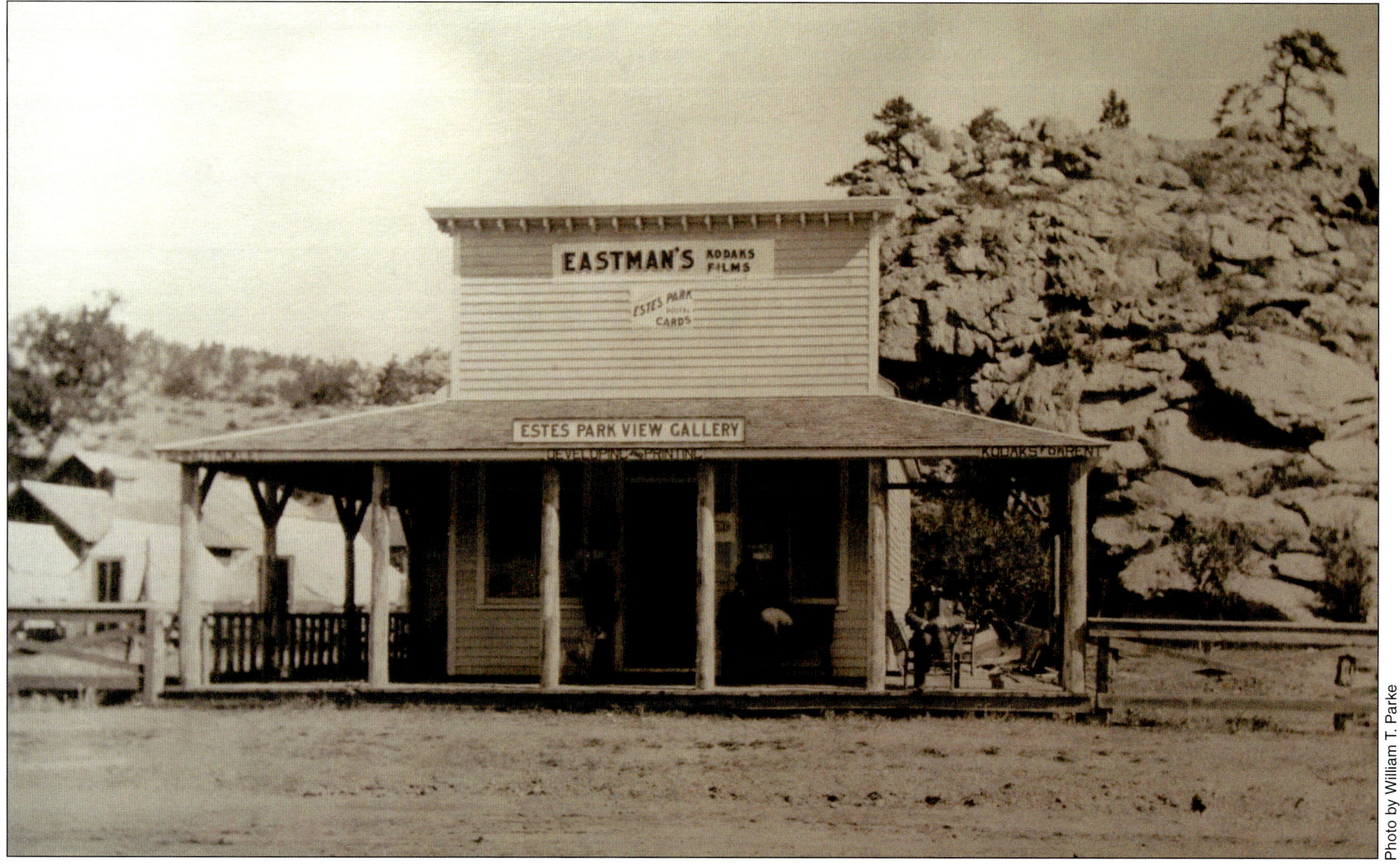

Photo by William T. Parke

William T. "Billy" Parke, an Indiana native, came to Colorado by way of Kansas and by the turn of the century had opened a small grocery store along lower Elkhorn Avenue. There, as an agent for the Colorado Telephone Company, he installed what was most likely the first telephone in Estes Park. In late 1901, William T. Parke sold the business to a young Irishman from Lyons named Samuel Service.

After leaving the grocery business, Parke turned to photography, became the town's first resident photographer, and soon was chafing to get back into the tourist business. In 1906, he completed construction of an art and curio store and studio near the corner of Elkhorn and Moraine Avenues. In addition to selling souvenirs, Parke distributed his own photographs and postcard views of Estes Park. Business was good, and in 1913, Parke expanded the building through

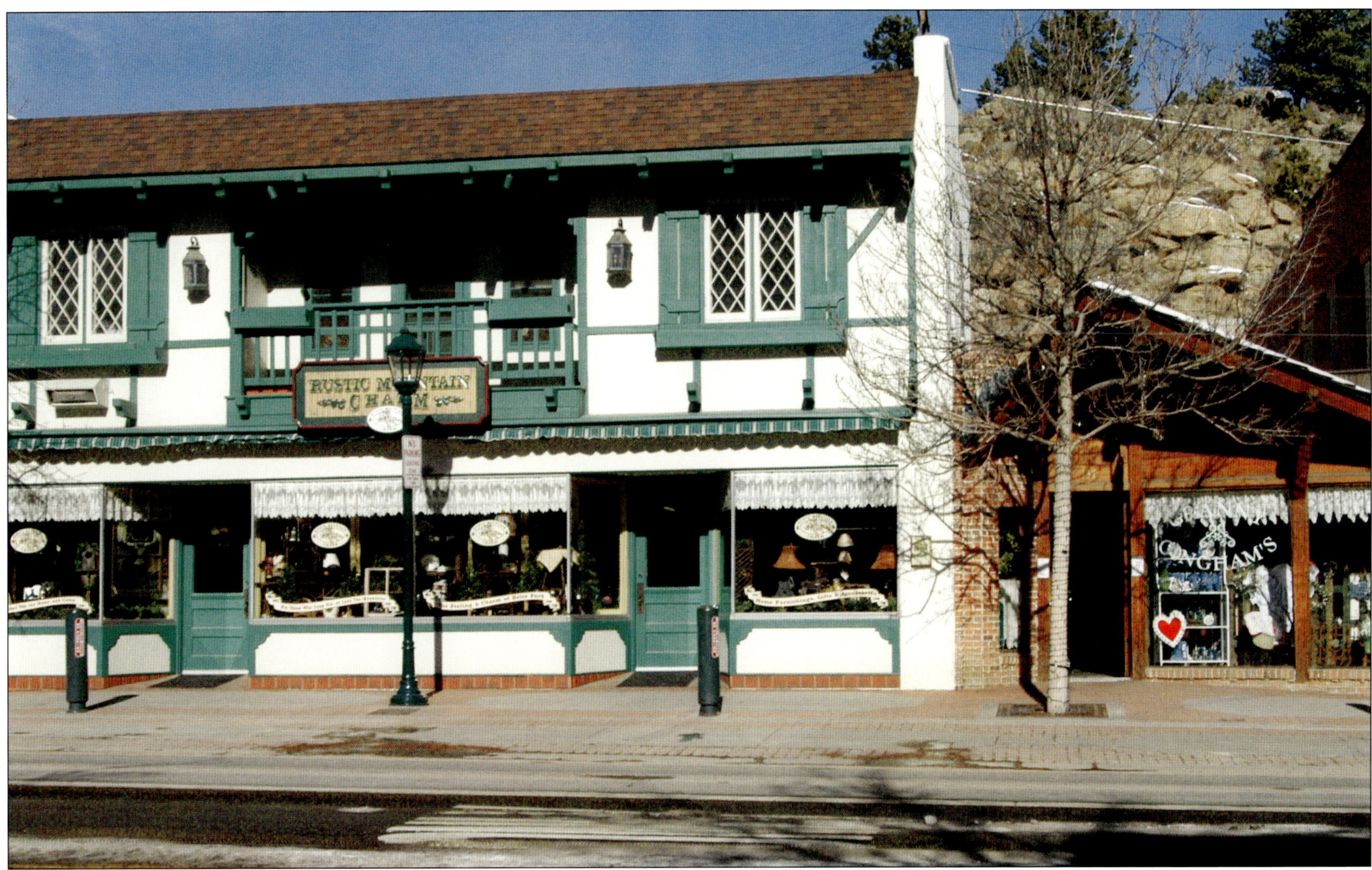

additions to the west and north, tripling its size. The new store survived the epic winter storm of December 1913 and was ready for the 1914 season. Parke became actively involved in the life of the town, and at the time of his death in 1924 still owned shares in the local bank, country club, and water company.

In 1921, Parke sold the store to John Baird of Denver, whose family would own the property for nearly half a century. In 1937, Baird extensively remodeled the original store, replacing the facade and porch with a two-story brick addition so that living quarters could be added above. In 1970, the building was sold to the Seybold family, its current owners. After 35 years in the souvenir business, the Seybolds closed their store and rented the building. Over the years, Estes Park has seen stores come and go. The Parke building, by contrast, has housed only four businesses in its century of existence.

38. Rocky Mountain Parks Transportation Company, circa 1910

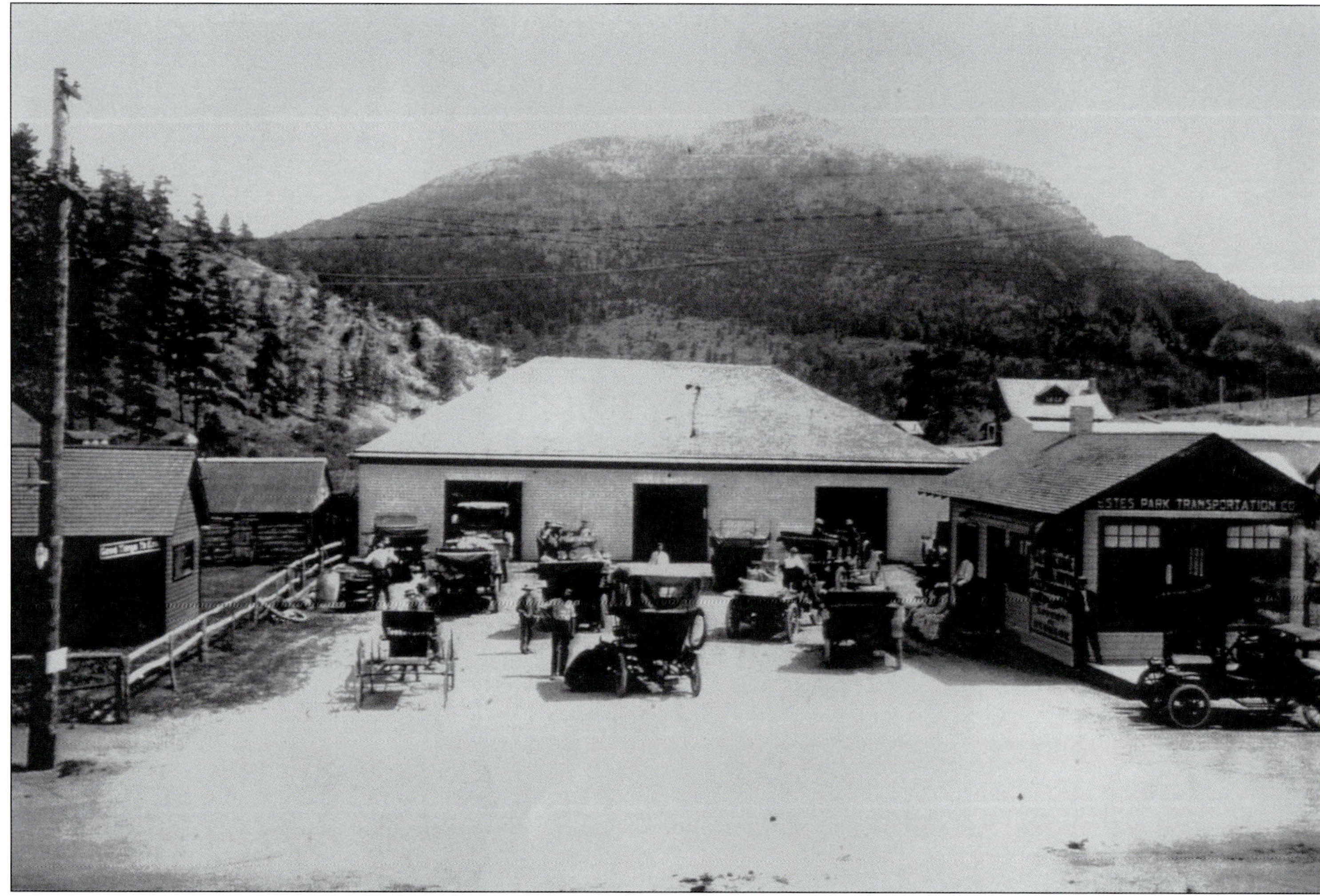

Photo by William T. Parke

The building that is now known as the Park Theatre Mall began modestly as the Estes Park Transportation Company. F. O. Stanley established the company in 1908 to bring passengers from Longmont and Lyons to Estes Park in anticipation of the 1909 opening of his splendid new hotel. Built across three lots on Elkhorn Avenue backing onto Fall River, the facilities initially consisted of the baggage and ticket office shown here, and space in the rear to park and service Stanley's steam automobiles, including the 12-seat Stanley Mountain Wagons, which revolutionized transportation in the region.

F. O. Stanley sold his company in 1916 to another transportation pioneer, Denver's Roe Emery. Emery then greatly expanded his Rocky Mountain Parks Transportation Company by buying out smaller competitors and investing in new equipment. By 1919, when he received an exclusive government franchise to carry tourist visitors into Rocky Mountain National Park, Emery had established a virtual monopoly.

Needing more room to house his growing tour bus fleet, Emery placed two buildings together and enclosed them as a new structure beneath a single roof,

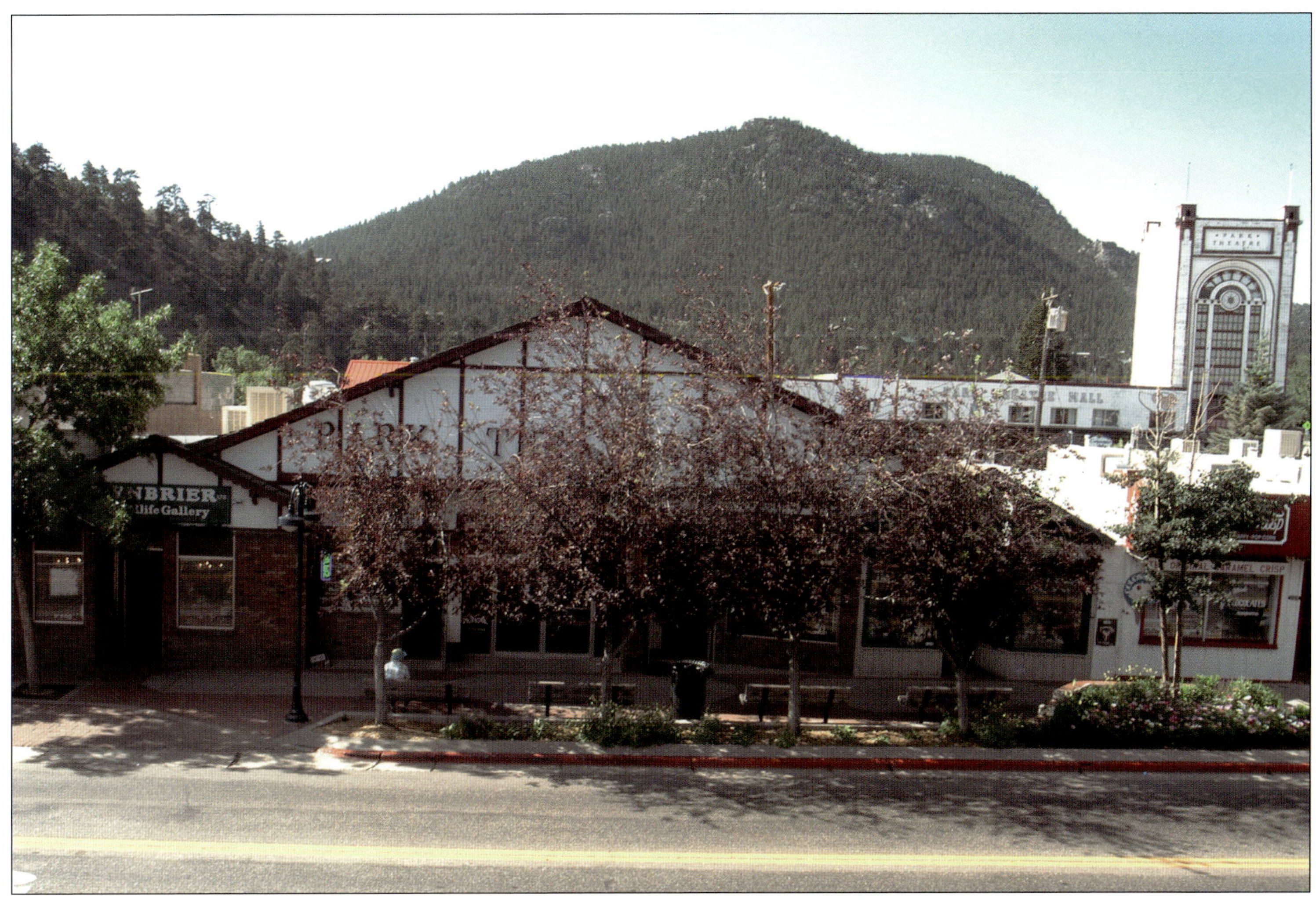

with a wide entrance opening onto Elkhorn Avenue. The concrete floor of the new building was extended back over Fall River to produce a warren-like structure containing the company's business offices, repair facilities, and parking area. It also contained dormitory space that housed Emery's corps of drivers, who brought passengers to Estes Park from the railroad station in Denver and the other gateway towns along the Front Range. According to local folklore, Emery created the landfill needed to support his new building by using the chassis of the Stanley Steamers he had purchased and then junked in favor of White Motor Company touring cars. F. O. Stanley, so the story goes, was anything but amused.

39. Hupp Hotel

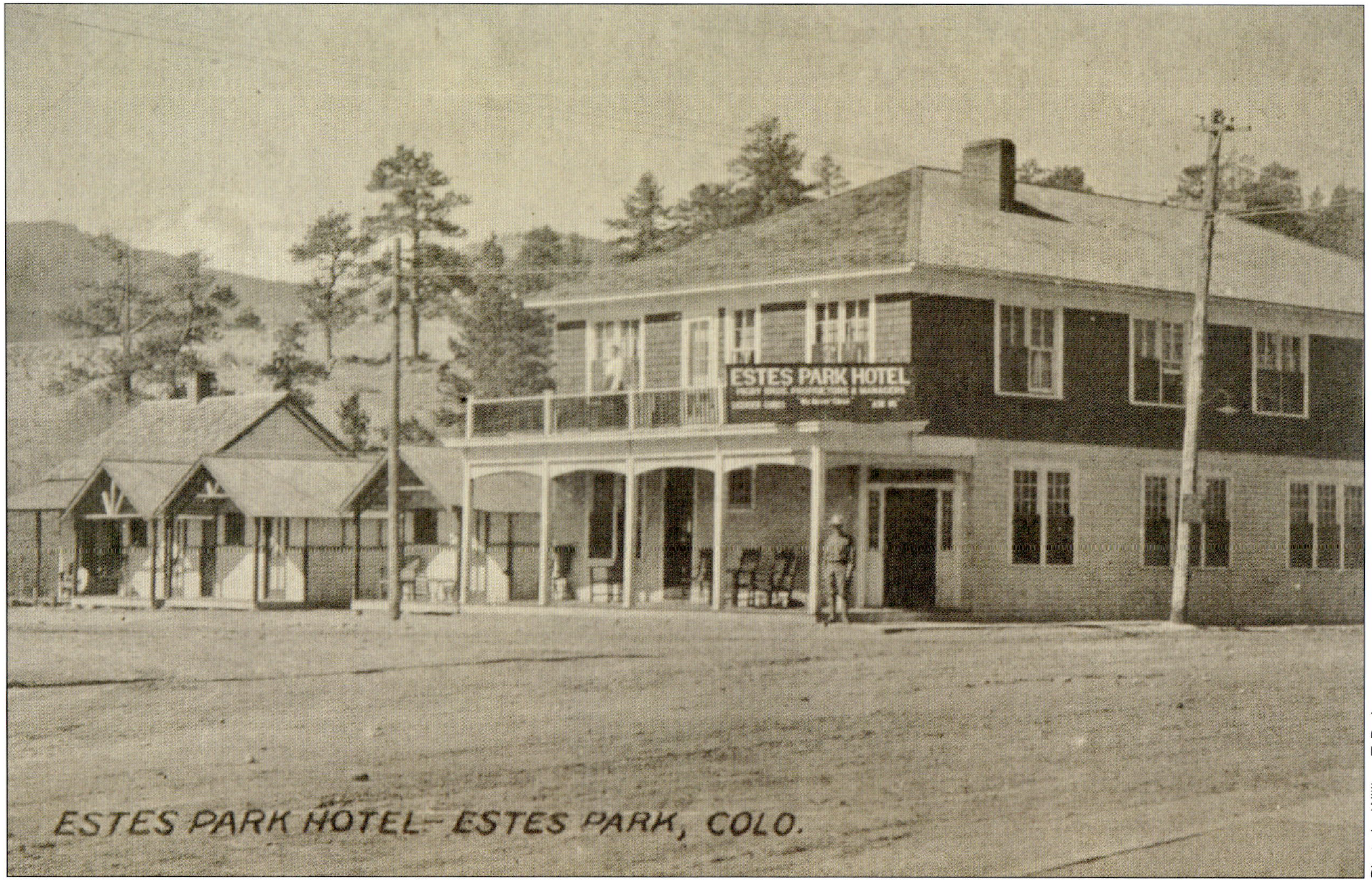

Photo by William T. Parke

Modernity seemed to arrive in Estes Park in 1906, when Josie Hupp opened her new two-story, 23-room hotel on the southwest corner of Elkhorn and Moraine Avenues. The location was choice, for "the Corners" and its group of small buildings comprised all there was of tiny Estes Park. Here stood John Cleave's frame house; his 8-by-12-foot post office; a community building that served as church, school, and meeting hall; a stage barn; and a small general store that was run in the summer ever since 1891 by Elizabeth Ann (E. M. A.) Foot and Jenny Chapin.

The Hupp Hotel had verandas on two sides, a large dining room, steam heat, and hot-and-cold running water. Unlike many other buildings along Elkhorn, it had its own basement. The first floor of the building was long ago converted to a gift shop, yet the basic structure of the old hotel is much the same.

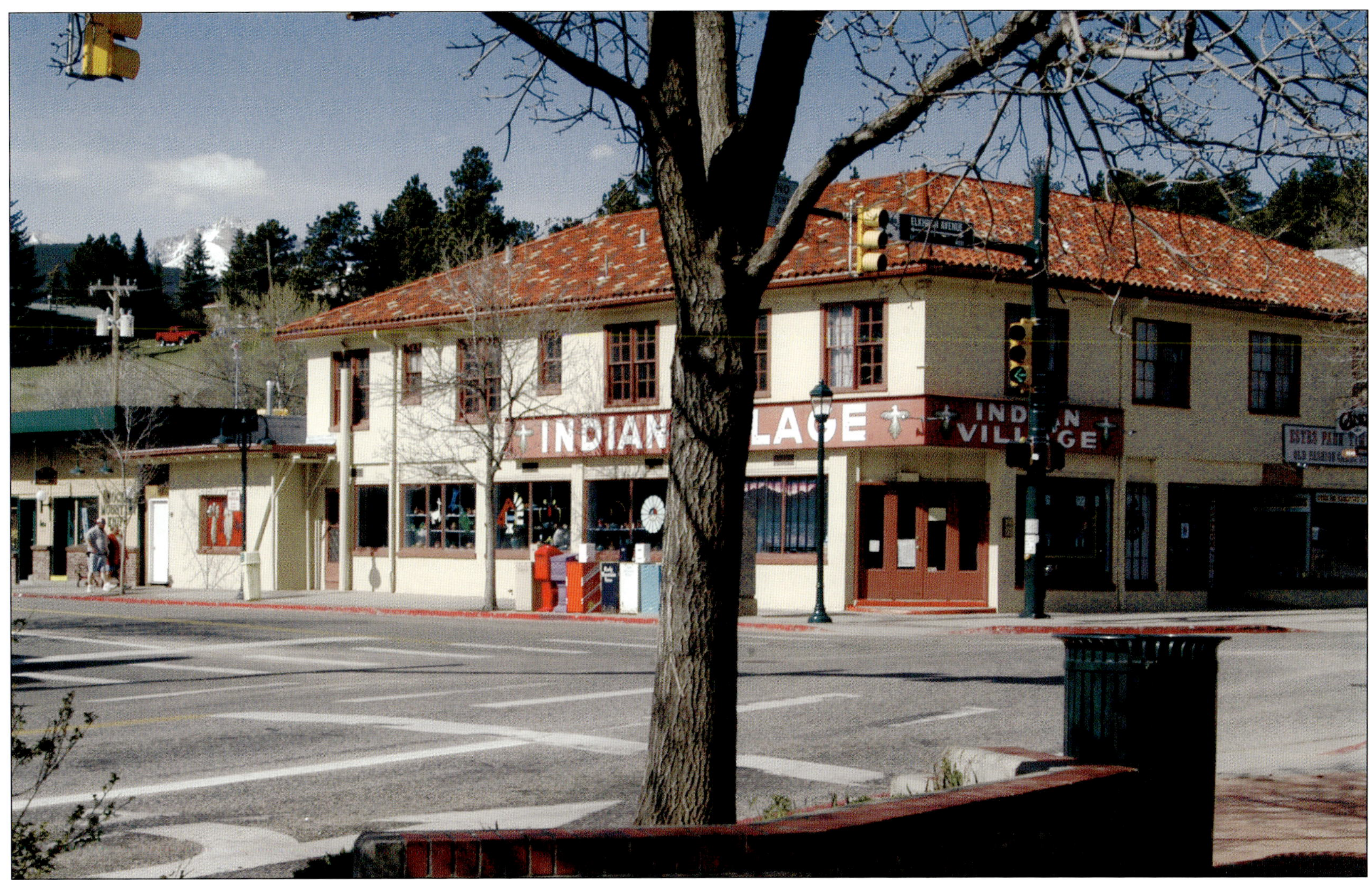

However, the hotel's name and ownership changes caused confusion for decades. The confusion began in 1908, when Josie Hupp purchased the new Manford Hotel (see p. 106), diagonally across the street from her Hupp Hotel. She promptly changed the Manford's name to the Hupp Annex, as it was known until 1932 through two changes of ownership, despite the fact that the old Hupp Hotel was now the Estes Park Hotel. Now there was a Hupp Annex but no Hupp Hotel. That year, Hupp Annex owner Anna May Derby leased the 15-room second floor of the original Hupp Hotel, now called the Somers Building. She chose to call the Hupp Annex the Hupp Hotel, and renamed the Somers Building the Hupp Annex, and so the two buildings had traded names.

If you are confused by all this, you are not alone. Today, the original Hupp Hotel is known as Miller's Indian Village Trading Post.

40. Manford Hotel, circa 1920

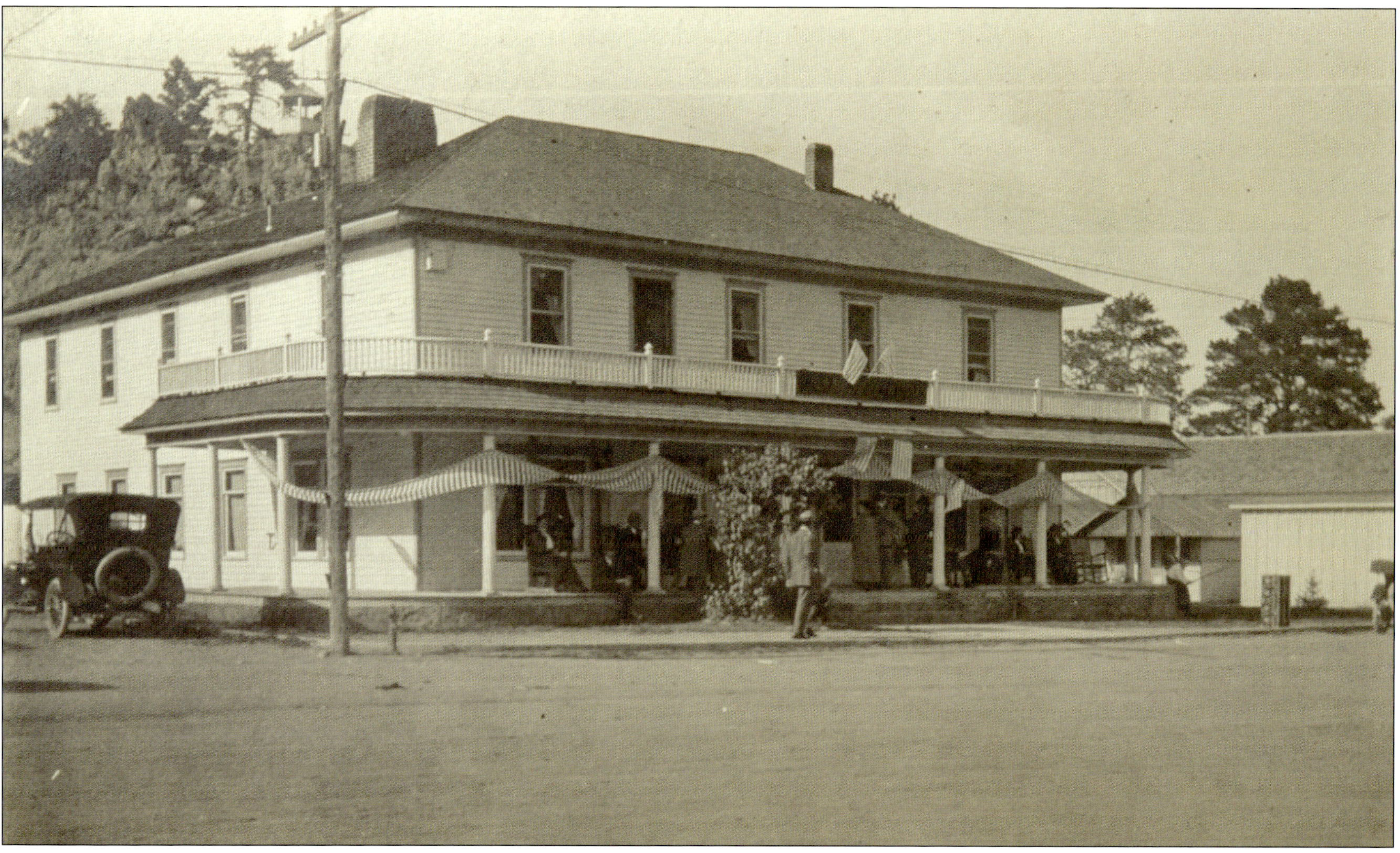

In 1908, early Estes Park businessman John Manford built the 21-room Manford Hotel, or Manford House. The new hotel was diagonally across from the Hupp Hotel on the northeast corner of what is now Big Horn Drive (then Anderson Lane) and Elkhorn Avenue. The house built in 1888 by postmaster John Cleave had originally occupied the site, but in 1907, John Manford paid Cleave $3,000 for it. He then moved the postmaster's house to the property's rear, where it remained, clearly visible in photographs, until it was finally removed in 1947.

Built on six lots, the Manford Hotel was bigger than its rival just across the street, containing on the first floor a large dining room and kitchen, a parlor, a gentleman's smoking room, and an office. The guest bedrooms were on the second floor. On the south and east exteriors of the building, early photographs

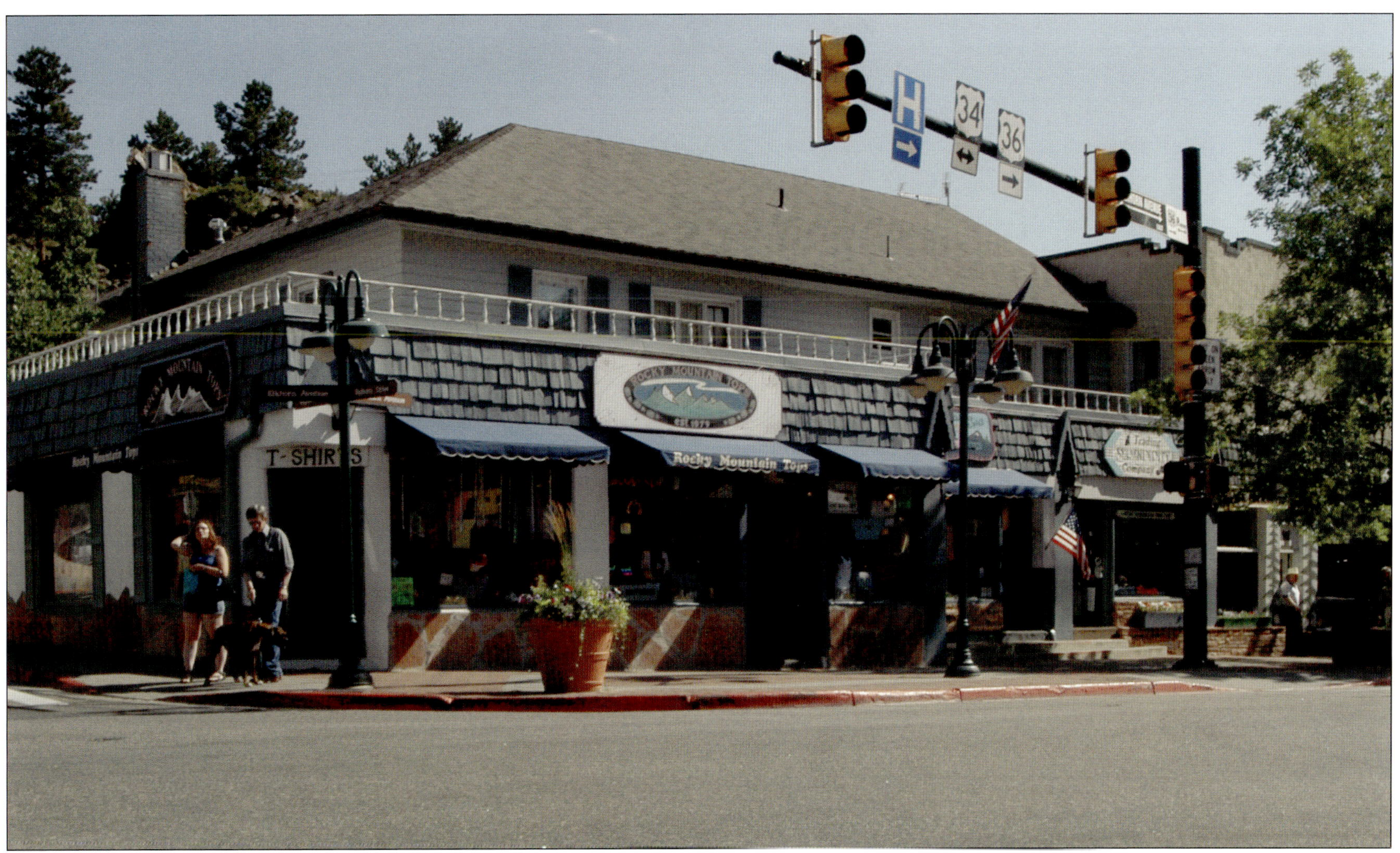

show open verandas. In those days, a row of tents was erected next to the hotel. The *Mountaineer*, Estes Park's first newspaper, noted in June 1908 that among the Manford's attractions was the "splendid view of the mountains" to be had from the hotel windows.

John Manford didn't own the hotel for long. In December 1908, after its first season, he sold it to competitor Josephine "Josie" Hupp for a reported $16,000. She changed the name to the Hupp Annex which started more than 20 years of confusion (see p. 104). In 1913, the hotel was sold to Cornelius H. Bond, who sold it four years later to William and Anna May Derby. The Derbys exchanged its original exterior wood for stucco, removed the verandas, introduced shops on the lower floor, and, in 1926–1927, built a large addition on the east side. All these later features are clearly visible in the contemporary photograph.

41. Estes Park Bank, circa 1909

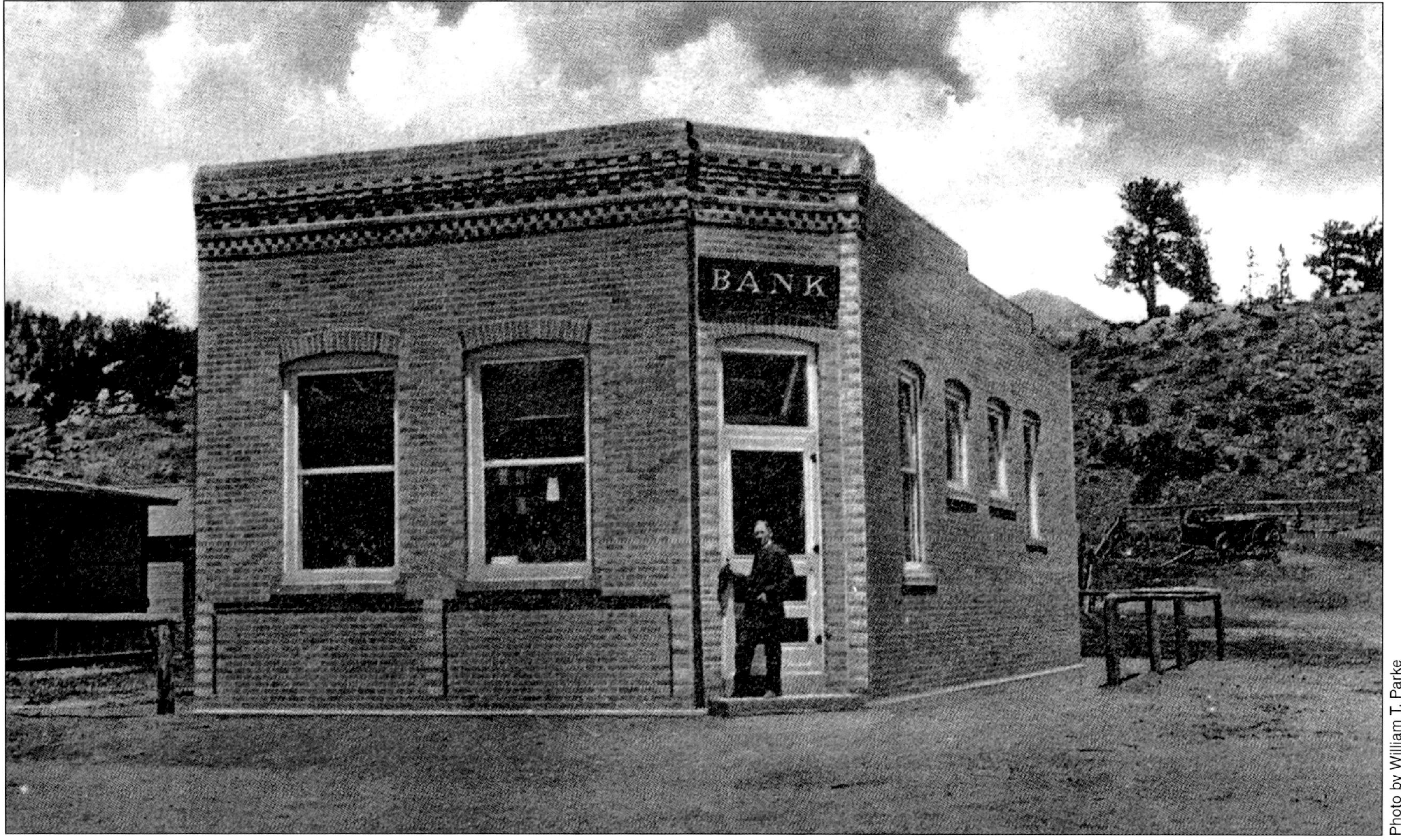

Photo by William T. Parke

The Estes Park Bank, the first brick structure ever built in Estes Park, stood at the northwest corner of Elkhorn Avenue and what is today Big Horn Drive. Across the street were the Hupp and Manford Hotels. Initially capitalized at $12,000, the bank was organized in early February 1908 by the 36 individuals who had agreed to purchase its 120 shares of stock. F. O. Stanley was elected president. Incorporation papers were filed on March 4, 1908.

Construction on the original 20-by-40-foot building began that spring on two lots purchased for $800 from the Estes Park Town Company. It stood on the site of Estes Park's first schoolhouse and community building, which had been moved several doors to the west and later became Fred Payne Clatworthy's gift shop (see p. 110). The cost of the new building was $1,627 and included the bank's 6-by-8-by-9-foot reinforced concrete vault with safety deposit boxes. The bank's

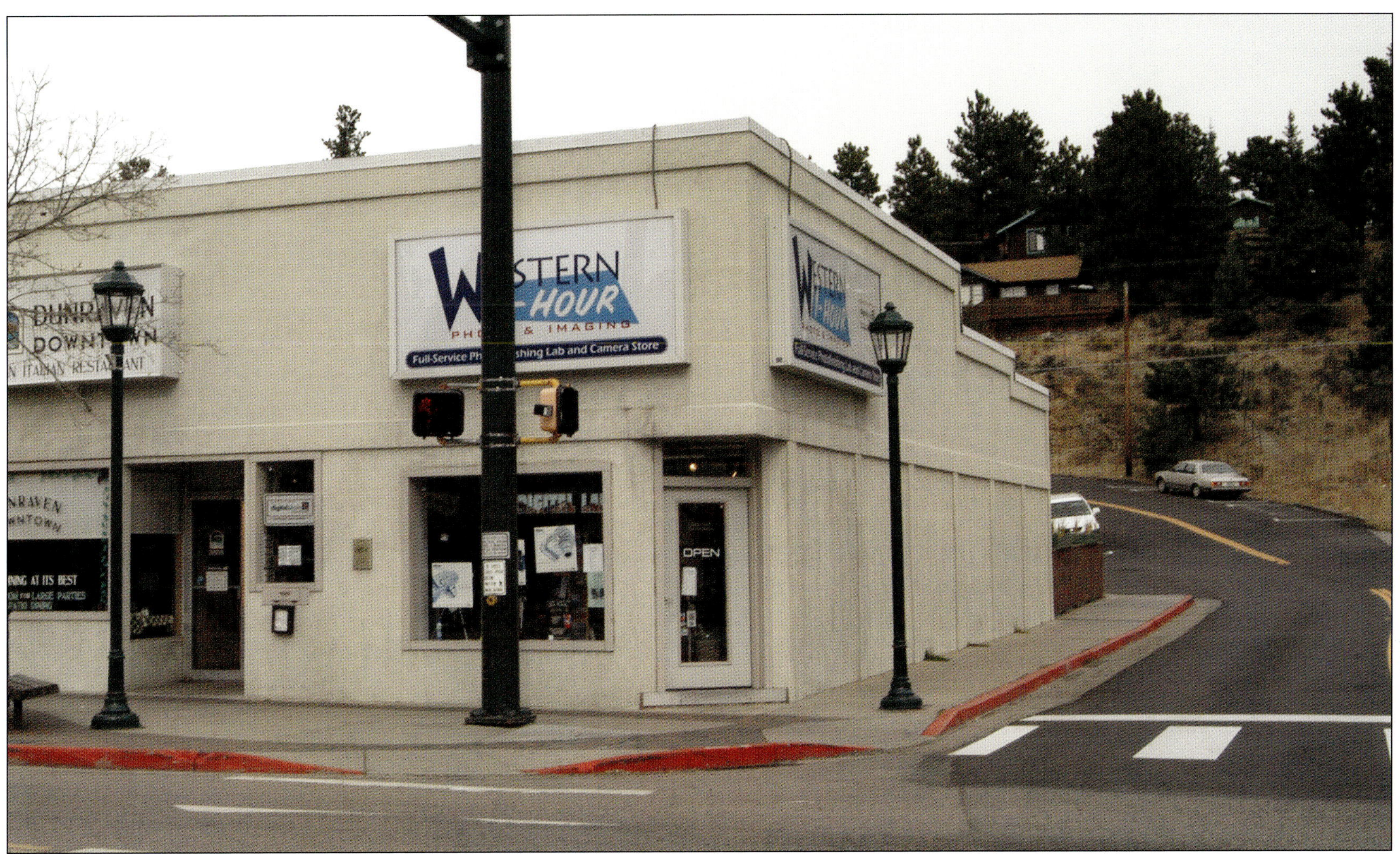

interior décor and fixtures included specially made polished oak desks, glass countertops, and iron grillwork. The Estes Park Bank first opened its doors for business on June 16, 1908. It was chartered by the State of Colorado as State Bank No. 37, the third oldest bank in Larimer County.

In 1910, the original building was enlarged with an addition to the west at a cost of $1,610. The building's subsequent tenants included the grocery businesses run by Harry Boyd and Ron Brodie. Today, it houses a photography store. The figure in the bank doorway in the early photograph is Charles Hanscomb. Like other early bank employees, he was paid 50 cents to $1 per day, a salary then thought to be a reasonable wage because of the low cost of living in Estes Park.

42. Ye Lyttel Shop, circa 1920

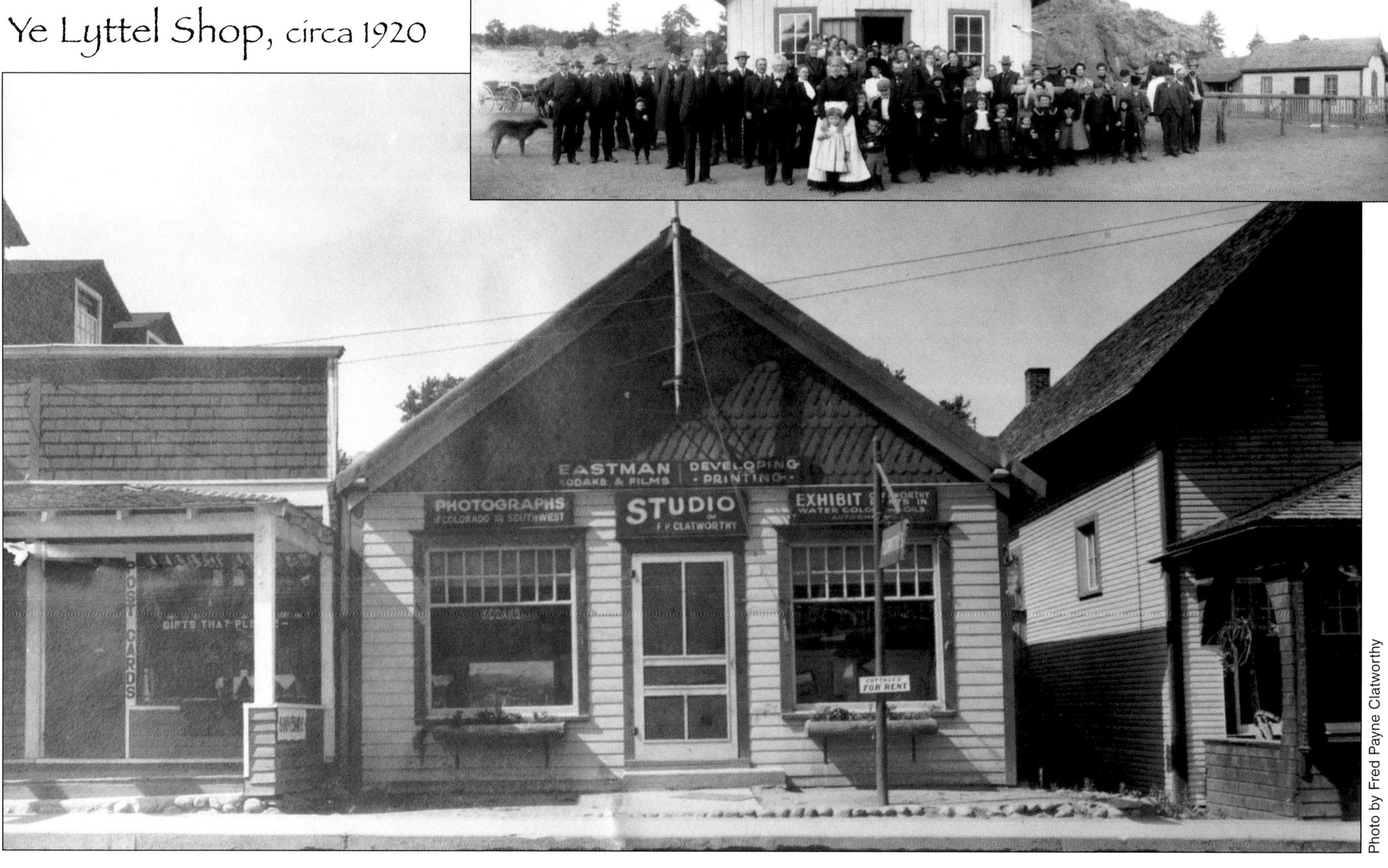

Photo by Fred Payne Clatworthy

Estes Park souvenir shops started popping up early. Fred Payne Clatworthy's Ye Lyttel Shop, at 115 West Elkhorn Avenue, was perhaps the most famous.

Clatworthy's lifelong love affair with the West began in 1900, when he and a friend rode bicycles from New York to California. He soon put aside his legal career to concentrate on photography.

Settling in Loveland in 1904, Clatworthy received a visit by his mother and sister from Ohio. This provided the occasion for a wagon trip up the newly opened Big Thompson Canyon. Clatworthy decided to try and make a living selling his photographs in Estes Park. His first studio was a tent on Elkhorn Avenue, soon replaced by a wood-frame building set on skids for easy movement.

The Ye Lyttel Shop was located just east of the original school-community building, which Clatworthy would later purchase and incorporate into his growing business. Later, he erected Estes Park's first tile building behind the store, to house a darkroom and safeguard his negatives and plates.

Clatworthy soon offered framed photographs as well as hundreds of postcards, many of them purchased as keepsakes. He sold items from stationery

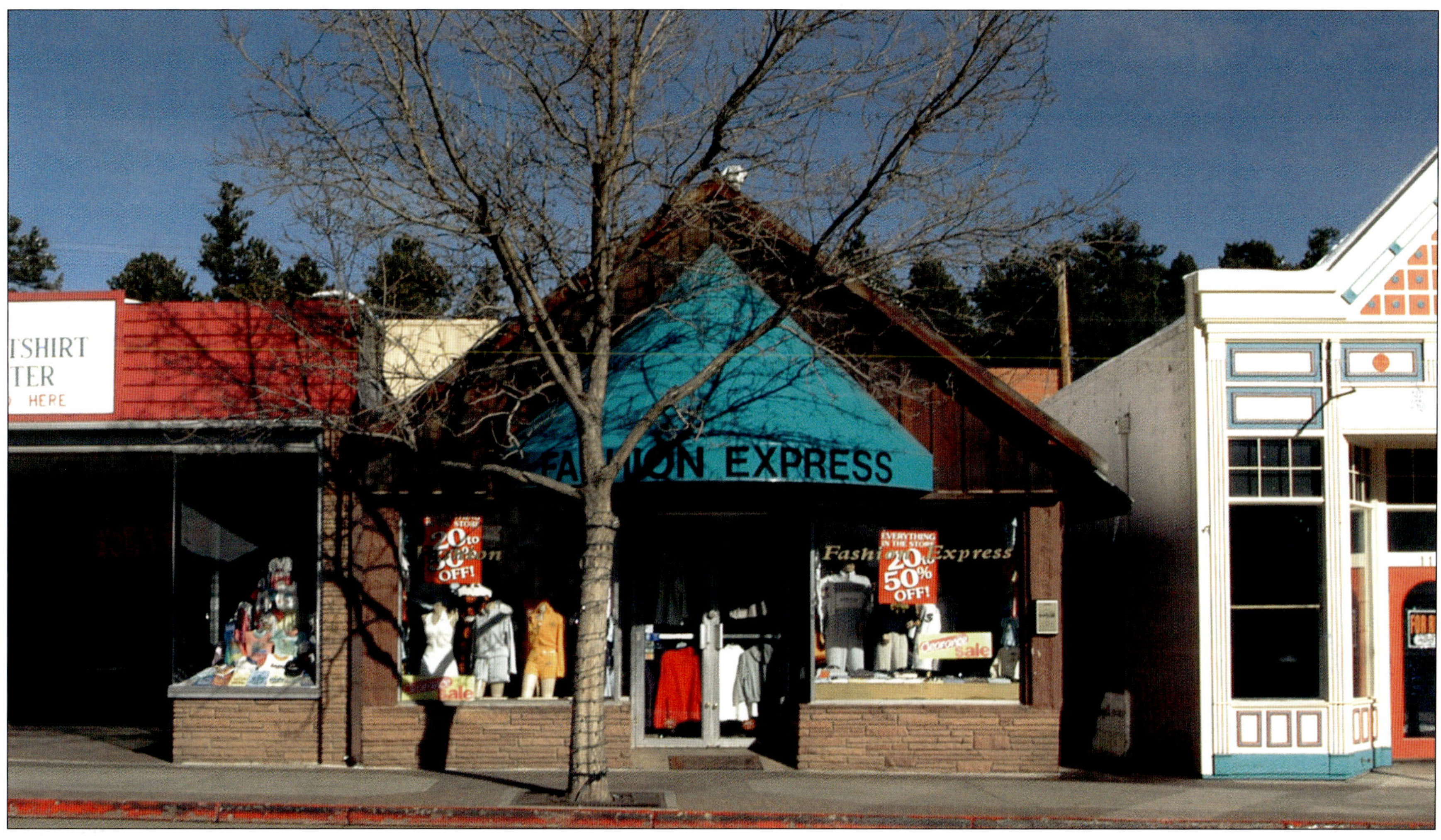

and photo albums to Navajo rugs and alabaster collectibles. Clatworthy's shop also offered photo developing because, by the century's first decade, amateur photography was in vogue among tourists.

Clatworthy sold both black-and-white views and hand-tinted photographs and became famous for pioneering the autochrome color photography process. Many of his later autochromes were published in *National Geographic*.

After the store was sold in 1930, Clatworthy moved his studio to his home on Cyteworth Road. His original building was later demolished to make room for a larger structure, although his adjacent store (the old community building-schoolhouse) still remains. The tile building that served as Clatworthy's darkroom also stands, with its back to Cleave Street.

43. Estes Park Church, circa 1910

Estes Park didn't have its own church until 1907. Early services were held in the tiny 40-by-22-foot community building located west of John Cleave's house; the building was also used as a meeting house and school. Organist Eleanor Hondius later recalled that a pioneering preacher, the Reverend Elkanah J. Lamb—an imposing black robe draping his lofty 6-foot-5-inch frame—delivered hour-long fire-and-brimstone sermons there.

After Estes Park was platted in 1905, it became clear that the village needed a permanent house of worship. Following a meeting that was held at the community building on New Year's Eve of 1907, a lot was purchased on West Elkhorn for $600 with a loan from the Presbyterian Board of Missions. Volunteers then completed the Presbyterian Church of Estes Park in 1909 for a cost of $4,000. The Reverend J. Mont Travis became its first pastor for an annual salary of $1,000. In 1914, a manse was built on Park Lane behind what is now Bond Park. (In 1992, that house

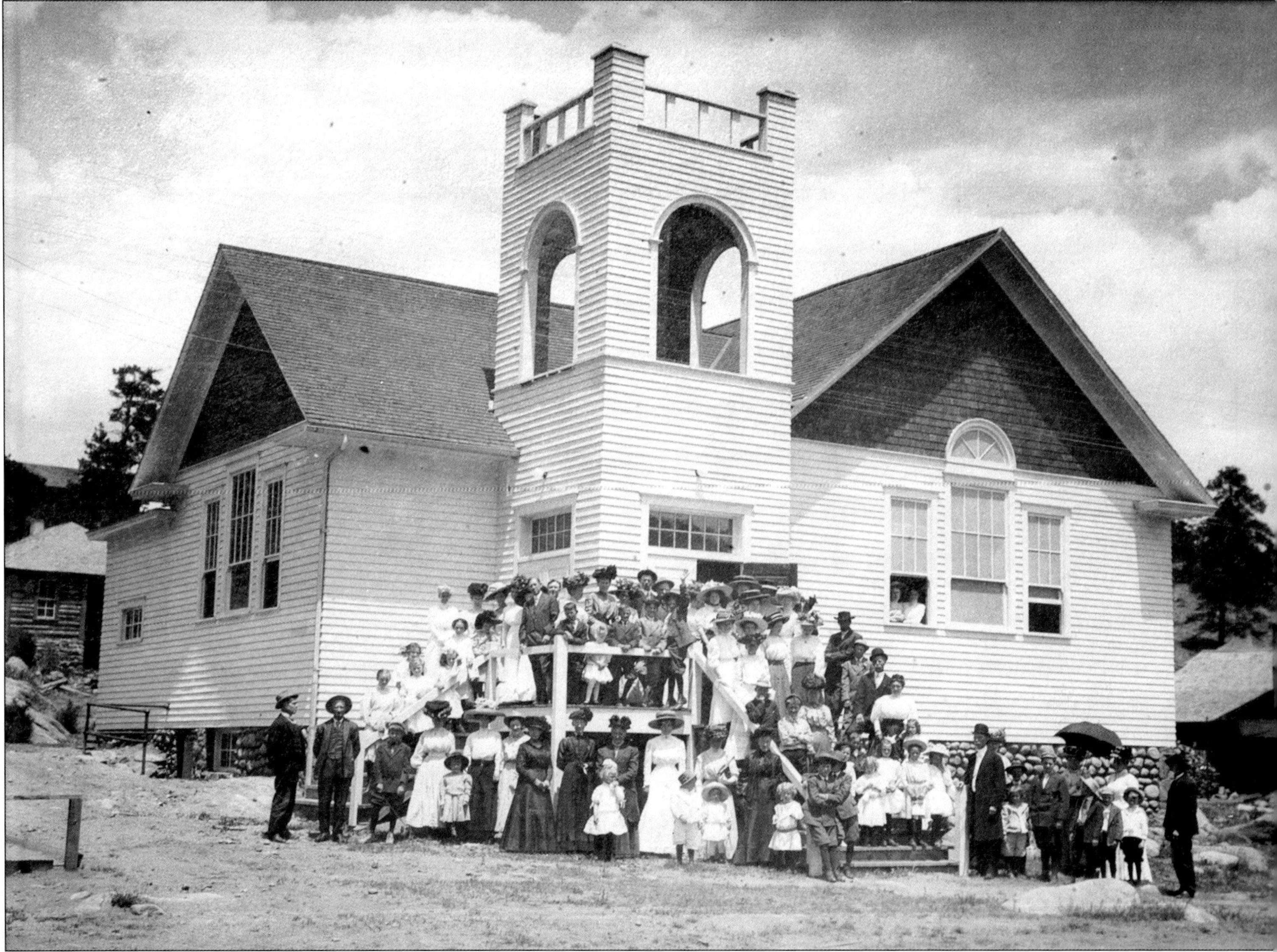

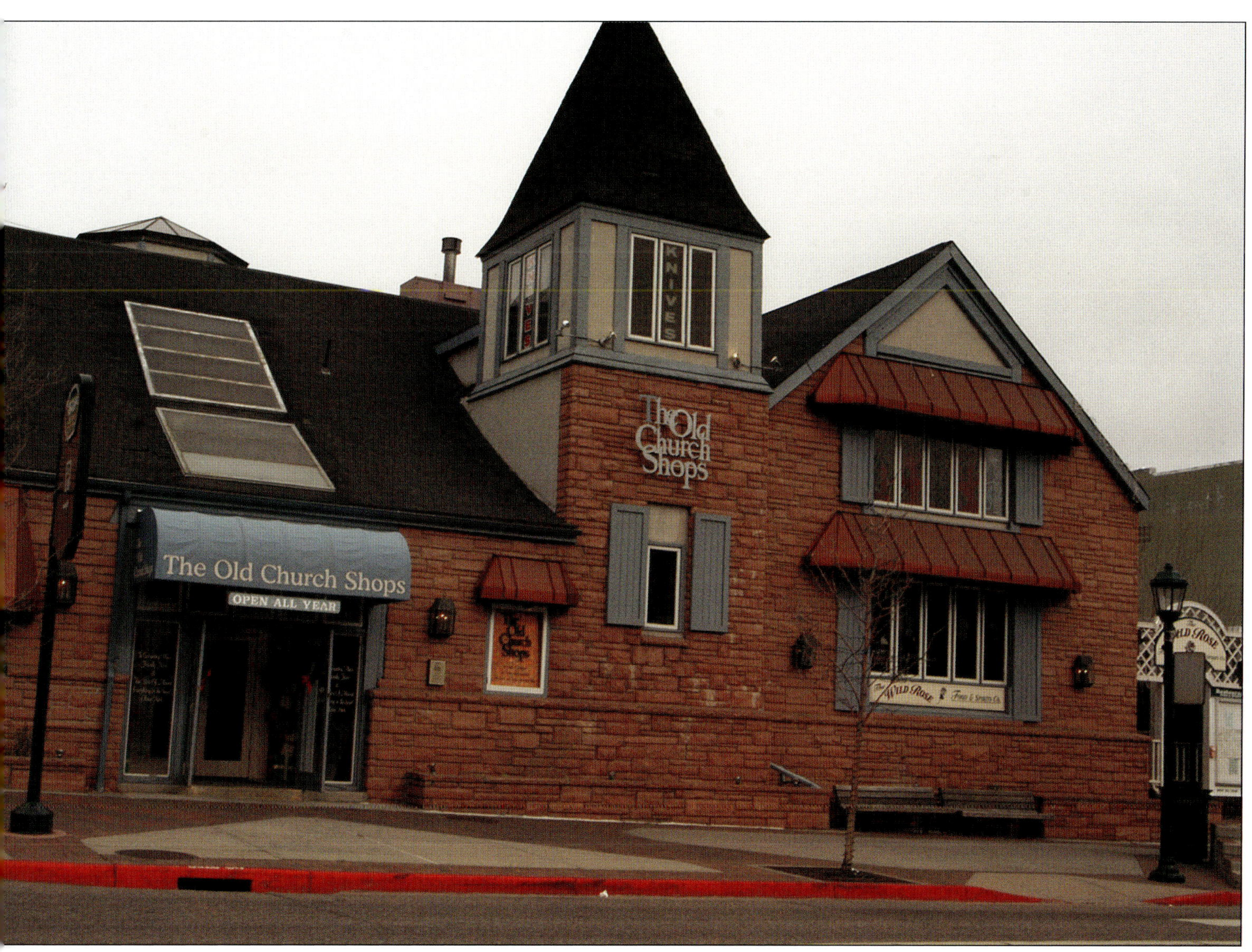

was moved to Wonderview Avenue and is now a private residence.)

In 1935, the original small white church was enlarged to meet the needs of its growing congregation, which for $13,000 added a Sunday school building, kitchen, classroom, and pastor's study. In 1959, with an expansion again inevitable, members decided to relocate the church, now called the Community Church, to a new 26-acre site that was located just north of the Estes Park Country Club. The new church's construction, however, didn't begin until 1981. The church had its first service there on August 15, 1982.

As shown in the contemporary photograph, the original expanded Estes Park Presbyterian Church has been remodeled and is now called The Old Church Shops, which houses boutiques and a restaurant.

44. Estes Park from the West End, circa 1917

In the years following its platting in 1905, taking photographs from atop the rocky outcropping at the west end of Elkhorn Avenue was a favorite way of capturing the progress of the new town. As the original view from the camera of Denverite Louis C. McClure illustrates, one could see virtually the entire village of Estes Park framed against Mount Olympus' looming presence to the east. In the contemporary photograph, a number of the buildings, particularly those seen on the left side of Elkhorn, still remain some 90 years later.

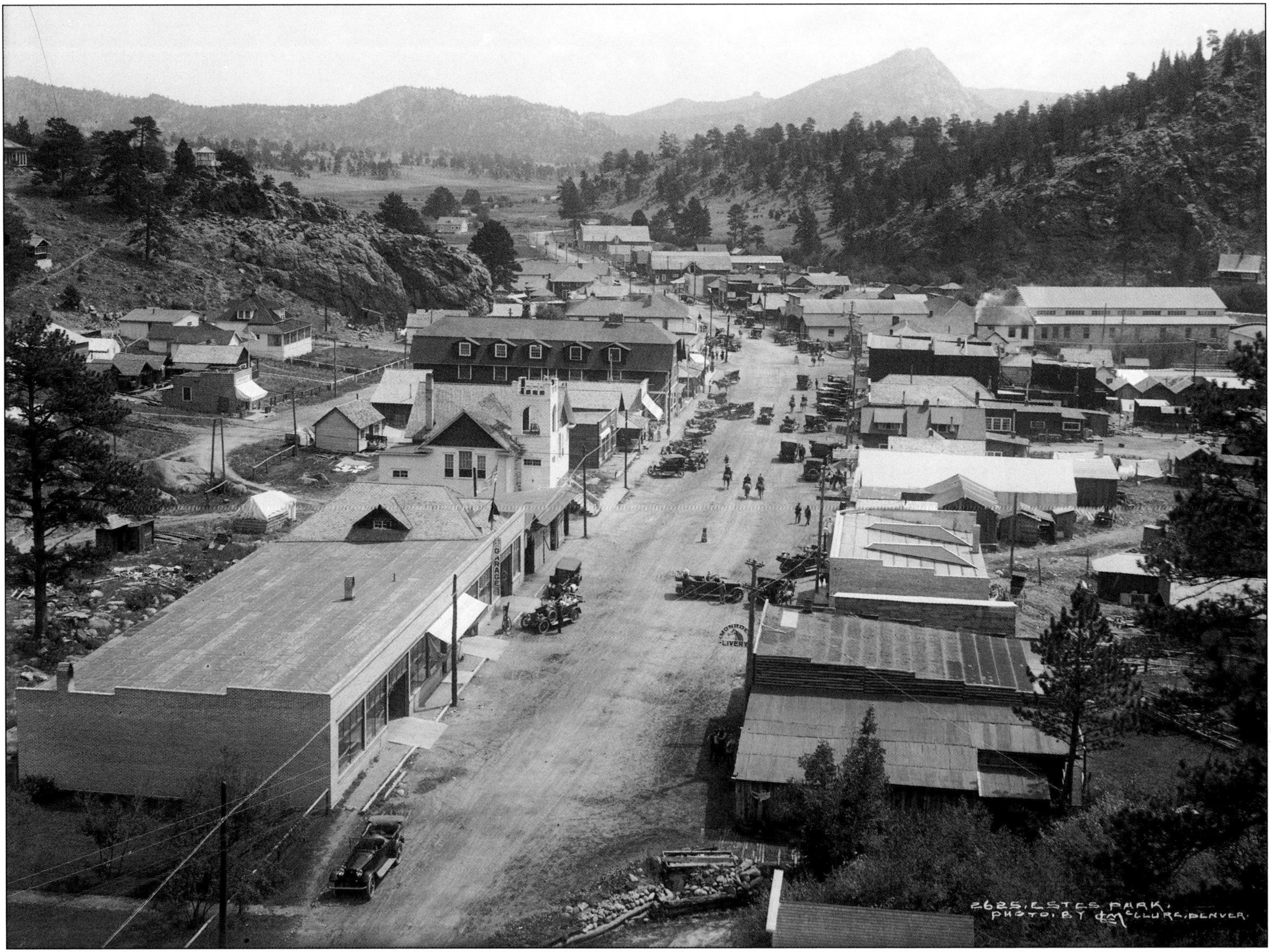

Photo by Louis C. McClure

Among the most prominent structures seen in the McClure photograph, beginning on the left, is the low-roofed garage of Daniel Osborn's Loveland-Estes Park Transportation Company, which, beginning in 1907, had pioneered automobile transportation in the Estes Park region. Osborn and his sons, Will, Otto, and Estes, stored their Stanley Steamer touring cars in this large 130-by-50-foot brick

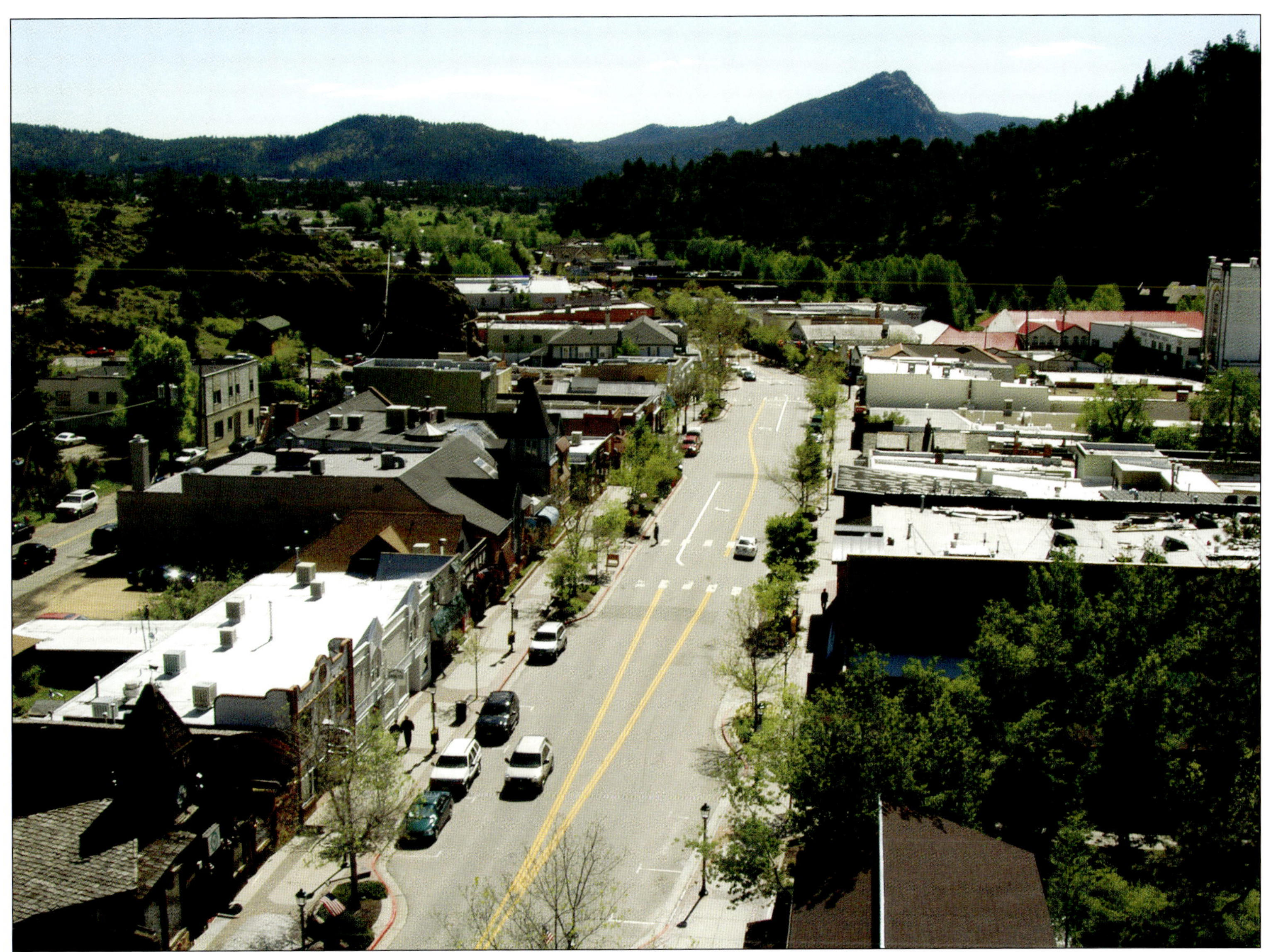

building, whose entrances can be clearly seen in the photograph. Next to the Osborn garage, separated by a lower building, is the community church, with its distinctive belfry. The large building beyond the church is the hotel that would be known for most of its life as the Sherwood. Farther down Elkhorn, one can make out the Hupp Annex.

On the right-hand side of the street, at the photographer's feet, is the Monroe Livery. Farther down Elkhorn is the rear of the original Hupp Hotel, and slightly beyond it, set well back from the street, is the large garage of F. O. Stanley's Estes Park Transportation Company, now in the hands of Roe Emery. Farther on down Elkhorn, one can make out the large barns of the Grubb and Stanley liveries—another reminder that despite the many automobiles along the street, in Estes Park come summer, the horse remained king.

45. Lewiston Hotel, circa 1935

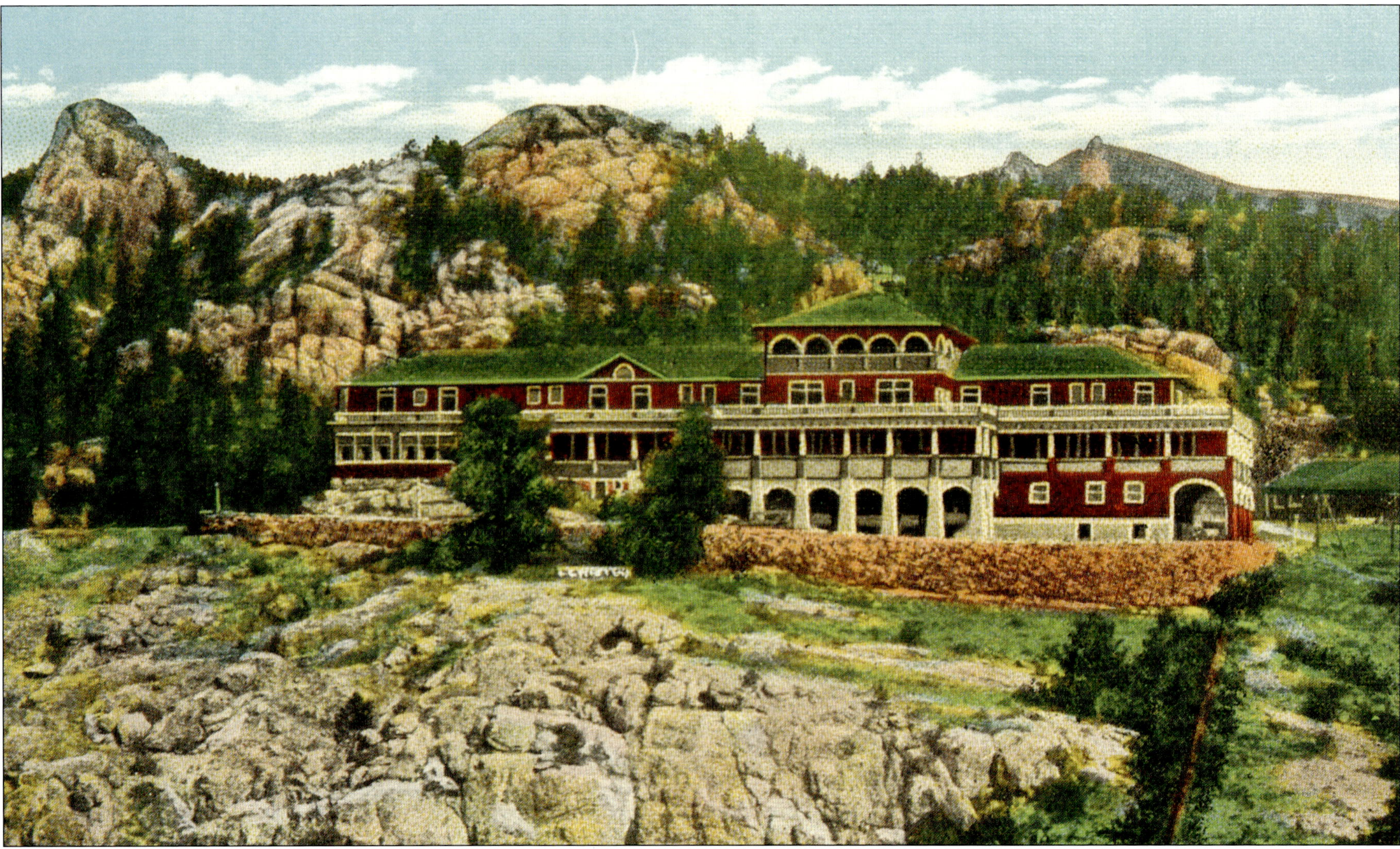

The Lewiston Hotel in its day rivaled the Stanley Hotel in elegance, amenities, and popularity. The Lewiston began modestly as the home of A. D. "Gus" Lewis, who arrived in Estes Park in 1912 and became cashier of the Estes Park Bank. When his wife Anita decided to enter the resort business, the Lewises added bungalows and tent houses. Then they began to enlarge the house itself, eventually expanding it to three stories. By 1920, it contained 70 rooms, each with its own hot-and-cold water, plus a third-floor ballroom with organ and adjacent roof garden. "The Lewiston needs no introduction," a 1924 advertisement proclaimed, "as it has entertained as its guests the most fastidious of the pleasure seeking public." The price: $50 per week.

The Lewiston became the centerpiece of A. D. Lewis' Lewiston Hotel Company, which for a time owned the Lewiston Chalets above Marys Lake,

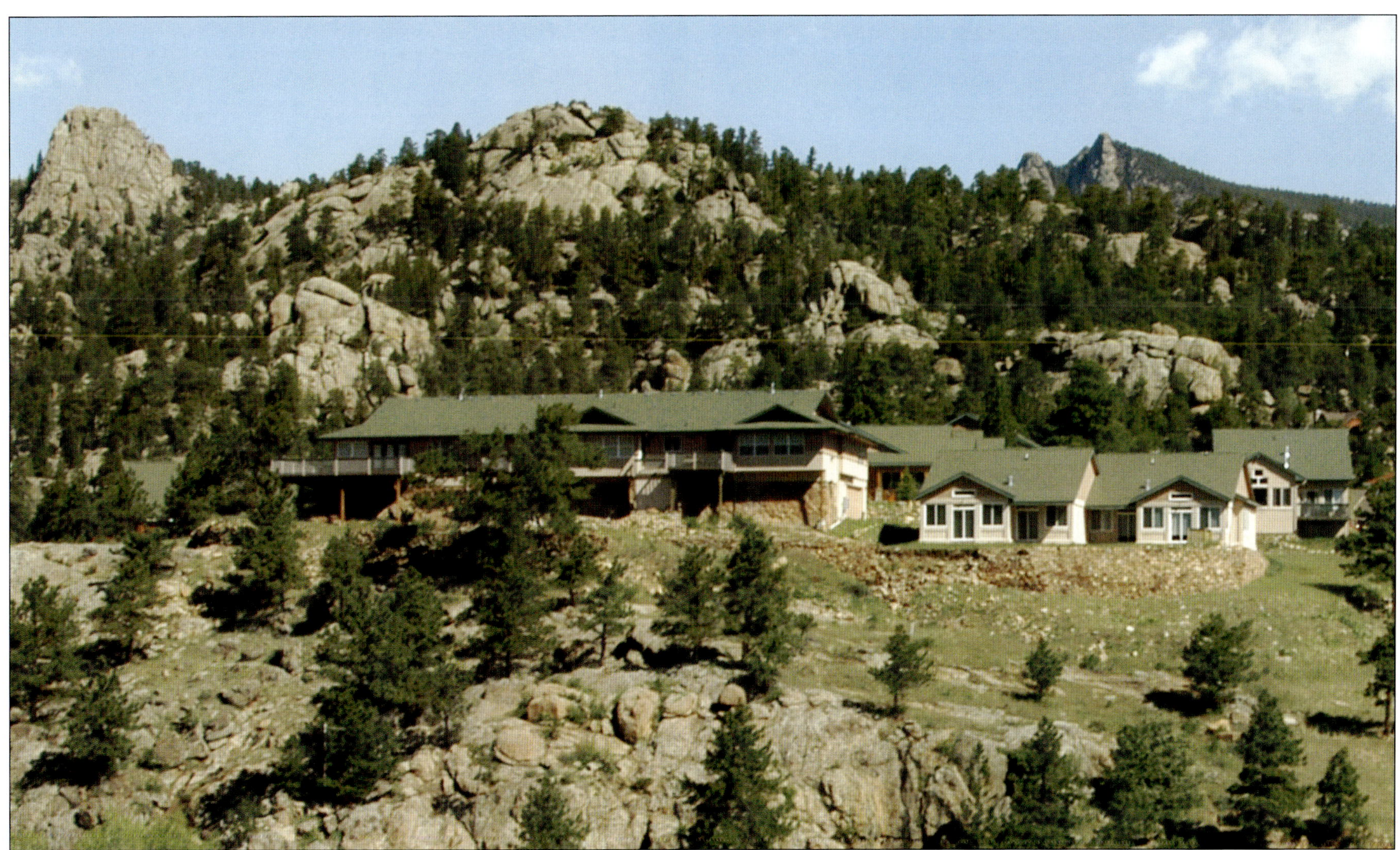

the Josephine Hotel on Elkhorn Avenue, the Lewiston Café in the original Hupp Hotel, where the company had offices, and the Grand Lake Lodge across the Continental Divide.

The Lewiston anchored the west end of Elkhorn Avenue until September 4, 1941, when a fire broke out in an overloaded attic flue and left the building in ruins. Members of the local football team left practice at the high school field and raced to the site. Team members were able to salvage a 5-gallon tub of ice cream, which they devoured as they watched the fire. The cost to rebuild the hotel, estimated at $320,000, was prohibitive during wartime, and the Lewises soon left for California. For many years, the stone verandas of the Lewiston remained as reminders of the grandeur of an earlier day. They have now been incorporated into the foundations of the townhouses that occupy the site.

46. Estes Park from Oldman Mountain, 1884

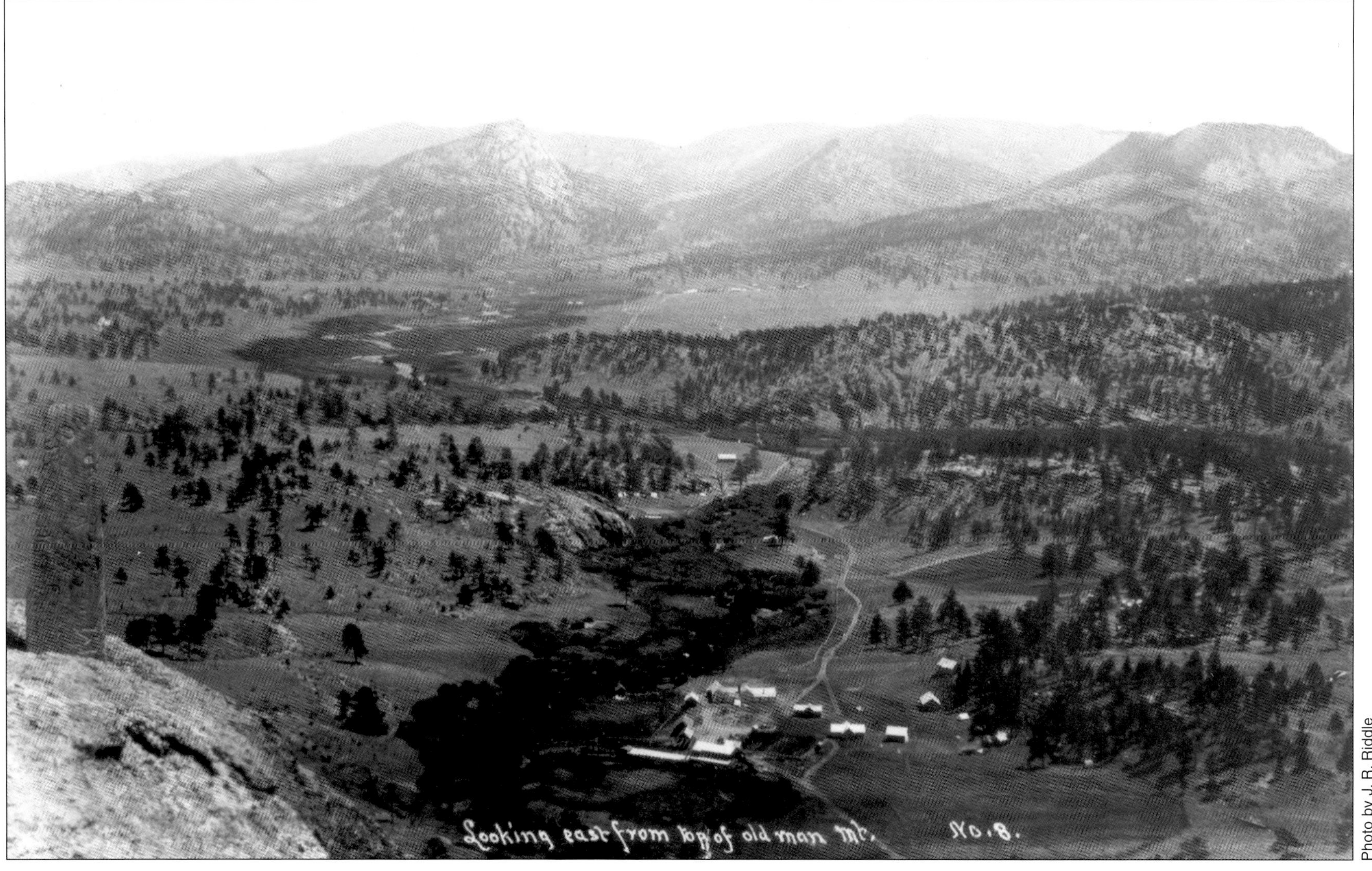

Photo by J. R. Riddle

Oldman Mountain, the granite knob west of the village of Estes Park, has a rich history dating back to ancient times. During the 1930s, pottery shards and other artifacts found around its base offered evidence of its use as a vision quest site by Estes Park's earliest residents. Several Arapaho who were brought back in 1914 to identify the Indian names of local landmarks called the mountain "Sitting Man," and reported that Indians often fasted atop it.

It was inevitable that Oldman Mountain would attract visiting tourists viewing the Estes Valley. The original 1884 photograph shown here provides one of the earliest views of the Estes Valley. The Elkhorn Lodge buildings (see p. 130) are visible to the lower right. At the top of the photograph, below Mount Pisgah, is the original Estes-Evans ranch (see p. 19), by then the Earl of Dunraven's. In the middle of the photograph, there are a few scattered cottages and an

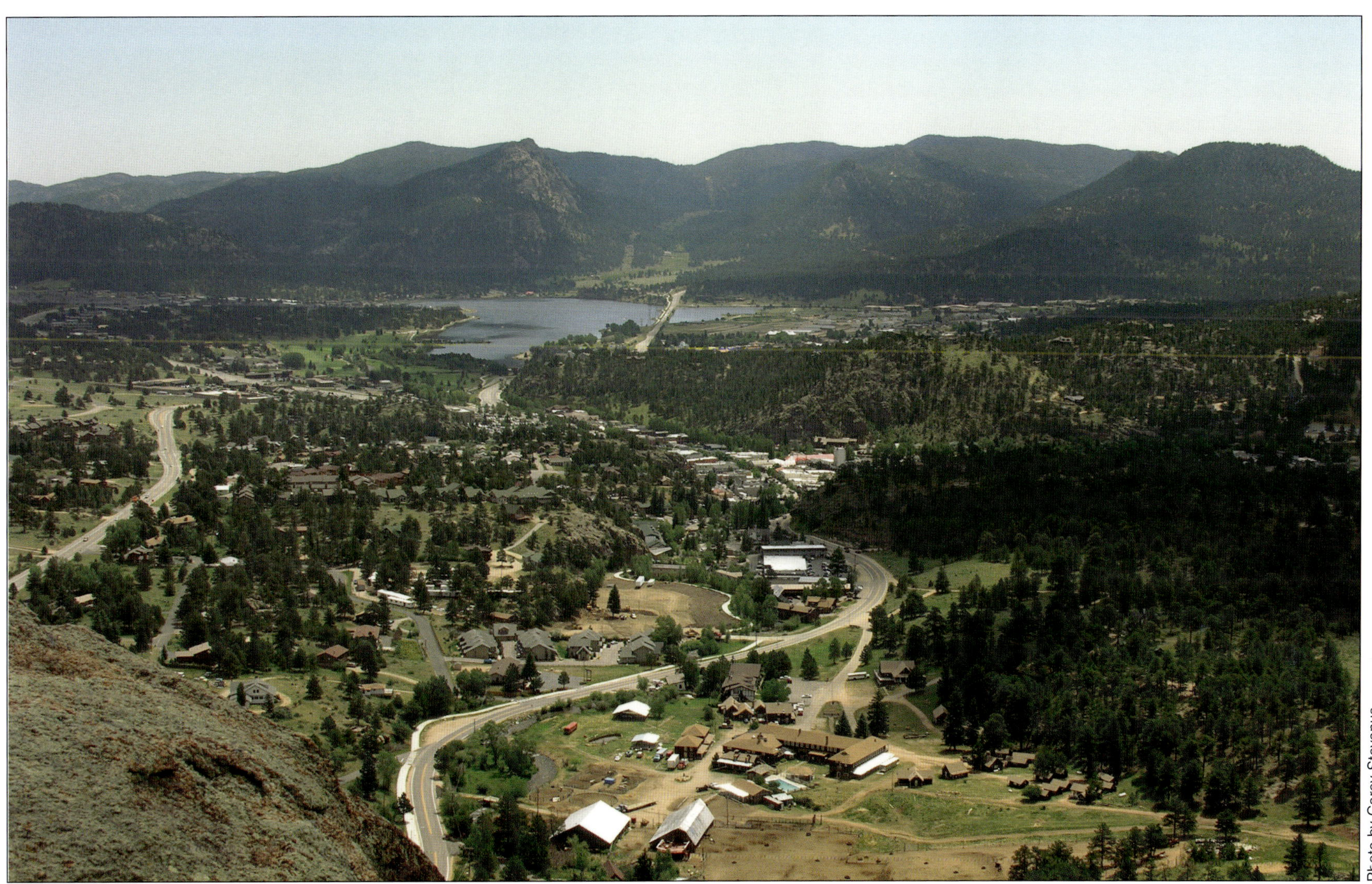
Photo by Carey Stevanus

unidentifiable large structure, possibly a barn or the community building. But the rest of the valley is undeveloped, a place of tranquility interrupted only by the dirt road leading east from the Elkhorn Lodge, and the meanderings of the Big Thompson River toward the Big Thompson Canyon.

The photograph also provides evidence of the ingenuity of the early climbers who have inscribed their names on a board shoved into a crevice on the summit.

The contemporary photograph records 120 years of growth. Where there was once a peaceful country road, there is a sprawling business community; where the Big Thompson flowed through open meadows, there is Lake Estes. Only the Elkhorn Lodge remains, looking not unlike it did in 1884, when an early photographer lugged his camera to the top of Oldman Mountain to capture a rare moment of Estes Park history.

47. Oldman Mountain Ski Site, circa 1930

In the 1920s and later, Oldman Mountain became one of the Estes Valley's major year-round tourist attractions. During the winter of 1923–1924, members of the Estes Park Group of the Colorado Ski Club built the region's first ski jump in an attempt to make Estes Park a winter sports center. This required a jumping facility to compete with those at Hot Sulphur Springs, Steamboat Springs, and Denver's Genesee Mountain.

In 1924, the new jump became the central attraction of the club's first annual All-Colorado Tournament, which attracted well-known professional jumpers including Lars and Anders Haugen and Barney Riley ("the Wild Irish Rose of Skidom"), as well as amateurs from ski clubs statewide. The Sunday crowd of 800 helped convince the *Rocky Mountain News* "that Americans can and will have winter sports in the Colorado mountains that are equal to and easier of approach than those staged in Switzerland."

Tournaments on Oldman Mountain were held in 1925 and 1926, the 1925 event coming on the day that Agnes Vaille froze to death on the Boulder Field of Longs Peak. The 1926 competition's second day attracted some 3,500 onlookers, said to be the largest crowd of people to attend a single event in Estes Park. In 1931, the first Annual Mid-Summer Ski Meet was added, timed to coincide with the beginning of the tourist season. Five hundred cubic yards of snow were brought down from Fall River Pass and spread by hand. It was a great success. Jumping events, summer and winter, continued intermittently, although by 1934 the area's focus had shifted to Rocky Mountain National Park's Hidden Valley ski area. The 1951 event was the last. The course, which is still visible from Fall River Road, has lapsed into decay, an all but forgotten reminder of a time when Estes Park aspired to be the "St. Moritz of America."

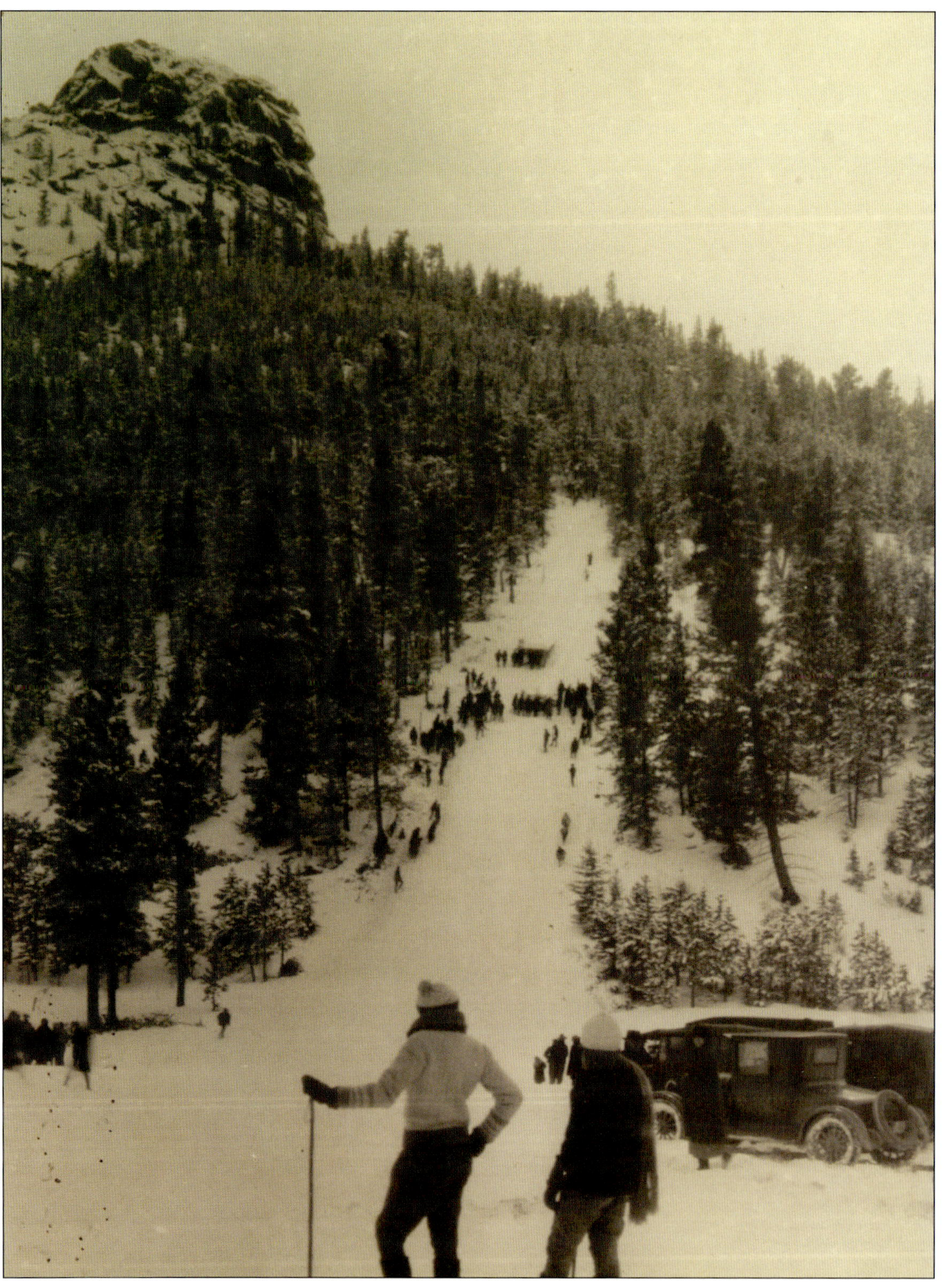

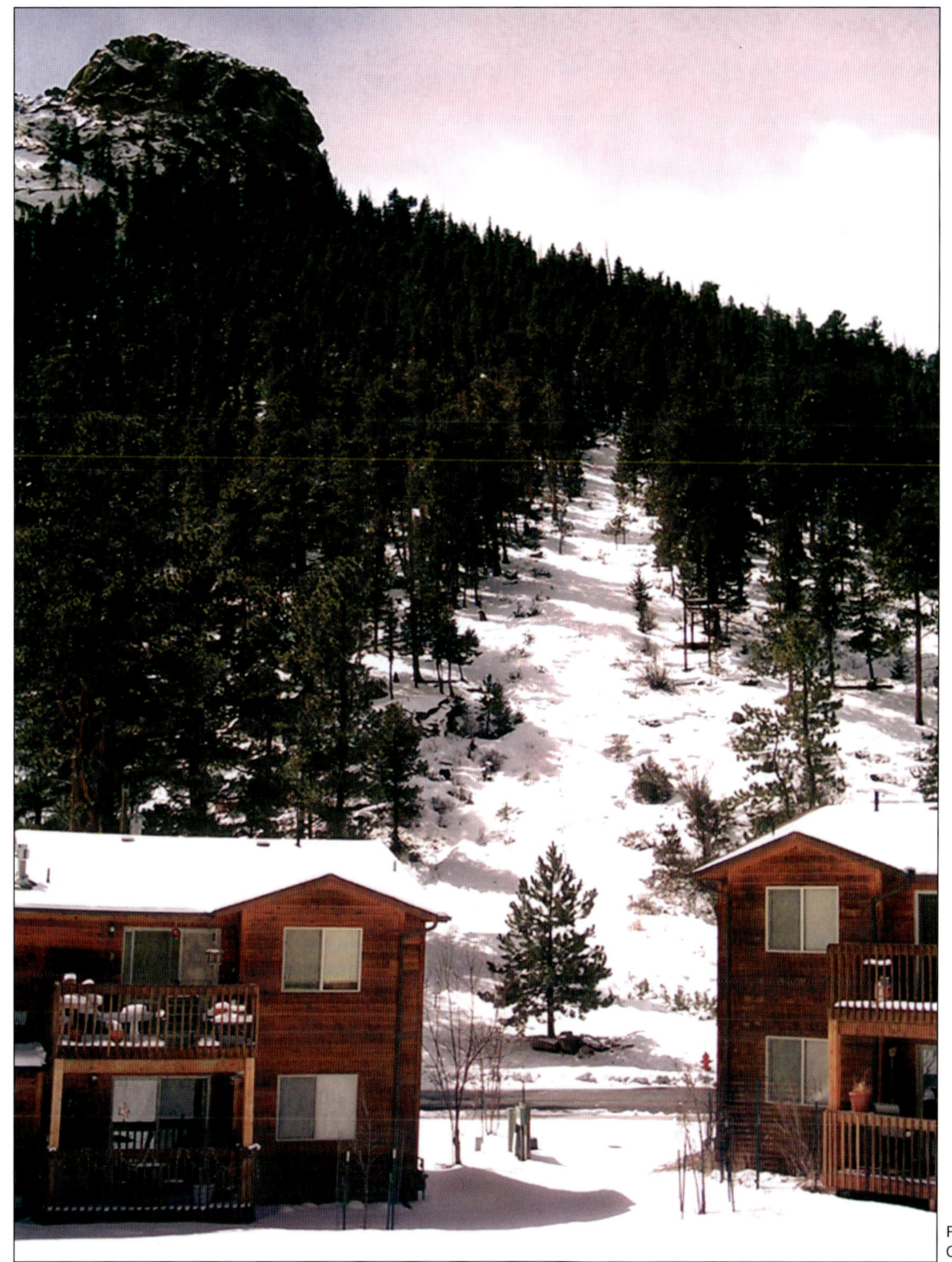

Photo by
Carey Stevanus

48. Crags Hotel, circa 1920

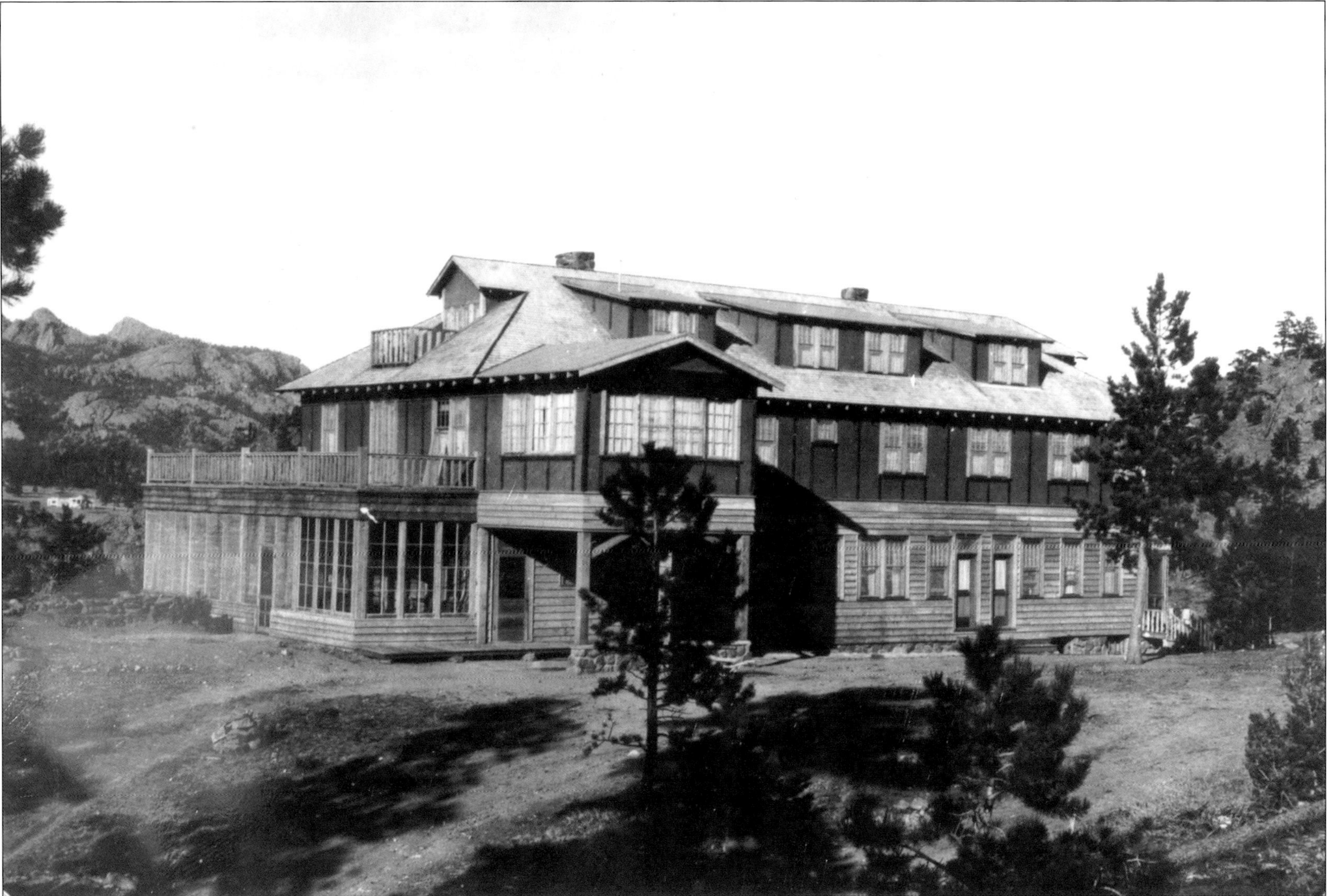

Photo by William T. Parke

The Crags Hotel, called "The House on the Hill," was built by Enoch Josiah "Joe" Mills, younger brother of famed naturalist and inn owner Enos A. Mills. Born on the family farm in Kansas, the younger Mills came west to Estes Park in 1899, making the last leg of the journey over the old Bald Mountain–Pole Hill Road from Loveland riding on a bicycle. Joe "Nuck" Mills spent three years at Colorado Agricultural College (today's Colorado State University), where he proved to be a gifted athlete, playing "on every C. A. C. team through every college contest." From the late spring of 1902 to the fall of 1903, he made his home in Estes Park, a period that he would write about in his charming fictionalized autobiography, *A Mountain Boyhood*, published in 1926.

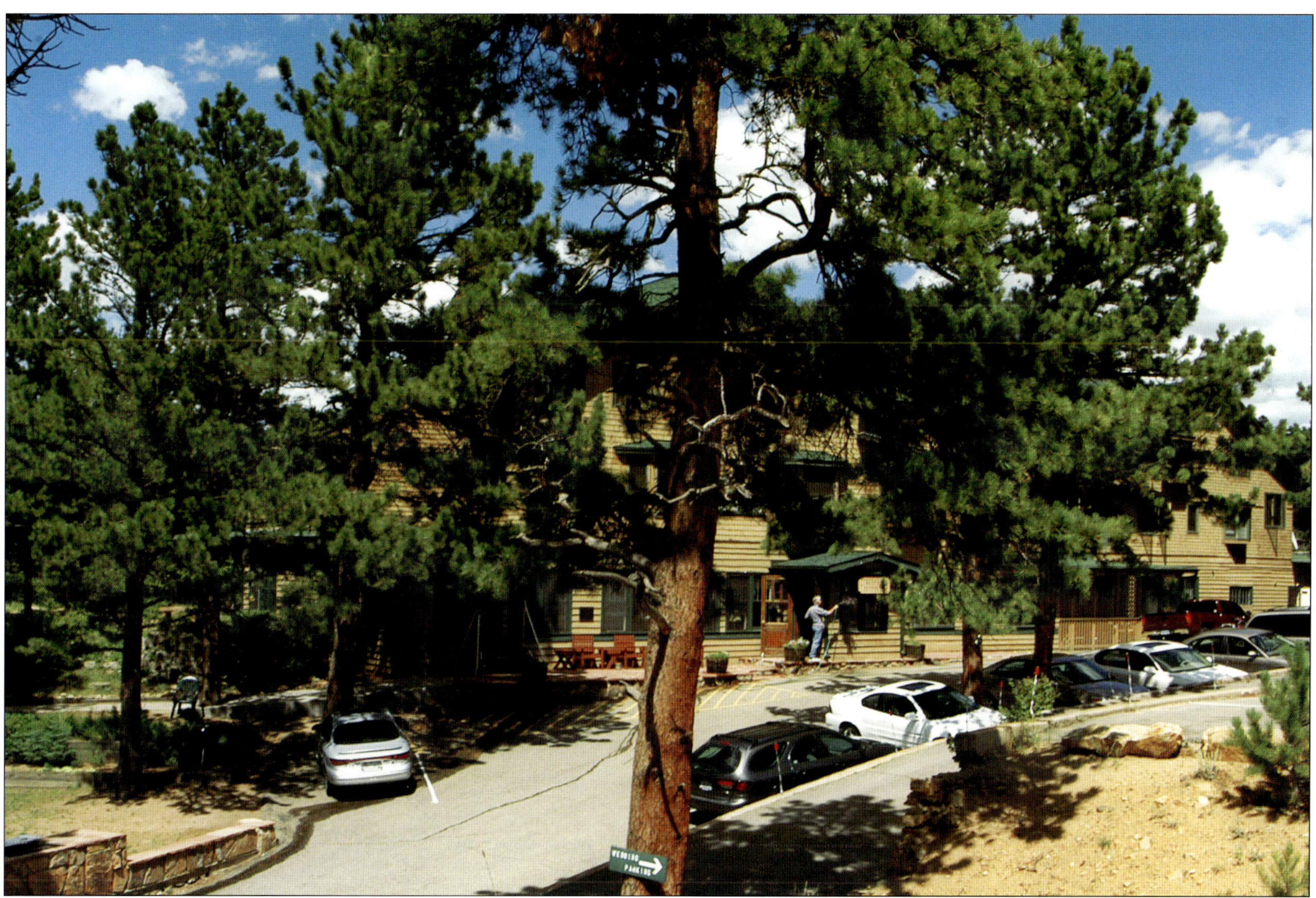

Mills transferred to the University of Denver, where he earned a degree and again starred in football and basketball. He then entered college coaching, a career that took him to Texas, where he became the athletic director at Baylor University. His heart, though, was in the mountains. In 1911, he brought Ethel, his wife of three years, back to Estes Park, where he began in the resort business by managing the Forks Hotel in nearby Drake. Yet, like his older brother, Joe Mills wanted a place of his own. He purchased land from F. O. Stanley on the lower slope of Prospect Mountain overlooking the village, and began construction of the 21-room frame hotel he called The Crags, which opened up for business on July 4, 1914. The main building was enlarged in 1917 and then a recreation hall was added in 1920. The hotel as we know it today is the result of a second expansion in 1923–1924, when the lobby and dining room were enlarged and enclosed by a wall of windows and additional guest rooms and cottages were added. Joe and Ethel Mills personally presided over The Crags, making it among the most popular resorts in Estes Park. Joe Mills was universally admired for the active role he played in local affairs as one of Estes Park's leading boosters, and his death in 1935 was mourned by the entire community. "He loved the region," the *Estes Park Trail* observed, "with a silent, unobtrusive love that was truly food for the inner man, and was moved to further and develop it by motives of the highest altruism." Ethel Mills continued to operate The Crags until 1946, when it passed into other hands.

The first of the original photographs of The Crags was taken about 1920, and the second about a decade later, by photographer Fred Payne Clatworthy from the hill behind his home off East Riverside Drive.

Crags Hotel, circa 1930

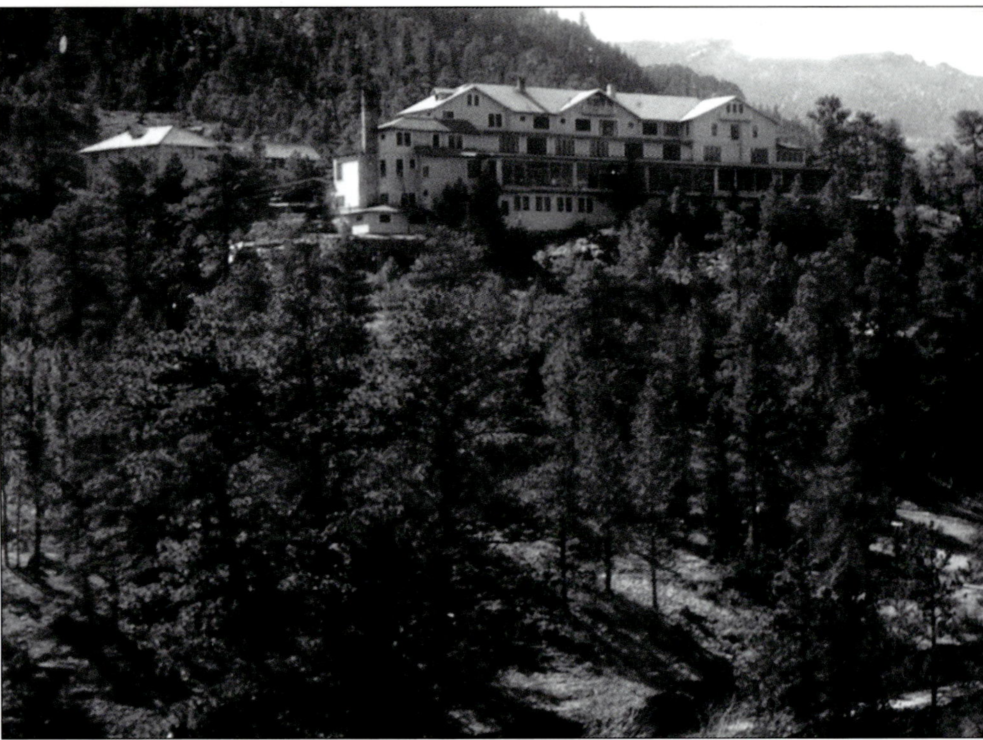

Photo by Fred Payne Clatworthy

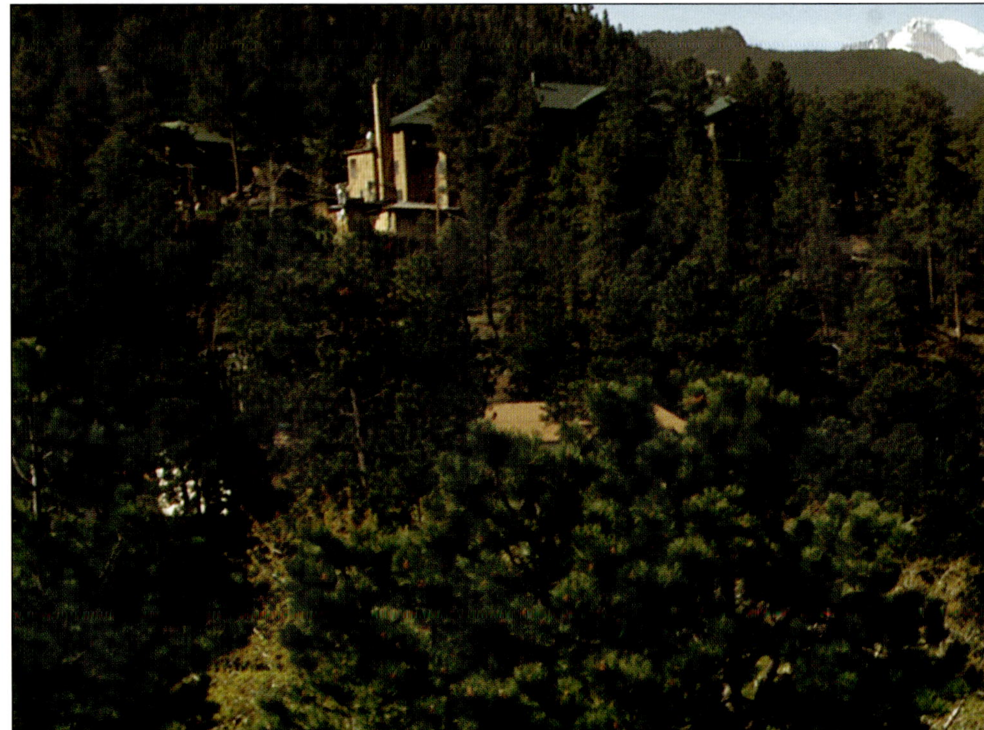

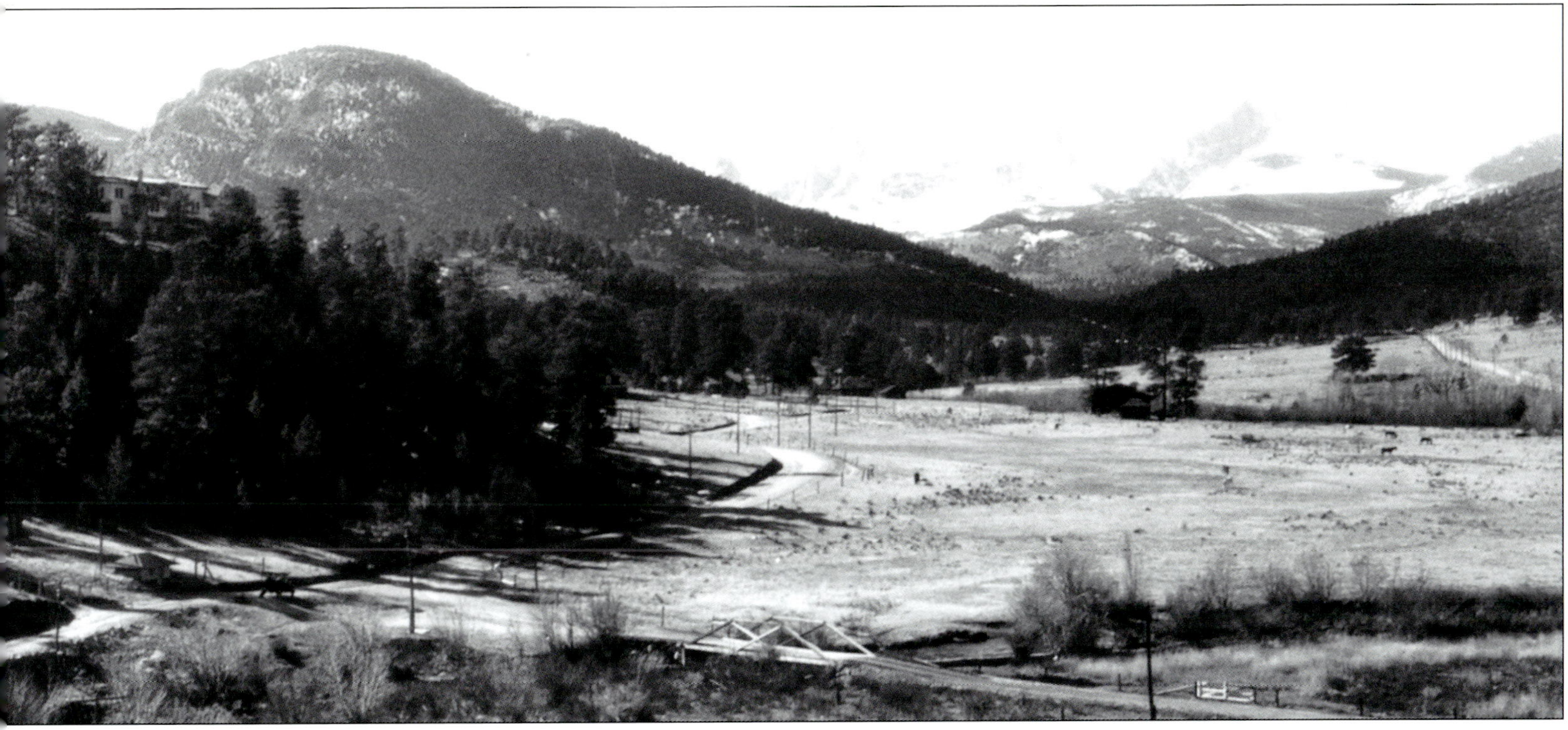

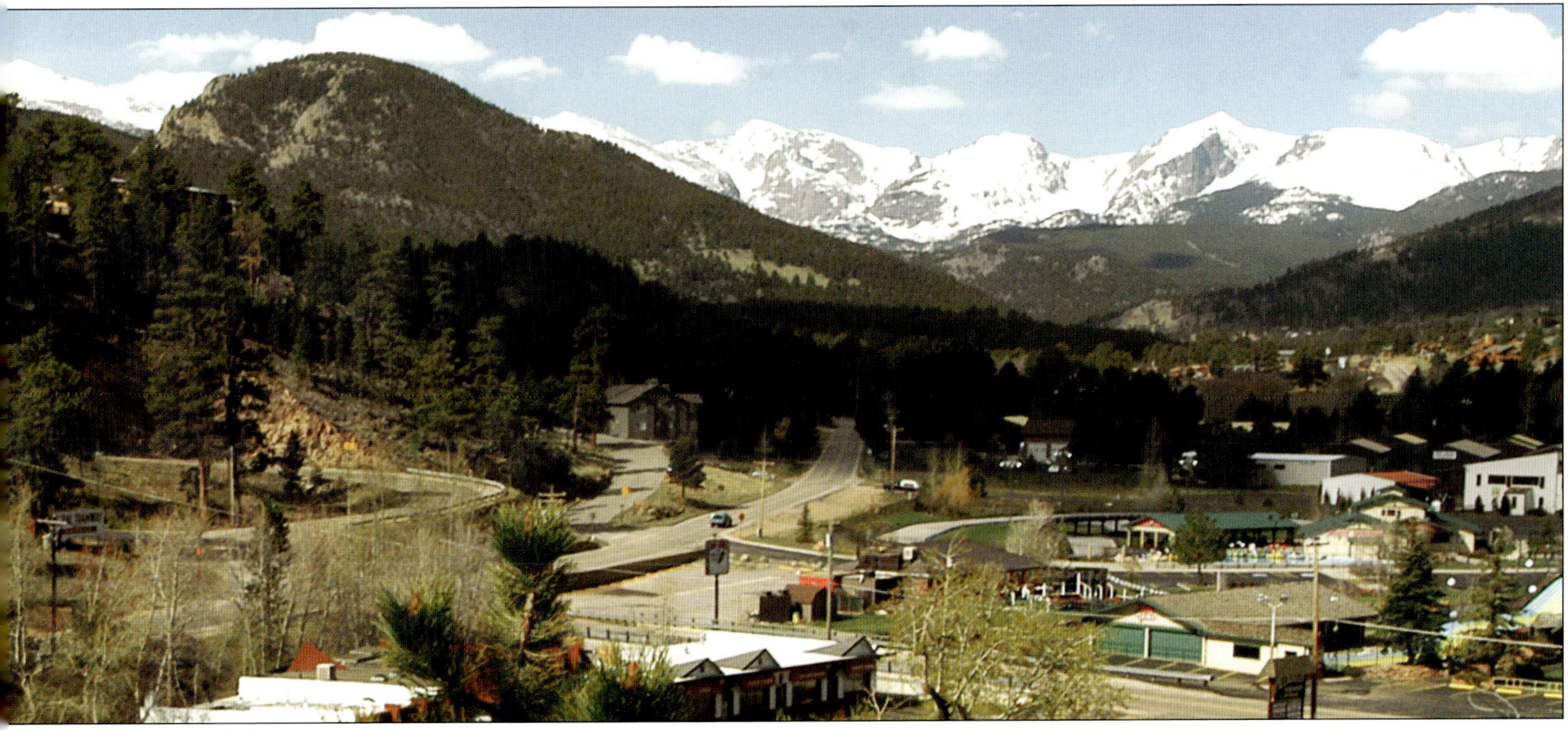

49. Boyd House

Just south of the corner of East Elkhorn Avenue and East Riverside Drive, in what is now Confluence Park, once stood the home of James and Fannie Boyd. Boyd had come to Estes Park shortly after the turn of the century, operating a blacksmith and wagon repair shop. The original photograph of about 1908 clearly shows that Boyd's shop, with its false facade, stood southeast of the house, facing directly onto East Riverside. Quite fortuitously, as it turned out, Sam Service's store and home (see p. 88) stood directly across Elkhorn Avenue. Boyd became friends with Sam and Sadie Service, met Sam's sister, Fannie, and married her in 1906. All four of these buildings are visible in the panoramic photograph of Estes Park taken in 1919 (see p. 80). What attracted us to the photo of the Boyd house reproduced here is that it contains an early view of the East Riverside area adjacent to the Big Thompson that is seldom seen in period photographs.

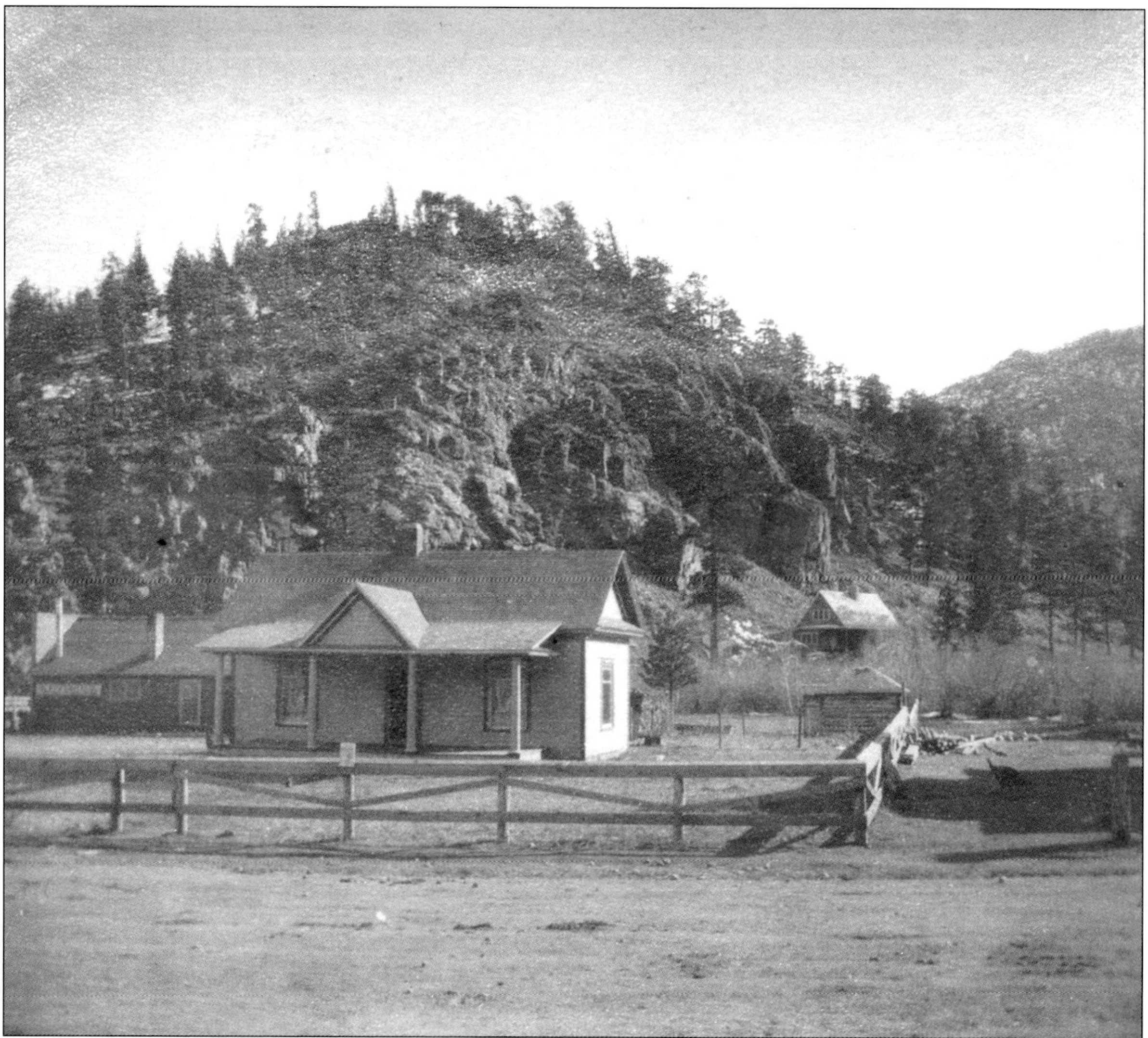

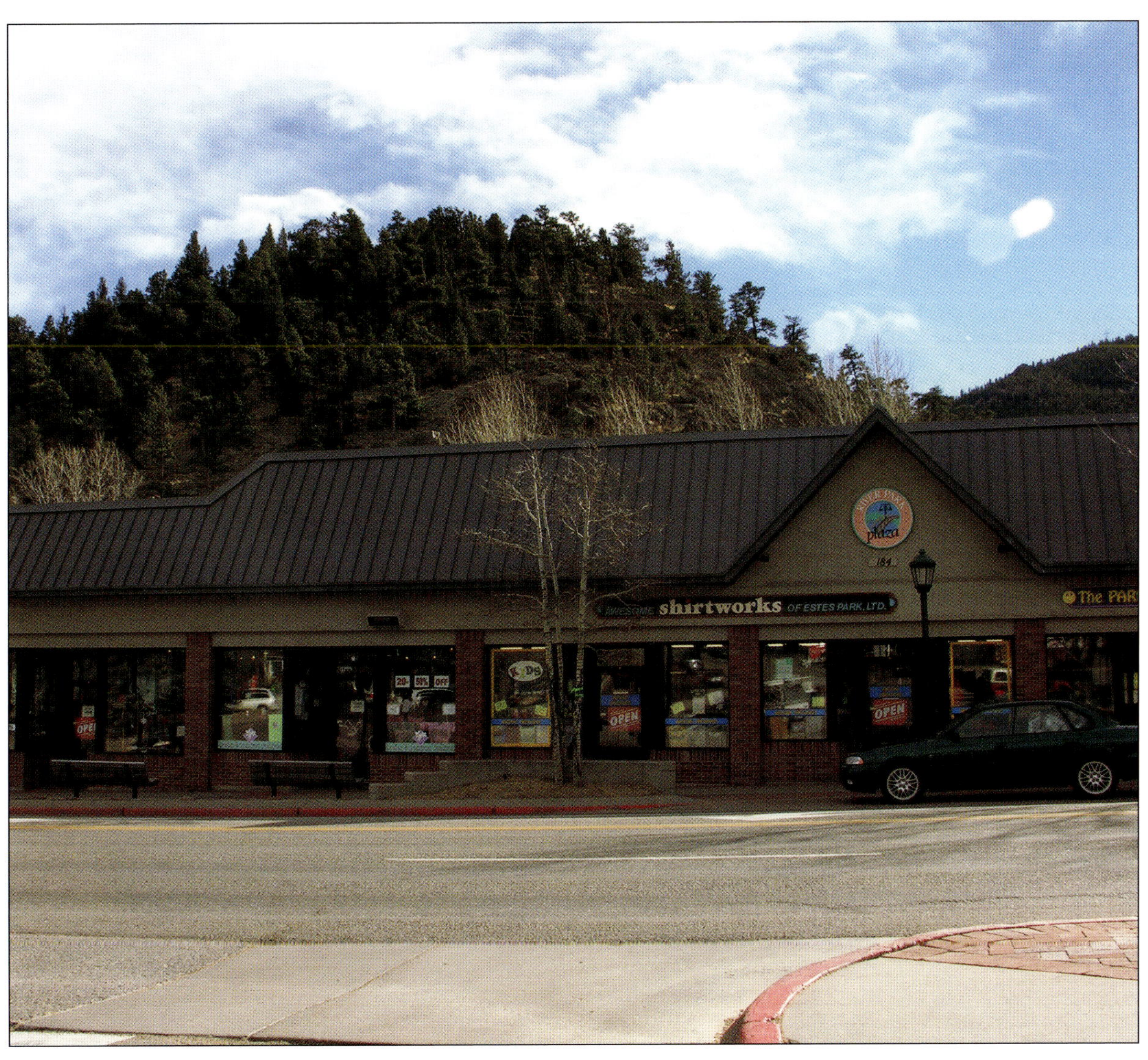

Photo by
Carey Stevanus

The Boyd's home became the victim of progress in 1925 when it was removed to make way for the Boyd building, seven fireproof brick and tile stores at the corner of Elkhorn and East Riverside covering almost five existing lots. In their day, they gave an impressive look of modernity and stability to the rustic village of Estes Park, whose early buildings were constructed mostly of wood and were a constant fire risk.

Like so many other historic structures in the Estes Park area, including the Bear Lake Lodge and the original church parsonage, the Boyd house was relocated rather than being destroyed. It now occupies a wooded lot on Big Horn Drive, where, enlarged and perched upon a new basement, it serves its current owners as a quaint bed and breakfast.

50. Stanley Hotel, 1908

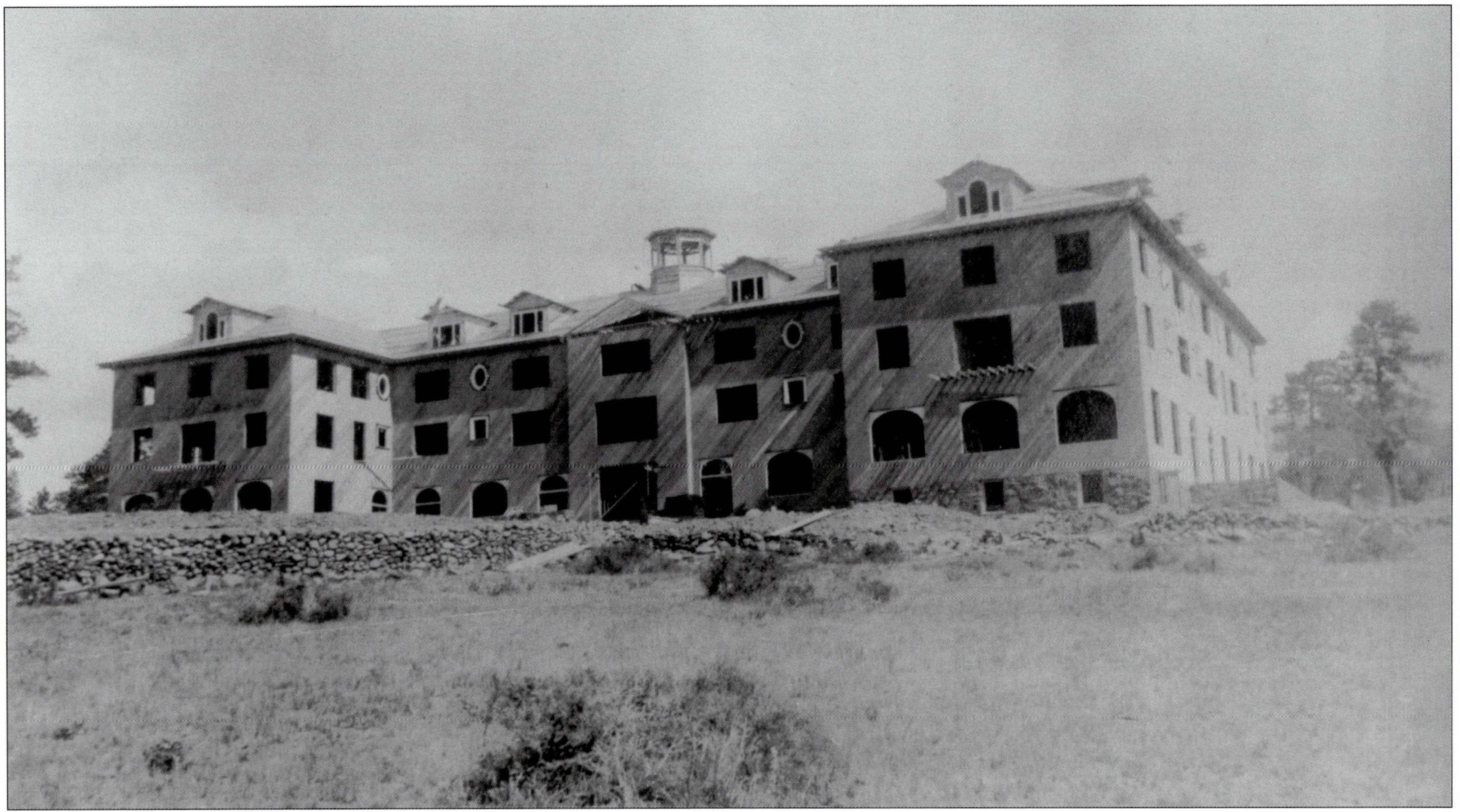

F. O. Stanley had no experience in the tourist business when he undertook the construction of the Stanley Hotel in 1907, yet over the next two years he built the finest hotel complex in northern Colorado. Stanley hired a Denver architect, but directed the project with his own preferences—including its Georgian architecture and original mustard yellow paint. Pictured here under construction in 1908, the complex included the 105-room central hotel; the adjacent Manor House (a miniature, winterized replica of the main building completed in 1910); the Casino (now Stanley Hall), with theater seating for 600 and a basement bowling alley; and the Carriage House, which contained a garage and machine shop. There were also employees' quarters, a laundry, ice-house, golf course, and later, even an airfield. Stanley's all-electric hotel opened for business in June 1909.

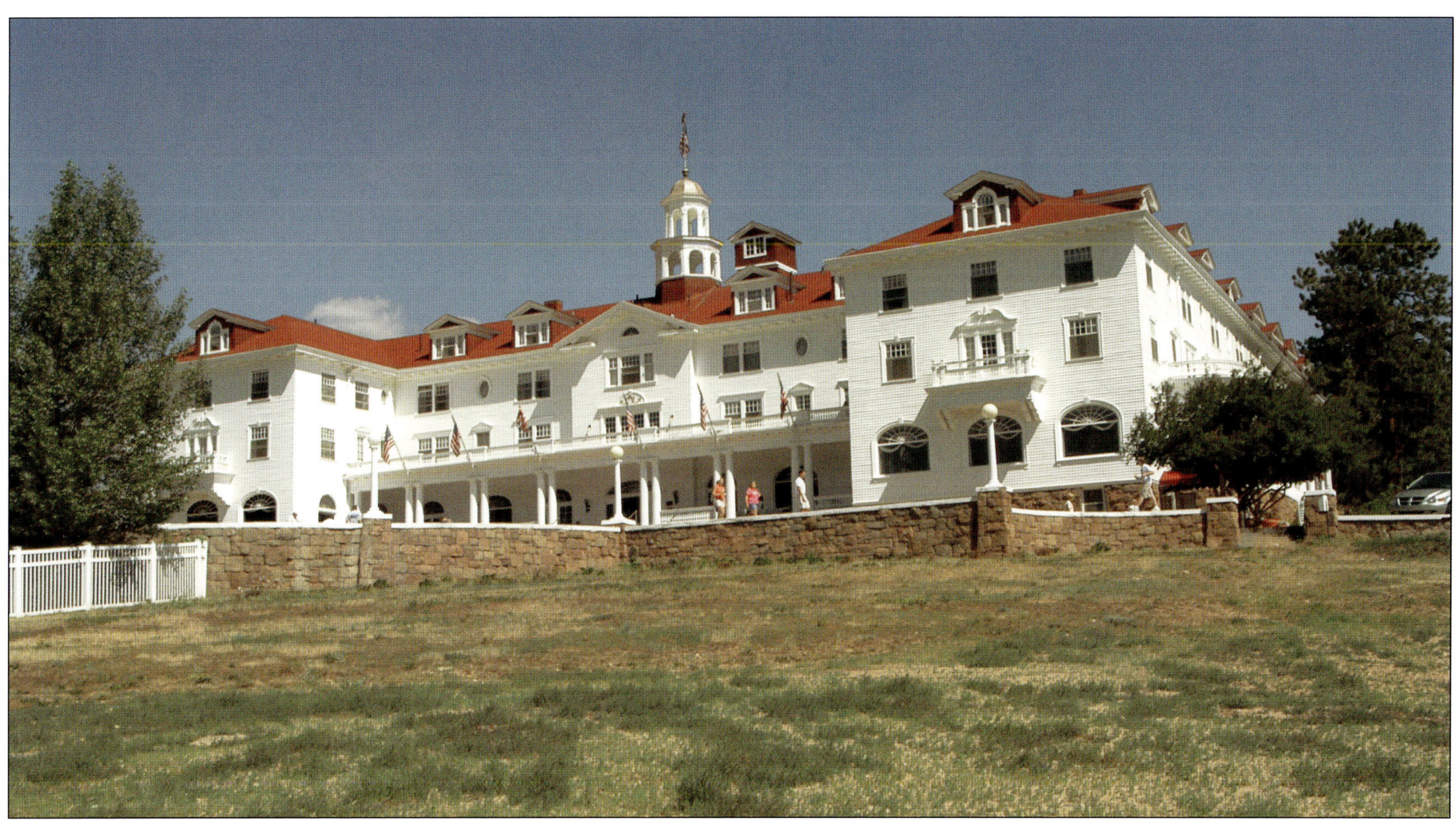

Stanley intended to call the hotel "The Dunraven," after the Irish earl. But news of the name caused widespread consternation. A petition in the form of a buckskin was quickly gathered. Among its 180 signatures were those of every hotel owner in Estes Park. "We, the undersigned," it stated, "appreciating the good work you have done in Estes Park, hereby petition that the building which will stand as a monument to its founder, shall be called 'The Stanley Hotel.'" Stanley acquiesced.

Stanley sold the hotel in 1929. The Stanley Hotel remains the jewel of Estes Park. Now painted white, and without its porte cochere, the Stanley stands proudly against the gray granite of Lumpy Ridge, a tribute to the vision and workmanship of its remarkable builder.

We found the spot where the original photograph was taken without much difficulty; you will note from the shadows on the third-story dormers that we arrived at almost exactly the same time on an equally sunny day.

51. Elkhorn Lodge, circa 1920

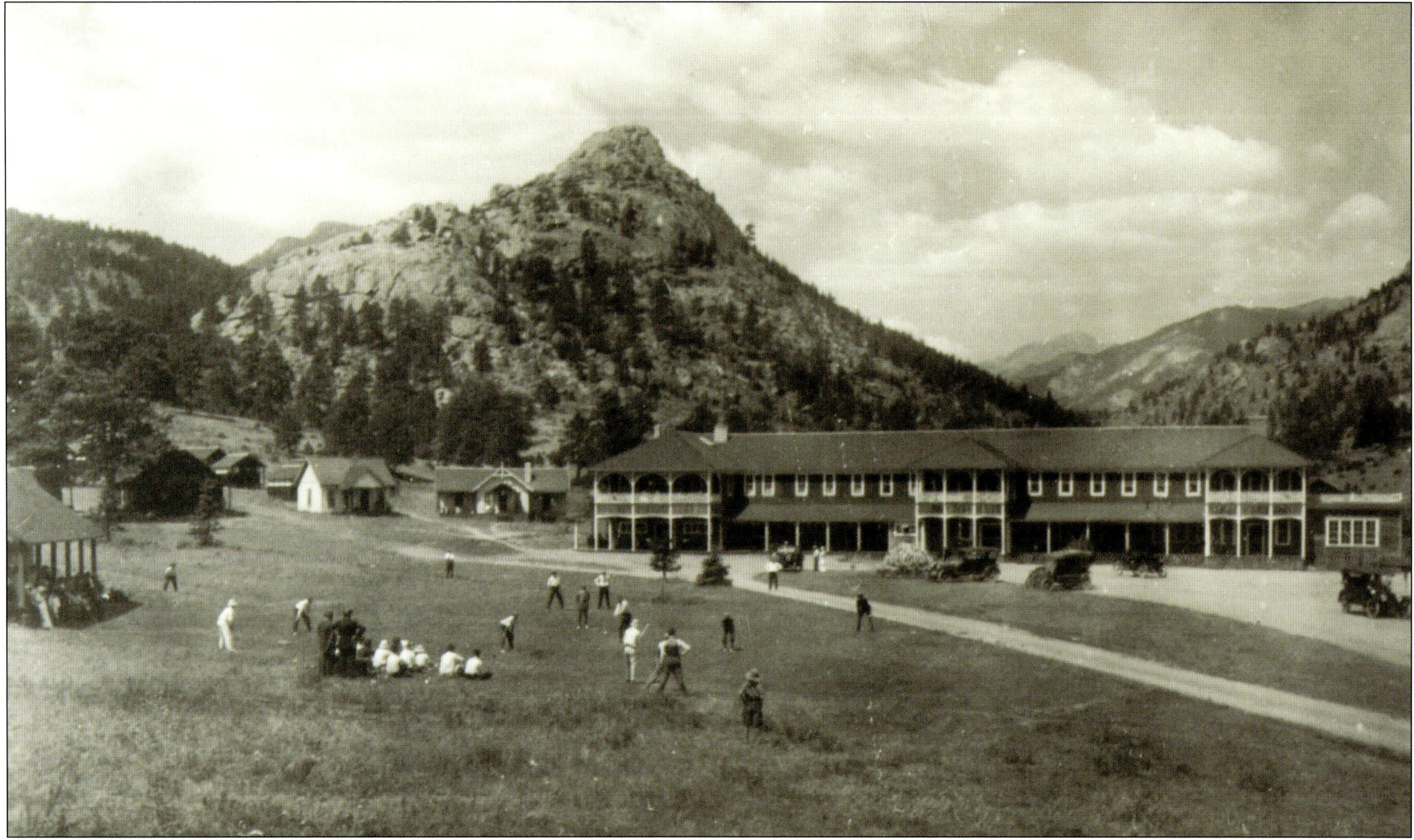

The Elkhorn Lodge, on Fall River west of Estes Park, was established by New York native William E. James, who first visited the Estes Valley on a hunting expedition in autumn 1874. The following May, James brought his family back to homestead near what is now known as McCreery Spring (see p. 70). In 1875, James established a second claim above the MacGregors' in Black Canyon. The following year, he swapped his original claim along Lumpy Ridge for the site on Fall River, and there built a modest cabin.

James tried to make a living as a stockman in Horseshoe Park, but soon began adding guest cabins and tent houses to his family's Fall River property. By 1880, their ranch, renamed the Elkhorn Lodge, could accommodate nearly 40. In 1884, one of the Elkhorn's cottages became the site of Estes Park's first school, under Dr. Judson Ellis, one of James' employees and lodgers. By 1891, the complex included nine cottages, and further enlargements followed through 1912, including a casino, a sizable stable, and a new main lodge with dining

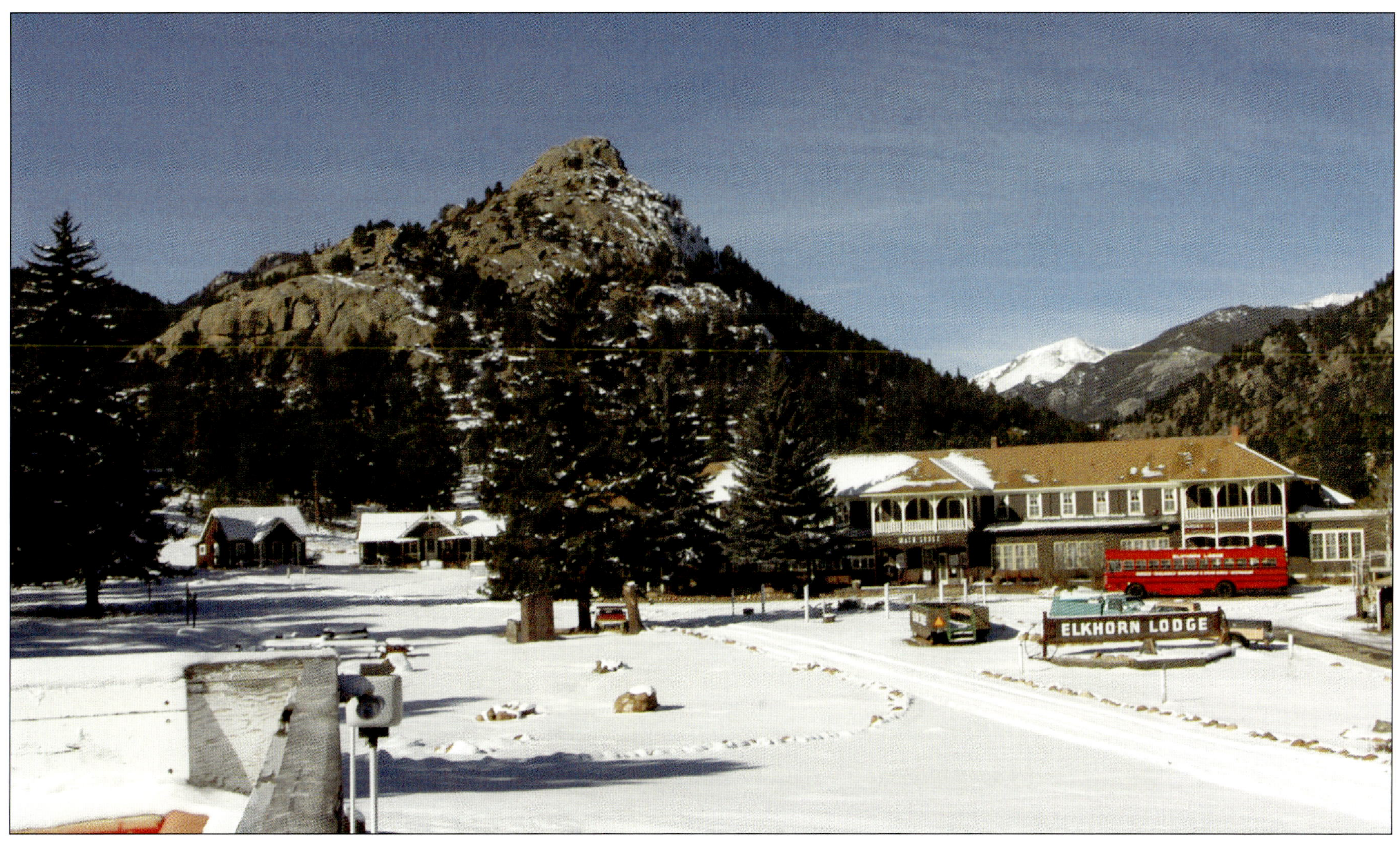

room, ballroom, and billiard room. Ultimately, the lodge's 33 buildings made it Estes Park's largest tourist establishment, while James' hunting trips resulted in the large pile of elk antlers that became one of its signature features.

After James' death in 1895, responsibility for running the Elkhorn Lodge fell to his widow, Ella McCabe James, and sons Howard and Homer. When Ella James died in 1917, Howard James and his wife Edna took over management, assisted by his sister, Eleanor James Hondius, the wife of rancher Pieter Hondius. In 1961, the James family sold the lodge to the first of a series of new owners who have served as stewards of one of Estes Park's most famous, historic, and important resort properties.

52. MacGregor Ranch, circa 1890–1920

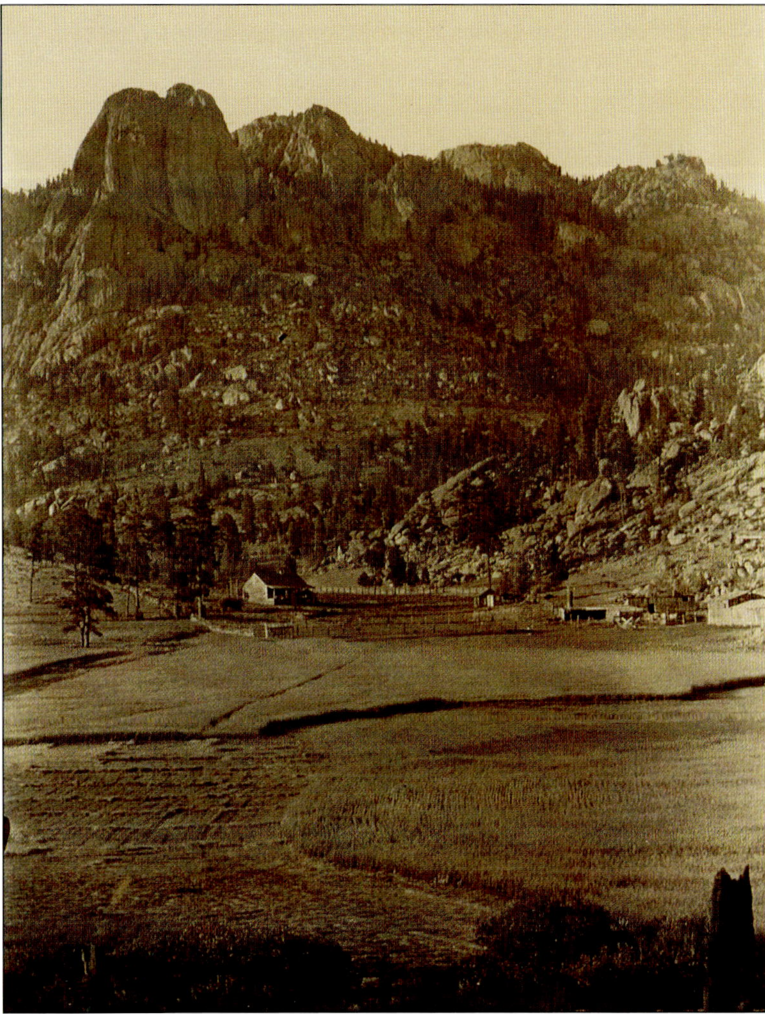

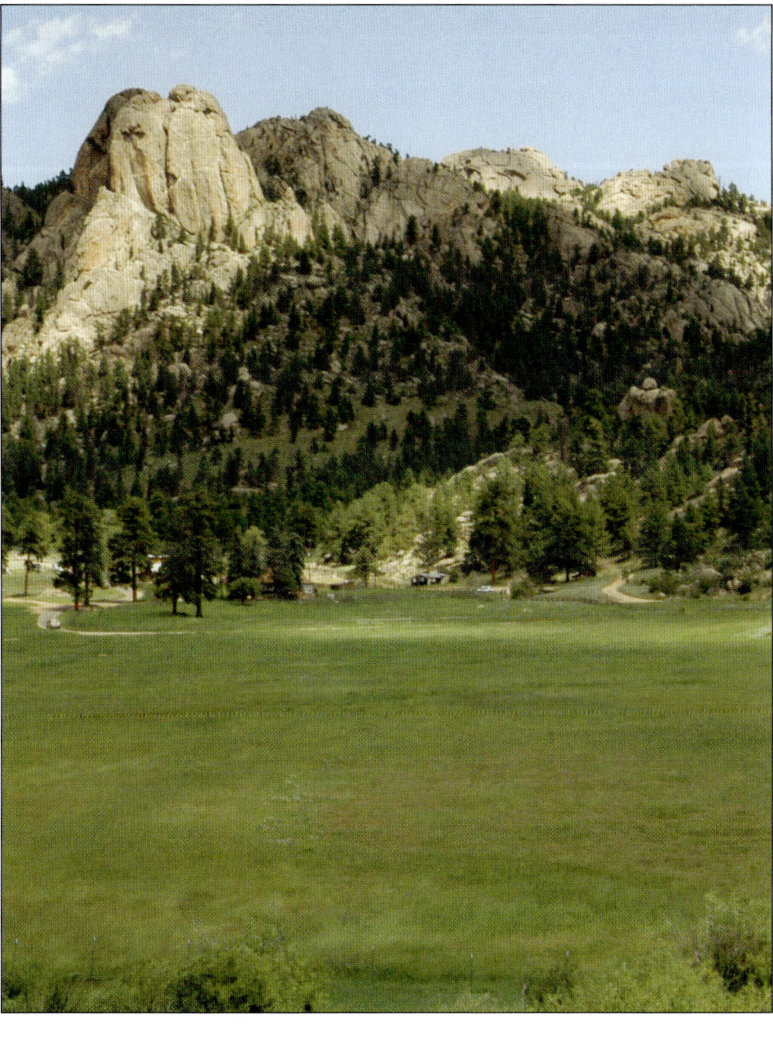

MacGregor ranch, situated at the mouth of the Black Canyon, is the oldest continuously operating ranch in the Estes Valley. It dates to late 1874 or early 1875, when a 160-acre claim by Black Canyon Creek was filed by Alexander Quiner MacGregor and his new wife, Clara. Although both were from Wisconsin, the MacGregors met in 1872 in Colorado. She had come to Colorado on a sketching trip that was organized by her art instructor, Henry Chapman Ford of Chicago. Somewhere along the way between Colorado Springs, South Park, and Estes Park, Clara crossed paths with Alexander MacGregor, 26, a Denver lawyer. He'd been admitted to the bar that year and was planning to form a partnership with Westbrook Decker, a judge. MacGregor seemed poised to make a name for himself in Colorado legal circles. Instead, he and Clara came to Estes Park to take up cattle ranching and farming, beginning a presence here that lasted three generations.

In late 1874, even before completing the first of what would be several houses, Alexander MacGregor carved for himself an essential part in the life of the future community. Realizing that the growth and development of Estes Park demanded better roads, he began construction of a toll road from Lyons. That road was opened for use in July 1875. The next year, when it became time to establish the first post office, MacGregor offered the use of a building at the ranch, with Clara serving as postmistress. From an early date, the MacGregors also opened their home and property to summer visitors by constructing a series of cabins and a dining hall on the north side of Black Canyon Creek.

The MacGregors prospered. By 1882, the original ranch house had been incorporated into a new one with rooms "fixed up in the latest style," today called the A. Q. House.

In the new century, responsibility for MacGregor ranch, which would grow to more than 2,000 acres, was assumed by Donald MacGregor, the second son,

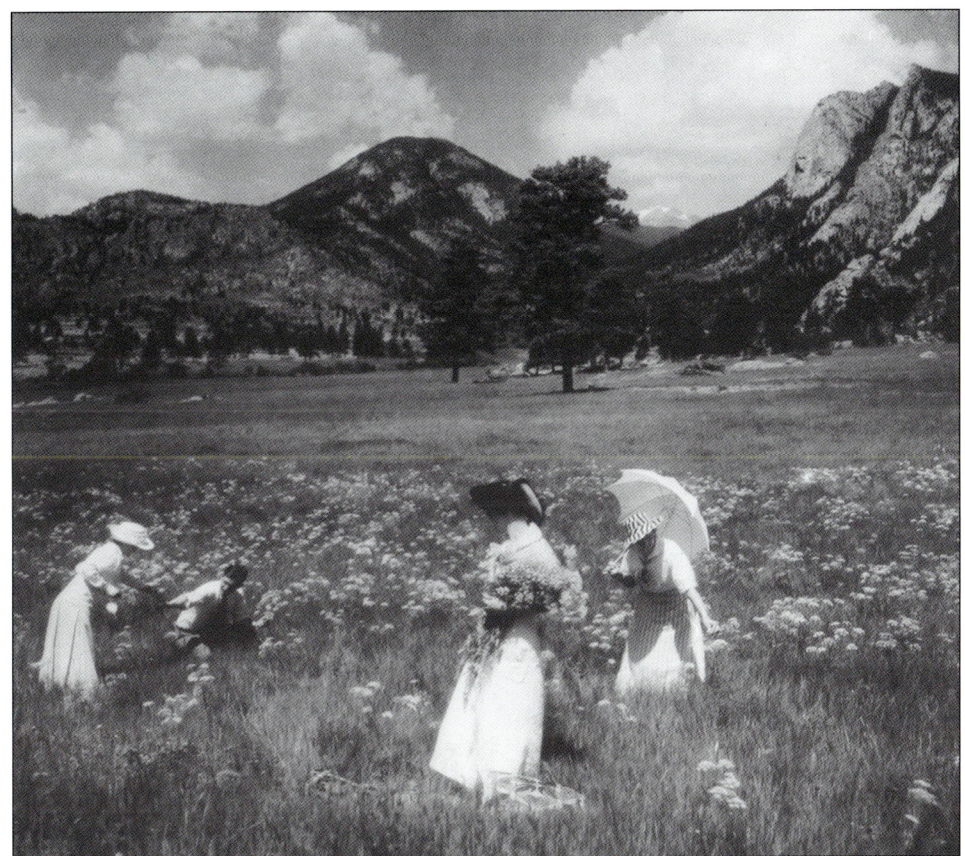

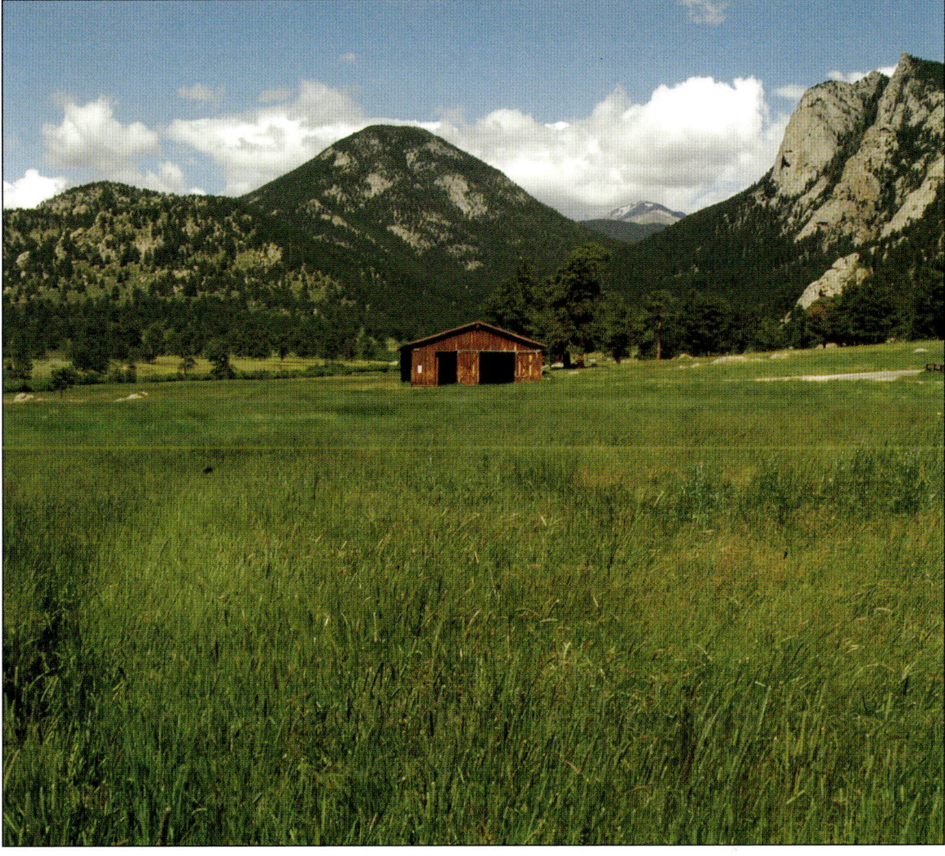

and his wife, Minnie Maude. Following their deaths, their only daughter, Muriel, ran the ranch. Muriel never married and devoted most of her life struggling to maintain the ranch. Muriel MacGregor passed away in 1973. Five years later, the Muriel L. MacGregor Charitable Trust, a private, nonprofit operating foundation, was formed to carry out her wish that her ranch and cattle should be kept together to serve educational purposes. Today, the MacGregor ranch, with its distinctive "XIX" brand, serves as a working cattle ranch, youth education center, and museum. Twenty-eight of the 43 buildings on the ranch are listed in the National Register of Historic Places.

As the photographs here suggest, MacGregor ranch and its Black Canyon setting have attracted many photographers. There is the photograph on p. 5, titled "We Three," in which the authors of this book posed in front of the A. Q. House in an effort to duplicate the original photograph of Alexander MacGregor and family taken by an unknown photographer about 1892. Of the other original photographs taken on the ranch between about 1890 and 1920, the first, an early photo, shows the ranch and its buildings beneath the rock outcropping of the Twin Owls, while the second photograph strikingly captures the flower-strewn pasture below the barns, where three women and a man are gathering bouquets. The final two are signature photographs making use of the ranch's trees, both taken by Fred Payne Clatworthy. The first image is of the so-called "Japanese Tree" and captures Longs Peak and the Front Range to the south. This view was an extremely popular one, for this distinctive tree also appears in photographs taken by Louis C. McClure, William T. Parke, and H. Bruce Wiswall. The second of the Clatworthy photos, capturing much the same scene, was shot from a location on the hillside to the north. Clatworthy, quite appropriately, titled this photograph "Between the Pines."

"The Japanese Tree"

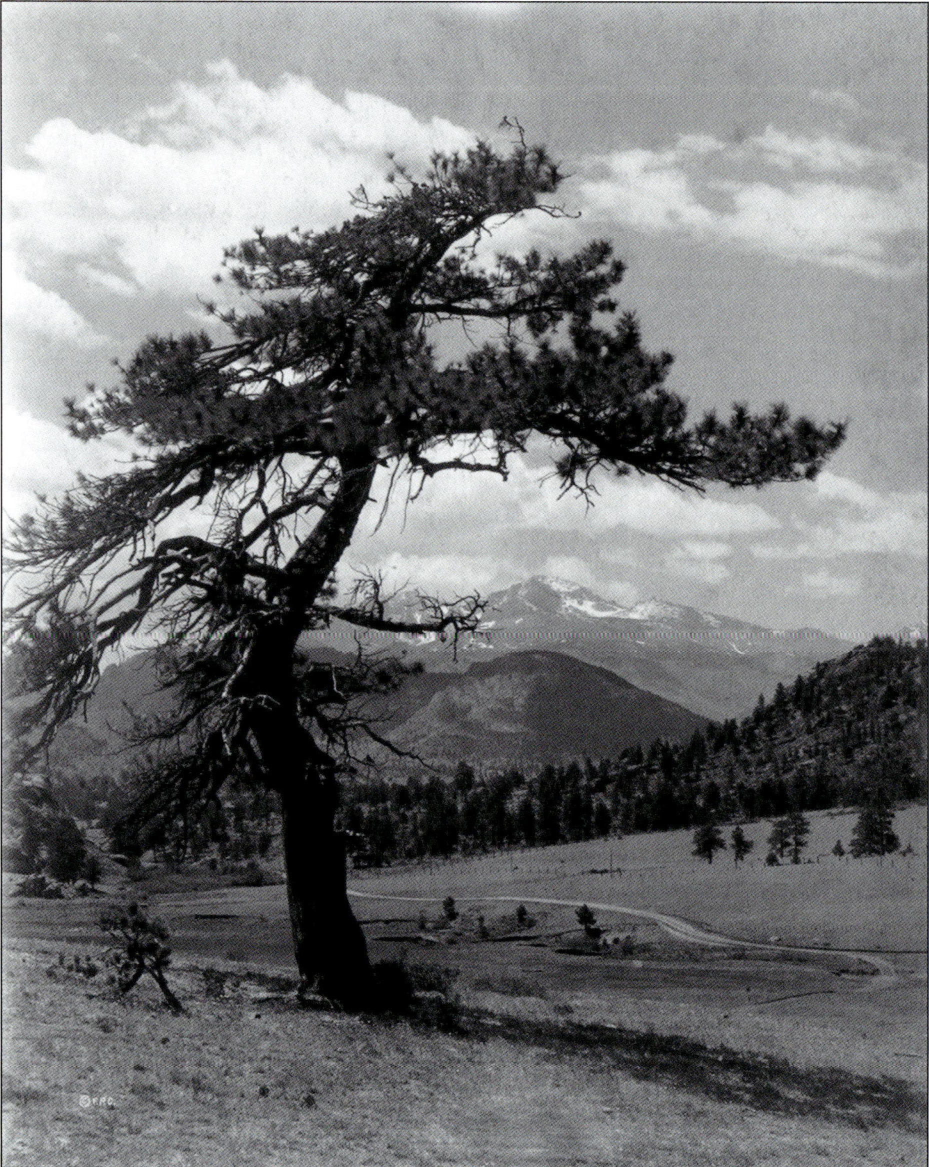

Photo by Fred Payne Clatworthy

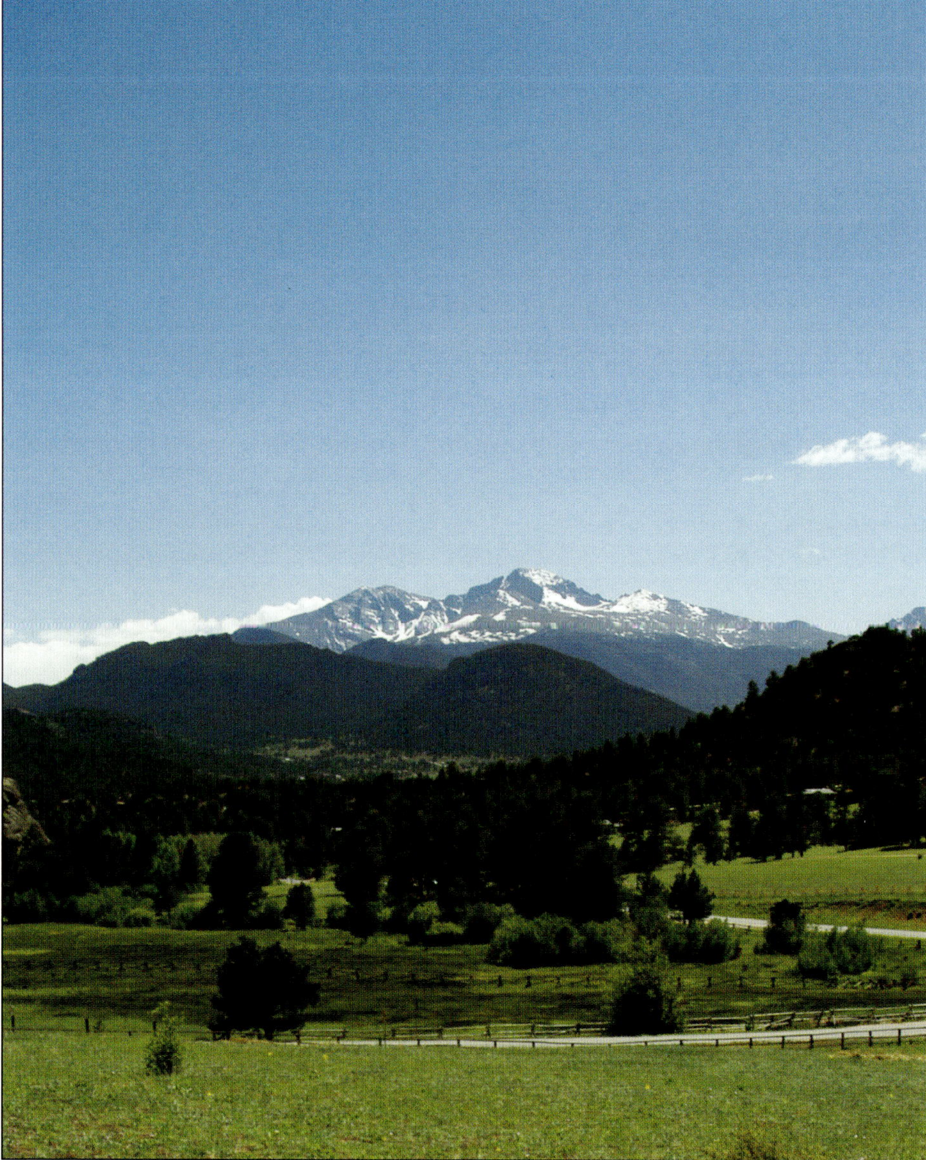

"Between the Pines"

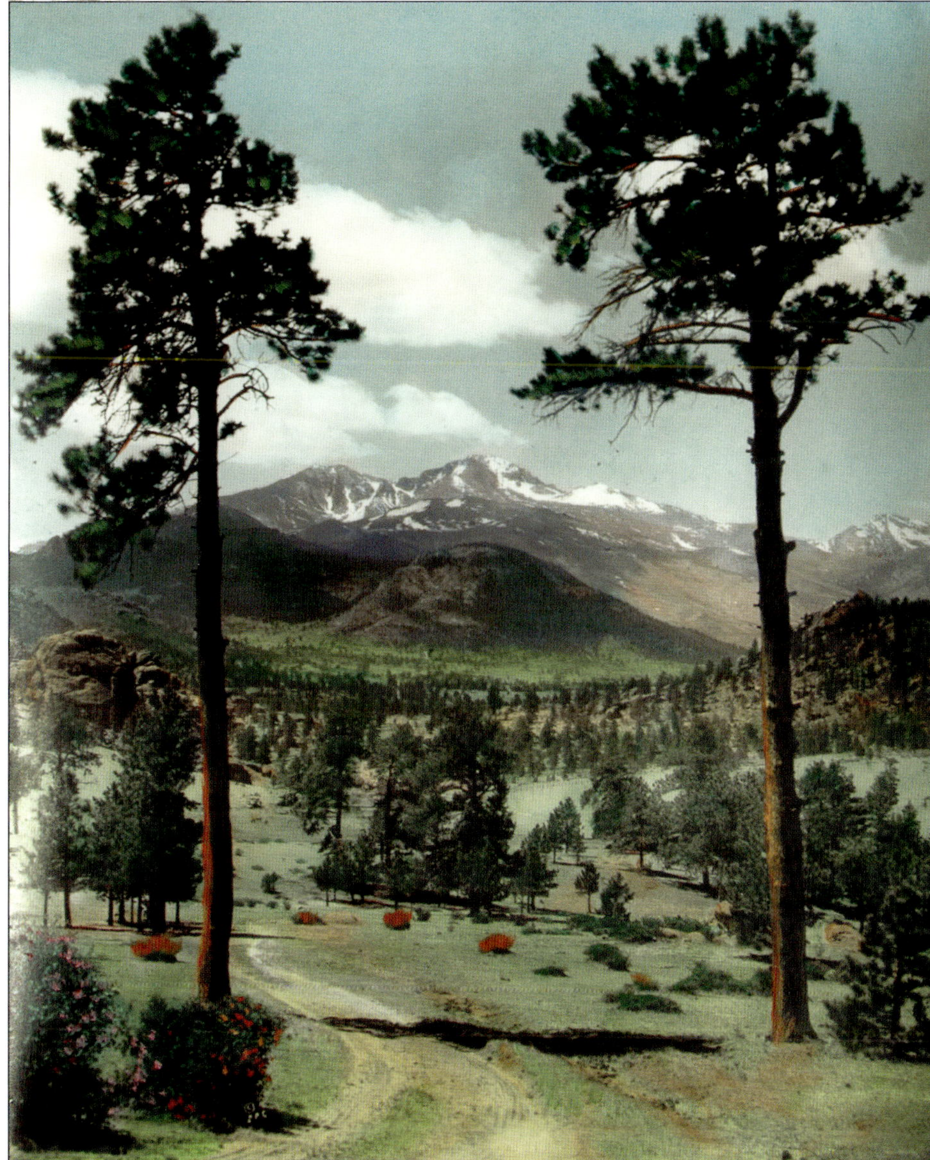

Photo by Fred Payne Clatworthy

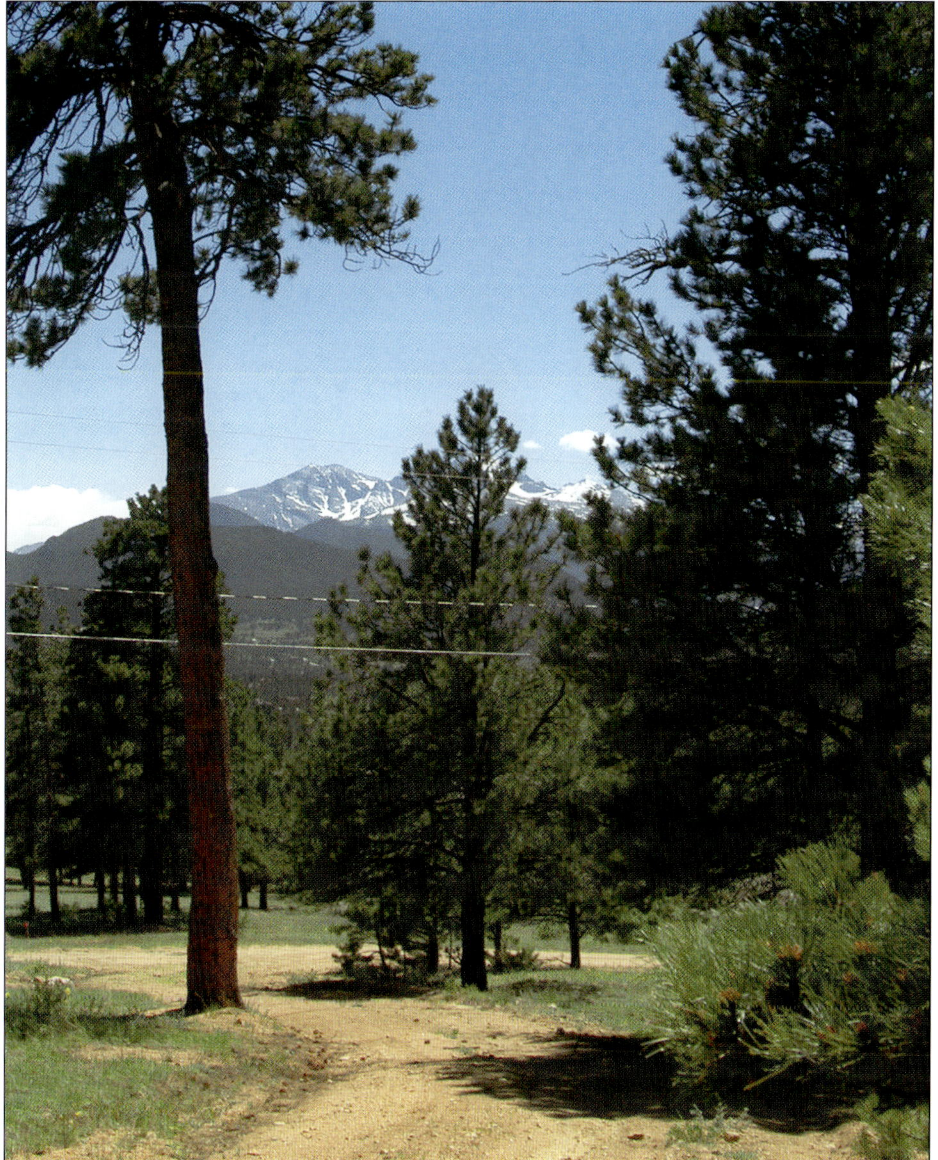

53. McGraw Ranch, circa 1922

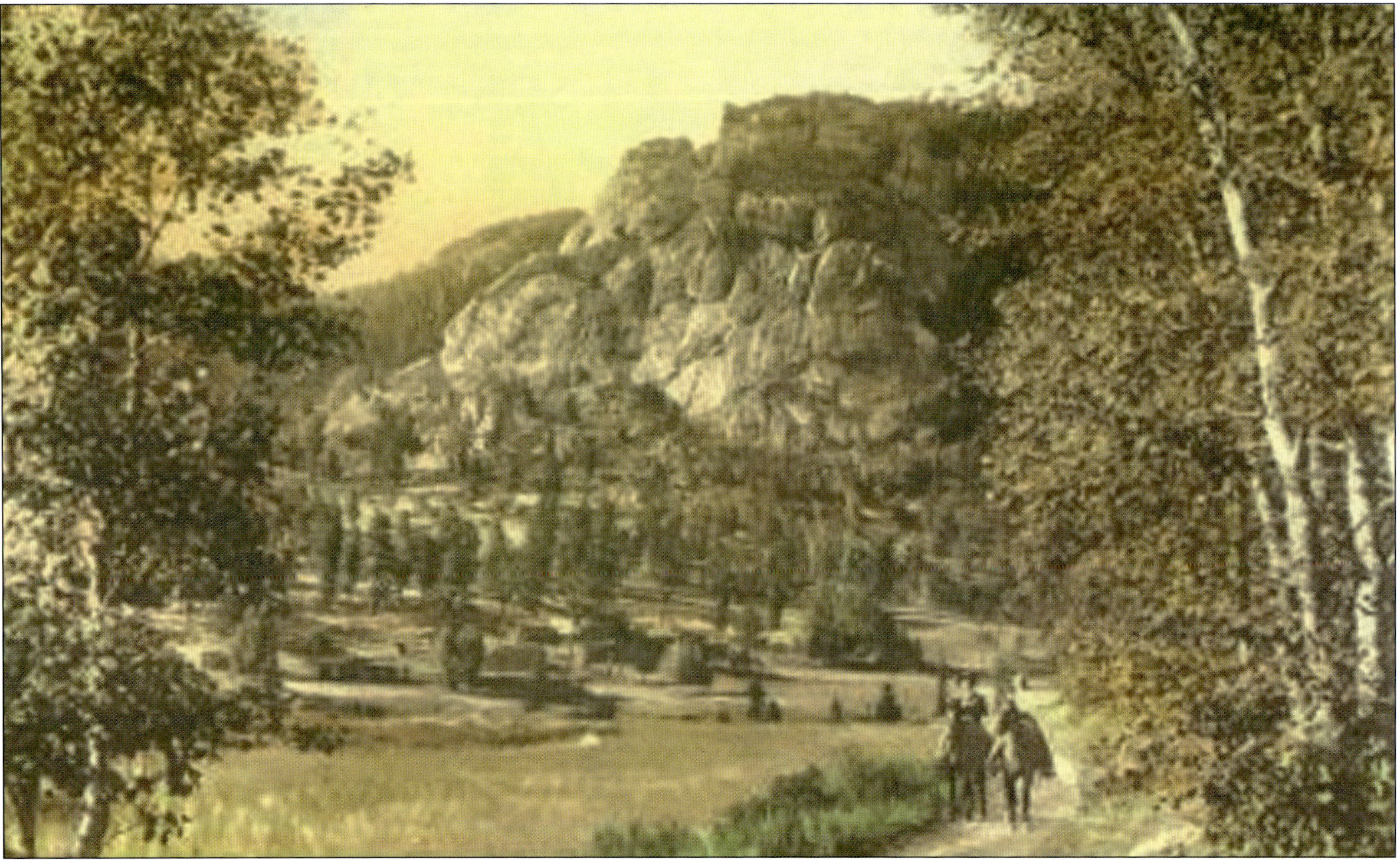

Photo by Fred Payne Clatworthy

The McGraw ranch on Cow Creek has had a long and complex history. It was homesteaded by Hank Farrar, a well-known hunter, who built a log house, a milk house, and a dirt-roofed shed on the property. Farrar subsequently took on a partner, Caleb A. "Cale" Cook. In 1884, the ranch was purchased by another Estes Park pioneer, Peter J. "P. J." Pauly Jr., who built a large barn, bunkhouse, and icehouse, laid out corrals, added a new room to the old cabin, and installed a pond and ditch system to support his sizable cattle operation. In 1897, Pauly's ranch was acquired by Hugo Miller, who, together with his cousin Henry C. Rouse of Cleveland, Ohio, had begun to purchase land in the area more than a decade before. Upon Rouse's death in 1907, Miller became the sole owner of the ranch, now sized well in excess of 1,000 acres. Miller and his wife Mary renamed it the Double Bar Y Ranch.

In 1908, because of his wife's failing health, Miller leased his property, which he was by then also operating as a small resort, to John J. McGraw, who had

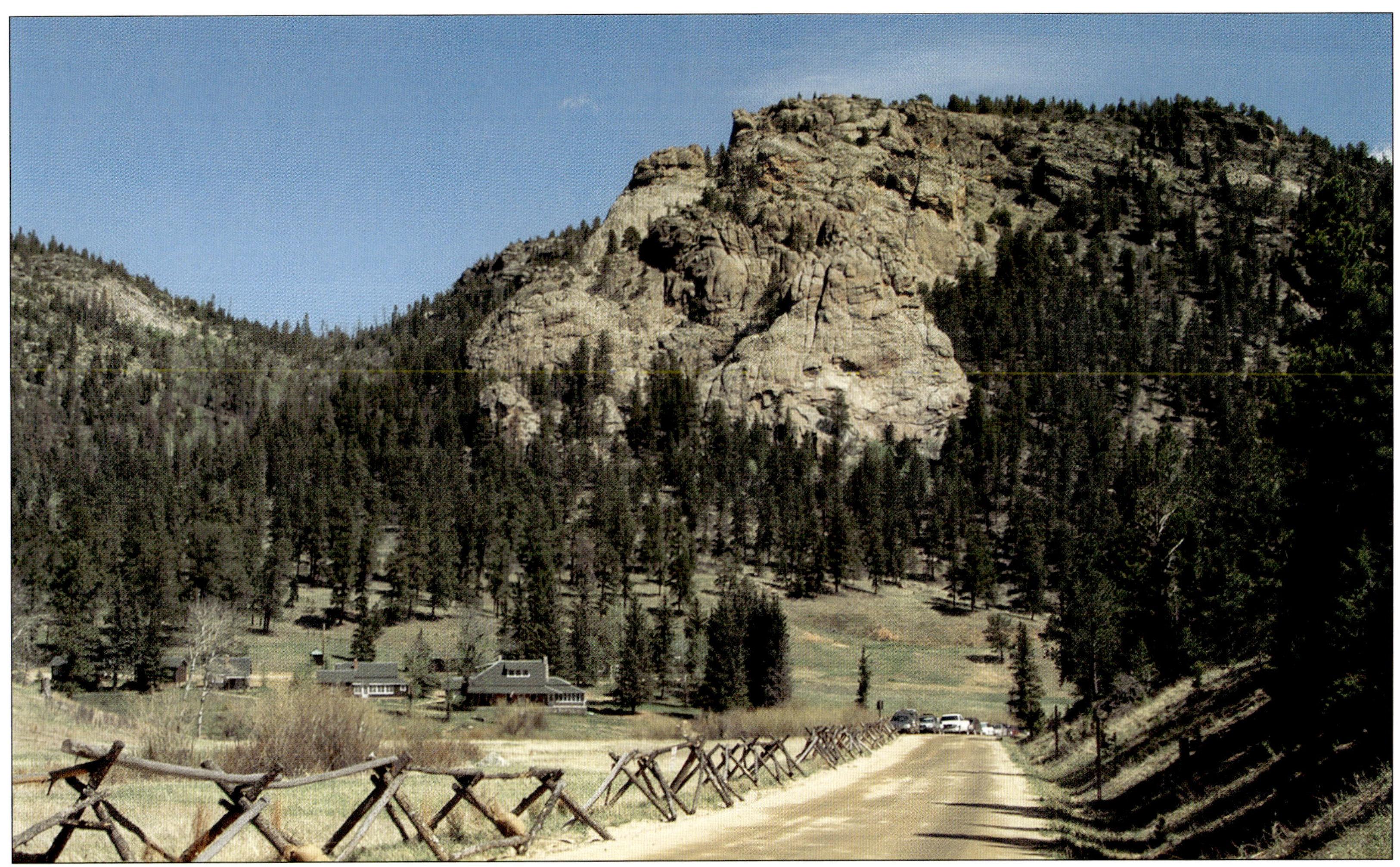

honeymooned in Estes Park two years before, met the Millers at church, and then visited the ranch. Although McGraw's lease ran for 25 years and had an option for another 25-year renewal, he purchased the ranch outright the next year for $16,000. After McGraw's death in 1917, his widow, Irene, stayed on to raise her four children and continue ranching. In 1936, two of her sons, John and Frank, began building a series of six guest cabins west of the lodge, converting the McGraw ranch into a dude ranch for those who wished to "rough it with ease." That summer the McGraw ranch became the focus of national attention when it hosted Kansas Governor Alfred "Alf" Landon and his family, both before and after his nomination as Republican candidate for the presidency.

Frank McGraw operated the ranch until 1979, when the ranch's core was sold and became the Indian Head Ranch. The McGraws in 1966 had sold 834 acres to the National Park Service, retaining a small parcel for themselves. In 1988, the Park Service acquired the rest of the property, some 220 acres, with

McGraw ranch, circa 1940

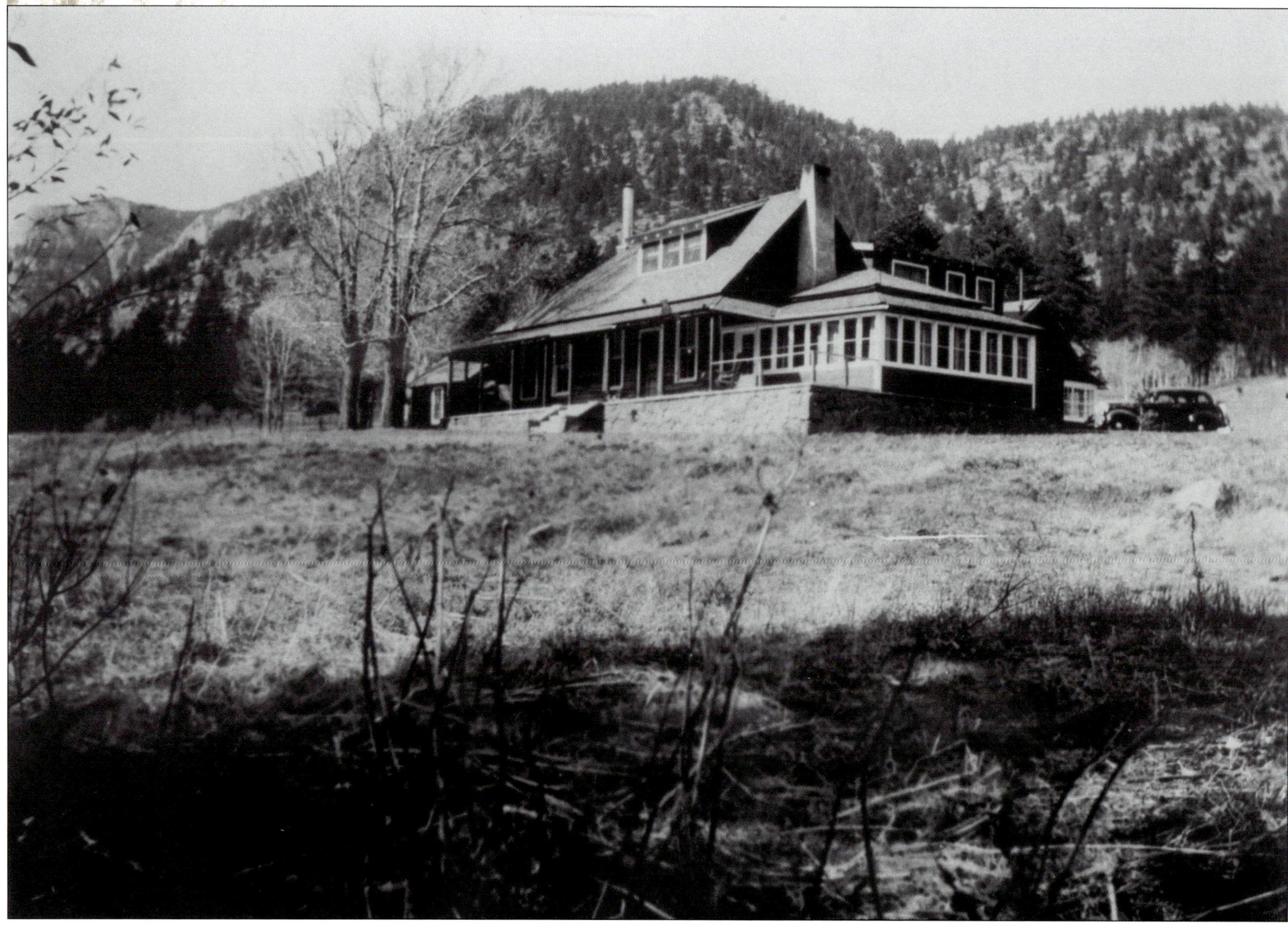

the intention of razing the buildings and returning the land to its natural state for elk habitat. Those plans were changed, however, after it was discovered under the National Historic Preservation Act that the ranch buildings had historical significance. The National Park Service has since stabilized the buildings, and, with the help of the State Historical Fund, restored them to the most significant period in ranch history, 1935–1955. The site is now used as a research center and

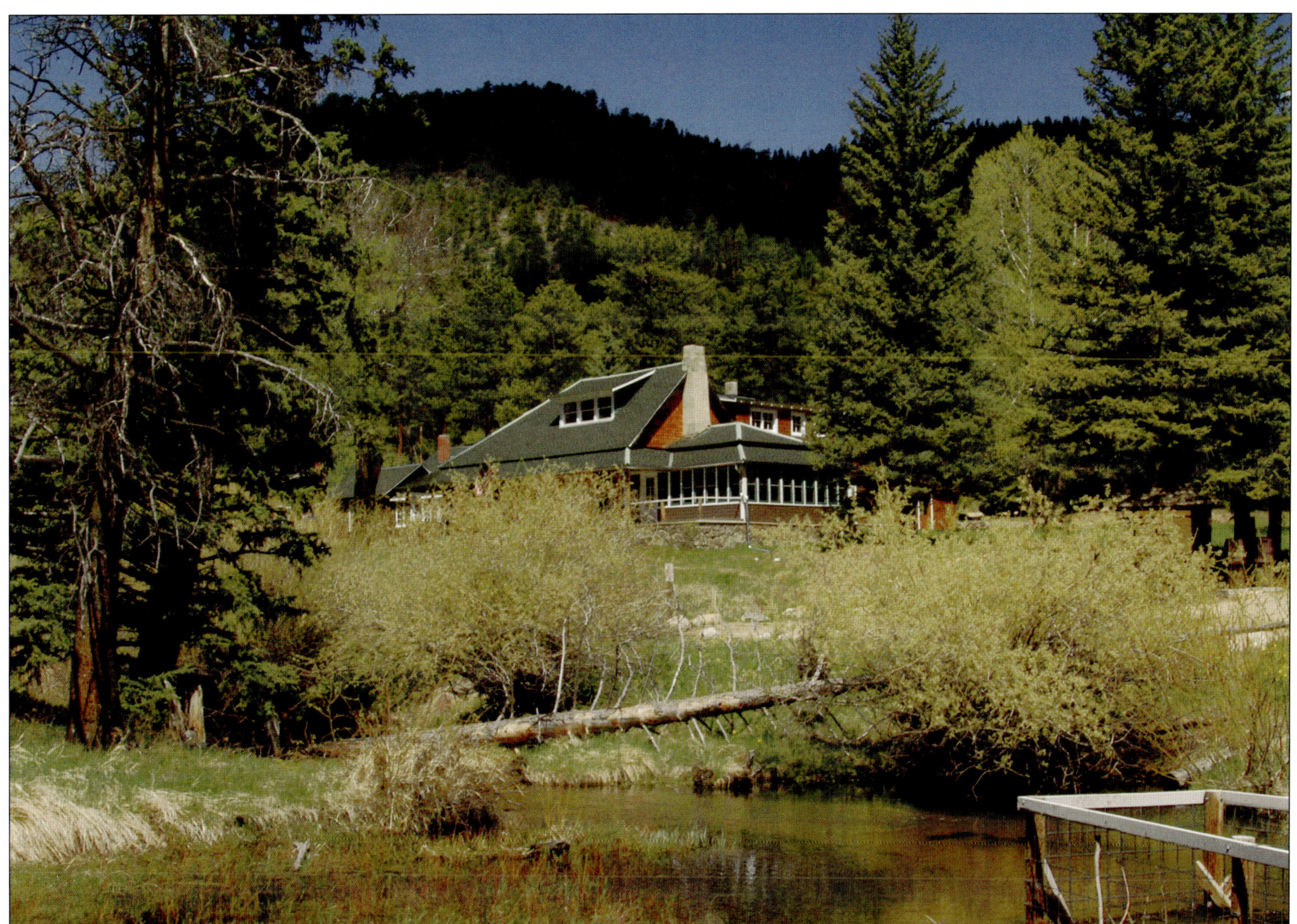

living quarters for scientists researching park resources. In 1998, the McGraw ranch was added to the National Register of Historic Places. The photographs here capture the ranch from two different perspectives: the first as Fred Payne Clatworthy photographed it from a distance as he stood on the approach road and looked down into the valley of Cow Creek; the second, a later close-up view of the ranch's main building, showing its recent renovation.

54. Rustic Hotel

The Rustic Hotel, on the rim of Devils Gulch some 5 miles northeast of Estes Park, was built by Shepherd "Shep" Husted and opened for tourists in 1901. Husted and his wife Clara had come to Estes Park in 1893, located land, and in 1896 built a small log homestead cabin on the site. A larger cabin, named "Shep," was erected close by a year later.

Deciding to enter the tourist business, the Husteds built additional cabins, and in 1900 began work on a two-story lodge building, designed by local architect Henry C. Rogers. F. O. Stanley—who was photographed driving his steam car to the Husted's during his first summer in the park in 1903—thought the view of the Front Range from the Rustic the finest in the park.

Although Shep personally served as the Rustic's manager, the hotel was not a financial success. Part of the reason had to do with Husted himself. His love of the mountains was always more alluring than housing and feeding tourists. Husted was happiest when out on the trail on horseback, guiding his guests to some remote lake or mountaintop. In 1907, he sold the hotel to devote his time and attention to the career as guide and lecturer that made him locally and regionally famous. Enos A. Mills, whose own feats as a local guide and mountaineer were legendary, pronounced Husted "the most capable guide I have known."

Following Husted's departure, the Rustic was managed for several seasons by W. G. Edwards and then sold in 1912 to veteran hotel man Charles E. Lester. (Lester had been managing the Estes Park Hotel at the time it was ruined by fire in August 1911 and was looking for a new opportunity). To signify his ownership and the hotel's new beginnings, it was renamed Lester's Hotel at the start of the 1913 season.

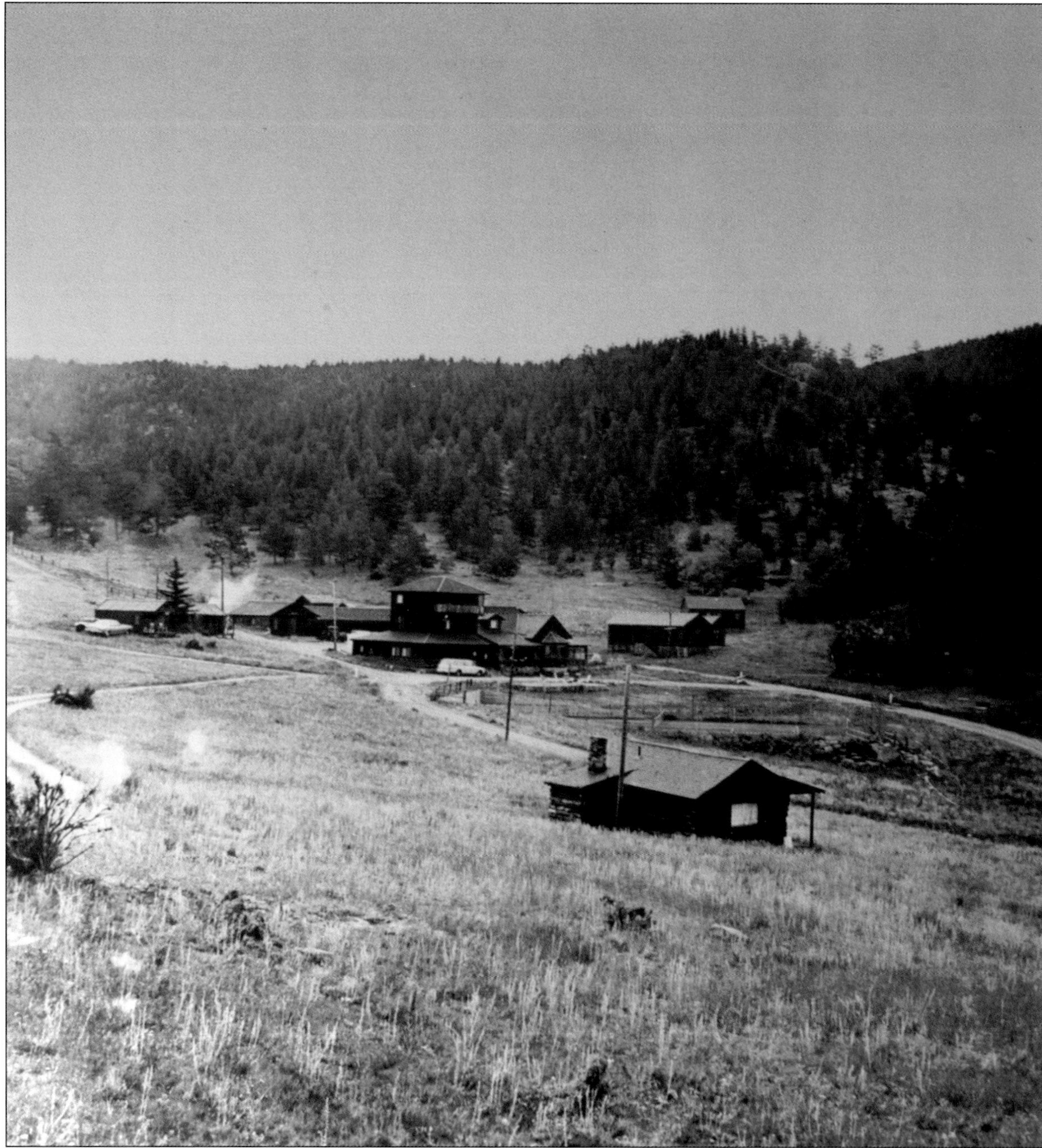

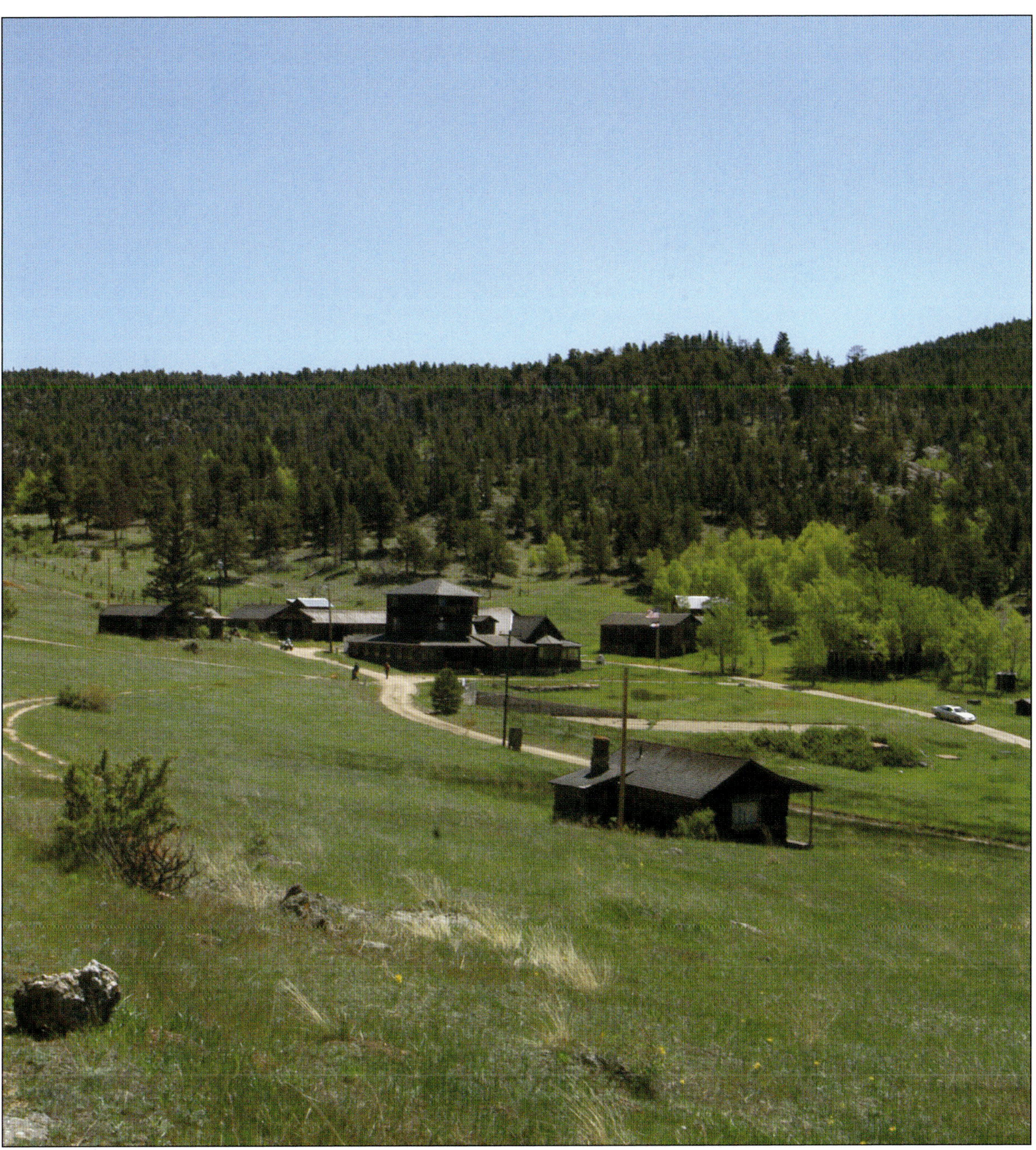

In the two decades that followed, Lester developed the property and expanded its facilities. By the 1920s, there was not only the main lodge with its stone fireplace, lounge, and amenities but 10 adjacent cottages, a tennis court, and a livery.

In 1933, Lester exited the hotel business because of ill health, selling the 200-acre property and its buildings to Julian Livingston of Denver for $12,000. In 1935, the property reopened to the public as the H Bar G Ranch. (The "H" stood, of course, for Shep Husted; the "G" was for Livingston's sister, Helen Gates.) The H Bar G operated as a dude ranch through the 1958 season, with a capacity of 52 guests. Later, it became the H Bar G Ranch for Girls, and then a youth hostel. Now closed to the public, the property remains in the hands of the Livingston family. Today, as the contemporary photographs show, its 1896 homestead cabin (in the lower middle of the first photograph) and its main building look much as they did when Shep Husted erected them more than a century ago.

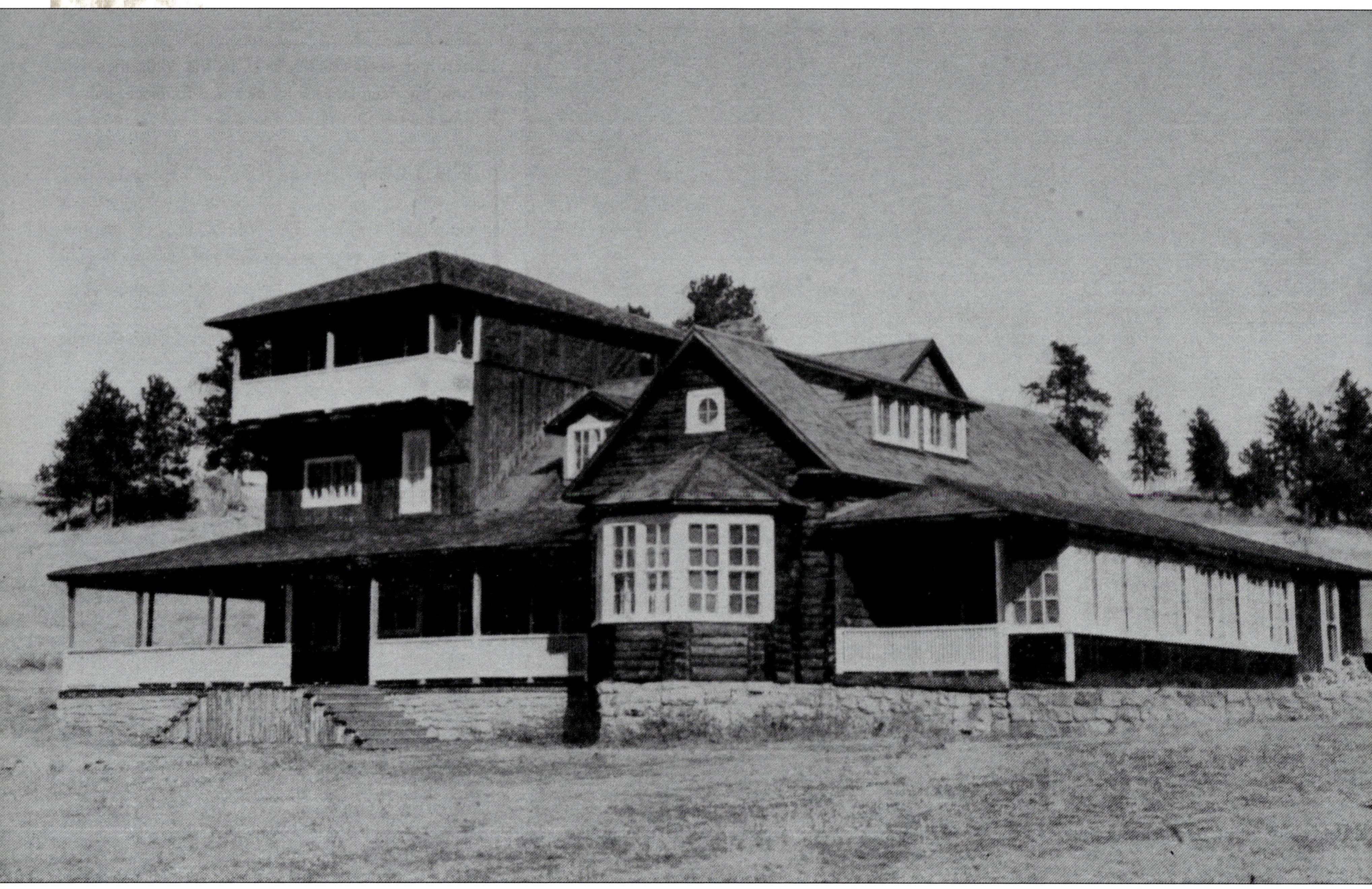

Photo by William T. Parke

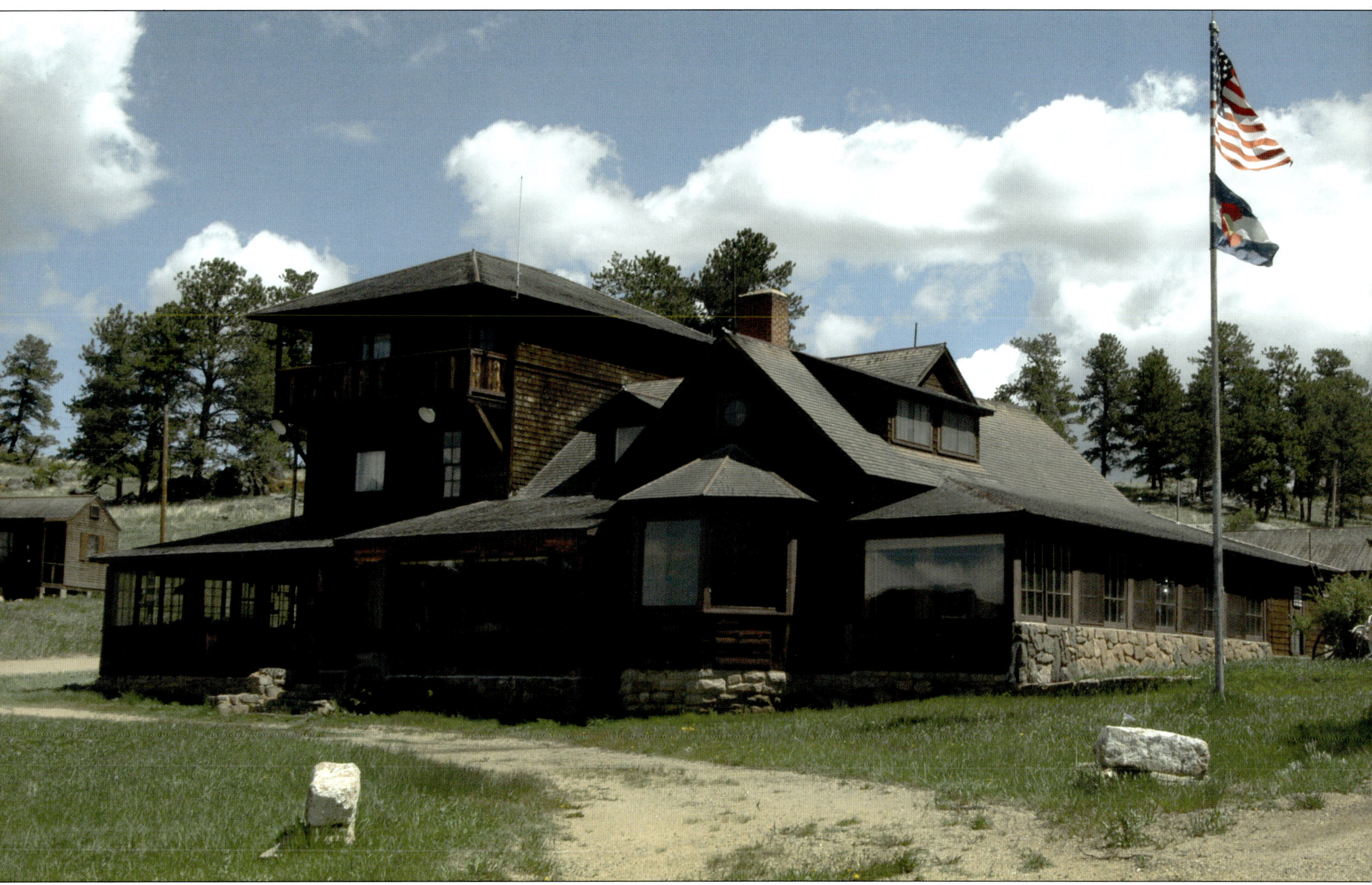

55. Olympus Lodge, circa 1930

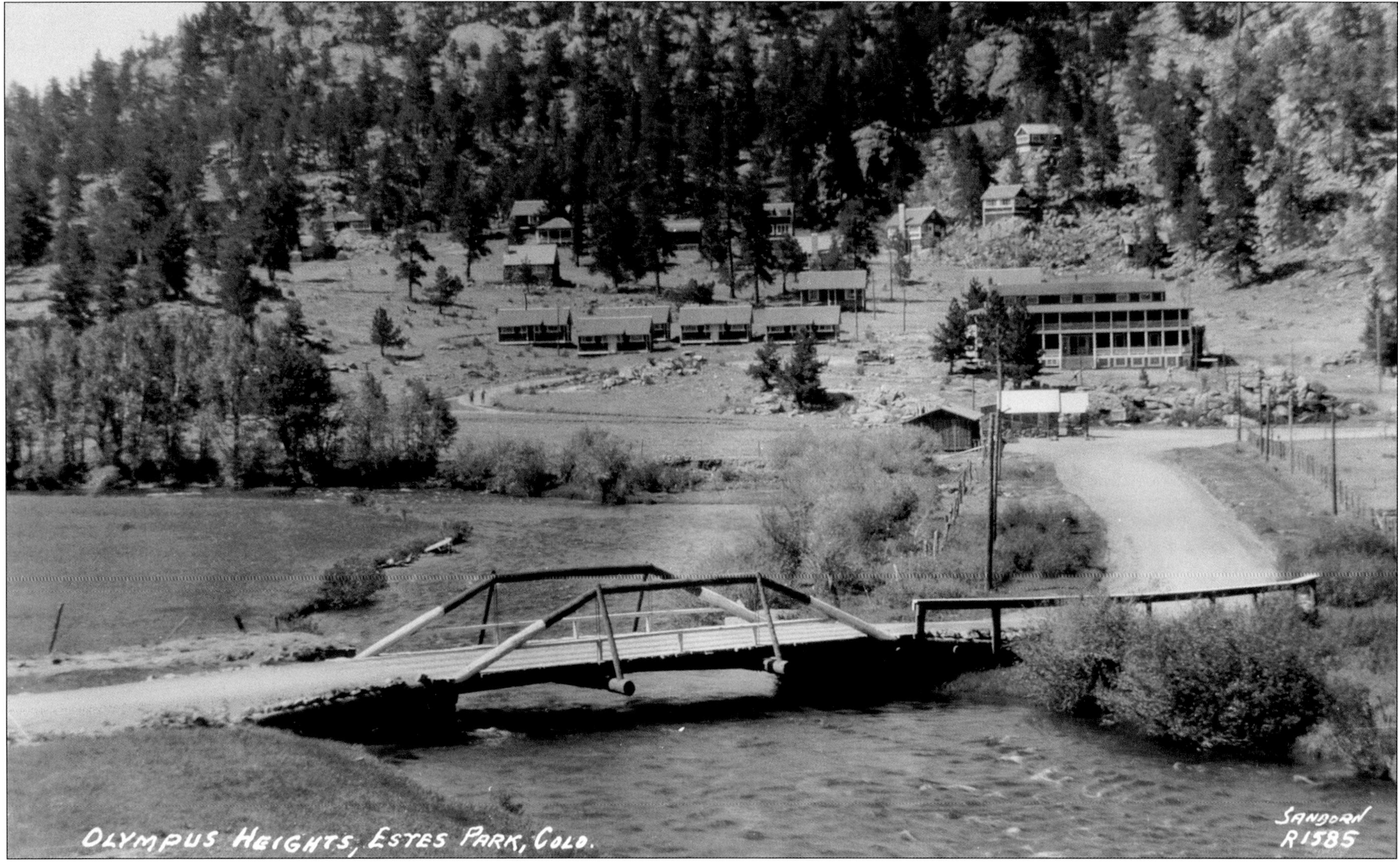

Photo by Sanborn Souvenir Company

Named for nearby 8,800-foot Mount Olympus, Olympus Lodge was the result of a group of Greeley educators who wanted to offer summer extension courses through the Colorado State Teacher's College at Greeley (today's University of Northern Colorado). Organizing in 1921 as the Greeley–Estes Park Outing Club, they purchased land near the entrance to Big Thompson Canyon for $10,000 to make that dream a reality. The lodge and cottages, visible in the original photograph, were built in 1923.

When summer school was in session, the lodge building served as headquarters, the cottages as student dormitories. Before and after summer school, Camp Olympus, as it was then known, was open to the tourist public, advertising itself as a "Delightful Inn and Pleasant Cottages." Several Greeley faculty members built cottages on the adjacent hillside.

As the contemporary photograph suggests, Olympus Lodge has changed its appearance considerably. In the mid-1930s, it lost much of its original seclusion

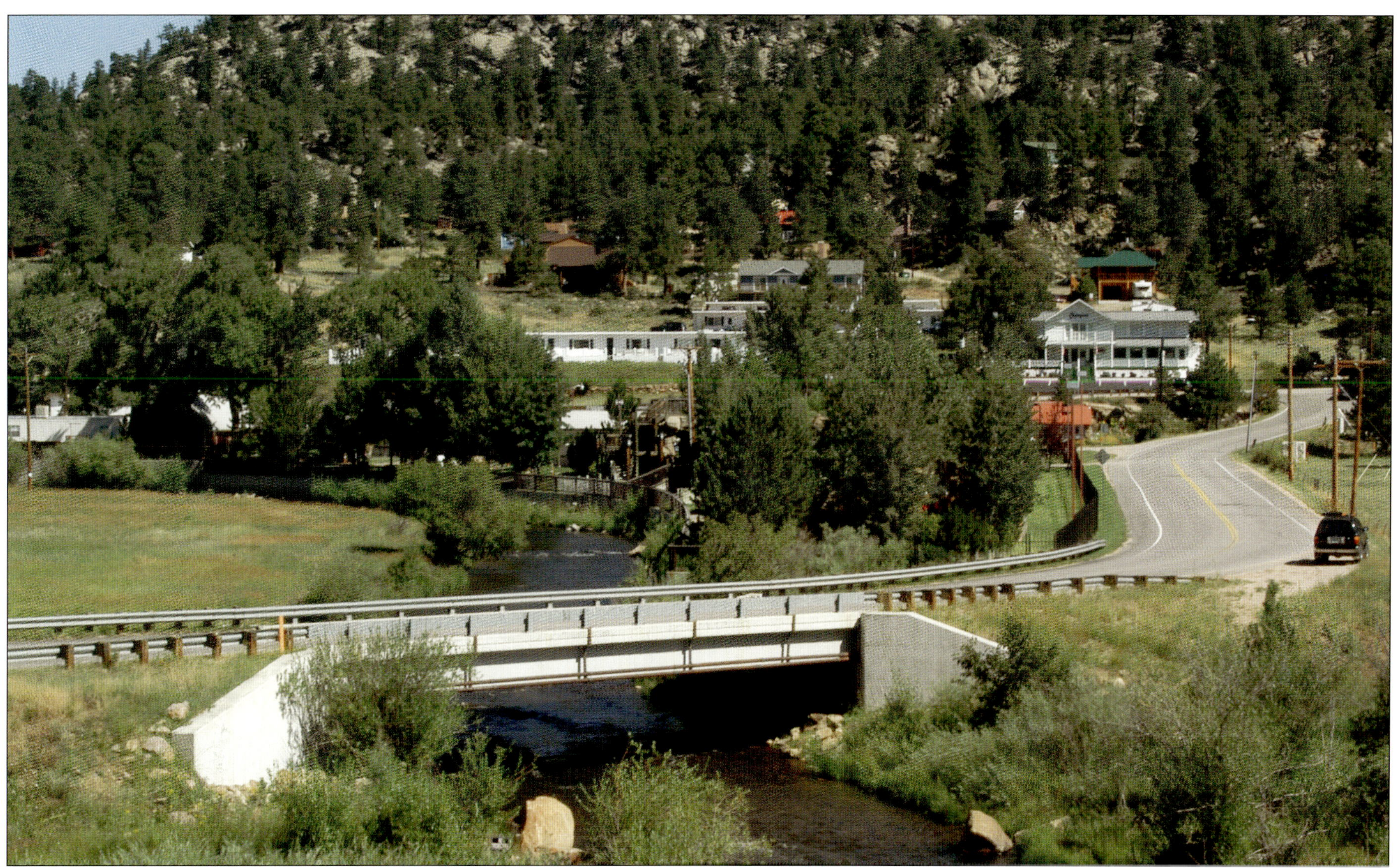

when what is now US 34 was rerouted directly in front of the lodge building. (Note how the highway now passes east–west above the small stone building immediately below the hotel, rather than below it, as it originally did.) The lodge building itself changed dramatically in 1951–1952, when new owners not only removed the third floor, but moved both kitchen and dining room from the first to the second floor to improve a view that had recently been affected by the construction of nearby Olympus Dam. It was at this time that the 12-unit motel (visible in the current photograph) and seven two-bedroom cottages were added. What has not substantially changed, however, even with the completion of the Colorado–Big Thompson Project, is the location of the bridge that crosses the Big Thompson River.

56. Crocker Ranch, circa 1900

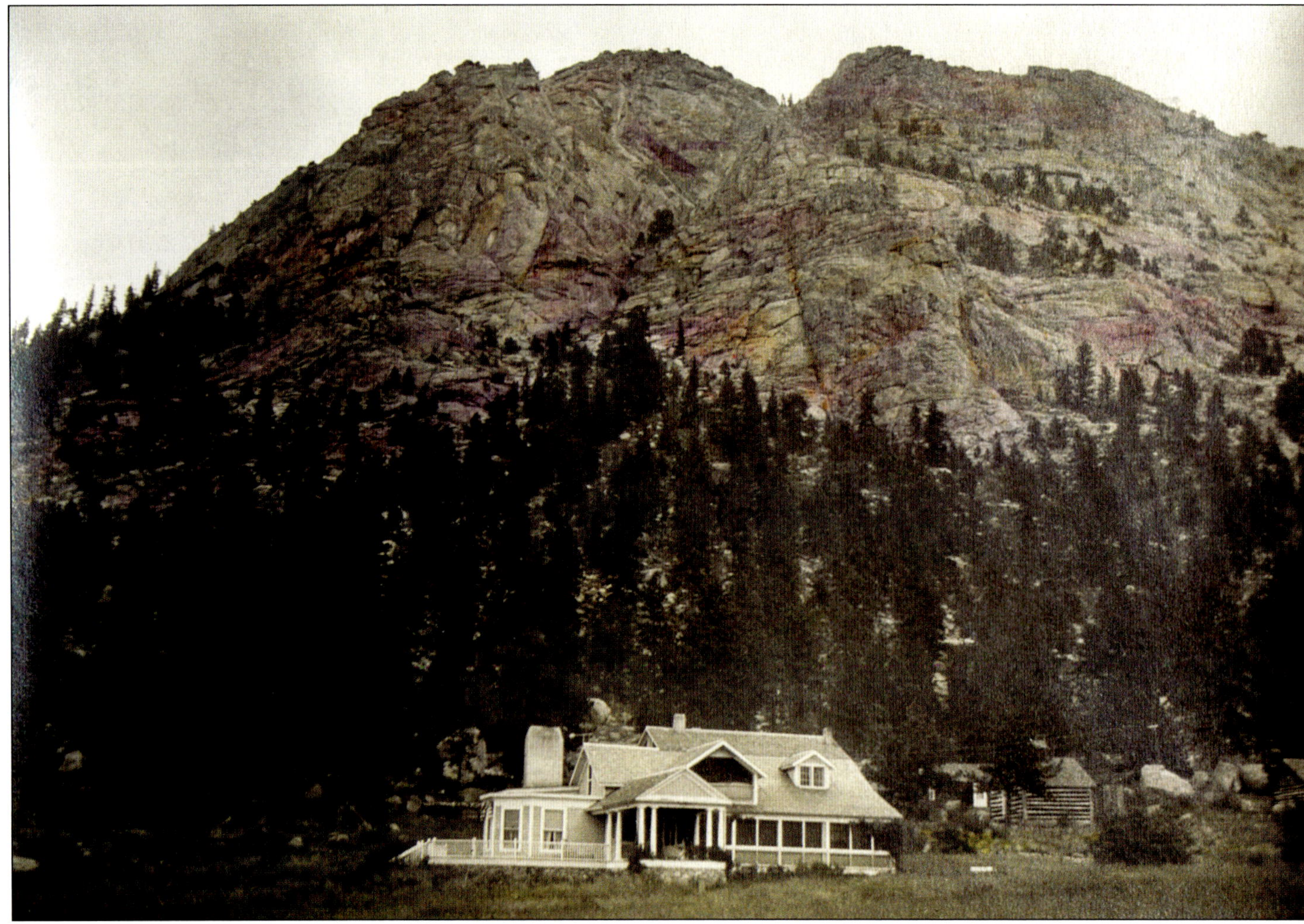

Photo by Albin Drott

The Crocker ranch, named for former owner Frank Crocker, lies in the valley below Mount Olympus and Park Hill. The property was first homesteaded by pioneer Israel Rowe. In 1877, Rowe built a log house on the property, where he raised a herd of cattle. In 1888, he sold his Mount Olympus Ranch, as it was then known, to New York's John Stuyvesant, who built a substantial new house for himself near the old Rowe cabin. In 1899, Stuyvesant's widow sold the property to Frank Crocker, whose cracker factory on Denver's Blake Street built in 1881 and now on the National Register of Historic Places, would eventually be acquired by the National Biscuit Company, making him a wealthy man.

Crocker made Estes Park his summer home until his death in 1932. His only daughter, Helene, married Arthur E. Pew of Philadelphia, the son of the founder of the Sun Oil Company. Following the death of Frank Crocker's widow, the ranch was subdivided and given to two of Helene's sons. Walter Crocker Pew received the "upper ranch" at the base of Mount Olympus. His brother, Arthur Edmund Pew Jr., got the "lower ranch" in Muggins Gulch, which was subsequently known as the Meadowdale Ranch (today's Harvest House). In the 1930s, the upper ranch was used to raise purebred Percheron draft horses.

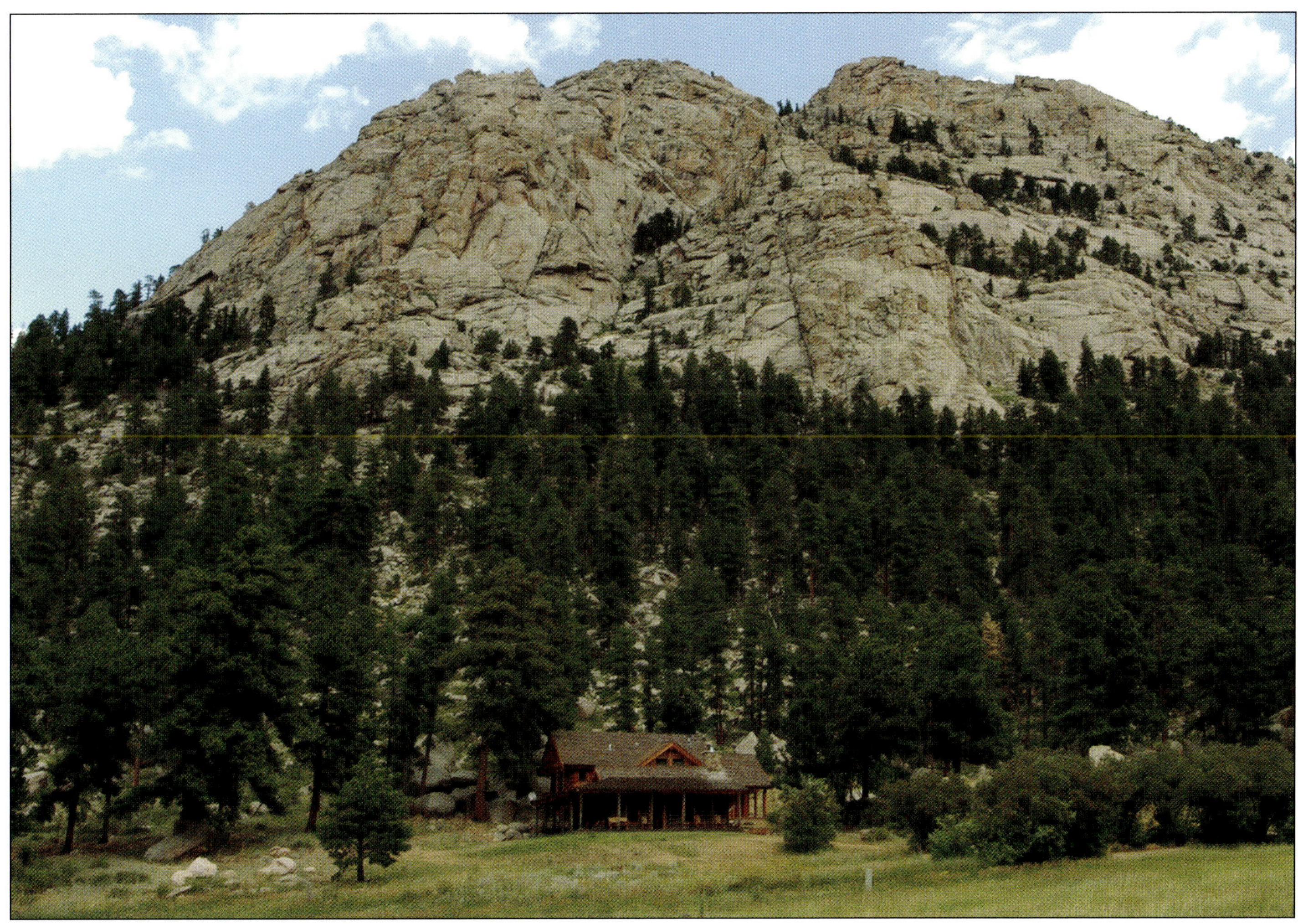

The Crocker ranch has other historical associations as well, for it was through the ranch property that Alexander MacGregor's original toll road of 1875 entered the Estes Valley. Its traces are still visible on ranch property, though Frank Crocker had the upper portion blasted to ensure privacy. The Crocker ranch remains today in private hands with a number of its historic buildings intact and well preserved.

The original photograph, taken about 1900, shows the house built by John Stuyvesant as subsequently remodeled and enlarged by Frank Crocker. To the rear of the house, though not visible in the photograph, is the homestead cabin of Israel Rowe from 1877. To the right are several of the ranch's outbuildings, including the blacksmith shop. The Stuyvesant-Crocker house was significantly damaged by rains accompanying the Big Thompson flood of July 1976 and has been removed, as the contemporary photograph indicates. What is visible in its place is Israel Rowe's original nine-room house, which has been modernized by the recent owners.

57. Estes Park Chalets, circa 1925

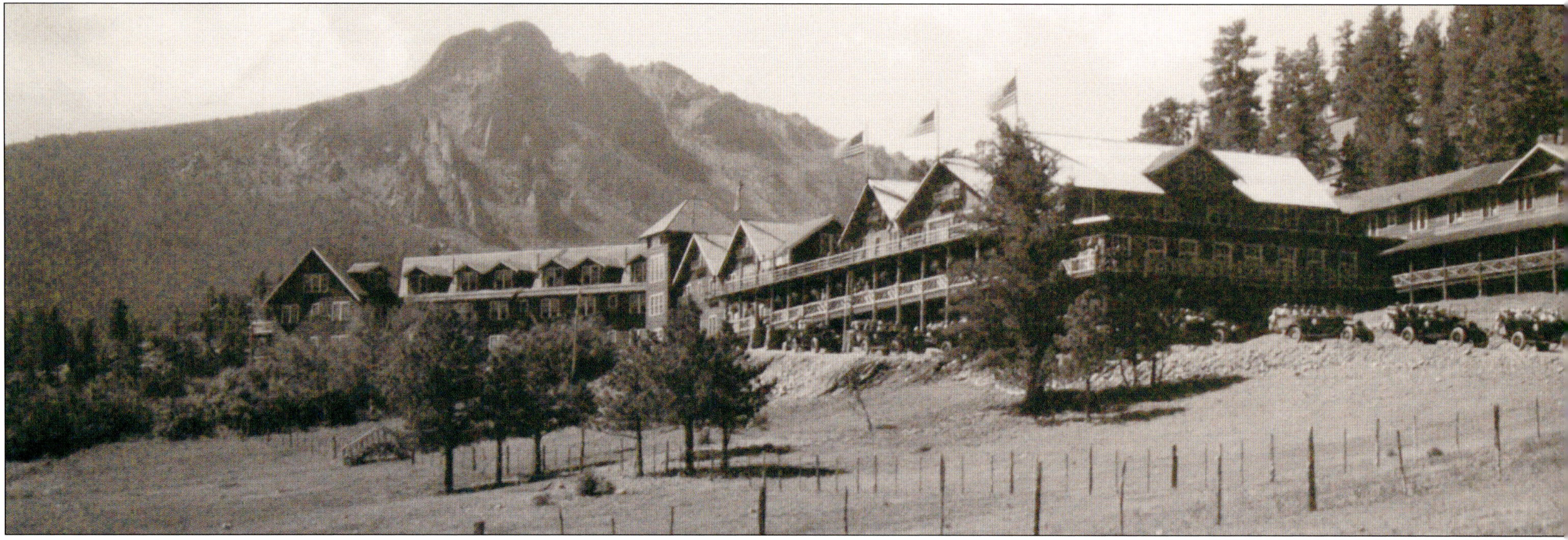

Photo by Fred Payne Clatworthy

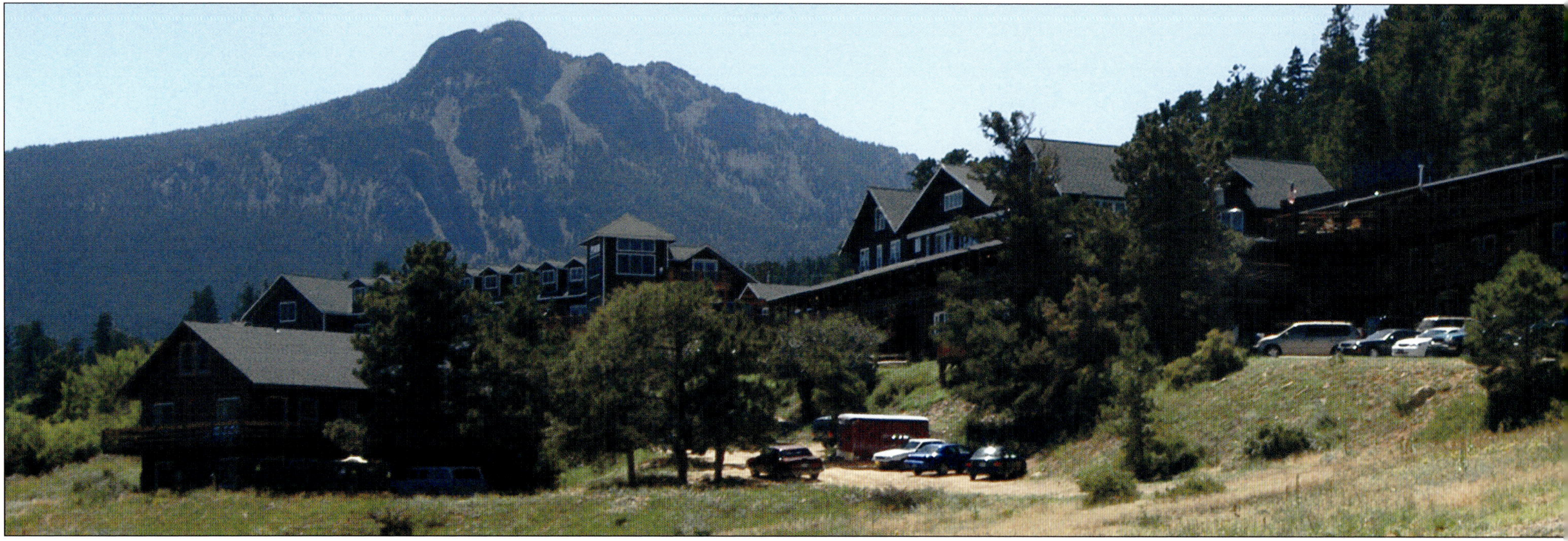

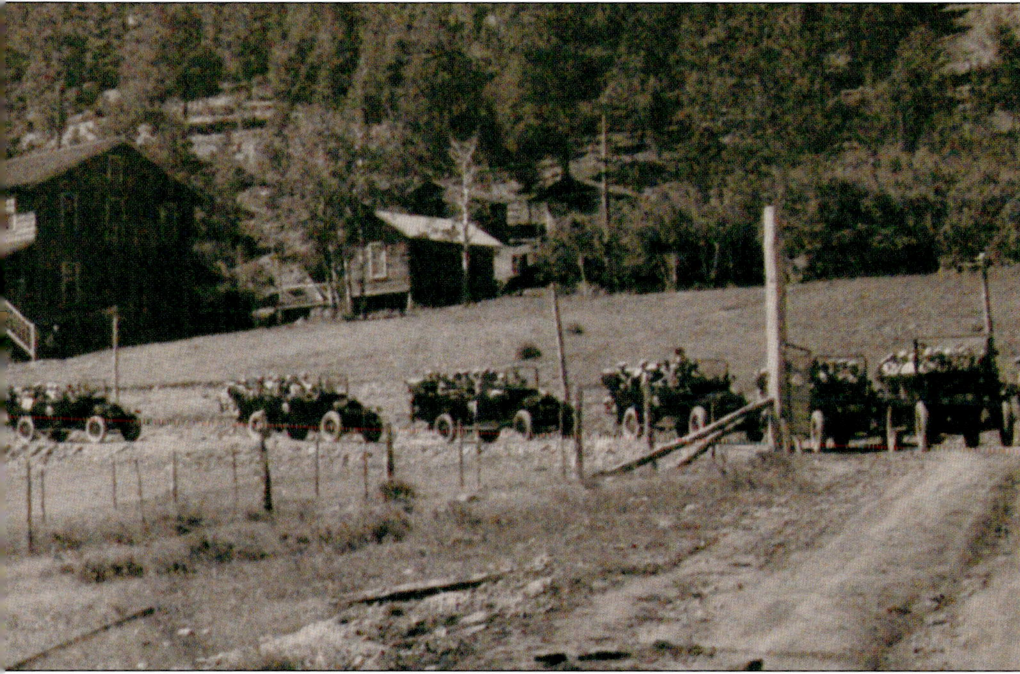

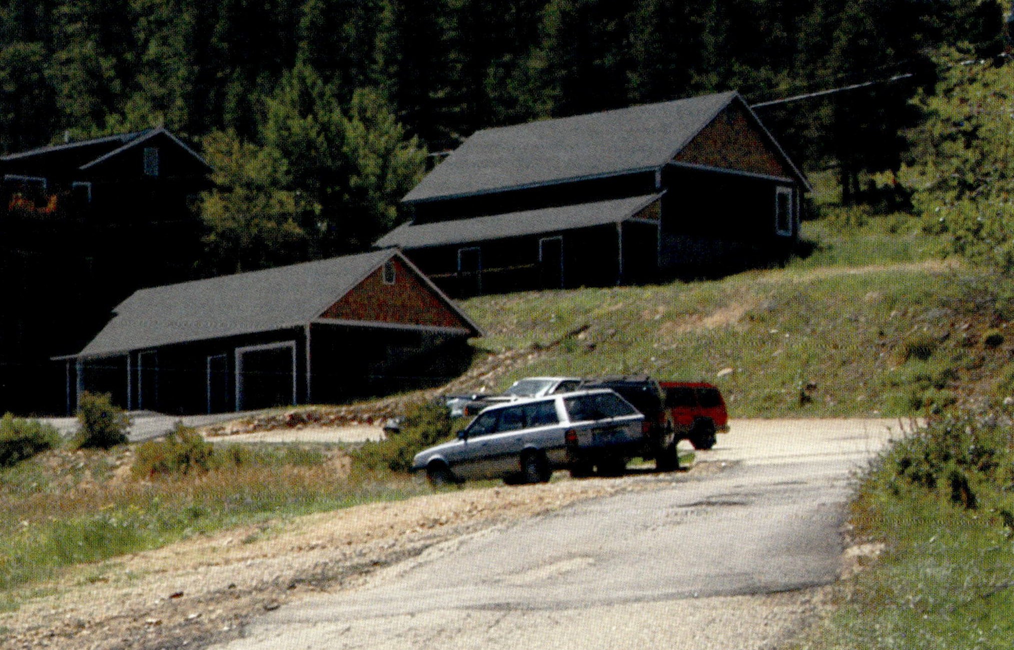

The Estes Park Chalets, the resort we know today as Marys Lake Lodge, began as the Rockdale Cottages, opened after the turn of the 20th century by John and Mary (Hupp) Jones, who had homesteaded south and east of Marys Lake. Their son-in-law, Charles Robbins, and his partner, Clarence Nevins, purchased the property and in 1913 added a small hotel.

The Rockdale was sold in 1915 to Claude Verry, who operated it through the 1919 season. That winter a windstorm greatly damaged the hotel. The site was then purchased by Estes Park hotel man A. D. "Gus" Lewis, who built an enlarged hotel, the Lewiston Chalets, which made use of Western-style Stick architecture and incorporated this style into the central structure of the old Rockdale Hotel.

In 1923, the chalets were sold to Roe Emery and his Rocky Mountain Parks Transportation Company. Emery renamed the hotel Estes Park Chalets, and then expanded its facilities so that it could handle some 300 guests, many of whom arrived on one of his popular Circle Tours, which brought visitors from Denver to Rocky Mountain National Park and over the new Fall River Road. (Emery's White Motor buses and the greatly expanded lodge are clearly visible in the original photograph.) When Emery retired in 1952, the hotel and other company assets, including Grand Lake Lodge, were sold to Ted and Isaac James, two other transportation pioneers. During the 1970s, the Estes Park Chalets' rooms were converted into condominiums. Then, on July 6, 1978, fire destroyed the hotel's south wing.

In recent years, new owners have brought the old lodge back to life, rebuilding the south wing and refurbishing the lounge, parlors, and dining rooms. In the 1980s, the Estes Park Chalets was given its present name, Marys Lake Lodge. It is now on the Colorado State Register of Historic Properties.

58. Ferguson's Highlands Hotel, circa 1885

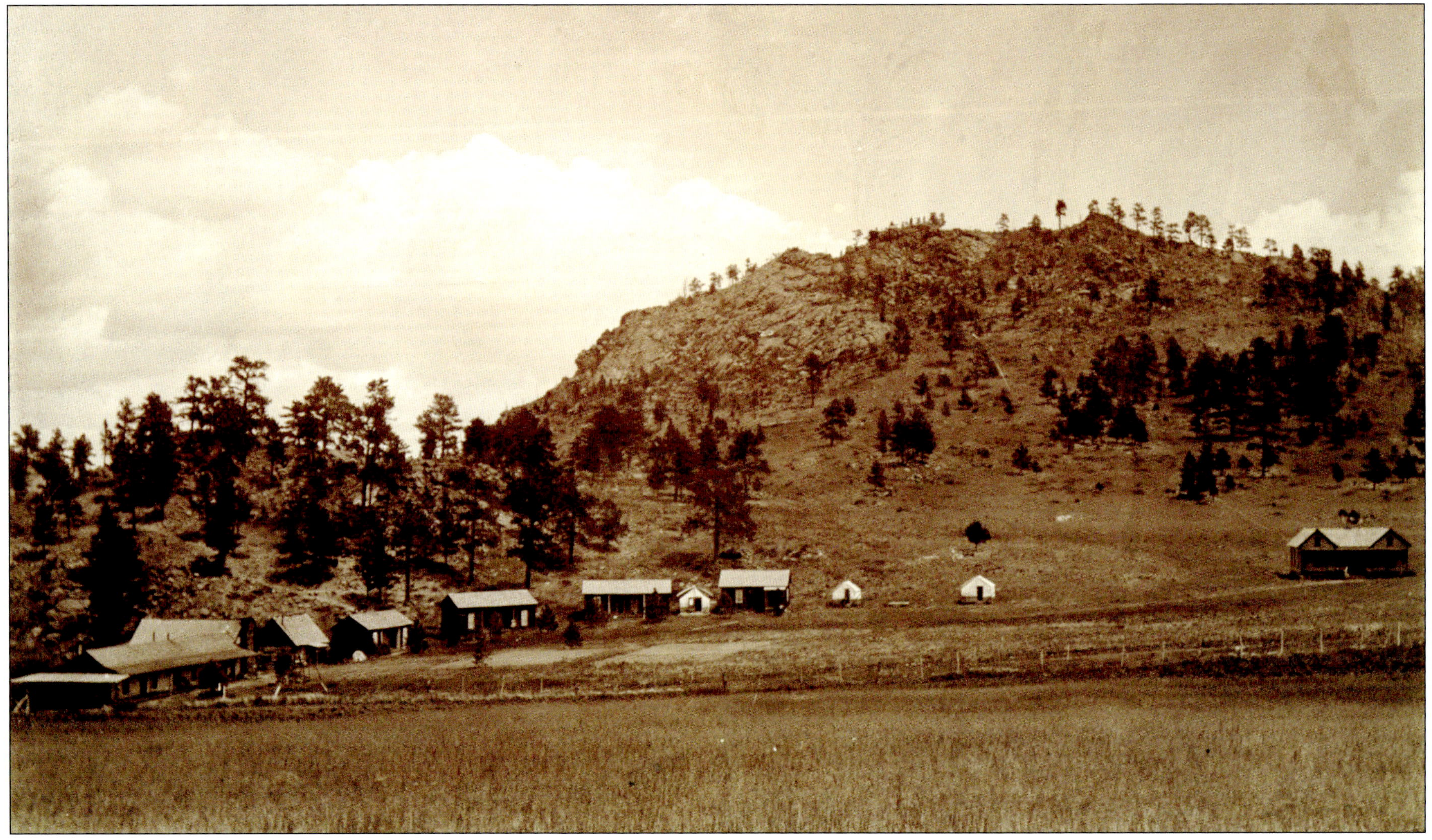

In 1875, Horace Ferguson, a Kentucky native who had been living in Evans, Colorado, south of Greeley, brought his family to a two-room, mud-chinked, dirt-roofed cabin northwest of Marys Lake, on land with a fine natural spring. As was often the case in early Estes Park, his homestead cabin evolved into a summer resort. By 1878, a kitchen and dining hall had been attached to the main building and the Fergusons could accommodate 60 guests in their five three-room log cabins and tent houses. The family called their rustic resort the "Highlands," because Horace Ferguson maintained that his ancestors could be traced back to Scotland's first monarch, King Fergus.

Connecticut druggist Frederick H. Chapin used the Highlands as his base of operations during his visits of the 1880s, taking early photographs of the resort. "From the cabins around Ferguson's ranch," he wrote, "a magnificent view is obtained of the great Mummy Range; and the sunset lights on the cliffs of Lily [Twin Sisters] Mountain, to the east, are indescribably beautiful."

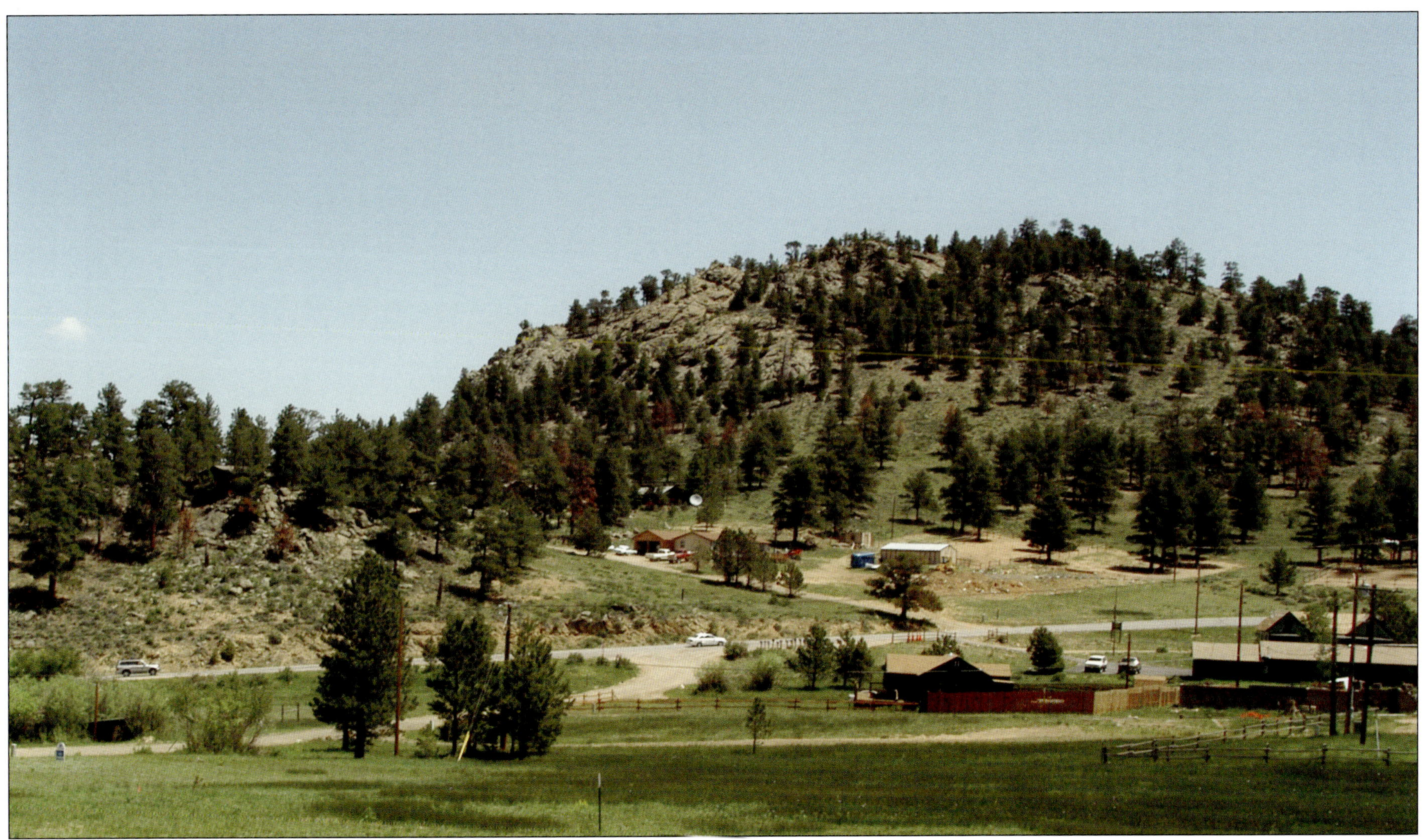

In 1881, William L. Hallett, an MIT graduate who had left engineering for ranching, built the Victorian gingerbread house shown here on three acres that Ferguson provided, and named it "Edgemont." The original road to Marys Lake, visible in the photograph, passed directly in front of the Hallett house. Hallett soon became an adept mountaineer, and he guided Chapin on many of the climbs recorded in Chapin's 1889 book, *Mountaineering in Colorado: The Peaks About Estes Park*.

Only the footings for the chimney of one of the original buildings remain to mark the Highlands' location. The spring that brought the Fergusons to the site, however, is still in evidence. So is Edgemont. Its dormers and roof are clearly visible in the contemporary photograph.

59. Baldpate Inn, circa 1922

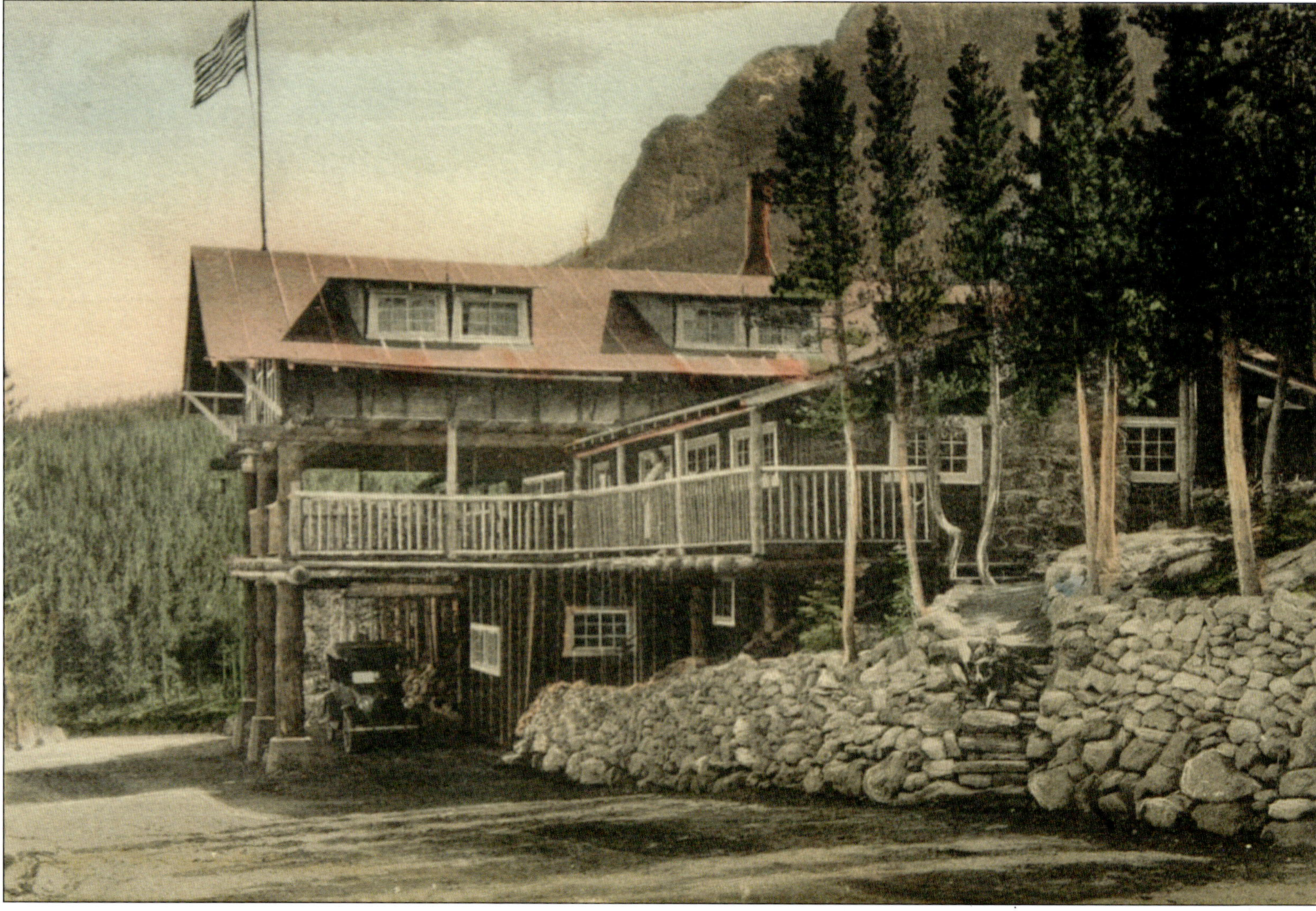

Photo by Fred Payne Clatworthy

Overlooking the Estes Valley, Baldpate Inn was built and opened in 1917 on the northern slope of Twin Sisters Mountain by English-born Gordon Mace and his wife Ethel. Together with Gordon's photographer brother, Charles Mace, they had homesteaded the land three years earlier. Using hand-hewn lumber from their own property, Gordon Mace did much of the construction work on the original three-story central wing, and employed popular Western-style Stick architecture—with its characteristic wood siding, gabled roof (compatible with heavy winter snows), wide overhanging eaves, and projecting porch—to achieve intimacy with the natural surroundings. Gordon Mace also crafted and built some of the inn's furnishings, including writing desks for the lobby and front porch.

An east wing, containing the dining room, was added in 1918; a two-story west wing was added in stages: the first story in 1921; the second story in 1935.

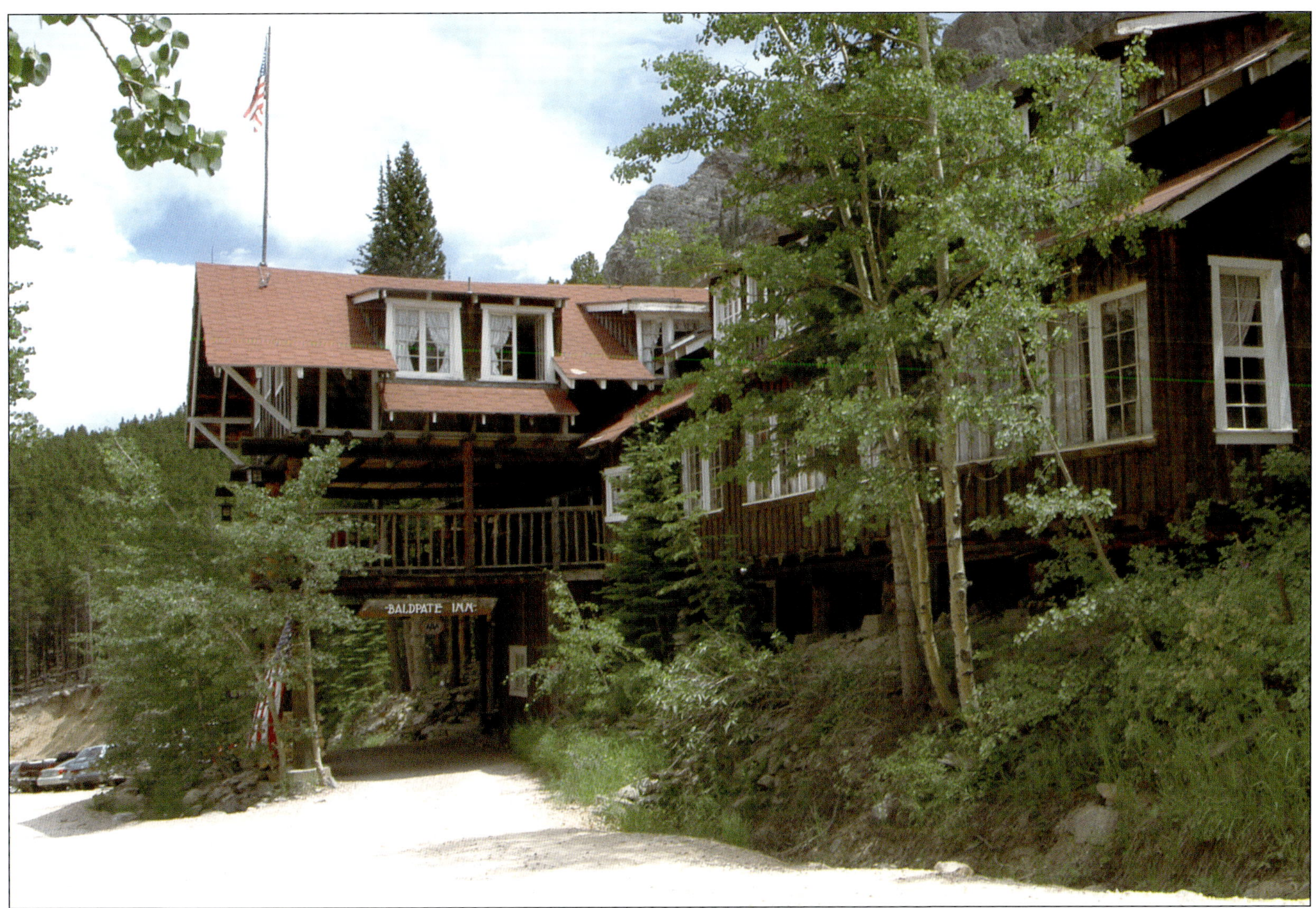

The inn's porte cochere and observation deck originally fronted onto the wagon road that Elkanah and Carlyle Lamb cut through the timber to reach their Longs Peak House in the Tahosa Valley in 1875–1876.

In its heyday, Baldpate Inn consisted of 12 buildings along the sloping hillside below the Mace's one-room homestead cabin. These included the main lodge and four cabins, a dance hall (the "Casino" built in the 1920s, where Harry James, Tommy Dorsey, and other big-name bands once performed), as well as a bathhouse, bunkhouse, icehouse, stable, garage, and horse shed. The inn's second floor contained 21 bedrooms and 12 baths.

The name for the inn, as well as the idea for its famous "Key Room" (shown on p. 154), which now houses thousands of keys from all over the world, came from the title of the 1913 mystery novel *Seven Keys to Baldpate*, by Earl

The "Key Room" of the Baldpate Inn, circa 1940

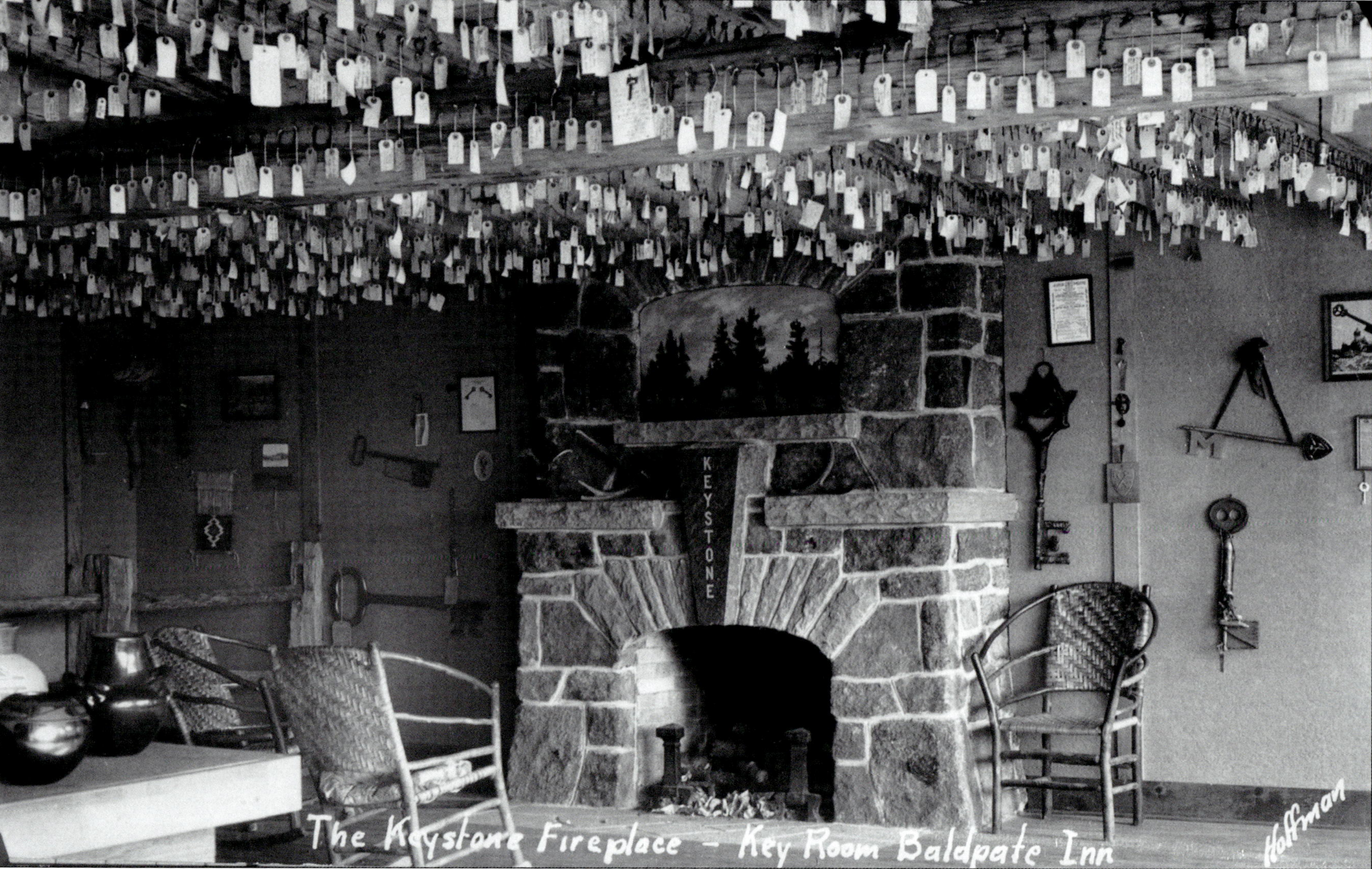

Photo by Hoffman

Derr Biggers which was soon dramatized by George M. Cohan for stage and screen. While the novel and adaptations were not set in Estes Park, they lent the hotel its distinctive name. According to tradition, Biggers, on his way to climb Longs Peak, suggested that the Maces call their new hotel Baldpate Inn.

The key room began when, instead of giving departing guests a small set of keys for a souvenir, the Maces suggested that guests might donate keys of their own. Still decorating the inn today, the collection includes keys from such varied places as the Philadelphia Mint, Westminster Abbey, Buckingham Palace,

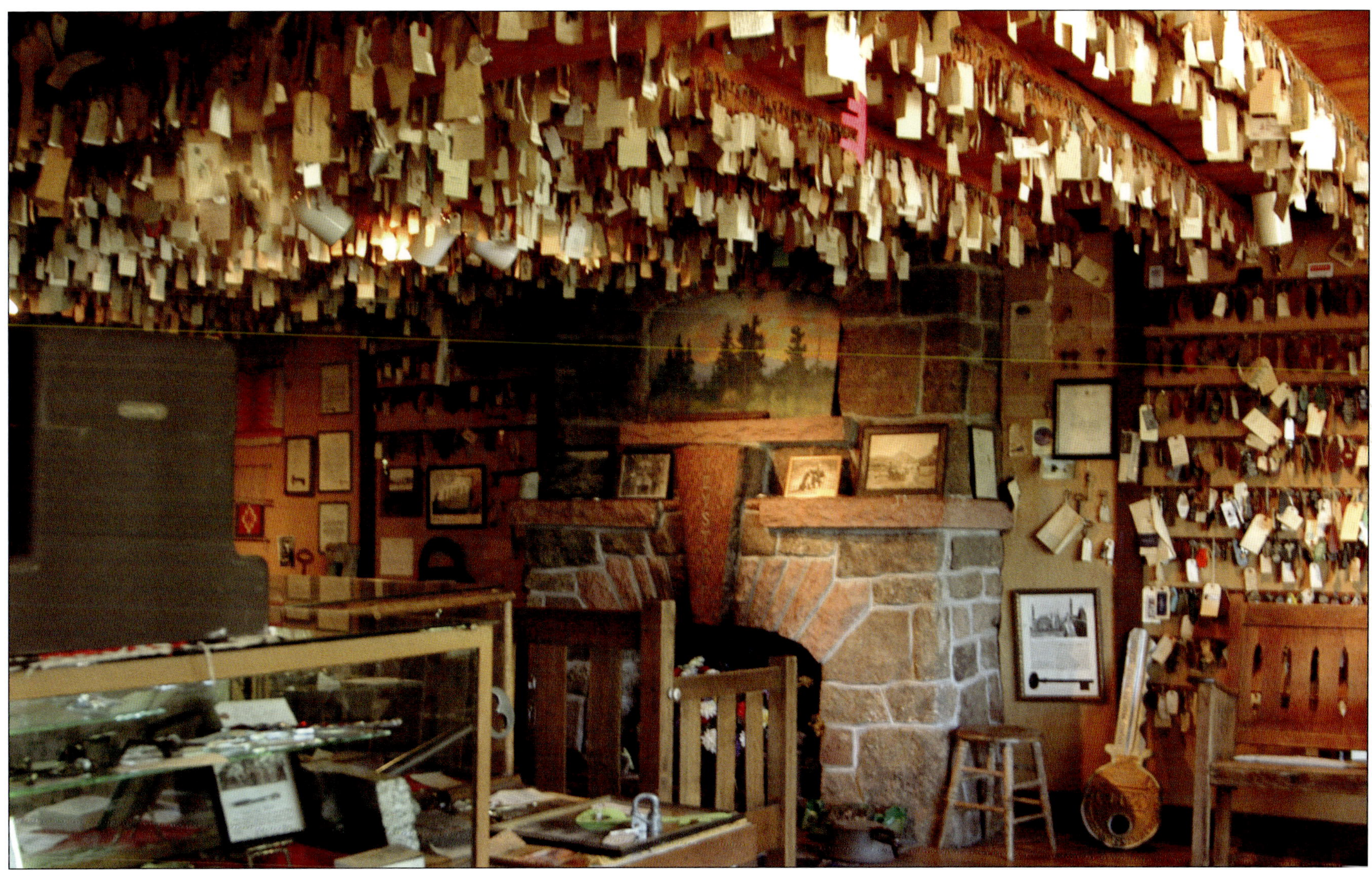

Mozart's wine cellar, Frankenstein's castle, the Nebraska State Capitol Building (new and old), and the first bank in Kentucky robbed by Frank and Jesse James. In 1923, Earl Derr Biggers himself presented the Maces with a key. Its inscription read: "This is the original key to Baldpate. All others are imitation." In keeping with the theme, seven wooden posts with a diminishing number of keys were installed at 1-mile intervals between Estes Park and the inn.

Baldpate Inn is now a bed and breakfast serving lunch and dinner. In 1996, it was entered in the National Register of Historic Places.

60. Wind River Ranch, circa 1910

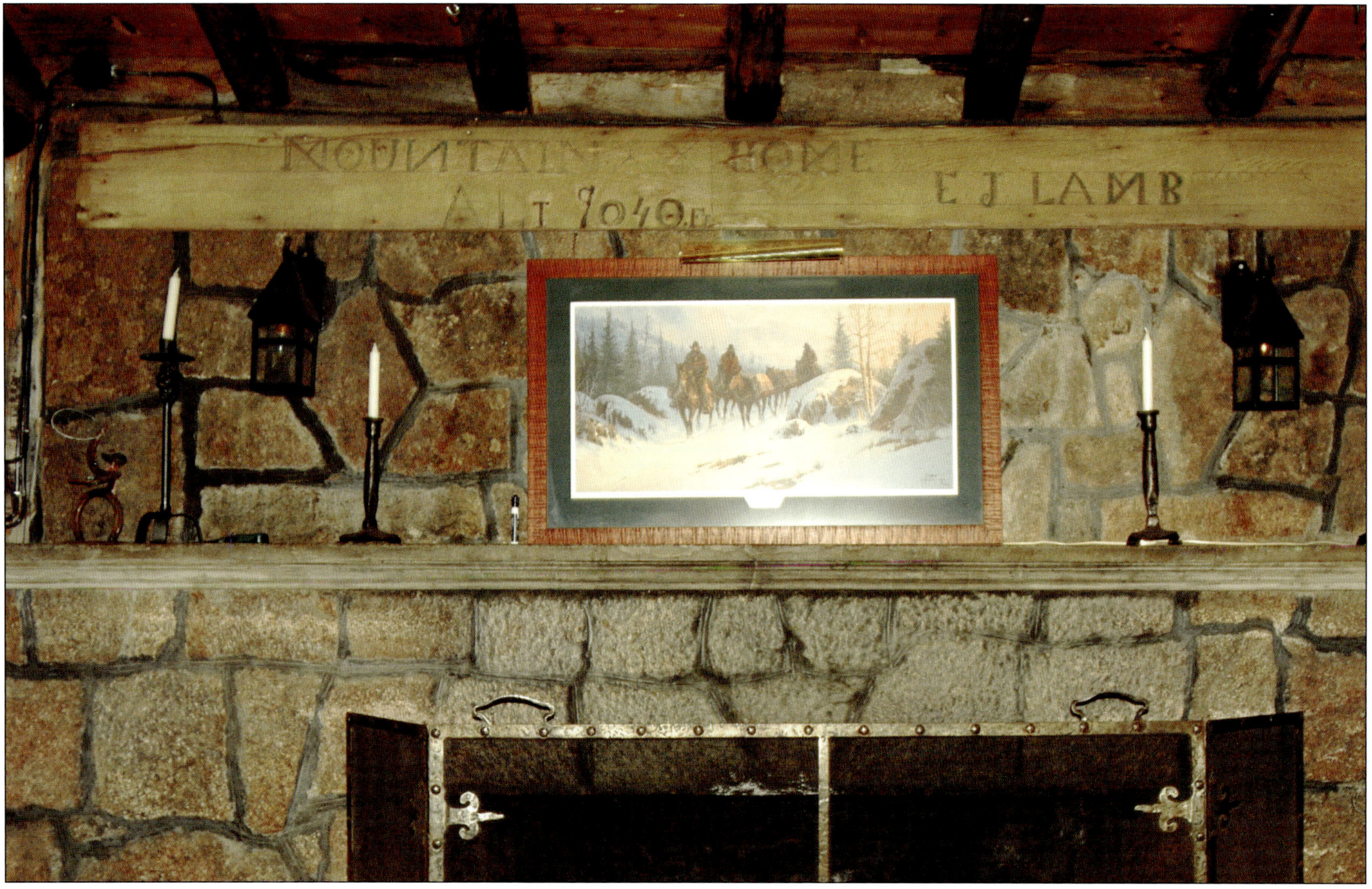

Wind River Ranch, at the northern end of the Tahosa Valley ("Tahosa" is a Kiowa word meaning "dwellers of the mountaintop"), began as the 1878 homestead property of the Reverend Elkanah J. Lamb, an itinerant minister for the Church of the United Brethren. The Lamb family also homesteaded land just to the south, at the base of Longs Peak. These original buildings were expanded and became Longs Peak House, a popular overnight way station for those bound for the peak (see p. 164). On their 160 acres at the head of Wind River (then known as "Lamb's Notch"), Lamb and his wife Jane built the two-story house (rephotographed here) and an adjacent barn, which they used for a small dairying and stock-raising operation. A larger barn, the one shown here in our contemporary photograph, was built in the late 1890s. In 1902, after their son Carlyle sold Longs Peak House to Enos A. Mills, the elder Lambs made Wind River their

Longs Peak from Wind River Ranch

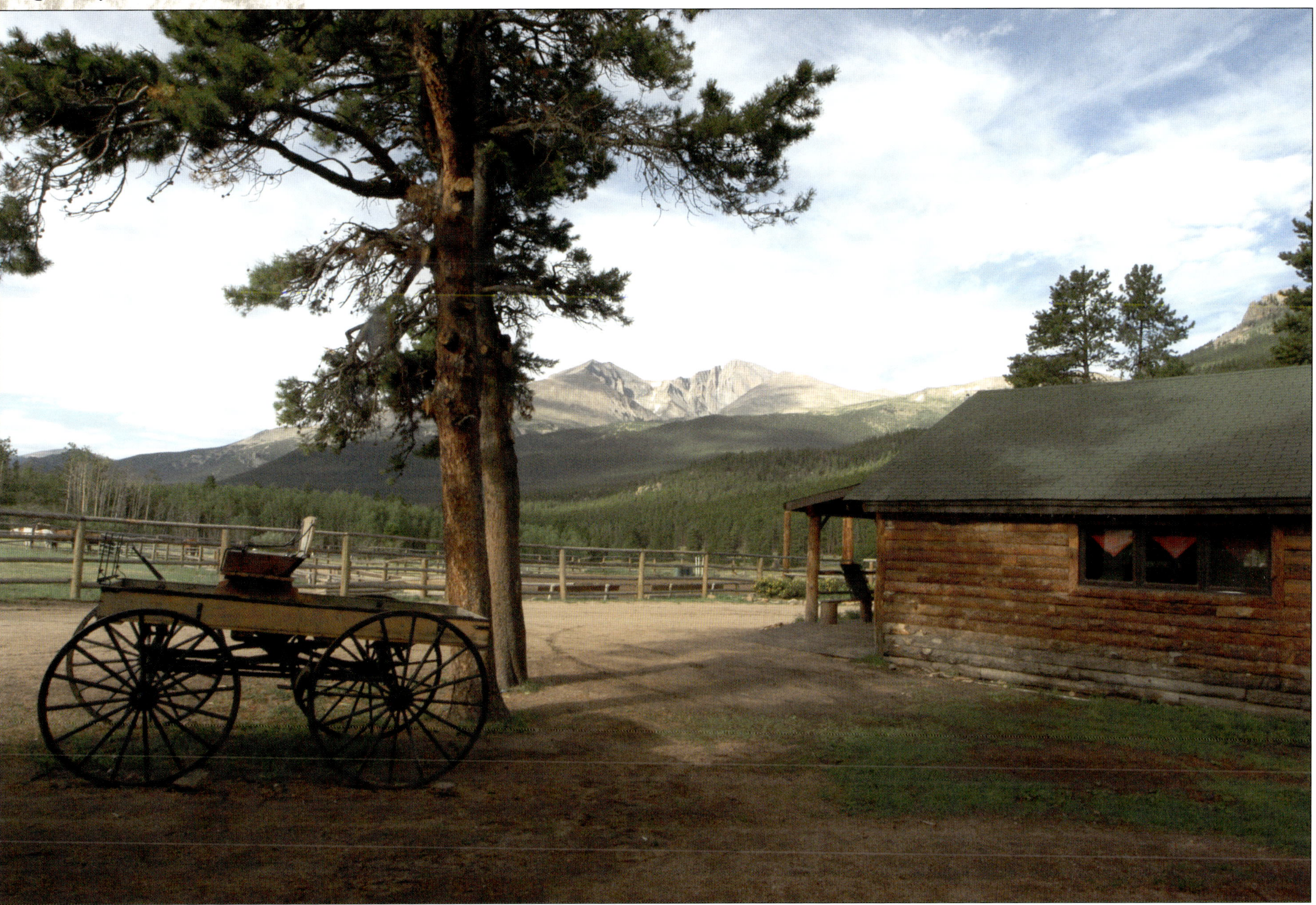

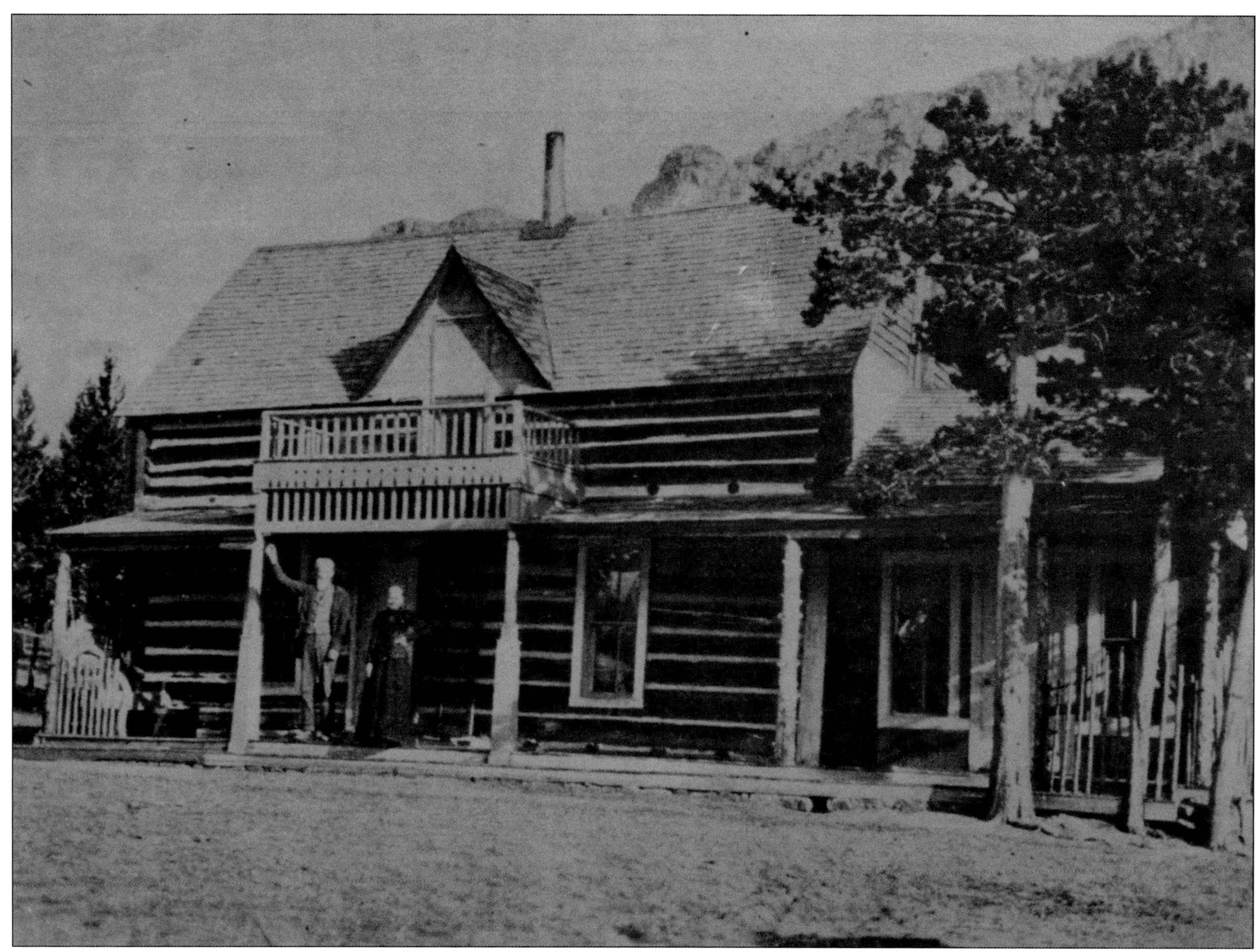

home, erecting a simple sign over the entrance gate that read "Mountain Home." That sign, reclaimed by friends and neighbors, was subsequently returned to Wind River Ranch, where today, as our first photo shows, it sits in a place of honor above the fireplace in the ranch library.

In 1911, the Lambs sold the property to John and Mary Belle King Sherman. John Dickinson Sherman, a prominent newspaperman, had come out from Chicago for reasons of health and decided to stay. It was while living at Wind River that Mary Belle King Sherman launched her career as a lobbyist for conservation through the General Federations of Women's Clubs. It would earn her the title "National Park Lady." The ranch was sold again in 1924, this time to Chicago doctor James Gay and his wife Bessy, who built seven cabins for use by family members and expanded the property to 525 acres by purchasing land

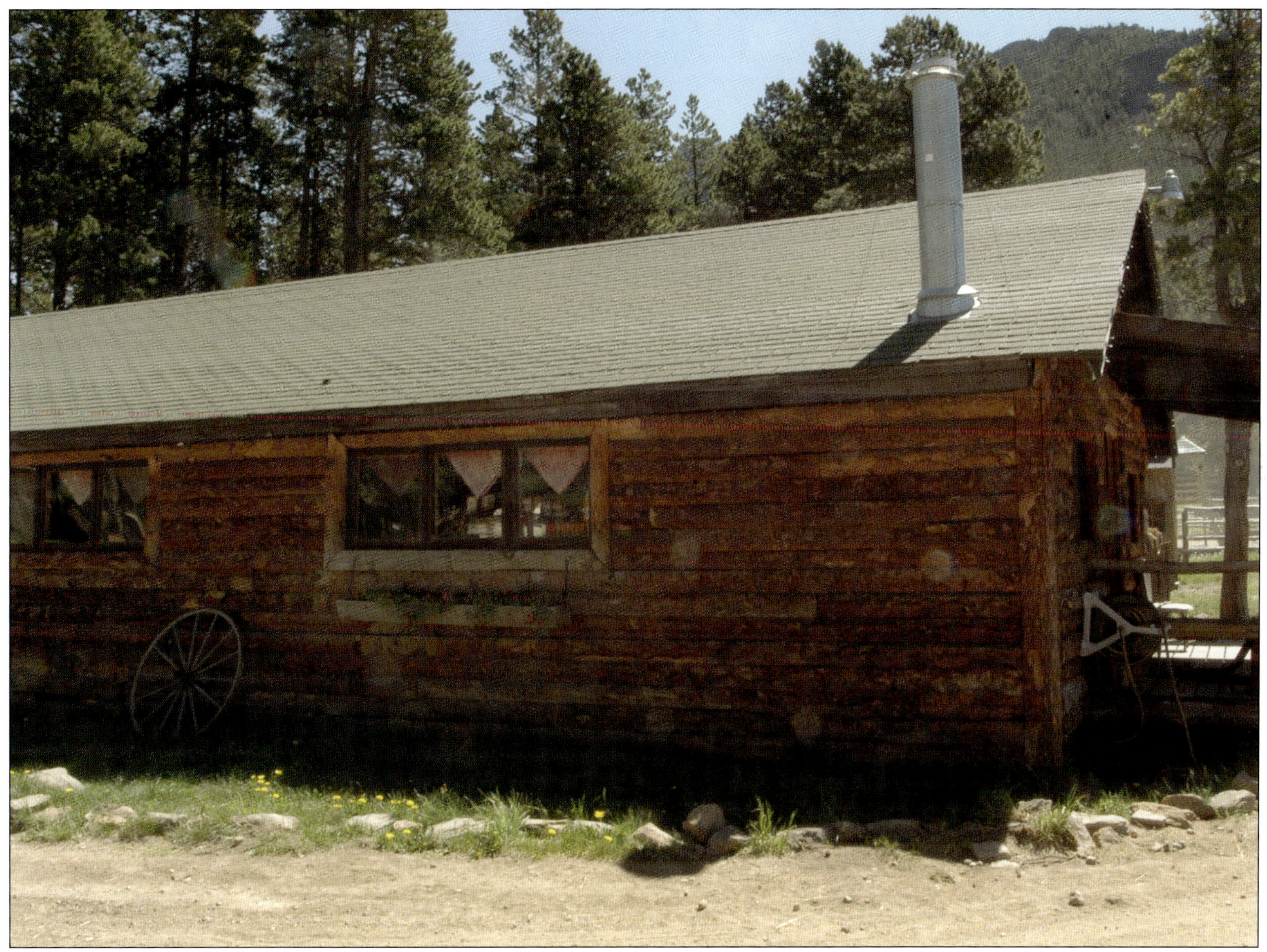

on both sides of today's Highway 7. Although it was the Gays' daughter and her husband who first began taking in paying guests, Wind River Ranch, as the property was by then known, did not become a full-fledged dude ranch until 1944, when it was purchased by the Robert Hutchinson family. The Hutchinsons expanded the number of cabins, built a recreation hall (photographed above), making use of the stone fireplace that had been part of the Lambs' "Mountain Home," and for nearly 30 years made Wind River one of the most successful and popular guest ranches in the Estes region, a tradition that has been continued by its subsequent owners.

61. Columbine Lodge, circa 1930

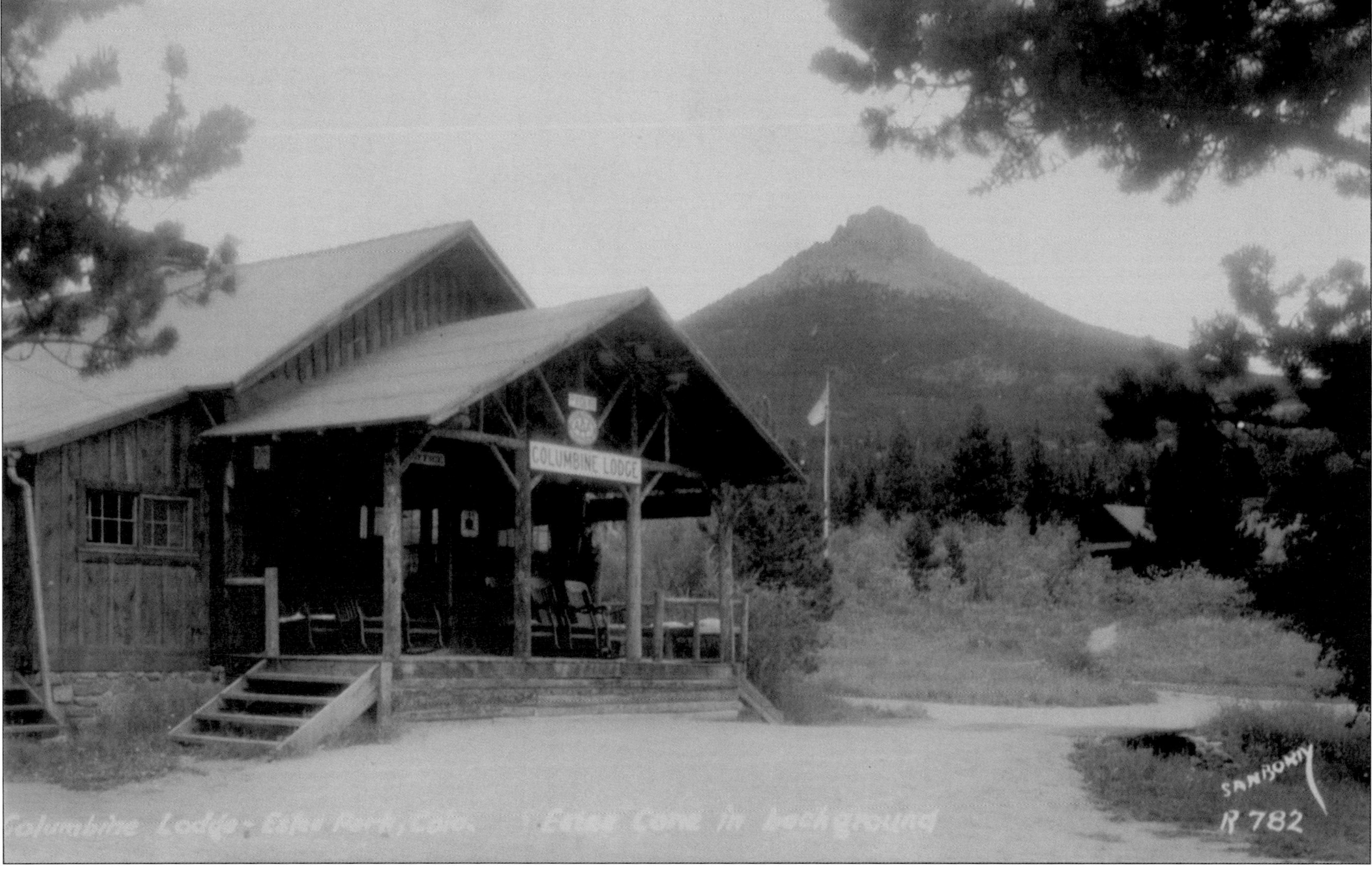

Photo by Sanborn Souvenir Company

Columbine Lodge in the Tahosa Valley, now called High Peak Camp and owned and operated by the Salvation Army–Intermountain Division, was built about 1908 by Harry Bitner, a former attorney from Michigan. It was sold in July 1913 to Edwin Gillette, who owned property and a summer home nearby. Three years later, in 1916, the Columbine was leased and then sold once again, this time to Charles H. Alexander, an experienced hotel man, who successfully operated the Columbine until 1944.

In its heyday, the Columbine Lodge consisted of a main lodge (or "Reception Hall"), a large dining hall, and a series of equally rustic cabins. A lot of the Columbine's charm lay in its picturesque setting, with a brook flowing directly beside the lodge itself. As one early brochure noted, "For those who delight in walking excursions, without hard climbing, a comprehensive system of several miles of picturesque trails has been completed, covering the western slope of Elkanah Valley, starting from 'The Columbines' and leading off, among the trees

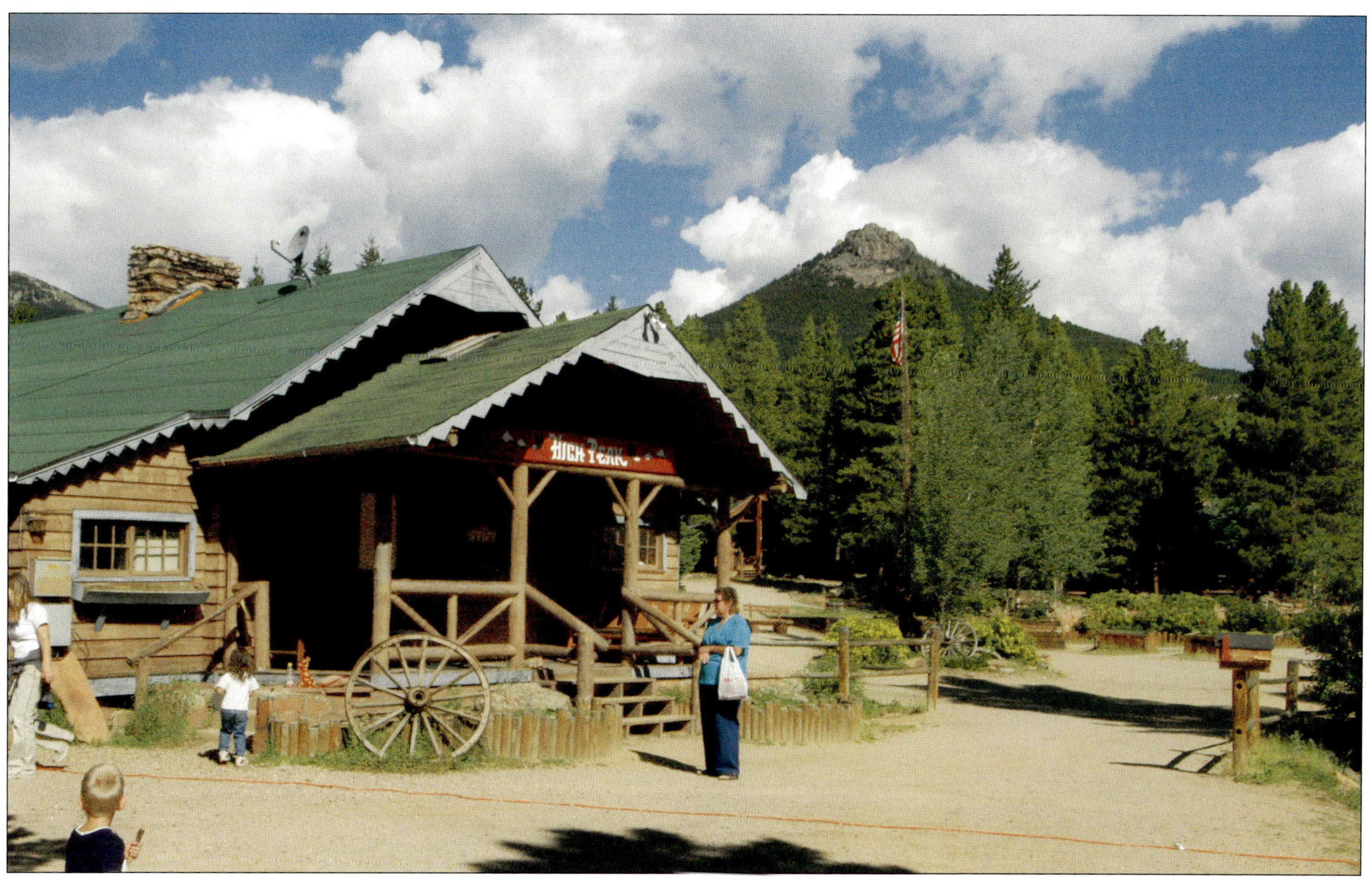

and flowers and along the streams to the Norwall Mine, Lion Gulch, Storm Pass and Estes Cone. On the eastern slope are good trails to the Twin Sisters, Cabin Rock and Peaceful Valley. The Beaver Colonies are within a short walking distance, to the south." The name "Elkanah Valley" refers to an active, if short-lived, attempt in 1915 by the Columbine's then-owner Edwin Gillette and his neighbors to have the valley named after its first resident, the Reverend Elkanah J. Lamb, whose family homesteaded the land that became both Longs Peak Inn (see p. 164) and Wind River Ranch (see p. 156). That name was rejected by the Colorado Geographic Board because of the opposition of another neighbor, Enos A. Mills.

62. Hewes-Kirkwood Inn, August 1937

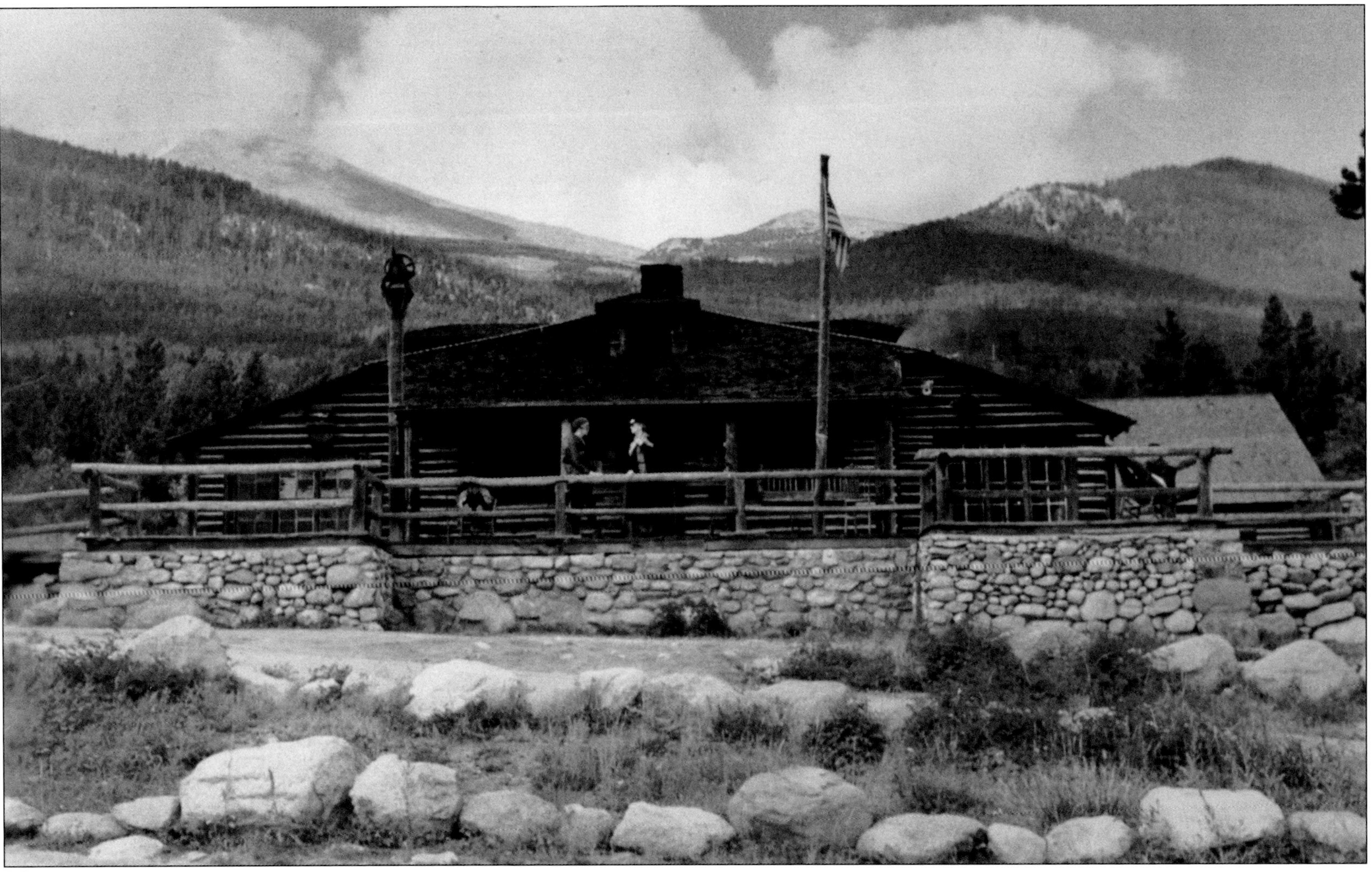

The Hewes-Kirkwood Inn began as Bleak House, the cabin of Mary Kirkwood, the widowed mother of poet-novelist Charles Edwin Hewes and his brother, Steve. In 1907, the family homesteaded 960 acres in the Tahosa Valley, along today's Highway 7, and operated the inn there for four decades.

The brothers first expanded Bleak House in 1913, adding a kitchen and a dining room, and building four single and three double cabins and eight tent houses. The Hewes-Kirkwood Hotel Ranch and Store opened for business on July 4, 1914. Mary Kirkwood took charge of the dining room with the help of her irrepressible maid, Julia Morrissey, while Steve Hewes worked as entertainer and guide, and Charlie Hewes served as "general utility man" and bookkeeper. "I worked like a demon," he recalled of that first summer.

In 1916, six new cabins were added nearby. This was followed in 1917 by a new dining room with an 18-foot ceiling and stone fireplace, giving the Heweses "a pretty complete little hotel," the configuration of which still survives.

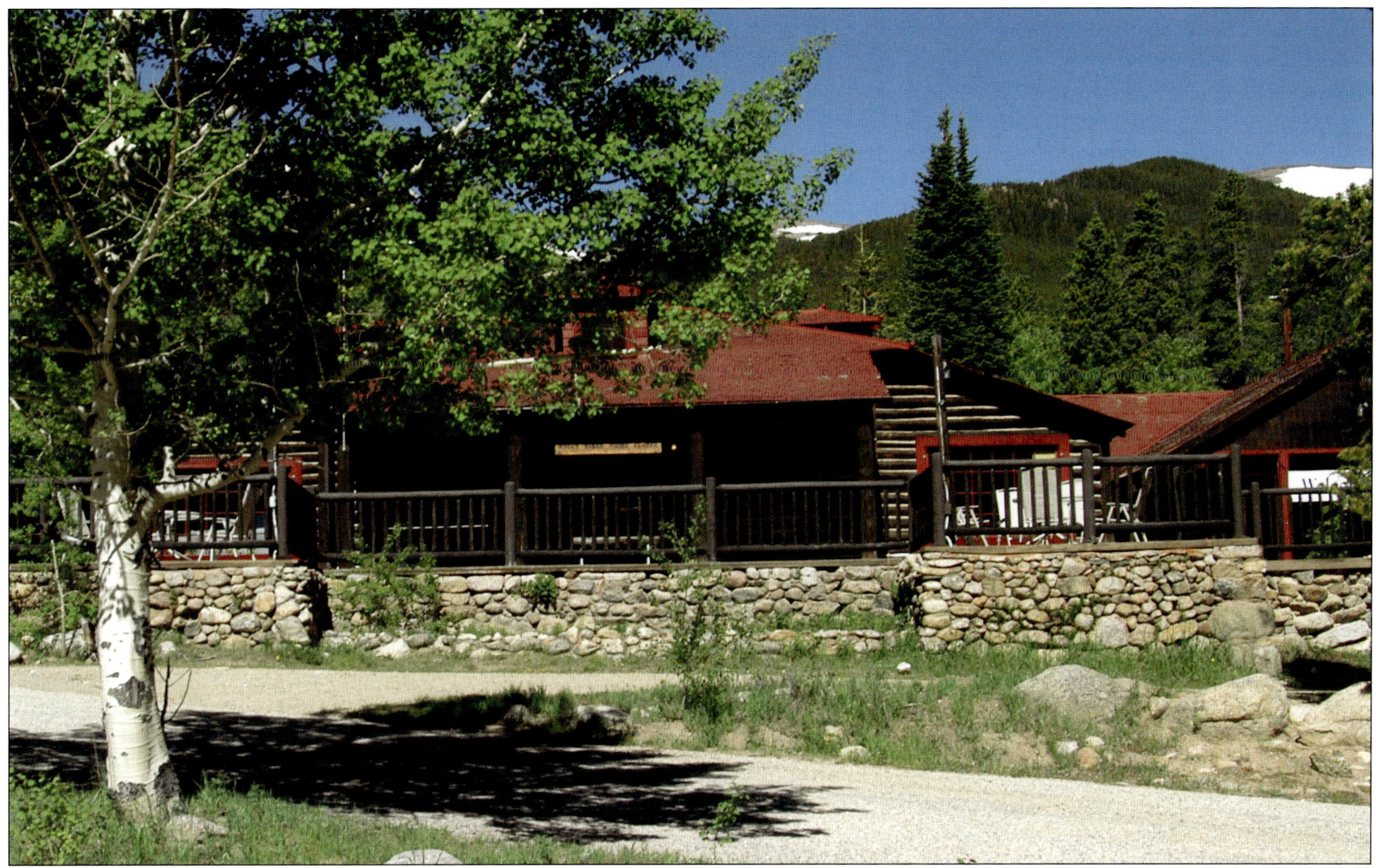

Charlie Hewes operated the inn through the Depression and World War II. In 1945, he sold the ranch to Paul W. Nesbit, a former ranger and mountain guide, with the understanding that he and the ever-loyal Morrissey could keep living there. Charlie Hewes died two years later.

In 1951, Nebraskan Beth Miller Harrod acquired the resort and turned the inn and its remaining 65 acres into Rocky Ridge Music Center, a summer music camp for young musicians. In 1994, Hewes-Kirkwood Inn was entered on the National Register of Historic Places. Mary Kirkwood's 1907 cabin, the 1917 dining room, and a number of original guest cabins have been restored through grants from the Colorado State Historical Fund.

The original photograph was taken in August 1937, and shows the expanded homestead cabin and the 1917 dining room at the rear.

63. Lambs Ranch and Longs Peak Inn, circa 1905

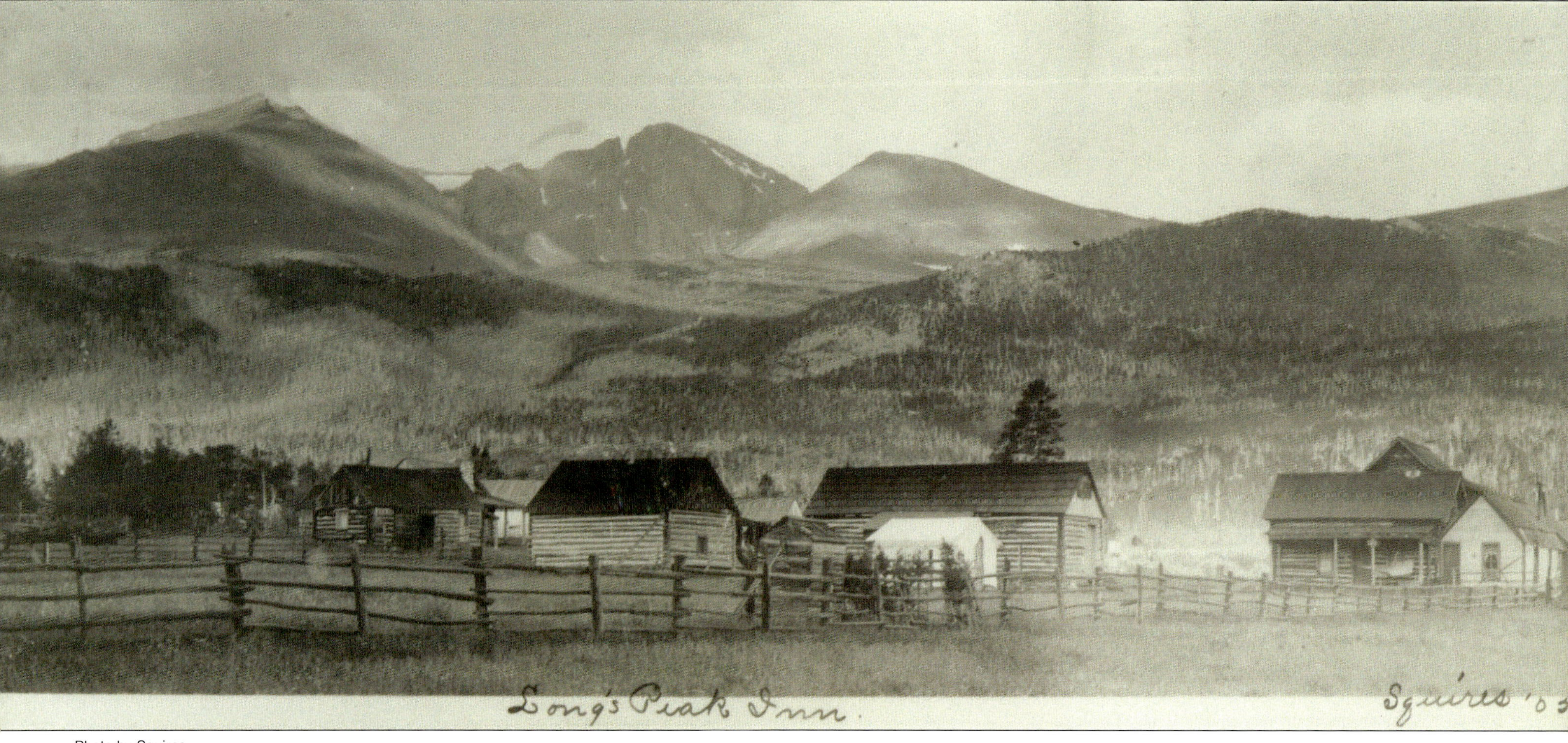

Photo by Squires

Both Lambs Ranch and its successor, the Longs Peak Inn, date from 1875, the year that the Reverend Elkanah J. Lamb, his wife Jane, and son Carlyle homesteaded at the base of Longs Peak. The elder Lamb had come to Estes Park four years earlier, staying at Griff Evans' ranch and also climbing Longs Peak. Beginning with a 12-by-14-foot cabin, father and son constructed the buildings that soon became Longs Peak House.

Enos A. Mills, whose father and Elkanah J. Lamb were cousins, arrived at the ranch in 1884. The next year he constructed a small tin-roofed homestead cabin nearby on the lower slopes of Twin Sisters Mountain. In 1902, Mills bought Lambs Ranch. A disastrous fire in 1906 destroyed the main lodge of Longs Peak Inn, as he had renamed the property. Mills rebuilt to his own specifications, using wind- or fire-killed trees, gnarled roots, and tree stumps. Beginning in 1909,

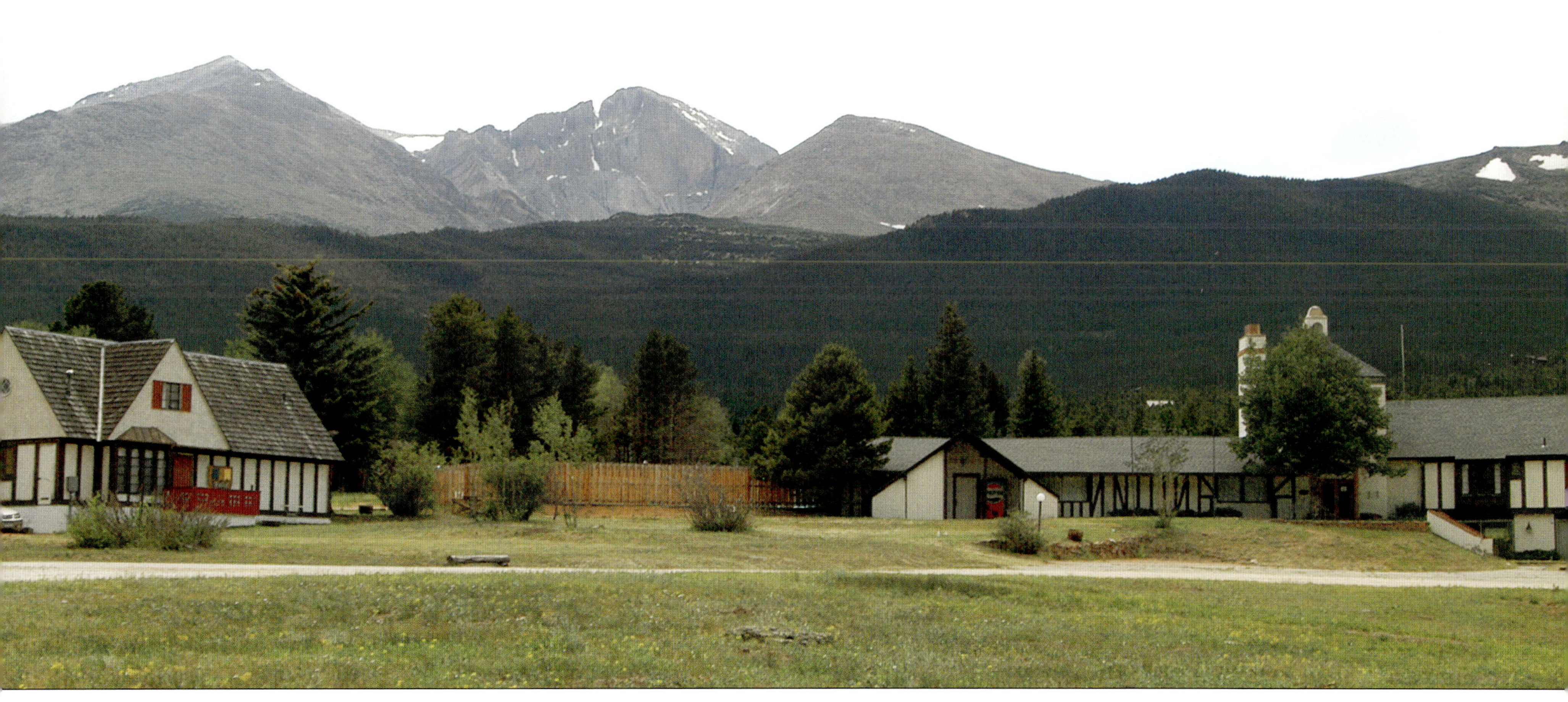

Mills made Longs Peak Inn his base of operations for his six-year battle for the creation of Rocky Mountain National Park. After Mills' sudden death in 1922, inn operations were taken over by his widow, Esther, who carried on the traditions he had established and fastidiously maintained. The inn was sold in March 1946; three years later, its main building again was destroyed by fire. Today, what remains of Longs Peak Inn is owned by the Salvation Army. The only authentic signs of its historic past are to be found in its cabins and outbuildings, a number of which were built by Enos A. Mills.

The original photograph of Longs Peak Inn was taken in 1905, before the disastrous fire of June 1906, and shows many of the buildings of the old Lambs Ranch, including, to the right, the house occupied by Carlyle Lamb.

64. Rocky Mountain National Park Dedication Site in Horseshoe Park, 1915

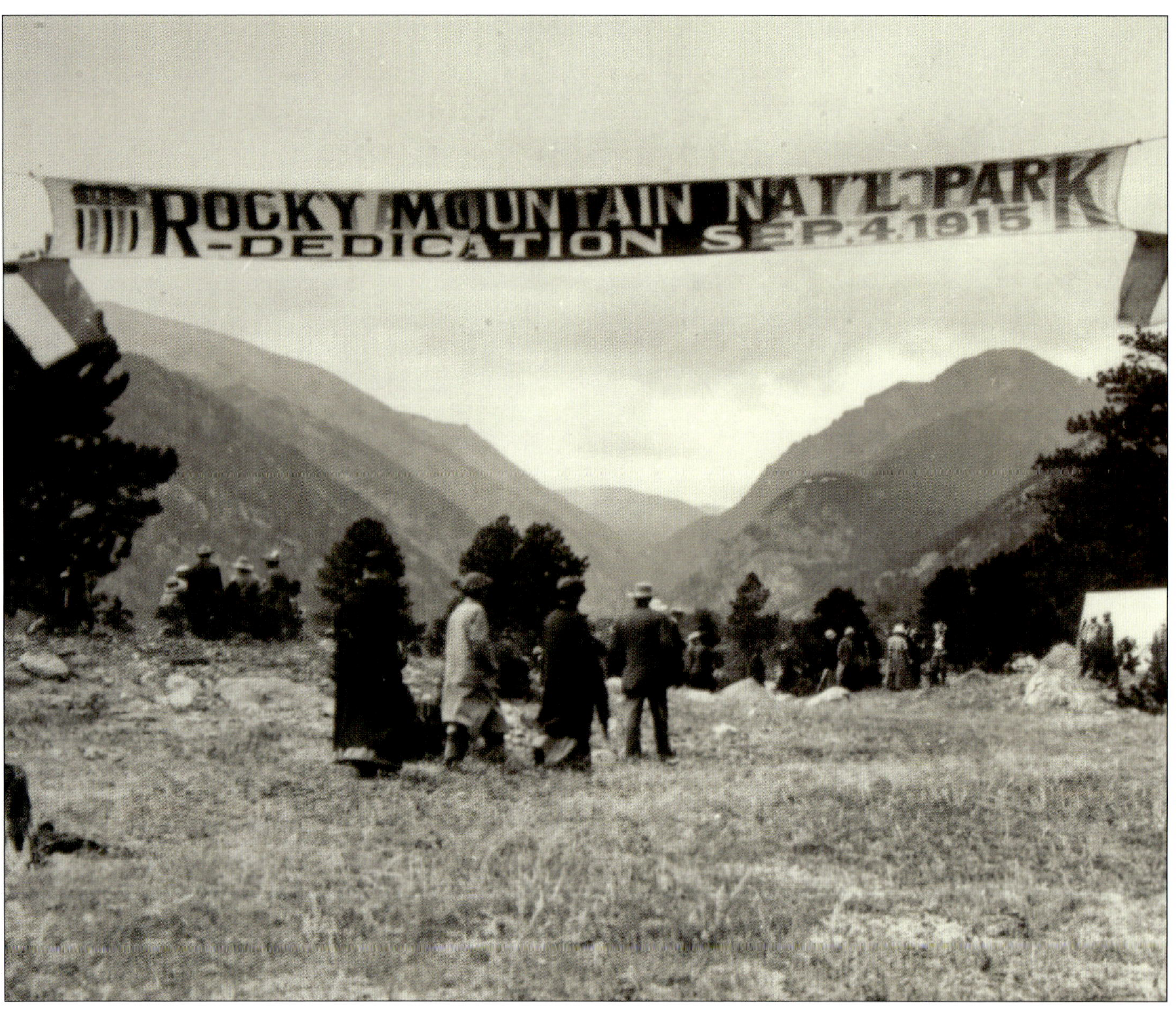

As shown in this original photograph, September 4, 1915, was an important day in Horseshoe Park. Rocky Mountain National Park, which had been created the previous January through an act of Congress, was to be dedicated. Though the day was cool and unpromising, the area near today's Lawn Lake Trailhead was crowded. People began to arrive early, particularly those who came from Denver and various valley towns. The Denver auto caravan, with such notables as Assistant Secretary of the Department of the Interior Stephen Mather, Colorado Governor George Carlson, and Congressman Edward Taylor, had left the headquarters of the Denver Motor Club at 7:30 a.m. Other cars joined up along the way. Similar groups came up from towns like Loveland, Longmont, and Fort Collins. Official ceremonies began at 2 p.m., and by that time some 267 automobiles were parked together along Fall River Road.

Elaborate preparations were made for the event. Hanging across the road, suspended from two pines and framing Endovalley, a big banner proclaimed the occasion and date. Members of the Estes Park Woman's Club and their husbands

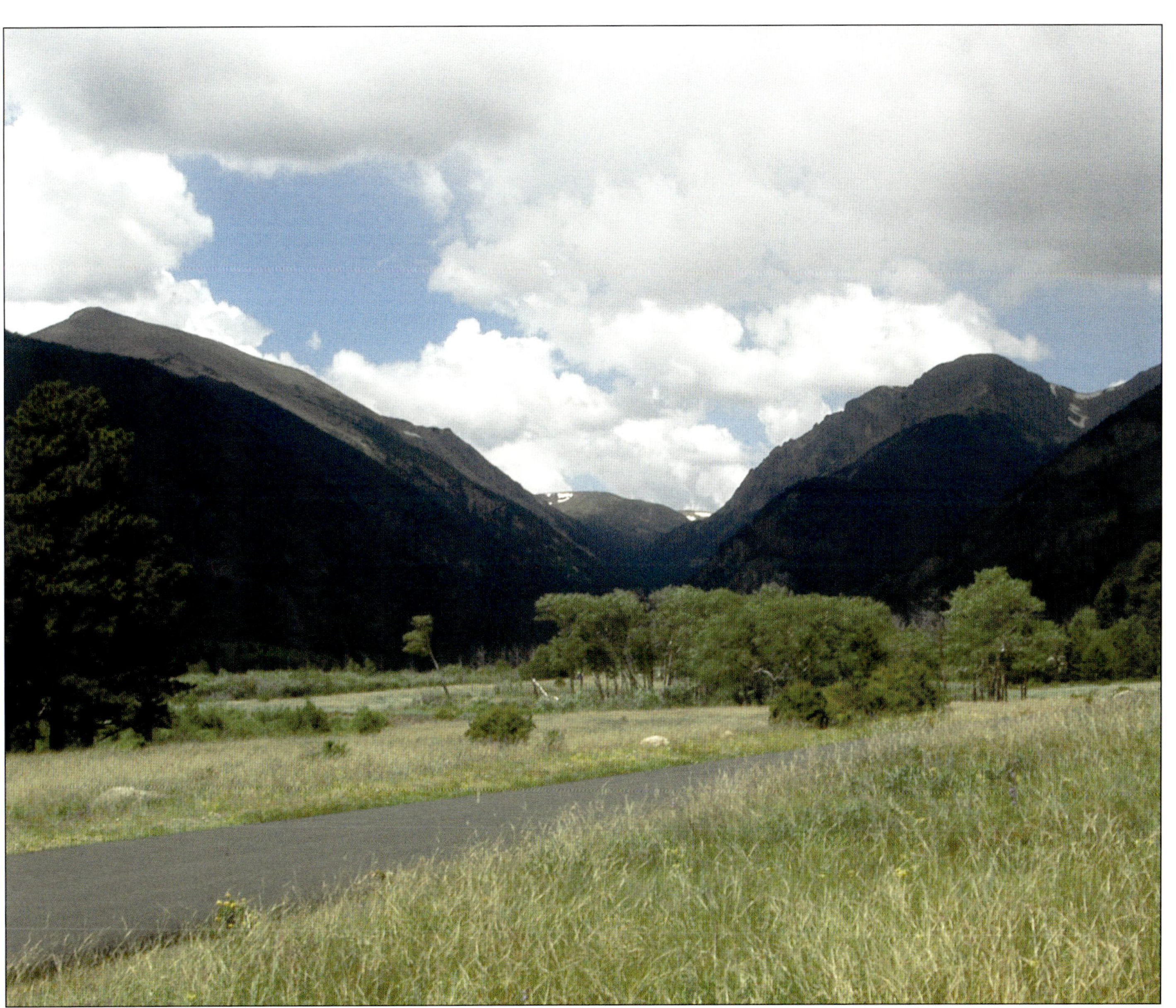

distributed box lunches as well as drinks. Governor Carlson and conservation-activist Mary Belle King Sherman took their lunches into the adjacent woods to enjoy them picnic-style near a large rock, where one of the photographers captured their image. Members of the 25-piece Fort Collins concert band serenaded. Enos A. Mills, already identified by the Denver press as the "father" of the new park, was the master of ceremonies and conducted the dedication by reading telegrams and introducing the dignitaries and guests.

In trying to retake one of the 1915 signature photographs—like the one that was taken from the small knoll just west of the banner site, showing cars parked out in the meadow and a small group of guests—we ran into a major perplexity. The scene ahead of us just didn't "look right." We finally realized that the location of the 1915 road has been changed. Today's road has been relocated just to the right of the original one, and this has changed slightly the contour of the land. The building that appears in the distance in the dedication photograph is Fall River Lodge, which had opened for business the previous July.

Rocky Mountain National Park dedication, September 4, 1915

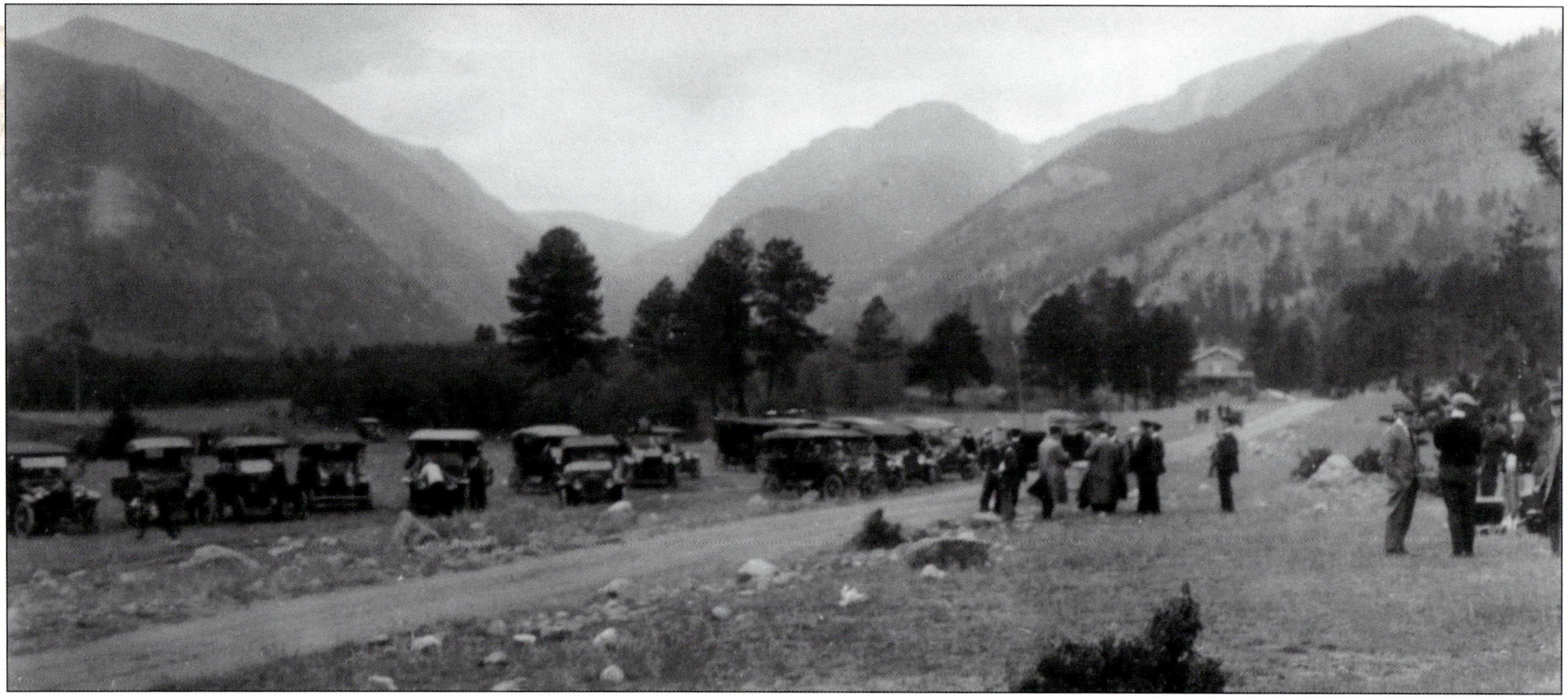

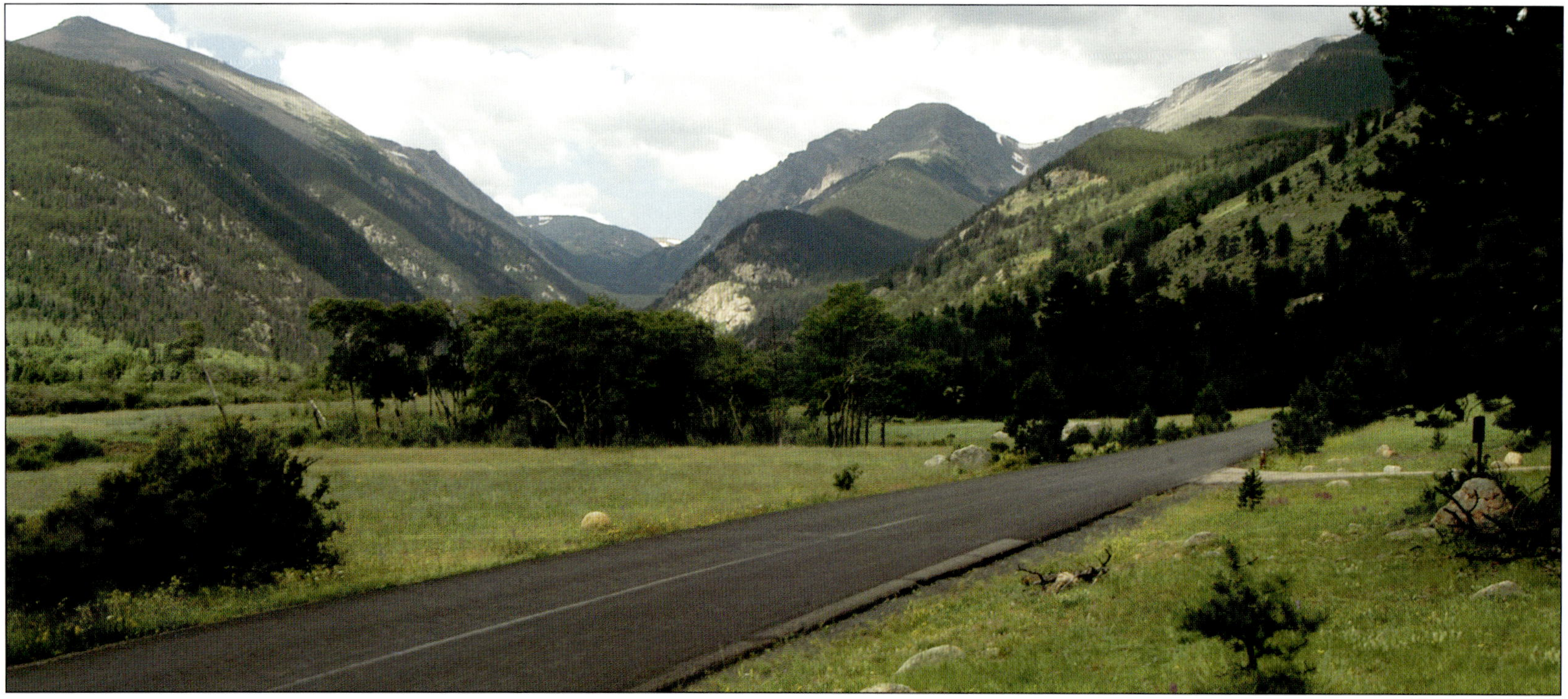

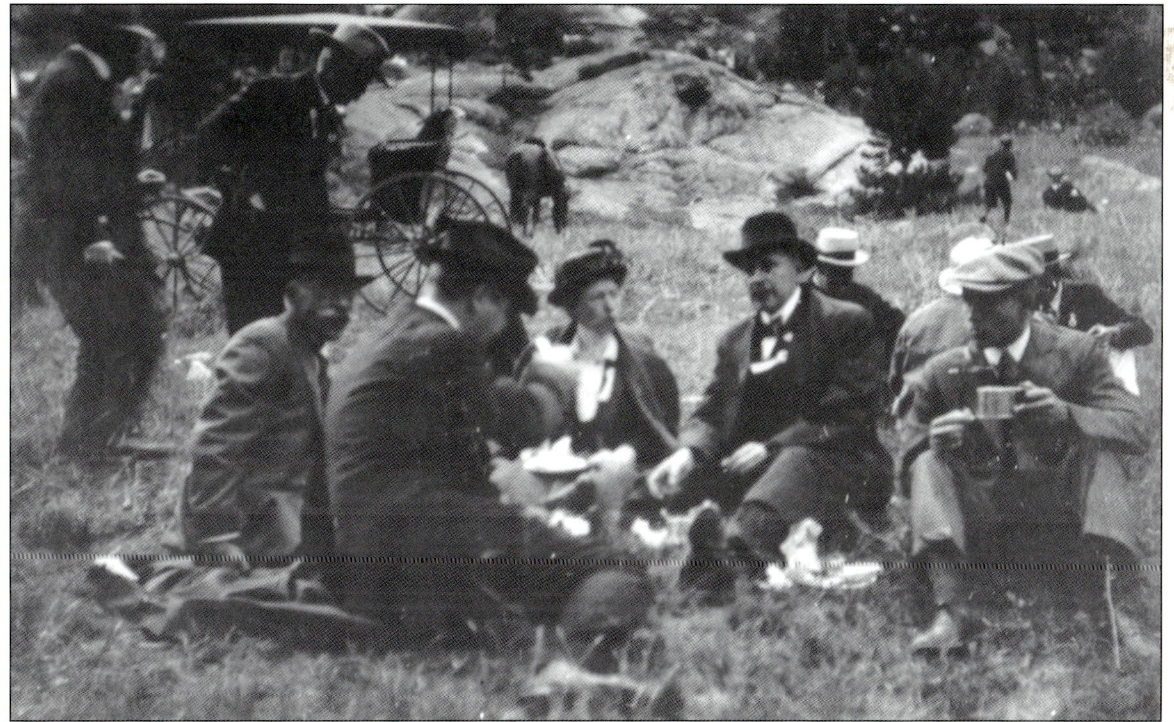

Picnickers in Horseshoe Park

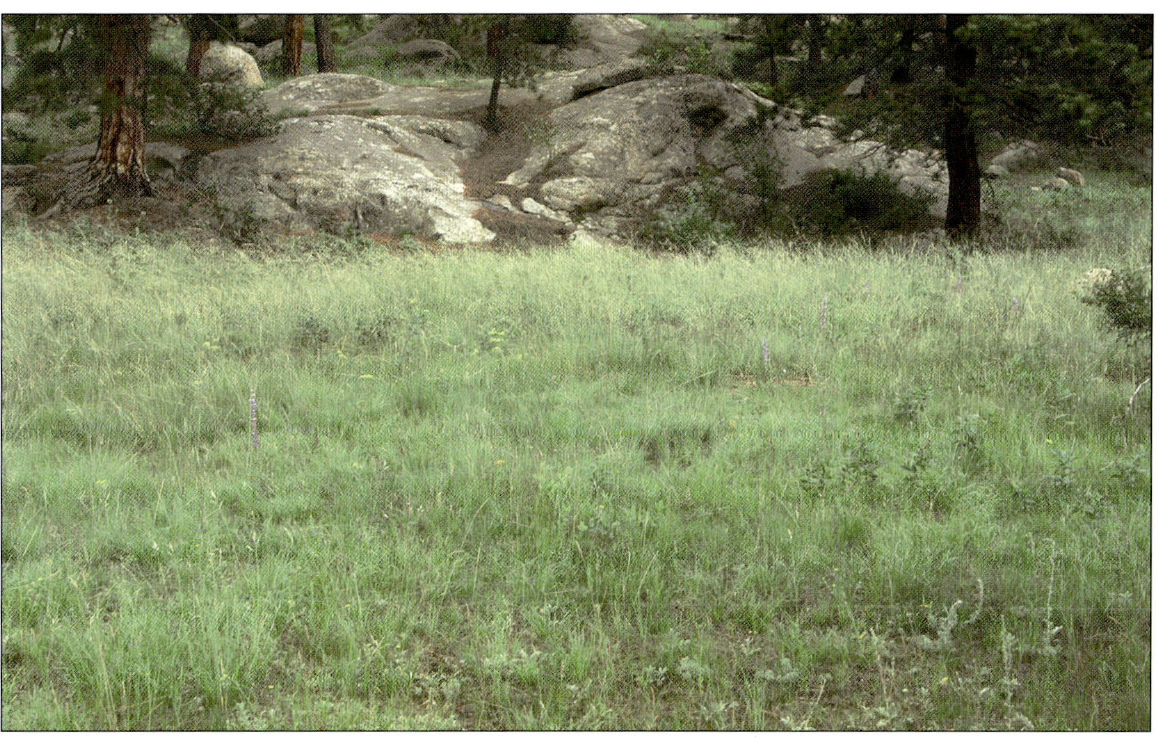

65. Fall River Lodge, circa 1930

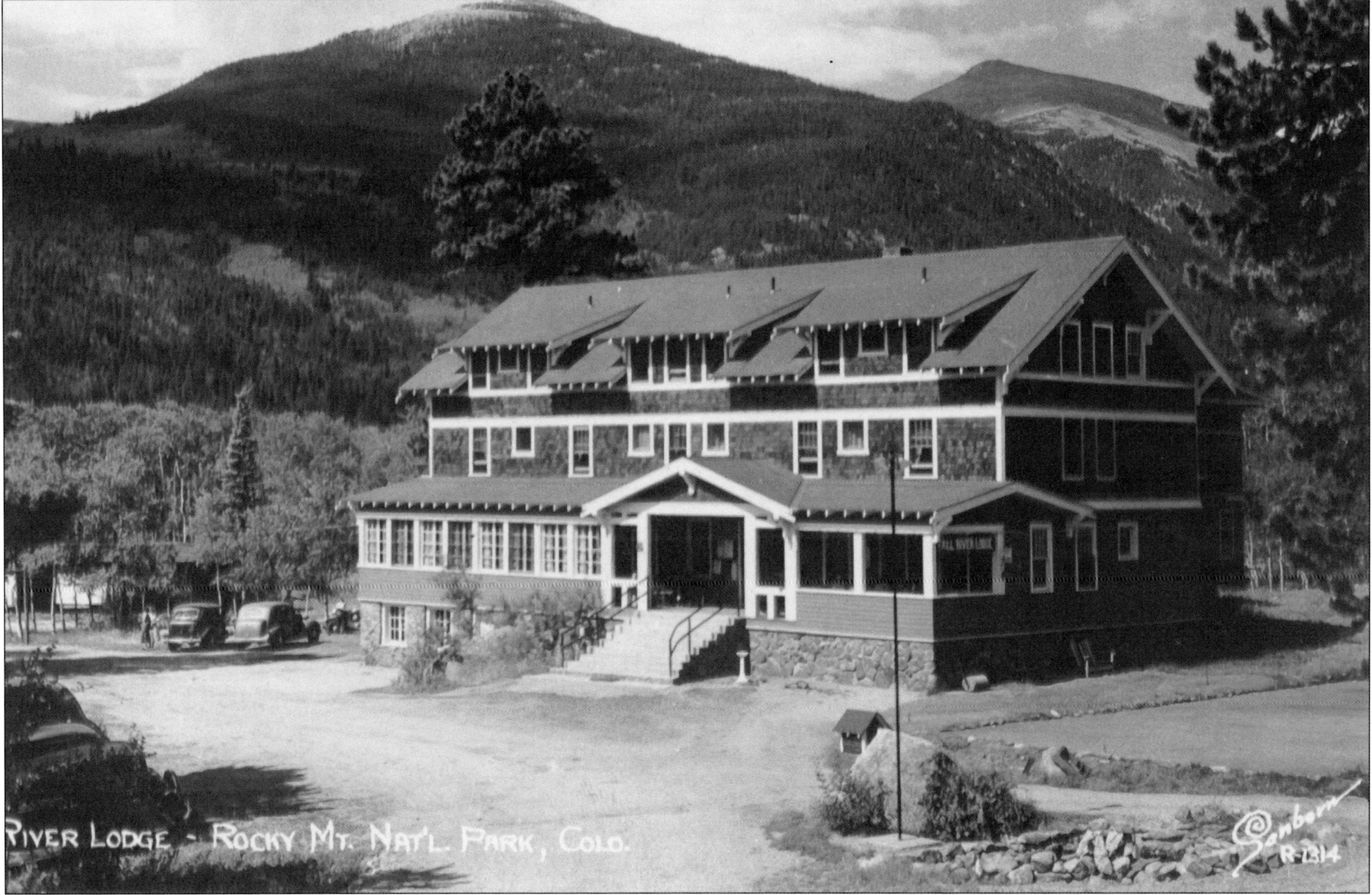

Photo by Sanborn Souvenir Company

The land on which Fall River Lodge and its outbuildings and cabins once stood, just west of the Lawn Lake Trailhead, was homesteaded in 1911 by Daniel and Minnie March. The timing was perfect for their new hotel, which was built just east of their homestead cabin (see p. 176) in the spring of 1915 and opened for business on July 3. Not only was their lodge ready to accept tourists in time for the park's inaugural season, but its buildings also dotted both sides of the new Fall River Road, then being extended across the Continental Divide to link the towns of Estes Park and Grand Lake. (Fall River Road would not officially open until September 1920.)

Some 13 one- and two-bedroom cabins—including the one photographed on p. 172—were added to Fall River Lodge in 1921, and over the next 25 years the March hotel was expanded into a complete resort complex with such amenities

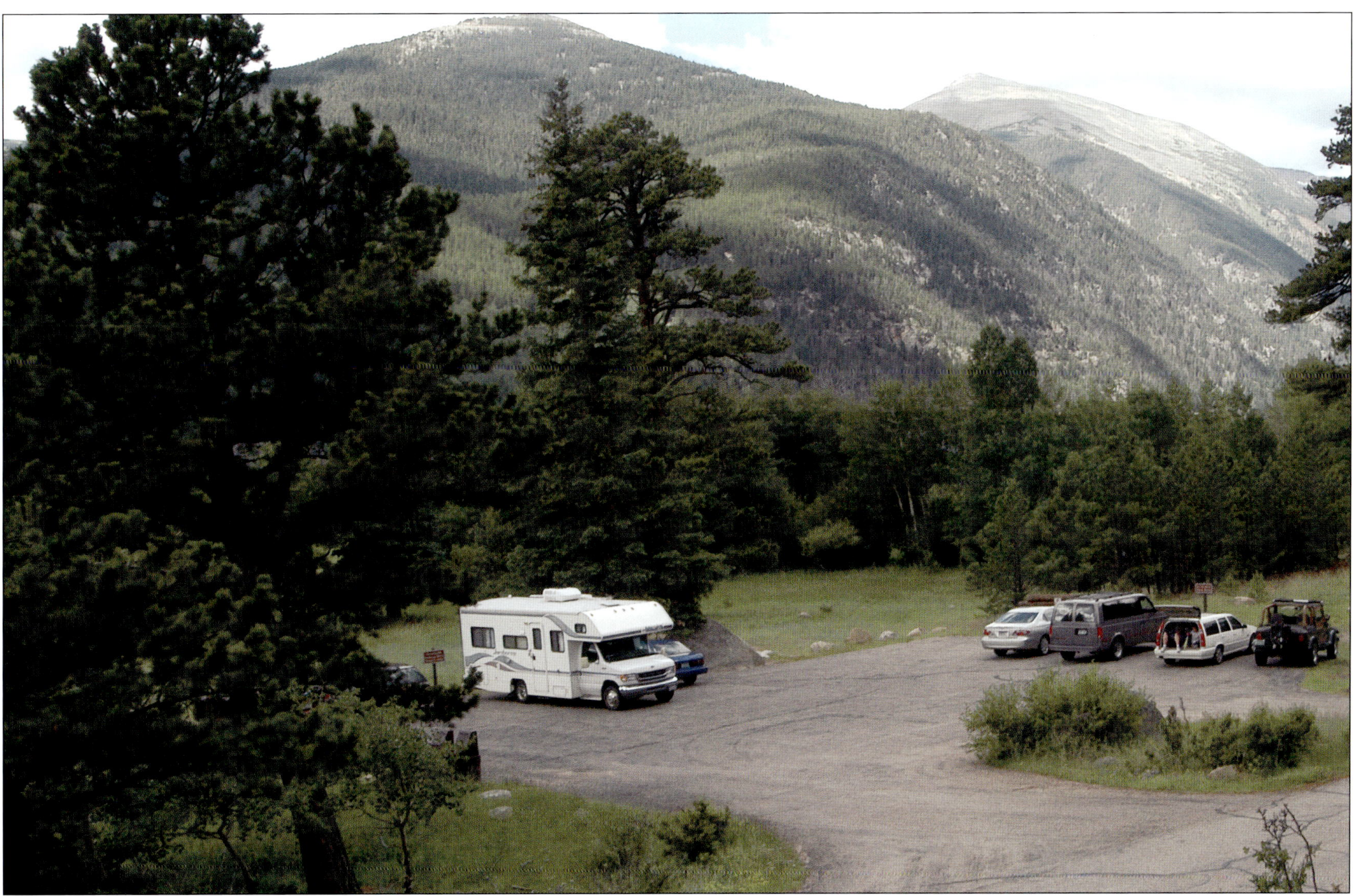

as a recreation hall and artificial lake. After Daniel March's death in 1923, his widow operated the lodge alone until October 1935, when she married popular longtime Estes Park merchant Sam Service. Following Service's death, Minnie sold the property to J. Russell McKelvey, a former employee. McKelvey was responsible for the lodge's final expansion in 1948, when he enlarged the dining room with an extension to the west.

Unlike neighboring Horseshoe Park Inn, with which it once shared both livery and power plant, Fall River Lodge survived through the difficult years of the Depression and World War II. The National Park Service later purchased the property from McKelvey in 1955 for $160,000 and operated it on a concession basis through the 1959 season, when negotiations for its continuing use broke down. The lodge and its buildings were razed in 1964.

Cabin at Fall River Lodge

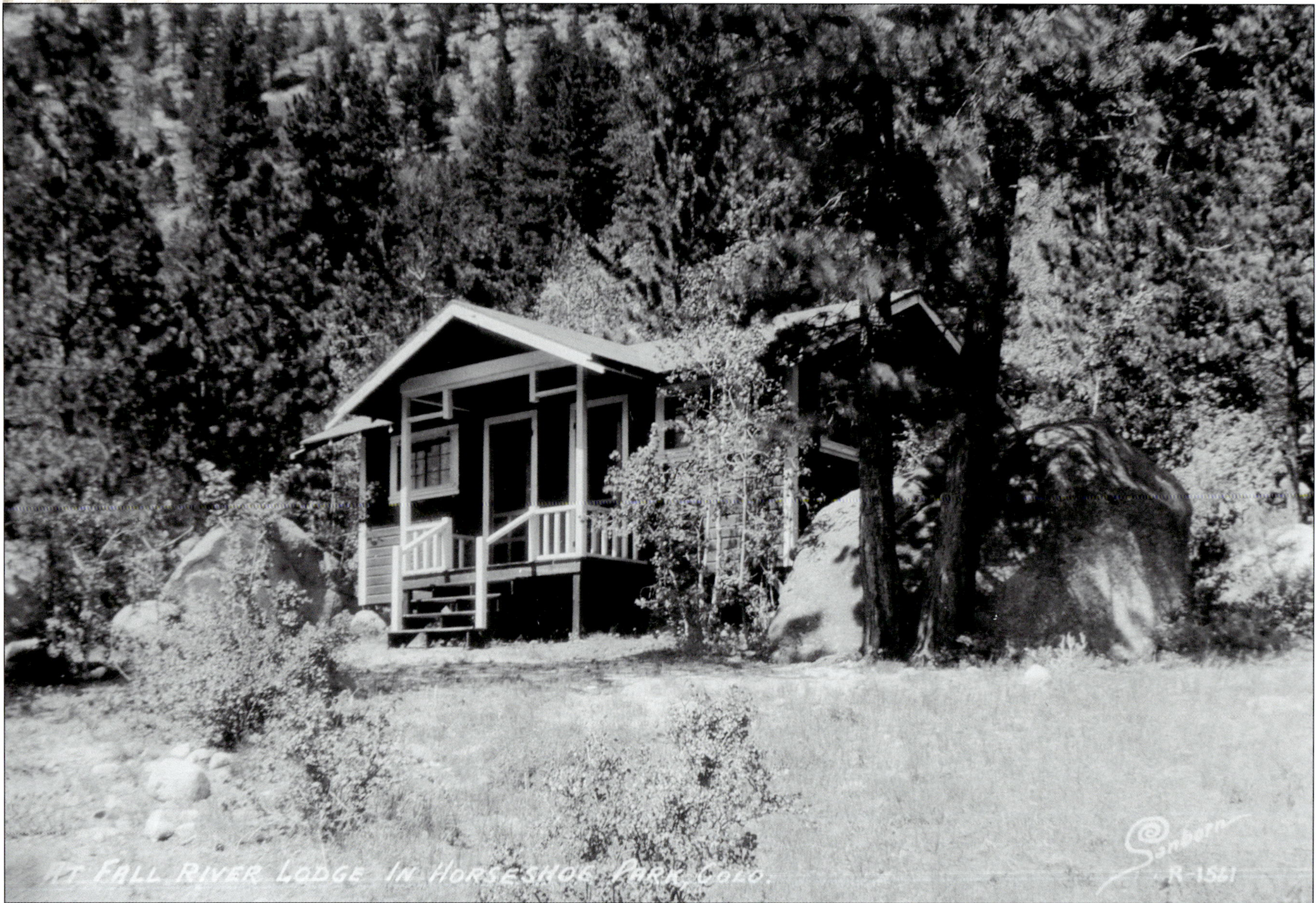

Photo by Sanborn Souvenir Company

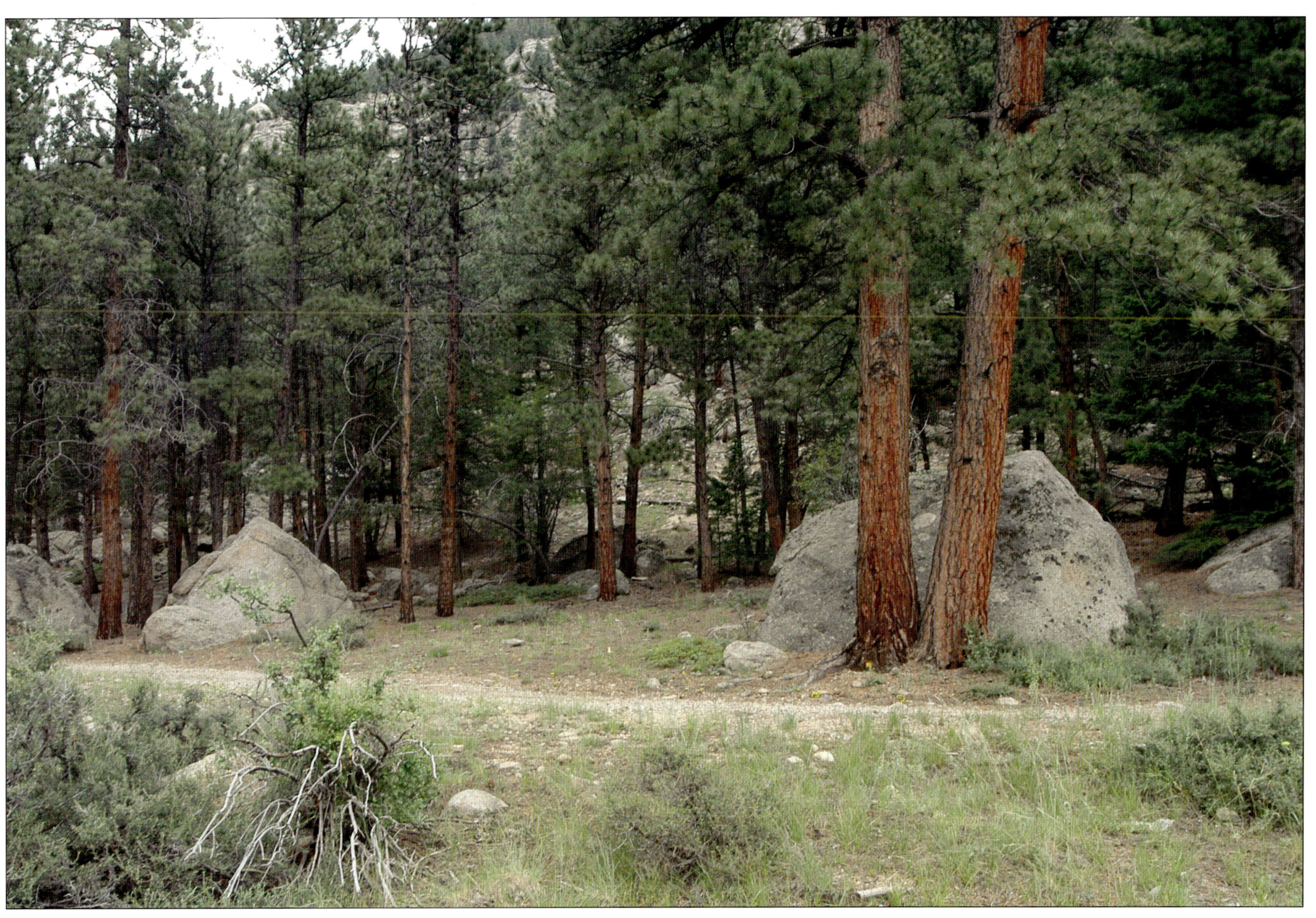

66. Convict Cabins, circa 1920

During the early stages of construction of the Fall River Road, convicts from the Colorado State Penitentiary at Cañon City and their supervisors lived in one- and two-room log huts east of the March homestead. The men, nicknamed "Tom Tynan's Boys" after their warden, worked under an 1899 law permitting convicted felons to shorten their jail sentences by helping construct roads. This arrangement proved quite advantageous for cash-strapped Larimer County, and was also said to exert a positive "moral and physical influence" upon the convicts by exposing them to the benefits of outdoor life.

Thirty-eight convicts began the work in August 1913, and by early September, some 3,000 feet of the new road had been built. Camp superintendent Thomas Lancaster had said that he expected to make good progress "before the snow flies." He was proven to be wrong. The severest snowstorm in the state's history roared in during the first five days of December. Work on the road came to a halt. For three weeks, Lancaster and his men continued to hunker down in their small cabins in Endovalley, under conditions that must have been far from comfortable. By December 23, 1913, 4 feet of snow covered the ground.

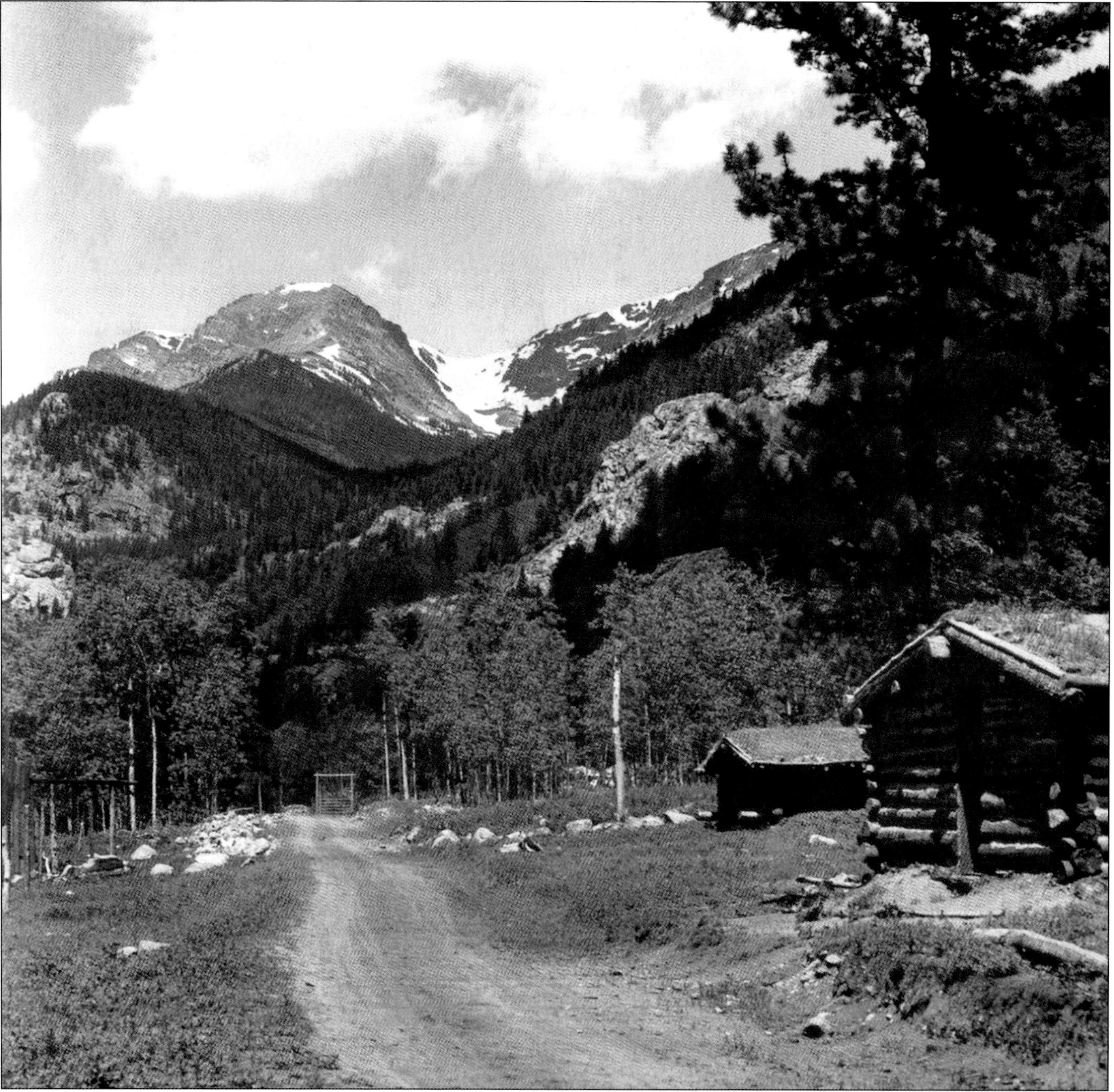

Photo by Fred Payne Clatworthy

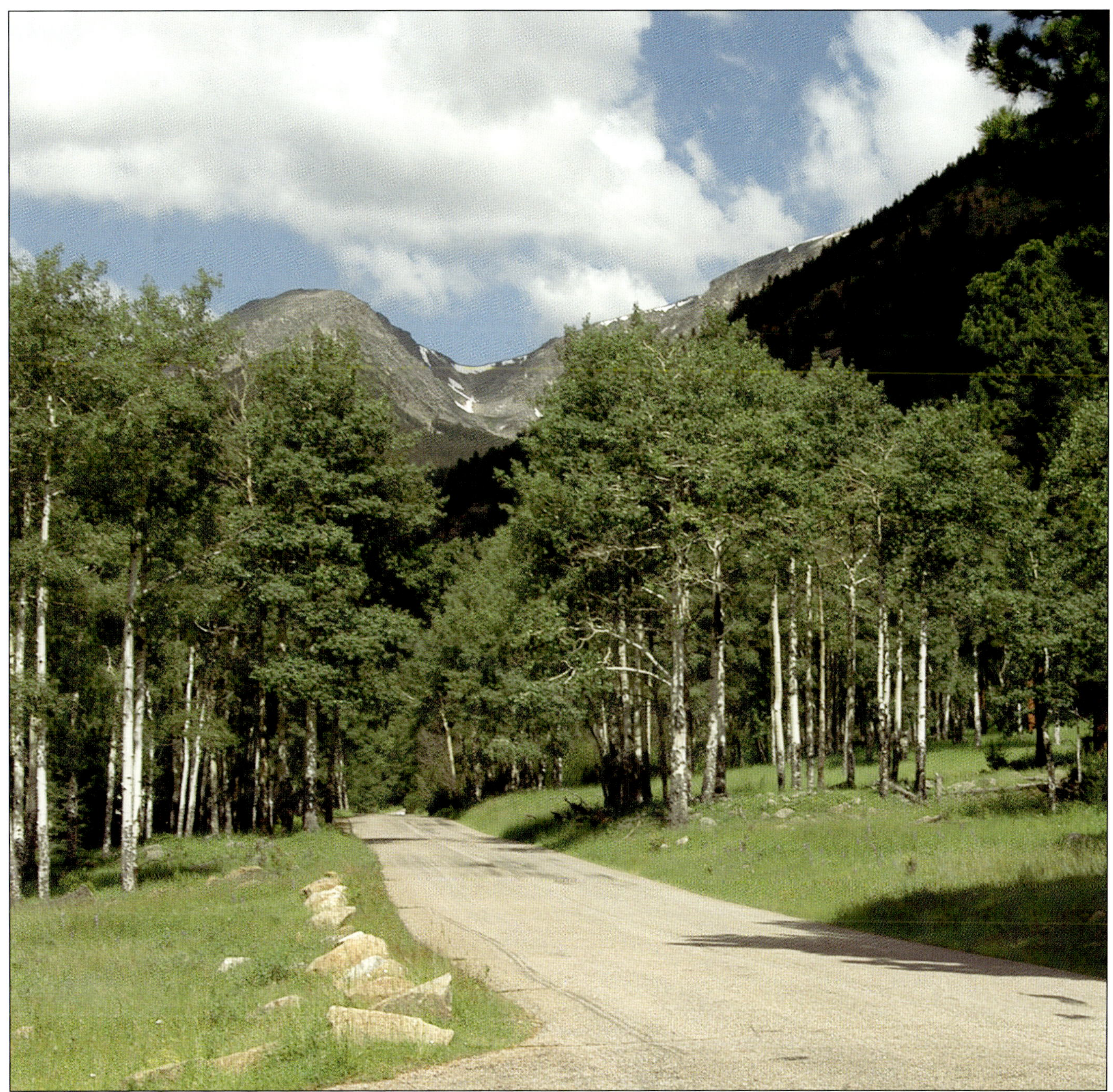

Because the road-building project went over budget, Lancaster's men did not resume work until February of 1914. Progress was agonizingly slow, and it would take another six years, until September 1920, to finish the new road to Middle Park, by which time the convict labor had given way to traditional road construction crews. The abandoned convict cabins on Fall River Road became a tourist attraction for travelers motoring on the new road, as well as a subject for photographers like Fred Payne Clatworthy. Today, all that is left to remind us of where Tom Tynan's Boys heroically endured the winter of 1913–1914 are a few rotting logs and foundations.

67. March Homestead Cabin, 1911

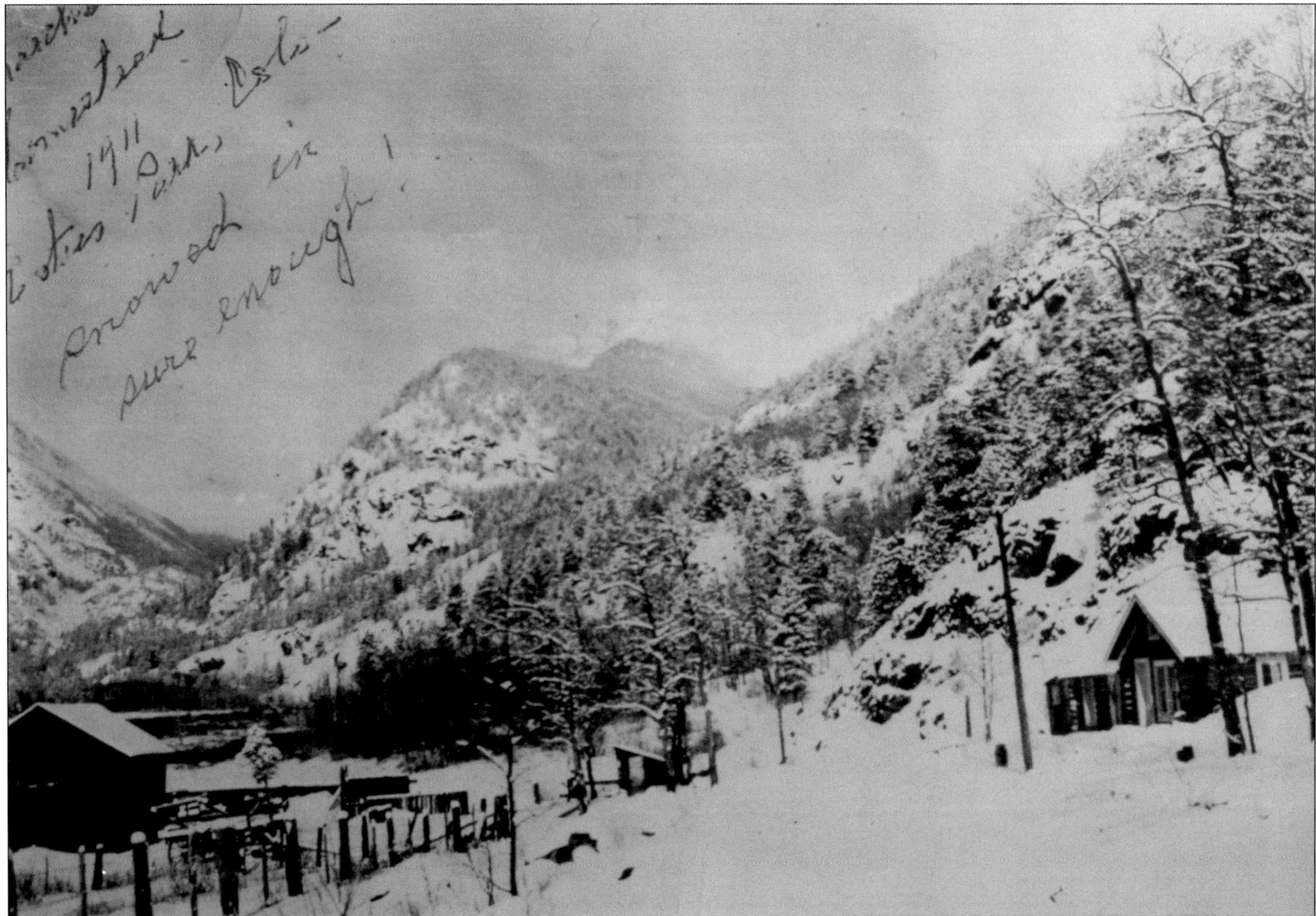

On this site, just west of the convict cabins, stood the homestead cabin that Daniel and Minnie March built in 1911. The adjacent river made their task quite a difficult one. Most of the tract they had chosen was swampy, willow-filled, and required draining before a house and barn could be built and the land fenced for livestock. The house and barn stood on opposite sides of what would become Fall River Road.

When convict labor to begin construction on the new road arrived in 1913, local residents were initially alarmed. The roadbed was within feet of the Marches' cabin door, and, Minnie later recalled, some found the prospect of having convict neighbors a disturbing one. The Marches, to the contrary, found the men kind and considerate, and indeed a blessing. During the great snow of December 1913, which cut Estes Park off from the world and paralyzed towns

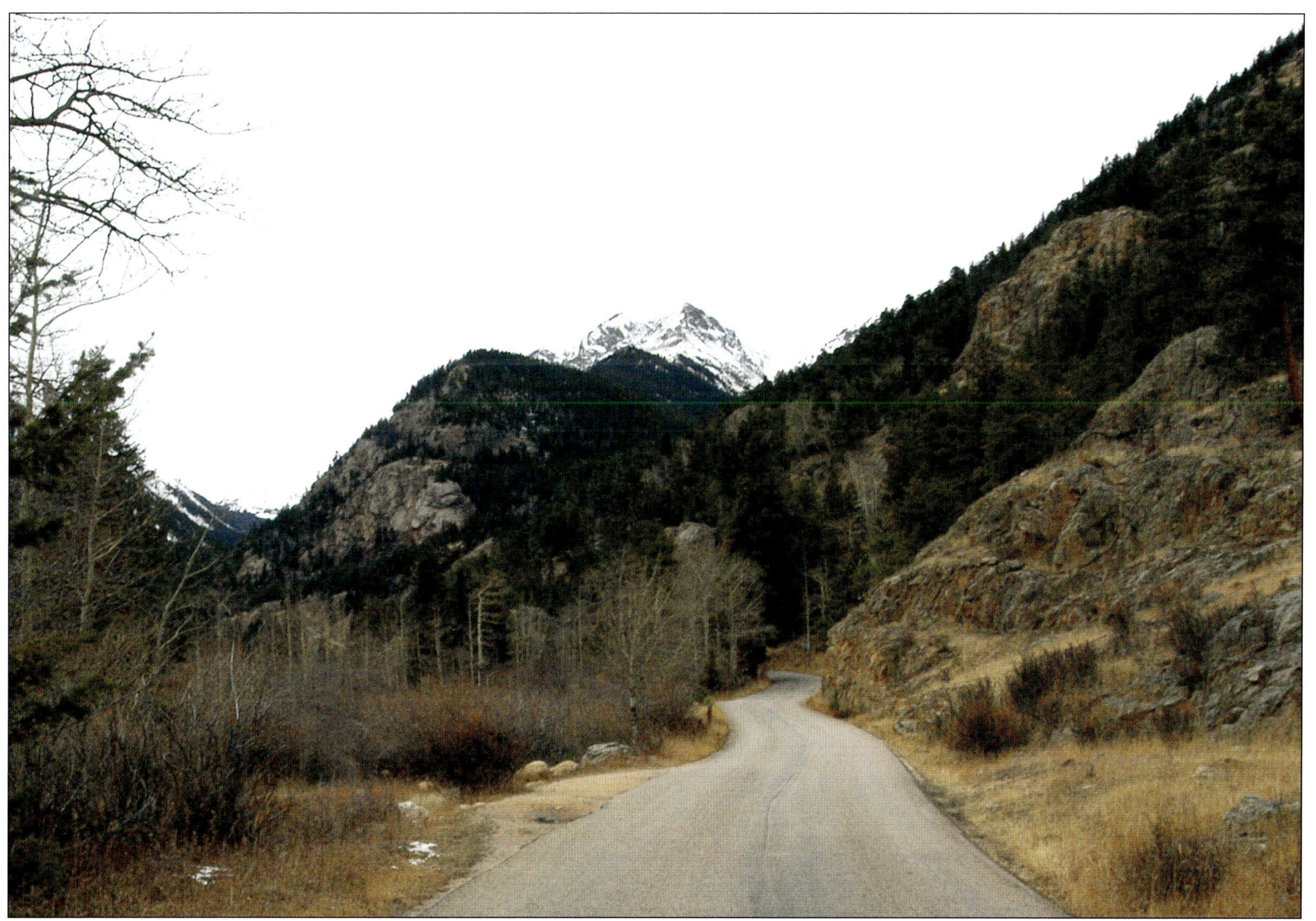

along the Front Range, the convicts brought a team of horses rigged with a sled of logs up from their winter camp, rescued the Marches, and carried them to the village 8 miles away. "At 10 o'clock in the morning we started for the Village," Minnie later wrote. "I rode in the saddle on Halley's back, and at times the snow was so deep I had to almost stand in the saddle to keep out of it. The big sorrel team broke trail for us all the way to the Village." Returning to their huts, the convicts remained "in residence" through what turned out to be one of the greatest snowstorms in Colorado history.

Today, a few stone footings mark the site of the March house and barn.

68. Cascade Lodge, circa 1930

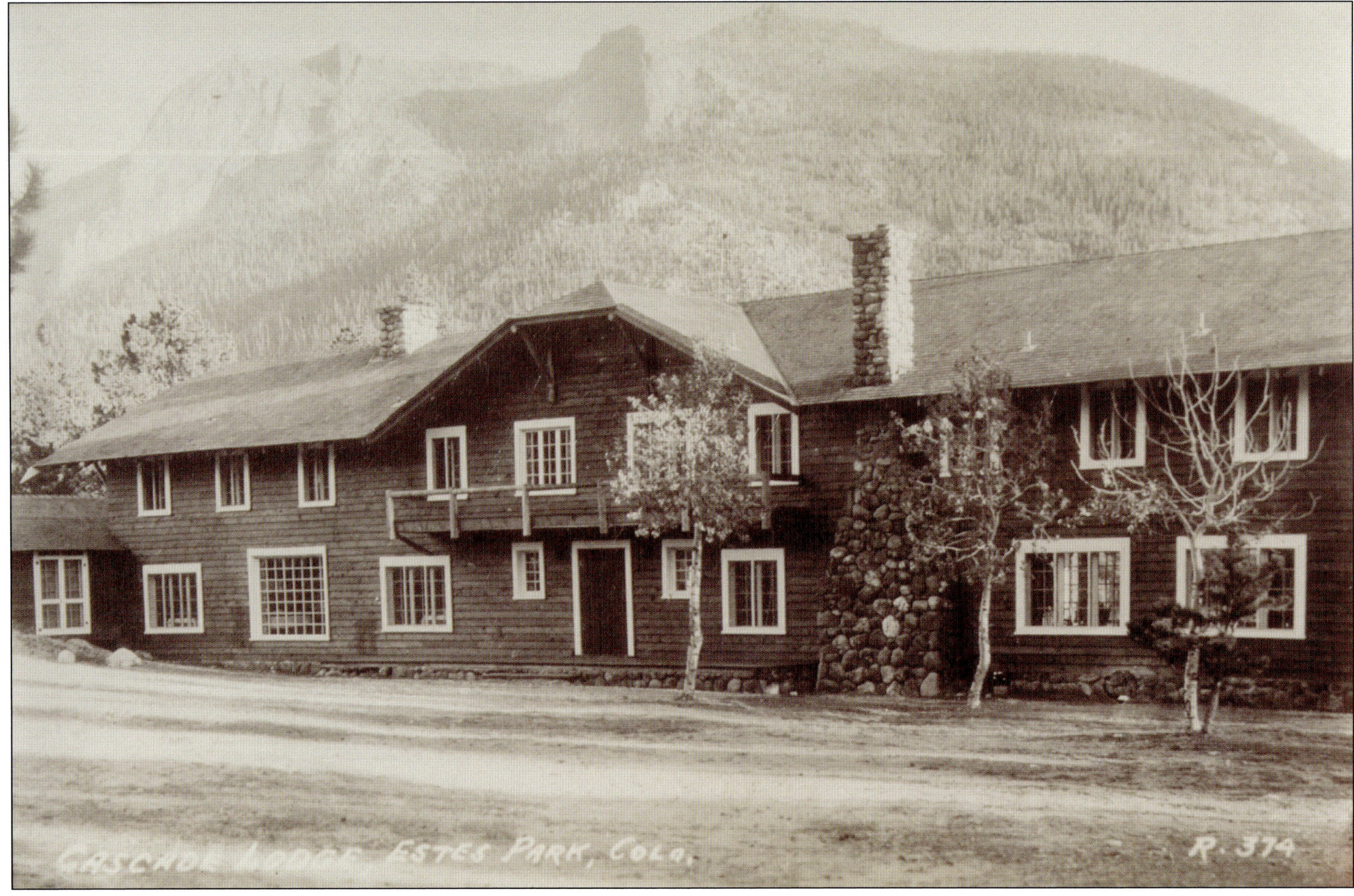

Photo by Sanborn Souvenir Company

The Cascade Lodge resort complex guarded Horseshoe Park's eastern entrance, some 5.5 miles west of Estes Park village. Completed and opened in 1925, it had an 18-room main building and surrounding cottages with room for 75 guests. The lodge building was sited on Fall River, just above Cascade Lake and its dam, which F. O. Stanley constructed in 1909 to divert water to his power plant below.

We know little about the lodge's original owner, but it was sold around 1929 to Anna May and William Derby, who during the early 1930s also acquired the old Manford Hotel on Elkhorn Avenue (see p. 106). Cascade Lodge came to an end on the morning of June 12, 1935, when the main lodge caught fire. By the time that firefighters could arrive, the blaze was out of control, leaving a charred structure burned beyond repair. Some 125 Civilian Conservation Corps workers camped nearby kept the fire from spreading to the wooded slopes.

Although the Derbys did not rebuild, Cascade Lodge continues on as guest cottages. In 1941, Kansas schoolteacher L. V. Davis and wife Hazel bought the

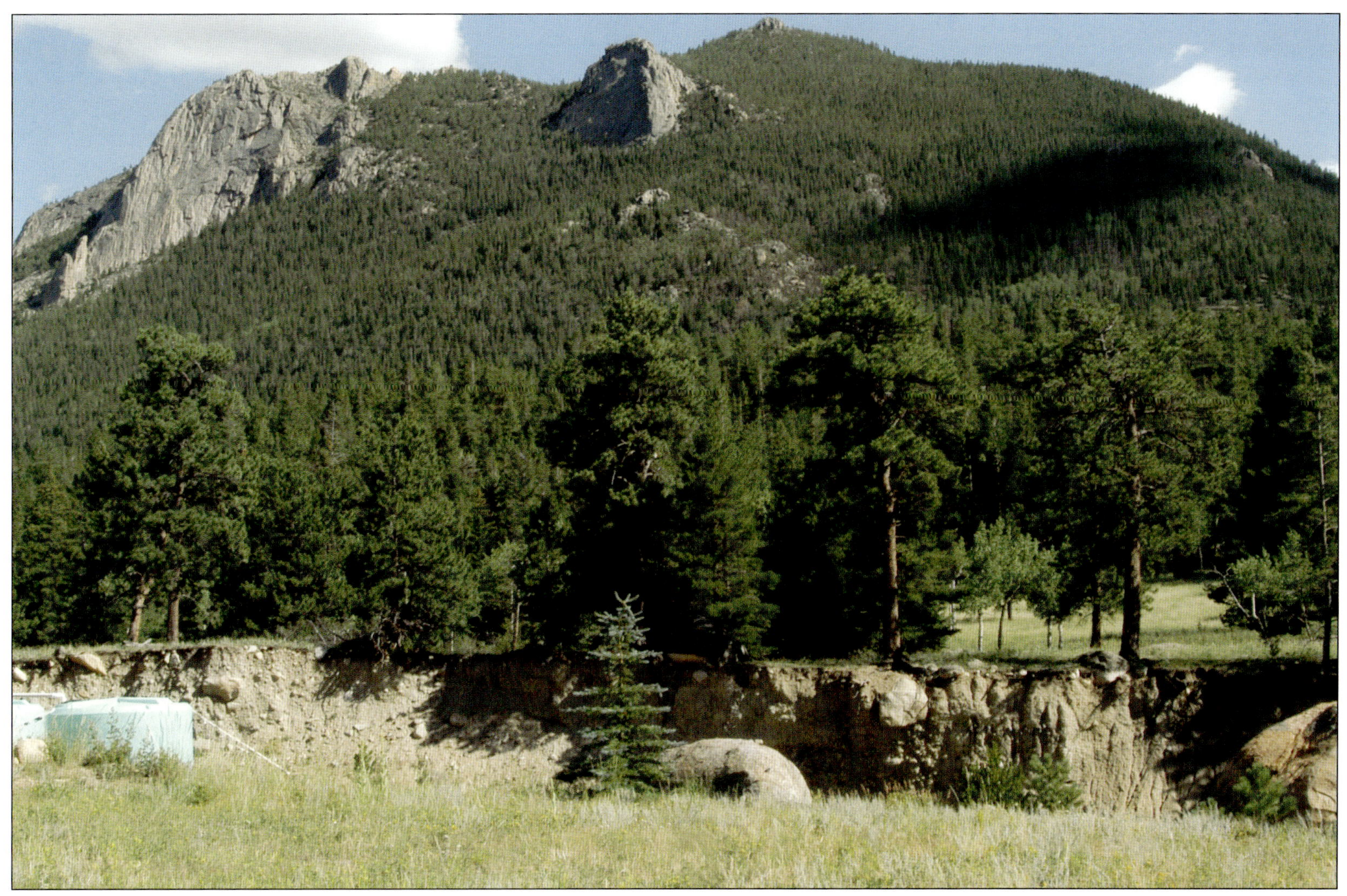

nine Cascade Cottages and added several more. Their daughters, Grace and Mary Lee, together with their husbands, still operate the family business—the only remaining commercial lodgings within Rocky Mountain National Park.

The recent photograph shows the devastation caused on July 15, 1982, when a wall of water, rushing through Horseshoe Park from the breached farmer's cooperative dam at Lawn Lake, destroyed Cascade Lake and its dam, gouging the banks of Fall River before rushing below to render Stanley's power plant and the nearby fish hatchery permanently inoperable. The Park Service prohibited rebuilding the Cascade Lake dam, leaving a gaping hole in the ground and the adjacent cottages without a water source.

69. Richmond Homestead and Horseshoe Inn, 1904

Photo by Louis C. McClure

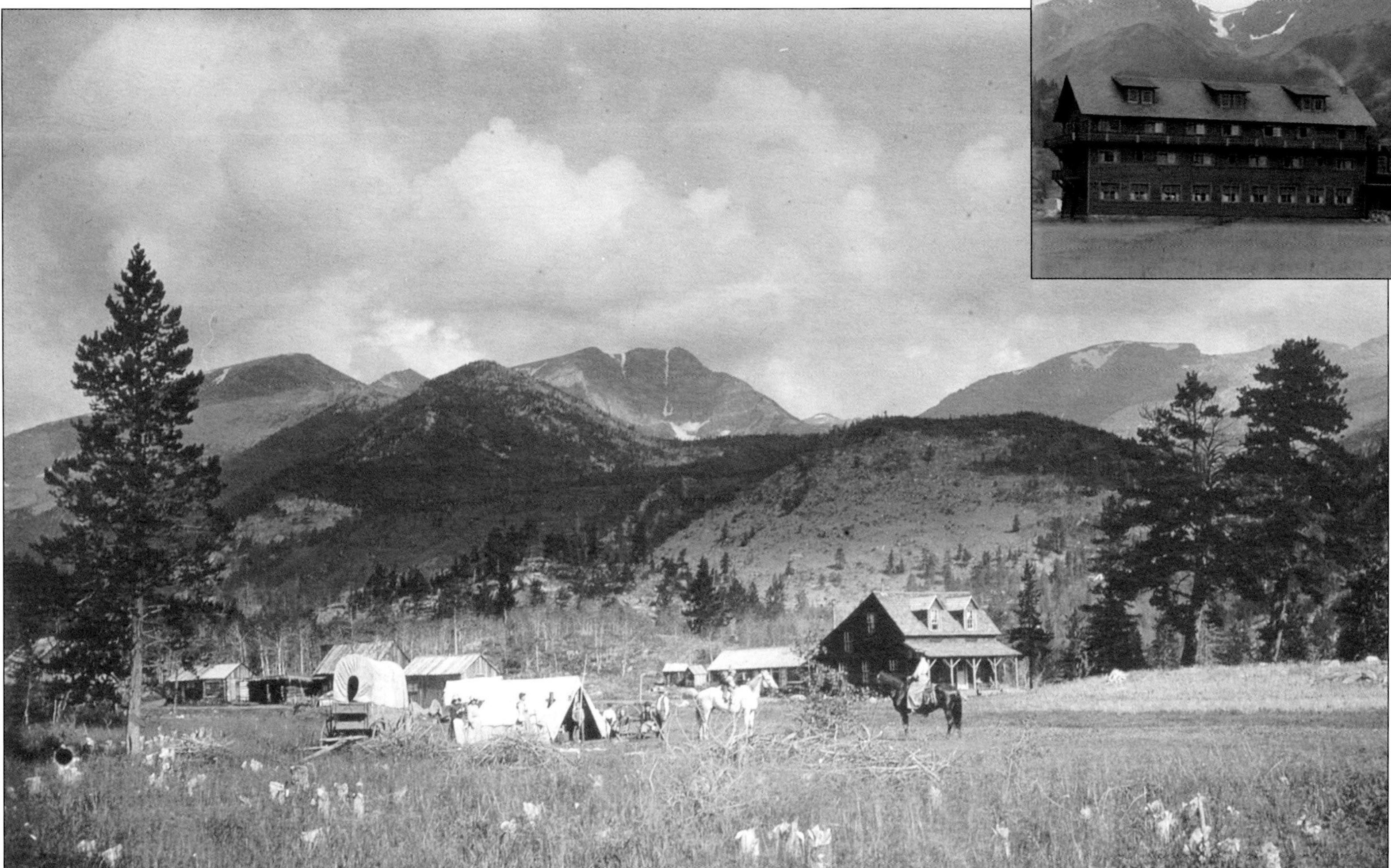

Photo by Fred Payne Clatworthy

It is difficult to imagine that this grassy knoll at the mouth of Endovalley in Horseshoe Park was the site of a large resort complex. Horseshoe Inn, like many guest ranches and hotels in the Estes region, began as a modest establishment. Massachusetts native William H. Ashton, his wife Grace, and daughter Ruth (to become a well-known botanist) came to Estes Park in 1905 on vacation, staying to purchase the ranch house and 160 acres in Horseshoe Park homesteaded in 1896 by blacksmith Ed Richmond.

After deciding to get into the tourist business, Ashton briefly flirted with a Chicago architect for plans. Frank Lloyd Wright produced a series of renderings for a lodge radically different from anything in the Estes region. The June 4, 1908, edition of the *Mountaineer*, Estes Park's new summer newspaper, described a 288-foot-long one-story building to accommodate 100 guests "that will seem part of the beautiful landscape, rather than a mar upon it, as so often the case with summer hotels."

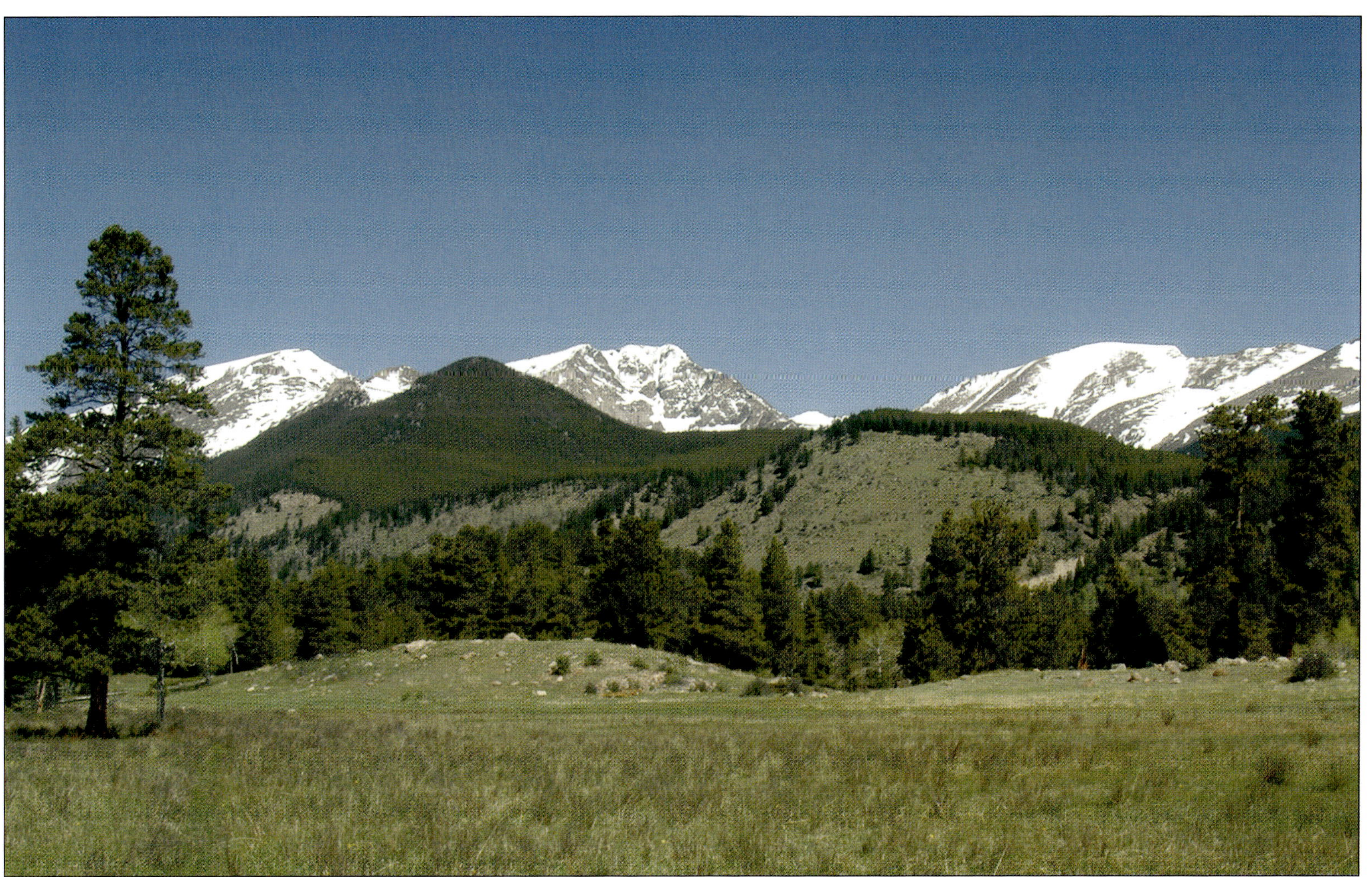

Wright's design was never used after all. For reasons unknown, but doubt less involving cost, Horseshoe Inn was built in the traditional Western Stick-style architecture, incorporating the original ranch house (as shown in Fred Payne Clatworthy's photograph) into the northwest section of the wooden two-story structure. Opened in June 1909, the lodge was enlarged over the years to four stories, with a three-story annex to the southwest.

Ashton sold Horseshoe Inn in 1915 to Harry Bradley and Claude Patrick, automobile dealers from Fort Collins, under whose direction major expansions were carried out. When the National Park Service began acquiring inholdings in October 1931, during the hardest years of the Depression, the Patricks, now the sole owners, were the first ones to sell, accepting $32,500 for the inn and its remaining acreage. Before year's end the buildings had been razed.

70. CCC Camp in Little Horseshoe Park

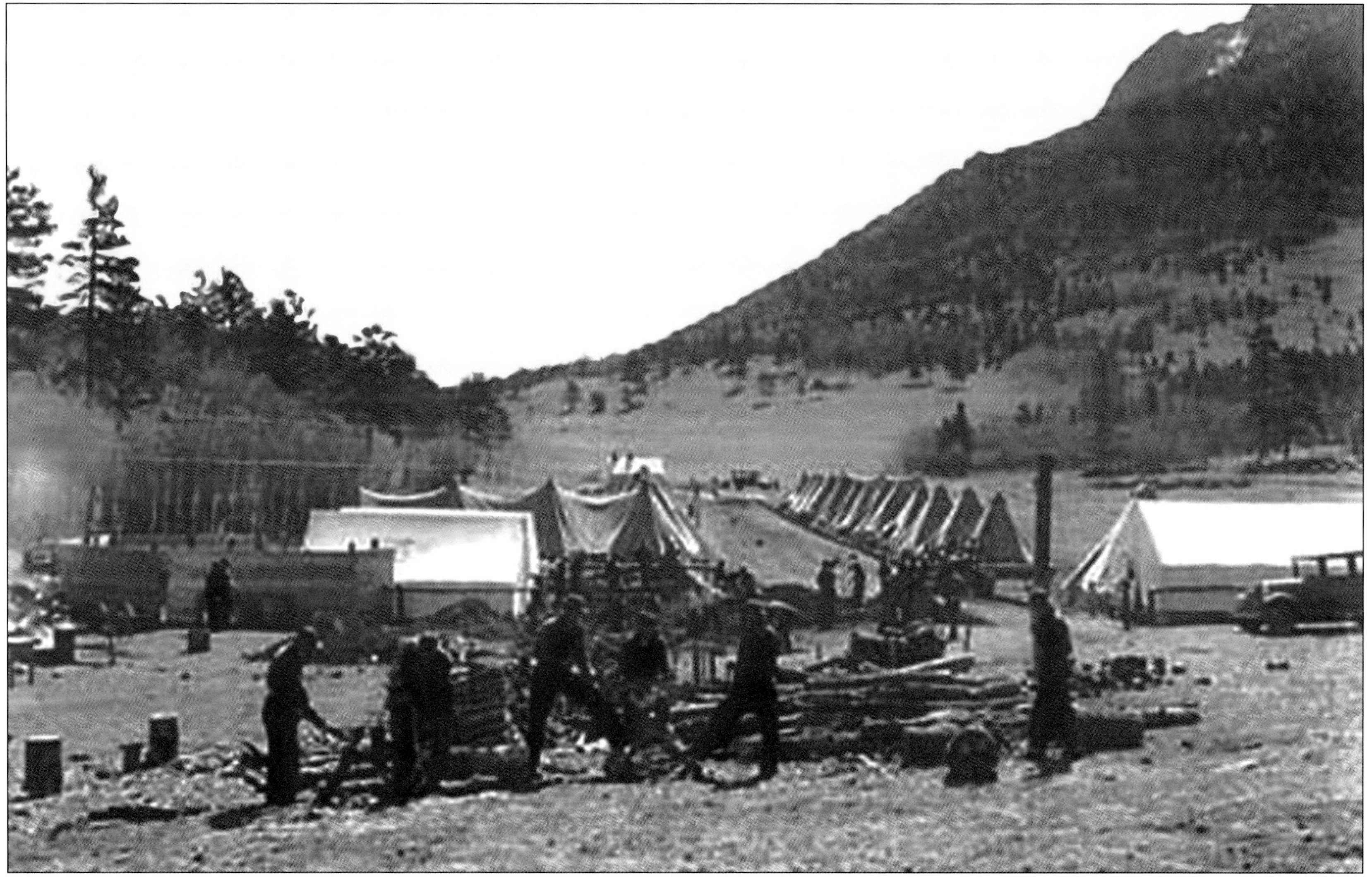

Of all Roosevelt's New Deal programs during the Depression, none proved more popular—or more important to the nation's parks and forests—than the Civilian Conservation Corps (CCC). Created on March 21, 1933, through the Emergency Conservation Work Act, the CCC built character, and provided educational, and job training for unemployed young men while battling the erosion and destruction of the nation's natural resources at a time when jobs were scarce or nonexistent. Camp N. P. 1-C, the first CCC camp in a national park west of the Mississippi, was established in Rocky Mountain National Park on May 15, 1933. Within days, some 200 recruits and the army officers who supervised them, having survived the initiation of a numbing spring snowstorm, were settled in their new home in Little Horseshoe Park.

Though Camp N. P. 1-C was a summer camp only, during the six years of its existence its contributions to Rocky Mountain National Park were enormous: "delousing the forest" from the extensive damage being done by the Black Hills

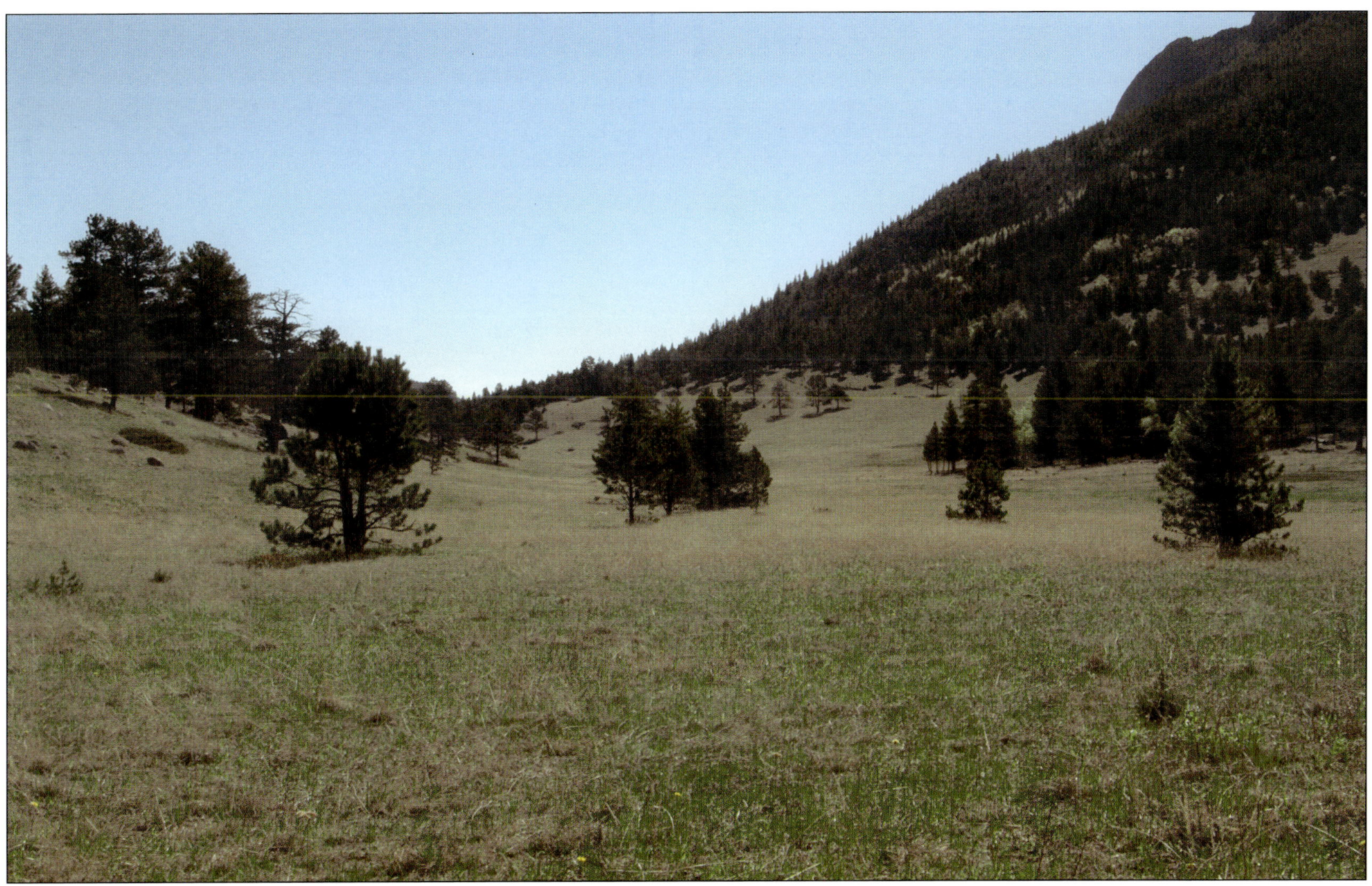

beetle, trail and campground maintenance and building, roadside cleanup, cutting and removing dead trees, landscaping, participating in research and rescue operations, and firefighting. It has been estimated that during its relatively short existence, Roosevelt's "Woodpecker Army" advanced the development of the nation's park system by as much as two decades.

As the contemporary photograph suggests, there are few signs in Little Horseshoe Park of the busy CCC camp that once stood in this tranquil place. The only reminder of the important park work accomplished by the young recruits is the plaque on the road from Deer Ridge Junction. But, coming back to Rocky Mountain National Park in later years, more than one member of that CCC generation recalled those days in Little Horseshoe Park as among the happiest and most altering of their lives.

71. Deer Ridge Chalet, circa 1940

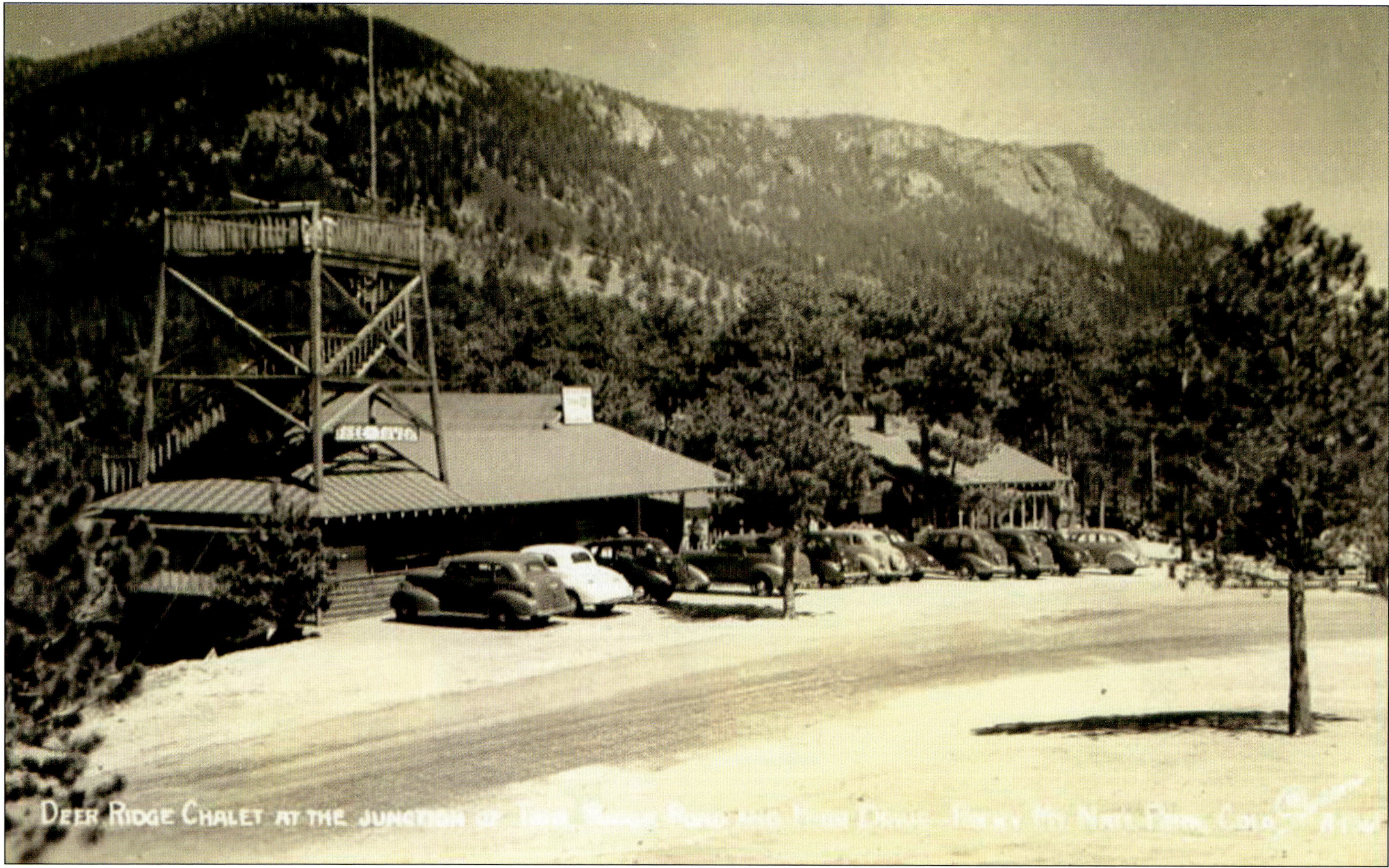

Photo by Sanborn Souvenir Company

On any summer day, Deer Ridge Junction—where Highways 34 and 36 meet—is a busy place. Motorists entering the park from Beaver Meadows can continue on to Hidden Valley, Trail Ridge, and Grand Lake or proceed on down into Horseshoe Park. Visitors park here to take the trail up Deer Mountain or take a picture of Longs Peak and its neighbors across the moraine. The bustling Deer Ridge Chalet once stood here, a popular tourist stop for more than four decades.

It began in 1917 when semiprofessional photographer and painter Orville W. Bechtel erected a lean-to at what was then the end of the road (High Drive), from which he sold postcards and lemonade. From here, rough trails led onward to Hidden Valley and Horseshoe Park. During the next decade, he expanded his operations by adding a restaurant, rustic cabins, and a filling station. In 1924, he opened a popular ski run on the north side of the road running down into

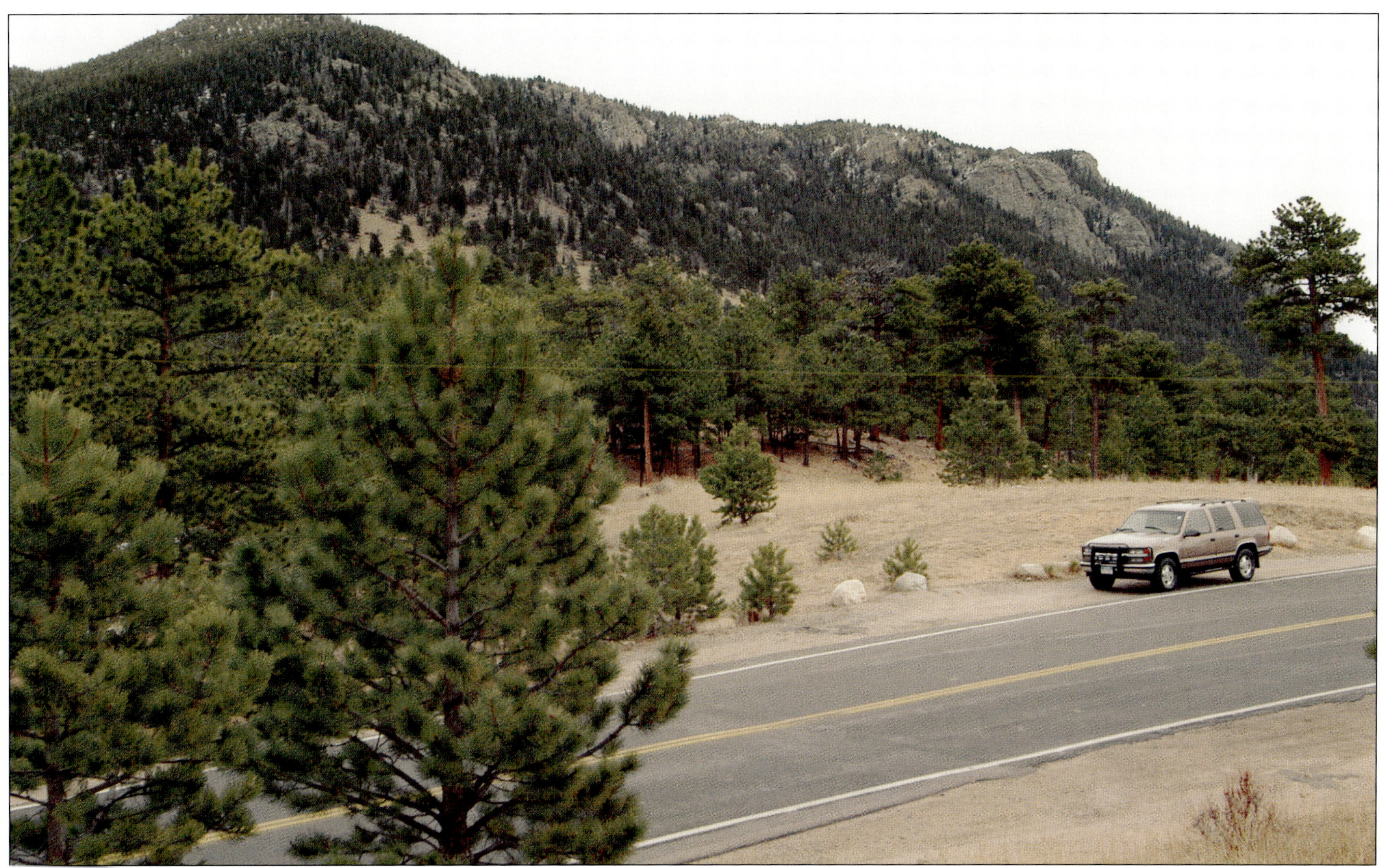

Little Horseshoe Park, with a shelter cabin at the top of the slope and later a toboggan run at one side.

In 1926, Bechtel sold the property to the Gustave Shubert family, who relocated most of the business to the northeast side of the road (where it sits in the original photograph) and constructed the large lodge called the Deer Ridge Chalet. They then added a 50-foot observation tower and a variety of other structures, including cabins, to take advantage of the new Trail Ridge Road, completed in 1933.

The government acquired the property in 1960, and the following year local contractors dismantled and removed the structures. The kitchen, dining room, and gift shop were moved to a site on Highway 7 and then reassembled to become the core building for Masonic Lodge No. 183.

72. Hupp Homestead, circa 1885

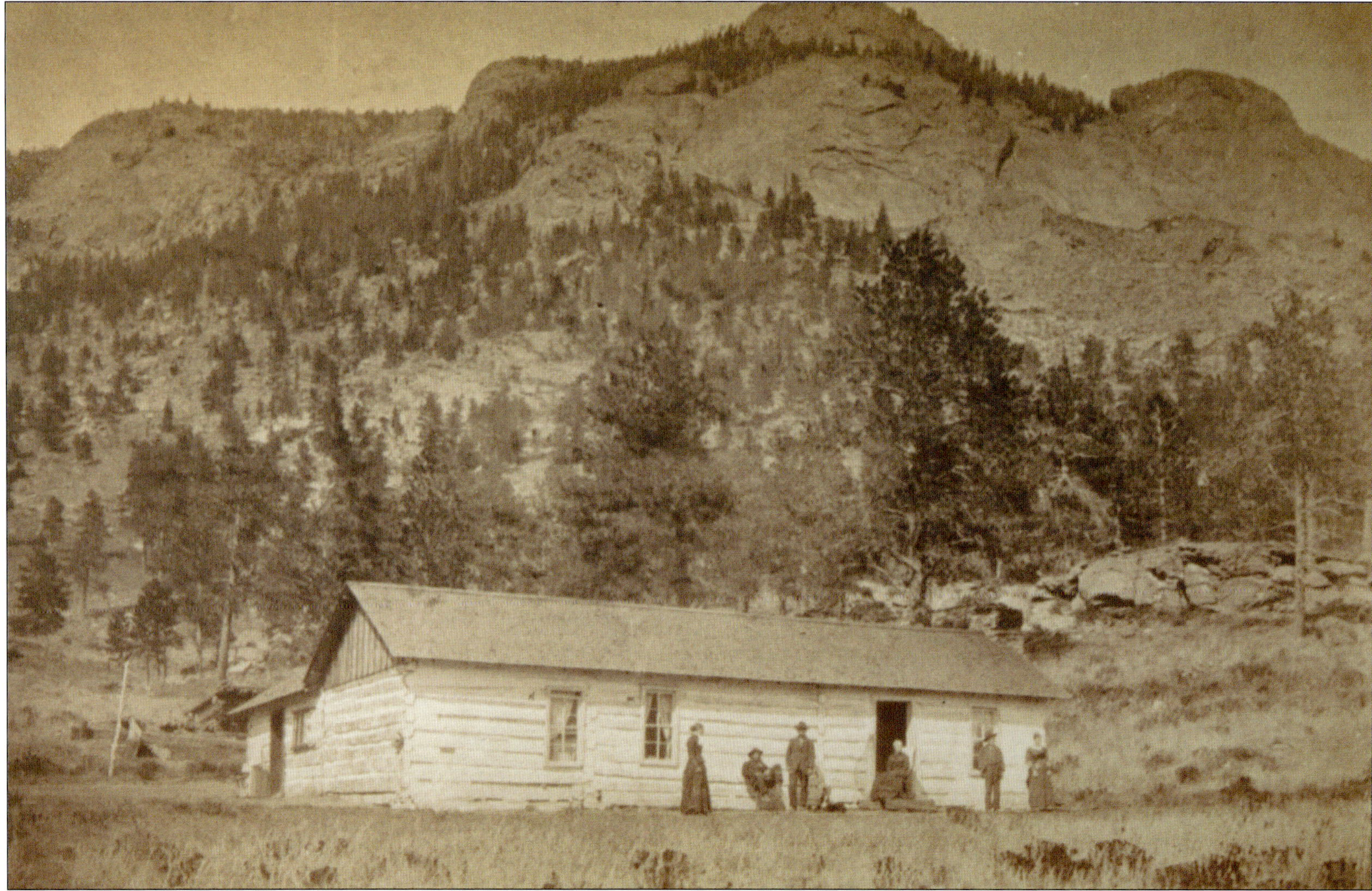

The photograph above shows the homestead cabin of John T. and Eliza Hupp. It was situated on the lower slope of Deer Mountain in lower Beaver Meadows. The Hupps came to Estes Park in August 1875 from Otterville, Missouri, where John Hupp and Horace Ferguson (see p. 150) ran a flour mill.

Here on a gentle hillside near a spring, the Hupps built the three-room, 38-by-16-foot hewn-log-and-frame house in the photograph (the figures posed in the current photograph are positioned to mark the location of the original house); later they enlarged the home with a 14-by-16-foot rear addition. They also improved the property by erecting post-and-pole fencing, a corral, root cellar, chicken house, milk house, and two slab-sided stables. Here, with their seven children, they grew potatoes, vegetables, hay, barley, and wheat, maintained a garden, and managed a small herd of 50 cattle.

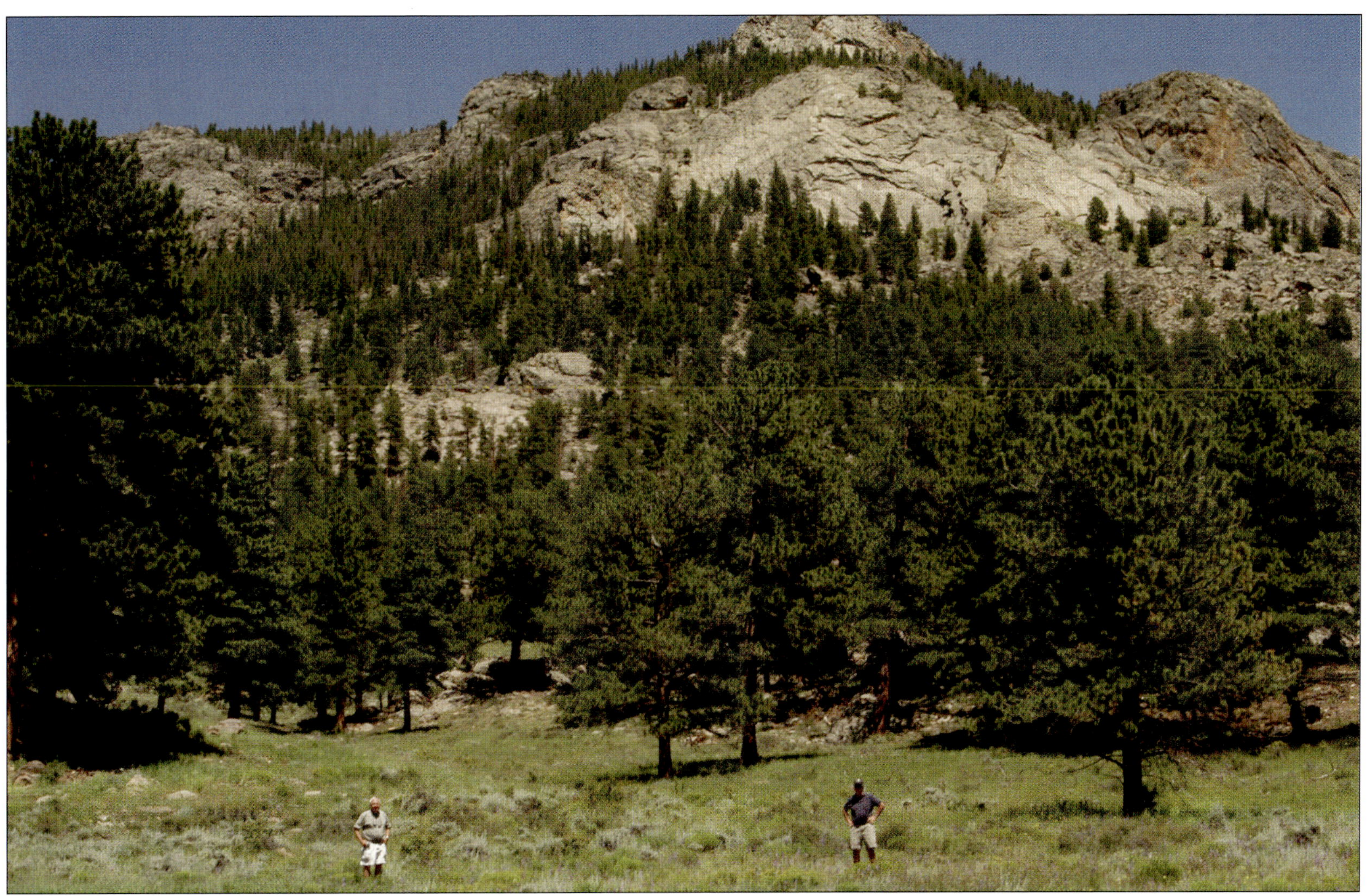

In October 1877, before these improvements were complete, John Hupp died, leaving Eliza to continue to farm and ranch. Several irrigation ditches that were used to water her 12 acres of crops are still visible on the south side of the road entering Beaver Meadows. In 1898, two years before her death, Eliza sold the homestead to her neighbor, Pieter Hondius. Eliza was presumably allowed to retain her home. In 1932, Hondius sold off the property to the National Park Service. To restore the terrain to its original condition and expand grazing land for a rapidly growing elk population, CCC workers quickly removed all buildings. John and Eliza Hupp and daughter Frances are buried near their homestead, and in July 1964, a permanent native granite headstone was erected to mark the spot.

73. Hondius Ranch, 1914

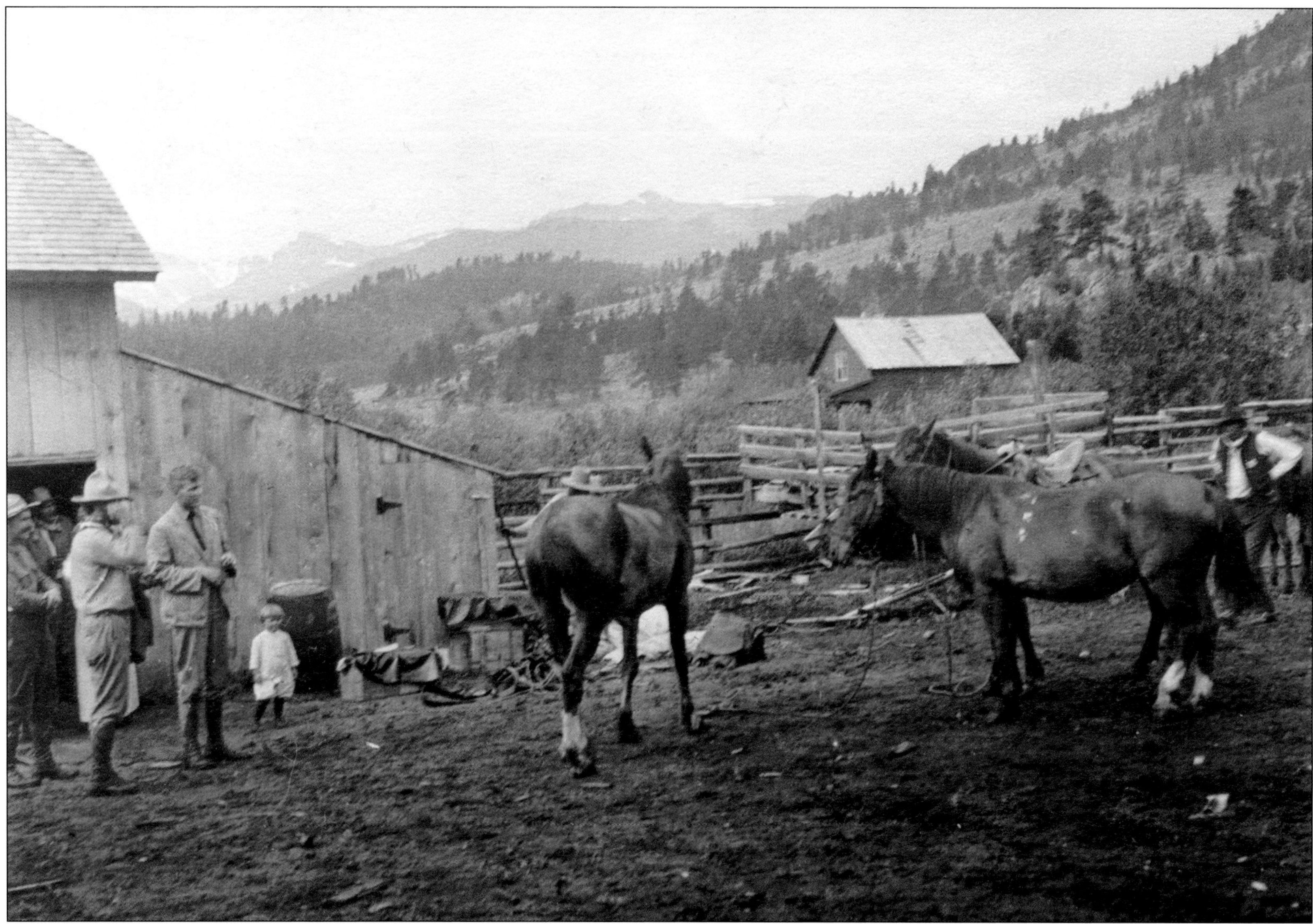

Among the "movers and shakers" of early Estes Park, none was more civic-minded or influential than Dutch-born Pieter Hondius. Coming to Estes Park by way of Denver in 1896 because of chronic asthma, Hondius stayed on to ranch and farm. Purchasing land in Horseshoe Park and in Beaver Meadows, Hondius built a house and barn at the upper end of Beaver Meadows. The barn, it was said at the time, was the largest in Larimer County.

Cattle gave way to other interests, beginning in 1904, when Hondius married Eleanor Estes James, daughter of the original owner of Elkhorn Lodge. This

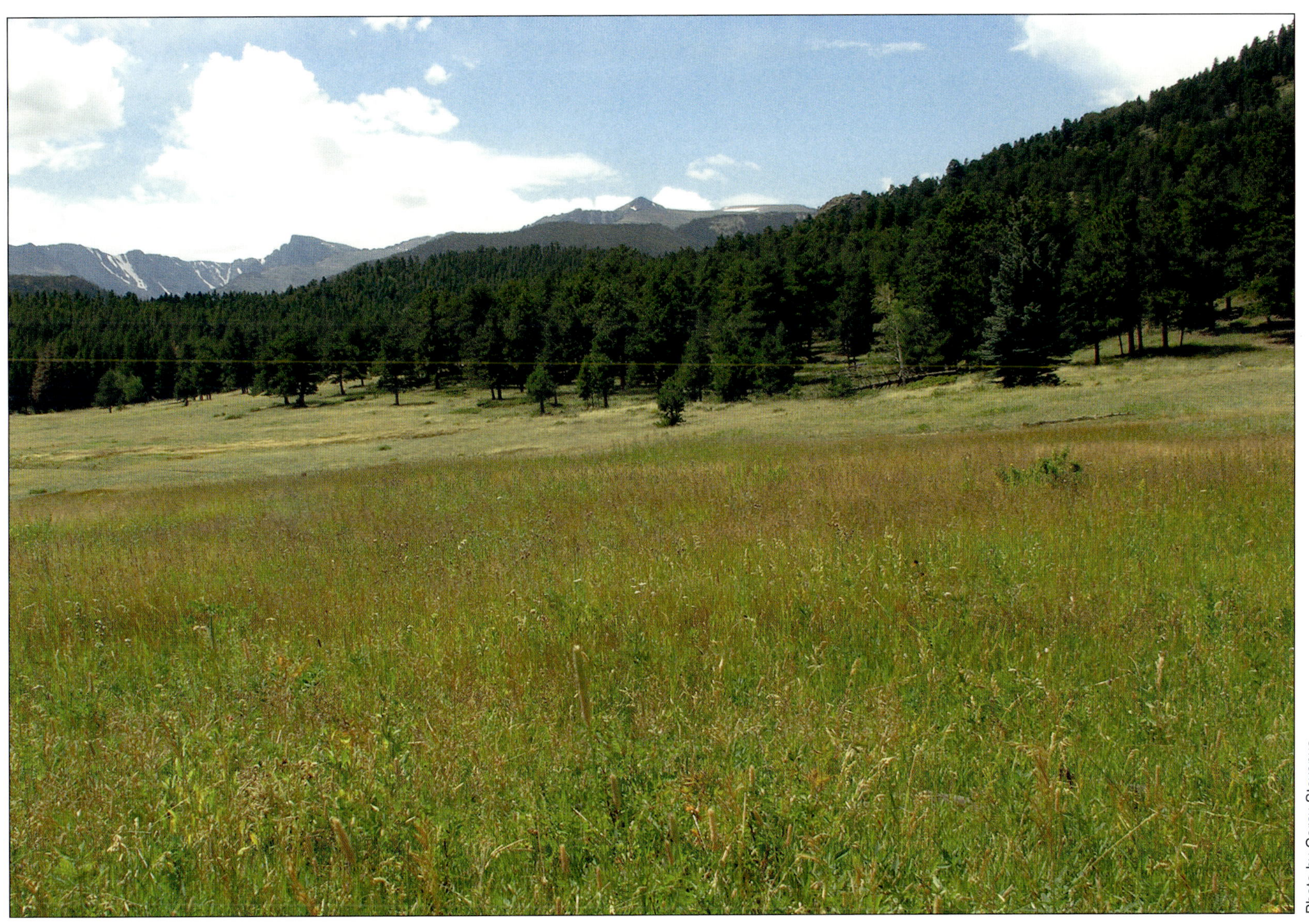
Photo by Carey Stevanus

event—together with such other ventures as the construction of the 6-mile Hondius Water Line, beginning in 1906, to sell water from Buck Creek in Upper Beaver Meadows to cabin owners in the High Drive area south of Deer Mountain—brought him into contact with other early leaders of the Estes Park community. Hondius became particularly active in the Estes Park Protective and Improvement Association, which raised money to build the new fish hatchery in 1907 (see p. 66), reintroduced elk to the region from Yellowstone in 1913 and 1915, and lobbied for the creation of a national park.

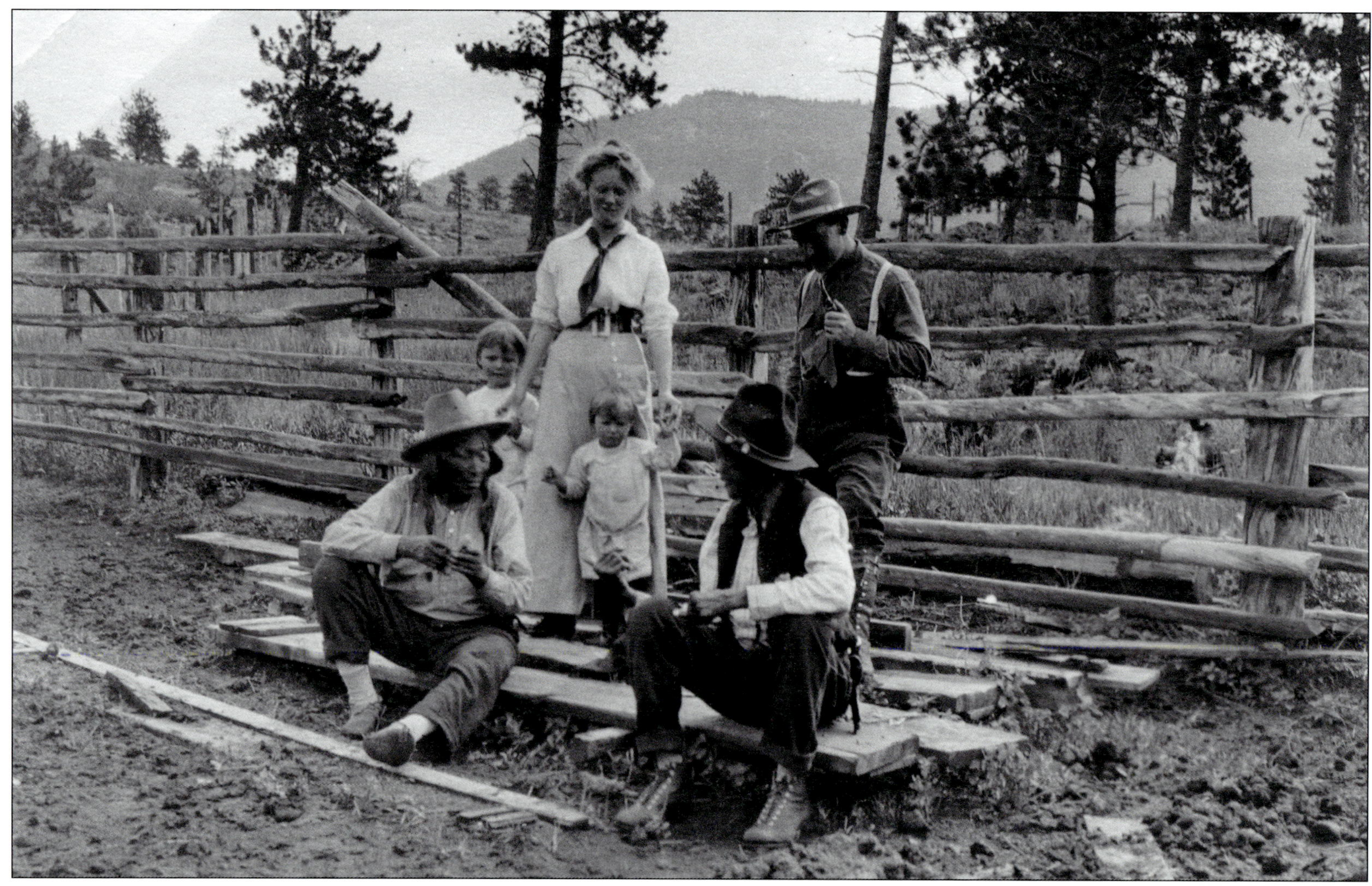

Hondius sold his 1,762-acre holdings in Beaver Meadows and Horseshoe Park to the National Park Service in 1932 for $140,720, then considered a princely sum. House, barn, and other outbuildings were soon removed and the site obliterated. All that remains today are a square of stones where the ranch house once stood, in the meadow across the stream from the present parking lot; a block of concrete near the Park Service's new latrine facility, which once held the gatepost for the barn's corral; and, back in the woods to the west, the unmistakable signs of the ditches and diversions that were part of the Hondius Water Line.

Also of interest on the rocky outcropping immediately southwest of the ranch house is the so-called "Indian Fort," a site identified in 1914 by the Arapaho brought back to the area under the auspices of the Colorado Mountain Club. According to 63-year-old Sherman Sage, the fort had been "the scene of a great battle between the Apaches and the Arapahos." Sage was only four at the

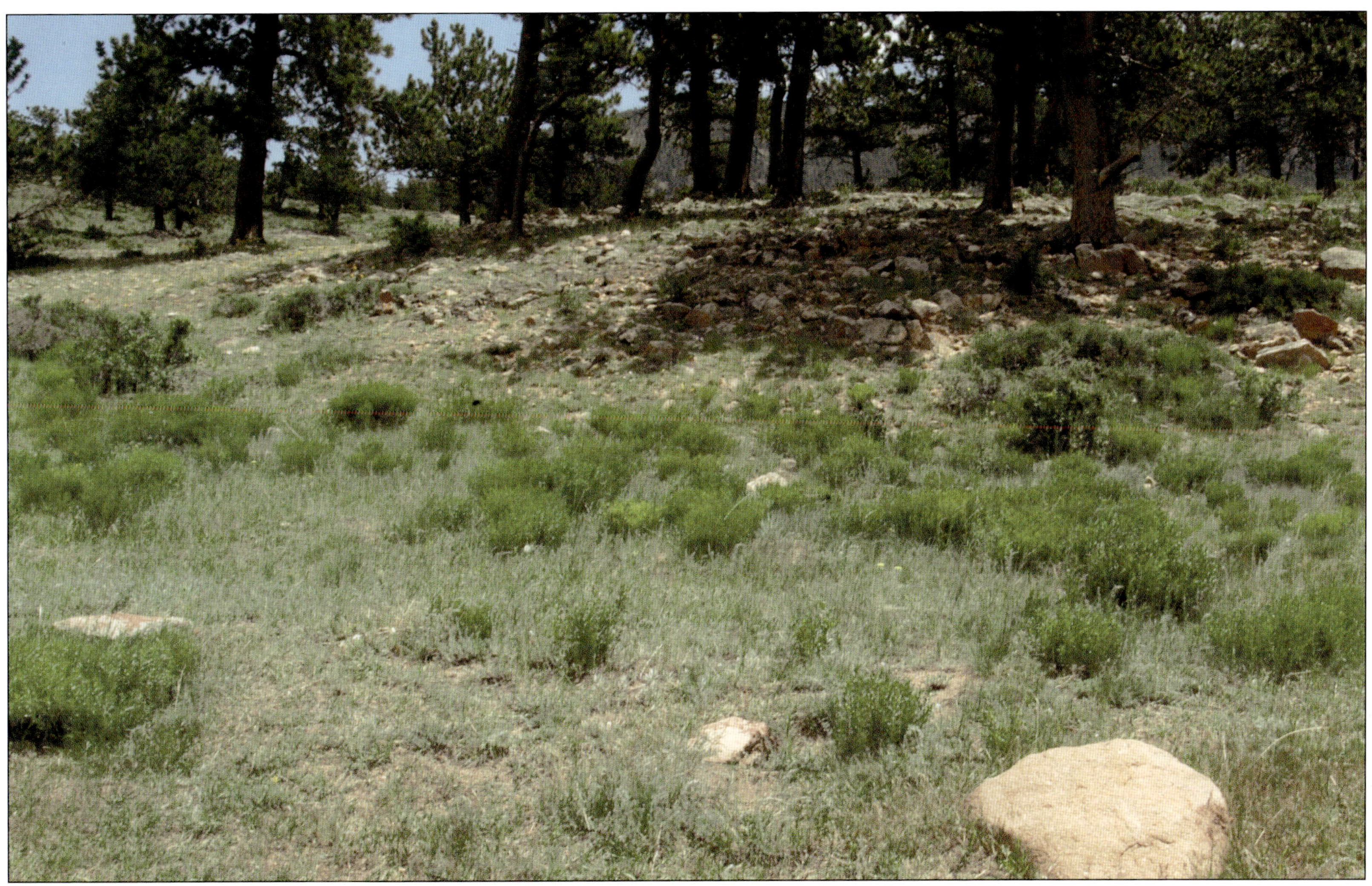

time—which would date the battle as having taken place in 1855. Retreating across Beaver Meadows to the rocky cliffs behind the Hondius ranch, so the story goes, the Apache made a last stand behind stones they had piled along the cliff to a height of 3 or 4 feet. Those stones were used a half century later as footings for the Hondius house.

The photographs of the Hondius ranch date from the day of that memorable visit. The first photograph, showing the two Arapaho standing in the corral, provides the only known view of the Hondius ranch house. The second historic photograph shows Sherman Sage and fellow Arapaho Gun Griswold seated by a fence at the ranch. The fence shown in the photograph stood on the right side of today's parking area.

74. Camping in Moraine Park, circa 1895

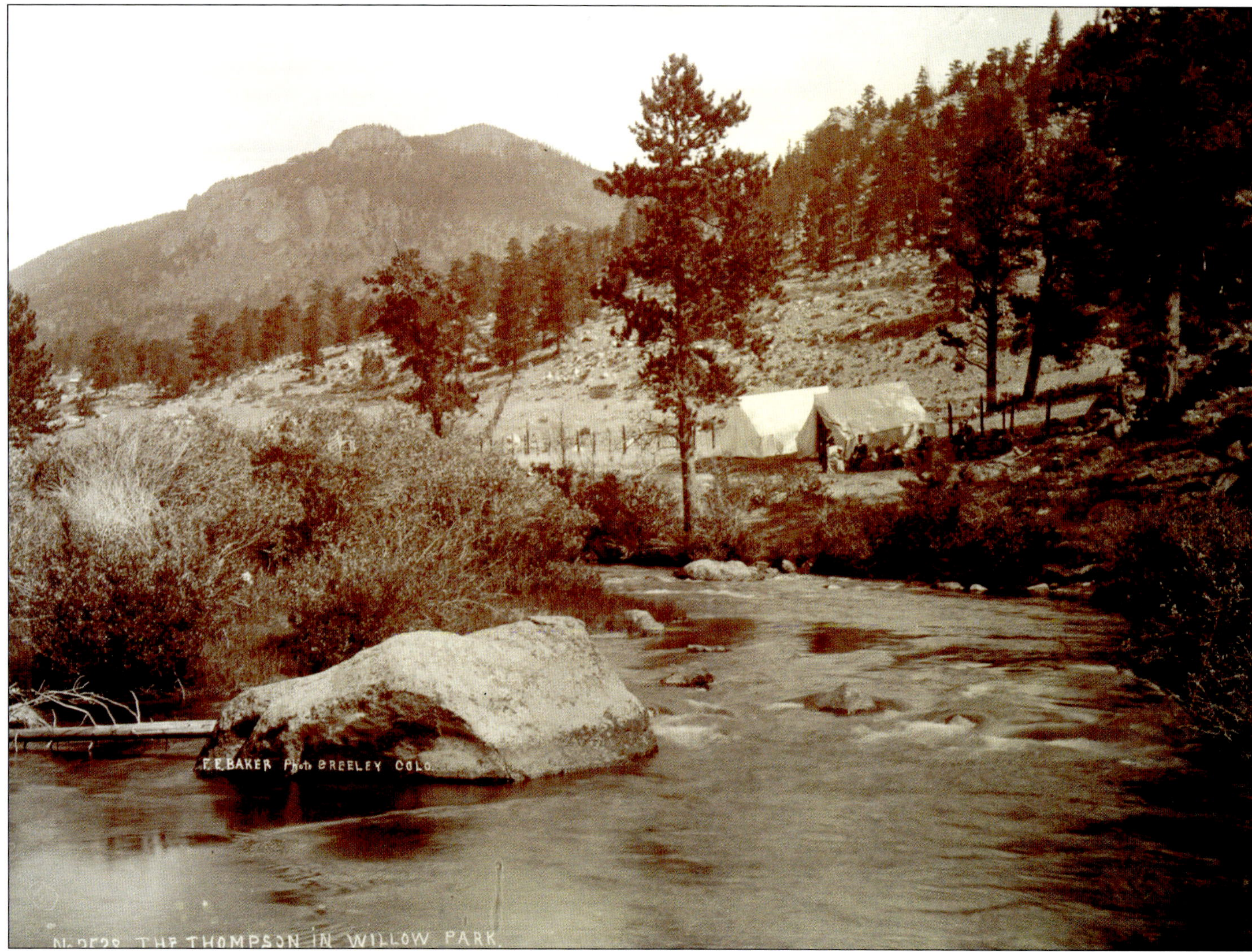

Photo by F. E. Baker

Moraine Park, or "Willow Park" as it was first called due to the willow bushes that lined the Big Thompson River, has always been popular. For many years a small community surrounded the post office and store run by Abner Sprague's mother, "Grandma Sprague." Moraine Park was also the site of lodges, guest ranches, and private cottages. With its view of Longs Peak, the Front Range, and Forest Canyon, Moraine Park has also attracted many photographers.

One was Frank E. Baker of Greeley, who took this original photograph across the Big Thompson. We know little about him other than he came to Greeley from South Pass, Illinois, in 1871, married in 1872, and spent the next three years in Greeley before returning to Illinois. In March 1893, Baker was back in Greeley, where he purchased the studio of M. E. Chase on Main Street, advertising himself as a "Photographer and View Artist." By the summer of 1895,

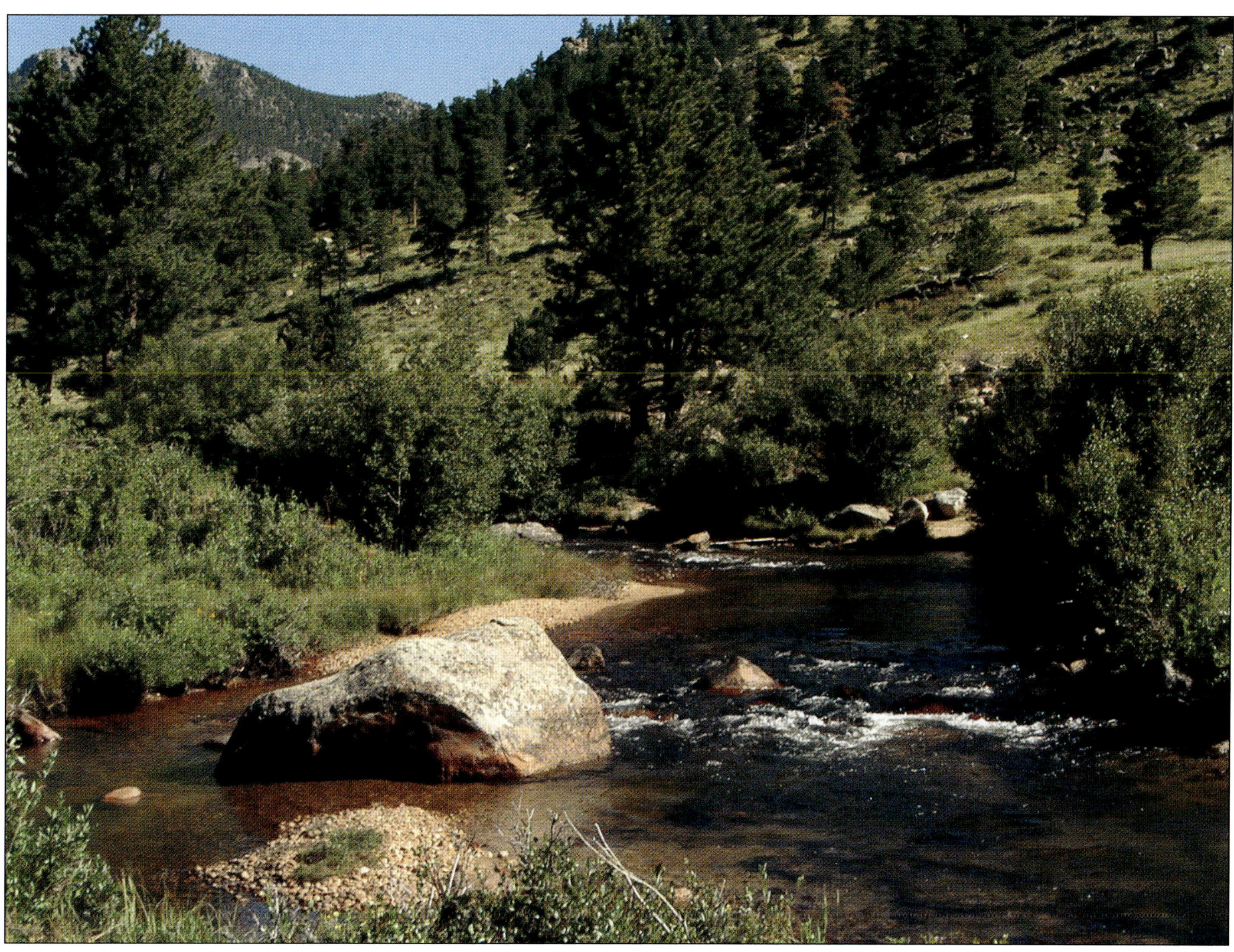

Baker was taking photographs in the Rocky Mountains, and in June 1896 he opened a photographic gallery in Estes Park. The following April he went to Chicago, leaving his son, photographer Bert D. Baker, in charge of his gallery, apparently never to return again. Much of our historical knowledge of early Estes Park's appearance is thanks to F. E. Baker's stunning sepia-color photographs of these early days of Colorado history.

Both the subject and Baker's artistry with the camera in skillfully capturing the effects of light and shadow attracted us to this photograph. The scene of tenting on the riverbanks, roughly where the road to Bear Lake is now, reminds us how early visitors often summered in Estes Park, pitching their tents in some scenic, sequestered spot to recreate, relax, fish, or, as in F. E. Baker's case, to take photographs.

75. Chapman Ranch, circa 1910

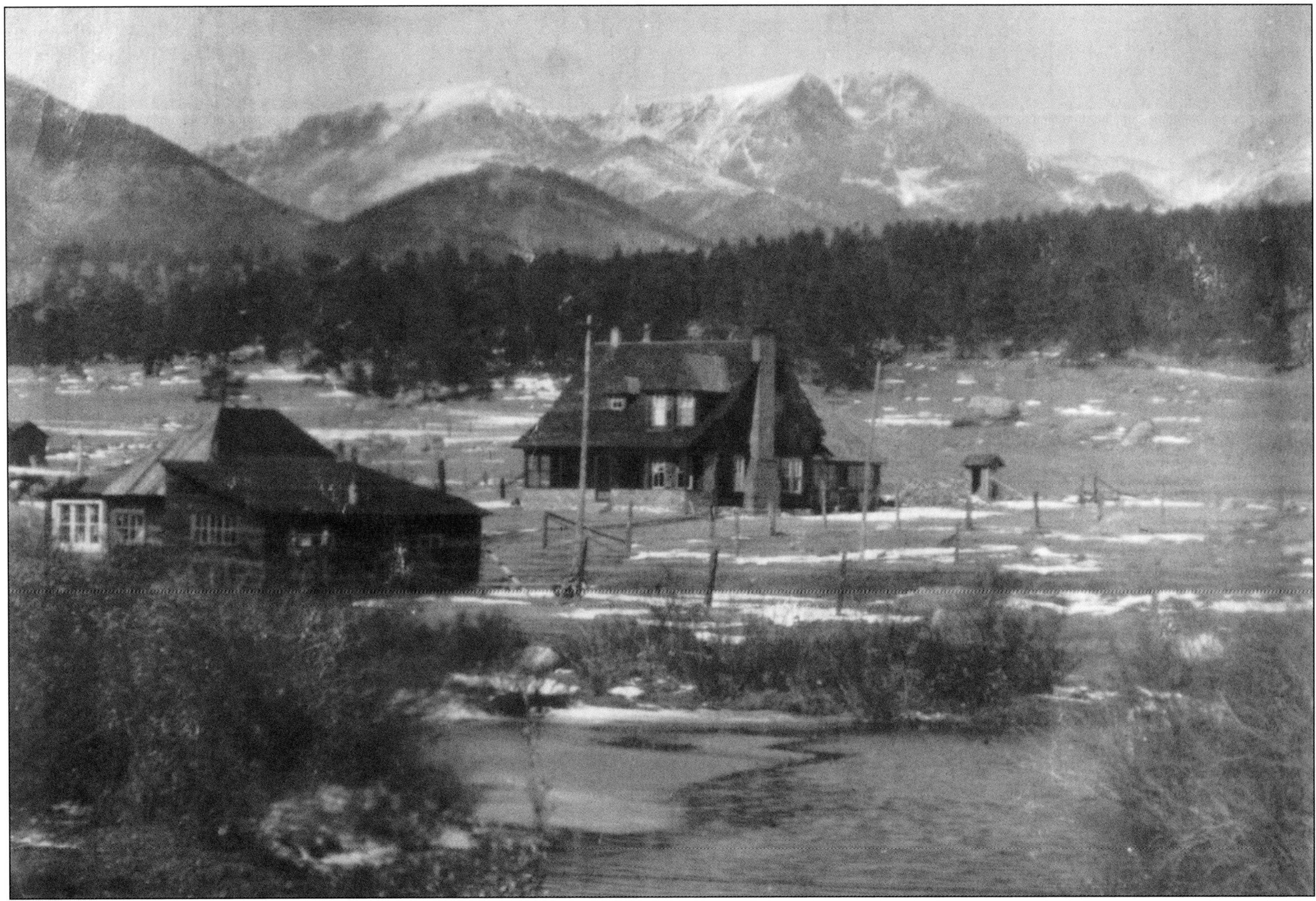

The Chapman Ranch in Moraine Park was once the home of Areanna Sprague Chapman, Abner Sprague's sister. "Arah" came from Illinois with the rest of the Sprague family and settled in the Big Thompson Valley east of Loveland. In 1871, she became the first teacher at Namaqua, a small settlement on the Big Thompson. The next year she met future husband Alson Chapman, who also became her brother's camping and climbing companion; when Abner Sprague made his first ascent of Longs Peak in 1874, Alson accompanied him.

Arah and Alson Chapman married in 1876 and made their home in the Big Thompson Valley. Alson died in 1890, and two years later Arah brought her sons, Charles and Alson, to Moraine Park, where they settled on 160 acres east of where her brother had built his homestead cabin in 1875. Her house and its Moraine Park setting have been rephotographed here. Arah built small rental cabins near the river; one of her 1889 renters was University of Kansas student William Allen White, future editor of the *Emporia Gazette* (see p. 198).

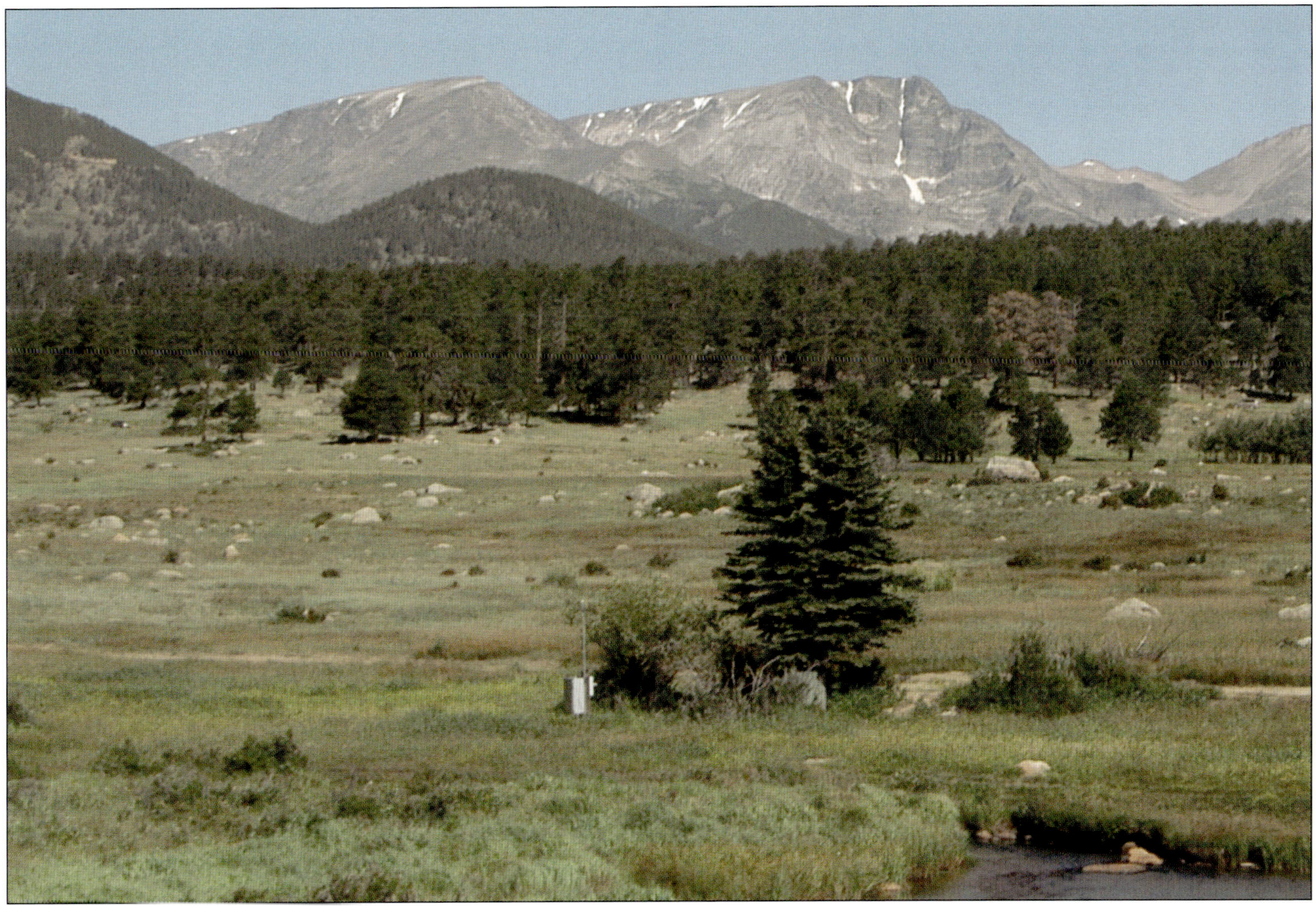

Nearby was the general store that Arah's mother, Mary Sprague, opened in the late 1870s. In 1880, the rear of the store became the Willow Park Post Office, the second in Estes Park. Mary Sprague served as postmistress until 1908, when Arah took over.

Arah Chapman sold her Moraine Park property to the National Park Service in 1932 for $23,630 and moved into a new home on upper Elkhorn Avenue. The Park Service, intent on restoring the land back to its original state, quickly burned the buildings—an act for which Arah never forgave the government. The fire was so intense that the shards of glass, still scattered near the original fireplace footings, fused together.

76. Eaton House, *circa* 1930

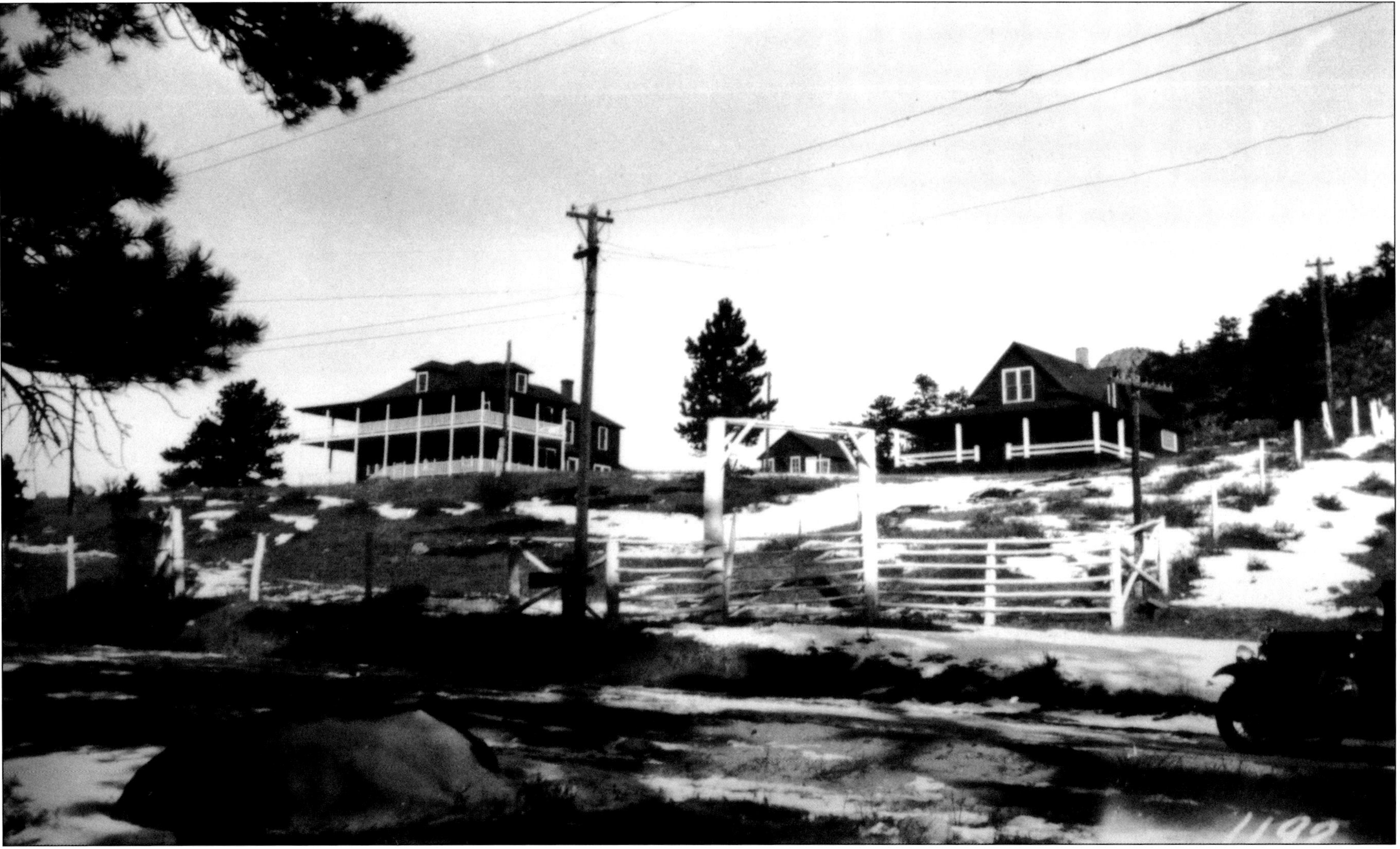

On this hillside below Eagle Cliff Mountain, overlooking Moraine Park and the Big Thompson River, and close by the road that until the 1960s was one of the two eastern entrances accessing Rocky Mountain National Park, once stood two imposing summer homes built by the Eaton and Kennedy families. Today, only a few traces of their footings and foundations remain. And strangely, given the prominence of both families, we know relatively little about either home.

The larger of the two homes shown in the historic photograph was the Eaton house, built sometime after 1906 on 6.57 acres of land purchased from the Chapman family by Bruce G. Eaton. He was the son of Benjamin Harrison Eaton, a wealthy Greeley farmer who had served as Colorado's 10th governor from 1885 to 1887 and was one of the state's most influential and prominent men. Bruce Eaton spent most of his life managing his father's extensive interests in

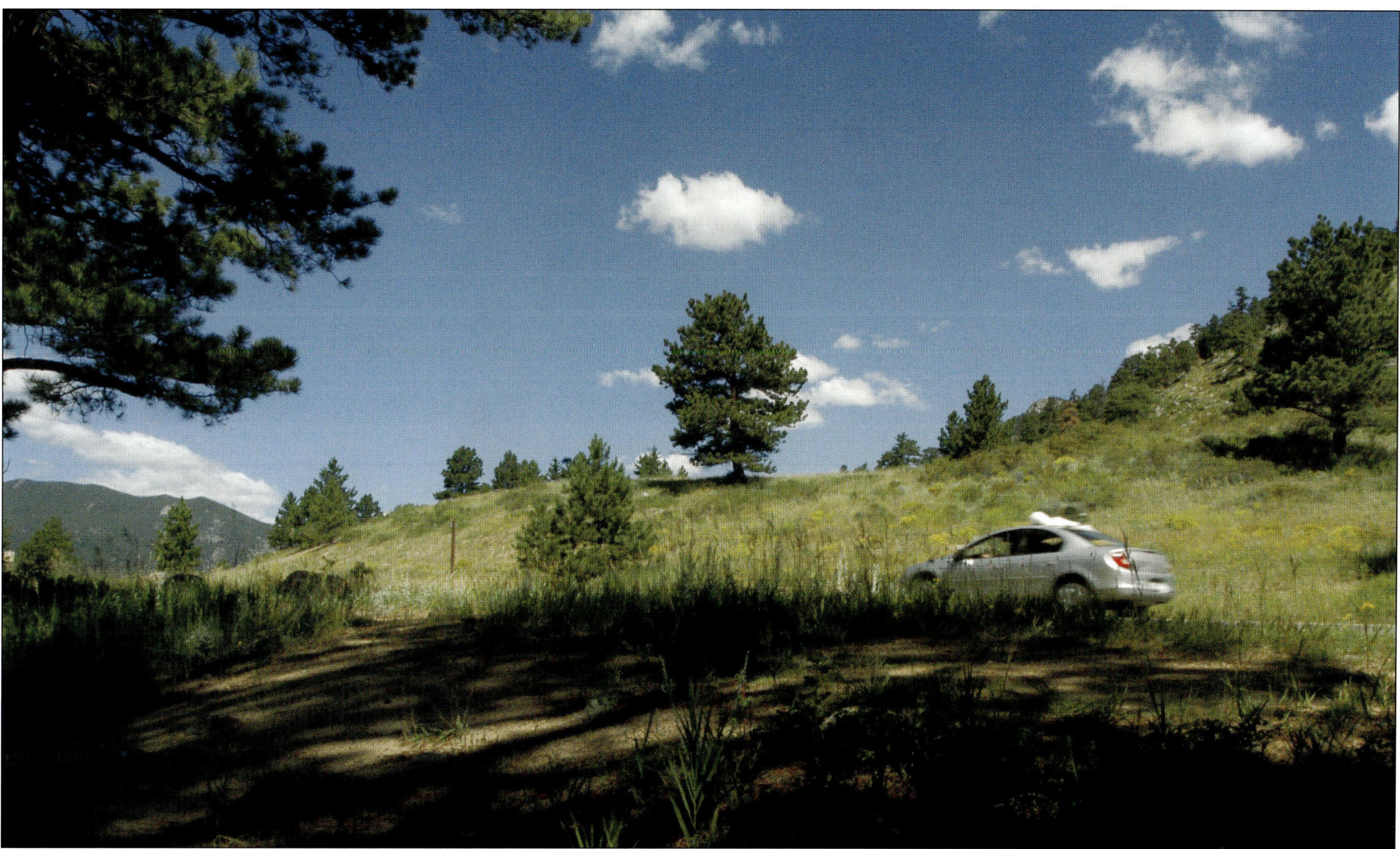

and around Eaton, Colorado, founded by his father in 1892, and his summers were spent in Estes Park, in the house with the large veranda photographed here. He also played a fairly active role in turn-of-the-century Estes Park affairs as a member of the Estes Park Protective and Improvement Association.

The Kennedy house, though difficult to make out in the photograph, predated its neighbor, as well as its other neighbors, the William Allen White cabin and The Scottage (see pp. 198 and 202). It was built by a Dr. Kennedy of Denver. Though the site of both houses today is somewhat remote, the road entering Moraine Park and Rocky Mountain National Park once climbed the hill in back of them.

77. William Allen White Cabin, circa 1965

From 1912 to 1943, this rustic one-bedroom, one-bath cabin that overlooked Moraine Park was the summer retreat of Emporia, Kansas, newspaper editor and author William Allen White. He attended the University of Kansas, and it was with a group of fellow KU students that he first came to Estes Park in the summer of 1889, living in a cabin in Moraine Park on the Big Thompson. The group also included future major general "Fighting Fred" Funston and future Missouri governor Herbert Hadley. "We were not a serious crowd," White would later write in his Pulitzer Prize–winning *Autobiography* (1946). "We lived simply, gaily. We had two rules, only two, as the laws of our republic: every man must clean his own fish, and no razor would be allowed in the camp."

On one occasion, Funston, apparently in a fit of what today we would call "conservationism," took a rifle and "marched down the road to where some advertising painters were smearing huge boulders with admonishings to use somebody's sarsaparilla," scaring them away with a combination of bravado and profanity. (His efforts, however, were only partially successful, for the lead paint advertisement on one of those boulders is still visible in the underbrush south of the William Allen White cabin close by the Big Thompson River, near today's bridge.)

When White married Sallie Lindsay in 1893, he returned to Moraine Park for his honeymoon. In 1912, now the established editor of the *Emporia Gazette*, White purchased this small, high-beamed cabin with a living room/dining area and large fireplace east of The Scottage (see p. 202). It had been built in the early years of the century by professor Arvin S. Olin, also of the University of Kansas. The cabin was too small for a growing family, even after the Whites added a bathroom and a 14-foot porch with cobblestone columns on three sides. To make room, White built two additional small bedroom cabins—one for son Bill, the other for daughter Mary—as well as a study for himself located a hundred feet up the hill, guaranteeing privacy.

Here in Moraine Park the Whites spent the happiest summers of their family life, a period that climaxed in tragedy, when in 1921 the vivacious 16-year-old Mary was fatally injured in Emporia. As she turned to greet a friend, her horse rode into the branch of a tree.

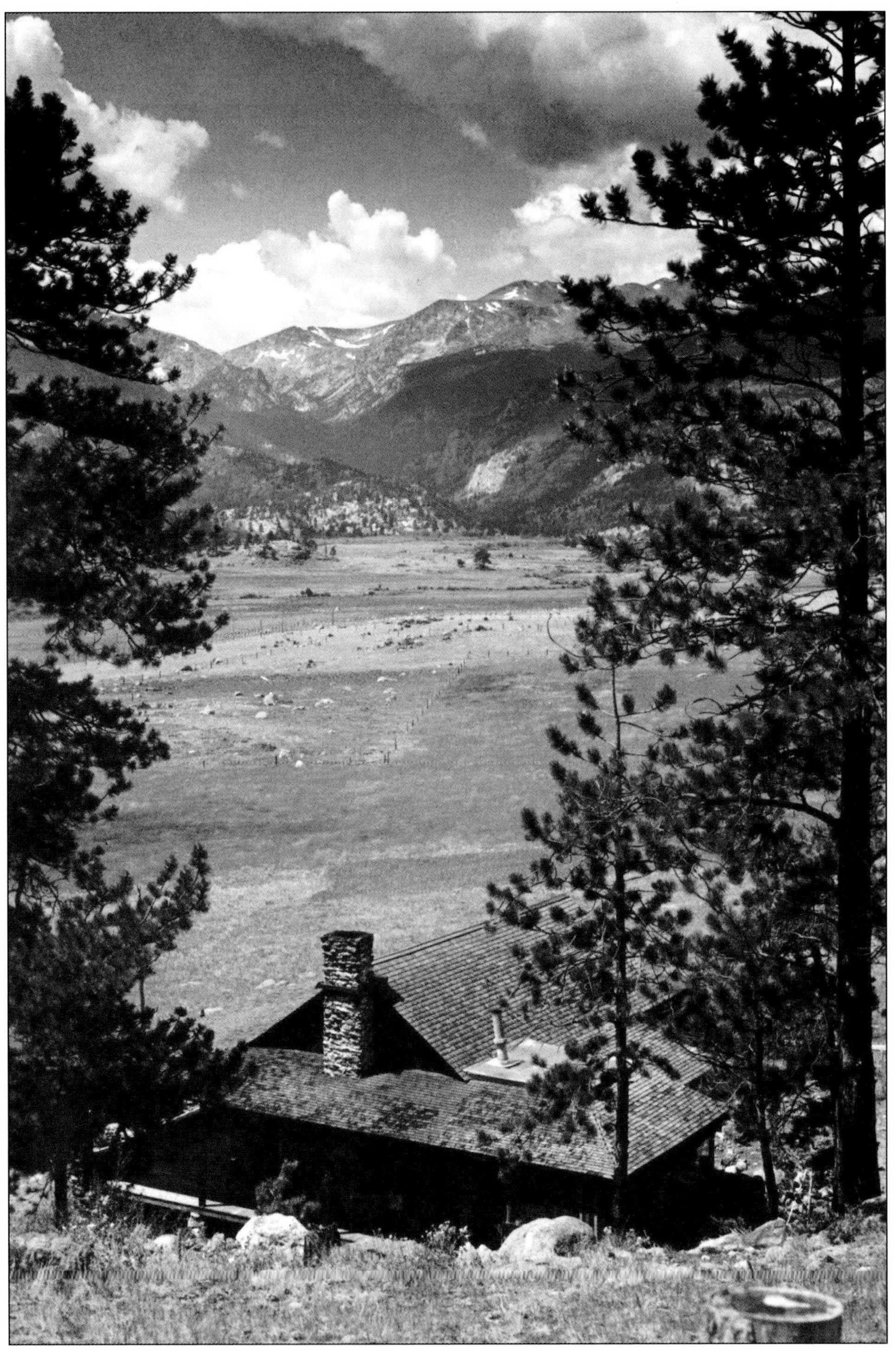

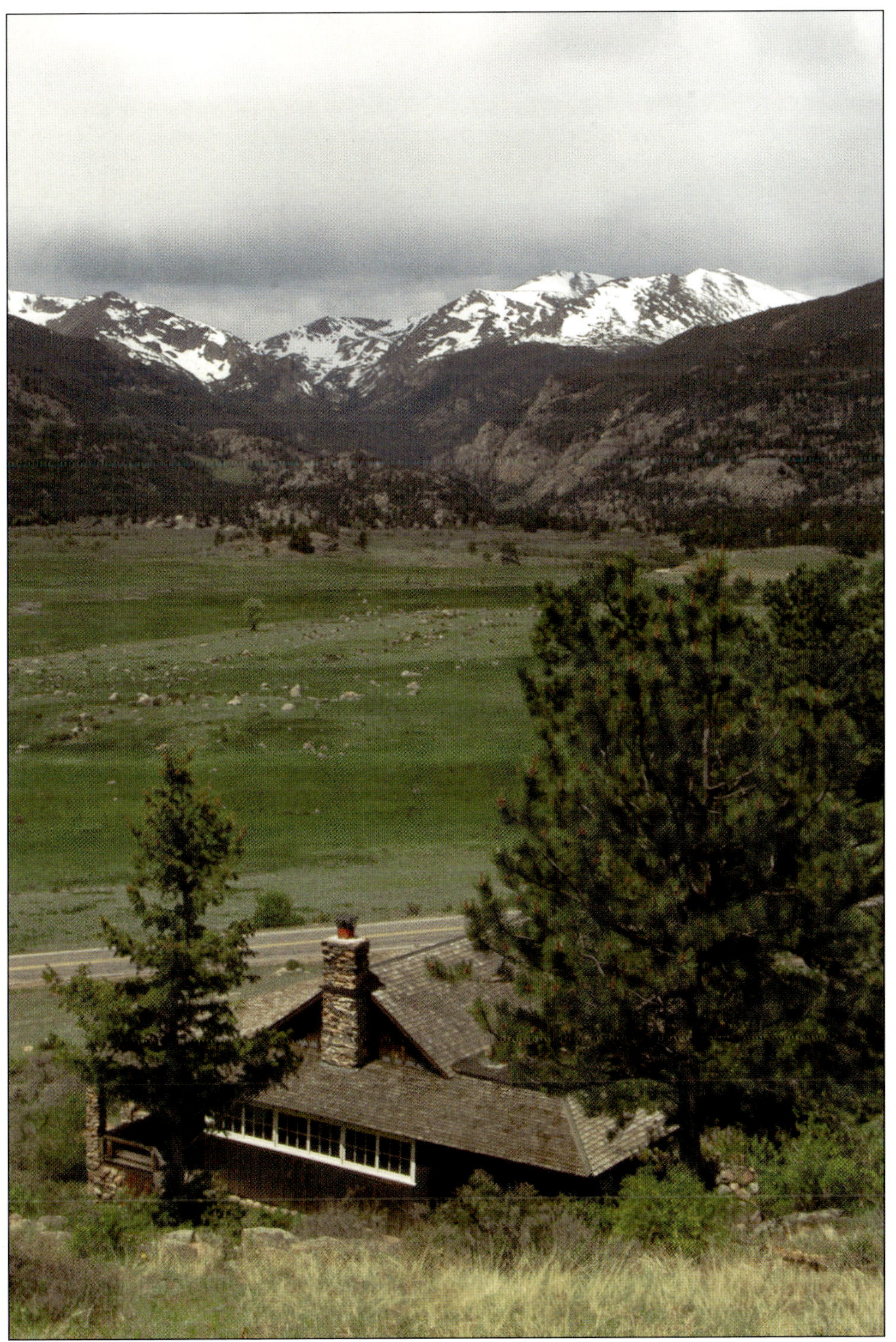

Despite grief that time never erased, the Whites returned to summer in Moraine Park. A staunch Republican who was not afraid to break with party on principle, or to use his position to vigorously oppose the intolerance of Kansas' powerful Ku Klux Klan, William Allen White was now nationally famous. He also used his summer cabin to entertain some of the best-known figures of his generation, while communicating with others by telephone and continuing to write about major issues facing the nation and the world.

The cabin remained in the White family up until 1972, when "Young Bill," William Lindsay White, decided to sell off the house and its contents to the National Park Service. It is today used to house visitors in the Park Service's Artist in Residence Program.

The photographs of the White cabin capture it as it was and is. The first, of the cabin and its Moraine Park vista, was taken from just inside the doorway of William Allen White's study on the hillside above. For the second photograph, we were fortunate enough to persuade Ferrel Atkins, a longtime seasonal ranger and an authority on William Allen White, to pose as the Kansas editor.

William Allen White and, opposite, Ferrel Atkins

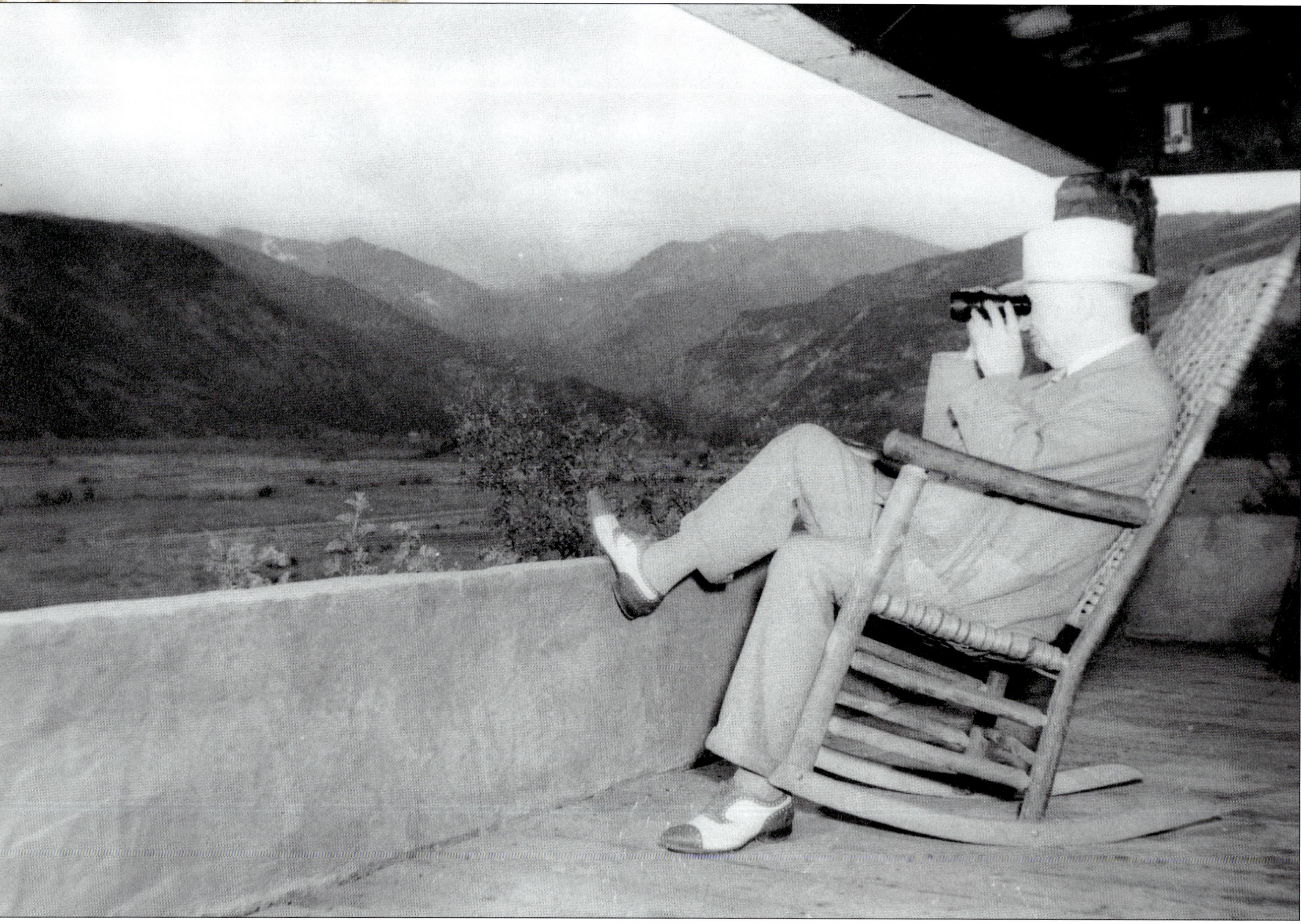

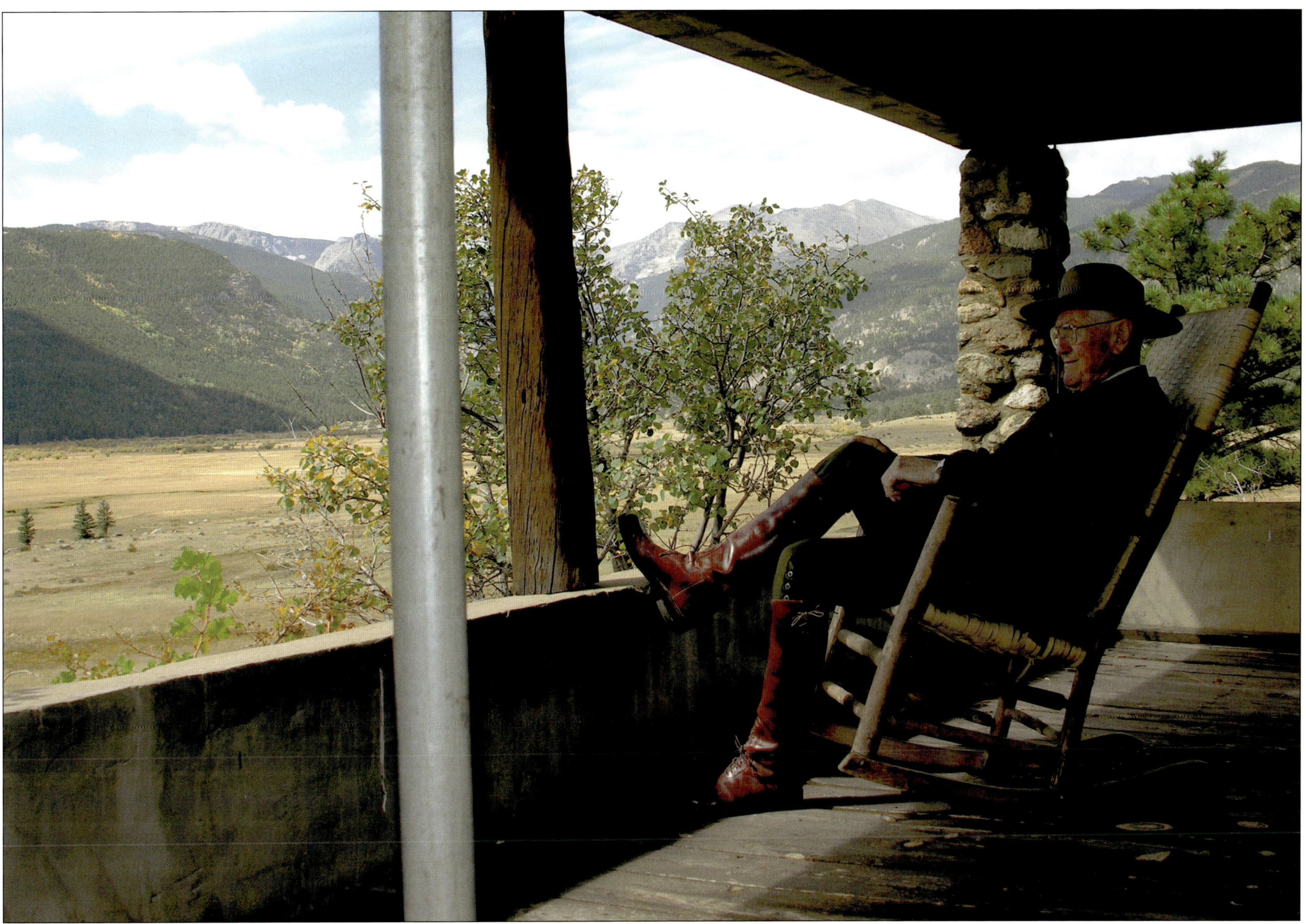

Photo by Carey Stevanus

78. The Scottage, circa 1905

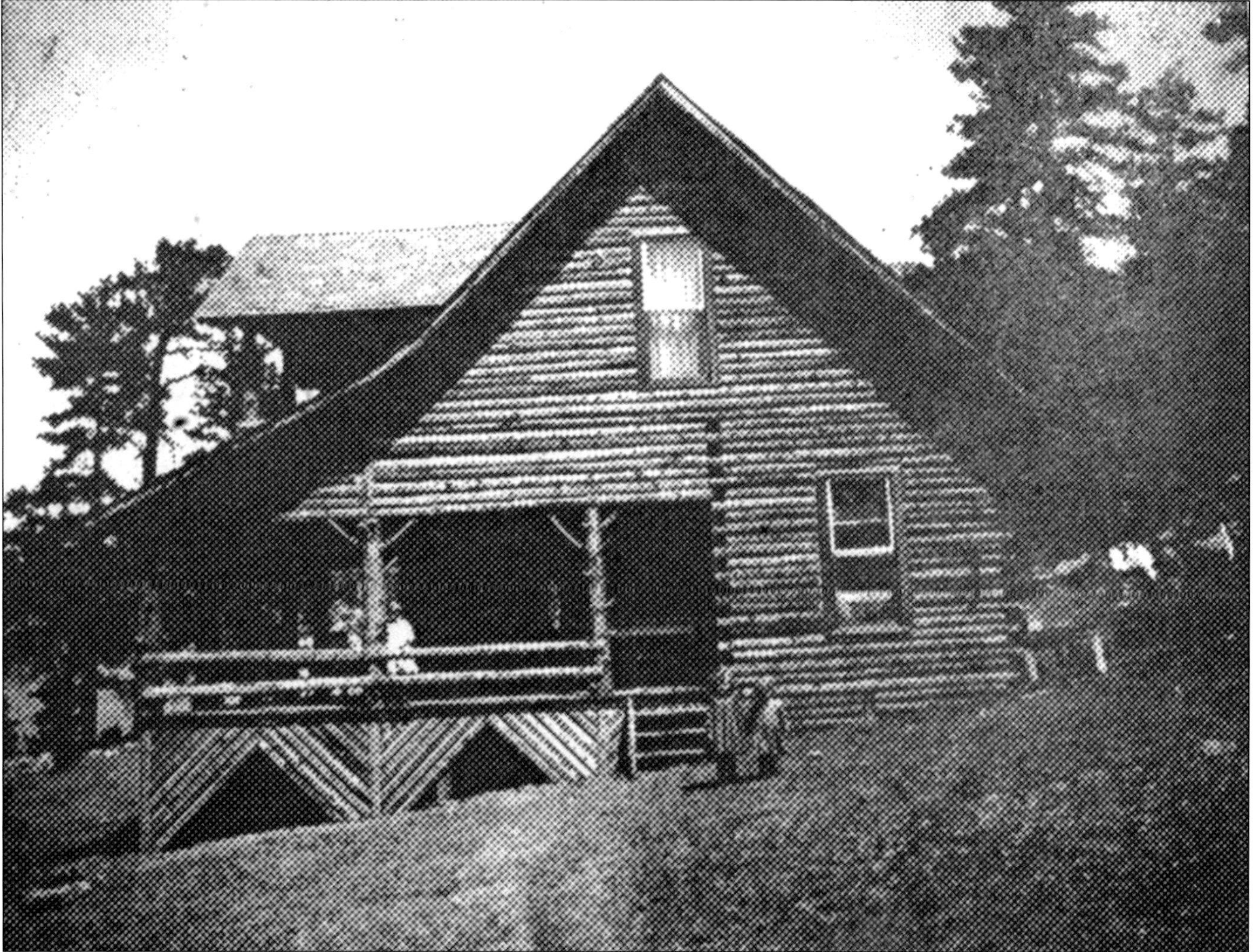

Standing south of the Moraine Park Visitor Center and named after its family of owners, "The Scottage" was built in 1899 for Charles F. Scott—Iola, Kansas, newspaperman, state civic leader, and Republican congressman. He had first visited Moraine Park in the late 1880s with a group of young people from Kansas that included Fred Funston, the future major general, and Vernon L. Kellogg, who would later become a distinguished entomologist at Stanford University. Presumably he returned in other summers, for Moraine Park had become a favorite destination of many associated with the University of Kansas, including Scott's friend and neighbor William Allen White.

In June 1893, Charles Scott married May Brevard Ewing, and in late 1898 or early 1899, he paid Fred Sprague $70 for 8 acres of hillside land on which to build a summer cottage for his wife and their children. The cottage, which the

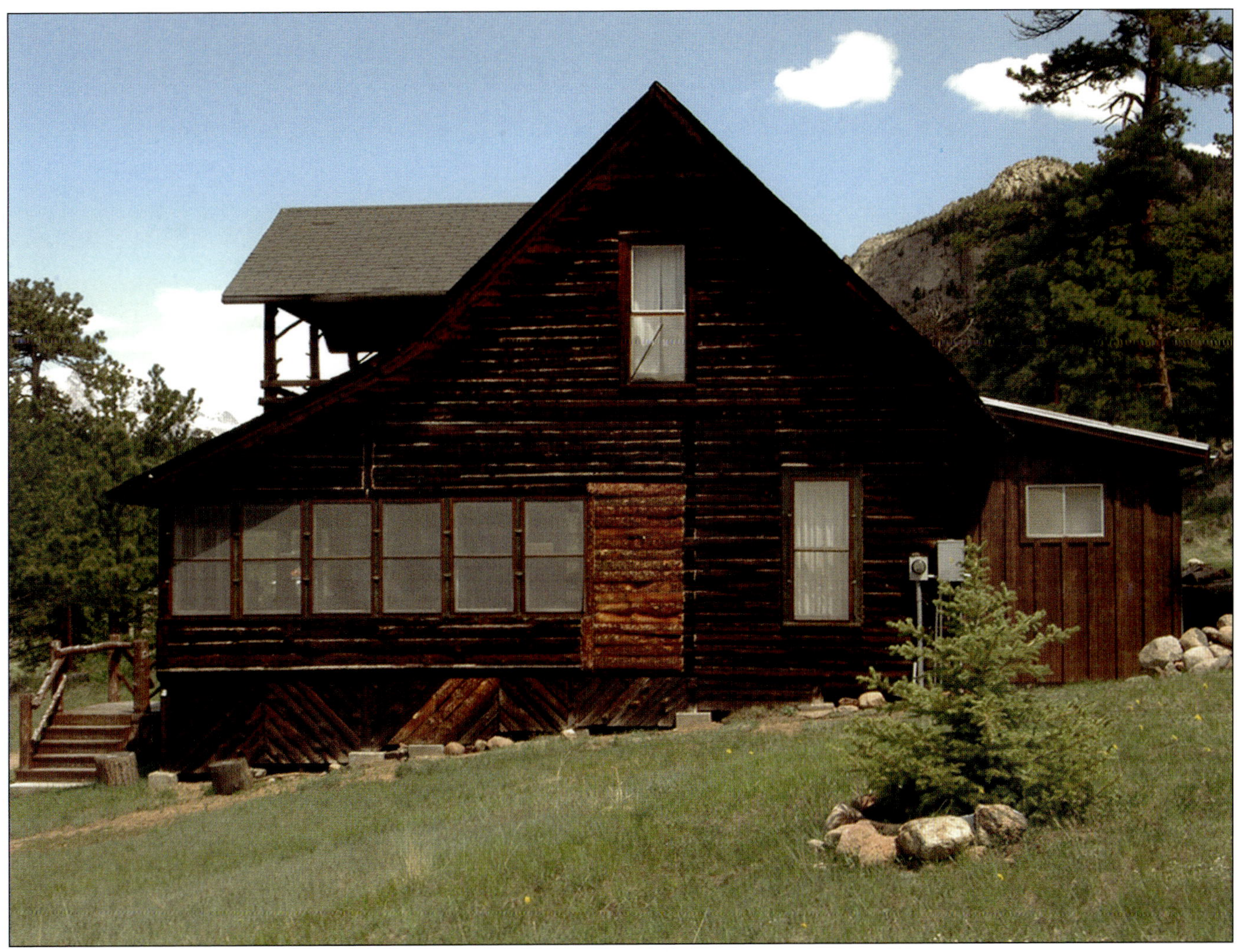

Scotts first occupied during the summer of 1900, originally had no back porch, pantry, or bathroom. These additions followed, together with a retaining wall at the rear of the house. The open side porch was also closed to become the dining porch. Later still, the back porch became a second bathroom, the side door and steps off the dining porch were removed, and the front wooden steps, which originally went straight down, were rebuilt to split at a landing. The changes to the front and side of the house are clearly visible in the photographs here, as is the fact that the lower front and side of the porch have been given a wooden facade.

The story of the Scott family and their long love affair with Moraine Park and their summer cottage has been told in a typescript manuscript titled "The Scottage: A Medley."

79. Moraine Lodge, circa 1925

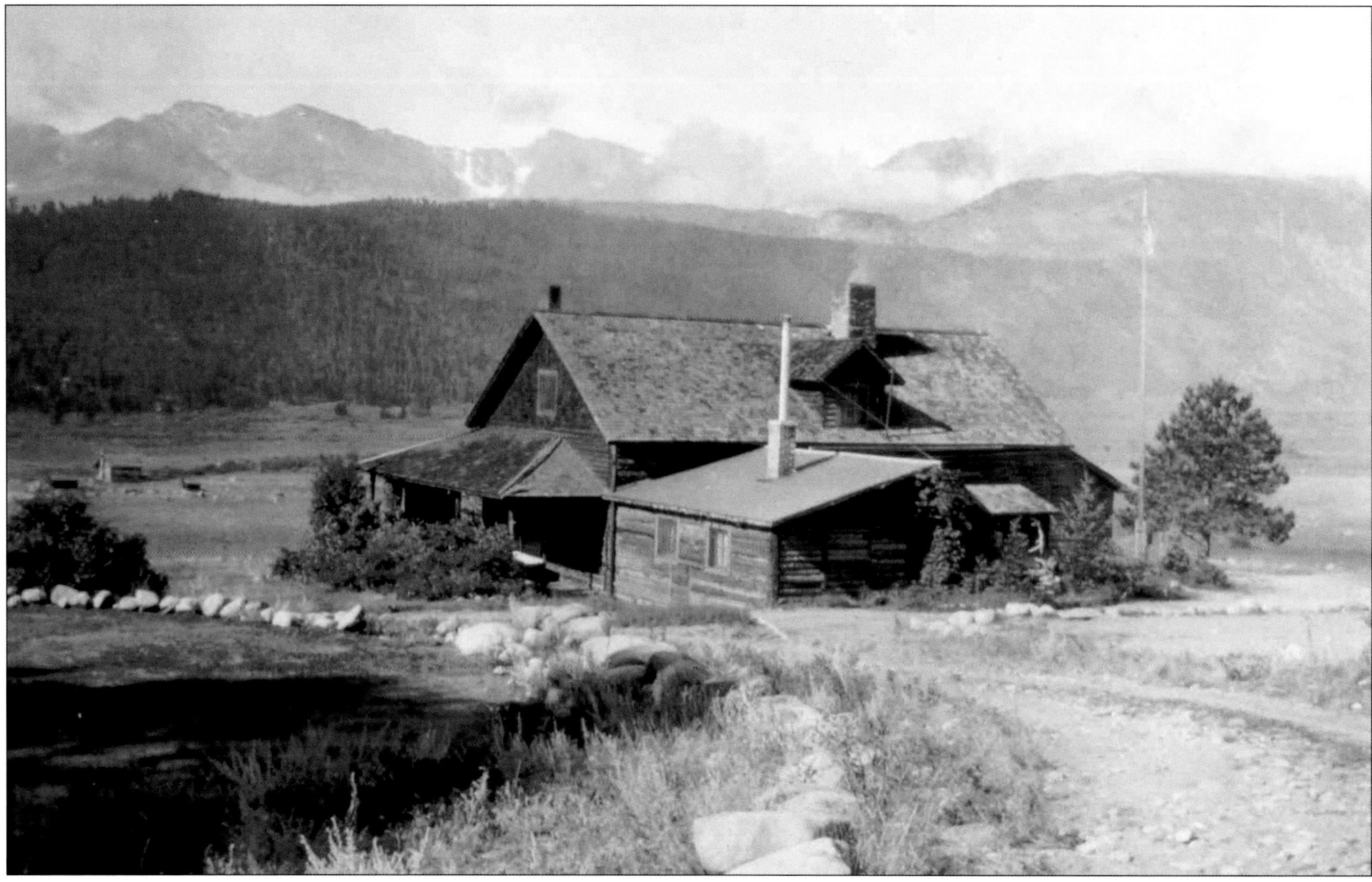

Today's visitors to Rocky Mountain National Park know the Moraine Lodge as the Moraine Park Visitor Center, whose building was once the lodge's recreation and assembly hall. Moraine Lodge began as the homestead of Mary Imogene Bates Greene, an Indiana native and recent divorcée who had come to Estes Park on vacation in August 1898. She purchased for $200 a choice 160-acre tract with a small cabin she named "Hillside."

By 1905, Mary MacPherson, since her marriage to William D. MacPherson, a Rocky Ford lumber dealer, decided to try the tourist business. "Hillside" expanded into Moraine Park Lodge, opening in June 1910 with main lodge and dining room, cabins, tent houses, and stable. William died in 1919, and Mary, who was active in local affairs, carried on. A large two-story log assembly hall below the main lodge was completed in 1923, containing a tearoom and business office.

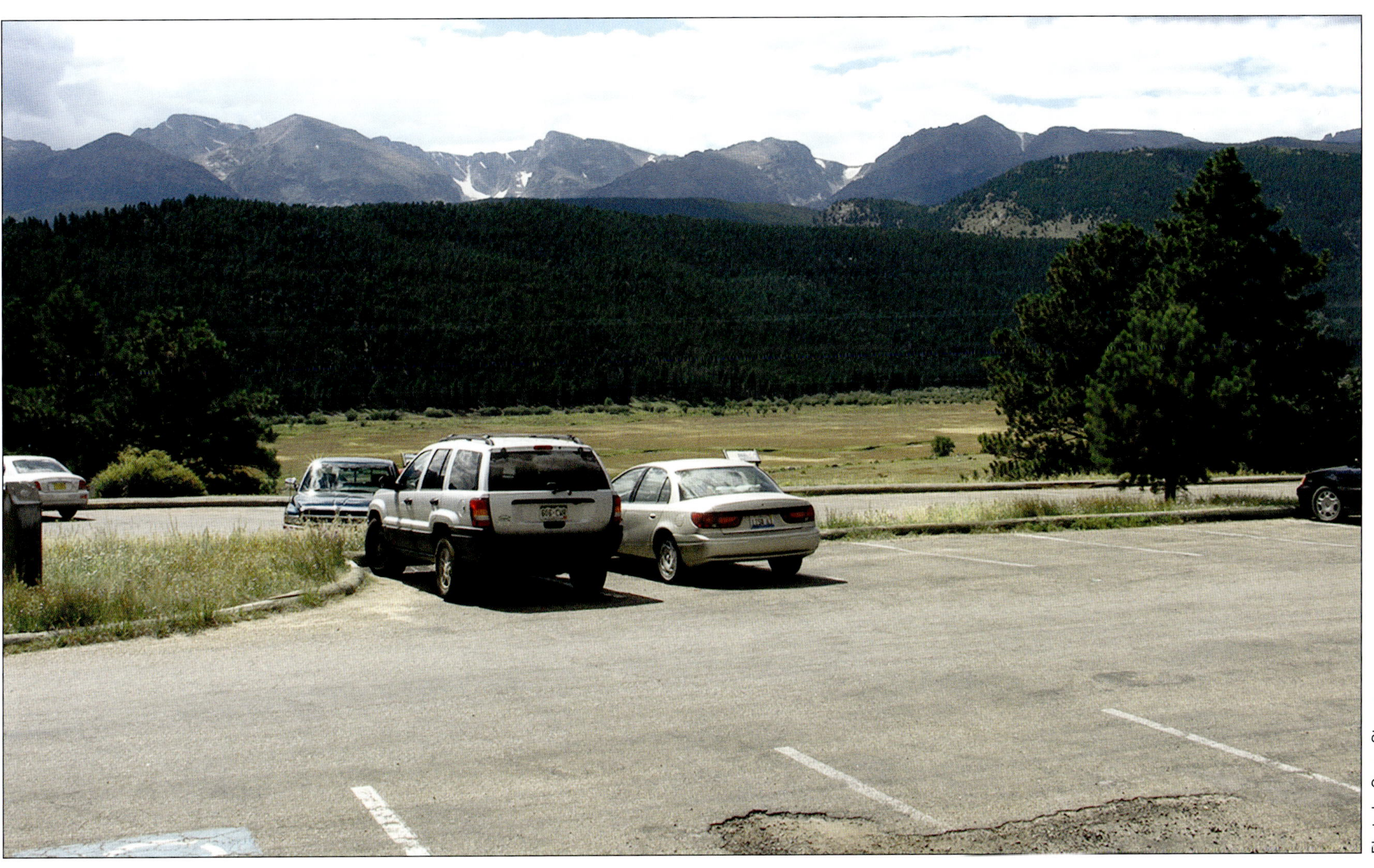

Photo by Carey Stevanus

Mary MacPherson, also known to her guests as "Mother MacPherson," was fatally injured in a Los Angeles car accident in 1928. In 1932, the National Park Service purchased the property for $30,125, and its buildings, with the exception of the recreation-assembly hall, were razed by CCC workers. Remodeled as a museum, that building opened in 1937, with Moraine Park's glacier-carved basin and its river being used to tell the geologic and human history of the national park. Close by, the CCC installed a 200-seat amphitheater for evening programs. The 1930s displays have been replaced, but the building still anchors the park's interpretive programs.

The original photos here come from the mid-1920s. As the contemporary photograph shows, the main lodge building stood in what today is a parking area for visitors to Rocky Mountain National Park.

Moraine Lodge

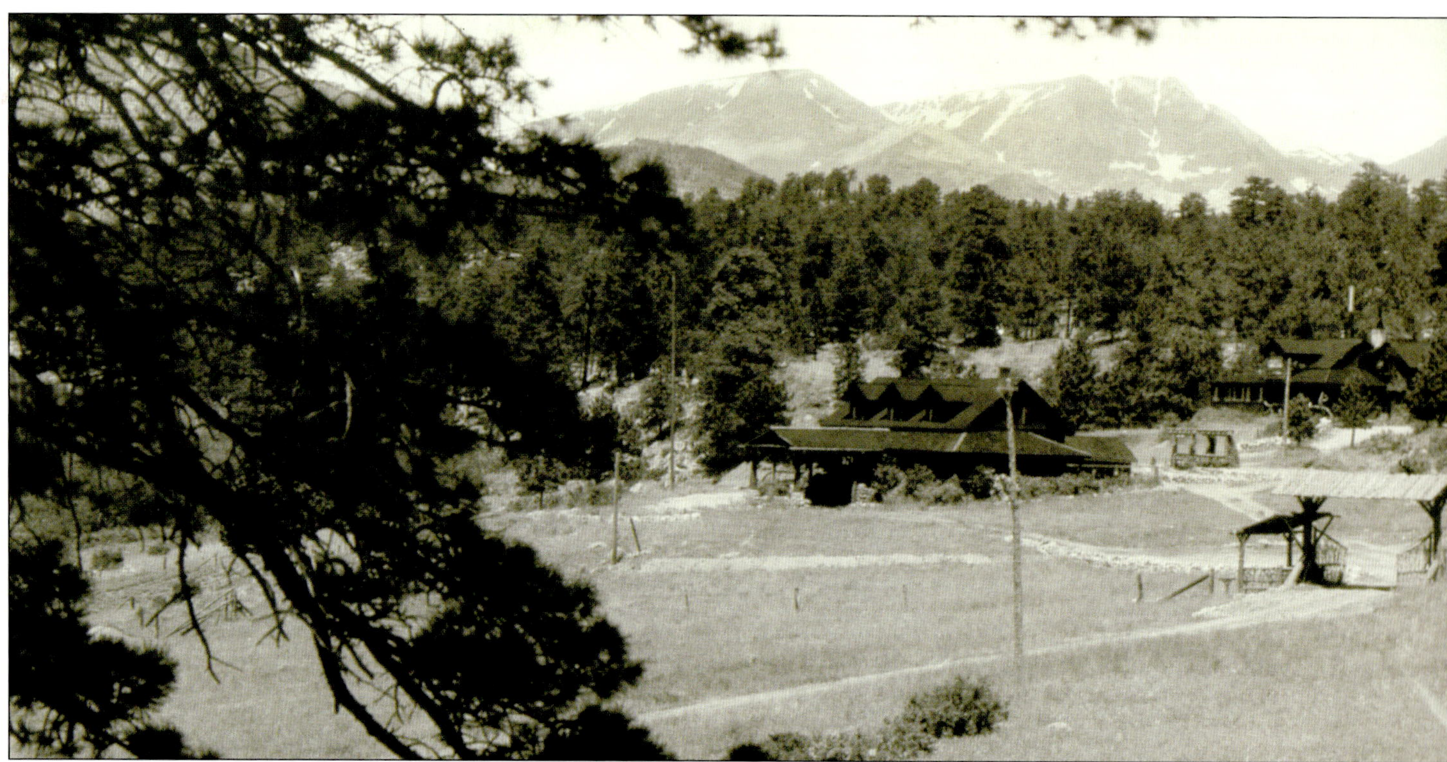

Photo by Fred Payne Clatworthy

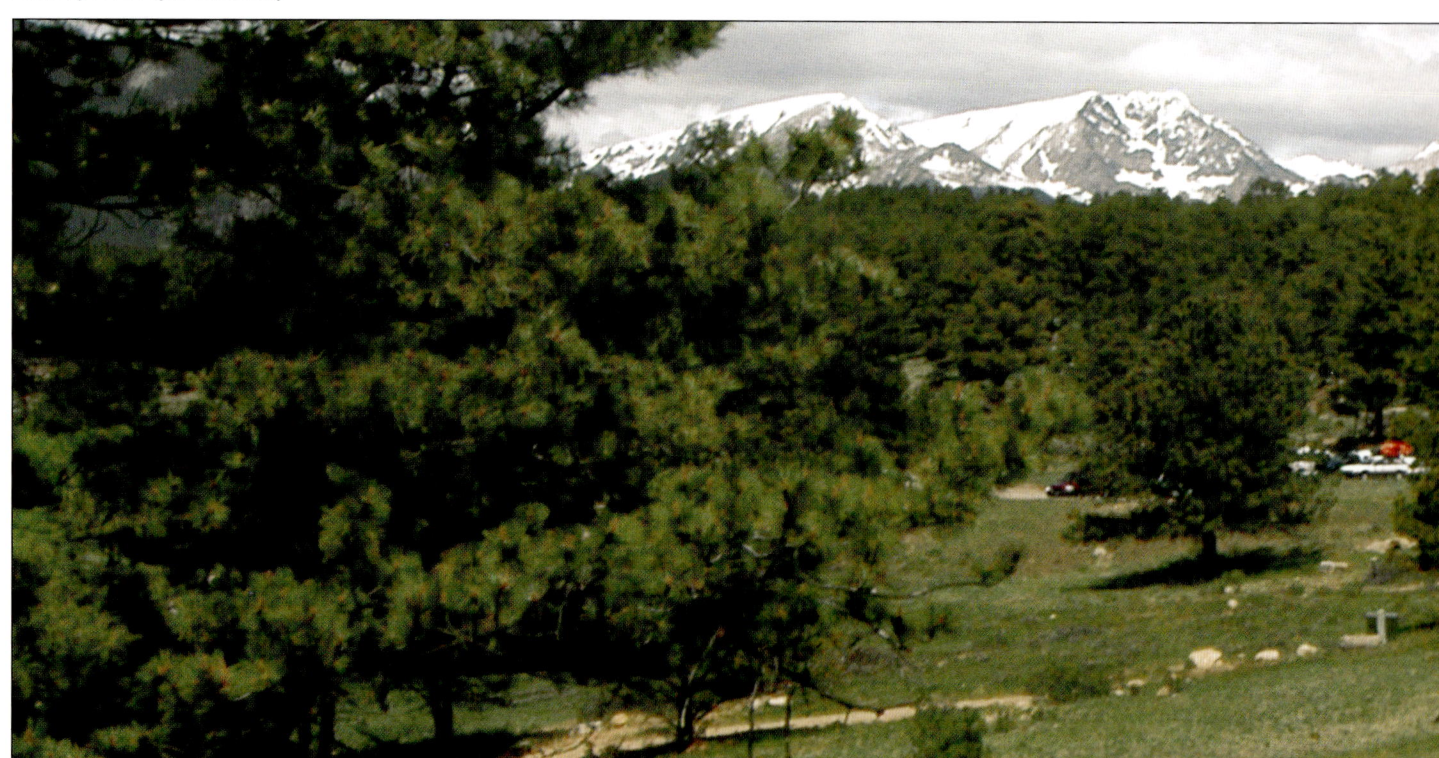

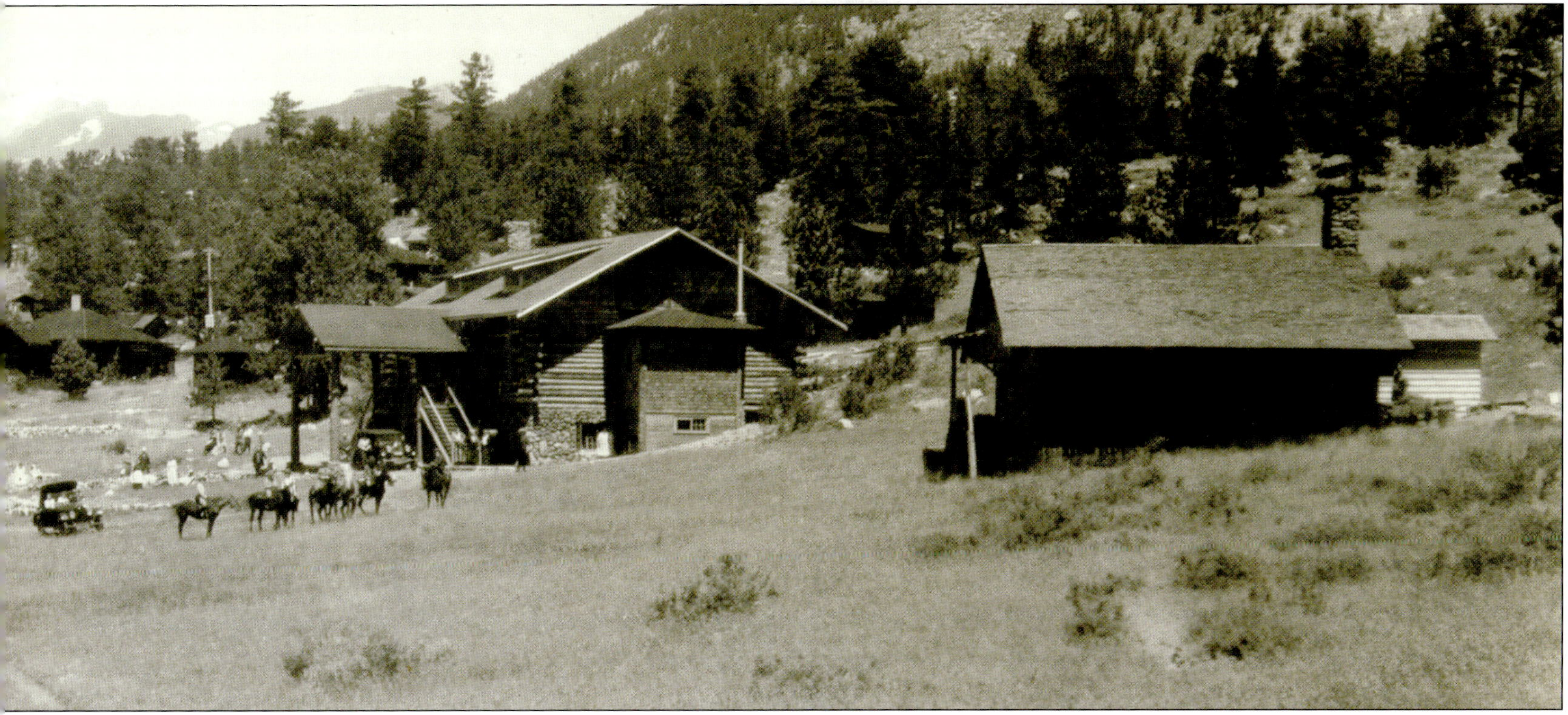

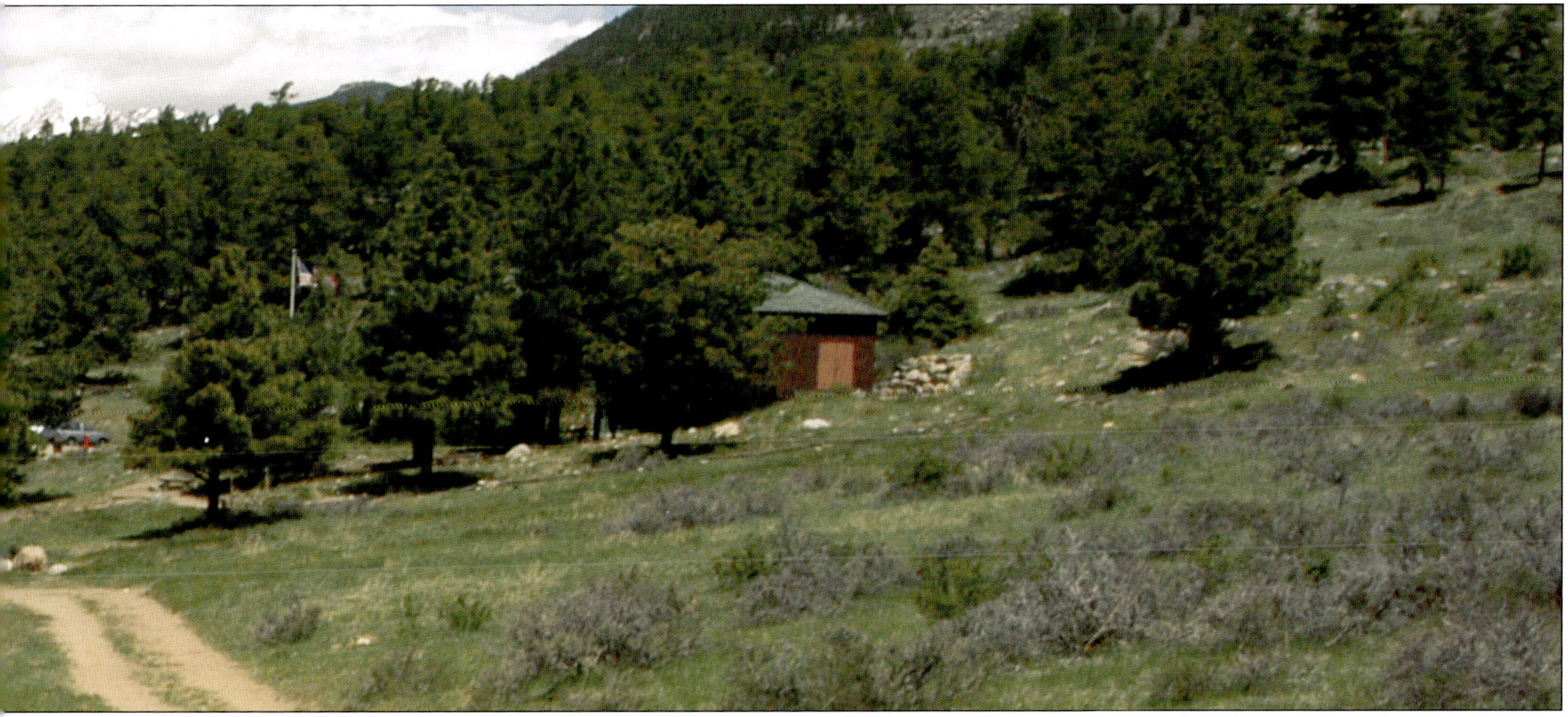

80. Sprague's Ranch and Stead's Ranch and Hotel, circa 1880

It all began with the 24-by-16-foot log cabin with a peat-covered pole roof (shown in the photograph below, though with the peat roof replaced). Pioneer Abner Sprague erected this homestead close by a fine spring on the north lateral moraine of Moraine Park, on which he had filed in May 1875. That spring, enclosed by the wooden spring house to the left of the homestead cabin in the original photograph, still flows down the hillside. Other members of the Sprague family—including his father Thomas Sprague, his younger brother Fred, and his sister Arah—also took out claims nearby, totaling 640 acres.

Though the Spragues had come to ranch and farm, they were soon in the tourist business. Thomas Sprague began by adding a series of rough-hewn log cabins to the ranch, and then built a main lodge containing guest rooms, dining room, and kitchen (a building that later was expanded to three stories). Other changes and enlargements followed, with most of them being done after 1904 when Abner Sprague and wife Alberta exited the tourist business in Moraine Park by selling his holdings to James Stead of Chicago, Illinois, who had become a partner two years before. Stead then changed the name to "Stead's Ranch." Later it would become "Stead's Ranch and Hotel."

Under Stead's management, the resort complex continued to expand. By 1920, in addition to the lodge, there were 27 guest cottages, employee housing, corral and barns, and other outbuildings. In time there would be even more cabins, a swimming pool and bath house, trout pond, tennis courts, an enlarged recreation hall, and a dining room capable of seating 250 guests. There would also be a nine-hole golf course built in the meadows along the Big Thompson, where the Spragues had grown timothy, maintained trout ponds, and grazed their cattle. Stead, a dairyman by profession, kept a herd of Guernsey milk cows on the property, branded with the same letter "S" that adorned the resort's hand-painted white china.

After Stead's death in 1931, his wife Dora enlisted her cousin Myra Lewis and her husband Will to manage the resort. In 1950, the hotel and its 791 acres were sold to Edgar M. Stopher, Alberta Sprague's nephew, for something less than

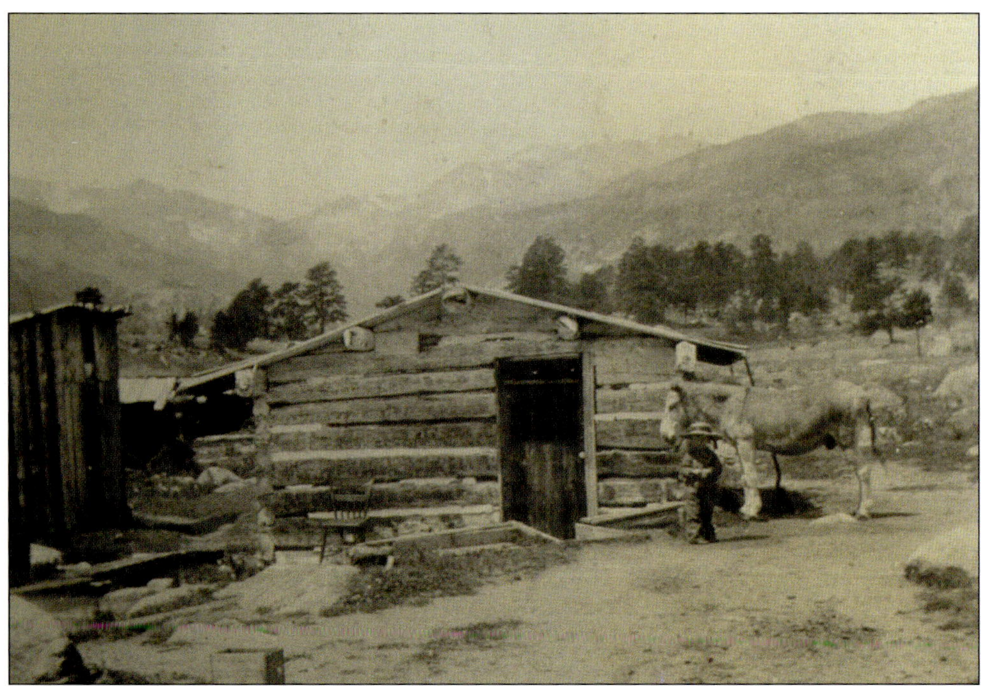

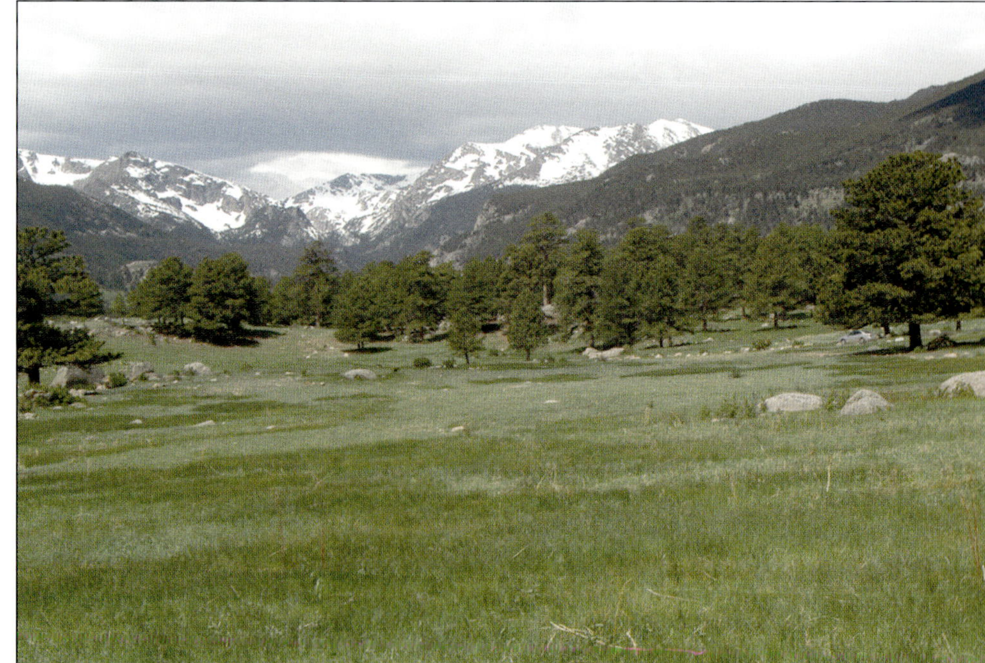

Stead's ranch, circa 1904

$100,000. Stopher oversaw the resort's final expansion. Upgrading and maintenance, however, became a continuing and expensive proposition and in 1962 Stopher accepted the Park Service's $750,000 purchase offer. The ranch buildings were soon torn down and the site obliterated.

The photographs here were taken well before the resort's final expansions. The view of the main lodge from the hillside was taken about 1904 by Fred Payne Clatworthy. The figure in the foreground is Clatworthy's mother, Emma. The photograph showing tourists sitting on the rock was obviously taken much earlier, about 1880. The photograph of the homestead cabin also dates from about 1880.

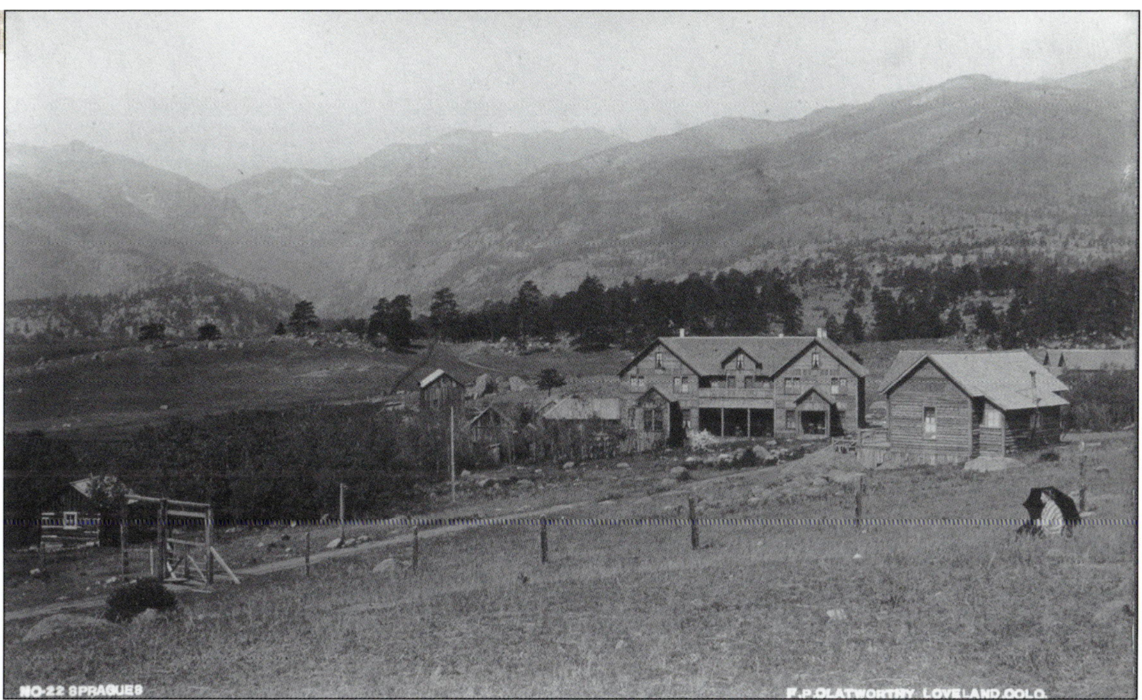

Photo by Fred Payne Clatworthy

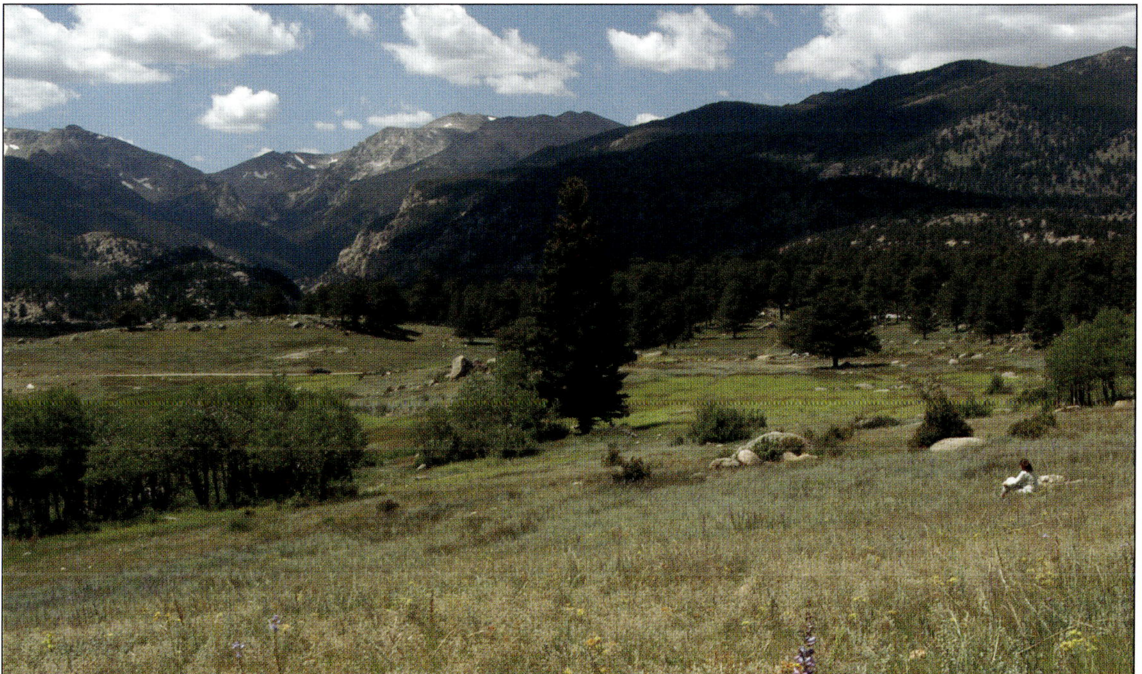

Sprague's ranch, circa 1880

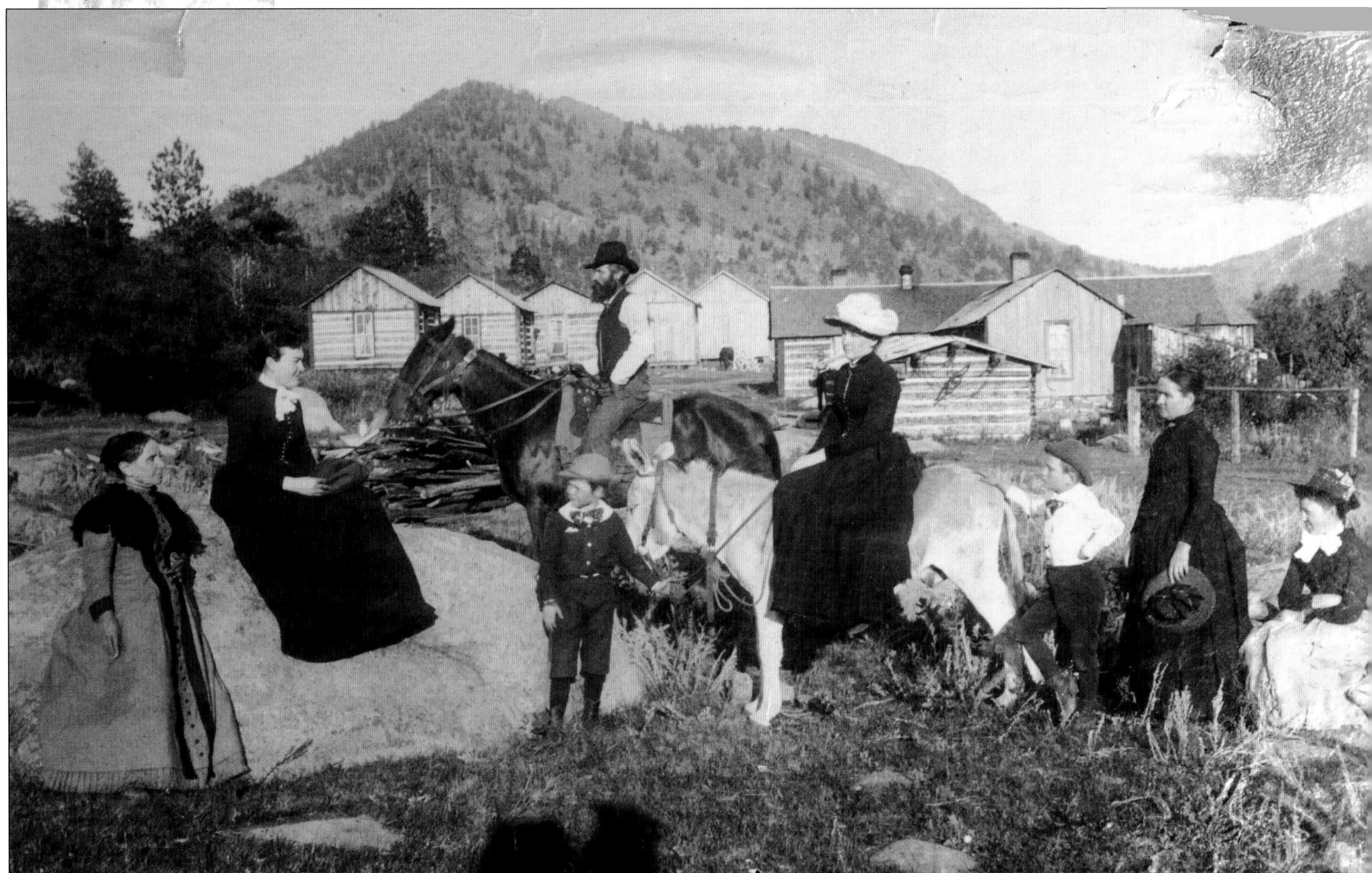

Photo by Williams

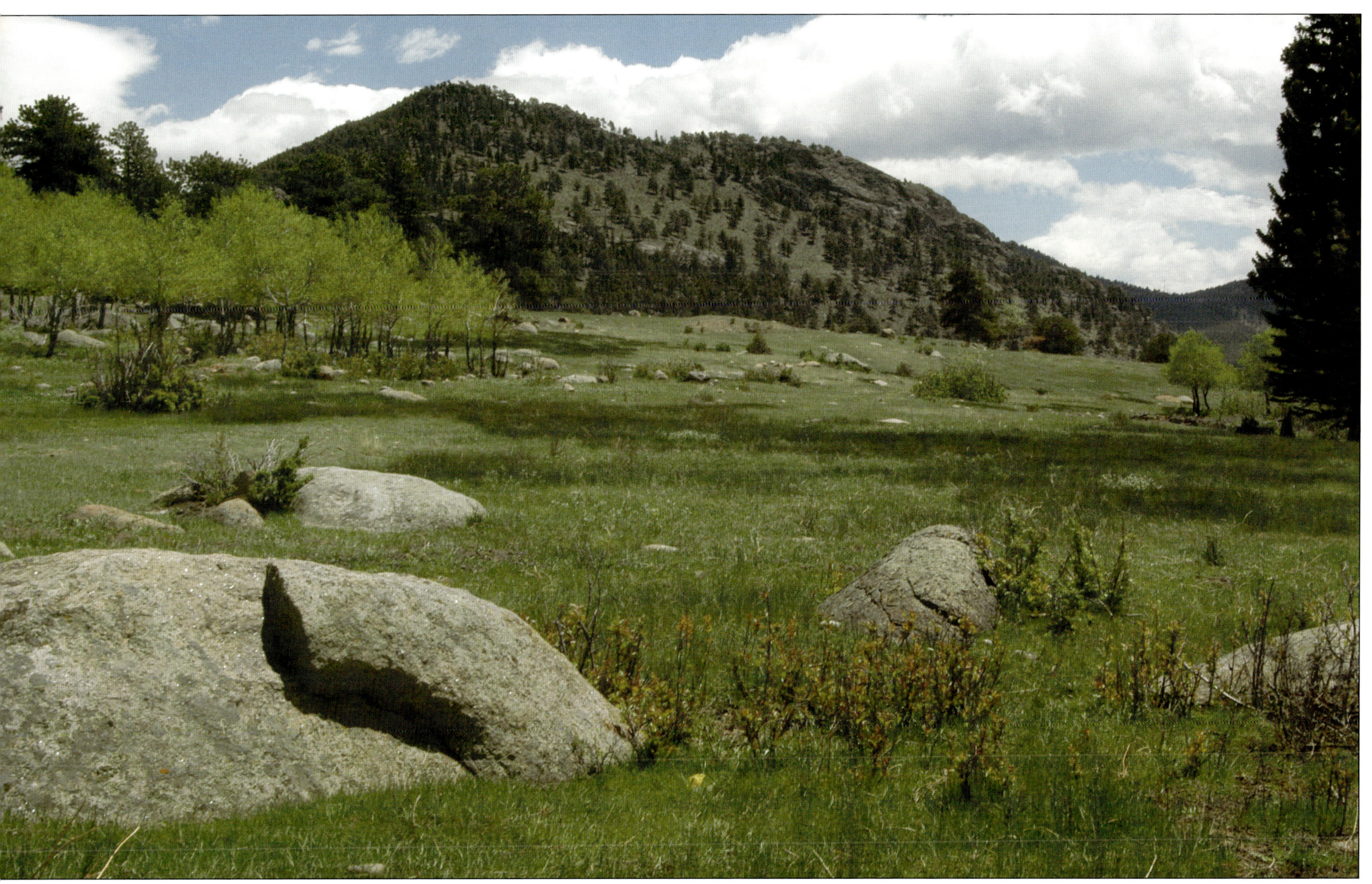

81. Brinwood Ranch and Hotel, circa 1930

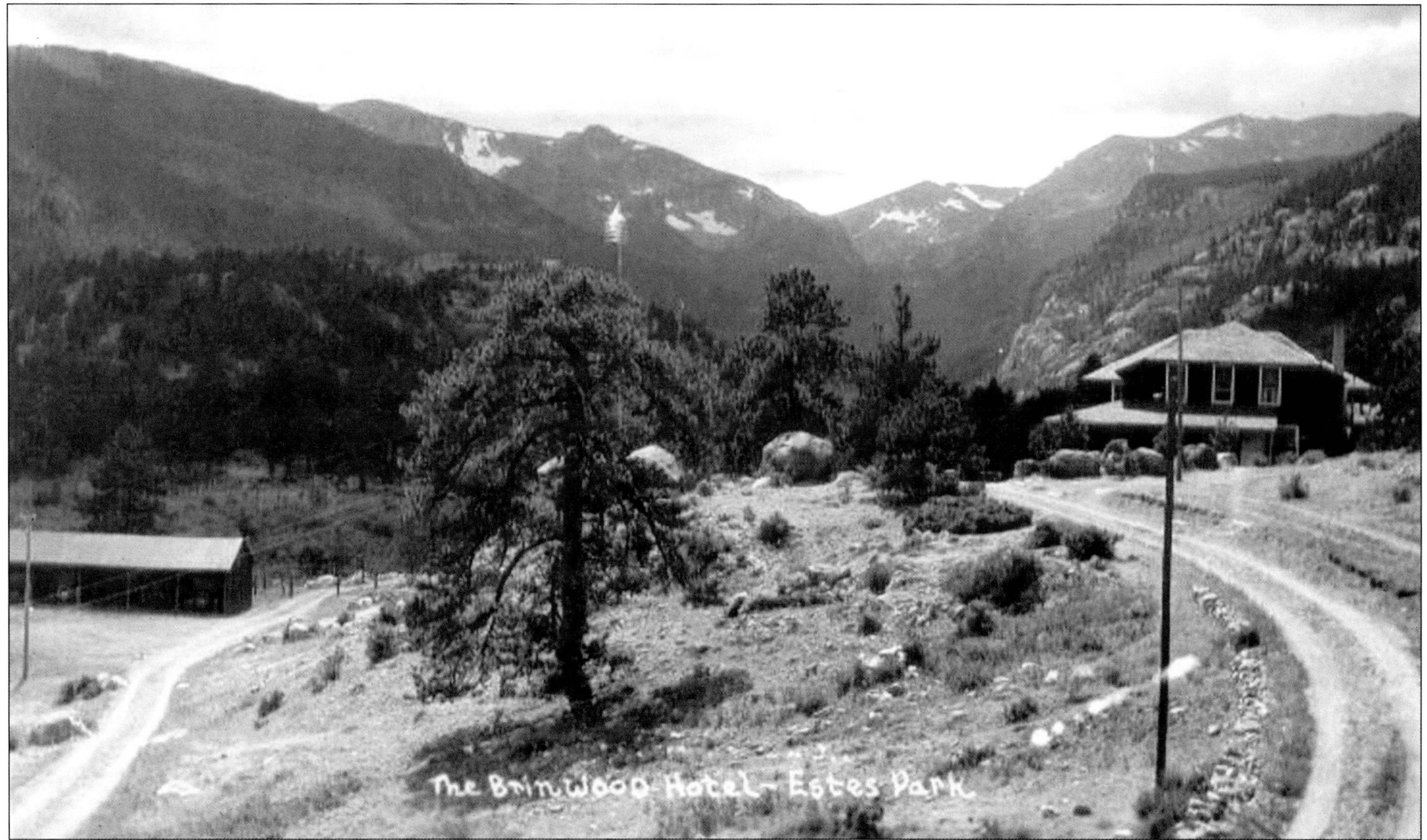

The Brinwood resort hotel once sat on the hillside at the upper end of Moraine Park, near today's Cub Lake Trailhead, on land homesteaded in 1879 by William Hunter Ferguson, son of pioneer Horace Ferguson (see p. 150). Hunter's younger brother James, their sister Sallie Ferguson Reed, and her husband Charles Reed acquired the site in 1909 to build a hotel. The location was excellent, for it could be accessed over a comparatively good road and was close to the trails leading to Cub Lake, The Pool, Marguerite Falls, and the popular Fern-Odessa region.

The Brinwood, later named the Brinwood Ranch and Hotel, remained in the Reed family for 47 years. The resort consisted of some 29 log-and-frame buildings on approximately 290 acres, with a capacity of 90 guests in its lodge and cottages. The most impressive of these buildings was the two-story lodge, with porches across the east and south sides (shown in the original photograph). Windows across the front looked down to Moraine Park and the Big Thompson River, and across to Longs Peak and its neighbors. Across the road, at the edge

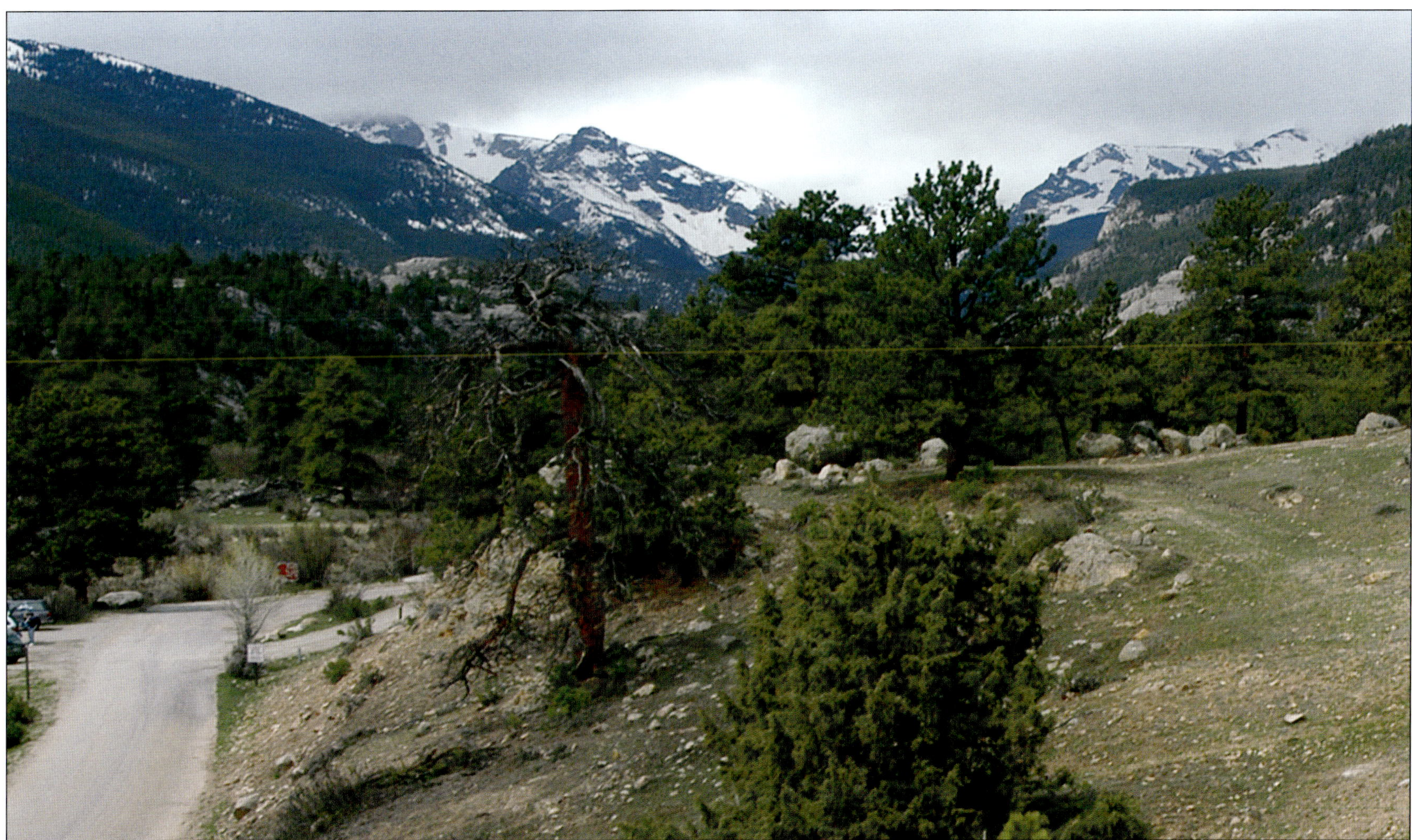

of a meadow, stood the parking lot, garage, barn, dairy, garden, and stables. (The garage site is today's parking lot.)

In 1932, the National Park Service acquired the Brinwood, with a provision that the hotel could operate under a 20-year lease. A park study of concession needs in the early 1950s showed hotel capacity was insufficient, so in 1959 the Brinwood was open to bids with the stipulation that at least $56,000 in repairs be made. There were no takers, for the next year its buildings were razed.

A footnote to history: The large pine tree on the hillside below the hotel (visible to the left in both photographs) is no more. Succumbing to age and a windstorm, it fell in the fall of 2005.

82. Forest Inn

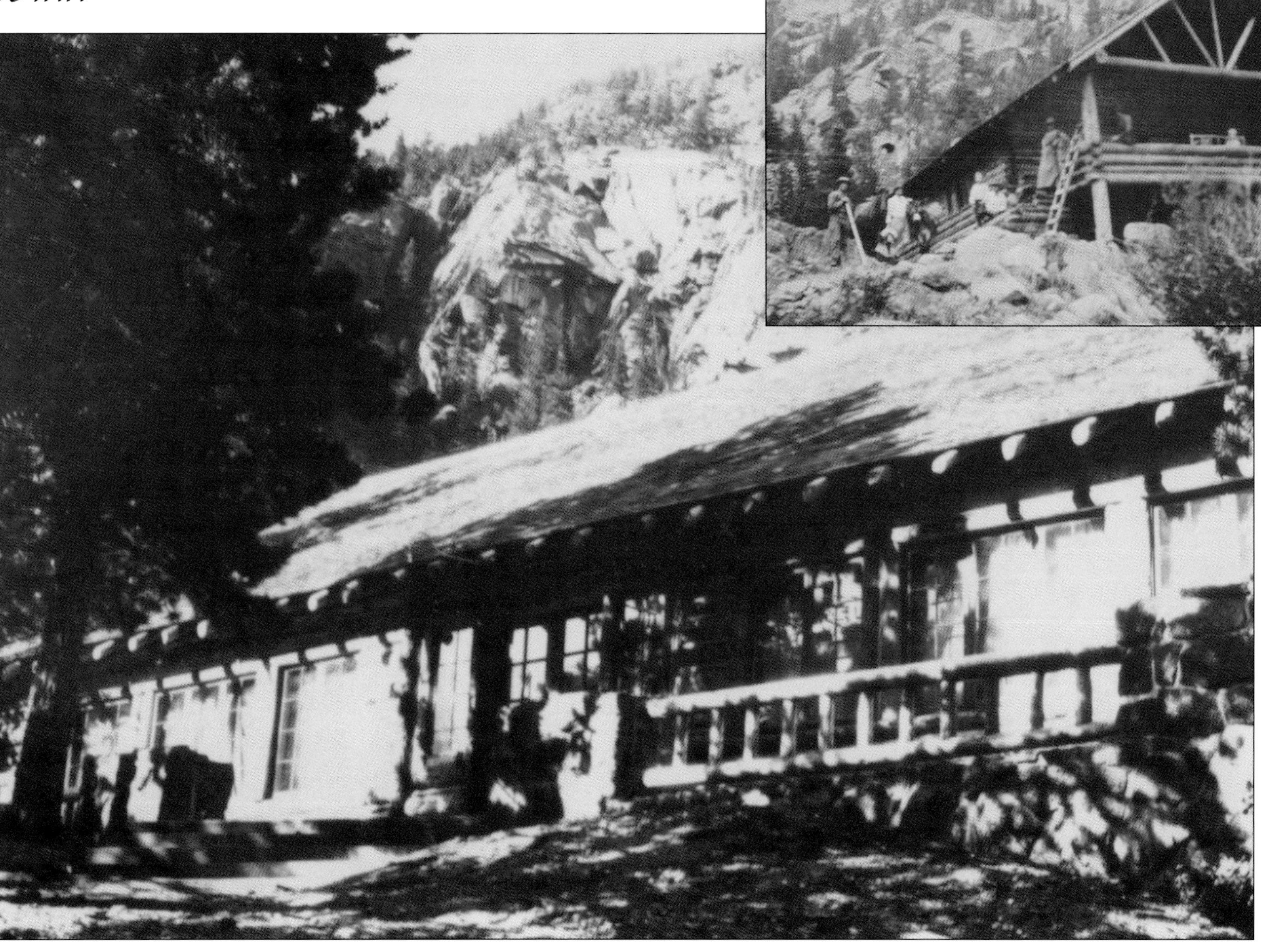

Many of the old historic lodges in and around Rocky Mountain National Park remained family-owned throughout their existence. The Frank Tecker family from Parks, Nebraska, ran the Forest Inn at The Pool for 35 years.

It began as a modest tent camp owned by brothers Clifford, Reed, and Lester Higby of Estes Park, who also operated a fledgling tent and cabin resort at Fern Lake (see p. 216). The Higbys didn't stay long. They sold both properties to photographer Frank W. Byerly, who in 1917 turned the site at The Pool over to his sister and her husband, Fannie and Frank Tecker. Anticipating that the trail from Moraine Park to The Pool and Fern Lake would become a road, Tecker built a substantial 56-by-24-foot main lodge (see inset above), giving his camp a capacity of 50. This log building stood above The Pool on a site looking down on today's trail; it burned to the ground in June 1919 following a lightning strike.

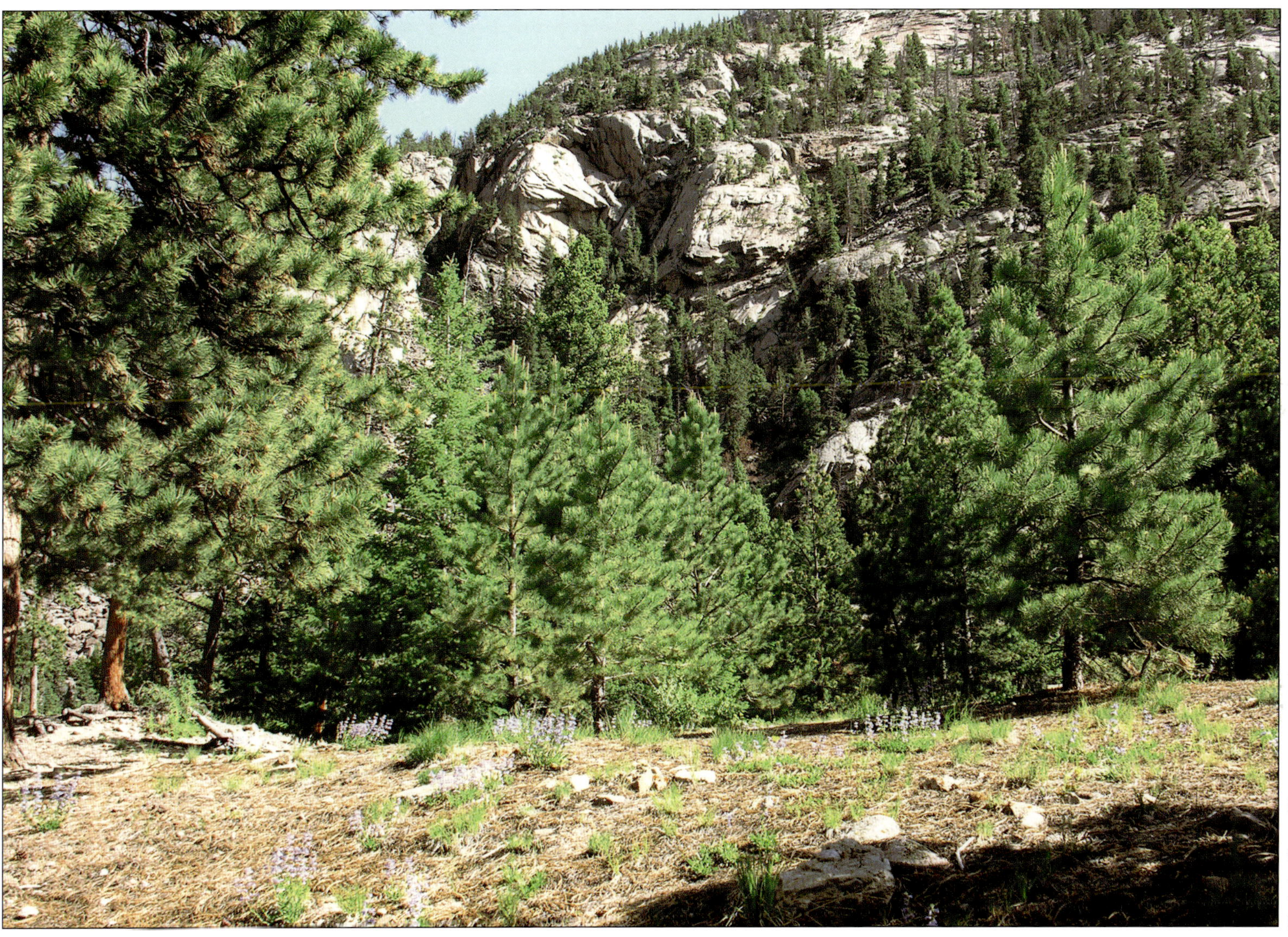

Phcto by Carey Stevanus

Undeterred, the Teckers continued to operate their camp without a main lodge until 1927, when a new and larger building, containing both dining room and lounge, was built farther up the hillside. Guests continued to be housed in substantial log cabins (like the one shown in the photograph on p. 214) and in a series of tent houses with stone floors and wooden walls.

Fannie Tecker died in 1931, but Frank and his son and daughter-in-law ran the resort until 1952, when in his 86th year he sold the property to the National Park Service for $14,000. At that time Forest Inn consisted of the lodge, one three-room cabin, two two-room cabins, five one-room cabins, and two tent houses. The buildings were razed in 1959.

83. Fern Lake Lodge, circa 1915

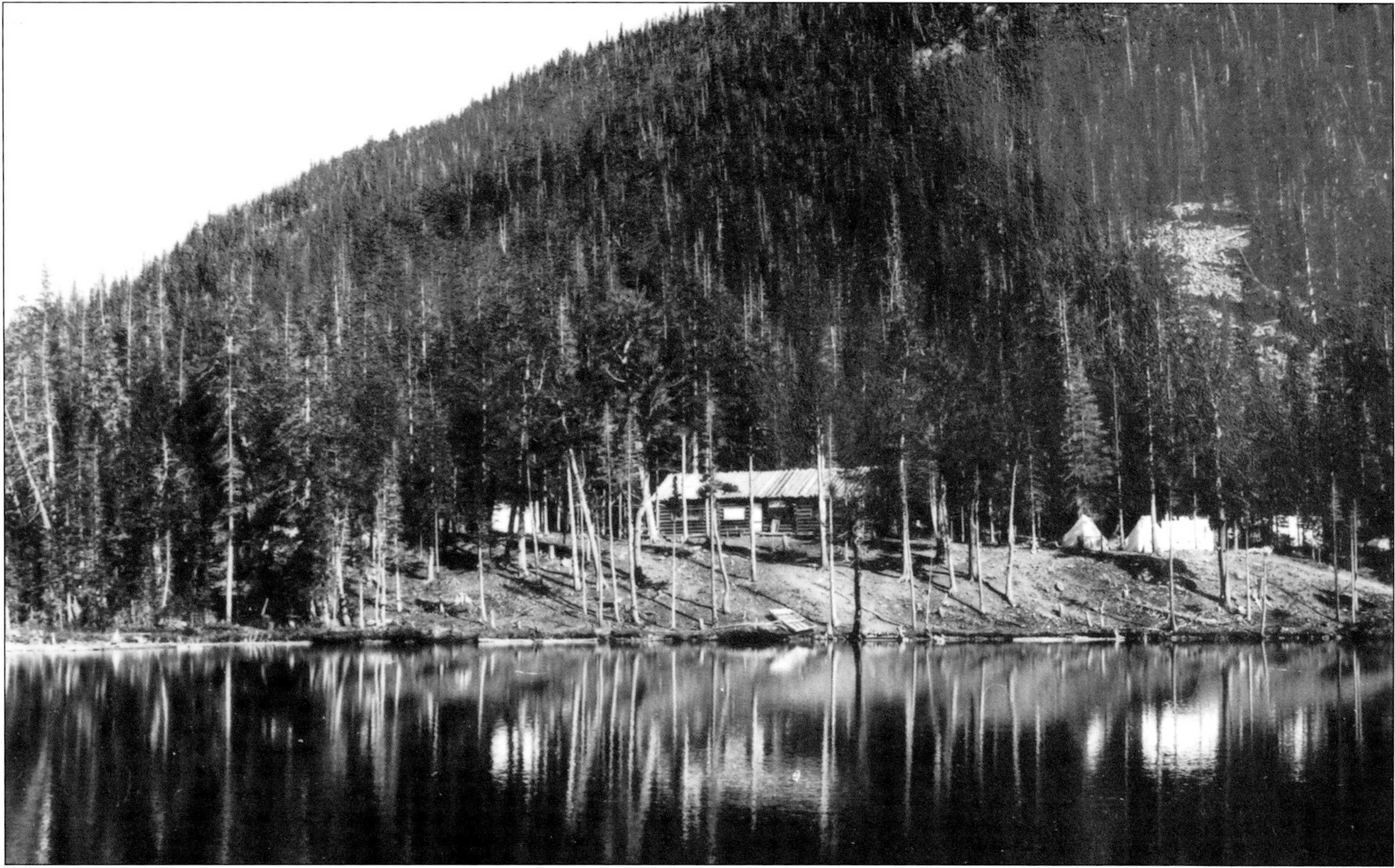

Photo by William T. Parke

Fern Lake Lodge was built by Dr. William J. Workman, a physician from Ashland, Kansas, who moved his practice to Denver in 1902 due to his wife's health. After a visit in 1898, Workman loved the wilderness of Estes Park, and shortly after coming to Denver he bought land in Moraine Park from Abner Sprague for a summer home. An avid outdoorsman and fisherman, Workman was soon exploring the nearby Fern-Odessa and Forest Canyon regions, where he named many of its most prominent features, including Fern Lake, Notchtop Mountain, Marguerite Falls, Grace Falls, the Little Matterhorn, Odessa Lake, and Lake Helene.

About 1910, Workman began building a fishing lodge of local lumber on the eastern shore of Fern Lake, not far from its outlet. It took some 10 weeks to hew logs to complete the building and its roof, which was made watertight by using curved logs. The lodge was initially a crude affair, with oiled paper on the windows and blankets covering the doors. The floor was made of log blocks set on end and fitted, and most of the furniture was also fashioned from logs.

In 1915, Workman sold the lodge to the Higby brothers, Clifford, Reed, and Lester. By 1917, it was in the hands of Frank W. Byerly. In later years the lodge

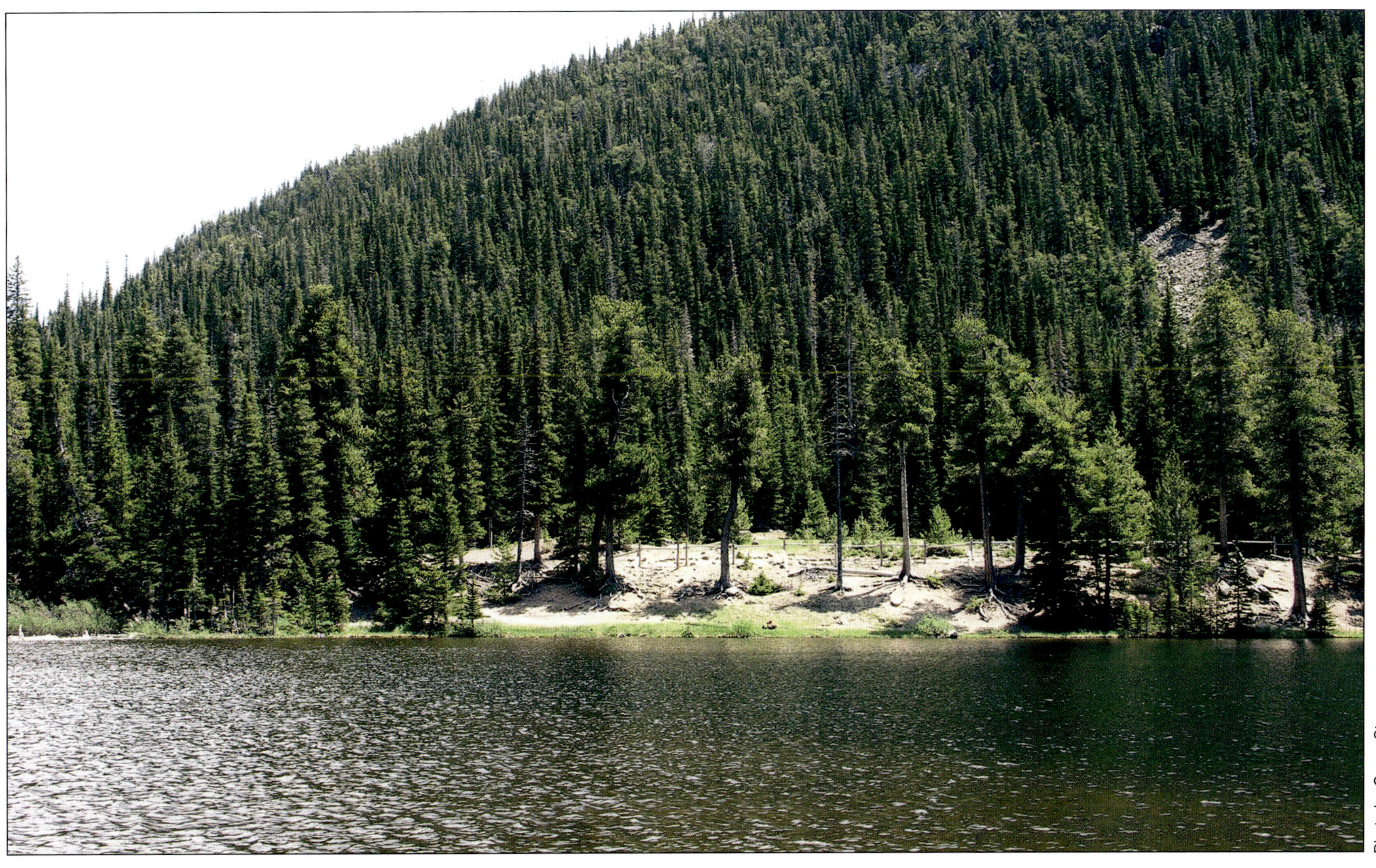
Photo by Carey Stevanus

was managed by Byerly's second wife, Edna B. Bishop, and her sons James and Charles. At first, Fern Lake Lodge was a summer camp, with guests housed in tents. This began to change in 1917, when Fern Lake became the site of the well-remembered annual February outings held by the Colorado Mountain Club (CMC), which lasted well into the 1930s. To accommodate the CMC, the storehouse was turned into a dormitory with two-deep bunks. Well-chinked log sleeping cabins were gradually built, and in 1922, Byerly added a new dining room to the lodge, featuring a large round table with a built-in lazy Susan. By that date the lodge and outbuildings were able to accommodate about 55 people in reasonable comfort.

Though Fern Lake Lodge stopped providing meals and overnight lodging after 1939, it remained open to serve light snacks through the 1950s. During the summer of 1958, it was managed by folksinger Judy Collins and her husband. Time and vandals, however, took their toll, and in 1976 the National Park Service burned the Fern Lake Lodge and removed its other buildings.

Fern Lake Lodge, circa 1930

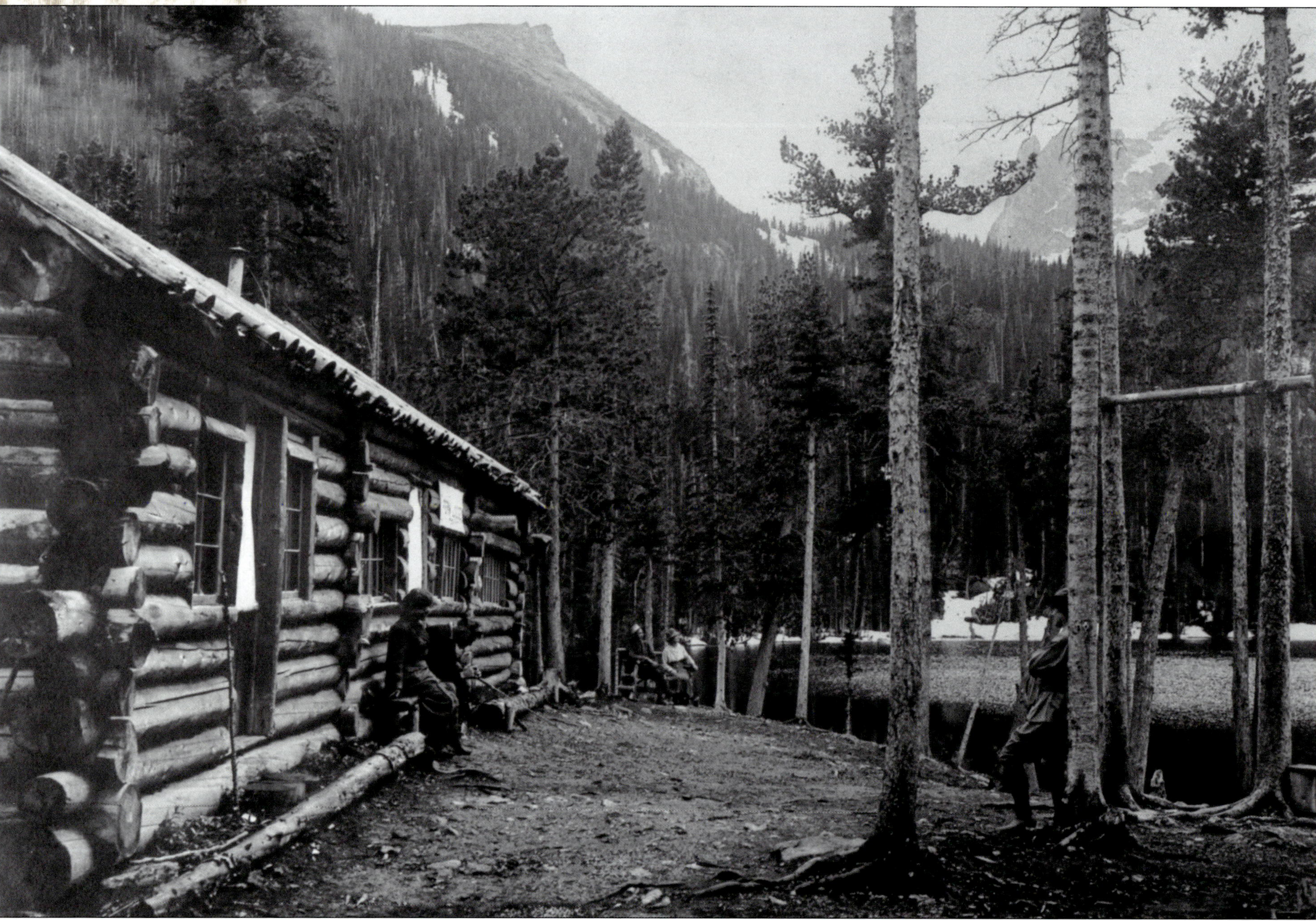

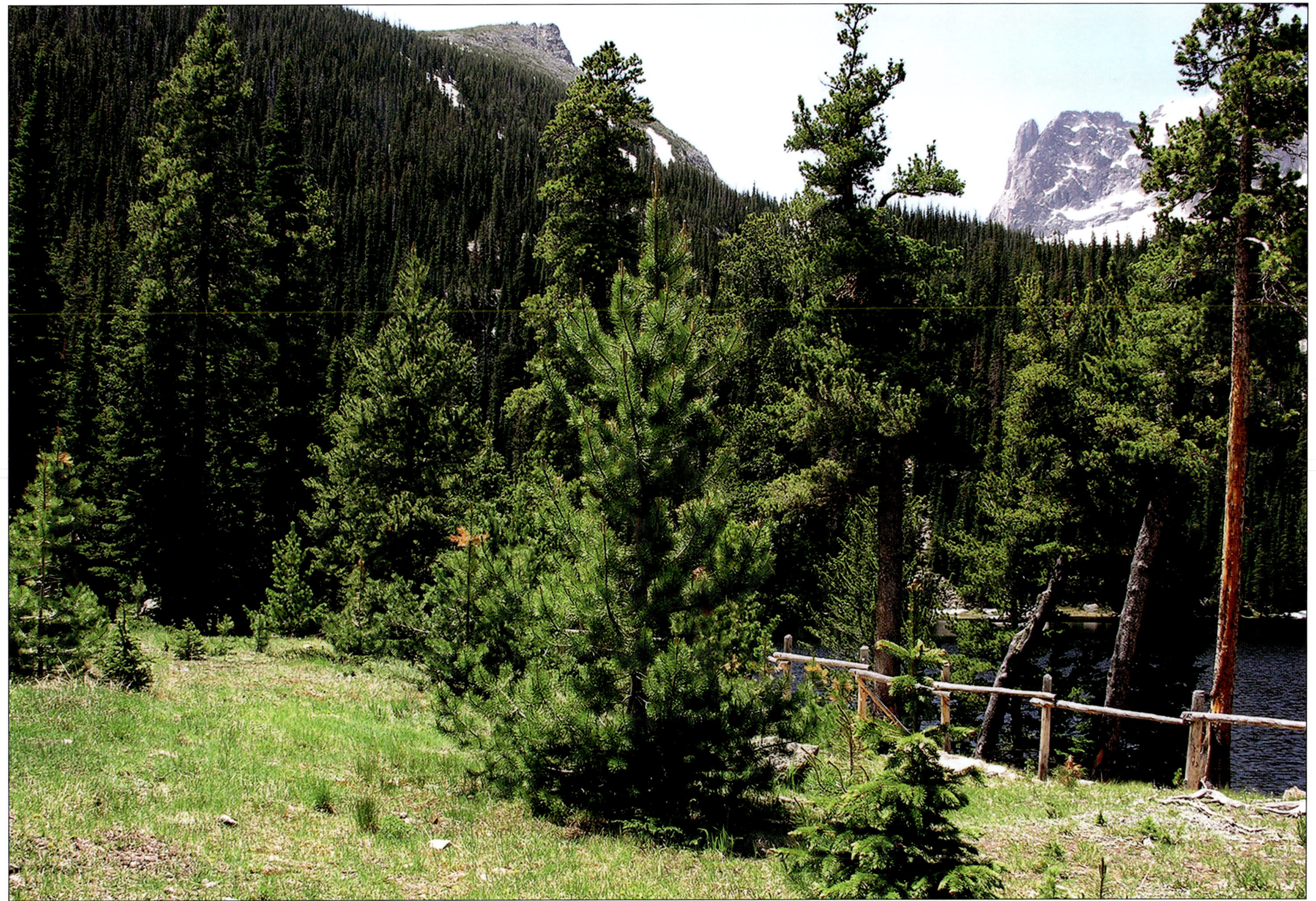

Photo by Carey Stevanus

84. CCC Camps in Hollowell Park

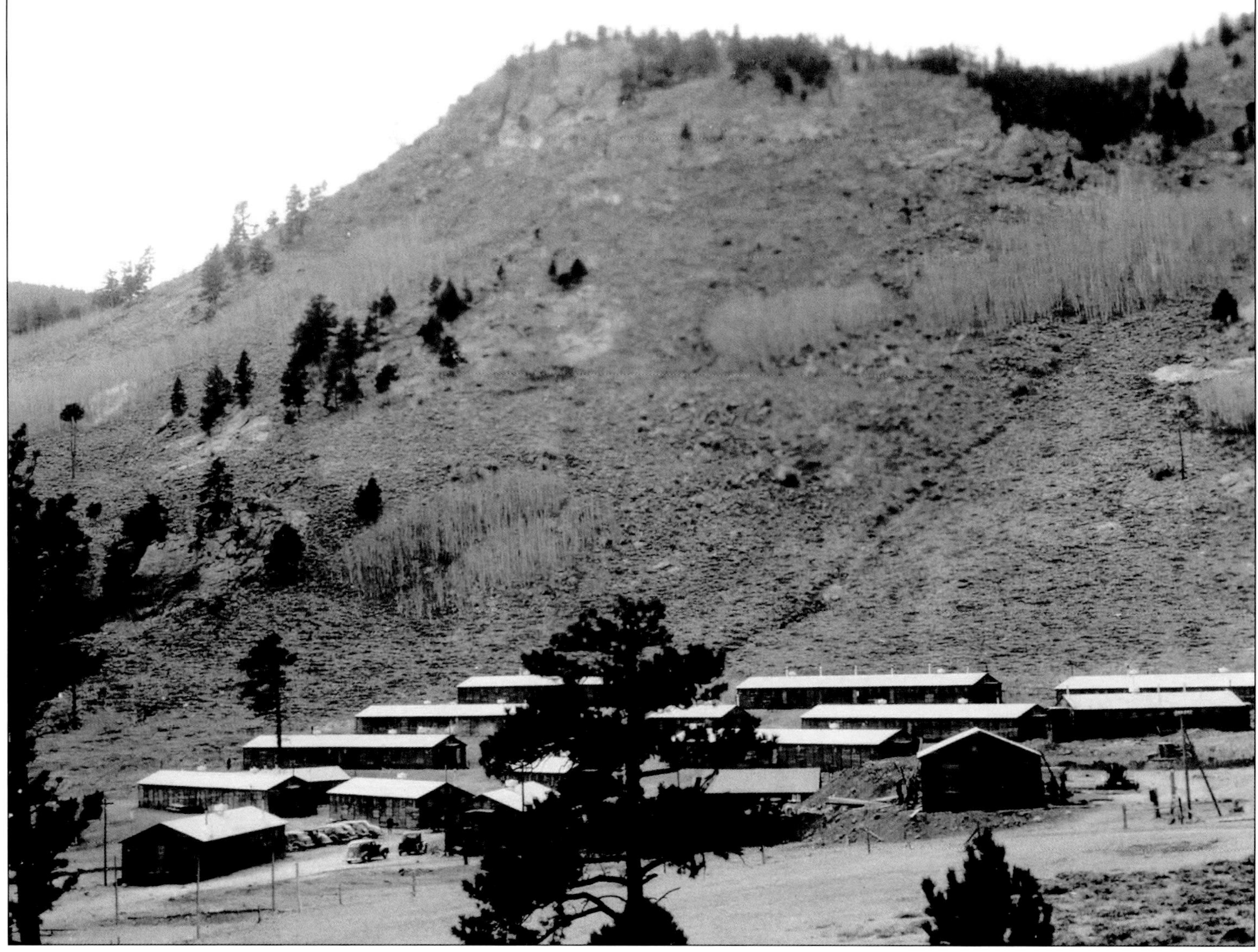

There were two permanent year-round Civilian Conservation Corps (CCC) camps in Hollowell Park, the grassy basin below Steep Mountain named after rancher George C. Hollowell of Loveland, who ranged cattle there along Mill Creek before the turn of the 20th century. The first of these, Camp N. P. 4-C, was established in stages beginning in April 1934. A mess hall and bathhouse were built first. That fall, after a summer during which the camp's first recruits were housed in hospital tents, other buildings were added, including a headquarters, recreation hall, five barracks (each built to house 50 men), a garage, and tool house.

A second camp in Hollowell Park, Camp N. P. 11-C, the one photographed here, was established in November 1939, during the final years of the CCC when Camp N. P. 1-C in Little Horseshoe Park was closed down (see p. 182).

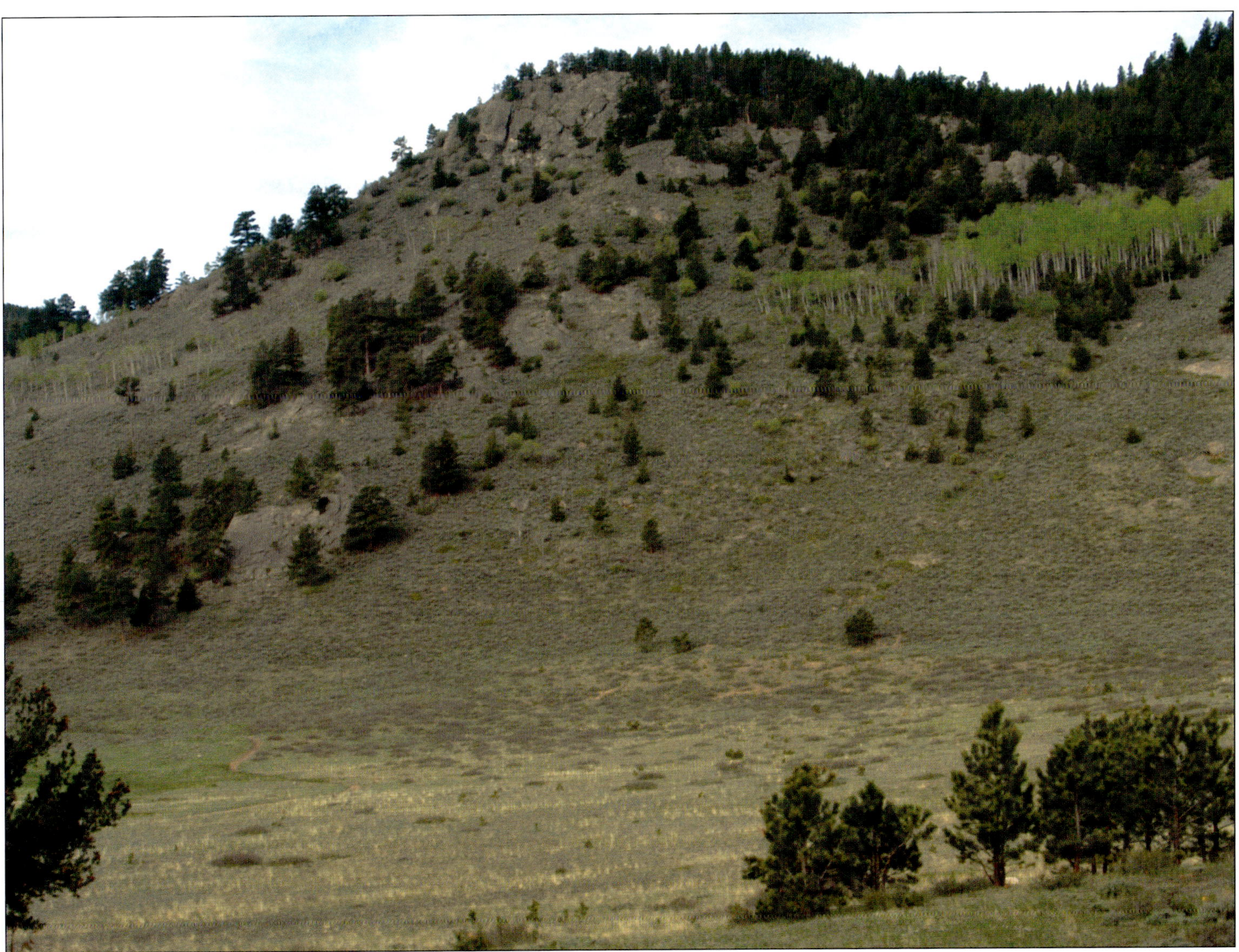

It was built in much the same way as its adjacent sister camp, making use of portable prefabs that could be easily removed.

The coming of World War II brought an end to the Civilian Conservation Corps. By the summer of 1940, with war going on in Europe and defense plants offering well-paying jobs, it became difficult to recruit young men for conservation work that "paid" only $25 a month. After December 7, 1941, the men of the CCC were needed for other things. Camp N. P. 4-C on Mill Creek, the oldest permanent camp in Rocky Mountain National Park, was closed in July 1941; Camp N. P. 11-C came to an end in October 1942. Their sites were then obliterated from the landscape.

85. Rocky Mountain Boys Camp, circa 1940

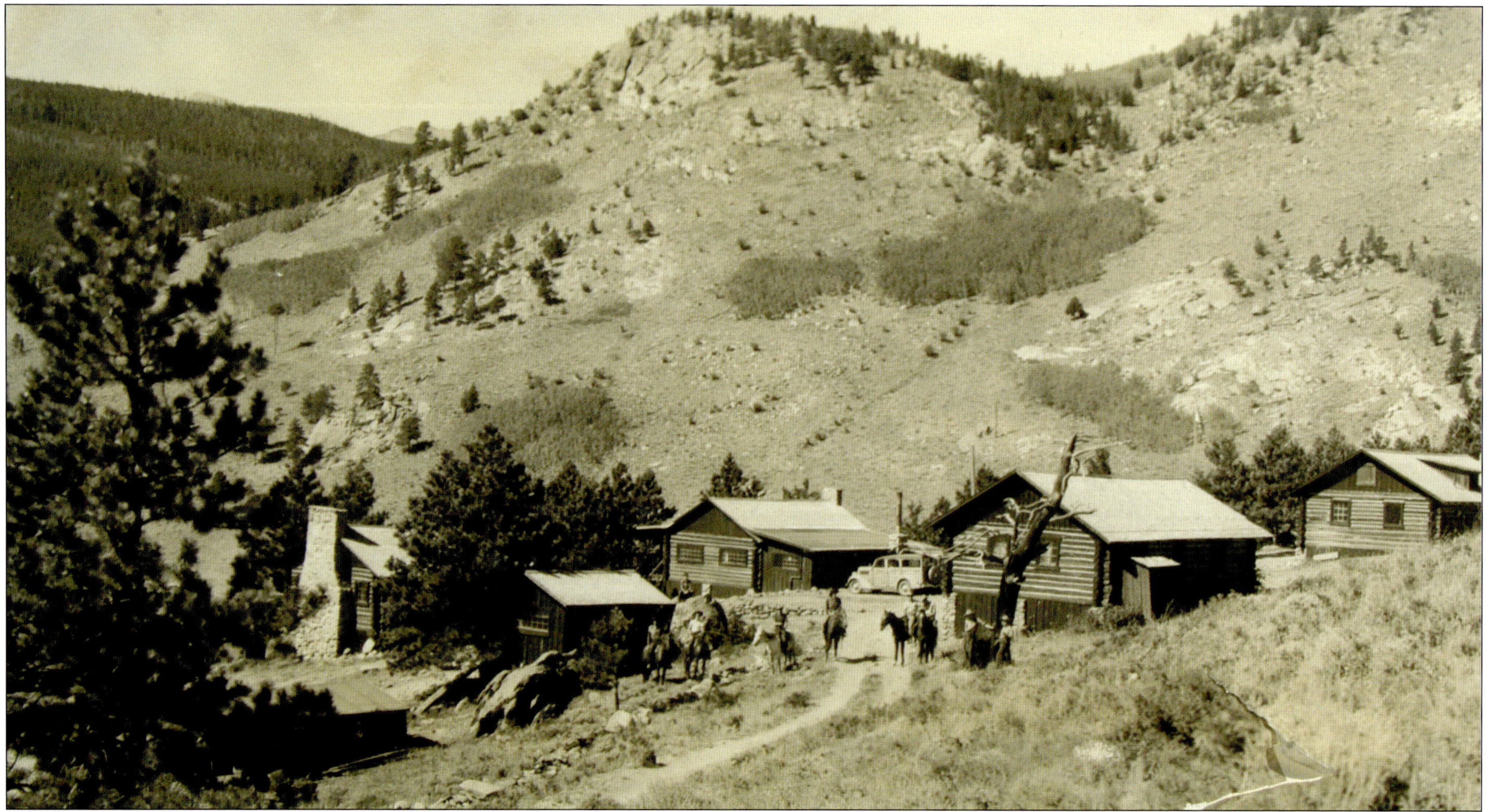

For more than 80 years, Cheley Colorado Camps have been synonymous with the Estes Park region (see p. 44). However famous, Cheley was not the first. In 1919, Reverend Harrison Anderson of Wichita, Kansas, along with the help of Reverend John Timothy Stone (see p. 60) and others, established the Rocky Mountain Boys Camp high on a moraine above Hollowell Park. Nearly 6 miles from Estes Park in the Mill Creek Valley, the 120 acres were purchased for use as "a riding camp exclusively for young gentlemen." Unapologetic in catering to the sons of the well-to-do, many from the Chicago area, the purpose of the camp, Stone announced, was "to help every boy to have a strong body and live a clean life, with a natural and true relationship to God and man." With an investment of $40,000, 12 log cabins were built. Of these, two were sleeping cabins. The largest building, the main lodge, containing dining hall and library, had a moss rock fireplace, piano, and Victrola. It was a comfortable place: Navajo and bearskin rugs covered the floors, while mounted animal heads adorned the walls.

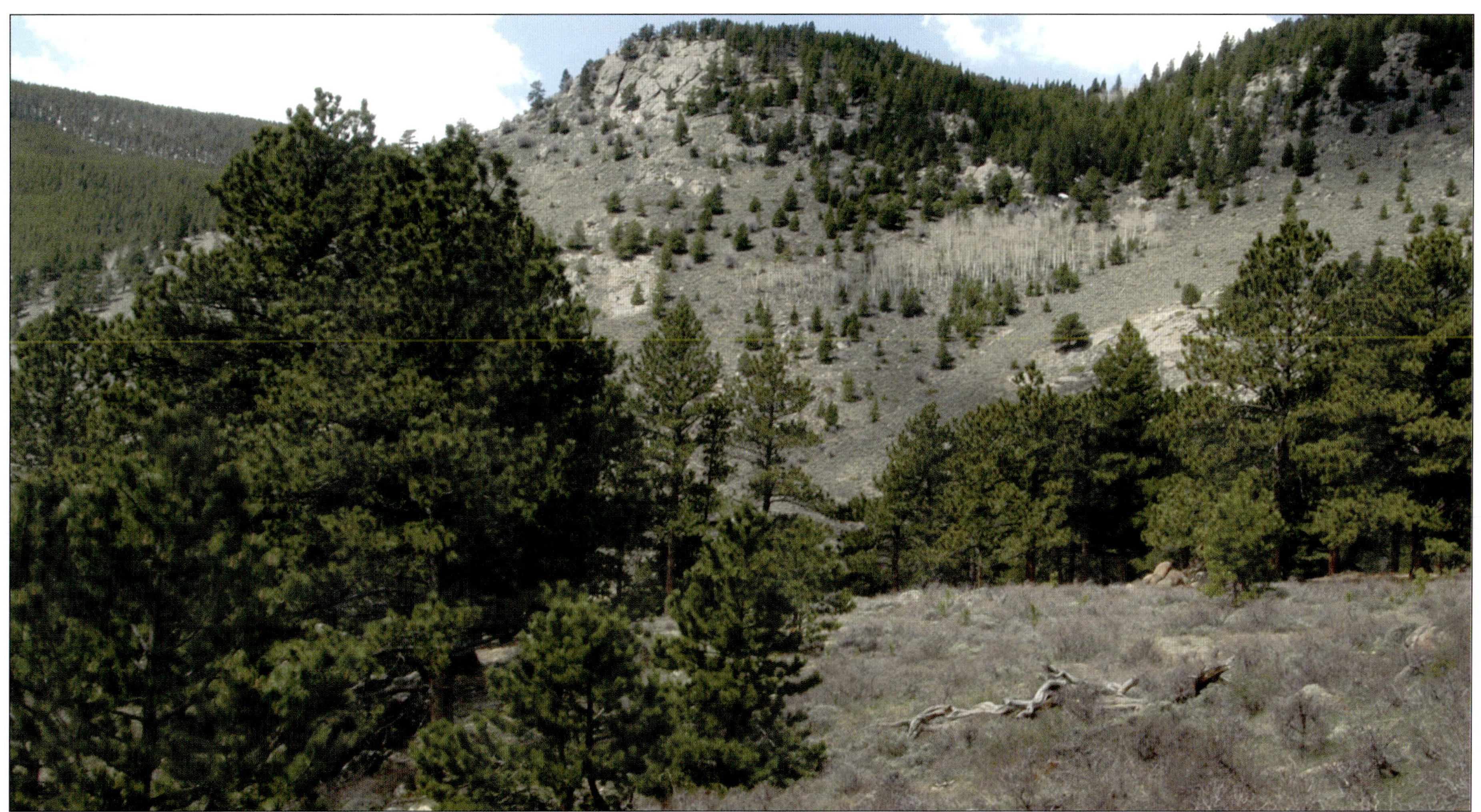

In November 1924, the camp was sold to a syndicate that included David C. Primrose, Frank H. Cheley, and Clifford Higby. Primrose, athletic director and coach at Macalester College, became director—a post he would occupy for some 27 years. He handled the athletic program, which included baseball, tennis, horseshoes, volleyball, and swimming. Higby, Estes Park resident and licensed national park guide, taught horsemanship and camping, while Cheley instructed the boys in such outdoor subjects as forestry and fishing. Primrose soon became sole owner.

The Rocky Mountain Boys Camp continued through the 1940s. In 1951, Primrose sold it to the National Park Service, which used the facilities as housing for summer rangers before razing them. All that remains on the site are cabin footings and signs of the road that once climbed the moraine to the camp.

86. Spragues Lodge, circa 1940

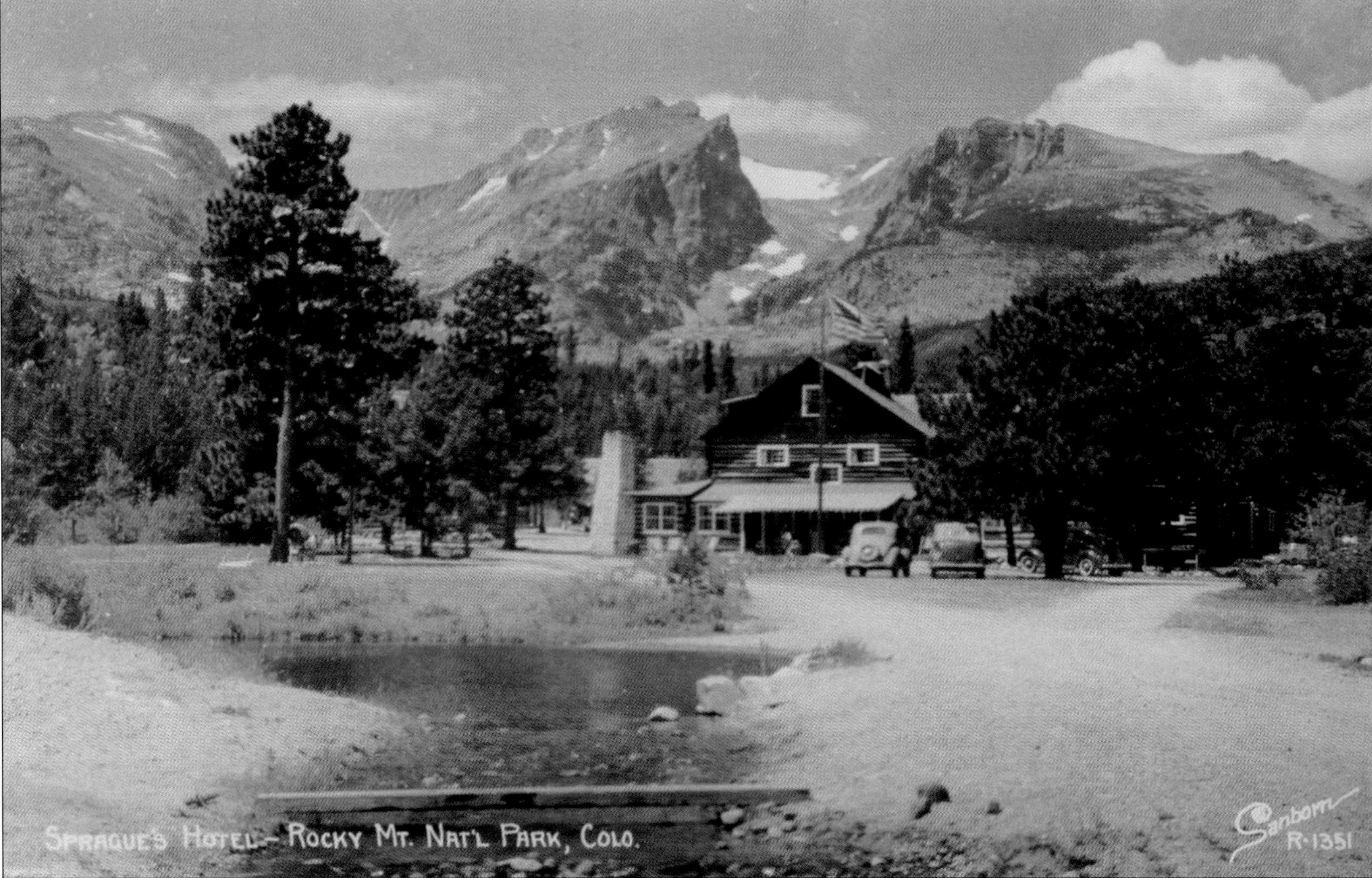

Photo by Sanborn Souvenir Company

Following the sale of his resort in Moraine Park to James Stead in 1904, Abner and Alberta Sprague moved to Loveland, where Abner formed an engineering partnership and served three elected terms as Larimer County surveyor. The allure of Estes Park and the mountains could not, however, be resisted and during the summer of 1908, Abner and his brother-in-law John Stopher completed a log cabin for the vacation use of both families in Glacier Basin near Glacier Creek, a tributary of the Big Thompson, on about 60 acres leased from the Forest Service. "I sought to prevent my homesickness for Estes Park and the mountains from becoming chronic," Sprague would later write. "Loveland was too tame and the country too flat for a 'hillbillie'.

In 1914, Abner and Alberta moved back to the mountains and decided to use the site in Glacier Basin to reenter the resort business. The original cabin

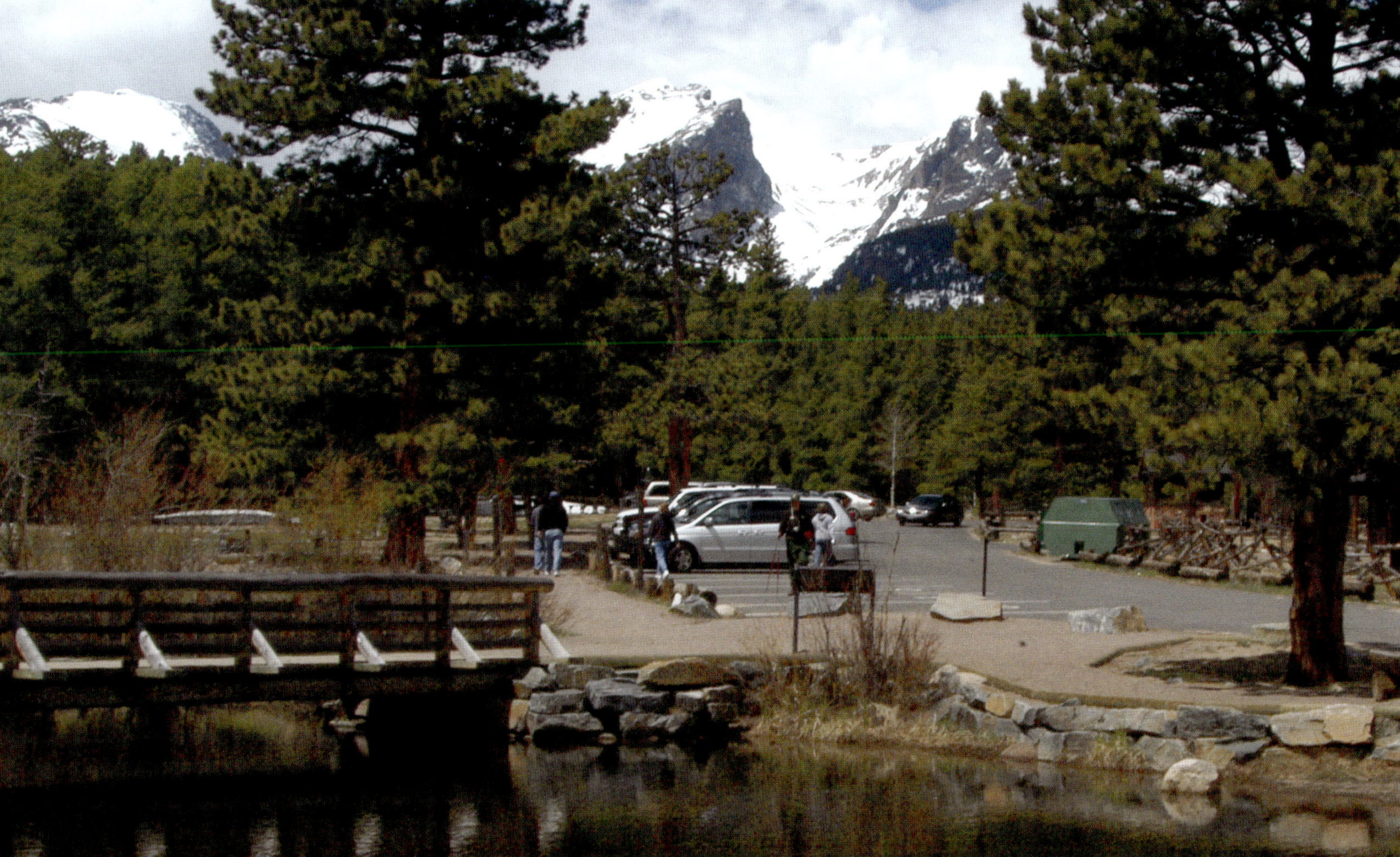

was expanded into a two-story main lodge and Abner constructed a trout lake. In 1916, the lodge was enlarged once more, its downstairs consisting of seven rooms (lounge with a stone fireplace, dining room, butler's pantry, bathroom, kitchen, and storerooms), with guest bedrooms on the second floor.

The government purchased Spragues Lodge in 1932 for $35,210, though Sprague was given a 20-year lease. Alberta Sprague's nephew Edgar Stopher purchased the lease in 1939, and over the next decade expanded the capacity of Spragues to about 85. A series of extensions followed. In 1957, because the government would let him neither improve nor expand operations, Stopher requested that his contract be terminated. All buildings but the livery were razed about 1960. In 2003–2004, the livery was relocated, leaving the entire site a picnic area.

87. Bear Lake and Bear Lake Lodge, 1916

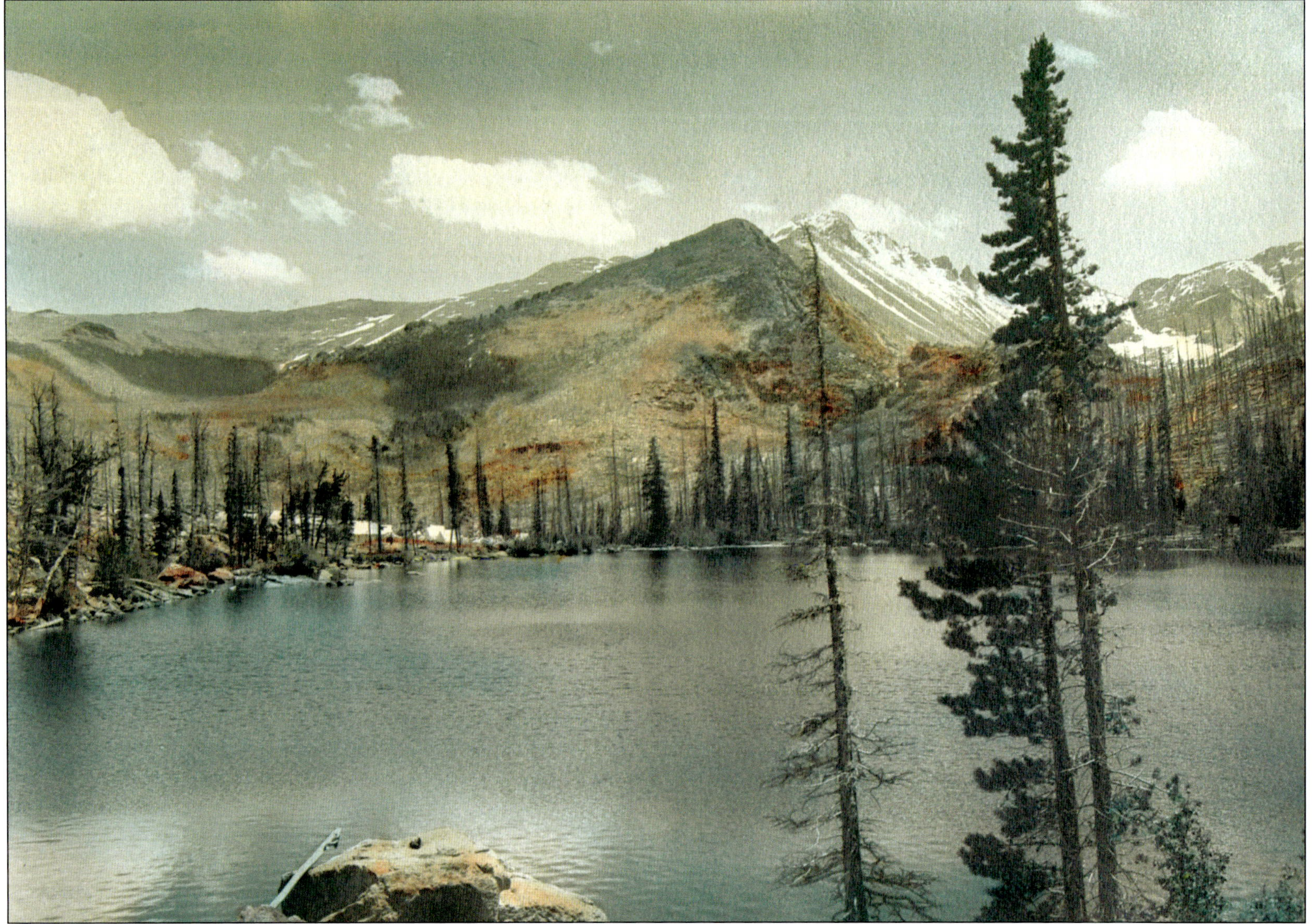

Though today's visitor to Bear Lake might find it difficult to believe, beginning in the early 1920s this picturesque place below Hallett Peak was once the site of two active summer colonies, the resort known as Bear Lake Camp (later Bear Lake Lodge) and the Bear Lake Trail School, a summer camp for boys that Frank H. Cheley (see p. 44) established in 1921. Though an auto road did not reach the lake until 1924, the attractions of Glacier Gorge and its string of lakes had been known for decades, and well before the turn of the century the lake was a popular destination for hikers and campers. One such party, failing to

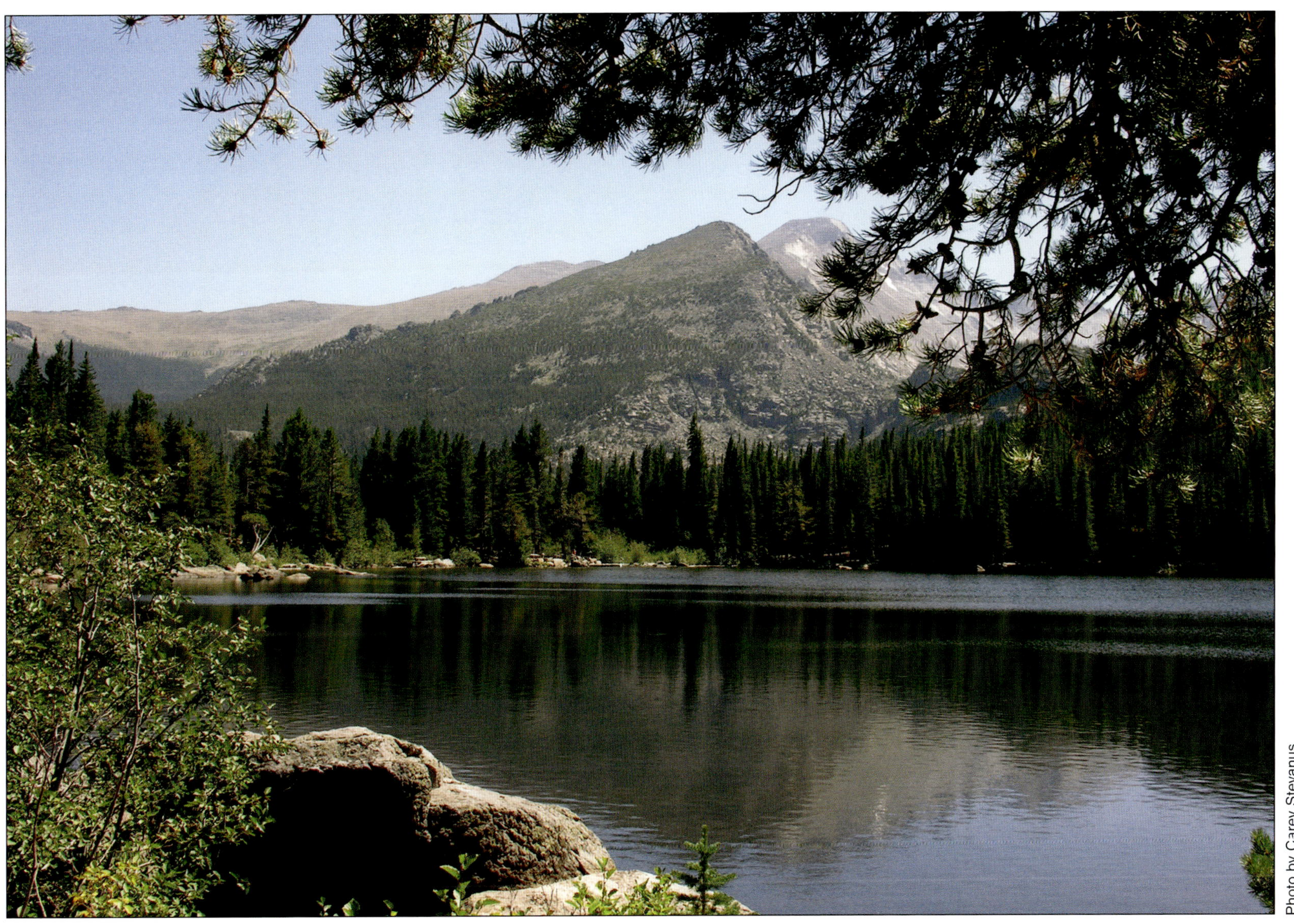

Photo by Carey Stevanus

extinguish its fire properly, had caused the great Bear Lake Fire of August 1900. The fire, which burned for several weeks, swept the entire Glacier Gorge region, in many places to timberline, leaving Bear Lake surrounded with vast areas of fire-killed trees for years.

The first tourist facilities at Bear Lake were built in 1915, by E. A. Brown. He received permission to found a summer resort and campground, for which he erected a 12-by-15-foot log kitchen near the lake's eastern shore and pitched a series of tents. By 1916, a second log building had been erected. These facilities

Bear Lake Lodge, circa 1940

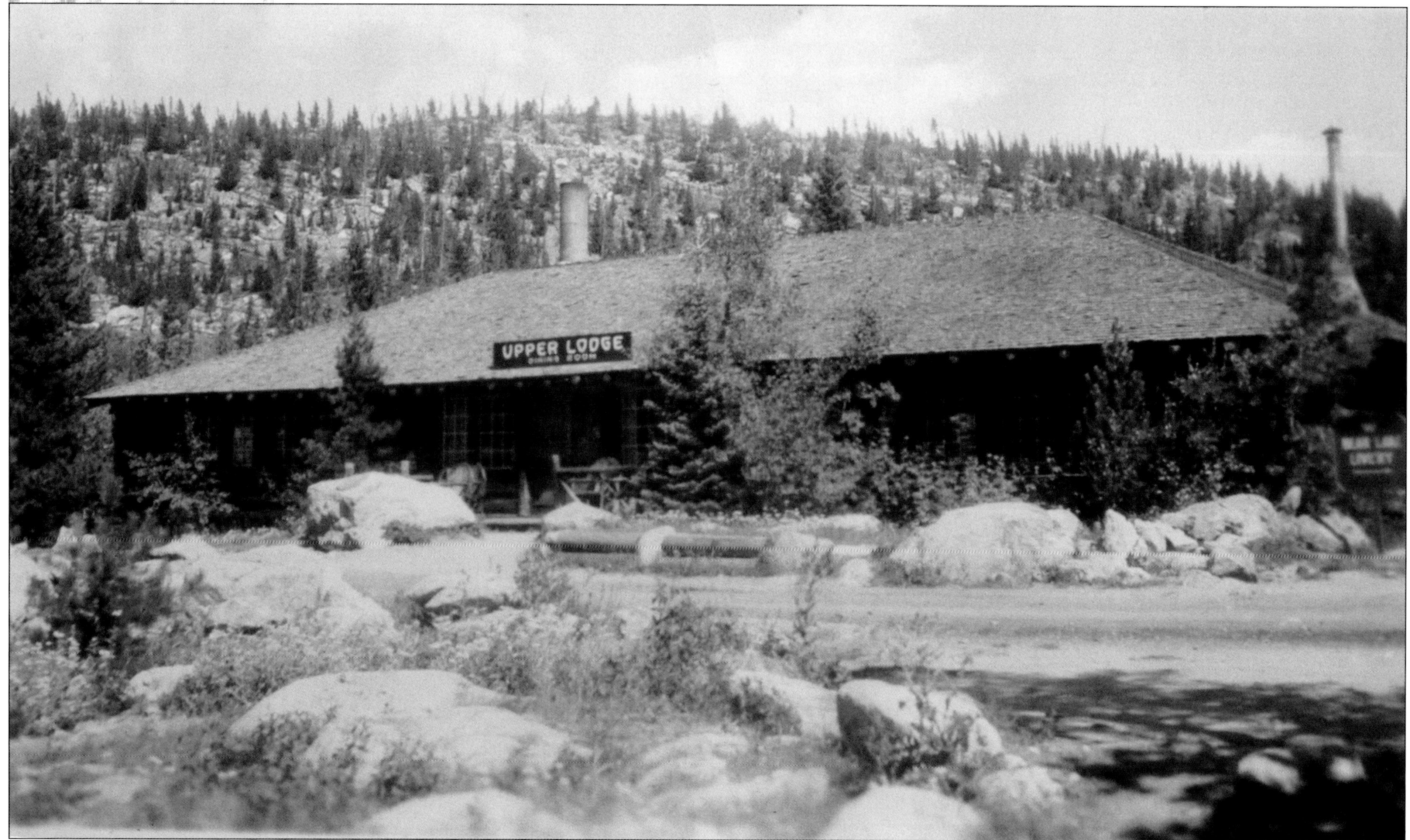

were enlarged during the early 1920s by Frank W. Byerly, who, having taken over Brown's interests under an arrangement with the National Park Service, built a 36-by-60-foot log building known as the Upper Lodge, with a dining room. That building site is shown in the "then" and "now" photographs here.

In 1923, Frank Cheley entered into an agreement with Byerly to use part of his resort as a boy's camp, with shared facilities. Cheley then constructed a two-story 36-by-60-foot administrative building that was named "Tip-Waken," two "barracks," and a director's cabin. These buildings stood in a row above the head of today's parking area.

Cheley kept his camp at Bear Lake until 1927, when, fearing the lake was becoming too crowded, he moved his camp to its present site. The Lower Lodge was then remodeled to become a gift shop, soda fountain, and recreation hall.

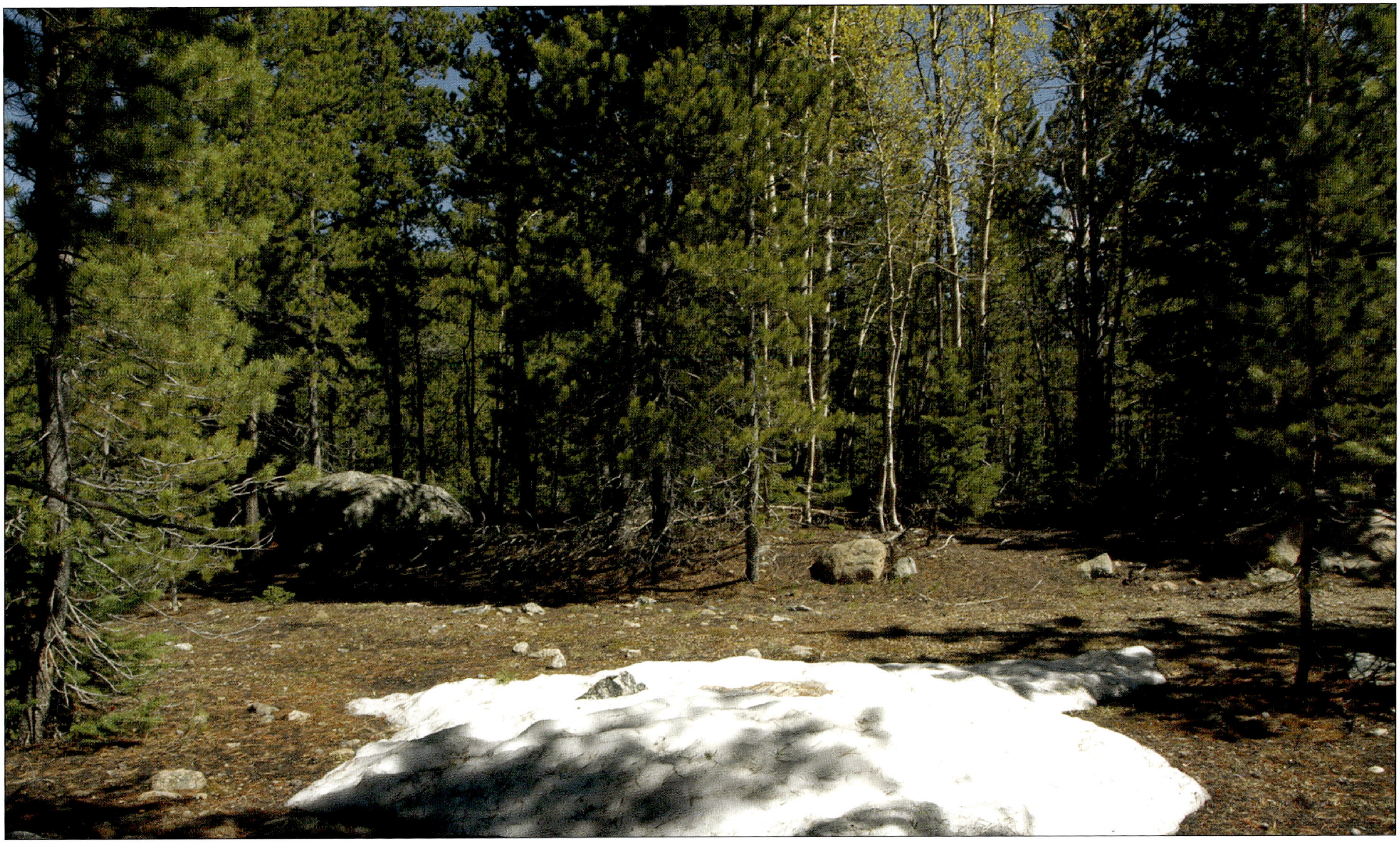

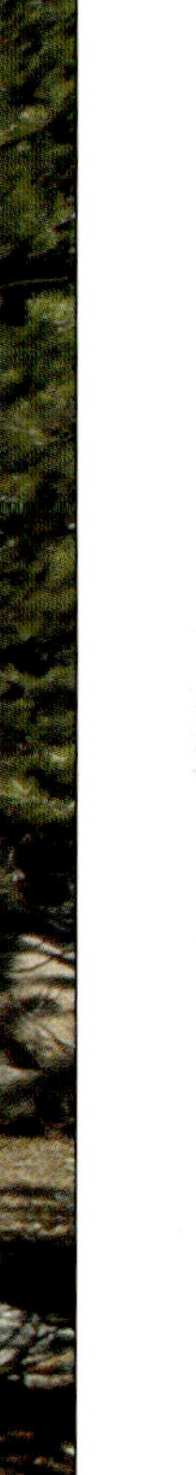

Acquired by the Park Service, Bear Lake Lodge continued to operate on a lease basis until 1958. The following year the Upper Lodge was moved to a campground outside of Estes Park and the rest of the buildings were torn down.

The first historic photograph, hand-tinted by an unknown photographer, was taken about 1916 from the north shore of the lake, looking back toward the area above today's parking lot and against the scenic backdrop of Longs Peak. Bordering the lake, surrounded by woods showing the unmistakable signs of the 1900 fire, is E. A. Brown's tent camp, soon to be replaced by Frank W. Byerly's and Frank H. Cheley's log buildings.

88. Old Fall River Road

After passing the 1915 park dedication site, Fall River Lodge, and the March homestead, Fall River Road, completed in 1920, left the floor of Endovalley and its wetlands to climb by way of 16 switchbacks to Fall River Pass, a distance of 9.4 miles. These switchbacks, together with the road's steep grade and tight and blind curves, created a challenge for early motorists, including the drivers of Roe Emery's Rocky Mountain Parks Transportation Company buses (see p. 102). Some vehicles could not negotiate the road at all because of low gear ratios and gravity-fed fuel systems. Other automobiles were forced to take some of the

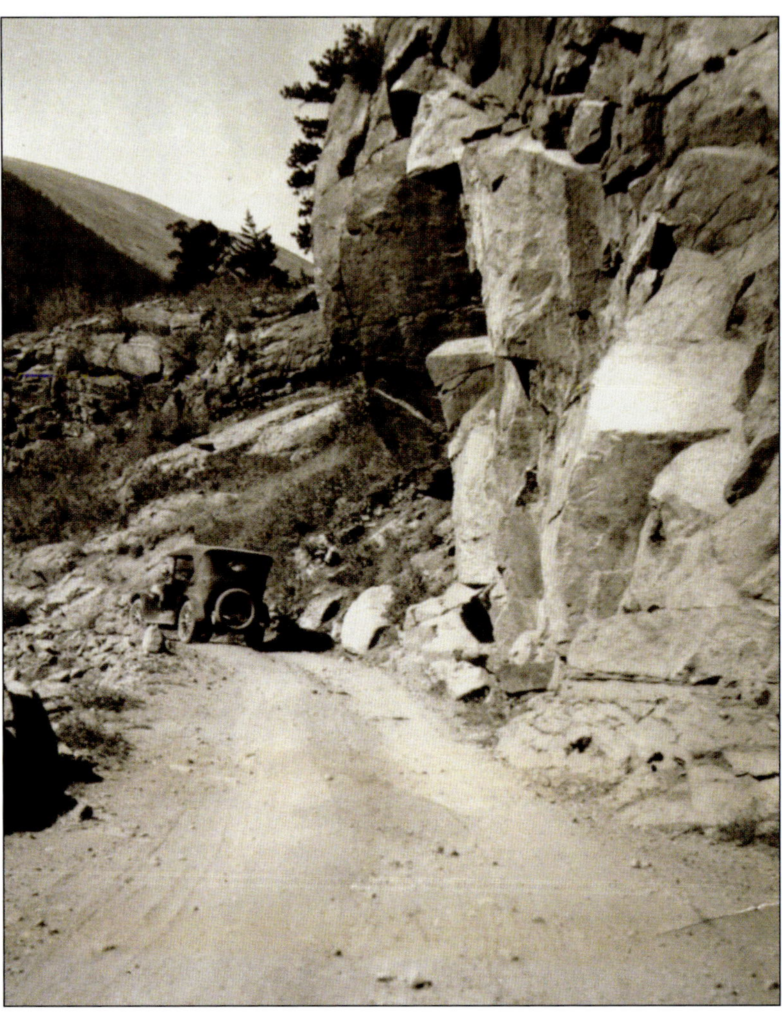

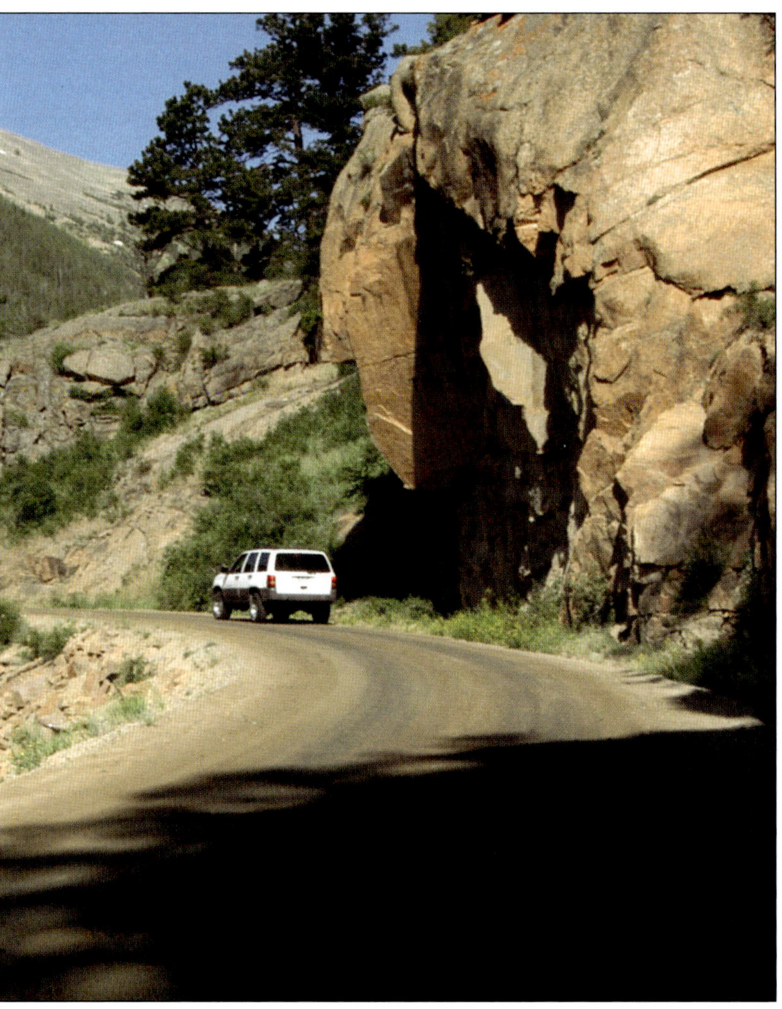

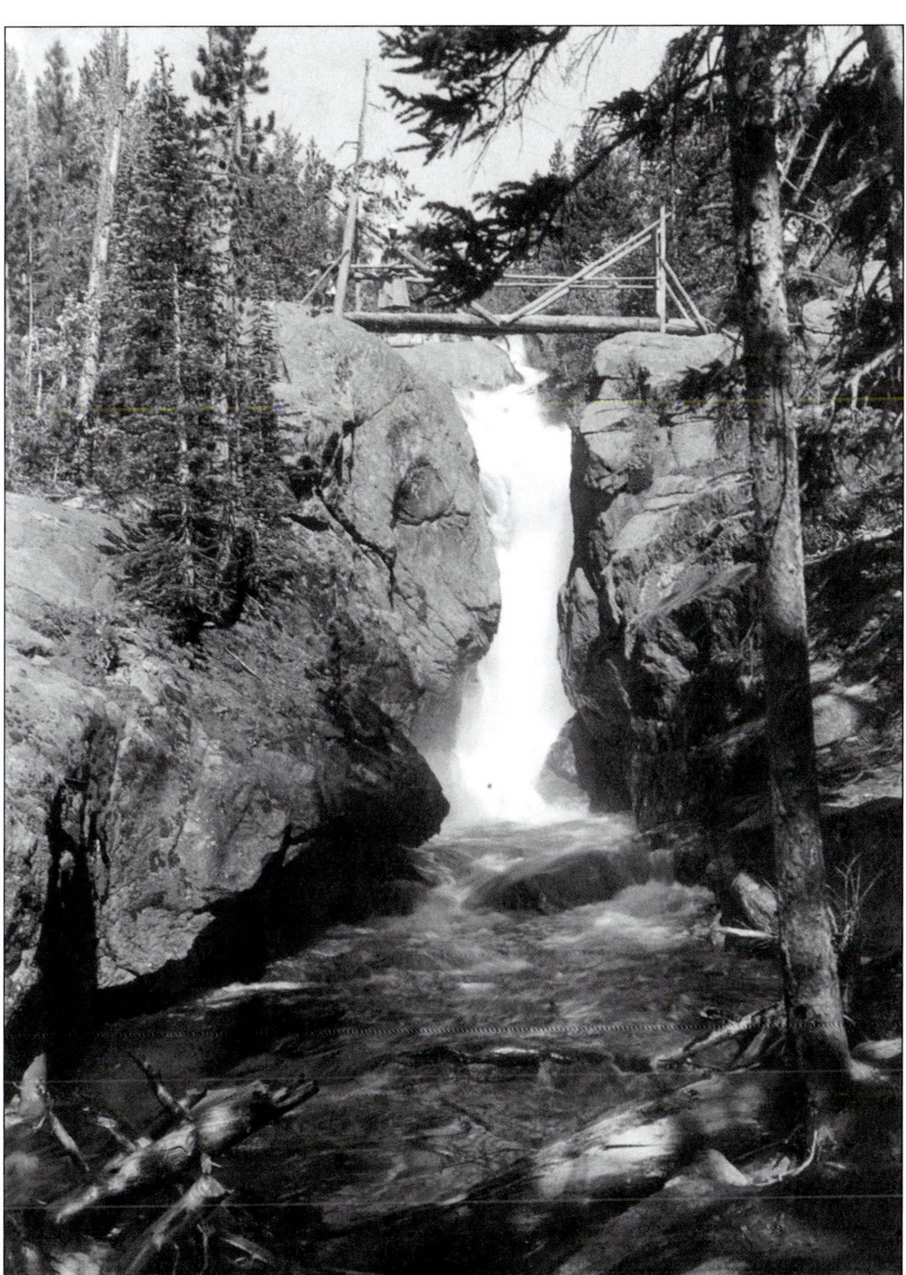

Photo by Fred Payne Clatworthy

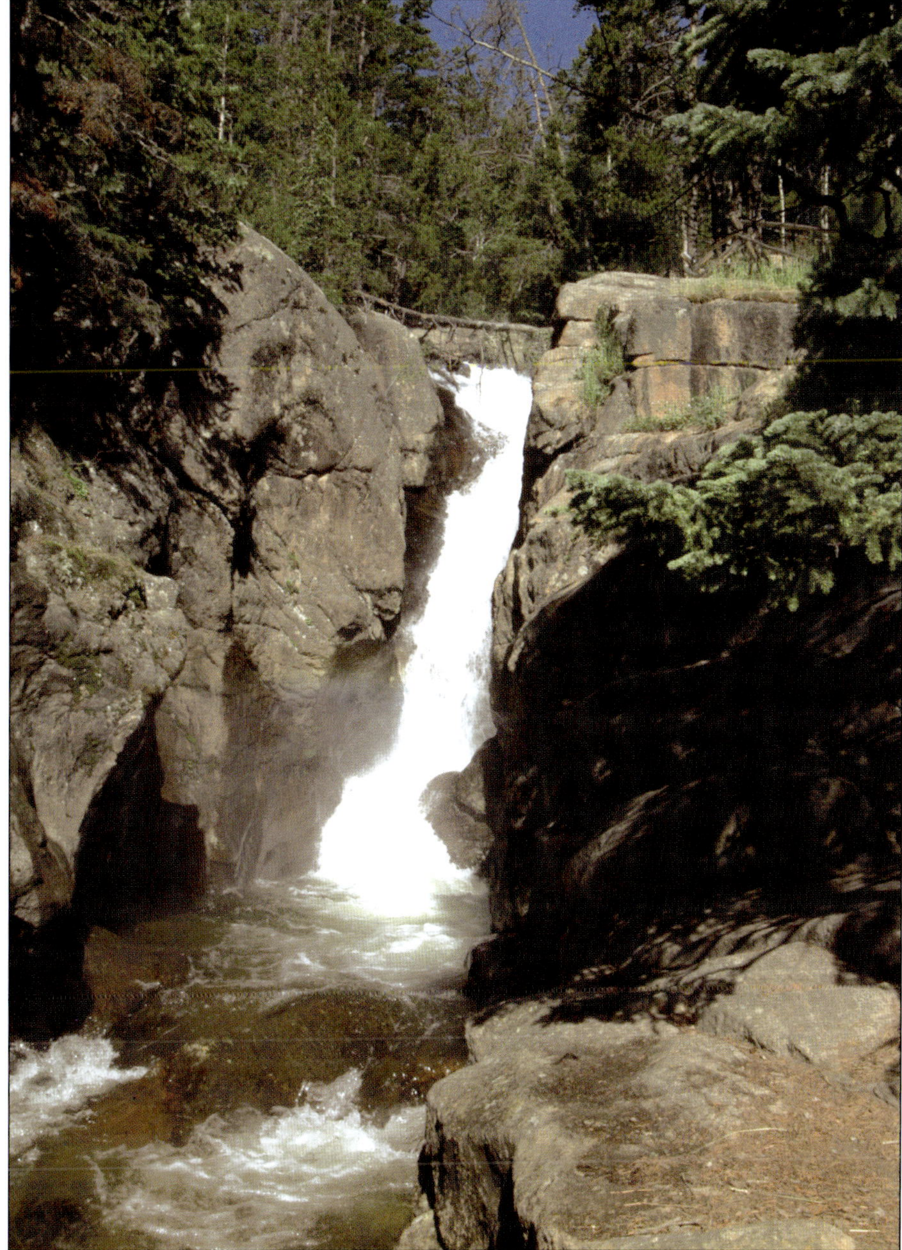

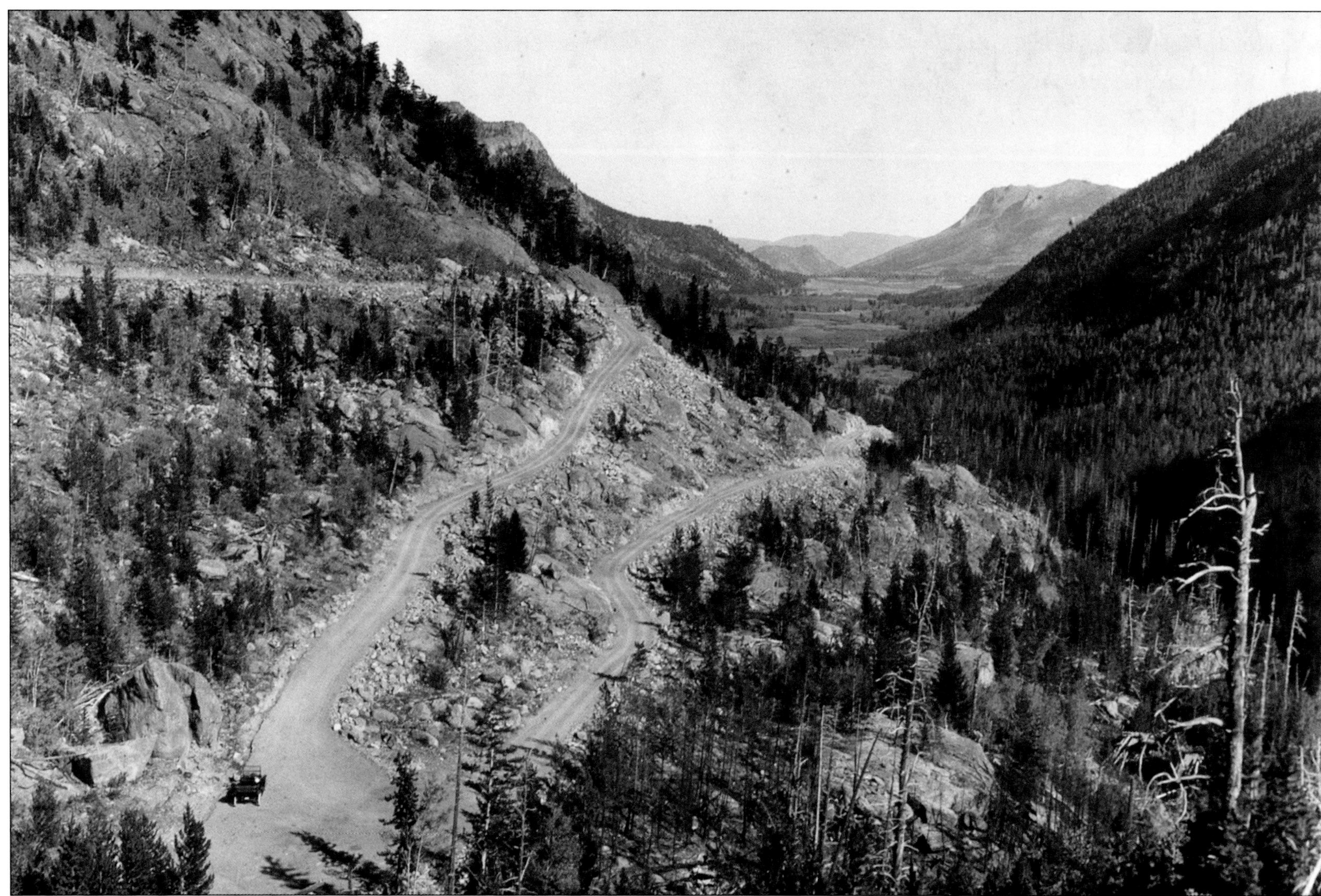

Photo by Fred Payne Clatworthy

switchbacks in reverse because their reverse gears had more power than their low ones. Despite difficulties such as these, the trip proved to be an enormously popular one, and many park visitors reported that the experience of navigating through the upper montane and subalpine life zones, though frightening, was very exhilarating and fun.

The completion of Fall River Road also made possible, for the first time, the Circle Tours, made famous by Roe Emery. These tours began and ended in Denver's railroad station. Arriving tourists would settle into one of Emery's buses and were then driven to Estes Park for an overnight stop. The following day, it was on to Middle Park and Grand Lake by way of Fall River Road, and

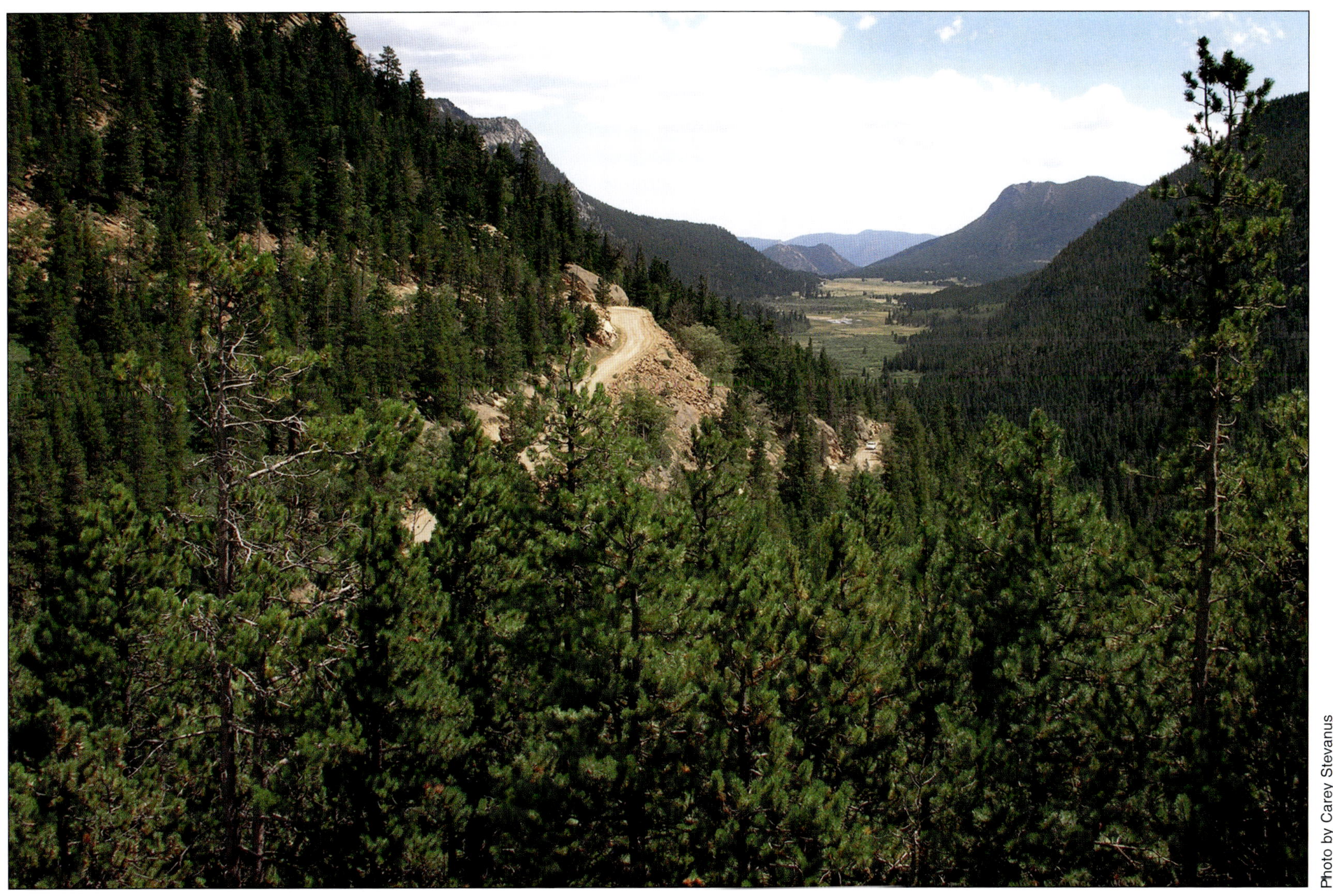

Photo by Carey Stevanus

back to Denver over Berthoud Pass. The opening of Fall River Road, along with the popularity of Emery's tours, had a major impact on the tourist industry in Estes Park. The village and Rocky Mountain National Park were no longer just final destinations. They became places of transit, stops on the journey to somewhere else.

Though considered in its first years little short of a marvel, Fall River Road was never satisfactory: It was difficult to open in spring from winter snows, difficult to maintain from sudden washouts and falling rock in spring and summer, and a challenge for drivers in any season. The decision to replace it with Trail Ridge Road in the mid-1920s was, therefore, greeted with almost-universal enthusiasm. Once Trail Ridge Road was completed in 1932, the decision was made to restrict travel on Fall River Road to one-way up-traffic only.

The Old Fall River Road experience is illustrated by these seven "then and now" pairs of photographs. The first one was taken just past the place in Endovalley where the road begins its ascent up the shoulder of Mount Chapin. The second photograph is of Chasm Falls, a favorite stop where 1920s tourists could cross a bridge to watch the falls below as they drop some 25 feet into a glacial pothole; the bridge was removed following an accident. The third photograph shows one of the road's many steep switchbacks, which more than one driver during the 1920s found intimidating. The fourth and fifth pairs of photographs were taken at Fall River Pass —the fourth looking southwest, taken from the end of what is today the Alpine Visitor Center parking lot, and the fifth, also looking southwest, of the old Fall River Pass Ranger Station, built in 1924. The sixth photograph shows Fall River Road as it passed beneath a series of huge upright boulders on the hillside above Poudre Lake at Milner Pass. Though the road was obliterated by Civilian Conservation Corps (CCC) workers once Trail Ridge Road was completed in 1932, its signs can still be seen in several places, including here. The seventh pair shows the rock formation known as Indian Head Rock. It is located just before Farview Curve on Trail Ridge Road. As the original photograph suggests, this large and distinctive outcropping once stood just above Old Fall River Road. The rock signaled to motorists that they were just about to start their rapid descent by means of switchbacks to the floor of the Kawuneeche Valley.

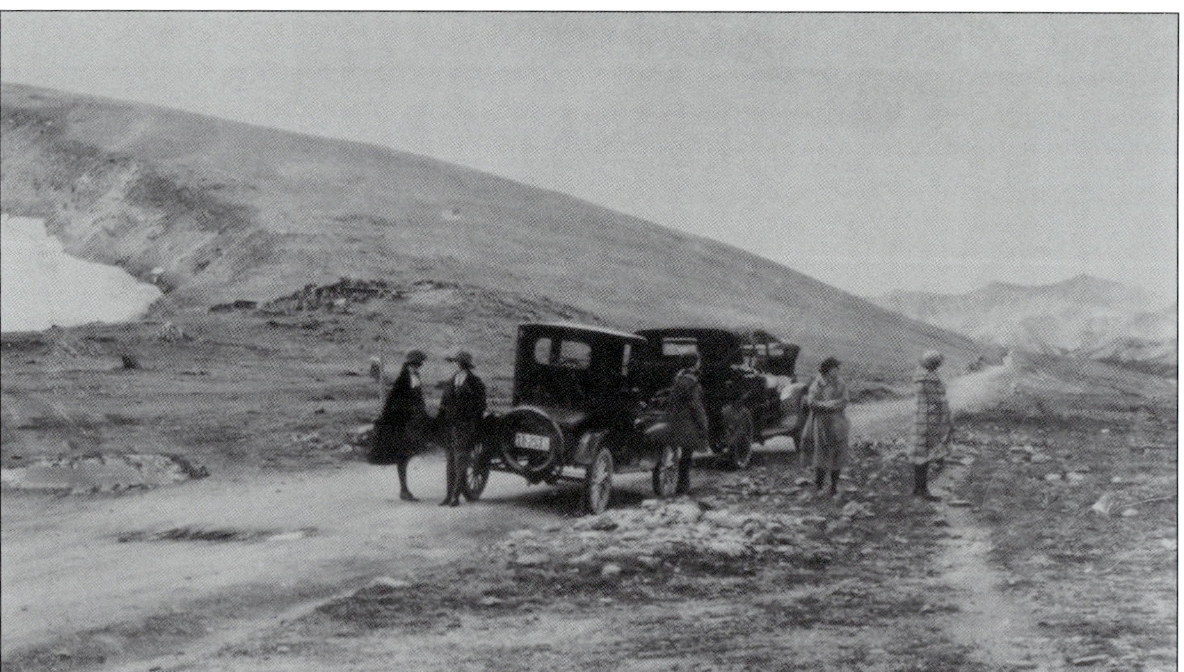

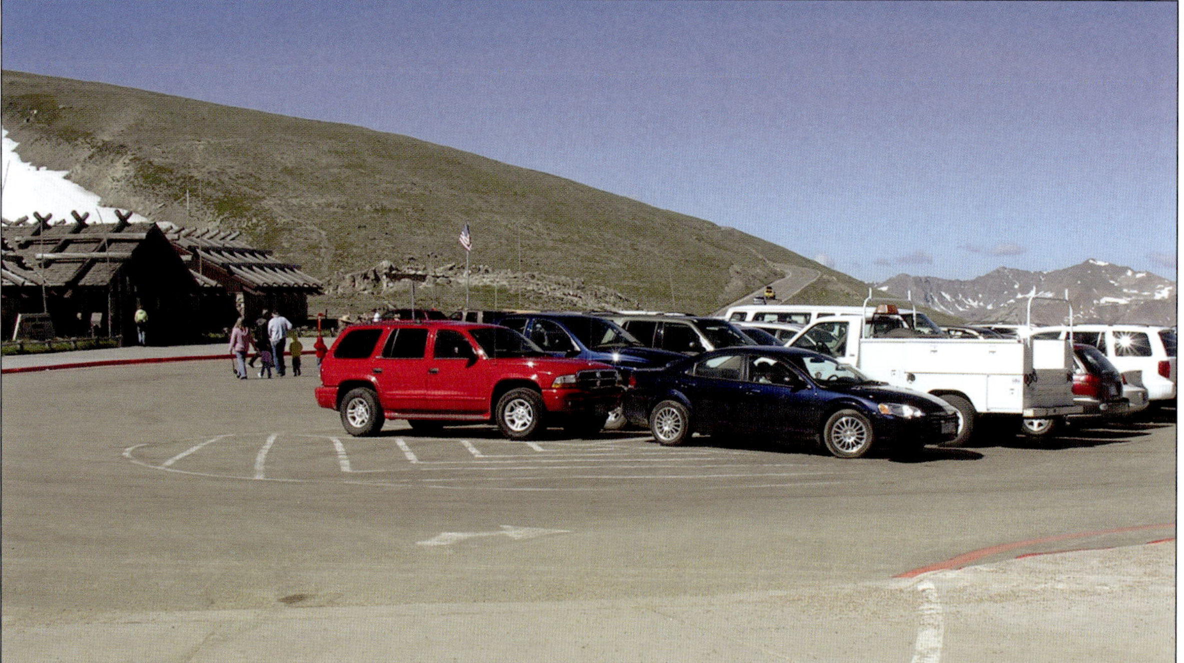

Photo by Carey Stevanus

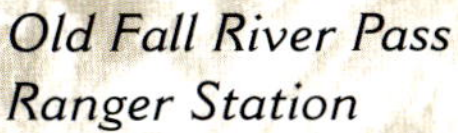

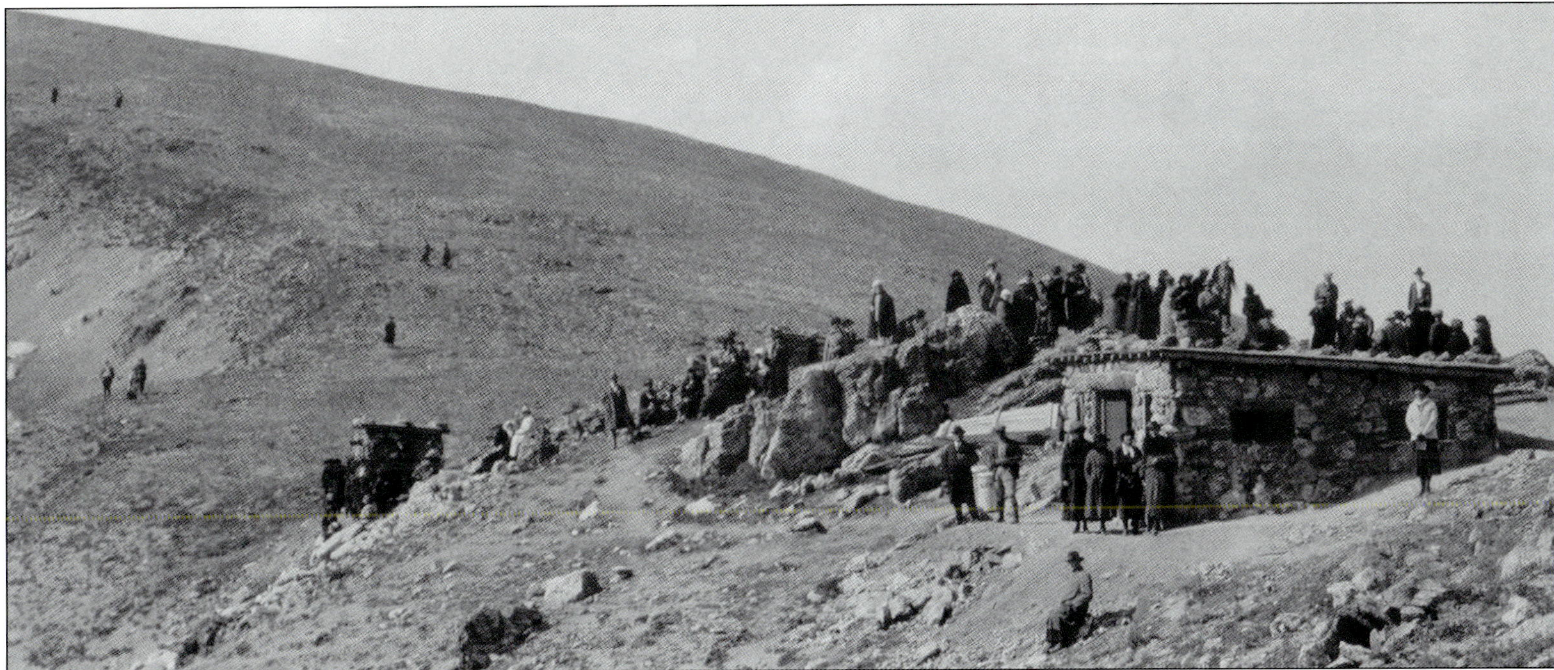

Photo by Fred Payne Clatworthy

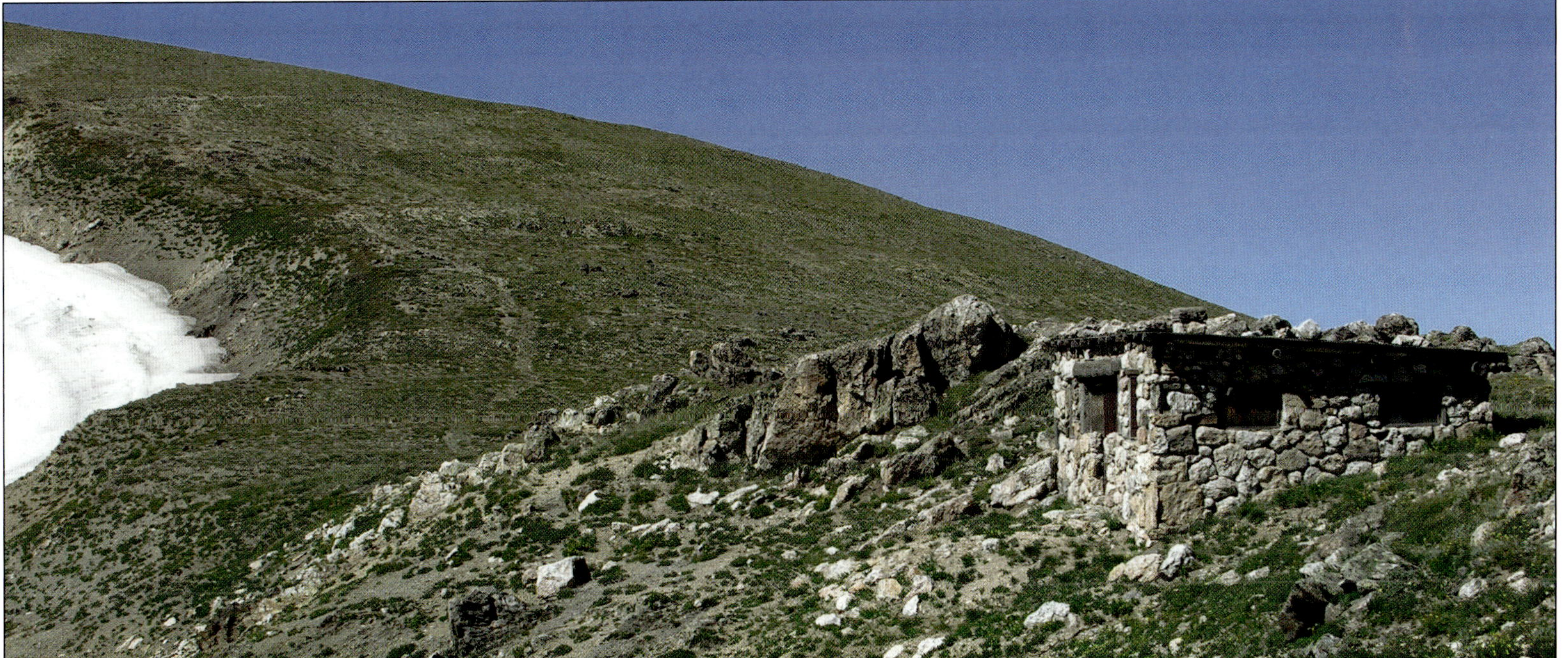

Photo by Carey Stevanus

Fall River Road above Poudre Lake

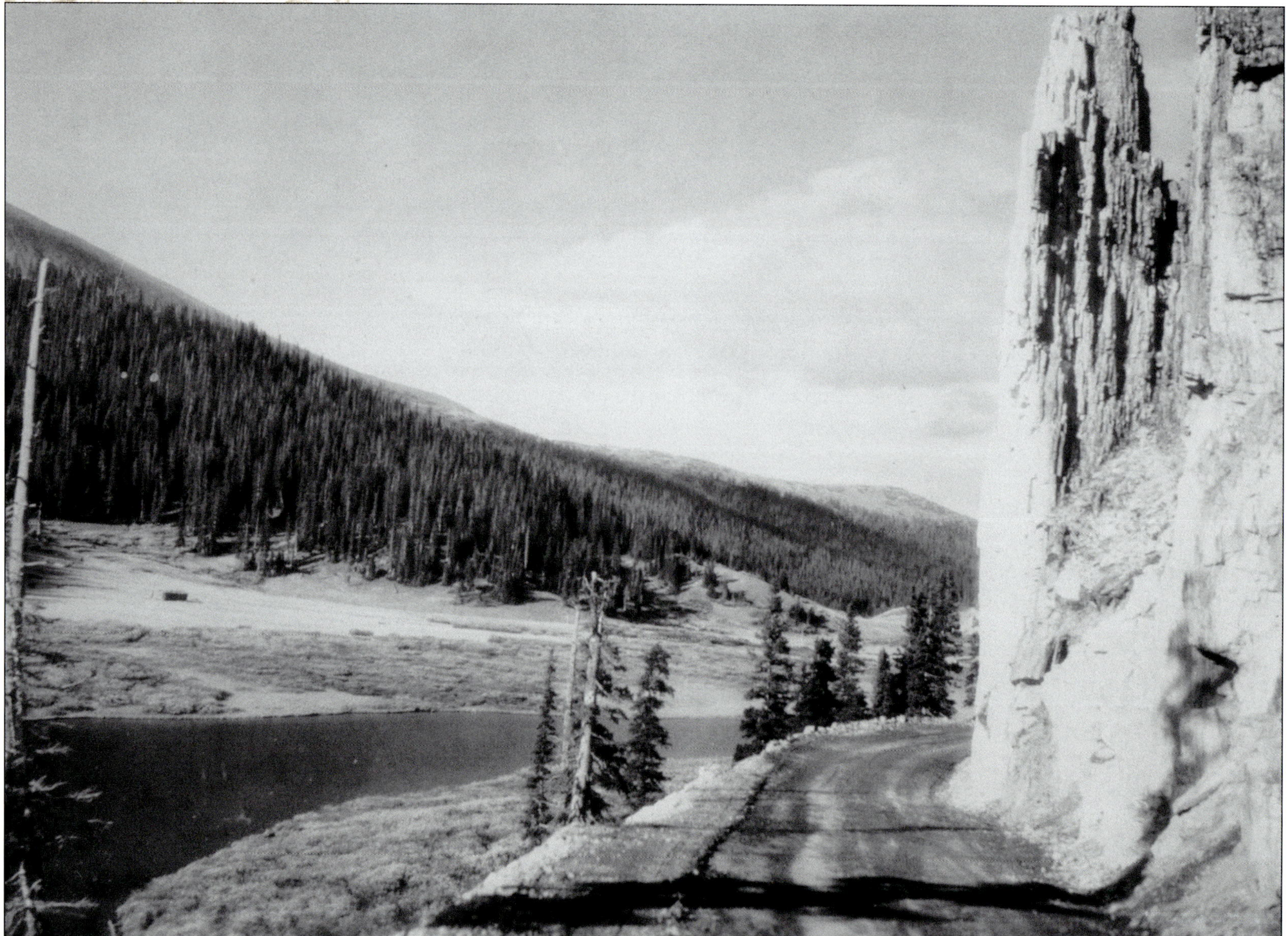

Photo by F. J. Francis

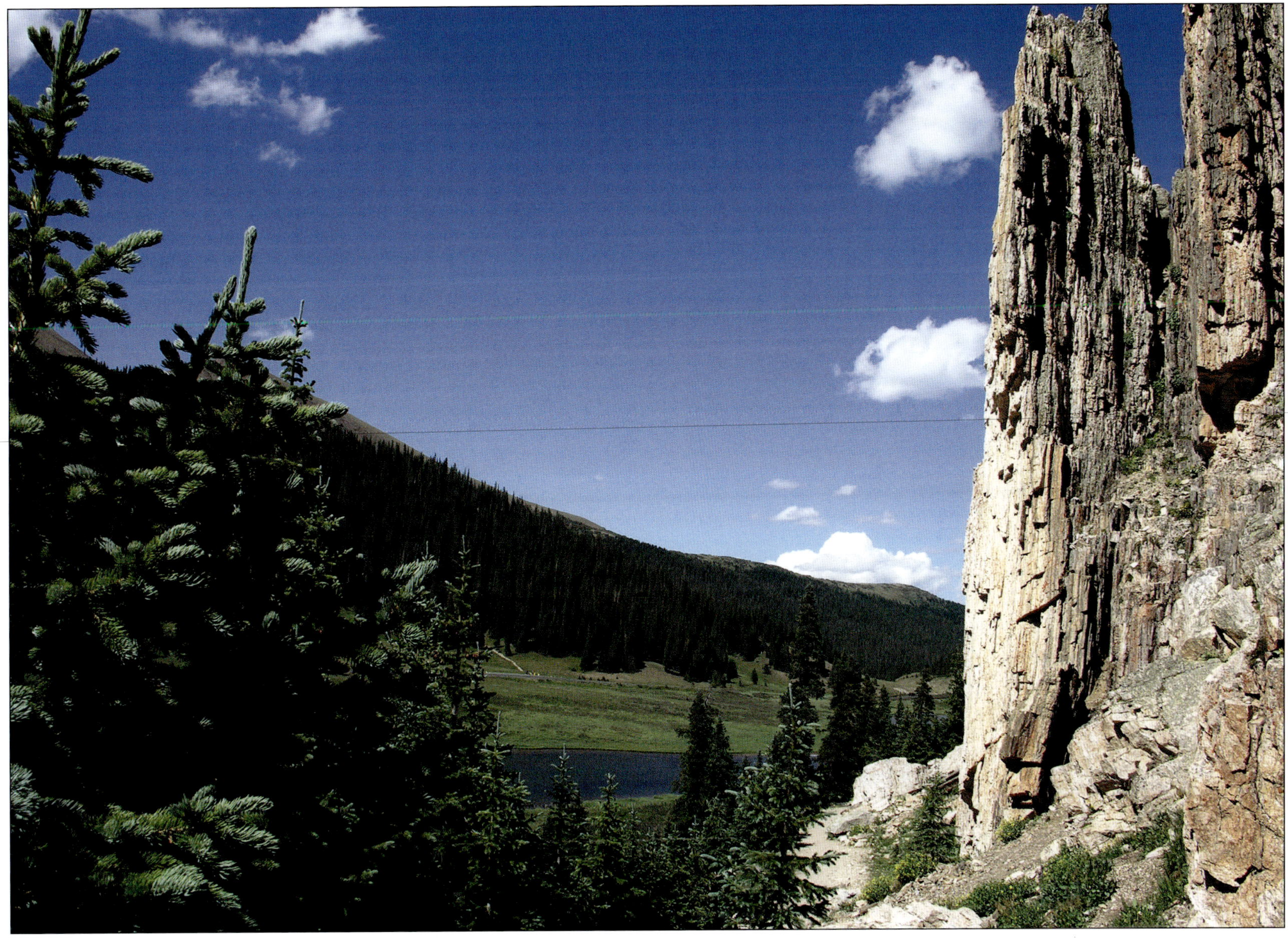

Photo by Carey Stevanus

Indian Head Rock above Old Fall River Road

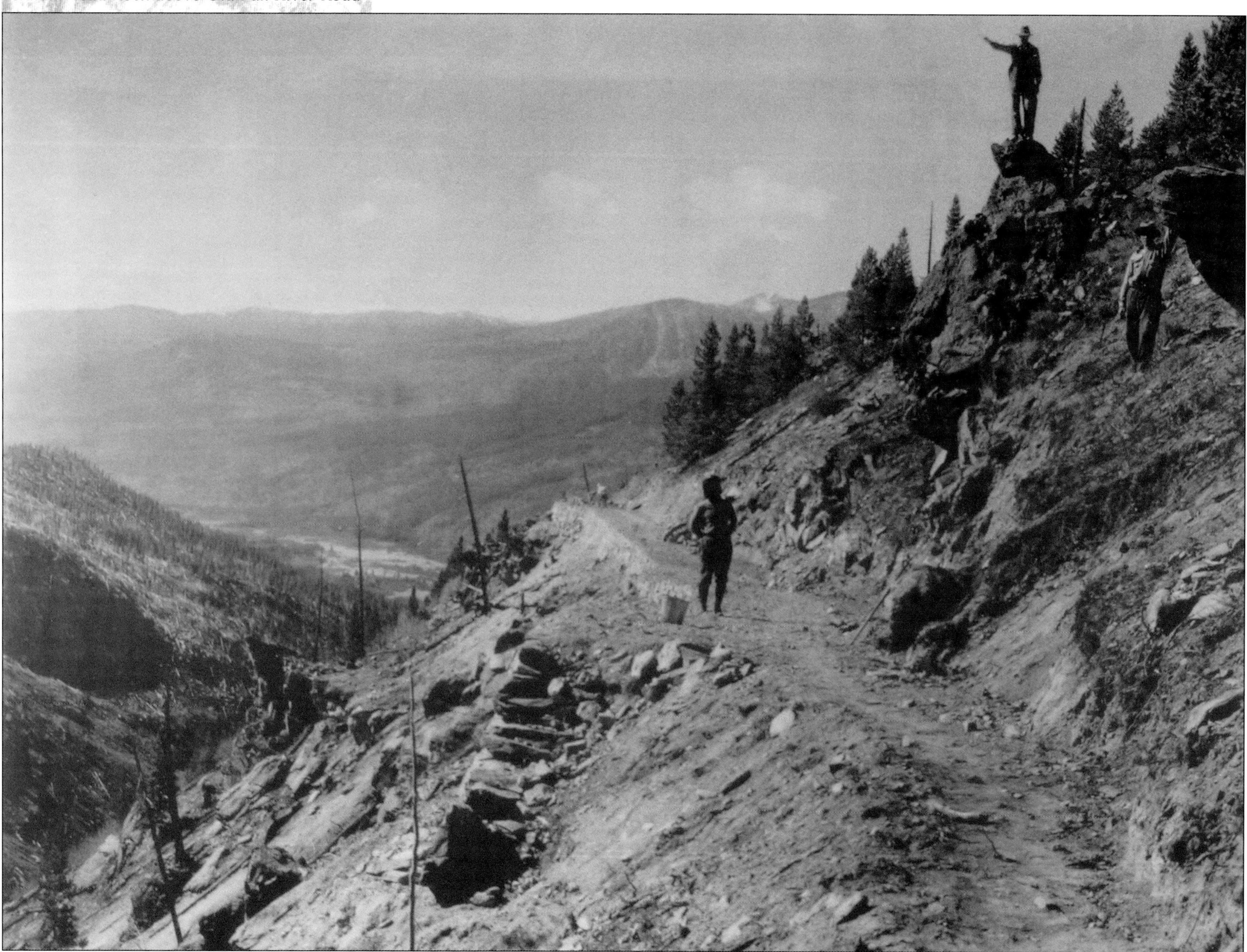

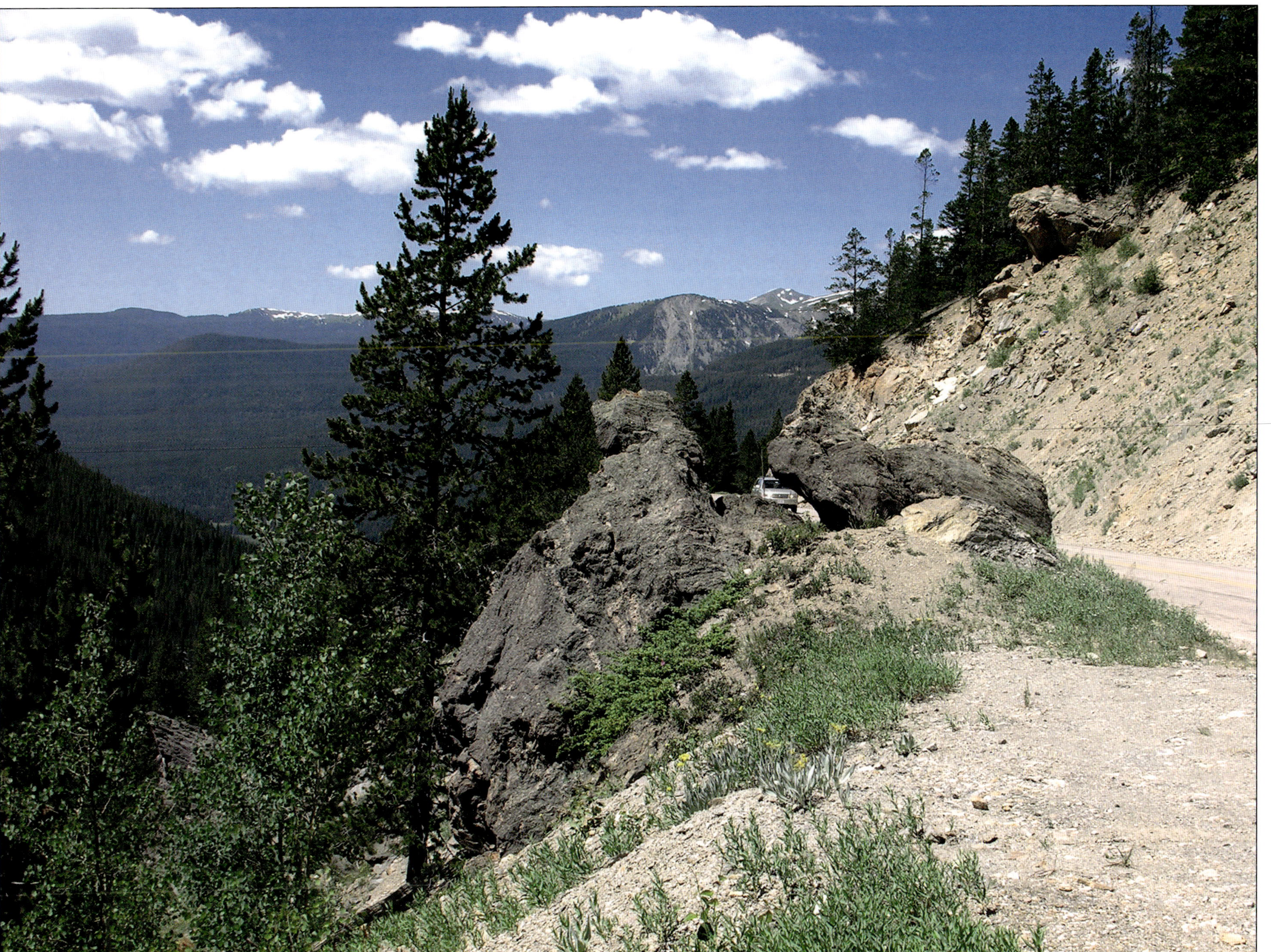

Photo by Carey Stevanus

89. Trail Ridge Road, circa 1940

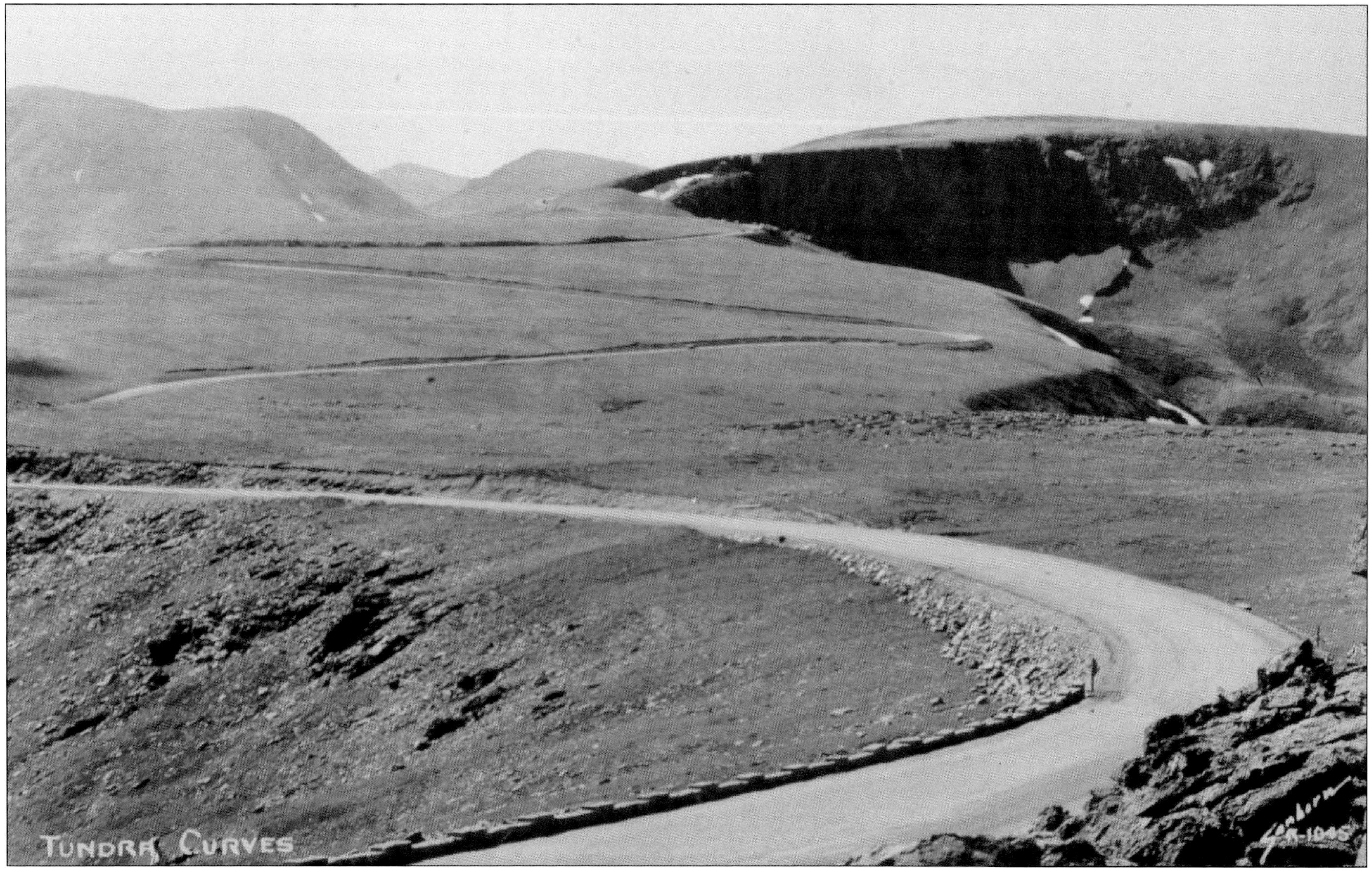

Photo by Sanborn Souvenir Company

Fall River Road formally opened for traffic in September 1920, seven long years after construction had begun. But for all the enthusiasm of its builders and early users, the road quickly became obsolete. It was difficult to maintain and keep open because of erosion, earthslides, and snow. It was equally difficult for cars and buses to negotiate safely because of its grade, tight curves, and switchbacks. Passing was difficult—in many places impossible—particularly given the volume of traffic, which increased each summer. Double-tracking was precluded because of the terrain and the expense involved.

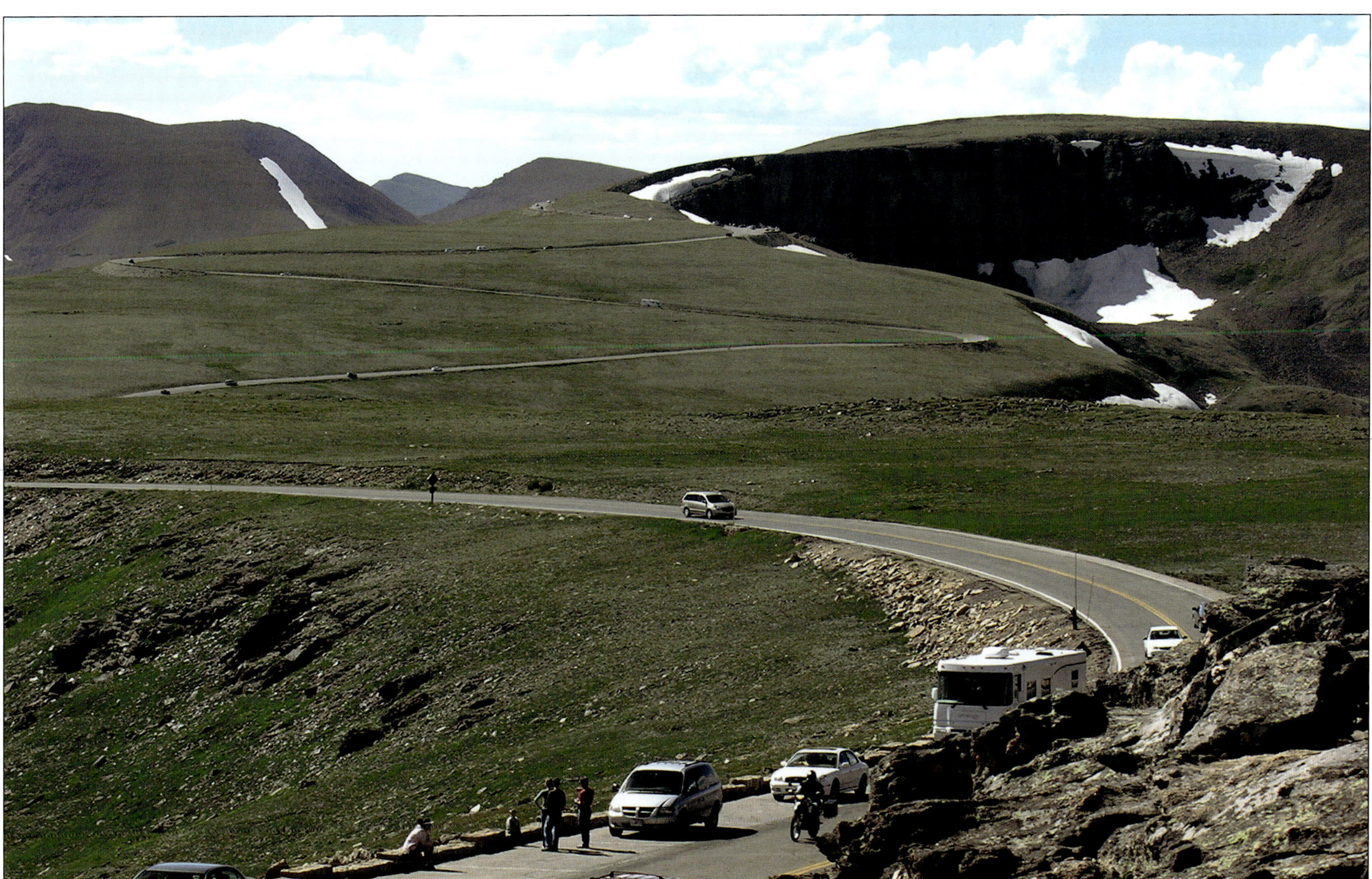

Photo by Carey Stevanus

As early as 1922, park superintendent Roger Toll suggested opening a new road to Grand Lake by way of the tundra on Trail Ridge, making use of a route that Native Americans followed while crossing to Middle Park. Planning did not actively begin, however, until the summer of 1926, when Toll and Stephen A. Wallace, a locating engineer from the Bureau of Roads, conducted a feasibility study. Wallace's report was enthusiastic. The route surveyed across Trail Ridge offered not only "unsurpassed mountain scenery" but would be easier to maintain and keep open and be far less congested.

Trail Ridge Road, August 1932

Bids were formally advertised in August 1929 for the first 17.2-mile section of the new road from Deer Ridge to Fall River Pass. Work on the 22-foot-wide road was begun by the veteran contractor William A. Colt, whose men took great care not to permanently damage the fragile terrain, using salvaged timber as cribbing to shield rock outcroppings adjacent to blasting areas. On the western side, crews began work in October 1930, directed by L. T. "Bill" Lawler of Butte, Montana, who extended the road from Fall River Pass to the upper Kawuneeche Valley.

One of the most challenging sections of the new road was at the Rock Cut (shown here), which required major blasting and the excavation of large boulders. The work done by Colt, Lawler, and their tough and resourceful men was heroic, given the altitude and the unpredictability of the weather, with its constant threat of sleet, snow, and electrical storms. Officially opened for travel in the summer of 1932, Trail Ridge Road, dubbed "the eighth wonder of the modern world," is the highest continuous paved highway in the United States—a road completed on time, within budget, and without the loss of a single life.

The first set of photographs is of Tundra Curves and was taken from above the road just west of the Rock Cut.

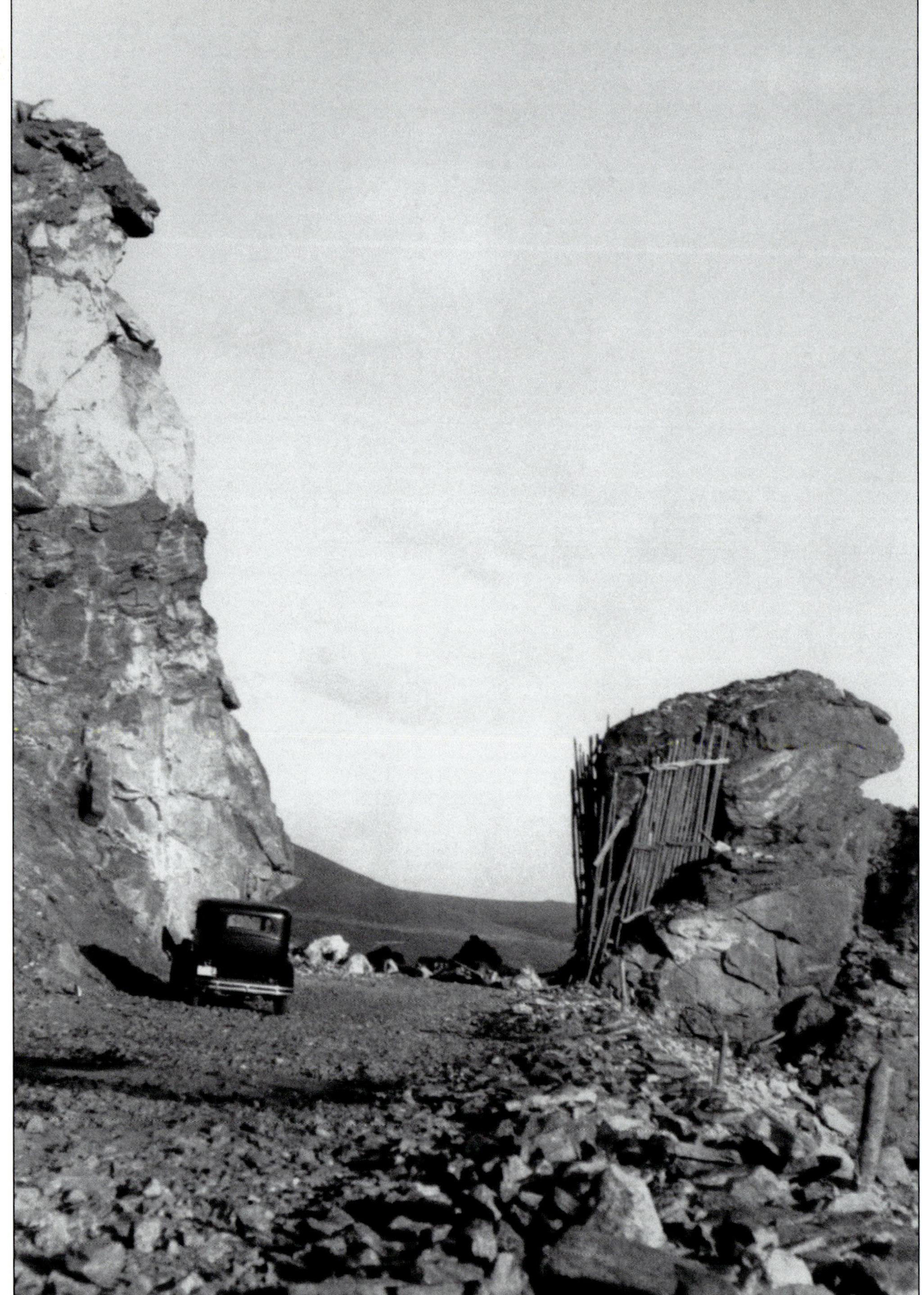

Photo by John McLaughlin

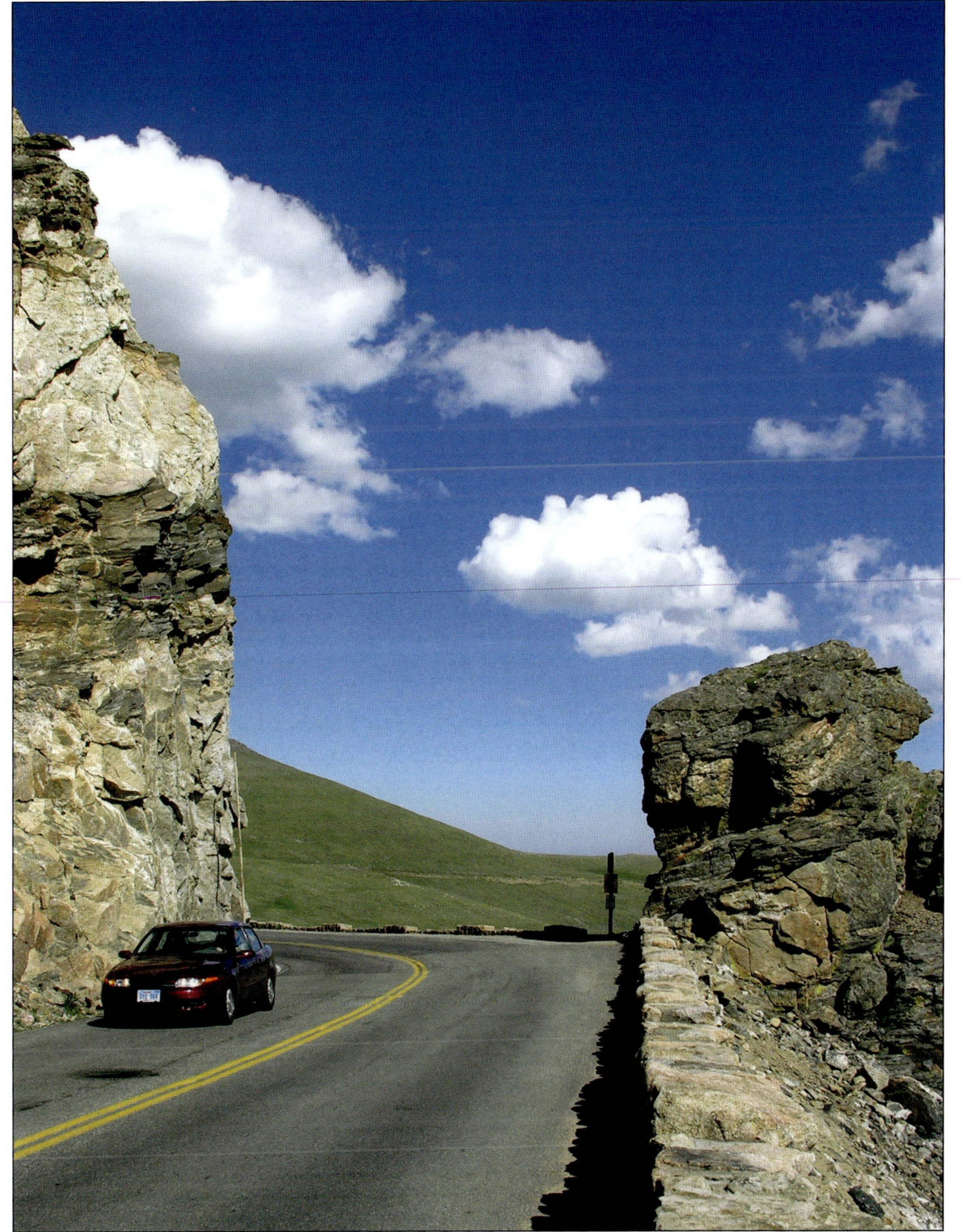

Photo by Carey Stevanus

90. Grand Lake, circa 1925

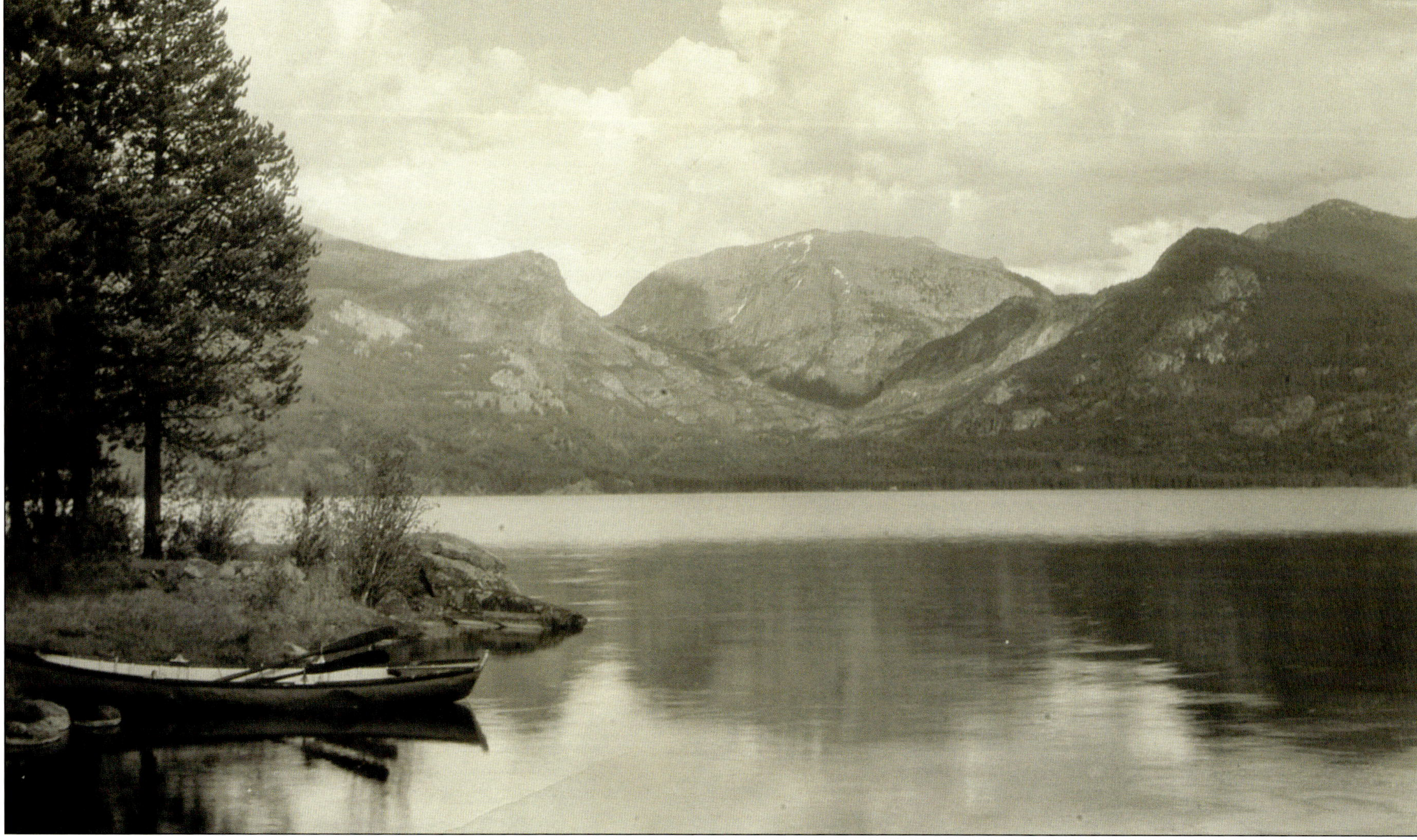

Photo by Fred Payne Clatworthy

Grand Lake's human history stretches back more than a thousand years, when its first seasonal residents began stopping by Colorado's largest natural lake to fish and hunt. Later there were the Arapaho and Cheyenne, who on occasion crossed the Continental Divide to hunt, and the Ute, who summered regularly in Middle Park into the late 1860s.

The town of Grand Lake developed with the mining boom of the early 1880s. Between 1881 and 1888, Grand Lake was important enough to be the county seat. When the boom collapsed, Grand Lake relaxed, becoming a very popular summer resort community, with hotels, restaurants, and businesses that served the tourist public.

Grand Lake's woods, shoreline, mountain vistas, and changing moods have always been popular subjects for the camera of amateur and professional alike. William Henry Jackson, during his days working with the Hayden survey and afterward, and his Denver contemporary William G. Chamberlain took early

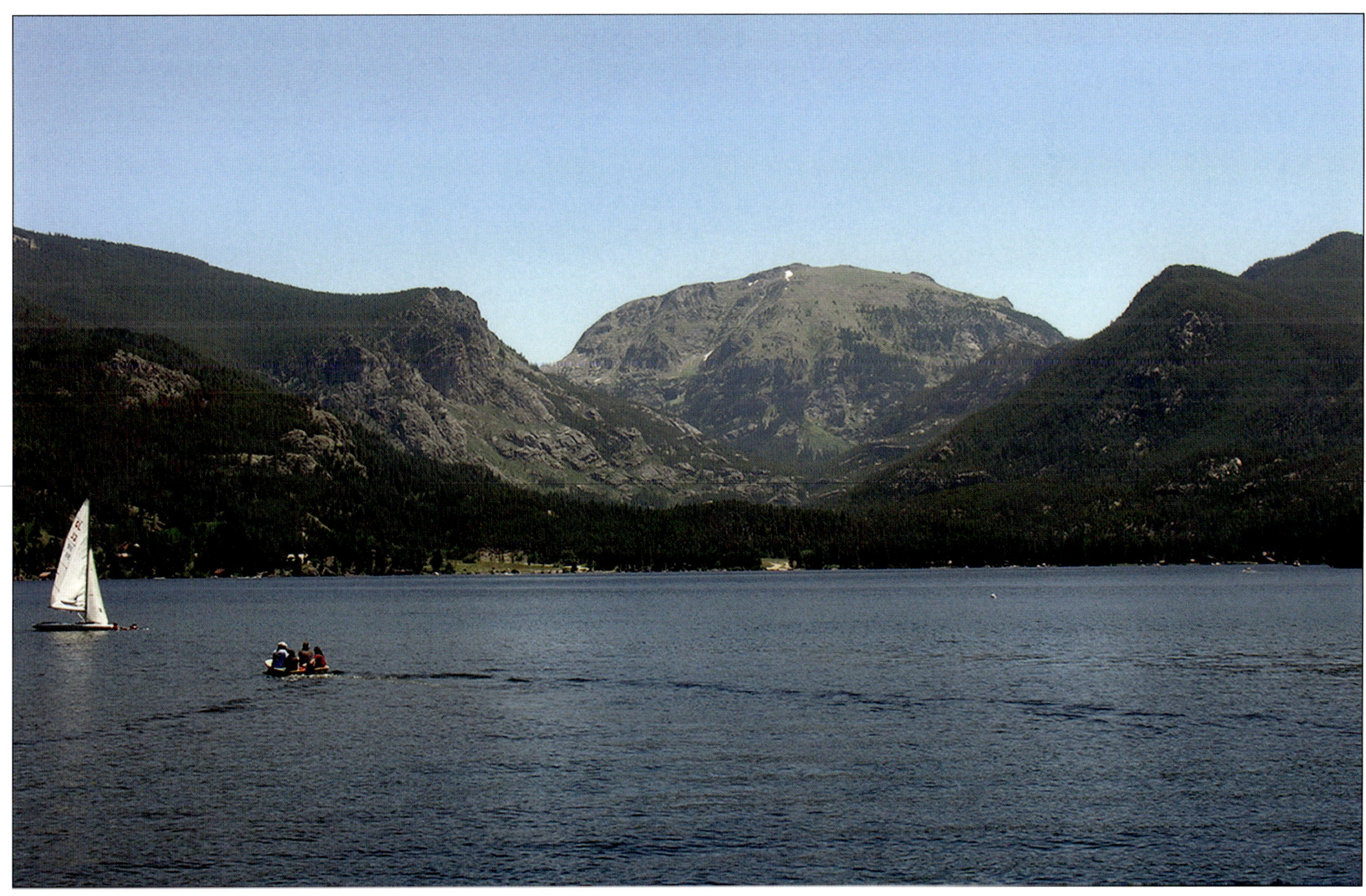

Photo by Carey Stevanus

photographs of the lake, as did professional photographers of the next generation like Denver's Louis C. McClure and Estes Park's Fred Payne Clatworthy.

Fred Payne Clatworthy took the original photograph from near today's Point Park on Grand Lake's western shore; this is the spot where the channel from Shadow Mountain Reservoir enters the lake, directly across from 12,007-foot Mount Craig, which old-timers still call "Old Baldy." Clatworthy positioned his camera on a bridge over what was then the outlet to the Colorado River. The major difference between the "then and now" photographs results from the fact that the bridge on which Clatworthy stood was located farther down the channel than the present one and the fact that the Colorado–Big Thompson transmountain project of the 1940s and '50s raised Grand Lake's level by as much as 8 feet, significantly altering the appearance of the inlet.

91. Grand Lake Lodge, circa 1922

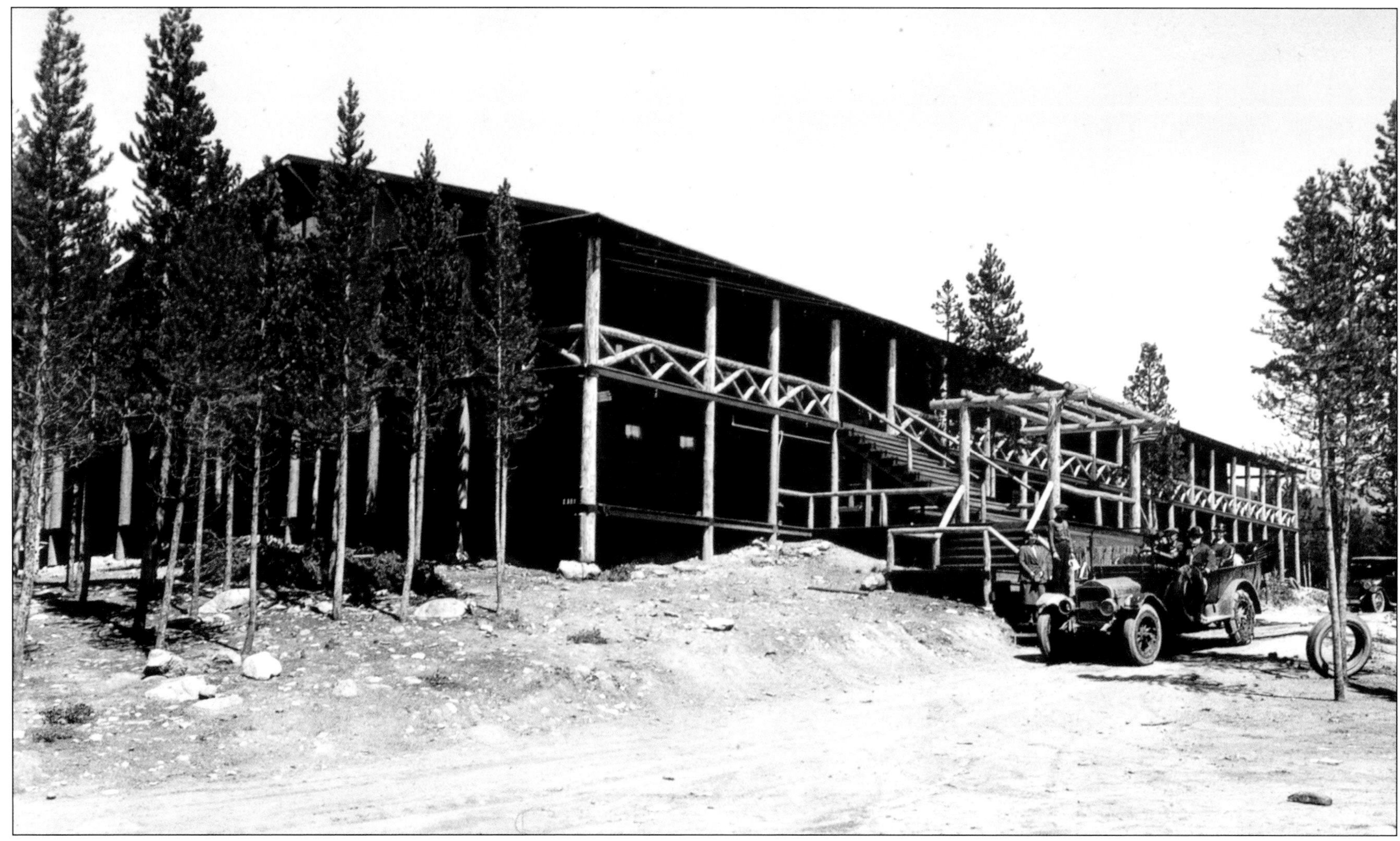

Though the completion of Fall River Road across the Continental Divide made it possible for Roe Emery and his Rocky Mountain Parks Transportation Company to establish their popular Circle Tours, Emery first needed lodging and dining facilities for his travelers. In anticipation, he struck a deal with A. D. Lewis to use his Lewiston Chalets near Marys Lake (see p. 148) as his first stop out of Denver. Emery also needed an overnight hotel on the west side of Fall River Road, so he invited Lewis to build a new lodge across the divide. In 1920, Lewis opened his Grand Lake Lodge on Park Service land above the lake, with a central dining lodge and cabins up the hillside.

Built of native lodgepole pine, Grand Lake Lodge, then and now, consists of a single open-ceiling room, whose massive timber crossbeams are supported by peeled log columns. The covered, log-railed front porch stretches along the entire length of the building to offer panoramic lake and mountain views. Over the years, the guest cabins to the rear increased to about 70.

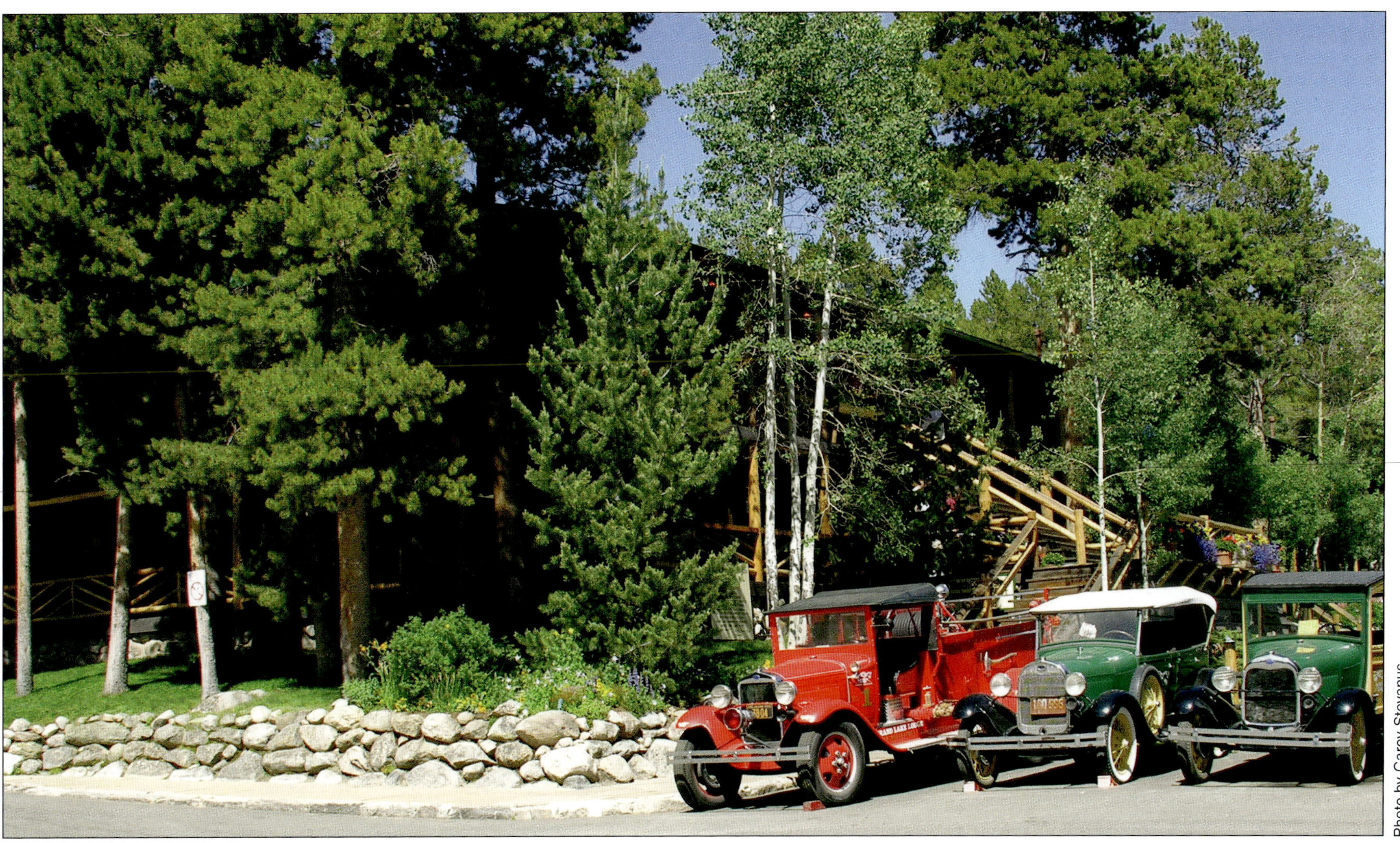

Photo by Carey Stevanus

In 1922 or 1923, Emery bought Grand Lake Lodge and the Lewiston Chalets, which he operated until 1953. They were then sold, with the rest of the Rocky Mountain Parks Transportation Company, to Ted and Isaac James, Nebraska brothers well established in the transportation business.

Thanks to negotiations by the Jameses in 1963, the 72-acre property was removed from Rocky Mountain National Park and Grand Lake Lodge escaped the fate of other historic guest resorts. It also survived a damaging 1973 fire. Employees' quick thinking saved most of the furniture and Navajo rugs as well as some of the taxidermy. Painstakingly restored by the Jameses, Grand Lake Lodge reopened in 1981, when the structure was added to the National Register of Historic Places.

92. Holzwarth Trout Lodge and Never Summer Ranch, circa 1930

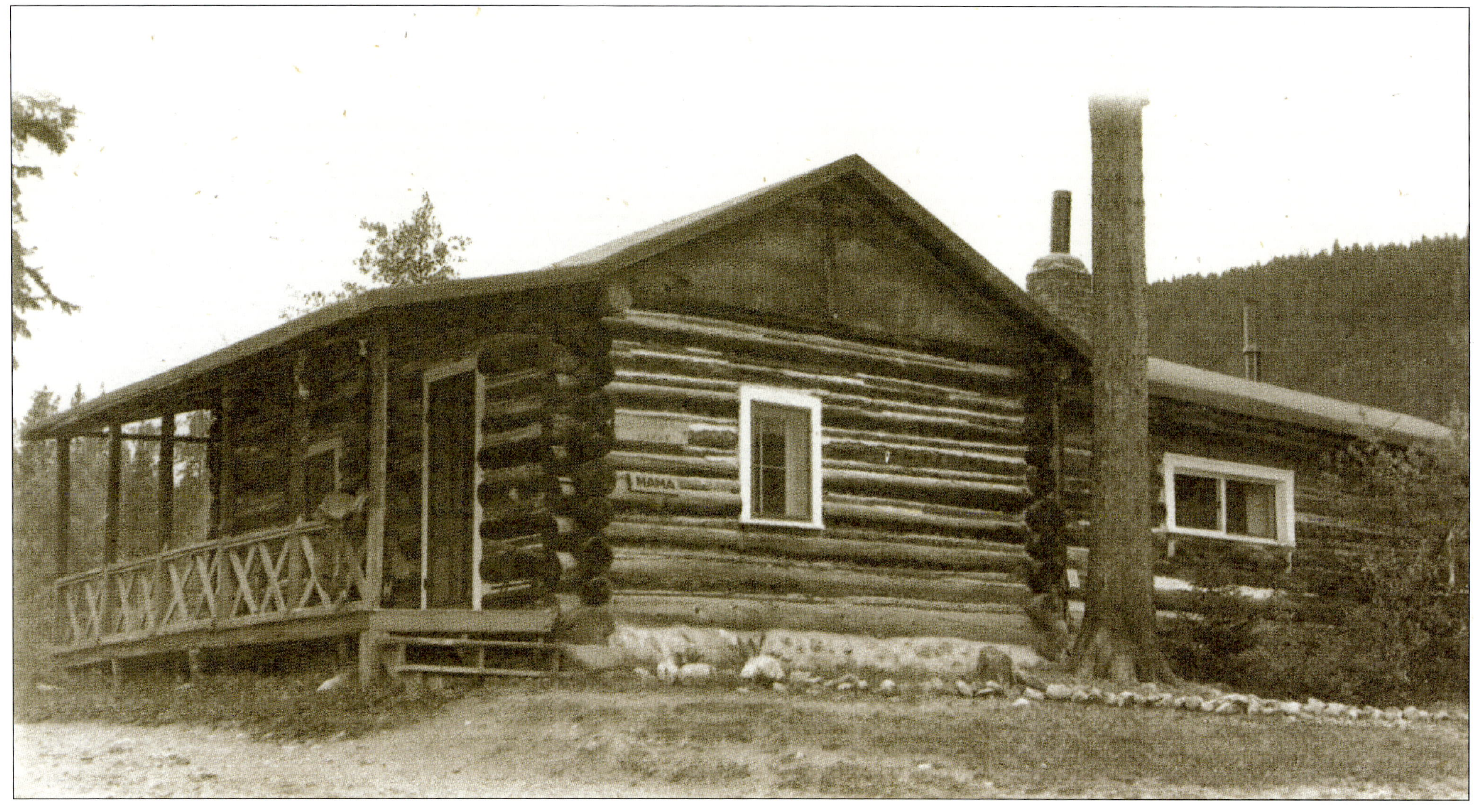

It was the summer of 1917 when John and Sophie Holzwarth gave up their lives in Denver—where until the coming of Prohibition in 1916, John (or Johnnie as he was universally known) had successfully operated a saloon and boarding house—to purchase a 160-acre homestead on the Colorado River north of Grand Lake. That summer saw the building of the one-room sod-covered "Mama Cabin" (shown here after subsequent expansions). A year later, in July 1918, they had purchased the adjacent Fleshuts ranch, increasing the size of their holdings that eventually would total more than 900 acres.

Though the Holzwarths originally intended to ranch the land, by 1920 they had discovered that with the proximity of the new national park there could be

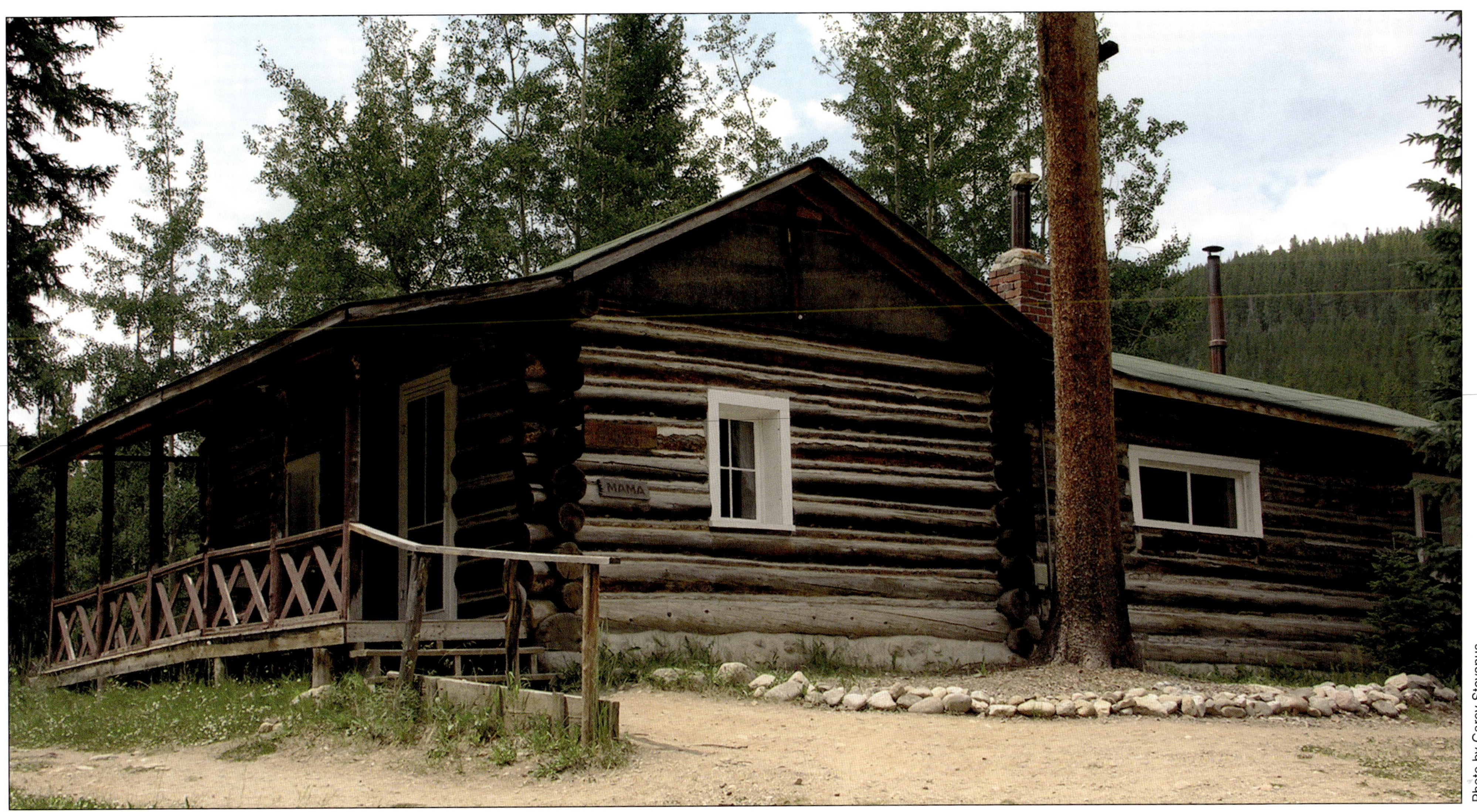

Photo by Carey Stevanus

more money to be made feeding, housing, and entertaining tourists than by raising cattle and growing hay. Additional cabins were constructed, the beginning of a building complex that would signal the birth of dude ranching in the Grand County area. Their new enterprise, the Holzwarth Trout Lodge, soon became a popular destination. The charge in the early days was $2 a day or $11 a week, which provided guests with three full meals a day, all the trout they could eat, and the use of a horse.

To better take advantage of nearby Fall River Road, in 1923 the Holzwarths shifted the bulk of the tourist operations to the east side of the Colorado River, first by making use of the Fleshuts homestead cabin and then by enlarging the

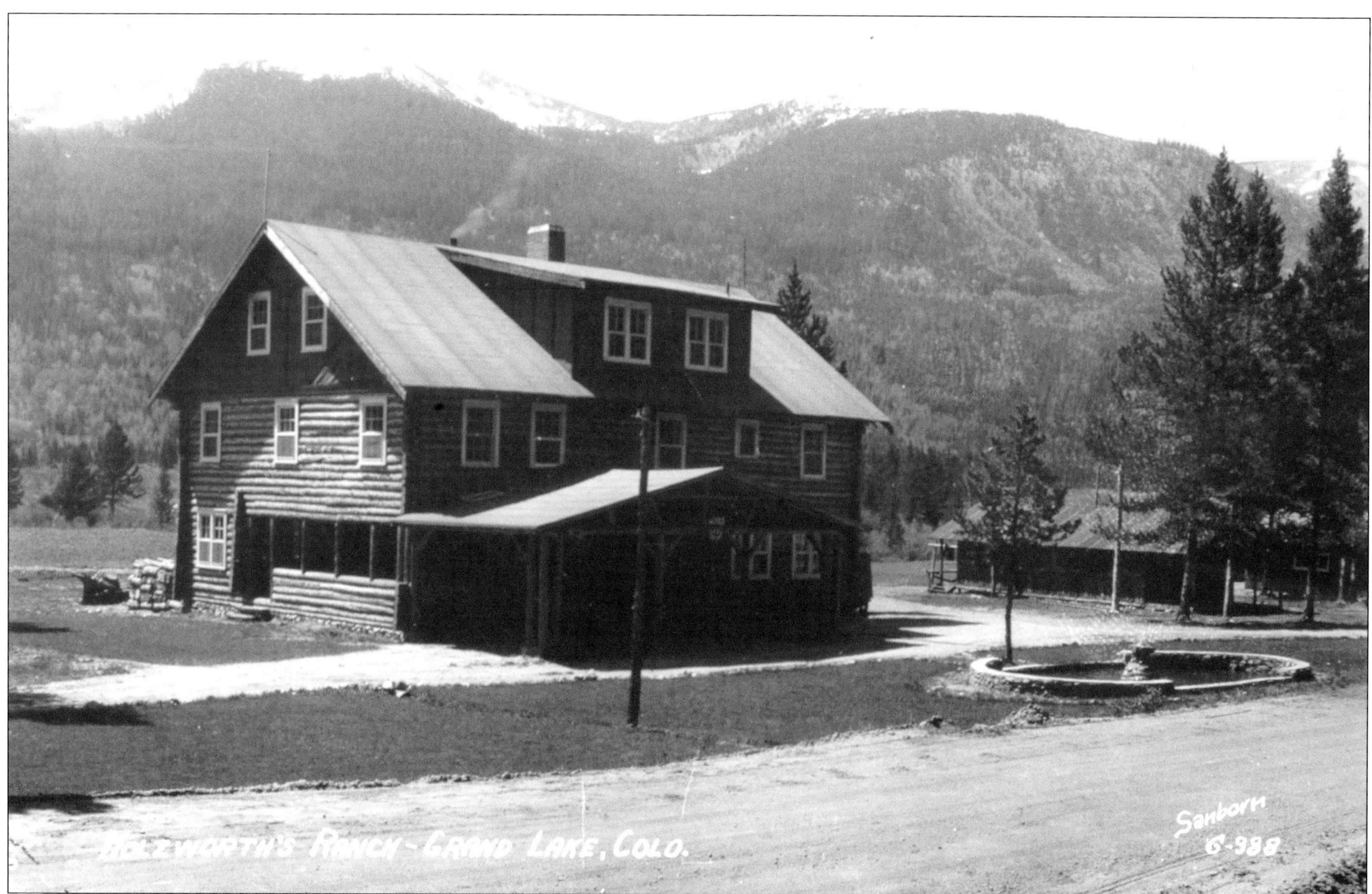

Photo by Sanborn Souvenir Company

site with the construction of new buildings. The first new cabin was built in 1924, and the main lodge was erected in 1929. The Holzwarths christened their new enterprise the Never Summer Ranch. The location of that grand lodge is rephotographed here.

In 1974, The Nature Conservancy purchased the section of the ranch west of the Colorado River containing the old Trout Lodge. The following year, on February 5, 1975, with the change of the park boundaries, the entire Holzwarth property was transferred over to the National Park Service. While all of the

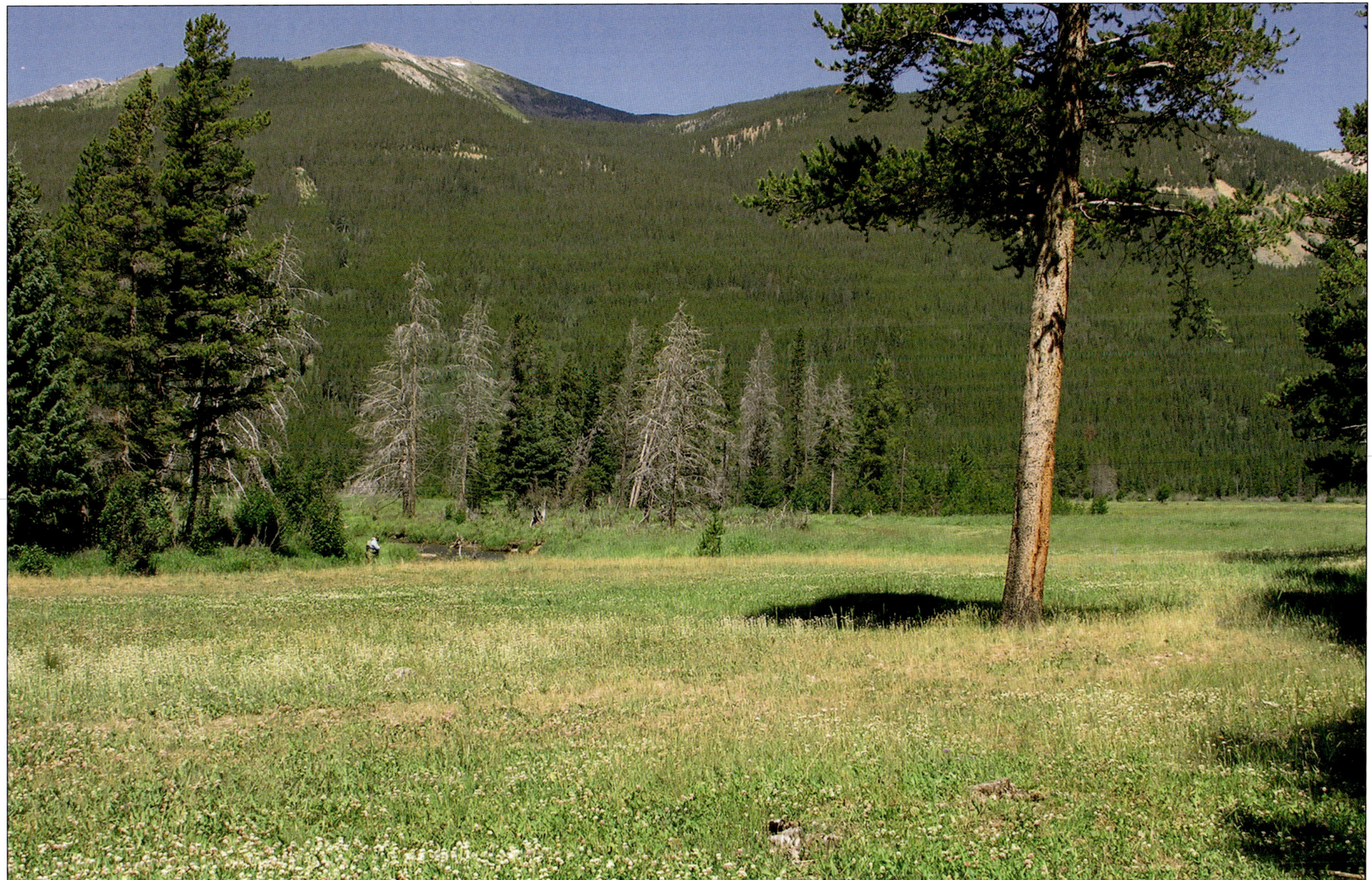

Photo by Carey Stevanus

Never Summer Ranch buildings except the Fleshuts cabin were soon razed, many of the historic structures of the old Trout Lodge—including the Mama Cabin, the icehouse, and John Holzwarth's taxidermy shop—still remain as the Holzwarth Trout Lodge Historic Site. During the summer the site is staffed by park volunteers and operated as an interpretive center, recalling the early ranching and tourist days in the Kawuneeche Valley.

93. Camp Wheeler (Squeaky Bob's), circa 1920

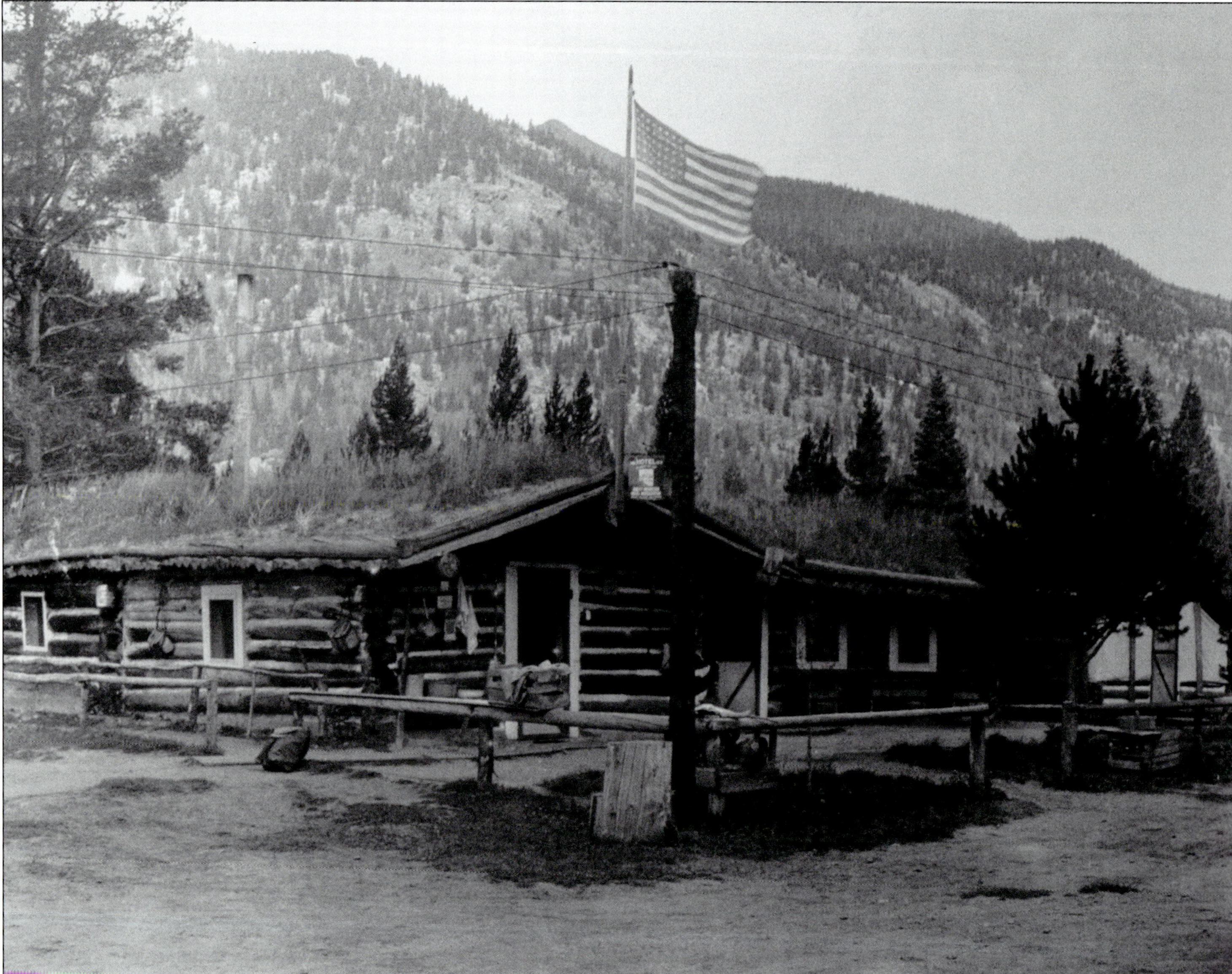

During the first ten years of Rocky Mountain National Park's existence, and for some years before, visitors to the north part of the Kawuneeche Valley and Grand Lake often made their destination the tent resort on the North Fork of the Colorado that was operated by Robert L. Wheeler, called "Squeaky Bob" for his falsetto voice. Camp Wheeler, also known as "Hotel de Hardscrabble" or simply "Squeaky Bob's," was where famous guide Shep Husted brought dudes he conducted on pack trips across the divide. President Theodore Roosevelt was also reported to be one of Bob Wheeler's guests.

In 1885, Wheeler came out to Colorado to visit his brother's cattle ranch in North Park, only to stay on for a decade as his partner. In 1900, following his service in the Spanish-American War and a brief mining interlude, Wheeler took up residence on a 160-acre homestead near the west end of Milner Pass. For a while he ran cattle, trapped, and did some prospecting. By 1908, he was in the resort business. Taking advantage of

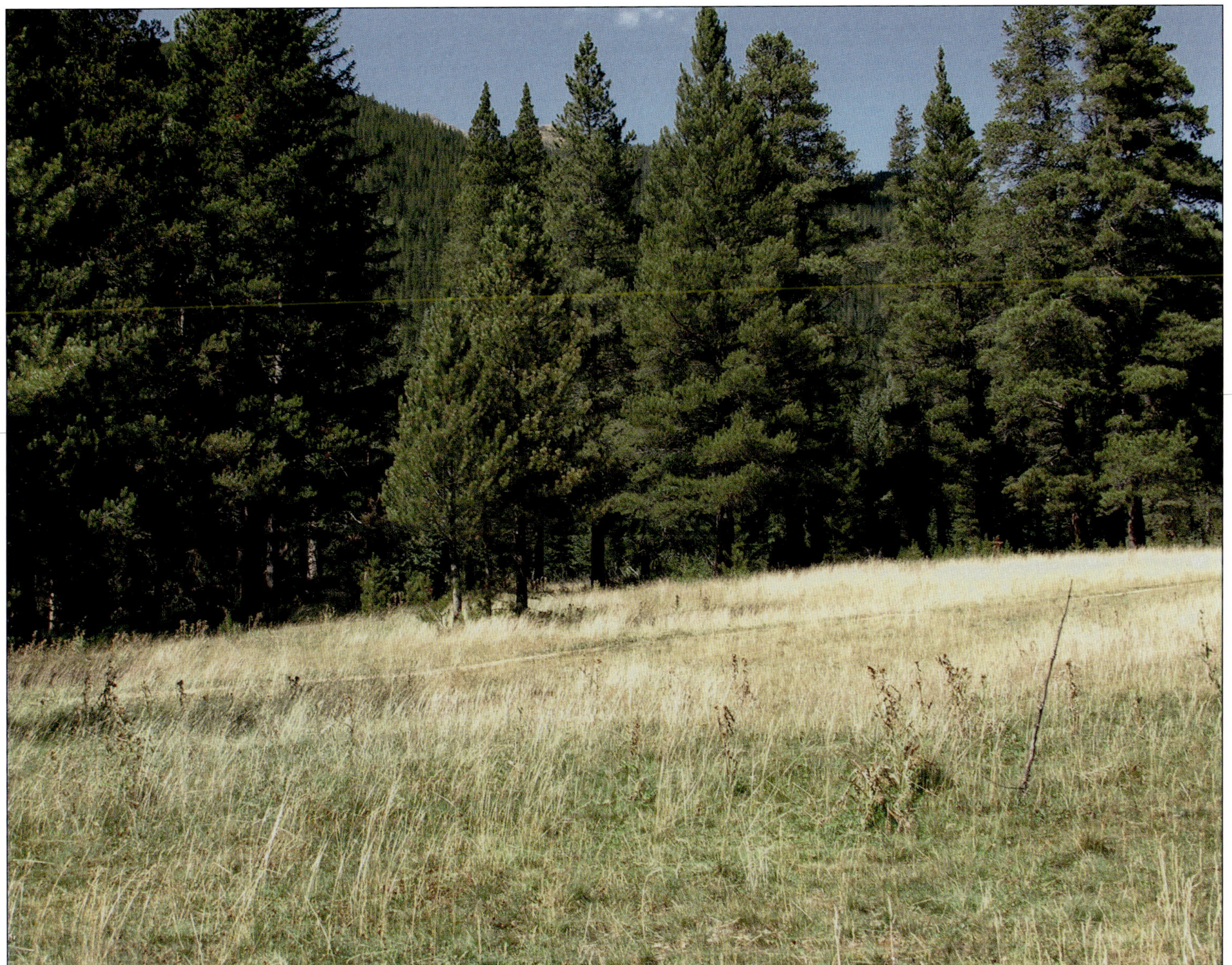

Photo by Carey Stevanus

a good location near the Estes Park–Grand Lake trail that went across Flattop Mountain, Wheeler erected four tent houses alongside his two-room log cabin, and he quickly found a ready clientele in both fishermen and hunters, as well as tourists in the summer. On each of his eventual 20 tent houses was a posted sign that read: "Blow your nose and clean your shoes. Use all the grub you need and leave things as you find them."

Due to problems with his heart, Wheeler sold his resort in 1926 for $24,000. The new owner renovated and enlarged the place and changed its name to Phantom Valley Ranch. The buildings were purchased by the National Park Service in the early 1960s and razed, returning the site to its original meadowland.

94. Lulu City, 1889

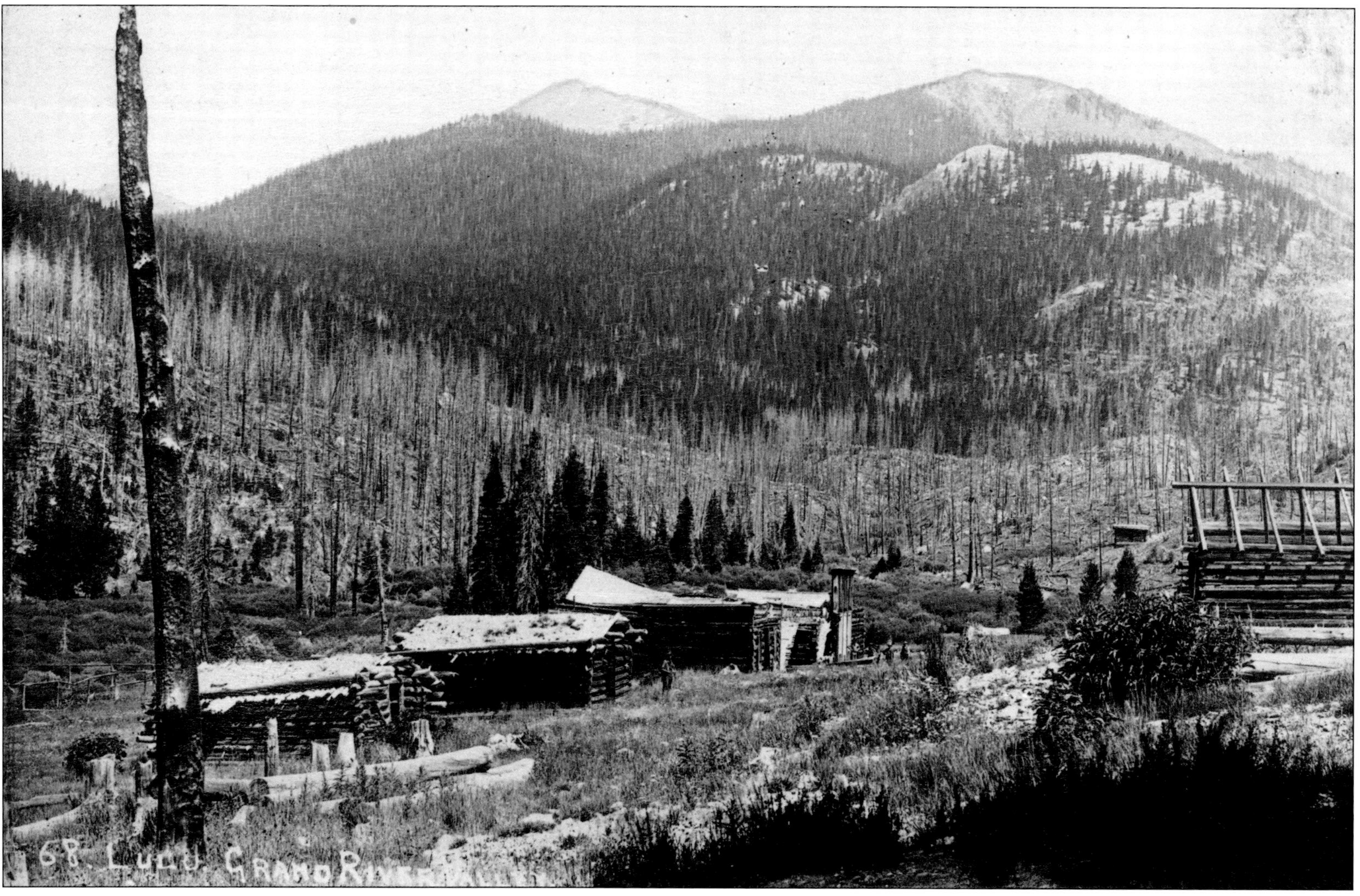

Not much is left of Lulu City. There was not much left in 1889 either, the date of one of the earliest surviving photographs of what had been only a decade earlier a vibrant, bustling mining camp located near the headwaters of the upper Colorado River. Lulu City was founded in 1879 after gold and silver were both discovered nearby. Hopes were fanned even more the following spring when it was wildly reported that surface outcroppings "surpassed anything known in mining history," and a mining boom followed.

Just who Lulu was is unclear. The most likely candidate is Lulu Burnett, the daughter of one of the town's founders. Others have suggested Lulu Stewart, the daughter of a mail carrier.

Tents and log cabins, followed by a general store and saloons, an assay office, land office, hotel, druggist, two lumber mills, several restaurants, and at least one brothel, marked the town's auspicious beginning. By 1881, the population had grown to about 500—in a county of some 2,000 people.

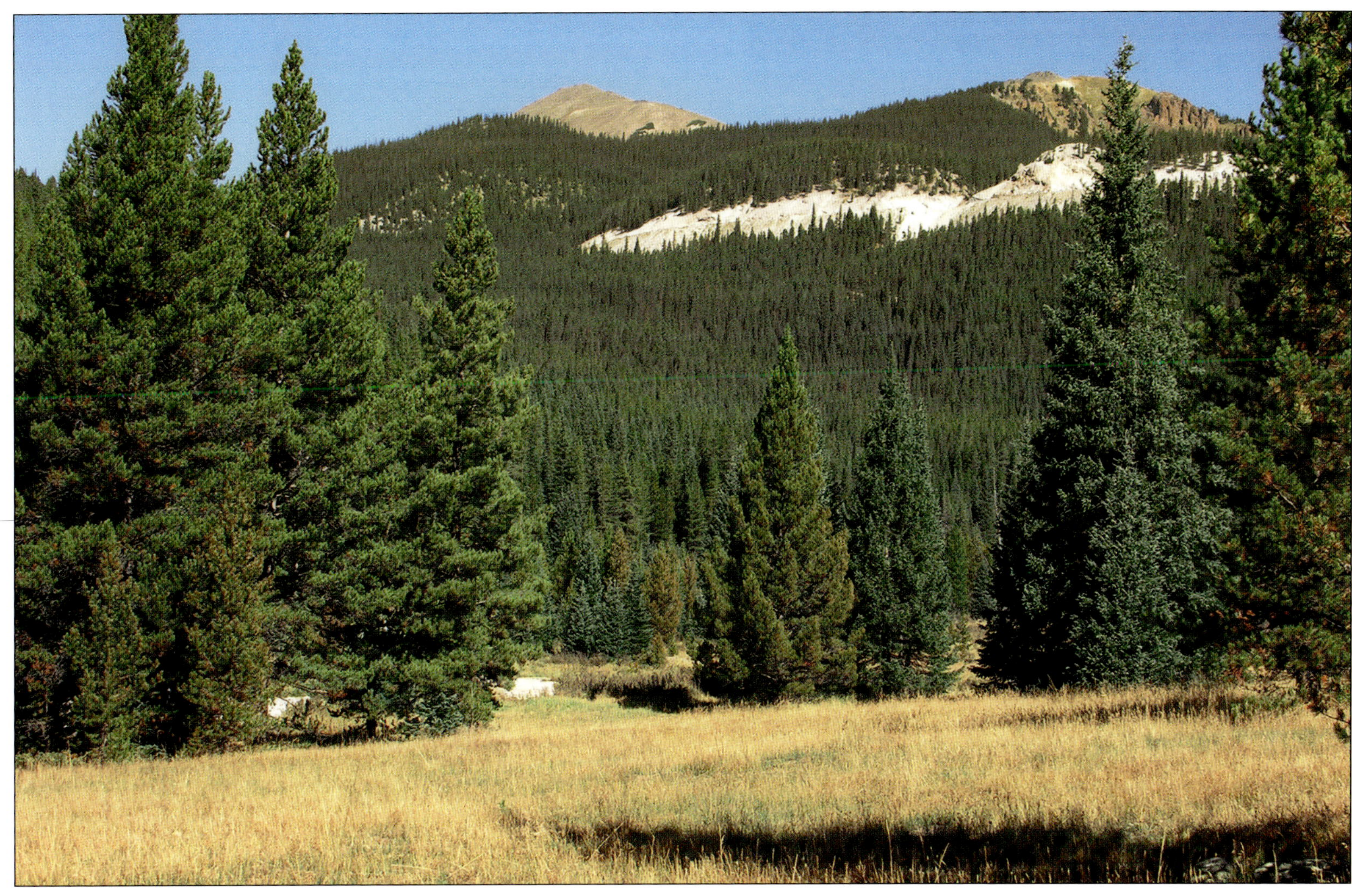

Photo by
Carey Stevanus

Though the nearby hills were scoured for paying ore, little gold and silver was found, and then only in pockets that proved to be of low grade. By 1884 or 1885, the boom was over, and Lulu City began its rapid decline (though some of the mines continued to operate sporadically into the 1890s). By 1886 the post office, established just six years before, had been discontinued; subsequent visitors reported finding dishes, clothing, and other belongings, suggesting that residents left quickly, taking as little as possible with them for their long trip back to "civilization."

Lulu City is now little more than a mountain meadow. The log buildings and other signs of settlement have long since disappeared, but the adjacent hillsides still bear mining scars, marking many of the places where miners once feverishly searched for gold and silver.

Longs Peak Region

95. Eugenia Mine, circa 1965

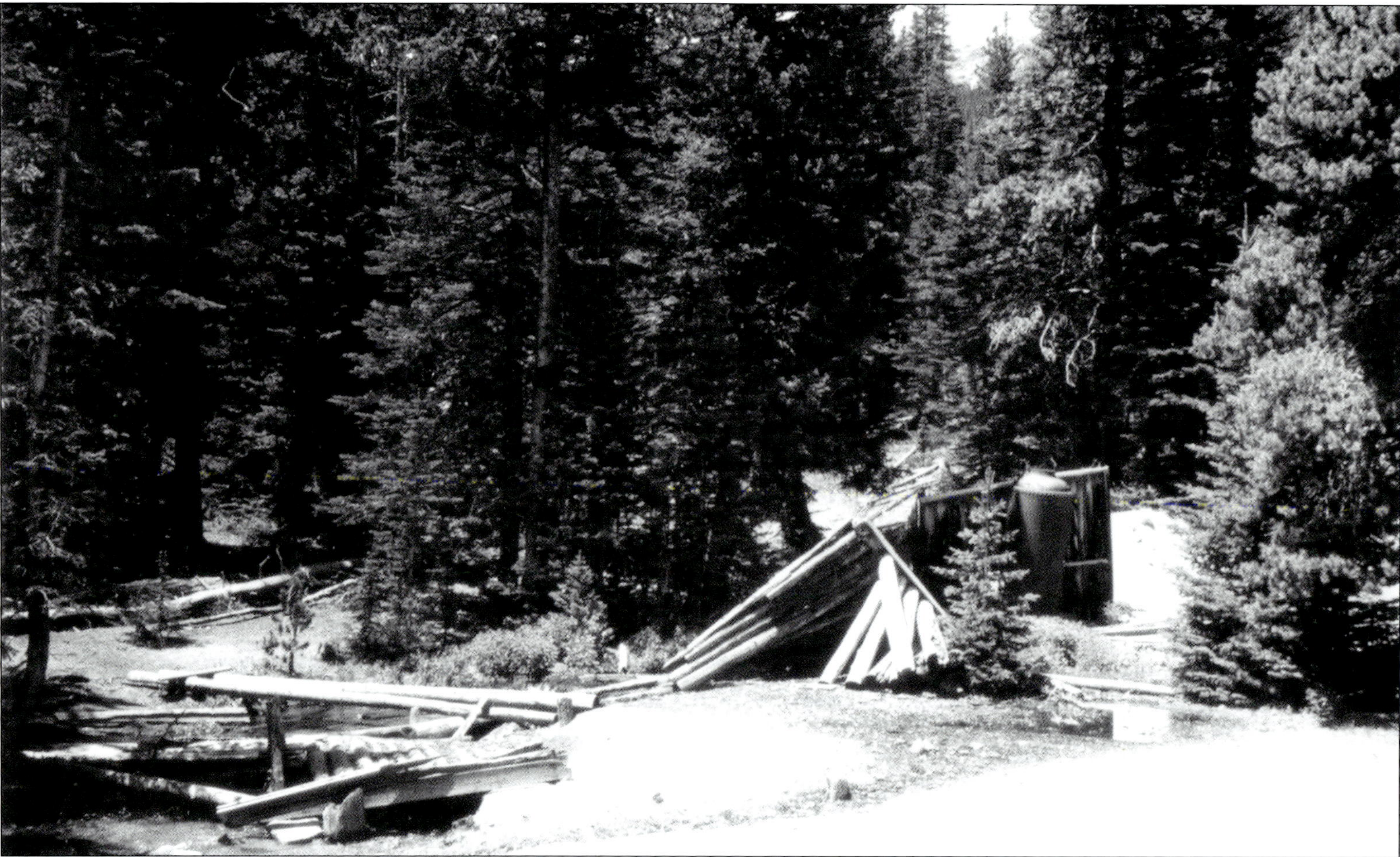

The gold and silver seekers who scoured Colorado's mountains and valleys for mineral wealth in the years following the 1858 discovery of gold in Little Dry Creek did not overlook the Estes Park region. Though the state's great mineral belt did not extend much above the gulches of Ward in Boulder County to the south, evidence of mining activity is apparent here, most often seen in the form of abandoned prospect holes.

Many of these efforts took place on the lower slopes of Longs Peak. The most successful was Battle Mountain's Eugenia Mine, near the Longs Peak Trail and the trail that today ascends up to Storm Pass. Also known as the Cudahy-Norwall Mine (after its owners) or the Amethyst Mine (after the area's quartz gemstones), the Eugenia Mine opened on September 23, 1905. "An enormous body of ore has been uncovered," the *Longmont Ledger* told its readers. "It runs

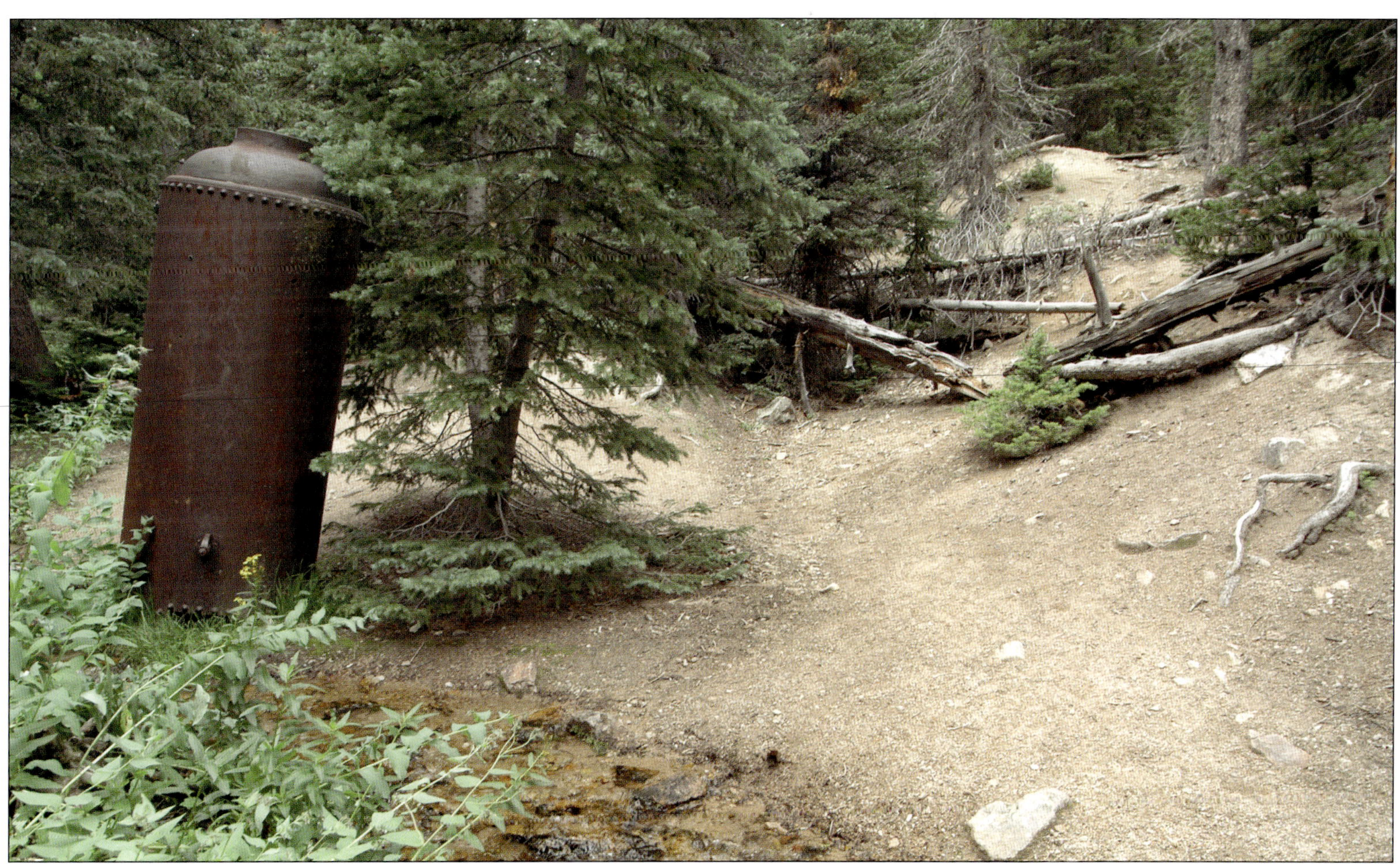

14 percent copper and from $6 to $18 in gold." Cabins were built near the mine shaft, a wagon road was cut through the woods to access the site, and for the next six or seven years the mine was worked seasonally by Carl P. Norwall and Dan Slaughter of Allenspark. By June 1910, the shaft that had been drilled into Battle Mountain had reached a reported depth of 1,500 feet, supposedly with "lots of ore in sight."

After about 1912, work was suspended and the site gradually fell into ruin. When the Park Service assumed responsibility, the entrance was collapsed for safety. The site, with its discarded boiler, talus pile, and cabin ruins, remains a popular hiking destination—a trip back to an era when men scoured the slopes of Longs Peak hoping to make their fortune.

96. Timberline Cabin, circa 1908

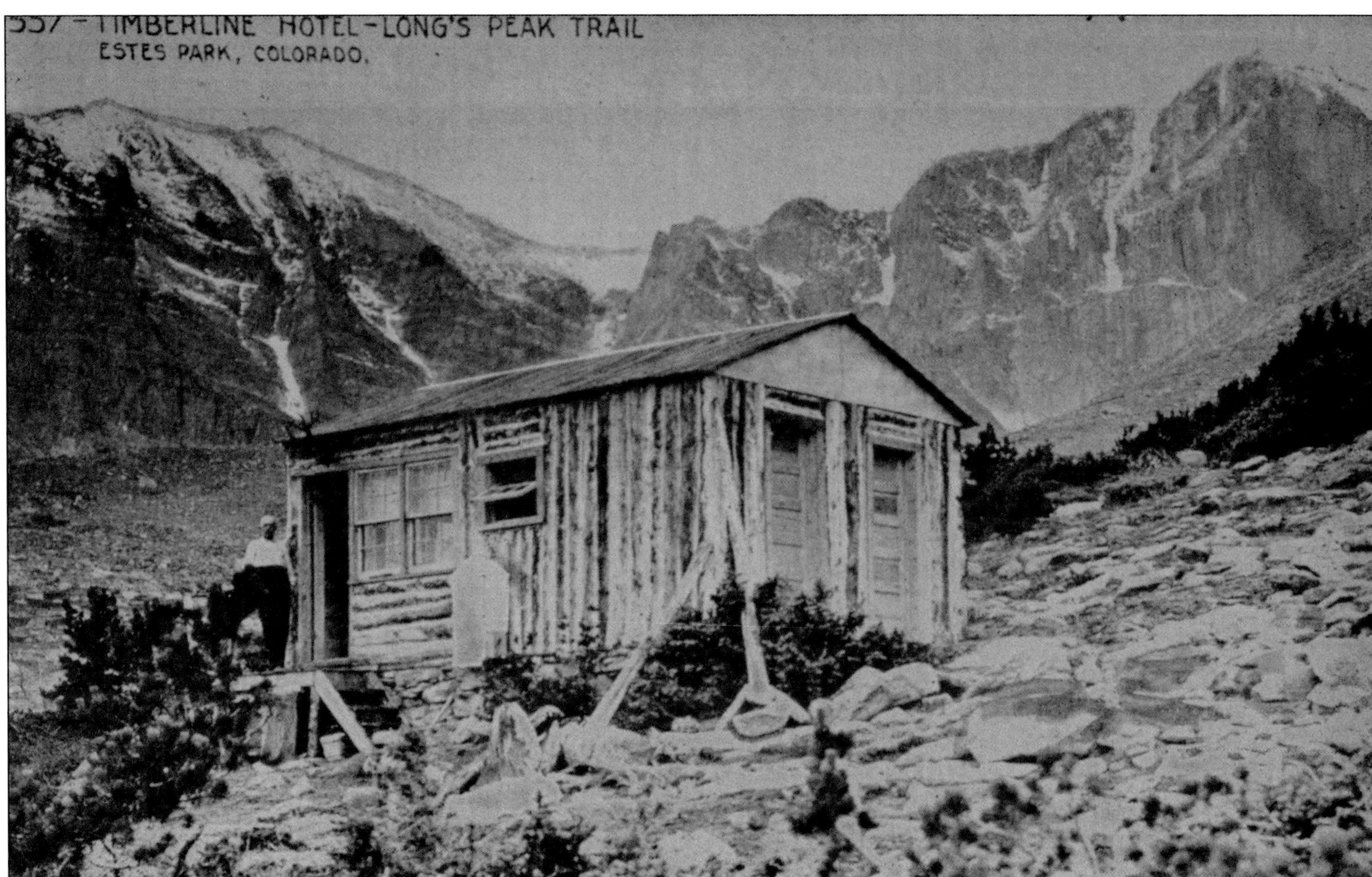

Photo by
William T. Parke

As Longs Peak climbers discovered, the 16-mile round-trip from the Tahosa Valley could be shortened considerably by camping overnight on or near the Boulder Field. A favorite spot was Jim's Grove, the stand of small spruce trees 4 miles up the trail named for "Rocky Mountain Jim"—James Nugent, who camped there with author Isabella Bird before their 1873 summit climb. Jim built a bonfire, around which he regaled Miss Bird with poetry of his own composition and "fearful Indian stories" before sending her to bed in a "bower of pines" with his saddle for a pillow.

In 1908, in an effort to offer better accommodations, intrepid mountaineer Enos A. Mills built Timberline Cabin, offering food and shelter to those bound for the peak. The wooden building, below Jim's Grove at some 11,400 feet, was about 12 by 24 feet in size. The east half contained kitchen, dining room, living

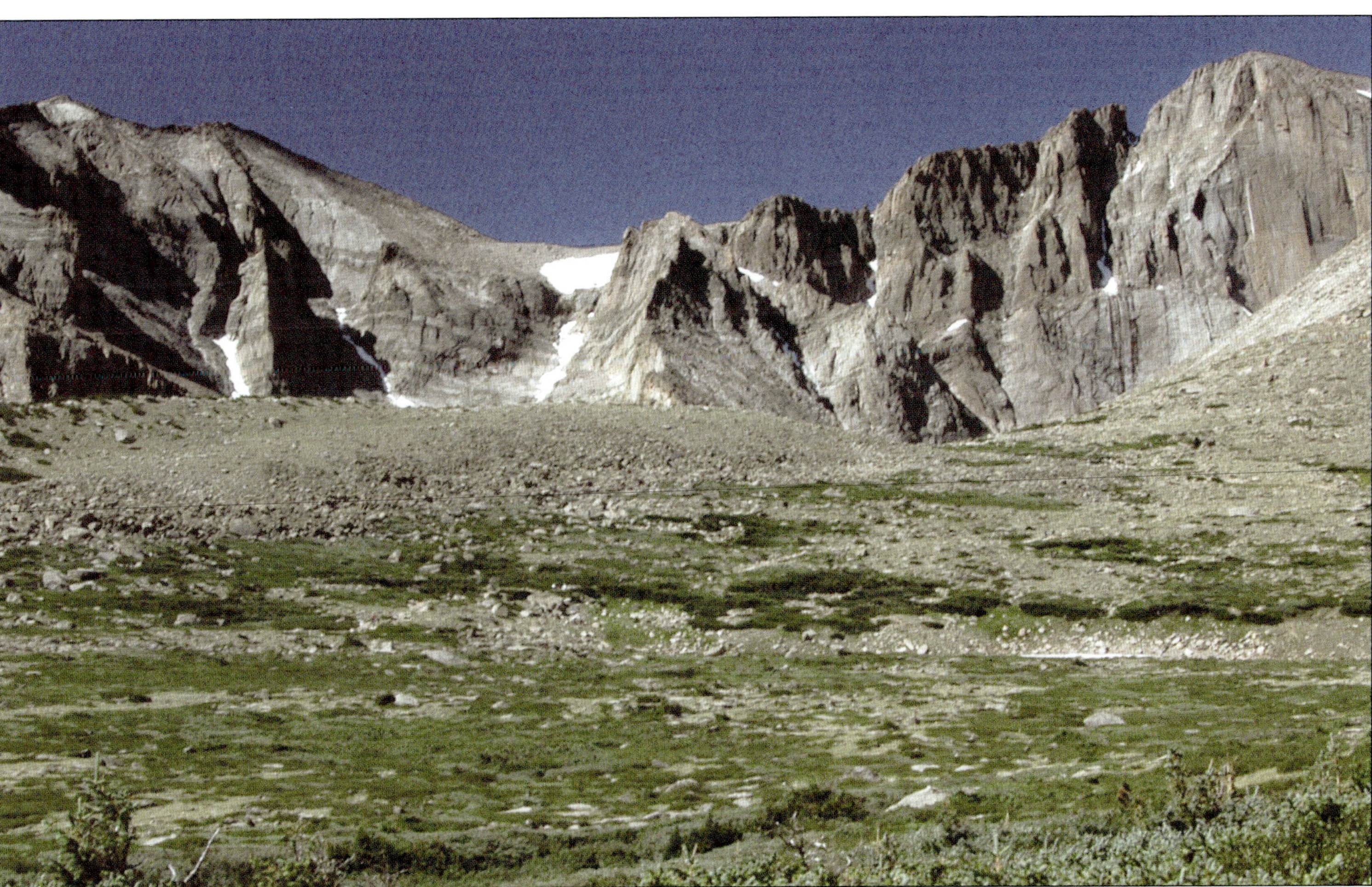

room, store room, and office; the north half held two bunkrooms, each with a series of 24-inch-wide wooden bunks built one above the other in three tiers. Mills rented them for $1 a night. In summer a resident cook provided meals for 75 cents.

Timberline Cabin had many visitors, even after it was closed and turned over to the National Park Service in 1924 by Enos Mills' widow. It was here in January 1925 that Agnes Vaille and guide Walter Kiener spent the night before departing on their ill-fated attempt to make the first wintertime ascent of the East Face. And it was here that the rescue party, which included park superintendent Roger Toll, Agnes' cousin, huddled before setting out to recover her body and find missing rescuer Herbert Sortland. By then the cabin had fallen into disrepair. It was subsequently removed and its site obliterated.

97. Agnes Vaille Shelter, October 1938

The Agnes Vaille Shelter, sitting just below The Keyhole at an elevation of 13,200 feet, stands as a stark and cold reminder of Longs Peak's greatest tragedy, the death on January 12, 1925, of Denverite Agnes Vaille, following the first successful wintertime ascent of the 1,630-foot East Face. Agnes' father, Frederick O. Vaille, founder and president of Denver's first telephone company, commissioned the shelter. The cylindrical structure was designed by Denver architects who, it is said, copied the design—with its conical beehive roof, narrow door, and two deeply recessed windows—from the Trullo rural architecture of southern Italy's Apulia region.

Construction began in August 1926 under the direction of Denver contractor Lars Laursen, who also built the Boulder Field Shelter Cabin that once stood below. The work was hard: Sand to mix the concrete had to be packed up in heavy 60-pound sacks by horse or by burro from the Longs Peak Campground below and then hand-carried across the giant granite slabs of the Boulder Field.

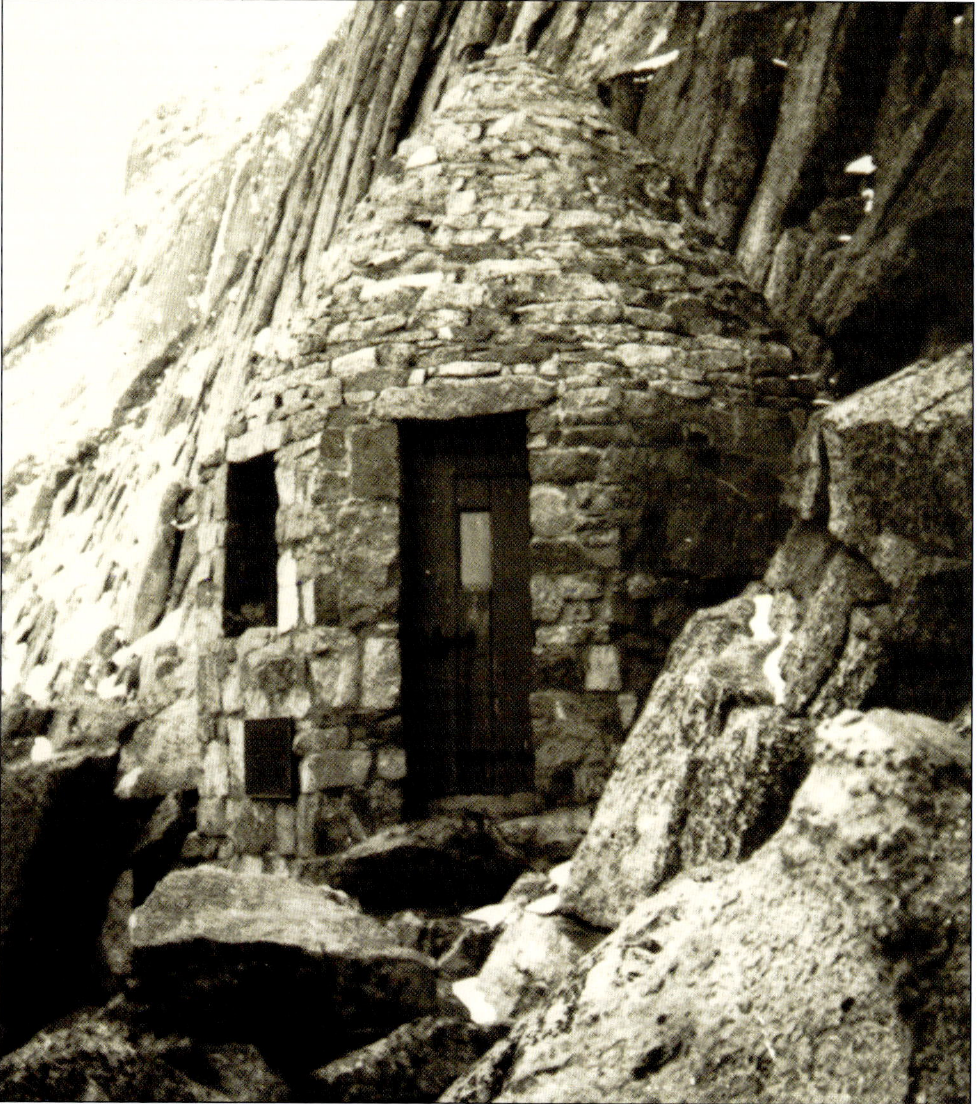

Photo by E. K. Field

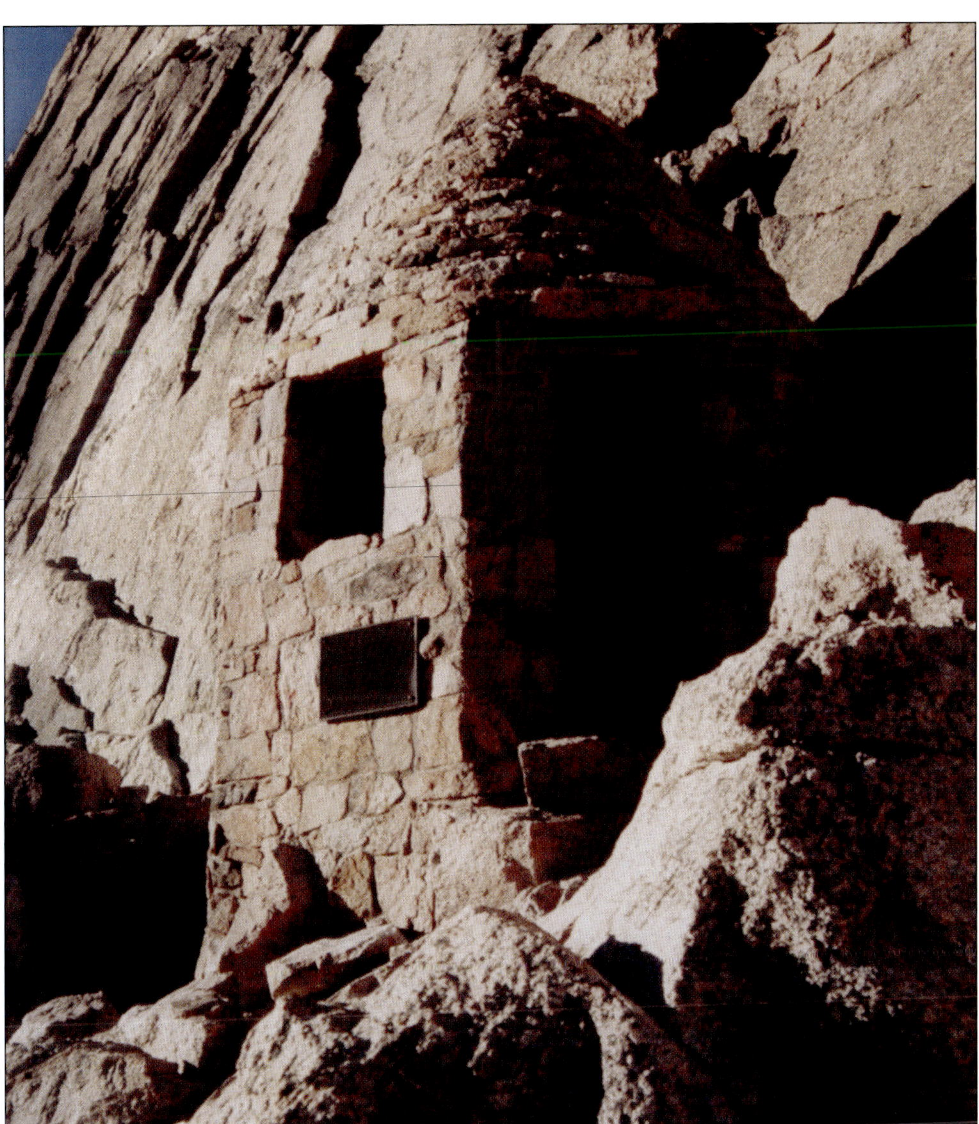

Since its completion in 1927, several generations of hikers coming and going through The Keyhole have sought refuge in the tiny hut to escape the wind, rain, hail, and snow. However, it is not, even in midsummer, a particularly cheery place, for as guide Harold Dunning noted many years ago, it was built on the wrong side of the mountain. Had the building been located on The Keyhole's west side, Dunning observed, it would have been out in the sunshine and far more hospitable and useful. In its present location, the hut serves more as monument than shelter, a memorial to the very human tragedy that took place on the Boulder Field below. It serves as a cautionary reminder to the unwary of the vagaries of nature in high places, which might well be its greatest service.

98. The Keyhole, circa 1910

The jagged cleft in the horizontal rocks above the Boulder Field on Longs Peak is known as The Keyhole. And it is here, as every veteran climber of the peak knows, that the hike ends and now the real climb begins, with serious exposure, elevation gain, and thin air to battle before the summit is reached. Once the climbers go through The Keyhole, they reach the top of a steep slope leading from near the summit far down to a precipice on its west side.

For many hikers unwilling or unable to go on, their day on the mountain ends here, having been content to look down from The Keyhole on the lakes of Glacier Gorge glimmering in their dark wooded setting far below. It is for this reason, among many, that The Keyhole has always been one of the most photographed places on Longs Peak, from the time of Frederick H. Chapin's visit of 1886 until the present. In fact, almost every well-known early Estes Park photographer—including F. E. Baker, Enos A. Mills, William T. Parke, and Fred Payne Clatworthy—has left several views of this impressive spot. A number of their photographs quickly became postcard views that found their way across the world, helping, in turn, to further publicize the region's grandest peak.

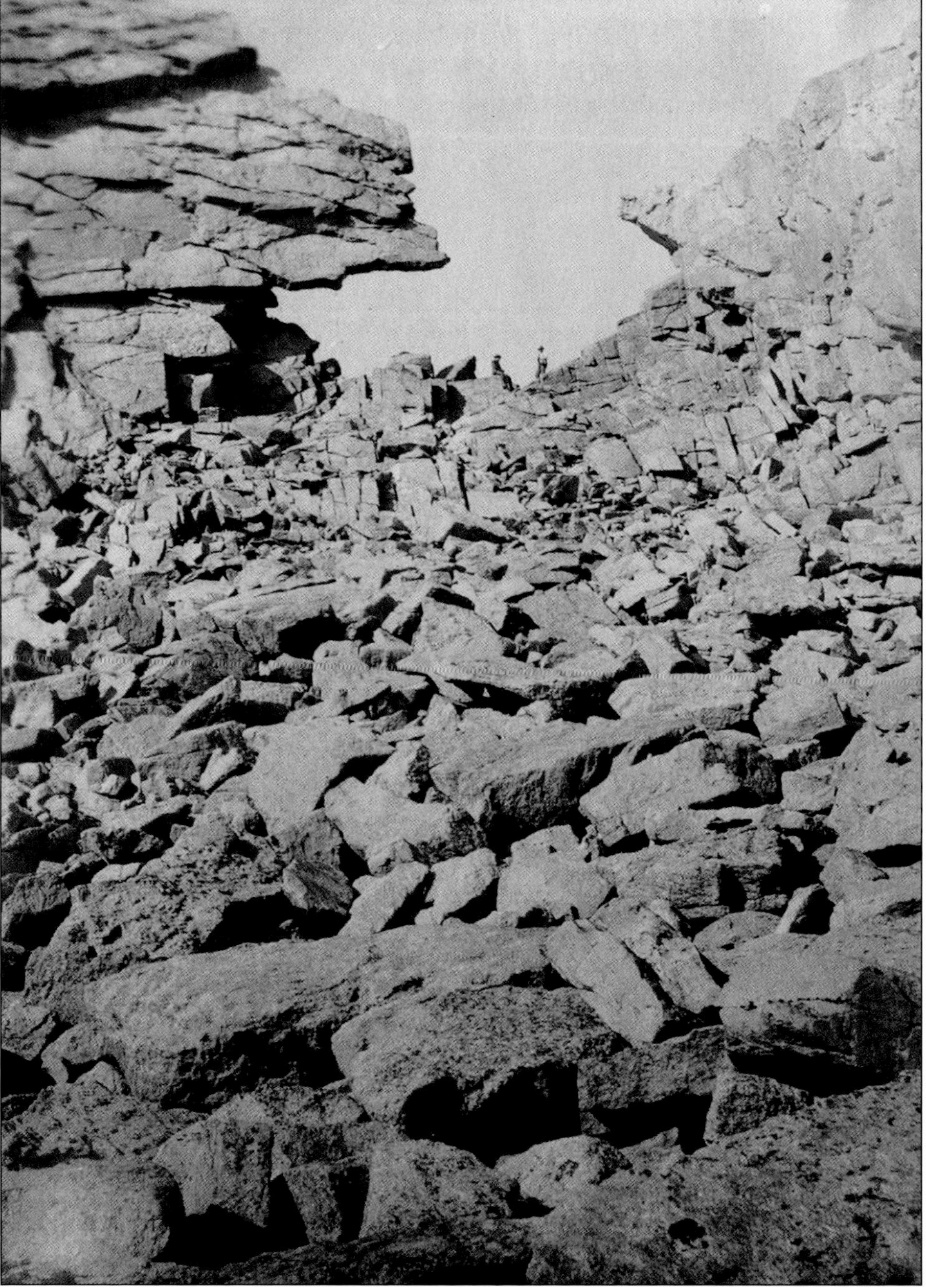

Photo by Fred Payne Clatworthy

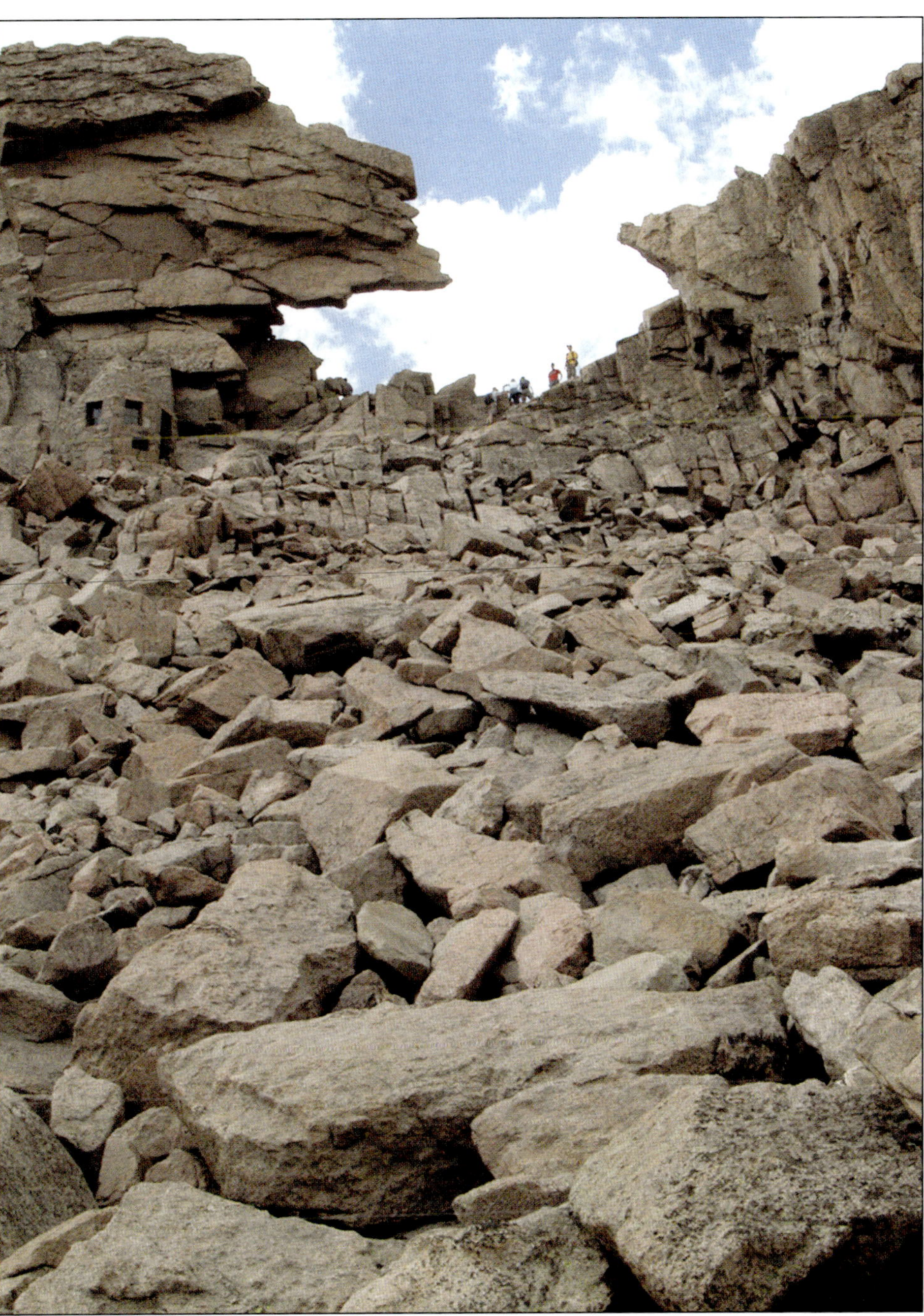

Site Locations and GPS Coordinates

Preface

See Site 52.

Estes Valley Scenes and Sites

1. **Estes Park from Park Hill:** N40°21'29", W105°27'26". Park Hill, at the head of the treeless draw known as Muggins Gulch, is between mile markers 3 and 4 at CR 122, where US 36 begins to descend toward Lake Estes.
2. **"Rocky Mountain Jim" Cabin Site:** Cabin site and spring are on private property 0.1 mile west of mile marker 6 on US 36.
3. **Estes Park from Mount Olympus:** Photograph taken from "Castle Rock" on the privately owned Crocker ranch.
4. **Estes-Evans-Dunraven Ranch:** 5) N40°22'5", W105°29'29"; 6) N40°22'12", W105°29'29"; 7) N40°22'12", W105°29'27"; 8) N40°22'11", W105°29'26". On lower Fish Creek Rd. 0.2 mile south of its junction with US 36; it is now submerged beneath the small arm of Lake Estes.
5. **Charles Partridge Adams House:** N40°21'57", W105°29'30". House was on what's now Sketch Box Ln., 0.4 mile south of the intersection of US 36 and Fish Creek Rd.
6. **Dunraven Cottage and Estes Park Hotel:** On Fish Creek Rd. 0.6 mile south of its junction with US 36.
7. **Estes Park Hotel:** Site is on private property on Fish Creek Rd., 0.9 mile from its junction with US 36 at Lake Estes.
8. **Estes Park Country Club:** N40°21'43", W105°29'52". On Golf Course Rd., off CO 7, 1 mile south of its junction with US 36.
9. **Front Range from Prospect Mountain:** N40°21'36", 105°31'15". Photographs taken from the south side of Prospect Mountain (the mountain on which the tramway operates) in the center of Estes Park. The original spot where Jackson took his photograph could not be located. The "now" shot was chosen to reflect the scenery that Jackson chose for his.
10. **Longs Peak from Dollar Lake:** Dollar Lake is most easily viewed from St. Francis of Assisi Parish, 3480 St. Francis Way. (St. Francis Way is a 0.1-mile spur to the right off Little Valley Rd. 0.8 mile from its junction with Fish Creek Rd.)
11. **Cheley Colorado Camps:** N40°19'1", W105°31'2". Entrance at the upper end of Fish Creek Rd. off CO 7.
12. **Marys Lake:** N40°20'36", W105°32'2". Off CO 7, some 3.5 miles from its intersection with US 36.
13. **Beaver Point:** N40°21'37", W105°32'34". On US 36, approximately 1.5 miles from the intersection of Elkhorn and Moraine Aves.
14. **Rocky Mountain National Park 1923 Headquarters:** N40°22'22", W105°31'27". On Moraine Ave. at the corner where US 36 curves west to follow the Big Thompson River to Rocky Mountain National Park's Beaver Meadows entrance.
15. **The Lone Pine:** N40°22'5", W105°34'39". Site is 2.2 miles west on High Dr. from Beaver Point, 0.1 mile beyond the blocked-off end of High Dr.
16. **The Y–Big Thompson Entrance to Rocky Mountain National Park:** N40°21'0", W105°34'5". 1.8 miles southwest on CO 66 from its junction with US 36, just before the bridge over the Big Thompson.
17. **Holland Inn:** N40°20'58", W105°34'7". 1.8 miles southwest on CO 66 from its junction with US 36, just before the bridge over the Big Thompson.
18. **YMCA of the Rockies:** N40°20'27", W105°34'21". 1.9 miles southwest on CO 66 from its junction with US 36.
19. **Mountainside Lodge:** N40°18'41", W105°36'16". Most easily reached by taking Mountainside Dr., the road on YMCA property that climbs Emerald Mountain.
20. **Wigwam Tea Room:** Wind River Trail begins 0.3 mile past the YMCA entrance, to the left.
21. **F. O. Stanley House:** Privately owned, Stanley's house is west of the Stanley Hotel at 415 W. Wonderview Ave.
22. **Estes Park Fish Hatchery:** N40°23'59", W105°34'52". Located on Fish Hatchery Rd. (a spur off Fall River Rd., 2 miles west of the junction of US 34 Bypass and US 34 Business) just past the bridge over Fall River, east of the Stanley Power Plant.
23. **Stanley Power Plant:** N40°24'37", W105°38'17". Located at the end of Fish Hatchery Rd., just west of the hatchery site.
24. **McCreery Cabin:** On private property off Devils Gulch Rd., 2.2 miles from its junction with US 34.
25. **North St. Vrain Road (Highway 36):** N40°14'25", W105°19'45". The site of the original photograph is just below mile marker 15 on US 36.
26. **South St. Vrain Road (Highway 7):** N40°19'7", W105°32'4". The rock cut is by the Lily Lake Trailhead, south of mile marker 5, below Lily Lake Visitor Center.
27. **Big Thompson Road (Highway 34):** 1) N40°25'39", W105°20'47"; 2) N40°25'16", W105°16'25"; 3) N40°25'13", W105°13'24". 1) Sheep Head Rock is at mile marker 75; 2) turn northeast off US 34 at the Dam Store onto CR 22H and drive 0.9 mile to the bridge; 3) the Dam Store is at mile marker 83 at the entrance to Big Thompson Canyon.

The Village

28. **Panoramic View:** Photo taken on private property to the right of the Christmas star on a steep, rocky hill at the junction of Elkhorn Ave. and Riverside Dr.
29. **Al Birch House:** N40°22'43", W105°31'12". The ruins are on the cliffs behind the Estes Park Municipal Building and Public Library. The ruins are visible from Elkhorn Ave. or from MacGregor Ave. at the eastern edge of Bond Park, where a plaque commemorates them. Access to this area is from the parking lot off Wonderview Ave.

30. **Estes Park from the Birch Ruins:** N40°22'36", W105°31'10". The Al Birch House ruins are above Elkhorn Ave. behind the municipal building (see Site 29).

31. **Sam Service Store:** N40°22'35", W105°31'17". 167 E. Elkhorn Ave. at the corner of Virginia Dr.

32. **Original 1915 Rocky Mountain National Park Headquarters:** N40°22'31", W105°30'19". Estes Park Museum, US 36 at 4th St.

33. **John Edward Macdonald Home and Store:** N40°22'34", W105°31'22". Macdonald Book Shop, 152 E. Elkhorn Ave.

34. **Josephine Hotel:** N40°22'35", W105°31'22". 134 E. Elkhorn Ave.

35. **Riverside Amusement Park:** N40°22'33", W105°31'17". Site was located at the municipal parking lot where Fall River joins the Big Thompson.

36. **National Park Hotel:** N40°22'35", W105°31'22". 145 E. Elkhorn Ave.

37. **William T. Parke Store:** N40°22'35", W105°31'22". 135 E. Elkhorn Ave.

38. **Rocky Mountain Parks Transportation Company:** N40°22'34", W105°31'23". The entrance to the Park Theatre Mall, named for the adjacent Park Theatre, is at 116 E. Elkhorn Ave. The other buildings that once made up the RMPTC complex are at 120, 112, and 110 E. Elkhorn Ave.

39. **Hupp Hotel:** N40°22'28", W105°31'22". 100 W. Elkhorn Ave. at the corner of Elkhorn and Moraine Avenues.

40. **Manford Hotel:** N40°22'33", W105°31'25". At the corner of E. Elkhorn Ave. and Big Horn Dr., from 101 to 129 E. Elkhorn Ave.

41. **Estes Park Bank:** N40°22'27", W105°31'23". Now Western 1-Hour Photo & Imaging, 101 W. Elkhorn Ave.

42. **Ye Lyttel Shop:** N40°22'34", W105°31'27". 115 W. Elkhorn Ave.

43. **Estes Park Church:** N40°22'34", W105°31'30". 157 W. Elkhorn Ave.

44. **Estes Park from the West End:** Photograph from a rock formation on private property on the north part of what is known as Davis Hill. The site overlooks the gentle curve at the west end of Estes Park.

45. **Lewiston Hotel:** The site, on private property, overlooks the Performance Park area at the upper end of Elkhorn Ave.

46. **Estes Park from Oldman Mountain:** N40°22'43", W105°32'35". Oldman Mountain, clearly seen west of town, is west of the Elkhorn Lodge off US 34.

47. **Oldman Mountain Ski Site:** N40°22'54", W105°32'34". The ski site is clearly visible as one drives west on US 34, just beyond the junction of US 34 Bypass and US 34 Business.

48. **Crags Hotel:** 1) N40°22'6", W105°31'25"; 2) N40°22'15", W105°31'17". 300 Riverside Dr., on the lower slope of Prospect Mountain.

49. **Boyd House:** On what is now Riverside Plaza near the corner of Elkhorn Ave. and East Riverside Dr. (house now relocated to 861 Big Horn Dr., just off of MacGregor Ave.).

Hotels, Lodges, and Ranches

50. **Stanley Hotel:** N40°22'53", W105°31'3". Visible from many places in Estes Park, the Stanley Hotel is easily reached by taking Wonderview Ave. at the junction of US 34 and US 36 and exiting up the hill at Steamer Pkwy.

51. **Elkhorn Lodge:** N40°22'39", W105°32'0". 600 W. Elkhorn Ave., 0.5 mile from the center of downtown (Elkhorn and Moraine).

52. **MacGregor Ranch:** The public is welcome to visit the ranch and its museum during regular business hours. MacGregor ranch is on private property located at 180 MacGregor Ln.. The ranch is reached from downtown Estes Park by driving north on MacGregor Ave. (Devils Gulch Rd.) 0.7 mile to the entrance on the curve.

53. **McGraw Ranch:** 1) N40°25'51", W105°30'6"; 2) N40°25'37", W105°30'1". At the end of McGraw Ranch Rd. off Devils Gulch Rd., 5.5 miles northeast of Estes Park.

54. **Rustic Hotel:** On private property on CR 61, about 0.8 mile from its junction with Dry Gulch Rd.

55. **Olympus Lodge:** N40°22'30", W105°29'13". Near the intersection of US 34 and Mall Rd.

56. **Crocker Ranch:** On private property off US 36 between mile markers 2 and 3.

57. **Estes Park Chalets:** N40°20'16", W105°31'50". Estes Park Chalets (Marys Lake Lodge) is just off the intersection of Marys Lake Rd. and CO 7.

58. **Ferguson's Highlands Hotel:** On private property at the junction of Marys Lake Rd. and Sutton Ln.

59. **Baldpate Inn:** N40°18'30", W105°32'4". Off CO 7 just east of Lily Lake and the Lily Lake Visitor Center, 7 miles south of Estes Park.

60. **Wind River Ranch:** 7 miles south of Estes Park between mile markers 7 and 8 on CO 7. Though open for summer visitors, the ranch is considered private property.

61. **Columbine Lodge:** High Peak Camp (Columbine Lodge) is on private property off CO 7, 8 miles south of Estes Park and 2 miles south of Lily Lake.

62. **Hewes-Kirkwood Inn:** 9 miles south of Estes Park off CO 7 and the road leading to the Longs Peak Campground and Trailhead. Now Rocky Ridge Music Center and private property.

63. **Lambs Ranch and Longs Peak Inn:** Longs Peak Inn site is on private property on CO 7, 9 miles from Estes Park.

Rocky Mountain National Park: East of Continental Divide

64. Rocky Mountain National Park Dedication Site in Horseshoe Park: 1–3) N40°24'20", W105°37'34". Site is adjacent to the Lawn Lake Trailhead, 2.2 miles west of the Fall River entrance.

65. Fall River Lodge: 0.3 mile west of Lawn Lake Trailhead (a parking area on the left side of the road helps identify the site).

66. Convict Cabins: N40°24'37", W105°38'28". The cabins were on both sides of Fall River Rd. approximately 1 mile west of the Lawn Lake Trailhead.

67. March Homestead Cabin: N40°24'42", W105°38'43". Site is 0.1 mile beyond that of the Convict Cabins, 1.1 mile west of the Lawn Lake Trailhead.

68. Cascade Lodge: N40°24'6", W105°36'15". The Cascade Cottages, and the site once occupied by Cascade Lodge, are next to US 34 as it enters Horseshoe Park, 0.8 mile from the Fall River entrance.

69. Richmond Homestead and Horseshoe Inn: N40°23'58", W105°37'38". Site is in an open area immediately west of the small parking area south of the Lawn Lake Trailhead; the parking area is 1.4 miles below Deer Ridge Junction.

70. CCC Camp in Little Horseshoe Park: N40°23'25", W105°36'34". Site is most easily reached via the old dirt road (now closed to traffic) that leads down into Little Horseshoe Park. It is to the right 0.6 mile down from Deer Ridge Junction.

71. Deer Ridge Chalet: N40°23'20", W105°36'40". The junction of US 34 and US 36 at Deer Ridge is 3 miles west of Rocky Mountain National Park Headquarters and Visitor Center.

72. Hupp Homestead: N40°22'11", W105°35'38". Site is on the road leading into Beaver Meadows, on the right approximately 0.2 mile from the entrance.

73. Hondius Ranch: 1) N40°22'14", W105°36'48"; 2) N40°22'21", W105°36'42". Sites are near the parking area at the end of the road into Beaver Meadows, 1.4 miles from the entrance.

74. Camping in Moraine Park: N40°21'9", W105°34'56". Site is just west of the Bear Lake Rd. bridge over the Big Thompson.

75. Chapman Ranch: N40°21'8", W105°35'37". Site is just west of the small parking lot along the Big Thompson below the Moraine Park Visitor Center, 1.5 miles from the beginning of Bear Lake Rd.

76. Eaton House: N40°21'2", W105°34'48". The Eaton and Kennedy houses stood on a hillside overlooking the Chapman Ranch (see Site 75), south of the William Allen White Cabin and just above the concrete bridge over the Big Thompson, 1.7 miles from the beginning of Bear Lake Rd.

77. William Allen White Cabin: 1) N40°21'15", W105°34'52"; 2) N40°21'14", W105°34'53". Site is 300 yards south of the Moraine Park Visitor Center, above Bear Lake Rd.

78. The Scottage: N40°21'17", W105°34'56". South of Moraine Park Visitor Center.

79. Moraine Lodge: 1) N40°21'20", W105°34'56"; 2) N40°21'32", W105°35'3". Site is now the Moraine Park Visitor Center parking lot.

80. Sprague's Ranch and Stead's Ranch and Hotel: 1) N40°21'22", W105°35'34"; 2) N40°21'24", W105°35'41"; 3) N40°21'24", W105°35'42". Site is just below the Moraine Park Campground, on the left where the road turns down toward the Cub Lake and Fern Lake Trailheads.

81. Brinwood Ranch and Hotel: N40°21'25", W105°37'03". Site is just east of the Cub Lake Trailhead, approximately 1.6 miles from Moraine Park Rd.

82. Forest Inn: N40°20'11", W105°39'33". The Pool is 2 miles from the Fern Lake Trailhead.

83. Fern Lake Lodge: N40°20'10", W105°40'32". Site is just above the lake's outlet, 3.8 miles from the Fern Lake Trailhead.

84. CCC Camps in Hollowell Park: N40°20'27", W105°36'26". The site of Camp N. P. 11-C in Hollowell Park is west of today's parking lot, 3.7 miles from the beginning of Bear Lake Rd. and 4.7 miles from the Beaver Meadows Visitor Center.

85. Rocky Mountain Boys Camp: N40°20'28", W105°36'26". Site is on the south lateral moraine above the parking area in Hollowell Park.

86. Spragues Lodge: N40°19'41", W105°35'45". Spragues Lake and the site of Spragues Lodge are off Bear Lake Rd., 3.2 miles below Bear Lake and 6.8 miles from the Beaver Meadows Visitor Center.

87. Bear Lake and Bear Lake Lodge: 1) N40°18'51", W105°38'40"; 2) N40°18'45", W105°38'51". Bear Lake is 9.4 miles from the Beaver Meadows entrance to the park.

Rocky Mountain National Park: West of Continental Divide

88. Old Fall River Road: 1) N40°24'53", W105°39'43"; 2) N40°24'59", W105°40'35"; 4) N40°26'20", W105°45'15"; 6) N40°25'27", W105°48'30"; 7) N40°23'52", W105°49'43". 1) Endovalley area starts 0.2 mile from where Old Fall River Rd. begins; 2) Chasm Falls, above which is its small parking area, is 1.4 miles from the beginning of Fall River Rd.; 3) switchbacks are just before the Chasm Falls parking area, 0.9 mile from the beginning of Fall River Rd.; 4) Fall River Pass is at the end of the old road, where it enters the Alpine Visitor Center area; 5) Fall River Ranger Station is directly south of the Alpine Visitor Center; 6) above Poudre Lake parking area; 7) 0.4 mile above Farview Curve.

89. Trail Ridge Road: N40°25'24", W105°44'59". Trail Ridge Road is the nearly 50-mile section of US 34 that crosses Rocky Mountain National Park between Estes Park and Grand Lake.

90. Grand Lake: N40°15'17", W105°49'35". Point Park is at the end of Cairns Ave. off Lake Ave. in Grand Lake.

91. Grand Lake Lodge: N40°15'17", W105°49'35". Grand Lake Lodge, off US 34, is 0.9 mile south of the Kawuneeche Visitor Center.

92. Holzwarth Trout Lodge and Never Summer Ranch: 1) N40°21'53", W105°51'14"; 2) N40°22'21", W105°51'42". 1) Mamas Cabin and Trout Lodge sites are a short walking distance from the Holzwarth Historic Site parking lot, 7.5 miles from Rocky Mountain National Park's Grand Lake entrance; 2) Never Summer Ranch site is 6.9 miles from the Grand Lake entrance.

93. Camp Wheeler (Squeaky Bob's): N40°24'24", W105°50'54". Camp Wheeler site is 0.5 mile north of the Colorado River Trailhead parking lot. The trailhead is 9.4 miles from Rocky Mountain National Park's Grand Lake entrance.

94. Lulu City: N40°26'40", W105°50'49". Lulu City site is reached via a 3.7-mile trail from the Colorado River Trailhead, which is 9.4 miles from Rocky Mountain National Park's Grand Lake entrance.

Rocky Mountain National Park: Longs Peak Region

95. Eugenia Mine: N40°16'57", W105°34'20". Site is 0.7 mile from the Longs Peak Ranger Station and the beginning of the Longs Peak Trail.

96. Timberline Cabin: N40°16'32", W105°35'25". Site is on the edge of Jim's Grove, about 3 miles up the Longs Peak Trail.

97. Agnes Vaille Shelter: N40°15'33", W105°37'14". On the left side of The Keyhole, about 5 miles up the Longs Peak Trail, past the Boulder Field.

98. The Keyhole: N40°15'33", W105°37'14". About 5 miles up the Longs Peak Trail, past the Boulder Field. It is visible through binoculars as far away as Fort Collins.

For Further Reading

Arps, Louisa Ward and Elinor Eppich Kingery. *High Country Names: Rocky Mountain National Park and the Indian Peaks.* Boulder: Johnson Books, 1994.

Bird, Isabella Lucy. *A Lady's Life in the Rocky Mountains.* London: John Murray, 1879.

Buchholtz, Curt W. *Rocky Mountain National Park: A History.* Boulder: Colorado Associated University Press, 1983.

Chapin, Frederick Hastings. *Frederick Chapin's Colorado: The Peaks about Estes Park and Other Writings.* Edited by James H. Pickering. Niwot, CO: University Press of Colorado, 1995.

Drummond, Alexander. *Enos Mills: Citizen of Nature.* Boulder: University Press of Colorado, 1995.

Dunning, Harold Marion. *Over Hill and Vale: In the Evening Shadows of Colorado's Longs Peak*, Vols. 1–3. Boulder: Johnson Publishing Company, 1956, 1962, 1971.

Foster, Lisa. *Rocky Mountain National Park: The Complete Hiking Guide.* Englewood, CO: Westcliffe Publishers, 2005.

Geary, Michael M. *A Quick History of Grand Lake Including Rocky Mountain National Park and the Grand Lake Lodge.* Ouray, CO: Western Reflections Publishing Company, 1999.

Gunn, John, ed. *Rocky Mountain Rustic: Historic Buildings of the Rocky Mountain National Park Area.* Estes Park, CO: Rocky Mountain Nature Association, 2004.

Knowlton, Lorna. *Weaving Mountain Memories: Recollections of the Allenspark Area.* Estes Park, CO: Estes Park Museum, 1989.

Melton, Jack R. and Lulabeth Melton. *YMCA of the Rockies: Spanning a Century.* Estes Park, CO: YMCA of the Rockies, 1992.

Musselman, Lloyd K. *Rocky Mountain National Park: Administrative History, 1915–1965.* Washington: U.S. Department of the Interior, National Park Service, 1971.

Osterwald, Doris B. *Rocky Mountain Splendor: A Mile by Mile Guide for Rocky Mountain National Park.* Lakewood, CO: Western Guideways, Ltd., 1989.

Pedersen, Henry F., Jr. *Those Castles of Wood: The Story of Early Lodges of Rocky Mountain National Park.* Estes Park, CO: Henry F. Pedersen Jr., 1993.

Pickering, James H. *America's Switzerland: Estes Park and Rocky Mountain National Park, The Growth Years.* Boulder: University of Colorado Press, 2005.

———, ed. *Early Estes Park: Historical Narratives*, Vols. 1–4. Estes Park, CO: Estes Park Museum/Alpenaire Publishing, 2004.

———. *In the Vale of Elkanah: The Tahosa Valley World of Charles Edwin Hewes.* Estes Park, CO: Estes Park Museum/Alpenaire Publishing, 2003.

———. *Mr. Stanley of Estes Park.* Kingfield, ME: Stanley Museum, 2000.

———. *"This Blue Hollow": Estes Park, The Early Years, 1859–1915.* Niwot, CO: University Press of Colorado, 1999.

Sprague, Abner E. *My Pioneer Life: The Memoirs of Abner E. Sprague.* Estes Park, CO: Rocky Mountain Nature Association, 1999.

Veblen, Thomas T. and Diane C. Lorenz. *The Colorado Front Range: A Century of Ecological Change.* Salt Lake City: University of Utah Press, 1991.

Willard, Beatrice Elizabeth and Susan Quimby Foster. *A Roadside Guide to Rocky Mountain National Park.* Boulder: Johnson Books, 1990.

Photography Credits

When known, information is included for each photographic pair as follows: contemporary photographer (CP); historic photographer (HP); source for historic photograph; and reference number for historic photograph.

Preface

A. Q. House at MacGregor Ranch: Skip Szilagyi (CP); MacGregor Charitable Trust

Introduction

1) Estes Park, circa 1903: Jill Bagley; **2) Estes Park, circa 1906:** C. A. Graves (HP); Estes Park Museum; **3) Estes Park village, circa 1923:** Paula Steige

Estes Valley Scenes and Sites

1. Estes Park from Park Hill: Mic Clinger (CP); Rocky Mountain National Park—NPS

2. "Rocky Mountain Jim" Cabin Site: 1) Mic Clinger (CP); **2)** Mic Clinger (CP); **3)** Mic Clinger (CP)

3. Estes Park from Mount Olympus: Mic Clinger (CP); William T. Parke (HP); Carey Stevanus

4. Estes-Evans-Dunraven Ranch: 1) William G. Chamberlain (HP); Denver Public Library, Western History Collection; X19337; **2)** William G. Chamberlain (HP); Denver Public Library, Western History Collection; X19303; **3)** William G. Chamberlain (HP); Dave Tanton, OldEstes; **4)** James H. Pickering; **5)** Mic Clinger (CP); Rocky Mountain National Park—NPS; **6)** Mic Clinger (CP); Rocky Mountain National Park—NPS; **7)** Mic Clinger (CP); Fred Payne Clatworthy (HP); Barbara Clatworthy Gish; **8)** Mic Clinger (CP); John Preston (HP); Rocky Mountain National Park—NPS;

5. Charles Partridge Adams House: 1) Mic Clinger (CP); **2)** Mic Clinger (CP)

6. Dunraven Cottage and Estes Park Hotel: Mic Clinger (CP); Estes Park Museum

7. Estes Park Hotel: 1) Mic Clinger (CP); F. E. Baker (HP); Estes Park Museum; **2)** Mic Clinger (CP); David Scarbrough, Mountain Time

8. Estes Park Country Club: Mic Clinger (CP); Fred Payne Clatworthy (HP); Barbara Clatworthy Gish

9. Front Range from Prospect Mountain: Mic Clinger (CP); William Henry Jackson (HP); Rocky Mountain National Park—NPS

10. Longs Peak from Dollar Lake: Mic Clinger (CP); William Henry Jackson (HP); Dave Tanton, Old Estes

11. Cheley Colorado Camps: Carey Stevanus (CP); Fred Payne Clatworthy (HP); Don and Carole Cheley

12. Marys Lake: Mic Clinger (CP); Frederick H. Chapin (HP); James H. Pickering

13. Beaver Point: Mic Clinger (CP); H. Raymond Gregg (HP); Rocky Mountain National Park—NPS

14. Rocky Mountain National Park 1923 Headquarters: Mic Clinger (CP); Rocky Mountain National Park—NPS

15. The Lone Pine: Mic Clinger (CP); Fred Payne Clatworthy (HP); Carey Stevanus

16. The Y–Big Thompson Entrance to Rocky Mountain National Park: Mic Clinger (CP); H. Raymond Gregg (HP); Rocky Mountain National Park —NPS

17. Holland Inn: Carey Stevanus (CP); Estes Park Museum

18. YMCA of the Rockies: Mic Clinger (CP); Fred Payne Clatworthy (HP); Lula W. Dorsey Museum

19. Mountainside Lodge: Mic Clinger (CP); Fred Payne Clatworthy (HP); Lula W. Dorsey Museum

20. Wigwam Tea Room: Carey Stevanus (CP); Rocky Mountain National Park —NPS

21. F. O. Stanley House: Mic Clinger (CP); Estes Park Museum

22. Estes Park Fish Hatchery: Mic Clinger (CP); Rocky Mountain National Park—NPS

23. Stanley Power Plant: 1) Mic Clinger (CP); **2)** Mic Clinger (CP); **3)** Mic Clinger (CP)

24. McCreery Cabin: James H. Pickering (CP); Estes Park Museum

25. North St. Vrain Road (Highway 36): Mic Clinger (CP); C. Byron Hall

26. South St. Vrain Road (Highway 7): Mic Clinger (CP); Sanborn Souvenir Company (HP); David Scarbrough, Mountain Time

27. Big Thompson Road (Highway 34): 1) Mic Clinger (CP); William T. Parke (HP); David Scarbrough, Mountain Time; **2)** Mic Clinger (CP); Louis C. McClure (HP); Denver Public Library, Western History Collection; MCC-2093; **3)** Mic Clinger (CP); Sanborn Souvenir Company (HP); David Scarbrough, Mountain Time

The Village

28. Panoramic View: Mic Clinger (CP); Miller Studio (HP); Mic Clinger/Estes Park Museum

29. Al Birch House: Mic Clinger (CP); Rocky Mountain National Park—NPS

30. Estes Park from the Birch Ruins: Mic Clinger (CP); Louis C. McClure (HP); Estes Park Museum

31. Sam Service Store: Mic Clinger (CP); Estes Park Museum

32. Original 1915 Rocky Mountain National Park Headquarters: Mic Clinger (CP); Rocky Mountain National Park—NPS

33. John Edward Macdonald Home and Store: Mic Clinger (CP); Paula Steige

34. Josephine Hotel: Mic Clinger (CP); Ray Davis/Estes Park Museum

35. Riverside Amusement Park: Mic Clinger (CP); Estes Park Museum

Louis C. McClure (1867–1957), one of Estes Park's early photographers, at work

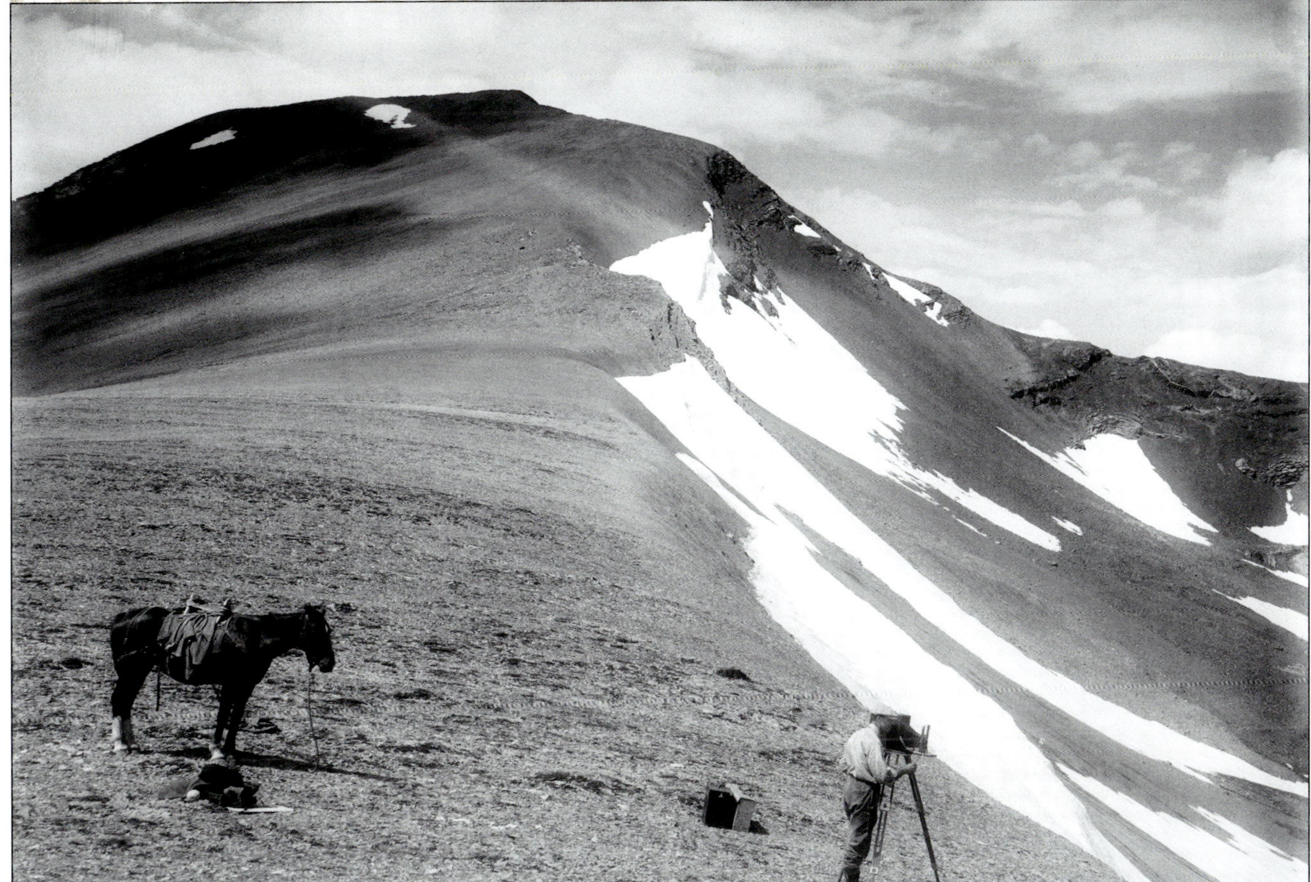

36. National Park Hotel: Mic Clinger (CP); Estes Park Museum

37. William T. Parke Store: Mic Clinger (CP); William T. Parke (HP); Estes Park Museum

38. Rocky Mountain Parks Transportation Company: Mic Clinger (CP); William T. Parke (HP); Estes Park Museum

39. Hupp Hotel: Mic Clinger (CP); William T. Parke (HP); David Scarbrough, Mountain Time

40. Manford Hotel: Mic Clinger (CP); Estes Park Museum

41. Estes Park Bank: Mic Clinger (CP); William T. Parke (HP); Estes Park Museum

42. Ye Lyttel Shop: Mic Clinger (CP); Fred Payne Clatworthy (HP); Barbara Clatworthy Gish

43. Estes Park Church: Mic Clinger (CP); George and Caprissa Frawley/ James H. Boyd Collection

44. Estes Park from the West End: Mic Clinger (CP); Louis C. McClure (HP); Denver Public Library, Western History Collection; MCC-2625

45. Lewiston Hotel: Mic Clinger (CP); Carey Stevanus

46. Estes Park from Oldman Mountain: Carey Stevanus (CP); J. R. Riddle (HP); Estes Park Public Library

47. Oldman Mountain Ski Site: Carey Stevanus (CP); Rocky Mountain National Park—NPS

48. Crags Hotel: 1) Mic Clinger (CP); William T. Parke (HP); Carey Stevanus; **2)** Mic Clinger (CP); Fred Payne Clatworthy (HP); Barbara Clatworthy Gish

49. Boyd House: Carey Stevanus (CP); George and Caprissa Frawley/ James H. Boyd Collection

Hotels, Lodges, and Ranches

50. Stanley Hotel: Mic Clinger (CP); City of Greeley Museums

51. Elkhorn Lodge: Mic Clinger (CP); Rocky Mountain National Park—NPS

52. MacGregor Ranch: 1) Mic Clinger (CP); Rocky Mountain National Park—NPS; **2)** Mic Clinger (CP); Rocky Mountain National Park—NPS; **3)** Mic Clinger (CP); Fred Payne Clatworthy (HP); Barbara Clatworthy Gish; **4)** Mic Clinger (CP); Fred Payne Clatworthy (HP); Barbara Clatworthy Gish

53. McGraw Ranch: 1) Mic Clinger (CP); Fred Payne Clatworthy (HP); David Scarbrough, Mountain Time; **2)** Mic Clinger (CP); Rocky Mountain National Park—NPS

54. Rustic Hotel: 1) Mic Clinger (CP); Estes Park Museum; **2)** Mic Clinger (CP); William T. Parke (HP); Carey Stevanus

55. Olympus Lodge: Mic Clinger (CP); Sanborn Souvenir Company (HP); David Scarbrough, Mountain Time

56. Crocker Ranch: Mic Clinger (CP); Albin Drott (HP); Leif and Heidi Johnson

57. Estes Park Chalets: Mic Clinger (CP); Fred Payne Clatworthy (HP); Barbara Clatworthy Gish

58. Ferguson's Highlands Hotel: Mic Clinger (CP); Estes Park Museum

59. Baldpate Inn: 1) Mic Clinger (CP); Fred Payne Clatworthy (HP); David Scarbrough, Mountain Time; **2)** Mic Clinger (CP); Hoffman (HP); David Scarbrough, Mountain Time

60. Wind River Ranch: 1) Mic Clinger (CP); **2)** Mic Clinger (CP); **3)** Mic Clinger (CP)

61. Columbine Lodge: Mic Clinger (CP); Sanborn Souvenir Company (HP); David Scarbrough, Mountain Time

62. Hewes-Kirkwood Inn: Mic Clinger (CP); Rocky Mountain National Park—NPS

63. Lambs Ranch and Longs Peak Inn: Mic Clinger (CP); Squires (HP); Rocky Mountain National Park—NPS

Rocky Mountain National Park: East of Continental Divide

64. Rocky Mountain National Park Dedication Site in Horseshoe Park: 1) Mic Clinger (CP); Rocky Mountain National Park—NPS; **2)** Mic Clinger (CP); Rocky Mountain National Park—NPS; **3)** Mic Clinger (CP); Rocky Mountain National Park—NPS

65. Fall River Lodge: 1) Mic Clinger (CP); Sanborn Souvenir Company (HP); David Scarbrough, Mountain Time **2)** Mic Clinger (CP); Sanborn Souvenir Company (HP); David Scarbrough, Mountain Time

66. Convict Cabins: Mic Clinger (CP); Fred Payne Clatworthy (HP); Barbara Clatworthy Gish

67. March Homestead Cabin: Mic Clinger (CP); Rocky Mountain National Park —NPS

68. Cascade Lodge: Mic Clinger (CP); Sanborn Souvenir Company (HP); David Scarbrough, Mountain Time

69. Richmond Homestead and Horseshoe Inn: 1) Mic Clinger (CP); Fred Payne Clatworthy (HP); Barbara Clatworthy Gish; **2)** Louis C. McClure (HP); Denver Public Library, Western History Collection; MCC-2632

70. **CCC Camp in Little Horseshoe Park:** Mic Clinger (CP); Rocky Mountain National Park—NPS

71. **Deer Ridge Chalet:** Mic Clinger (CP); Sanborn Souvenir Company (HP); David Scarbrough, Mountain Time

72. **Hupp Homestead:** Mic Clinger (CP); Estes Park Museum

73. **Hondius Ranch: 1)** Carey Stevanus (CP); Estes Park Museum; **2)** Mic Clinger (CP); Estes Park Museum

74. **Camping in Moraine Park:** Mic Clinger (CP); F. E. Baker (HP); Estes Park Museum

75. **Chapman Ranch:** Mic Clinger (CP); Rocky Mountain National Park—NPS

76. **Eaton House:** Mic Clinger (CP); Rocky Mountain National Park—NPS

77. **William Allen White Cabin: 1)** Mic Clinger (CP); Emporia State University; **2)** Carey Stevanus (CP); Emporia State University

78. **The Scottage:** Mic Clinger (CP); Mickey Lynn

79. **Moraine Lodge: 1)** Carey Stevanus (CP); Estes Park Museum; **2)** Mic Clinger (CP); Fred Payne Clatworthy (HP); Rocky Mountain National Park—NPS

80. **Sprague's Ranch and Stead's Ranch and Hotel: 1)** Mic Clinger (CP); Rocky Mountain National Park—NPS; **2)** Mic Clinger (CP); Fred Payne Clatworthy (HP); Barbara Clatworthy Gish; **3)** Mic Clinger (CP); Williams (HP); Rocky Mountain National Park—NPS

81. **Brinwood Ranch and Hotel:** Mic Clinger (CP); David Scarbrough, Mountain Time

82. **Forest Inn:** Carey Stevanus (CP); Rocky Mountain National Park—NPS; Inset: Hal and Doris Tecker

83. **Fern Lake Lodge: 1)** Carey Stevanus (CP); William T. Parke (HP); Rocky Mountain National Park—NPS; **2)** Carey Stevanus (CP); Rocky Mountain National Park—NPS

84. **CCC Camps in Hollowell Park:** Mic Clinger (CP); Rocky Mountain National Park—NPS

85. **Rocky Mountain Boys Camp:** Mic Clinger (CP); Dave Primrose

86. **Spragues Lodge:** Mic Clinger (CP); Sanborn Souvenir Company (HP); David Scarbrough, Mountain Time

87. **Bear Lake and Bear Lake Lodge: 1)** Carey Stevanus (CP); Carey Stevanus; **2)** Mic Clinger (CP); Rocky Mountain National Park—NPS

Rocky Mountain National Park: West of Continental Divide

88. **Old Fall River Road: 1)** Mic Clinger (CP); Rocky Mountain National Park—NPS; **2)** Mic Clinger (CP); Fred Payne Clatworthy (HP); Barbara Clatworthy Gish; **3)** Carey Stevanus (CP); Fred Payne Clatworthy (HP); Barbara Clatworthy Gish; **4)** Carey Stevanus (CP); Rocky Mountain National Park—NPS; **5)** Carey Stevanus (CP); Fred Payne Clatworthy (HP); Barbara Clatworthy Gish; **6)** Carey Stevanus (CP); F. J. Francis (HP); Rocky Mountain National Park—NPS; **7)** Carey Stevanus (CP); Rocky Mountain National Park—NPS

89. **Trail Ridge Road: 1)** Carey Stevanus (CP); Sanborn Souvenir Company (HP); David Scarbrough, Mountain Time; **2)** Carey Stevanus (CP); John McLaughlin (HP); Rocky Mountain National Park—NPS

90. **Grand Lake:** Carey Stevanus (CP); Fred Payne Clatworthy (HP); Barbara Clatworthy Gish

91. **Grand Lake Lodge:** Carey Stevanus (CP); Rocky Mountain National Park—NPS

92. **Holzwarth Trout Lodge and Never Summer Ranch: 1)** Carey Stevanus (CP); Rocky Mountain National Park—NPS; **2)** Carey Stevanus (CP); Sanborn Souvenir Company (HP); David Scarbrough, Mountain Time

93. **Camp Wheeler (Squeaky Bob's):** Carey Stevanus (CP); Rocky Mountain National Park—NPS

94. **Lulu City:** Carey Stevanus (CP); Denver Public Library, Western History Collection; 05315

Rocky Mountain National Park: Longs Peak Region

95. **Eugenia Mine:** Mic Clinger (CP); Rocky Mountain National Park—NPS

96. **Timberline Cabin:** Mic Clinger (CP); William T. Parke (HP); Carey Stevanus

97. **Agnes Vaille Shelter:** Mic Clinger (CP); E. K. Field (HP); Rocky Mountain National Park—NPS

98. **The Keyhole:** Mic Clinger (CP); Fred Payne Clatworthy (HP); Barbara Clatworthy Gish

Photography Credits

Louis C. McClure: Denver Public Library, Western History/Genealogy Department, #Mcc 1779

Acknowledgments

No project as ambitious as this one could have been accomplished without a great deal of help from people who shared our interest and enthusiasm. We would like to thank Westcliffe Publishers for bringing this book to life, especially publishers John Fielder and Linda Doyle, editors Jenna Browning and David Lewis, designer Carol Pando, as well as Craig Keyzer, Barrett Webb, and Jennifer Jahner. Thanks also go to Ferrel Atkins, for many years a seasonal ranger at Rocky Mountain National Park, whose knowledge of the history of the park and the region around it, much of it gained first-hand, is unsurpassed; Betty Kilsdonk, director of the Estes Park Museum, and staff members Becky Latanich, Lisel Goetze Record, and J. J. Rutherford; Sybil Barnes, who serves as local history librarian at the Estes Park Public Library and as librarian for the Rocky Mountain National Park library in McLaren Hall; Rocky Mountain National Park rangers Joan Childers, Christy Baker, Michael Edwards, Sue Langdon, Cynthia Langguth, Judy Visty, and Cheri Yost, who gave us access to the materials, sites, and facilities under their care; Jack Melton, director of the Dorsey Museum at the YMCA of the Rockies, who with his wife Lulie has preserved so much of the history of that important institution; and Dave Lively, president of the Grand Lake Museum. We would also like to acknowledge a number of others who graciously made their family photographs and personal collections available to us, gave us access to their property and buildings so that new photographs could be taken, or otherwise offered help and information. They include Eric Adams, Tom Adams, Paul Arguien, Jill Bagley, Tom Brown, Carole and Don Cheley, Grace and Lou Davis, Ray A. Davis, Kyle and Cindy Ford, Peggy A. Ford, Caprissa and Eric Frawley, Dorothy Scott Gibbs, Barbara Clatworthy Gish, Kathy George, Kim Glover, Dale Hatcher, Frank Hix, Helen and Pieter Hondius, Ken Jessen, Jon and Deyn Johnson, Leif and Heidi Johnson, Orpha Kendall, Mickey Lynn, Don McIntyre, Bill McNamara, Carol Nussbaumer, Melba and Charles Orshek, Dave Primrose, David Scarbrough, Grace and Richard Sipe, Lois Smith, Paula Steige, Skip Szilagyi, David Tanton, Doris and Hal Tecker, Nancy P. Thomas, Gladys Thompson, and Kyle and Randy Wolff. We also thank Patricia Pickering, who helped throughout in ways both large and small. All of you have been instrumental in making the completion of this project possible.

About the Photographer

Mic Clinger, a resident of Parker, Colorado, is an avid photographer, mountaineer, and outdoorsman with a love of history, particularly the history of Estes Park and Rocky Mountain National Park, where he has climbed and photographed extensively. This is his first book.

About the Authors

James H. Pickering, a longtime summer resident of Estes Park, is a professor of English at the University of Houston, where he has also served as dean, provost, and president. He has published 18 books on Colorado and the Rocky Mountain West, including the prize-winning *"This Blue Hollow": Estes Park, The Early Years, 1859–1915* (1999) and *America's Switzerland: Estes Park and Rocky Mountain National Park, The Growth Years* (2005). In these two volumes he traces the history and development of Estes Park and Rocky Mountain National Park from the arrival of Joel Estes in October 1859 through the end of World War II. Other titles include the first full-scale biography of automobile pioneer F. O. Stanley, *Mr. Stanley of Estes Park* (2000); *In the Vale of Elkanah: The Tahosa Valley World of Charles Edwin Hewes* (2003); *The Ways of the Mountains: Thornton Sampson, Agnes Vaille and Other Tragedies in High Places* (2003); four volumes of *Early Estes Park Narratives* (2004); and *Enos Mills' Colorado* (2006).

Ohio native, Kent State University graduate, and full-time Estes Park resident Carey Stevanus is a lifelong student of history and fan of black-and-white photography. Throughout her career, these interests have led to her working in places as diverse as an Estes Park "old-time portrait studio," the historic Estes Park Chalets (Marys Lake Lodge), and a senior center where the daughter of historic photographer Fred Payne Clatworthy resides. Aside from her writing duties, she contributed images from her vintage postcard and photograph collection, as well as her original contemporary photographs, to this project. With this book, her hope is to inspire readers to help preserve more of Estes Park's historic structures and the stories they have to tell.

International Standard Book Numbers:
ISBN-10: 1-56579-532-6
ISBN-13: 978-1-56579-532-7

Editors: Jenna Samelson Browning and David Lewis

Design: Carol Pando

Production Manager: Craig Keyzer

Published by:
Westcliffe Publishers, Inc.
P.O. Box 1261
Englewood, CO 80150

Printed in China by: C & C Offset Printing Co., Ltd.

Library of Congress Cataloging-in-Publication Data:

Pickering, James H.
Estes Park and Rocky Mountain National Park then & now / text by James H. Pickering and Carey Stevanus ; contemporary rephotography by Mic Clinger.
p. cm.
Includes bibliographical references.
ISBN-13: 978-1-56579-532-7
ISBN-10: 1-56579-532-6
1. Estes Park (Colo.)--Pictorial works. 2. Rocky Mountain National Park (Colo.)--Pictorial works. 3. Estes Park (Colo.)--History--Pictorial works. 4. Rocky Mountain National Park (Colo.)--History--Pictorial works. 5. Repeat photography--Colorado--Estes Park. 6. Repeat photography--Colorado--Rocky Mountain National Park. I. Stevanus, Carey. II. Clinger, Mic. III. Title.
F782.L2P54 2006
978.8'68--dc22
2006005145

For more information about other fine books and calendars from Westcliffe Publishers, please contact your local bookstore, call us at 1-800-523-3692, or visit us on the Web at ***westcliffepublishers.com.***

The authors and publisher of this book have made every effort to ensure the accuracy and currency of its information. Nevertheless, books can require revisions. Please feel free to let us know if you find information in this book that needs to be updated, and we will be glad to correct it for the next printing. Your comments and suggestions are always welcome.

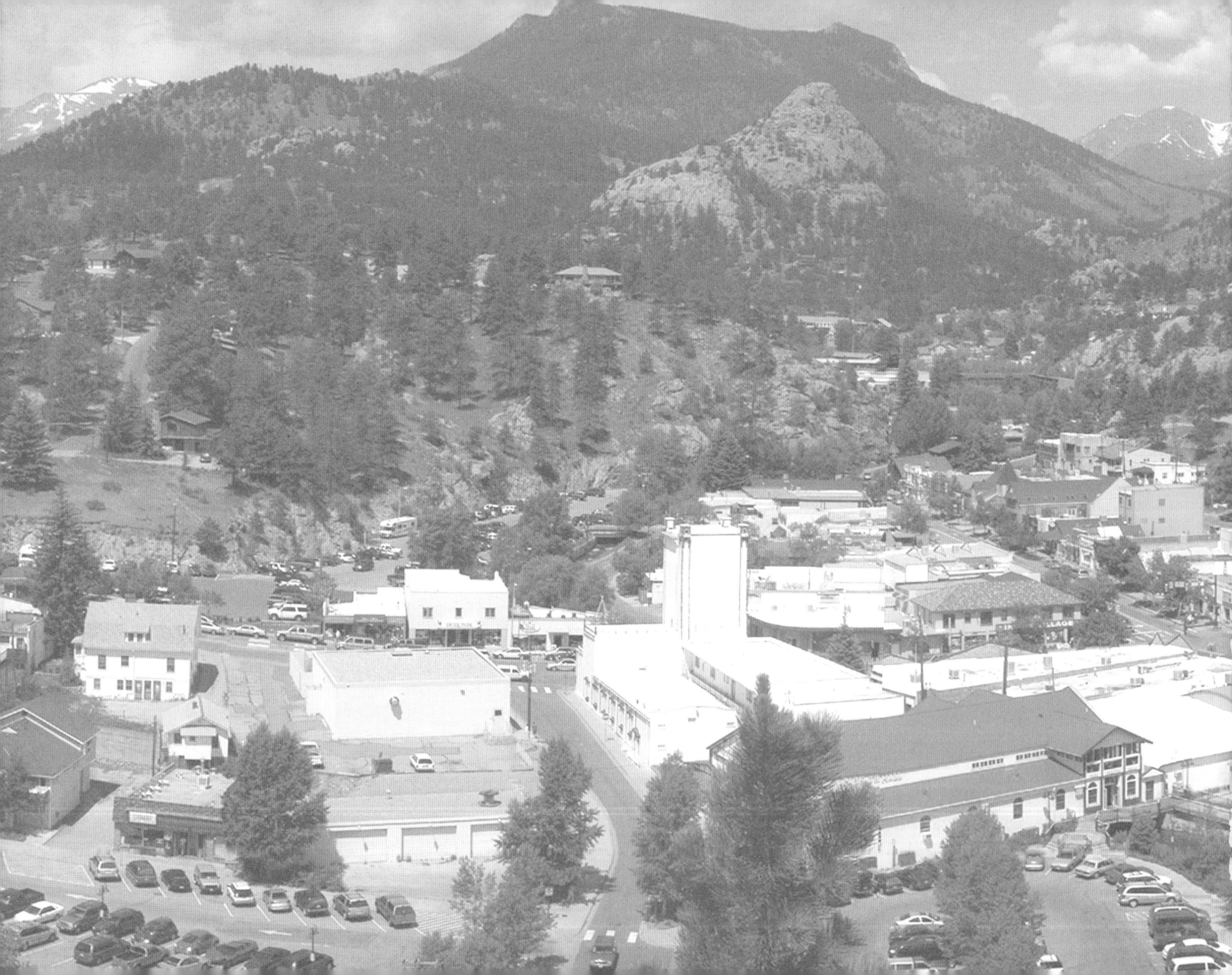